American Red Cross

FIRST AID

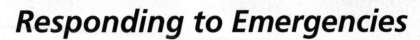

Responding to Emergencies

Third Edition

American Red Cross

FIRST AID

Responding to Emergencies

Third Edition

Important certification information

American Red Cross certificates may be issued upon successful completion of a training program, which uses this textbook as an intergral part of the course. By itself, the text material does not constitute comprehensive Red Cross training. In order to issue ARC certificates, your instructor must be authorized by the American Red Cross, and must follow prescribed policies and procedures. Make certain that you have attended a course authorized by the Red Cross. Ask your instructor about receiving American Red Cross certification, or contact your local chapter for more information.

American Red Cross

StayWell

StayWell

Printed in the United States of America

Composition by Graphic World
Printing/Binding by Banta

StayWell
1100 Grundy Lane
San Bruno, CA 94066

Library of Congress Cataloging in Publication Data

American Red Cross first aid responding to emergencies.
        p.   cm.
    Includes bibliographical references.
    Includes index.
    ISBN 1-58480-101-8
    1. First aid in illness and injury.   2. Medical emergencies.
1. American Red Cross.
    [DNLM: 1. Emergencies—programmed instructions.   2. First Aid—programmed instructions.   WA 18 A152]
RC86.7.A477   1995
616.02'52—dc20
DNLM/DLC
for Library of Congress   95-13642
                                                    CIP

02   03   04   05   /   9   8   7   6   5   4   3

This text is dedicated to the thousands of paid and volunteer staff of the American Red Cross who contribute their time and talent to supporting and teaching life-saving skills worldwide. And to the thousands of course participants and other readers who have decided to be prepared to take action when an emergency strikes.

This 3rd Edition of the First Aid—Responding To Emergencies text has been updated with the latest in life-saving CPR techniques and information. The text and related program meet the Emergency Cardiovascular Care (ECC) Guidelines 2000 while still maintaining the features and benefits of previous editions. Many of these features have been developed through input from instructors and students.

Look inside and note the vivid chapter opening images and thought-provoking scenarios. Notice that each chapter includes a list of Key Terms, Application Questions, End-of-Chapter Study Questions, and informative skills sheets and health check boxes. Each of these features helps course takers apply their training to their everyday lives. Informative sidebars provide additional topical information and resources that enhance this already information-packed learning resource. These features, combined with a comprehensive instructor's manual and video set, provide educational institutions the opportunity to provide the latest and best life-saving training available.

This text is part of an integral training program with certification available from your local American Red Cross chapter. CPR certification is valid for 1 year while first aid certification is valid for 3 years. Contact your local American Red Cross at www.redcross.org for more information on how you can receive American Red Cross life-saving certification.

For more information on American Red Cross Health & Safety Services training and products, visit www.redcross.org/services/hss

Acknowledgments

This textbook is the third edition of **American Red Cross First Aid—Responding to Emergencies.** We have endeavored to improve and polish this text and course to meet the recent Emergency Cardiovascular Care (ECC) Guidelines 2000. Many individuals shared in the development and revision process in various supportive, technical, and creative ways. Each edition could not have been developed without the dedication and support of paid and volunteer staff.

Members of the development teams at the American Red Cross national headquarters responsible for designing the course and writing this book include the following: First edition—M. Elizabeth Buoy Morrissey, MPH, Development Team Leader; Lawrence D. Newell, EdD, NREMT-P and S. Elizabeth White, MAEd, ATC, Project Managers; Martha F. Beshers, Elizabeth Peabody, and Joan Timberlake, Editors; Elaine P. McClatchey, Rebekah Jecker Calhoun, MSEd, and Marian F.H. Kirk, Analysts; Ella Holloway and Jane Moore, Administrative Support.

Second Edition—Paul Stearns III, Project Team Leader; S. Elizabeth White, MAEd, Project Manager; C.P. Dail, Jr., Senior Associate; Martha F. Beshers, Ann P. Dioda, Michael Espino, Jose Salazar, MPH, NREMT-B, and Patricia Appleford Terrell, Associates; Jane Moore, Specialist; and Betty Williams Butler, Administrative Assistant.

The following Red Cross national headquarters paid and volunteer staff provided guidance and review for the second edition: Susan M. Livingstone, Vice President, Health and Safety Services; Jean Wagaman, Director, Program and Customer Support; Earl Harbert, Manager, Contracts and Finance; Jeff Hoke, Risk Management; Zora Travis Salisbury, EdD, Manager, HIV/AIDS Education; Karen J. Peterson, PhD, Senior Associate, HIV/AIDS Education; and Rhonda Starr, Senior Associate, Educational Development.

Third Edition—Don Vardell, Director; Susan Thurner, Manager; Marc Madden, Associate; Saunderia Smith, Administrative Assistant II, Research & Product Development; Connie Harvey; Communications Manager; Ted Crites, CHES, Senior Associate, Health, Safety & Community Services; Amanda Land, Product Line Manager, Communication & Marketing.

The StayWell/Krames Editorial, Production, and Marketing/Sales Team for this third edition included: Nancy Monahan, Vice President; Reed Klanderud, Marketing Director; Paula Batt, Sales Director; Shannon Bates, Senior Project Manager.

Special thanks (second edition) go to Kathleen Scogna, Development Editor; Rick Brady, Daniel F. Cima, Jeanette C. Ortiz Osorio, Mark Wieland, and Ed Wheeler, Photographers; Rolin Graphics, Illustrators; Larry Didona, Cover and Interior Opener Designer; and to Terry Georgia for her creative efforts in producing the photographs for the cover, part openings, and chapter openings. For the third edition, special thanks go to Mark Spann, Project Coordinator; Liz Rudder, Design Manager; Kathy Tindell, Developmental Editor, Jane Moore, Desktop Publisher, and Jean Neiner, Vice President Sales, Krames Communications for her visionary leadership, her dedication to the mission of the Red Cross, and her tireless commitment to improving customer service and product quality.

Guidance and review were also provided by members of the American Red Cross First Aid—Responding to Emergencies *second edition Advisory Committee:*

Raymond A. Cranston
Educational Development
    Volunteer Chairperson
Commanding Officer, Traffic
    Safety Unit
Farmington Hills Police
    Department
Farmington Hills, Michigan

Deborah Radi
Advisory Committee Chairperson
    and Safety Programs Manager
American Red Cross
Greater Minneapolis Area
    Chapter
Minneapolis, Minnesota

Arthur L. Grist, Sr.
Associate Professor Emeritus
University of Southern Illinois at
    Edwardsville

Second Vice President Illinois State
    Service Council
Instructor Trainer
American Red Cross
Madison County Chapter
Edwardsville, Illinois

Laird Hayes, EdD
Professor, Physical Education and
    Athletics
Orange Coast College
Costa Mesa, California
Instructor
American Red Cross
Orange County Chapter
Santa Ana, California

Nancy S. Maylath, HSD
Associate Professor of Health
    Education
Department of Health Promotion

University of Toledo
Toledo, Ohio

Anthony Musculino, BA
Faculty, Fingerlakes Community
    College
Instructor Trainer
American Red Cross
West Ontario County
    Chapter
Canandaigua, New York

Kimberly D. Wright, MS
Director of Aquatics; Instructor,
    Health & Physical Education
Bridgewater College
Bridgewater, Virginia
Instructor
American Red Cross
Rockingham County Chapter
Harrisonburg, Virginia

External review was provided by the following organizations and individuals:

**American College of Emergency
    Physicians**
Dallas, Texas

Jane W. Ball, RN, Dr PH
Program Director, Pediatric
    Emergency Education and
    Research Center
Emergency Trauma Services
Children's National
    Medical Center
Washington, D.C.

Stuart A. Balter, MA, ATC, EMT-D
Head Athletic Trainer/Instructor
Athletics and Physical Education
    Departments
Hudson Valley Community College
Troy, New York
Emergency Medical Technician
Sand Lake Ambulance
Sand Lake, New York

Zilpha T. Bosone, PhD
Chairperson, Medical Affairs
    Committee of the IAC
Audiology and Speech Pathology
    Services
Veterans Administration Medical
    Center
Washington, D.C.

Dr. Dayna S. Brown, MA, AB
Assistant Professor; Health,
    Physical Education and
    Recreation
Morehead State University
Morehead, Kentucky

Les Chatelain, MS, BS
Director of Emergency Programs,
    Health Education
    Department
University of Utah
Salt Lake City, Utah

Susan T. Dempf, PhD
Director of Graduate Studies in
    Physical Education
Canisius College
Buffalo, New York

Dean W. Dimke, BA
Health and Safety Specialist for the
    State of Kentucky
American Red Cross
Louisville, Kentucky

William W. Forgey, MD
Board Member and Editor
Practice Guidelines Wilderness
    Medical Society (WMS)
Crown Point, Indiana

Susan J. Grosse
Milwaukee High School
    of the Arts
Milwaukee, Wisconsin

Kristen M. Haydon
Director, Health Services
American Red Cross
Dallas Area Chapter
Dallas, Texas

**Douglas M. Hill, DO, FACOEP,
    FACEP**
Co-Director, Emergency
    Department
North Suburban Medical
    Center
Denver, Colorado
Director, First Aid School
Colorado Mountain School
Golden, Colorado
Professor of Emergency Medicine
University of Health Sciences
College of Osteopathic Medicine
Kansas City, Missouri
Board of Directors
American College of Emergency
    Medicine
Dallas, Texas

Joyce Holbrook Huner, BS, MSEd
Professor; Health and Physical
  Education
Macomb Community College
Clinton Township, Michigan

Richard C. Hunt, MD, FACEP
Associate Professor and Vice Chair
Department of Emergency
  Medicine
East Carolina University
Greenville, North Carolina

**Lisa Anne Johnson, MS, BSEd,
  EMT-P**
Aquatic Director; Health, Physical
  Education, and Recreation
Illinois State University
Normal, Illinois

Carolyn Kennedy
Director Special Projects
Girl Scouts of the USA
New York, New York

Louise Feasel Lindenmeyer, BA
Professor; Health, Physical
  Education
Shoreline Community College
Seattle, Washington

Carol G. McKenzie, PhD
Professor; Physical Education
California State University, Los
  Angeles
Los Angeles, California
Instructor Trainer/Standards
  Committee
Safety Services Department
American Red Cross
Los Angeles Chapter
Los Angeles, California

Marshall J. Meyer, MS
Assistant Director, Health and
  Safety
American Red Cross
Oregon Trail Chapter
Portland, Oregon

Richard "Chip" Myers
Shenandoah Mountain Rescue
  Group
Vienna, Virginia

**National Association of Emergency
  Medical Services Physicians**
Pittsburgh, Pennsylvania

**National Diabetes Information
  Clearinghouse**
Bethesda, Maryland

**Lawrence D. Newell, EdD,
  NREMT-P**
Newell Associates, Inc.
Ashburn, Virginia
Adjunct Professor; Emergency
  Medical Technologies
Northern Virginia Community
  College
Annandale, Virginia

Laurie O'Brian
American Camping Association
Martinsville, Indiana

Catherine E. Rossilli, BS, MACE, MA
Assistant Professor, Head Coach
Kinesiology
Westmont College
Santa Barbara, California

Daniel R. Ruth
Associate Director
Council Services Division
Boy Scouts of America
Irving, Texas

Marge Scanlin
Division Director
American Camping Association
Martinsville, Indiana

Tom Schmitz, BA, NREMT
Instructor Trainer
American Red Cross
Greater Minneapolis Area Chapter
Minneapolis, Minnesota

**Barbara Ann Smink, RN, BSN,
  MSEd**
School Nurse, Health Occupation
  Teacher
Boerne Independent School
  District
Boerne High School
Boerne, Texas

**Rose Ann Soloway, RN, MSEd,
  ABAT**
Administrator
American Society of Poison
  Control Centers
Washington, D.C.

David L. Weld
Executive Director
American Lyme Disease
  Foundation, Inc.
Somers, New York

Renée Woodward-Few
Director, Education and
  Information
Epilepsy Foundation for the
  National Capital Area
Washington, D.C.

*Special thanks go to the Institute of Medicine of the National Academy of Sciences,
members of a special committee to advise the American Red Cross, for their extensive
review and guidance in the development of the first edition, which forms the foundation of this second edition.*

Contents

WHY YOU SHOULD TAKE THIS COURSE

People need to know what to do in an emergency before medical help arrives. Since you, the citizen responder, are the person most likely to be first on the scene of an emergency, it is important that you know how to recognize emergencies and how to respond. This course will prepare you to make appropriate decisions regarding first aid care and to act on those decisions.

The first critical step in any emergency depends on the presence of someone who will take appropriate action. After completing this course, you should be able to—

• Recognize when an emergency has occurred.
• Follow the emergency action steps, *Check-Call-Care,* for any emergency.
• Provide care for injury or sudden illness until professional medical help arrives.

This course clarifies when and how to call for emergency medical help, eliminating the confusion that is frequently a factor in any emergency. This course also emphasizes the importance of a safe, healthy lifestyle. The Healthy Lifestyles Awareness Inventory, which your instructor will provide, provides a means for you to evaluate your lifestyle, determine how you can improve it, and help prevent lifestyle-related illness and injury.

HOW YOU WILL LEARN

Course content is presented in various ways. The textbook, which will be assigned reading, contains the information that will be discussed in class. Your instructor has the option to use videos, transparencies, and slides to support class discussions and other activities. These audiovisuals emphasize the key points that you will need to remember when making decisions in emergencies and will help you provide appropriate care. They also present skills that you will practice in class. Participating in all class activities will increase your confidence in your ability to respond to emergencies.

The course design allows you to frequently evaluate your progress in terms of skills competency, knowledge, and decision making. Certain chapters in the textbook include directions for skill practice sessions that are designed to help you learn specific first aid skills. Some of the practice sessions require practice on a manikin. Others give you the opportunity to practice with another person. This will give you a sense of what it would be like to care for a real person in an emergency situation and help reduce any concerns or fears you may have about giving care. Your ability to perform specific skills competently will be checked by your instructor during the practice sessions.

Your ability to make appropriate decisions when faced with an emergency will be enhanced as you participate in the class activities. Periodically, you will be given situations in the form of scenarios that provide you the opportunity to apply the knowledge and skills you have learned. These scenarios also provide an opportunity to discuss with your instructor the many different situations that you may encounter in any emergency.

REQUIREMENTS FOR COURSE COMPLETION CERTIFICATE

When this course is taught by a currently authorized American Red Cross instructor, you will be eligible for an American Red Cross course completion certificate. In order for you to receive an American Red Cross course completion certificate, you must—

• Perform specific skills competently and demonstrate the ability to make appropriate decisions for care.
• Pass a final written examination with a score of 80 percent or higher.

The final written examination is designed to test your retention and understanding of the course material. You will take this examination at the end of the course. If you do not pass the written examination the first time, you may take a second examination.

If this course is taught at a college or university, there may be additional academic requirements, such as attendance and grading, that your instructor will explain to you.

TEXTBOOK

This textbook has been designed to facilitate your learning and understanding of the knowledge and skills required to effectively respond to emergency situations. The following pages graphically point out how to use this text to your best advantage.

Photographs, drawings, charts, and graphs appear in all chapters, which illustrate skills, concepts, and anatomical features.

What You Should Learn

At the beginning of each chapter is a numbered list of objectives. Each item describes something you should know or be able to do after reading the chapter and participating in class activities. Read this list carefully, and refer back to it as you read the chapter. These objectives form the basis for test questions on the final exam.

CHAPTER 5

Breathing Emergencies

WHAT YOU SHOULD LEARN

After reading this chapter, you should be able to—

1. Describe the breathing process.
2. Identify ten signs and symptoms of respiratory distress.
3. Describe the care for a person experiencing respiratory distress.
4. Identify two common childhood illnesses that may cause respiratory distress.
5. Describe the purpose of rescue breathing.
6. Describe when and how to provide rescue breathing for an adult, child, and infant.
7. Describe when and how to use breathing devices.
8. Describe special considerations for rescue breathing.
9. Identify five causes of choking for adults, children, and infants.
10. Describe the care for conscious and unconscious choking for adult, child, and infant victims.
11. Define the key terms for this chapter.

After reading this chapter and completing the class activities, you should be able to demonstrate—

1. How to provide rescue breathing for adult, child, and infant victims.
2. How to care for conscious adult, child, and infant choking victims.
3. How to care for unconscious adult, child, and infant choking victims.
4. How to make appropriate decisions when given an example of an emergency situation in which a person may be experiencing respiratory distress or arrest.

85

It's a warm spring day. You and your friend, Kevin, are playing basketball on the public courts in the park. The ten-year-old next door, Steve, has tagged along. As you and Kevin attempt to play one-on-one, Steve tries to steal the ball. At one point, he is successful, and, dribbling the ball, he dashes to the far end of the court. You and Kevin become angry. You chase Steve. Suddenly, Steve stops in his tracks. He lets the ball go and brings his hands to his chest, gasping and making a strange wheezing sound. As you run to him, you see Steve is really having trouble breathing. As Steve struggles to catch his breath, you and Kevin try to decide what to do.

Scenarios

Every chapter opener contains a brief scenario that presents an event involving some aspect of the chapter content. The story in the scenario will be used to answer the Application Questions in the chapter.

Key Terms

A list of key terms with their definitions appears on the front page of each chapter. You need to know these key terms and their meanings to understand the material in the chapters. These key terms are printed in boldface italics the first time they are explained in the chapter and also appear, defined, in the Glossary. Some key terms are listed in more than one chapter because they are essential to your understanding of the material presented in each. The pronunciation of certain terms is provided, and a pronunciation guide is included in the glossary. • • • • • ➤

342 MEDICAL EMERGENCIES

Introduction

When you hear the term substance abuse, what thoughts flash through your mind? Narcotics? Cocaine? Marijuana? Because of the publicity they receive, we tend to think of illegal (also known as illicit or controlled) drugs when we hear of substance abuse. In the United States today, however, legal (also called licit or noncontrolled) substances are among those most often misused or abused. Such legal substances include nicotine (found in tobacco products); alcohol (found in beer, wine, and liquor); and over-the-counter medications, such as aspirin, sleeping pills, and diet pills.

The term substance abuse refers to a broad range of improperly used medical and nonmedical substances. Substance abuse costs the United States tens of billions of dollars each year in medical care, insurance, and lost productivity. Even more important, however, are the lives lost or permanently impaired each year from injuries or medical emergencies related to substance abuse or misuse.

This chapter will teach you about common forms of substance misuse and abuse, how to recognize these problems, and how to care for its victims. In an emergency caused by substance abuse or misuse, the immediate care you give can save a life.

Key Terms

Addiction: The compulsive need to use a substance. Stopping use would cause the user to suffer mental, physical, and emotional distress.

Cannabis products: Substances, such as marijuana and hashish, that are derived from the *Cannabis sativa* plant; can produce feelings of elation, distorted perceptions of time and space, and impaired motor coordination and judgment.

Dependency: The desire or need to continually use a substance.

Depressants: Substances that affect the central nervous system to slow down physical and mental activity, such as tranquilizers and sleeping pills.

Drug: Any substance, other than food, intended to affect the functions of the body.

Hallucinogens (ha LOO sin ə genz): Substances that affect mood, sensation, thought, emotion, and self-awareness; alter perceptions of time and space; and produce hallucinations and delusions. Also known as psychedelics.

Inhalants: Substances inhaled to produce a mood-altering effect, such as glue and paint thinners.

Medication: A drug given therapeutically to prevent or treat the effects of a disease or condition or otherwise enhance mental or physical well-being.

Narcotics: Drugs prescribed to relieve pain.

Overdose: An excess use of a drug, resulting in adverse reactions ranging from and including mania and hysteria to coma and death; specific reactions include changes in blood pressure and heartbeat, sweating, vomiting, and liver failure.

Stimulants: Substances that affect the central nervous system and increase physical and mental activity.

Substance abuse: The deliberate, persistent, excessive use of a substance without regard to health concerns or accepted medical practices.

Substance misuse: The use of a substance for unintended purposes or for intended purposes but in improper amounts or doses.

Tolerance: Condition in which the effects of a substance on the body decrease as a result of continual use.

Withdrawal: The condition produced when a person stops using or abusing a substance to which he or she is addicted.

• Splint an injury in the position in which you find it. Do not move, straighten, or bend the injured part.

• Splint the injured area and the joints above and below the injury site.

• Check for proper circulation (feeling, warmth, and color) before and after splinting.

Keep the victim as comfortable as possible, and avoid overheating or chilling. Monitor breathing and signs of circulation. Chapter 11 describes splinting in detail.

CHAPTER 10 Musculoske[...]

to the head or spine; and poss[...] juries that may be difficult to t[...] erly, such as to the back, hips, an[...] legs, or that you are unable to adequately immobilize. Remember that fractures of large bones and severe sprains can bleed severely and are likely to cause shock.

Some injuries are not serious enough for you to call EMS personnel but still require professional medical care. If you decide to transport the victim yourself to a medical facility, follow the general rule: "When in doubt, splint." Always splint the injury before moving the victim. If possible, have someone drive you so that you can continue to provide care. (See Chapter 2 for information on transporting a victim.)

MIND AT WORK

3. What can Rita's sister do to make her more comfortable?

4. Should her sister call EMS personnel before providing care for Rita? Why or why not?

CONSIDERATIONS FOR TRANSPORTING A VICTIM

Some musculoskeletal injuries are obviously minor and do not require professional medical care. Others are not minor and may require you to call EMS personnel. If you discover a life-threatening emergency or think it likely one might develop, call EMS personnel and wait for help. Always call EMS personnel for any injury involving severe bleeding; suspected injuries

SUMMARY

Sometimes it is difficult to tell whether an injury is a fracture, dislocation, sprain, or strain. Since you cannot be sure which type of injury a victim might have, always care for the injury as if it is serious. If EMS personnel are on the way, do not move the victim. Control any bleeding first, wearing gloves or using appropriate barriers. Take steps to minimize shock and monitor breathing and signs of circulation. If you are going to transport the victim to a medical facility, be sure to immobilize the injury before moving the victim.

Answers to Application Questions

MIND AT WORK

1. Rita could have a serious shoulder injury, possibly injuring the bones, muscles, ligaments, and tendons. She might also have injured her neck and back.

2. Rita is obviously in pain—moaning and holding her shoulder. She repeatedly hit her shoulder while falling. She seems unable to get up. She appears unable to move her left arm.

3. Help her find the most comfortable position; keep her from moving her head, neck, and back as much as possible; immobilize her upper extremity and apply ice to the injured area; pre-

vent her from becoming chilled or overheated to delay the onset of shock and keep her comfortable until EMS personnel arrive.

4. Although the injury does not appear to be life-threatening—the victim is conscious, breathing, has signs of circulation, and is not bleeding severely—Rita may well have a fracture or dislocation and could also have injured her head, neck, or back. Call EMS personnel immediately. Then make Rita as comfortable as possible, taking care not to move her head, neck, and back. Watch for signs and symptoms of shock.

Application Questions

• • • • • • • • •

Application Questions, designated with a yellow and black caution bar and a Mind at Work icon, challenge you to apply the information you have learned and build a solution. The questions are based on the scenario that appears on the chapter-opening page. These questions challenge you to apply the information you have been learning to a real-life situation. Answers to the Application Questions are found at the end of the chapter.

FACTS ABOUT HIV AND AIDS

The Disease:
AIDS stands for acquired immune deficiency syndrome. It is caused by the human immunodeficiency virus (HIV). When the virus gets into the body, it damages the immune system, the body system that fights infection. People infected with HIV may not feel or appear sick. About half the people infected with HIV develop AIDS within 10 years after becoming infected. Eventually, the weakened immune system makes the body vulnerable to certain other types of infections.

How the Disease Is Transmitted:
The virus enters the body in three basic ways:
• Through direct contact with the bloodstream. Example: Sharing a needle with an HIV-infected person to inject drugs into the veins.
• Through the mucous membranes lining body openings, such as the rectum and vagina. Example: Having sex with an HIV-infected person—male or female—without using a latex condom.
• During pregnancy or delivery, or while breastfeeding. Example: Being infected as an unborn child or shortly after birth by an HIV-infected mother.

Since 1985, all donated blood in the United States has been tested for HIV. As a result, the risk of HIV infection from a blood transfusion is very low.

Unless broken or cut, the skin helps to protect against HIV infection. There are no documented cases of HIV having been transmitted by saliva, urine, feces, vomit, or tears.

Prevention:
Your behavior may put you at risk for HIV. You greatly reduce your risk by not sharing injection drug equipment and not having oral, anal, or vaginal sex without a latex condom.

First Aid Precautions:
The likelihood of HIV transmission during a first aid situation is very low. Always give care in ways that protect you and the victim from disease transmission. If possible, use latex gloves, a resuscitation mask, or other types of barriers, and wash your hands before and after giving care. Avoid touching or being splashed by another person's body fluids, especially blood. Make sure your first aid kit contains disposable latex gloves to put on before providing care and waterless antiseptic hand cleaners to wash with afterwards.

Testing:
If you think you may be at risk for HIV infection, get tested. A blood test will tell whether your body is producing antibodies in response to the virus. If you are not sure whether you should be tested, call your doctor, the public health department, or the HIV/AIDS hot line listed below. In the meantime, do not participate in activities that put anyone else at risk.

Hot Line:
If you have questions, call the National HIV/AIDS hot line at 1-800-342-AIDS, 24 hours a day, 7 days a week, or the VIH/SIDA hot line (Spanish) at 1-800-344-7432, 8 a.m.–2 a.m., EST, 7 days a week. TTY/TDD service is available at 1-800-243-7TTY, Monday–Friday, 10 a.m.–10 p.m., EST, or call your state health department.

TO LEARN MORE ABOUT HIV/AIDS,
CO...
AMERICA...

Sidebars

Feature articles called sidebars enhance the information in the main body of the text. They appear in most chapters and are easily recognizable because of their stylized icons. They present historical and current information and events that relate to the chapter content. You will not be tested on any information presented in these sidebars as part of the American Red Cross course completion requirements.

Tables

Tables, on a yellow background, are included in many chapters. They concisely summarize important concepts and information and may aid in studying.

TABLE 16-1

Caring for Bites and Stings

Insect Bites and Stings	Tick Bites	Spider Bites	Scorpion Stings	Snakebites	Marine Life Stings	Domestic and Wild Animal Bites	Human Bites
Signs and Symptoms:	**Signs and Symptoms:**	**Signs and Symptoms:**	**Signs and Symptoms:**	**Signs and Symptoms:**	**Signs and Symptoms:**	**Signs and Symptoms:**	**Signs and Symptoms:**
Stinger may be present	Bull's eye, spotted, or black and blue rash around bite or on other body parts	Bite mark or blister	Bite mark	Bite mark	Possible marks	Bite mark	Bite mark
Pain		Pain or cramping	Local swelling	Severe pain and burning	Pain	Bleeding	Bleeding
Local swelling	Fever and chills	Nausea and vomiting	Pain or cramping	Local swelling and discoloration	Local swelling	Pain	Pain
Hives or rash	Flulike aches	Difficulty breathing and swallowing	Nausea and vomiting				
Nausea and vomiting		Profuse sweating or salivation	Difficulty breathing or swallowing				
Breathing difficulty		Irregular heartbeat	Profuse sweating or salivation				
			Irregular heartbeat				
Care:	**Care:**	**Care:**	**Care:**	**Care:**	**Care:**	**Care:**	**Care:**
Remove stinger; scrape it away with card or knife	Remove tick with tweezers	If black widow or brown recluse—call EMS personnel immediately to receive antivenin and have wound cleaned	Wash wound	Wash wound	If jellyfish—soak area in either vinegar, alcohol, or baking soda paste	If wound is minor—wash wound, control bleeding, apply a dressing, and get medical attention as soon as possible	If wound is minor—wash wound, control bleeding, apply a dressing, and get medical attention as soon as possible
Wash wound	Apply antiseptic and antibiotic ointment to wound		Apply a cold pack	Immobilize bitten part and keep it lower than the heart	If stingray—immobilize and soak area in nonscalding hot water until pain goes away.	If wound is severe—call EMS personnel or local emergency number, control bleeding, and do not wash wound	If wound is severe—call EMS personnel or local emergency number, control bleeding, and do not wash wound
Cover wound	Watch for signs of infection		Get medical care to receive antivenin	Call EMS personnel or local emergency number	Clean and bandage wound		
Apply a cold pack	Get medical attention if necessary		Call EMS personnel or local emergency number	Minimize victim's movement	Call EMS personnel or local emergency number, if necessary		
Watch for signs and symptoms of allergic reactions; take steps to minimize shock if they occur							

335

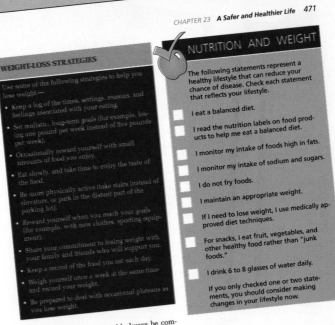

CHAPTER 23   A Safer and Healthier Life   471

WEIGHT-LOSS STRATEGIES

Use some of the following strategies to help you lose weight—

- Keep a log of the times, settings, reasons, and feelings associated with your eating.
- Set realistic, long-term goals (for example, losing one pound per week instead of five pounds per week).
- Occasionally reward yourself with small amounts of food you enjoy.
- Eat slowly, and take time to enjoy the taste of the food.
- Be more physically active (take stairs instead of elevators, or park in the distant part of the parking lot).
- Reward yourself when you reach your goals (for example, with new clothes, sporting equipment).
- Share your commitment to losing weight with your family and friends who will support you.
- Keep a record of the food you eat each day.
- Weigh yourself once a week at the same time and record your weight.
- Be prepared to deal with occasional plateaus as you lose weight.

NUTRITION AND WEIGHT

The following statements represent a healthy lifestyle that can reduce your chance of disease. Check each statement that reflects your lifestyle.

☐ I eat a balanced diet.

☐ I read the nutrition labels on food products to help me eat a balanced diet.

☐ I monitor my intake of foods high in fats.

☐ I monitor my intake of sodium and sugars.

☐ I do not fry foods.

☐ I maintain an appropriate weight.

☐ If I need to lose weight, I use medically approved diet techniques.

☐ For snacks, I eat fruit, vegetables, and other healthy food rather than "junk foods."

☐ I drink 6 to 8 glasses of water daily.

If you only checked one or two statements, you should consider making changes in your lifestyle now.

Weight loss or gain should always be combined with regular exercise—another part of a healthy lifestyle. Any activity—walking to the bus, climbing the stairs, cleaning house—uses calories. You even burn off a few while you sleep. The more active you are, the more calories you use. Activity allows you to eat a few more calories and still maintain body weight.

Your eating habits should change as you grow older. A person who eats the same number of calories between the ages of 20 to 40 and maintains the same level of activity during this time will be considerably heavier at 40 than at ... It is more important as you grow older to eat ...

Fitness

Many of us would like to be more fit. In general, fitness involves cardiorespiratory endurance, muscular strength, muscular endurance, and flexibility. You do not need to take part in sports, such as tennis, basketball, or soccer, to achieve health-related fitness. You can achieve fitness for health purposes by taking part in such activities as walking, jogging, swimming, cycling, hiking, and weight training, among others.

Exercise

... pain, no gain" theory is not a good ... exercise. In fact, experiencing pain ... ns you are exercising improperly. ... the health benefits of exercise ... somewhat uncomfortable, but not

---

Boxes

Boxes contain information that may be useful or of interest to you. They appear throughout the textbook.

Health Check Box

Health Check Boxes are easily recognizable because of their apple icon. They provide you with an opportunity to assess your understanding and practice of healthy behaviors.

CHAPTER 1   Help Can't Wait   19

STUDY QUESTIONS

1. Match each term with the correct definition.

    a. Citizen responder   d. Rehabilitation
    b. First responder   e. Hospital care providers
    c. EMT-Paramedic   f. EMS dispatcher

    _____ Often the first person on the scene trained to provide a higher level of emergency care, such as a law enforcement officer, fire fighter, or lifeguard.

    _____ The "eyes and ears" of the physician at an emergency scene; provides the highest level of out-of-hospital care, such as administering medications or intravenous fluids.

    _____ The staff that assume responsibility for the care of the injured or ill person while in the hospital.

    _____ The person who receives the call for help and determines what help is needed at the scene.

    _____ The process of returning the victim to his or her previous state of health.

    _____ Someone who recognizes an emergency and decides to act; the first link in the chain of survival.

2. Using all of the terms in Question 1, organize the six links of the EMS system components in the most effective order.

    a.

    b.

    c.

    d.

    e.

    f.

3. What potential indicators of an emergency do you find in each scenario that follows? Circle the five indicators.

    a. *I was fixing sandwiches and talking with Mrs. Roberts from next door, who had come by to borrow a book. Three-year-old Jenny was in the next room playing with some puzzles and singing to herself. As Mrs. Roberts got up to leave, I realized that I wasn't hearing any sounds. "Jenny," I called. No answer. I called louder. Nothing. I went into the room, but Jenny wasn't there. Suddenly, I heard a loud thump and a shriek from upstairs.*

Study Questions

At the end of each chapter are a series of Study Questions designed to test your retention and understanding of the chapter content. Completing these questions will help you evaluate how well you understand the material and also help you prepare for the final written examination. The answers to Study Questions are found in Appendix A of the text. Write the answers in your textbook and use additional paper, if necessary.

Skill Sheets

Learning specific skills that you will need to provide appropriate care for victims of sudden illness or injury is an important part of this course. Illustrated skill sheets at the end of certain chapters give step-by-step directions for performing specific skills. ● ● ● ● ● ● ● ● ● ● ● ● ● ● ➤

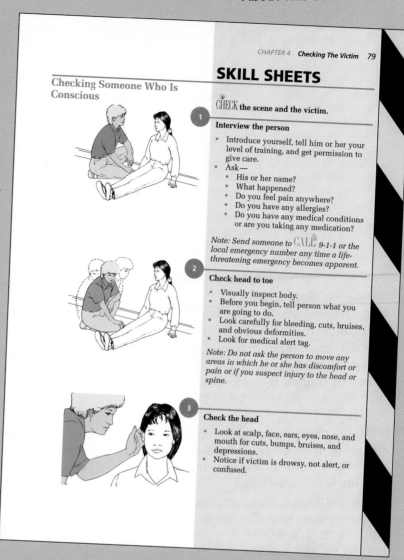

CHAPTER 4 *Checking The Victim* 79

SKILL SHEETS

Checking Someone Who Is Conscious

CHECK the scene and the victim.

1

Interview the person

• Introduce yourself, tell him or her your level of training, and get permission to give care.
• Ask—
  • His or her name?
  • What happened?
  • Do you feel pain anywhere?
  • Do you have any allergies?
  • Do you have any medical conditions or are you taking any medication?

Note: Send someone to CALL 9-1-1 or the local emergency number any time a life-threatening emergency becomes apparent.

2

Check head to toe

• Visually inspect body.
• Before you begin, tell person what you are going to do.
• Look carefully for bleeding, cuts, bruises, and obvious deformities.
• Look for medical alert tag.

Note: Do not ask the person to move any areas in which he or she has discomfort or pain or if you suspect injury to the head or spine.

3

Check the head

• Look at scalp, face, ears, eyes, nose, and mouth for cuts, bumps, bruises, and depressions.
• Notice if victim is drowsy, not alert, or confused.

HOW TO USE THIS TEXTBOOK

You should complete the following five steps for each chapter to gain the most from this course:

1. Read the chapter objectives before reading the chapter.
2. As you read the chapter, keep the objectives in mind. When you finish, go back and review the objectives. Check to see that you can meet them without difficulty.
3. Review figures and illustrations. Read captions and labels.
4. Answer the Application Questions as you read the chapter. Check your answers with those at the end of the chapter. If you cannot answer or do not understand the answers given, ask your instructor to help you with concepts or questions with which you are having difficulty.

5. Answer the Study Questions at the end of each chapter. Mark or write your answers in the text to facilitate your review or study. Answer as many questions as you can without referring to the chapter. Then review the information covering any questions you were unable to answer, and try them again. Check your responses to the questions with the answers in Appendix A. If you have not answered a question appropriately, reread that part of the chapter to ensure that you understand why the answer is correct. This exercise will help you gauge how much information you are retaining and which areas you need to review. If, after rereading that part of the chapter, you still do not understand, ask your instructor to help you.

HEALTH PRECAUTIONS AND GUIDELINES DURING FIRST AID TRAINING

The American Red Cross has trained millions of people in first aid and CPR (cardiopulmonary resuscitation) using manikins as training aids. According to the Centers for Disease Control (CDC), there has never been a documented case of any disease caused by bacteria, a fungus, or a virus transmitted through the use of training aids, such as manikins used for CPR.

The Red Cross follows widely accepted guidelines for cleaning and decontaminating training manikins. **If these guidelines are adhered to, the risk of any kind of disease transmission during training is extremely low.**

To help minimize the risk of disease transmission, you should follow some basic precautions and guidelines while participating in training. You should take precautions if you have a condition that would increase your risk or other participants' risk of exposure to infections. Request a separate training manikin if you—

- Have an acute condition, such as a cold, a sore throat, or cuts or sores on the hands or around your mouth.
- Know you are seropositive (have had a positive blood test) for hepatitis B surface antigen (HBsAg), indicating that you are currently infected with the hepatitis B virus.
- Know you have a chronic infection indicated by long-term seropositivity (long-term positive blood tests) for the hepatitis B surface antigen (HBsAg)* or a positive blood test for anti-HIV (that is, a positive test for antibodies to HIV, the virus that causes many severe infections including AIDS).
- Have a type of condition that makes you unusually likely to get an infection.

If you decide you should have your own manikin, ask your instructor if he or she can provide one for you to use. You will not be asked to explain why in your request. The manikin will not be used by anyone else until it has been cleaned according to the recommended end-of-class decontamination procedures. Because the number of manikins available for class is limited, the more advance notice you give, the more likely it is that you can be provided a separate manikin.

GUIDELINES

In addition to taking the precautions regarding manikins, you can further protect yourself and other participants from infection by following these guidelines:

- Wash your hands thoroughly before participating in class activities.
- Do not eat, drink, use tobacco products, or chew gum during classes when manikins are used.

* A person with hepatitis B infection will test positive for the hepatitis B surface antigen (HBsAg). Most persons infected with hepatitis B will get better within a period of time. However, some hepatitis B infections will become chronic and will linger for much longer. These persons will continue to test positive for HBsAg. Their decision to participate in CPR training should be guided by their physician.

After a person has had an acute hepatitis B infection, he or she will no longer test positive for the surface antigen but will test positive for the hepatitis B antibody (anti-HBs). Persons who have been vaccinated for hepatitis B will also test positive for the hepatitis antibody. A positive test for the hepatitis B antibody (anti-HBs) should not be confused with a positive test for the hepatitis B surface antigen (HBsAg).

- Clean the manikin properly before use. For some manikins, this means vigorously wiping the manikin's face and the inside of its mouth with a clean gauze pad soaked with either a solution of liquid chlorine bleach and water (sodium hypochlorite and water) or rubbing alcohol. For other manikins, it means changing the rubber face. Your instructor will provide you with instructions for cleaning the type of manikin used in your class.

- Follow the guidelines provided by your instructor when practicing skills such as clearing a blocked airway with your finger.

PHYSICAL STRESS AND INJURY

Training in first aid and CPR requires physical activity. If you have a medical condition or disability that will prevent you from taking part in the practice sessions, please let your instructor know.

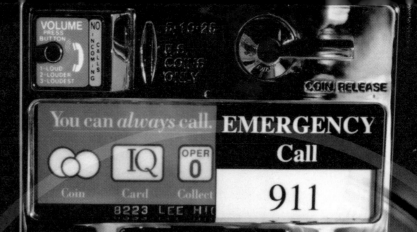

PART ONE

INTRODUCTION

*H*elp Can't Wait

WHAT YOU SHOULD LEARN

After reading this chapter, you should be able to—

1. Identify the six parts of the EMS system.

2. Describe the function of each part of the EMS system.

3. Describe your role in the EMS system.

4. Identify the most important action you can take in a life-threatening emergency.

5. List the five common barriers to action that may prevent people from responding to emergencies.

6. Identify seven ways bystanders can help at the scene of an emergency.

7. Define the four conditions that have to be present for a disease to be transmitted in a first aid situation.

8. Define the key terms for this chapter.

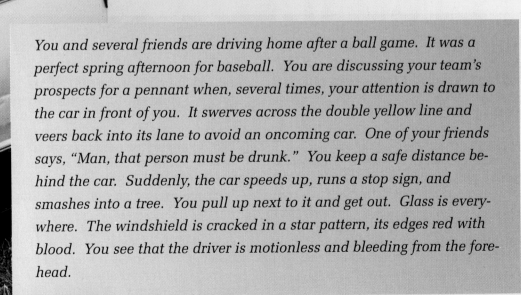

You and several friends are driving home after a ball game. It was a perfect spring afternoon for baseball. You are discussing your team's prospects for a pennant when, several times, your attention is drawn to the car in front of you. It swerves across the double yellow line and veers back into its lane to avoid an oncoming car. One of your friends says, "Man, that person must be drunk." You keep a safe distance behind the car. Suddenly, the car speeds up, runs a stop sign, and smashes into a tree. You pull up next to it and get out. Glass is everywhere. The windshield is cracked in a star pattern, its edges red with blood. You see that the driver is motionless and bleeding from the forehead.

Introduction

An emergency can happen at any time or at any place. An *emergency* is a situation demanding immediate action. The goal of this course is to train you in the basics of first aid that will help you recognize and respond to any emergency appropriately. Your response may help save a life.

THE CITIZEN RESPONDER AND THE EMS SYSTEM

The *emergency medical services (EMS) system* is a network of community resources and medical personnel that provides emergency care to victims of injury or sudden illness. Think of the EMS system as a chain made up of several links. Each link depends on the others for success. When the EMS system works correctly, a victim moves through each link in the chain, beginning with the actions of a responsible citizen and ending with care being provided to attempt to restore the victim to health (Fig. 1-1).

The Citizen Responder

As a citizen responder, you are the first and most crucial link in the EMS system. The *citizen responder* is someone who recognizes an emergency and decides to help. Ideally, everyone would know first aid. *First aid* is the immediate care given to a victim of injury or sudden illness until more advanced care can be obtained. But even if not trained in first aid, the citizen responder can provide critical help in any emergency.

The citizen responder must first recognize that the illness or injury that has occurred is an emergency. He or she must then activate the EMS system, either by dialing 9-1-1 or a local emergency number or by notifying a bystander or a nearby first responder, such as a police officer. The sooner someone activates the EMS system, the sooner more advanced medical help arrives, increasing the victim's chance of survival and recovery.

The EMS Dispatcher

The second link in the EMS system is the dispatcher who works in an emergency communi-

Key Terms

Citizen responder: A layperson (someone who does not have special or advanced medical training or skill) who recognizes an emergency and decides to help.

Emergency: A situation requiring immediate action.

Emergency medical services (EMS) professionals: Trained and equipped community-based personnel often dispatched through a local emergency number who provide emergency care for ill or injured victims.

Emergency medical services (EMS) system: A network of community resources and medical personnel that provides emergency care to victims of injury or sudden illness.

Emergency medical technician (EMT): A person who has successfully completed a state-approved emergency medical technician training program. The different levels of EMTs include the EMT-Basic and EMT-Paramedic.

First aid: Immediate care given to a victim of injury or sudden illness until more advanced care can be obtained.

First responder: A person trained in emergency care who may be called upon to provide such care as a routine part of his or her job.

Good Samaritan laws: Laws that protect people who willingly give first aid without accepting anything in return.

Injury: Damage that occurs when the body is subjected to an external force, such as a blow, a fall, a collision, an electrical current, or to extremes of temperature.

Medical emergency: A sudden illness requiring immediate medical attention.

Pathogen (PATH ă jen): A disease-causing agent; also called a microorganism or germ.

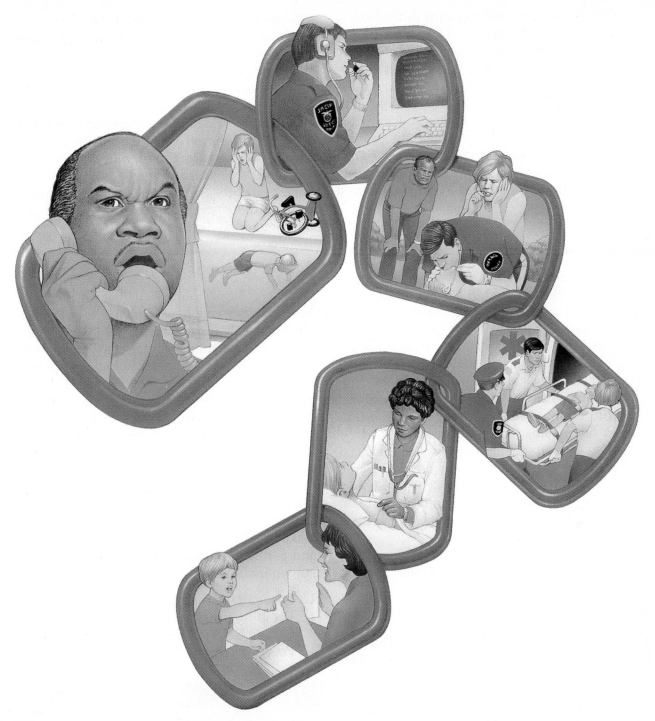

Figure 1-1 The EMS system is a network of community resources that provide emergency care.

cations center. The dispatcher receives the call and quickly determines what help is needed. He or she then dispatches the appropriate professionals. Some dispatchers are trained to give the caller instructions about how to help until EMS personnel arrive.

The First Responder

The first responder is the third link in the EMS system. The ***first responder*** is usually the first person to arrive on the scene who is trained to provide a higher level of care. First responders are often the first people you turn to for help at the scene of an emergency. They may be fire fighters, law enforcement officers, lifeguards, industrial safety officers, or people with similar responsibility for the safety or well-being of the community. Because of the nature of their jobs, they are often close to the scene and have the necessary supplies and equipment to provide care. First responders provide a critical transition between a citizen responder's basic level of care and the care provided by more advanced EMS professionals.

The Emergency Medical Technician (EMT)

The **emergency medical technician (EMT)** is the fourth link in the EMS system. Depending on the level of training and certification, the EMT is capable of providing more advanced emergency care and life-support techniques. In most of the United States, ambulance personnel are certified at least at the EMT-Basic level.

EMT-Paramedics are highly specialized EMTs. In addition to performing basic life-support skills, paramedics can administer medications and intravenous fluids, provide advanced airway care, and perform other advanced lifesaving techniques. They are trained to handle a wider range of conditions. Paramedics function at the highest level of out-of-hospital care. At the scene of the emergency, they serve as the "eyes and ears" of the hospital emergency physician through direct phone or radio contact.

Hospital Care Providers

The first four links of the EMS system give victims of injury or sudden illness the best possible out-of-hospital medical care. The fifth link of the EMS system, **hospital care providers,** begins once the victim arrives at a hospital or other medical facility and the emergency department staff take over care. Many different professionals, including emergency physicians, nurses, and other health care professionals, then become involved as needed.

Rehabilitation

The sixth and final link of the EMS system is **rehabilitation.** The goal of rehabilitation is to return the victim to his or her previous state of health. After the victim has been moved from the emergency department, other health care professionals work together to treat and rehabilitate the victim. These professionals include family physicians, consulting specialists, social workers, and physical therapists.

The six parts of the EMS system are linked together like a chain—a chain of survival for the victim. The stronger the chain, the better the chance that a victim of injury or sudden illness will be returned to his or her previous state of health. All the links should connect to provide the best possible care to victims of injury or sudden illness.

Your Role in the EMS System

Once you have recognized that an emergency has occurred and have decided to act, calling emergency medical services (EMS) professionals is the most important action you and other citizen responders can take. **Emergency medical services professionals** are trained and equipped to provide emergency care. Early arrival of EMS personnel increases the victim's chances of surviving a life-threatening emergency. Without the involvement of citizen responders, the EMS system cannot function effectively. Furthermore, a citizen responder trained in first aid can give help in the first few minutes of an emergency that can save a life or make the difference between complete recovery and permanent **disability.** Your role in the EMS system includes—

1. Recognizing that an emergency exists.
2. Deciding to act.
3. Calling EMS professionals.
4. Providing first aid until help arrives.

> **MIND AT WORK**
>
> 1. As citizen responders, what immediate steps could you and your friends who witnessed the car crash take?

RECOGNIZING EMERGENCIES

Recognizing an **emergency** is the first step in responding. A **medical emergency** is a sudden illness that requires immediate medical attention, such as a heart attack. An **injury** is damage to the body from an external force, for example, such as occurs with a fall or extremes of temperature. Some injuries can be serious enough to be considered emergencies. Emergencies can happen to anyone—a friend, family member, stranger, or you. They can happen anywhere—on the road, or at home, work, or play. Some emergencies are more obvious than others. You may become aware of an emergency from certain indicators. Common indicators include unusual noises, sights, odors, and appearance or behavior (Table 1-1).

Unusual Noises

Noises are often the first indicators that call your attention to an emergency. Some noises that may indicate an emergency include—

- Noises that indicate someone is in distress, such as screaming, yelling, moaning, crying, and calling for help, or silence when there should be noise.
- Alarming, often recognizable noises, such as breaking glass, crashing metal, screeching tires.
- Abrupt or loud noises that are not identifiable, such as collapsing structures or falling ladders.

Unusual Sights

Unusual sights that indicate a possible emergency can go unnoticed by the unaware observer (Fig. 1-2, *A-D*). Examples of sights that may indicate an emergency include—

- A stopped vehicle on the roadside, especially in an unusual position.
- An overturned pot on the kitchen floor.
- A spilled medicine container.
- Downed electrical wires.
- Sparks, smoke, or fire.

Unusual Odors

Many odors are part of our everyday lives, such as gasoline fumes at gas stations, the smell of

A

B

C

D

Figure 1-2   **A-D,** Unusual sights may indicate an emergency.

Figure 1-3 Unusual appearance may indicate an emergency.

chlorine at swimming pools, or smoke from a bonfire. However, when these and other odors are stronger than usual, not easily identifiable, or otherwise seem inappropriate, they may indicate an emergency. Always put your own safety first if you are in a situation in which you smell an unusual or very strong odor, since many fumes are poisonous. An unusual odor on a person's breath may also be a clue to an emergency situation. A person experiencing a diabetic emergency, for example, may have a characteristic breath odor that can be mistaken for the smell of alcohol. You will learn about diabetic emergencies in Chapter 14.

Unusual Appearance or Behavior

It may be difficult to tell if someone's appearance or behavior is unusual, particularly if he or she is a stranger. However, certain behaviors or appearances could indicate an emergency (Fig. 1-3). For example, if you see someone collapse to the floor, he or she obviously requires your immediate attention. You will not know if your help is needed, however, until you approach the person. He or she may merely have

slipped. On the other hand, the person may be unconscious and need immediate medical assistance. Other behaviors and appearances that could indicate an emergency may be less obvious. They include—

- Breathing difficulty.
- Clutching the chest or throat.
- Slurred, confused, or hesitant speech.
- Confused or unusual behavior.
- Sweating for no apparent reason.
- Uncharacteristic skin color—pale, flushed, or bluish skin.
- Inability to move a body part.

TABLE 1-1	
Recognizing Emergencies	
Emergency Indicators	Signals
Unusual noises	Screams, yells, moans, or calls for help Breaking glass, crashing metal, screeching tires Abrupt or loud unidentifiable sounds, silence
Unusual sights	Things that look out of the ordinary— A stalled vehicle An overturned pot A spilled medicine container Broken glass Downed electrical wires
Unusual odors	Odors that are stronger than usual Unrecognizable odors
Unusual appearance or behavior	Unconsciousness Difficulty breathing Clutching the chest or throat Slurred, confused, or hesitant speech Unexplainable confusion or drowsiness Sweating for no apparent reason Uncharacteristic skin color

These and other appearances and behaviors may occur alone or together. For example, a heart attack may be indicated by chest pain alone, or chest pain may be accompanied by sweating and breathing difficulty.

DECIDING TO ACT

You have already learned that citizen involvement is crucial in an emergency situation. Every year, countless people recognize and respond to emergencies. Some phone for help, some comfort the victim or family members, some give first aid to victims, and still others help keep order at the emergency scene. People can help in many ways. *But in order to help, you must act.*

Figure 1-4 Bystanders can help you respond to emergencies.

Barriers to Action

Sometimes people simply do not recognize that an emergency has occurred. At other times, people recognize an emergency but are reluctant to act. People have various personal reasons for hesitating or not acting. These reasons are called barriers to action. Common reasons people give for not acting include—

- The presence of bystanders.
- Uncertainty about the victim.
- The nature of the injury or illness.
- Fear of disease transmission.
- Fear of not knowing what to do or of doing something wrong.

Thinking about these things now and mentally preparing yourself will help you to respond more confidently in an actual emergency.

Presence of bystanders

Bystanders can cause confusion at an emergency scene. It may not be easy to tell if anyone is providing first aid. Always ask if help is needed. Do not assume, just because a crowd has gathered, that someone is caring for the victim. You may feel embarrassed about coming forward in front of strangers. Do not let this feeling deter you from offering help when needed. You may be the only one at the scene who knows first aid. If someone else is already giving care, offer to help.

Ensure that the crowd do not endanger themselves or the victim. Sometimes you may need to ask bystanders who are not helping to back away and give the victim and rescuers ample space. Bystanders, however, can be of great help in an emergency (Fig. 1-4). You can ask them to call for an ambulance, meet and direct the ambulance, keep the area free of unnecessary traffic, or help you give first aid. You can instruct bystanders who are willing to help to perform the necessary techniques or help you perform them. You might send them for blankets or other supplies. Bystanders may have valuable information about what happened or the location of the nearest phone. A friend or family member who is present may know if the victim has a medical condition. Bystanders can also help comfort the victim and others at the scene.

Uncertainty about the victim

Since most emergencies happen in or near the home, you are more likely to give care to a friend or family member than to a stranger (Fig. 1-5, p. 12). However, this is not always the case. You may not know the victim and may feel uncomfortable with the idea of touching a stranger. Sometimes you may hesitate to act because the victim may be much older or younger than you, be a different gender or race, not speak English or the same language you speak,

Honoring Our Heroes:
The Red Cross's Certificate of Merit

March 3, 1994 seemed like any ordinary day at the Child Development Center in Traveler's Rest, South Carolina. Parents arrived early in the morning to drop off their children on their way to work. One little boy, age 9 months, had a slight fever, but his mother thought he just had the sniffles. Shortly after she left, however, the staff of the day-care center noticed his fever was worsening. As they thought about calling the child's mother, the baby's fever suddenly spiked to 104 degrees F and, as the staff watched in horror, the little boy stopped breathing. Panicked and shaking, one staff member scooped the boy into her arms and carried the limp, feverish child into director Ann Vaughn's office.

Ms. Vaughn quickly assessed the situation using the skills she learned in a Red Cross course. She determined that he wasn't breathing, so she started rescue breathing. After a few puffs of air, the child revived. EMS arrived shortly thereafter and transported the baby to the hospital.

The baby whom Ms. Vaughn saved is now almost 3 years old and is still coming to the day-care center. For her lifesaving efforts, the Red Cross honored Ms. Vaughn with the Certificate of Merit. Recalling that fateful day in March, Ms. Vaughn says, "At the time it was frightening, but I just did what I had to do."

The Certificate of Merit is the American Red Cross's highest honor that it awards to citizens. The Red Cross confers this certificate on individuals not part of the community's ordinary emergency medical system who save or sustain a victim's life with skills learned in a Red Cross Health and Safety course.

Although the survival of the victim is not a criterion for eligibility for the award, nominees for the award must have performed every possible lifesaving skill prior to the victim's receiving medical care. Sometimes team certificates are awarded. In this case, each member of the team must contribute directly to the lifesaving act.

The Certificate of Merit program began in 1911 and was originally a cash award given annually to four railway workers who performed first aid. The next year, in 1912, the Red Cross decided to recognize four individuals from the general public who performed exemplary first aid skills. In 1915, water safety skills and rescues were included in the certificate criteria. From 1912 to 1925, the Red Cross gave cash awards to 66 individuals.

In 1928, the Red Cross reevaluated its cash award program. Because the cash awards could be given only to a few individuals a year and because the rescuers did not receive any lasting reminder of the award, the Red Cross decided to eliminate the cash award and institute the present-day Certificate of Merit. The certificate is signed by the President of the United States, who is also the honorary chairman of the American Red Cross (a tradition begun in 1913 by William Howard Taft), and often awarded in a local ceremony. Over 12,000 individuals have received a Certificate of Merit since 1911.

What kinds of people receive Certificates of Merit? A brief scan of the list of honored individuals for the past year reveals that honorees come from all walks of life, are of all ages, from 4 to 76, and perform their life-

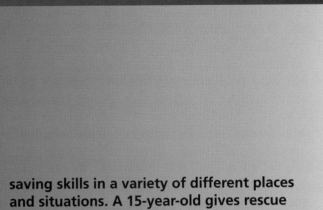

saving skills in a variety of different places and situations. A 15-year-old gives rescue breathing to her father, who suffers a stroke at home. A day-care worker gives abdominal thrusts to a 5-year-old who is choking on food during lunch. A woman controls bleeding, manages for shock, and monitors breathing and signs of circulation for a victim of a gas station stabbing. During a water emergency, a man frees a companion from underneath an overturned canoe, splints the victim's broken leg, provides care for hypothermia, and manages for shock.

Perhaps the one common element in all these cases is that the rescuer provided life-saving skills in an emotionally charged situation. These individuals demonstrate that life-sustaining first aid care can be rendered even when the emergency threatens the life of a loved one, a child, or a badly injured stranger. A Red Cross training course can give you the practical skills you need to help a person in danger and can equip you to handle an emergency even when you are frightened or panicked.

"Doing what you have to do," as Ms. Vaughn says, can mean the difference between life and death. And the Certificate of Merit provides proof that many people, just like you and me, save lives every day.

have a disabling condition, or be a crime victim.

Sometimes victims of injury or sudden illness may act strangely or be uncooperative. The injury or illness, stress, or other factors, such as the influence of alcohol or other substances, may make people act offensively. Do not take such behavior personally. Remember, an emergency can cause even the nicest person to be angry or unpleasant. If the victim's attitude or behavior keeps you from caring for him or her, you can still help. Make sure the EMS system has been activated, manage bystanders, and attempt to reassure the victim. If at any time the victim's behavior becomes a threat to you, withdraw from the immediate area.

Nature of the injury or illness

An injury or illness may sometimes be very unpleasant to handle. The presence of blood, vomit, unpleasant odors, or torn or burned skin is disturbing to almost everyone. You cannot predict how you will respond to these and other factors in an emergency. Sometimes you may need to compose yourself before acting. If you must, turn away for a moment and take a few deep breaths. Then provide care. Remember that this situation is an emergency—help can't wait. If, however, you are still unable to provide first aid because of the appearance of the injury, you can help in other ways. You can ensure your safety and the safety of victims and bystanders, call for EMS personnel, reassure the victim, and manage bystanders.

Fear of disease transmission

Professional rescuers and citizen responders alike are increasingly concerned about contracting a disease while giving emergency care. But although diseases can be transmitted in a first aid situation, the actual risk is far smaller than you may think.

Giving first aid in and of itself will not cause you to become infected with a disease. All of the following conditions have to be present for you to become infected:

- The injured or ill person must be infected with a disease.
- The rescuer providing first aid must be exposed to an infected person's body substances, such as blood, saliva, vomit, urine,

*take your time & do it right

Figure 1-5   You may need to respond to an emergency involving someone whom you do not know.

feces, and infected airborne droplets from a cough or sneeze.

- The rescuer must come in contact with infected body substances through breaks or cuts in his or her skin or through the mucous membranes of the mouth or eyes.
- There must be a sufficient amount of body substances that contain enough *pathogens,*

disease-causing microorganisms, to cause infection.

If any one of these conditions is absent, disease transmission is not possible (Fig. 1-6). In some instances, you may know the person's health status and be aware of risks of infection. You may find yourself in an emergency situation, however, in which you do not know what risks of infection may exist. Although you should take steps to protect yourself against the possibility of disease transmission, you should also act to reduce the risk of disease transmission from you to the victim. Assume that all emergency situations that involve contact with body substances have a potential for disease transmission between the victim and rescuer. Examples of such situations are those that require controlling bleeding or when an ill or injured person has vomited.

Preventing disease transmission

Diseases that can pass from one person to another are called infectious diseases and develop when pathogens invade the body. **Bacteria** and **viruses,** the most common pathogens that cause disease, do so by infecting cells and damaging or destroying them. When enough cells are damaged or destroyed to disrupt

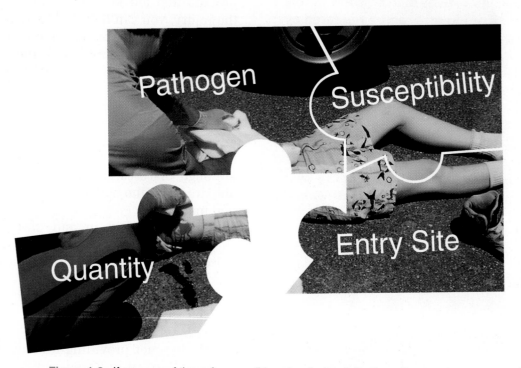

Figure 1-6   If any one of these four conditions is missing, infection will not occur.

FACTS ABOUT HIV AND AIDS

The Disease:
AIDS stands for acquired immune deficiency syndrome. It is caused by the human immunodeficiency virus (HIV). When the virus gets into the body, it damages the immune system, the body system that fights infection. People infected with HIV may not feel or appear sick. About half the people infected with HIV develop AIDS within 10 years after becoming infected. Eventually, the weakened immune system makes the body vulnerable to certain other types of infections.

How the Disease Is Transmitted:
The virus enters the body in three basic ways:
• Through direct contact with the bloodstream. Example: Sharing a needle with an HIV-infected person to inject drugs into the veins.
• Through the mucous membranes lining body openings, such as the rectum and vagina. Example: Having sex with an HIV-infected person—male or female—without using a latex condom.
• During pregnancy or delivery, or while breast-feeding. Example: Being infected as an unborn child or shortly after birth by an HIV-infected mother.

Since 1985, all donated blood in the United States has been tested for HIV. As a result, the risk of HIV infection from a blood transfusion is very low.

Unless broken or cut, the skin helps to protect against HIV infection. There are no documented cases of HIV having been transmitted by saliva, urine, feces, vomit, or tears.

Prevention:
Your behavior may put you at risk for HIV. You greatly reduce your risk by not sharing injection drug equipment and not having oral, anal, or vaginal sex without a latex condom.

First Aid Precautions:
The likelihood of HIV transmission during a first aid situation is very low. Always give care in ways that protect you and the victim from disease transmission. If possible, use latex gloves, a resuscitation mask, or other types of barriers, and wash your hands before and after giving care. Avoid touching or being splashed by another person's body fluids, especially blood. Make sure your first aid kit contains disposable latex gloves to put on before providing care and waterless antiseptic hand cleaners to wash with afterwards.

Testing:
If you think you may be at risk for HIV infection, get tested. A blood test will tell whether your body is producing antibodies in response to the virus. If you are not sure whether you should be tested, call your doctor, the public health department, or the HIV/AIDS hot line listed below. In the meantime, do not participate in activities that put anyone else at risk.

Hot Line:
If you have questions, call the National HIV/AIDS hot line at 1-800-342-AIDS, 24 hours a day, 7 days a week, or the VIH/SIDA hot line (Spanish) at 1-800-344-7432, 8 a.m.–2 a.m., EST, 7 days a week. TTY/TDD service is available at 1-800-243-7TTY, Monday–Friday, 10 a.m.–10 p.m., EST, or call your state health department.

TO LEARN MORE ABOUT HIV/AIDS, CONTACT YOUR LOCAL AMERICAN RED CROSS CHAPTER.

the body's vital functions, serious illness can result.

Many bacteria can live outside the body and do not depend on other organisms for life. The number of bacteria that infect humans is very small, but some can cause serious infections. These infections can be treated, however, with medications called antibiotics. Viruses depend on other organisms to live. Since few medications are effective against viruses, the immune system, the body system that protects against infection, is the major protection against viral infection.

In situations that require first aid, diseases can be transmitted by touching, breathing, and biting. If you touch an infected person's blood or other body substances, such as saliva, urine, or feces, and the pathogens in that person's blood or other body substances pass into your body, you can become infected (Fig. 1-7, *A*). Pathogens can pass into the body through breaks or cuts in the skin and the **mucous membranes** of the eyes, nose, and mouth. You can also be infected if you touch an object that has been soiled by the blood or other body substance of an infected person (Fig. 1-7, *B*).

Airborne infection can occur when an infected person sneezes or coughs and the pathogens are inhaled by another person (Fig. 1-7, *C*). Most of us are exposed to such pathogens every day in our jobs, on the bus, or in a crowded restaurant. Fortunately, exposure to these pathogens is usually not adequate contact for a disease to be transmitted. Furthermore, the diseases that are most likely to pass from one person to another through airborne infection, such as the common cold, are generally not life threatening.

American Mosquito Control Association

Figure 1-7 **A,** Direct contact transmission, **B,** indirect contact transmission, **C,** airborne transmission, and **D,** vector transmission are the four ways pathogens can enter the body.

Animals and insects can pass diseases through bites (Fig. 1-7, *D*). Infected dogs, cats, cattle, foxes, and other animals, both wild and domestic, can transmit rabies. In a first aid situation, however, it is unlikely you will be bitten.

When a break or tear in the skin causes bleeding, both the rescuer and the victim are exposed to the risk of disease transmission. Both the hepatitis B virus (HBV) and the human immunodeficiency virus (HIV), which causes AIDS, are transmitted through blood-to-blood contact. By following some basic guidelines, however, you can help reduce the possi- bility of disease transmission when giving first aid. These guidelines are described in Chapter 4.

Fear of not knowing what to do or of doing something wrong

We all respond to emergencies in different ways. Whether we are trained or untrained, some of us are afraid we will do the wrong thing and make the situation worse. If you are unsure about what to do, call 9-1-1 or the local emergency number. *The worst thing to do is nothing.*

What Everyone Should Know about
GOOD SAMARITAN LAWS

What laws protect you when you help in an emergency situation?

Most states have enacted Good Samaritan laws. These laws give legal protection to people who willingly provide emergency care to ill or injured persons without accepting anything in return.

When citizens respond to an emergency and act as a reasonable and prudent person would under the same conditions, Good Samaritan immunity generally prevails. This legal immunity protects you, as a rescuer, from being sued and found financially responsible for the victim's injury. For example, a reasonable and prudent person would—

- Move a victim only if the victim's life was endangered.
- Check the victim for life-threatening emergencies before providing further care.
- Summon professional help to the scene by calling 9-1-1 or the local emergency number.
- Ask a conscious victim for permission before giving care.
- Provide care only to the level of his or her training.

- Continue to provide care until more highly trained personnel arrive.

Good Samaritan laws were enacted to encourage people to help others in emergency situations. They require that the "Good Samaritan" use common sense and a reasonable level of skill, not to exceed the scope of the individual's training in emergency situations. They assume each person would do his or her best to save a life or prevent further injury.

People are rarely sued for helping in an emergency. However, the existence of Good Samaritan laws does not mean that someone cannot sue. In rare cases, courts have ruled that these laws do not apply when an individual rescuer's response was grossly or willfully negligent or reckless or when the rescuer abandoned the victim after initiating care.

Good Samaritan laws vary from state to state. If you are interested in finding out about your state's Good Samaritan laws, contact a legal professional or your state Attorney General's office, or check with your local library.

Sometimes people worry that they might be sued for giving first aid. Do not be overly concerned about this. Lawsuits against those who give emergency care are highly unusual and rarely successful. Most states have enacted **Good Samaritan laws** that protect people who willingly give first aid without accepting anything in return.

If Not You, Who?

In most states, a **layperson** has no legal duty to help victims in emergencies. Yet obviously, we would want to be helped if we were injured or suddenly ill. People will always have feelings that make them hesitate or fail to help. Barriers to action are personal and very real to the people who experience them. The decision to act is yours alone. Your decision to respond to emergencies should be guided by your own values, as well as by knowledge of the risks that may be present in various rescue situations.

MIND AT WORK

2. As you approach the victim of the car crash, you begin to feel faint and nauseated and are not sure you can proceed any farther. How can you still help?

3. The evening TV news reported that the approximate time of the crash you witnessed was 4:50 p.m., that EMS help did not arrive until 5:25 p.m., and that the victim did not arrive at the hospital until 6:30 p.m. What might have happened along these links in the chain of survival to cause this delay in reaching the victim and getting him to the hospital?

PREPARING FOR EMERGENCIES

If you are prepared for unforeseen emergencies, you can help ensure that care begins as soon as possible–for yourself, your family, and your fellow citizens. First aid training provides you with both the knowledge and skills necessary to respond confidently to emergency situations. Your training will help you to focus on the most important aspects of care by giving you a basic plan of action that can be used in any emergency. By knowing what to do, you will be bet-

ter able to manage your fears and overcome barriers to action. Your training will enable you to respond more effectively in your role as a citizen responder.

You can be ready for most emergencies if you do the following things now:

- Keep important information about you and your family in a handy place, such as on the refrigerator door and in your automobile glove compartment (Fig. 1-8). Include your address, everyone's date of birth, medical conditions, allergies, and prescriptions and dosages. List physicians' names and phone numbers.

- Keep medical and insurance records up to date.

- Find out if your community is served by an emergency 9-1-1 telephone number. If it is not, look up the numbers for police, fire department, EMS, and poison control center (PCC). Emergency numbers are usually listed in the front of the telephone book. Teach children how to call for help as soon as they are old enough to use the telephone.

- Keep emergency telephone numbers listed in a handy place, such as by the telephone, and in your first aid kit. Include the home and office phone numbers of family members, friends, or neighbors who can help. Be sure to keep both the list and the telephone numbers current.

- Keep a first aid kit readily available in your home, automobile, workplace, and recreation area (Fig. 1-9). Store each kit in a dry place and replace used contents regularly. A first aid kit should contain the following:

Figure 1-8 Keep important information in handy places, such as in your car's glove compartment.

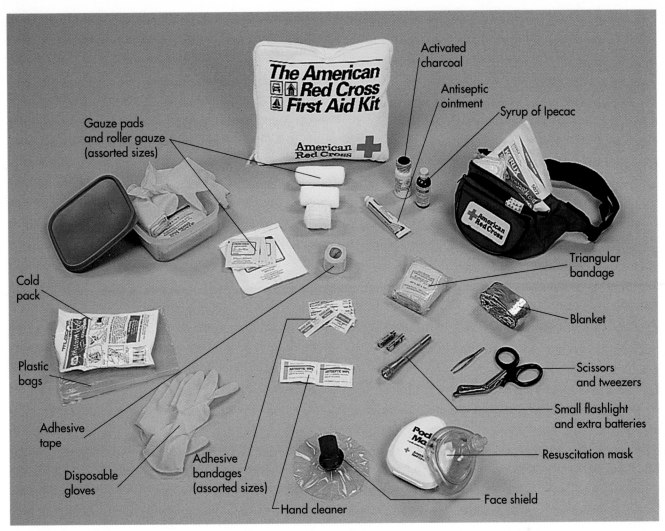

Figure 1-9 It is important to keep a well-stocked first aid kit in your home, automobile, workplace, and recreation area.

a. Sterile gauze pads (dressings), 2- and 4-inch squares to place over wounds
b. Roller and triangular bandages to hold dressings in place or to make an arm sling
c. Adhesive bandages in assorted sizes
d. Scissors and tweezers
e. Ice bag or chemical ice pack
f. Disposable latex gloves
g. Flashlight, with extra batteries in a separate bag
h. Antiseptic wipes
i. Resuscitation mask or face shield
j. Other items as suggested by your physician

• Learn and stay practiced in first aid skills, such as cardiopulmonary resuscitation (CPR).

• Make sure your house or apartment number is easy to read. Numerals are easier to read than spelled-out numbers. Report any downed or missing street signs to the proper authorities.

• Wear a medical alert tag if you have a potentially serious medical condition, such as epilepsy, diabetes, heart disease, or allergies (Fig. 1-10). A medical alert tag, usually worn on a necklace or bracelet, provides important medical information if you cannot communicate. Family members should also wear medical alert tags if necessary.

You will never see the emergencies you prevent. However, emergencies can and do happen, regardless of attempts to prevent them.

Figure 1-10 Medical alert tags can provide important medical information about the victim.

SUMMARY

You, the citizen responder trained in first aid, play a critical role by being the first link in the chain of survival. Your actions can help save the life of a victim of injury or sudden illness. You need to recognize that an emergency has occurred and decide to act. The most important action you can then take is to call EMS personnel. Then overcome any barriers to action and provide care for the victim.

In the following chapters, you will learn how to manage different kinds of emergencies. You will learn emergency action steps you can apply to any emergency situation and how to care for both life-threatening and nonlife-threatening conditions.

Answers to Application Questions

1. One person can find a phone and call EMS personnel; another can look around for a nearby first responder. Someone can begin to provide first aid.

2. Although you may feel ill and be incapacitated by the sight of blood or cries of pain, you can still help. If possible, turn away for a moment and try to control your feelings. If you are still unable to proceed, make sure EMS personnel have been called. Then find other ways to help, such as asking bystanders to assist you or helping keep the area safe.

3. People delayed calling EMS personnel; the caller gave an incorrect location of the crash; the ambulance was held up in traffic. EMS professionals may have had to cut the victim out of the car; the location of car was hazardous; they had to use special equipment; a helicopter may have had to be called and would have had to land; the hospital was far away.

STUDY QUESTIONS

1. Match each term with the correct definition.

    a. Citizen responder
    b. First responder
    c. EMT-Paramedic

    d. Rehabilitation
    e. Hospital care providers
    f. EMS dispatcher

    ___B___ Often the first person on the scene trained to provide a higher level of emergency care, such as a law enforcement officer, fire fighter, or lifeguard.

    ___C___ The "eyes and ears" of the physician at an emergency scene; provides the highest level of out-of-hospital care, such as administering medications or intravenous fluids.

    ___E___ The staff that assume responsibility for the care of the injured or ill person while in the hospital.

    ___F___ The person who receives the call for help and determines what help is needed at the scene.

    ___D___ The process of returning the victim to his or her previous state of health.

    ___A___ Someone who recognizes an emergency and decides to act; the first link in the chain of survival.

2. Using all of the terms in Question 1, organize the six links of the EMS system components in the most effective order.

    a. A - Citizen Resp.
    b. B - 1st Resp. ⟵) possibly
    c. F- EMS Disp. ⟵
    d. C- EMT Par.
    e. E- Hospital
    f. D- Rehabil.

3. What potential indicators of an emergency do you find in each scenario that follows? Circle the five indicators.

    a. *I was fixing sandwiches and talking with Mrs. Roberts from next door, who had come by to borrow a book. Three-year-old Jenny was in the next room playing with some puzzles and singing to herself. As Mrs. Roberts got up to leave, I realized that I wasn't hearing any sounds. "Jenny," I called. No answer. I called louder. Nothing. I went into the room, but Jenny wasn't there. Suddenly, I heard a loud thump and a shriek from upstairs.* Sounds

b. *I was on the bus headed for work. A man from the back of the bus came down the aisle, and as he passed me, I noticed that he was moving unsteadily. He stumbled and almost fell on me. Then he turned and headed back up the aisle. It was cold in the bus, but I noticed he was sweating and looked very pale. "I don't know where I am," I heard him mumble to himself.*

4. What barriers to giving care could apply in each situation?

a. _____

b. _____

5. In what ways could bystanders help?

a. _____

b. _____

6. Match each term with the best correct phrase.

a. First aid
b. Calling EMS personnel immediately
c. Medical emergency
d. Barriers to action
e. Indicator of an emergency
f. Citizen response
g. Emergency
h. EMS system

___G___ A situation that requires immediate action.

___H___ A network of community resources and medical personnel that provides emergency care to victims of injury or sudden illness.

___A___ The immediate care given to a victim of injury or sudden illness until more advanced care can be obtained.

___B___ The most important action you can take in a life-threatening emergency.

___C___ A sudden illness requiring immediate medical attention.

___E___ A spilled medicine container.

___F___ Recognizing an emergency and deciding to act.

___D___ Reasons for not acting or for hesitating to act.

7.   Circle six indicators of an emergency given in this scenario.

On your way to the grocery store from the parking lot, you hear the loud screech of tires and the crash of metal. You turn around and head in the direction of the sound. As you reach the corner of the parking lot, you notice that across the street a car has struck a telephone pole, causing it to lean at an odd angle. Wires are hanging down from the pole. Another vehicle is stalled in the middle of the street.

In question 8, circle the letter of the correct answer.

8.   Disease transmission from a victim to a rescuer requires four conditions to be present. Which of the following is one of these four?

a. The victim must be infected with the disease.
b. The rescuer must be exposed to the infected victim's body substance.
c. There must be enough body substance that contains the pathogen to cause infection.
d. All of the above.

Answers are listed in Appendix A.

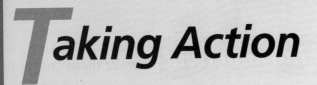

CHAPTER 2

Taking Action

WHAT YOU SHOULD LEARN

After reading this chapter, you should be able to—

1. Identify the three emergency action steps and describe each.

2. Identify four important questions to be answered when checking the emergency scene.

3. Explain what you should do if an unsafe scene prevents you from reaching the victim.

4. List the three things you must tell the victim to get permission to give care.

5. Explain when and how to call EMS personnel.

6. List the four conditions considered life threatening in an emergency situation.

7. Define the key terms for this chapter.

You are driving to your Dad's house on a Sunday morning. You and your father are going out to lunch. You arrive about 5 minutes early. After knocking on the door several times, you become concerned when no one answers. You unlock the door, stick your head inside, and yell for your father. No answer. Stepping back outside, you see that the garage door is closed, and that your Dad's antique car is nowhere in sight. "Maybe he's working on the car in the garage," you think. You open the garage door. The sight that greets you fills you with dread. Your Dad is lying on the garage floor. You run over to him and shake him, but he doesn't move. You are frightened and feel cold all over. Your hands tremble uncontrollably. "What should I do?," you think.

Introduction

An emergency scene can be overwhelming, terrifying, and at the least, confusing. It poses questions that demand immediate answers—What should I do first? Where can I get help? What can I do to help the ill or injured person? Remembering and following three basic steps will help ensure you respond to any emergency effectively.

Key Terms

Consent: Permission to give care, given by the victim to the rescuer.

Emergency action steps: Three basic steps you should take in any emergency—*Check-Call-Care.*

Implied consent: A legal concept that assumes a person would consent to receive emergency care if he or she were physically able to do so.

Signs of circulation: Normal breathing, coughing or movement in response to initial rescue breaths, or presence of carotid or brachial pulse in an unconscious victim.

TAKING ACTION

The **emergency action steps** are the three basic steps you should take in any emergency. These steps include—

- *Check* the scene and the victim.
- *Call* 9-1-1 or the local emergency number.
- *Care* for the victim.

Check the Scene and the Victim

The *Check* step has two parts—checking the scene and checking the victim. Do not skip over the check of the scene in your rush to get to the ill or injured person, or you may also become a victim.

Checking the scene

Before you can help the victim, you must make sure the scene is safe for you and any by-standers. Take time to check the scene and answer these questions:

1. Is the scene safe?
2. What happened?
3. How many victims are there?
4. Are bystanders available to help?

Look for anything that may threaten your safety and that of the victim and bystanders. Examples of dangers are downed power lines, falling rocks, traffic, a crime scene, a hostile crowd, violent behavior, fire, smoke, dangerous fumes, extreme weather, and deep or swiftly moving water (Fig. 2-1). *If any of these dangers are threatening, do not approach the victim. Retreat and call 9-1-1 or the local emergency number immediately.* Do not risk becoming a victim also and creating more work for EMS professionals. Leave dangerous situations to professionals, such as fire fighters and police officers, who have the training to deal with them. Once they make the scene safe, you can offer to help.

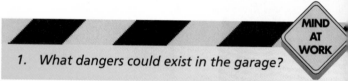

1. What dangers could exist in the garage?

MIND AT WORK

Find out what happened. Look around the scene for clues about what caused the emergency and the type and extent of the victim's injuries. You may discover a situation that requires your immediate attention. As you approach the victim, take in the whole picture. Nearby objects, such as shattered glass, a fallen ladder, or a spilled bottle of medicine, might tell you what happened (Fig. 2-2, p. 26). If the victim is unconscious, your check of the scene may be the only way to tell what happened.

When you check the scene, look carefully for more than one victim. You may not spot everyone at first. For example, in a car crash, an open door may be a clue that a victim has left the car or was thrown from it. If one victim is bleeding or screaming loudly, you may overlook another victim who is unconscious. It is also easy in any emergency situation to overlook an infant or a small child. Ask anyone present how many people may be involved. If you find more than one victim, ask bystanders to

Figure 2-1 Check the scene for anything that may threaten your safety and that of the victims and bystanders. Can you identify the hazards shown above?

help you care for them. Bystanders may be able to tell you what happened or help in other ways. A bystander who knows the victim may know whether he or she has any medical problems or allergies. If no bystanders are close by, shout for someone who can help you.

As you move closer to the victim, continue to check the scene to see if it is still safe. At this point, you may see other dangers that were not obvious to you from a distance. You may also see clues to what happened or victims and bystanders you did not notice before.

Figure 2-2   If the victim is unconscious, nearby objects may be your only clue to what has happened.

Figure 2-3   Check for life-threatening conditions, such as unconsciousness, when you first discover a victim.

Checking the victim

As a rule, do not move a victim unless an immediate danger, such as fire, flood, poisonous fumes, hazardous traffic patterns, or an unstable structure, threatens you and the victim. If danger is immediate, try to move the victim as quickly and as carefully as possible, without making the situation worse. If no immediate danger exists, tell the victim not to move. Tell bystanders not to move the victim.

If you find the victim has any immediately life-threatening conditions, you must call EMS personnel immediately or send someone else to call. The four conditions considered immediately life threatening in an emergency situation are unconsciousness, no breathing or difficulty breathing, no signs of circulation, and severe bleeding (Fig. 2-3). Checking for life-threatening conditions is described in Chapter 4.

MIND AT WORK

2. What specific factors in the garage could influence your decision to move or not move your Dad?

Identify yourself as a person trained in first aid. Try not to alarm the victim. Position yourself close to the victim's eye level (Fig. 2-4). Speak calmly and confidently. Identify yourself, explain that you have first aid training, and ask if you can help. Your words can re-

assure the victim that a caring and skilled person is offering help.

Get permission to provide care. Before giving first aid to a conscious adult victim, you must get the victim's permission to give care. This permission is referred to as ***consent.*** A conscious victim has the right to either refuse or accept care. To get consent you must tell the victim—

1. Who you are.
2. Your level of training.
3. What it is you would like to do.

Only then can a conscious victim give you consent. Do not give care to a conscious victim who refuses it. If the conscious victim is an infant or child, get permission to provide care from the supervising adult, if possible.

If the victim is unconscious or unable to respond because of the illness or injury, consent is implied. ***Implied consent*** means you can assume that if the person could respond, he or she would agree to be cared for. Consent is also implied for an infant or child if a supervising adult is not present or immediately available.

Call EMS Personnel

Your top priority as a citizen responder is to get professional help to the victim as soon as possible. The EMS system works more effectively if you can give information about the victim's condition when the call is placed. This infor-

Figure 2-4   When talking to the victim, position yourself close to the victim's eye level and speak in a calm and positive manner.

mation helps to ensure that the victim receives proper medical care as quickly as possible. By calling 9-1-1 or the local emergency number, you put into motion a response system that rushes the correct emergency care personnel to the victim. For situations in which no phone is available or EMS response time will be over 30 minutes as a result of distance, see Chapter 22.

When to call

At times, you may be unsure if EMS personnel are needed. For example, the victim may say not to call an ambulance because he or she is embarrassed about creating a scene. Your first aid training will help you make the decision. As a general rule, call EMS personnel for any of the following conditions:

- Unconsciousness or altered level of consciousness
- Breathing problems (no breathing or difficulty breathing)
- Persistent chest or abdominal pain or pressure
- No signs of circulation
- Severe bleeding
- Severe burns
- Vomiting blood or passing blood in feces or urine
- Poisoning or suspected poisoning
- Seizures, severe headache, or slurred speech
- Injuries to head, neck, or back
- Broken bones or suspected broken bones

Special situations also warrant calling EMS personnel for assistance. These include—

- Fire or explosion.
- The presence of poisonous gas.
- Downed electrical wires.
- Swiftly moving or rapidly rising water.
- Motor vehicle collisions.
- Victims who cannot be moved easily.

These conditions and situations make up by no means a complete list. It is beyond anyone's ability to provide a definitive list, since exceptions always exist. Trust your instincts. If you think there is an emergency, there probably is. Do not lose time calling untrained people, such as friends or family members. Call EMS personnel for professional medical help immediately. These professionals would rather respond to a non-emergency than arrive at an emergency too late to help.

Making the call

You may ask a bystander to call the emergency number for you. Tell him or her the victim's condition. For example, tell the bystander, "Call 9-1-1. Tell them the victim is not breathing." If you find that the victim is unconscious, do not delay calling EMS personnel. Unconsciousness is a sign of a serious injury or illness. Sending someone else to make the call enables you to stay with the victim to check breathing and circulation and provide needed care (Fig. 2-5).

When you tell someone to call for help, you should do the following:

1. Give the caller the EMS telephone number. This number is 9-1-1 in many communities. Tell the caller to dial "O" (the Operator) only if you do not know the emergency number in the area. Sometimes the emergency number is listed on pay phones and on the inside front cover of telephone directories (Fig. 2-6).
2. Tell the caller to give the dispatcher the necessary information. Most dispatchers will ask—
   a. The exact address or location and the name of the city or town. Be prepared to give the names of nearby intersecting streets (cross streets or roads), landmarks, the name of the building, the floor, and the room number.
   b. The telephone number from which the call is being made.

c. The caller's name.

d. What happened—for example, a motor vehicle collision, a fall, a fire, sudden onset of chest pain.

e. How many people are involved.

f. The condition of the victim(s)—for example, unconsciousness, chest pain, trouble breathing, bleeding.

g. The help (care) being given.

3. Tell the caller not to hang up until the dispatcher hangs up. It is important to make sure the dispatcher has all the information needed to send the right help to the scene. The EMS dispatcher may also be able to give the caller instructions on how best to care for the victim until help arrives.

4. Tell the caller to report to you after making the call and tell you what the dispatcher said.

If you are alone **Call First**, that is, 9-1-1 or the local emergency number before providing care for—

- An unconscious adult victim or child 8 years or older.
- An unconscious infant or child known to be at a high risk for heart problems.

If you are alone, provide 1 minute of care, then **Call Fast** for—

- An unconscious adult victim less than 8 years old.
- Any victim of submersion or near drowning.

Figure 2-6 Local emergency numbers are easily found.

- Any victim of arrest associated with trauma.
- Any victim of drug overdose.

If you are nowhere near a telephone, you will have to make a decision whether to go look for help or to stay with the victim, give care, and use whatever means you can to attract help. If you must leave to get help, do whatever you can to make the victim comfortable. For more information on these situations, see Chapter 22.

With your first aid training, you can do two important things that can make a difference to a seriously ill or injured person's chance of survival and return to health—call EMS personnel as quickly as possible and give care for life-threatening problems. If you are confused or unsure of what care to give, call the local emergency number immediately.

Figure 2-5 Sending someone else to call the emergency number will enable you to stay with the victim.

MIND AT WORK

3. *After checking the scene in the garage, what would you do next? Why?*

Hundreds of Millions Served

The 9-1-1 service was created in the United States in 1968 as a nationwide telephone number for the public to use to report emergencies and request emergency assistance. It gives the public direct access to a Public Service Answering Point that is responsible for taking the appropriate action. The numbers 9-1-1 were chosen because they best fit the needs of the public and the telephone company. They are easy to remember and dial, and they have never been used as an office, area, or service code (National Emergency Number Association).

When should you call 9-1-1? Call 9-1-1 whenever life or property is threatened or if injury is possible (Stanton W). Fire and motor vehicle crashes are obvious emergencies that require using 9-1-1. But you should also call 9-1-1 for other situations that threaten life or property or those that may cause injury, such as a dangerous animal running loose, a downed electrical line, a burglary, or an assault.

Hundreds of millions of people call 9-1-1 each year. The majority of calls, approximately 80 percent of 9-1-1 calls, pertain to law enforcement. Fire and EMS comprise the rest. EMS professionals alone respond to more than 19 million 9-1-1 calls each year.

What advantages does 9-1-1 offer? It was designed to save time in the overall response of a public safety agency (for example, fire, police, EMS) to a call for help (National Emergency Number Association). This includes the time it takes a citizen responder to telephone the correct agency or agencies for help. For example, imagine that a house is on fire in your neighborhood and your neighbor has been seriously burned. You run to call for help. Whom should you call first—the fire department to come and put out the fire so that no one else is hurt, the ambulance so that the EMTs can attend to your neighbor, or the police to help secure the area?

Without 9-1-1 service, you may need to place separate calls to all three agencies.

With 9-1-1 service, regardless of your needs, you make only one call. When the call comes in, a 9-1-1 dispatcher answers the call, listens to the caller, gathers needed information, and dispatches help. All 9-1-1 calls are recorded on tape.

Perhaps one of the most exciting lifesaving advances in computer technology in the past few years has been the development of the enhanced 9-1-1 system. This system uses Computer-Aided Dispatch (CAD). As soon as a call comes in, CAD automatically displays the telephone number, address, and name in which the phone is listed. So, even if the caller is unable to remain on the line or to speak or if the call is disconnected, the dispatcher will have enough information to send help.

The latest advance in 9-1-1 system development is the use of CAD units in police cars, fire engines, and ambulances. By the time these personnel start their vehicles, the built-in CAD units provide them with the location information. These CAD units are also used to send messages, establishing a vital communication link among the caller, the dispatcher, and the field unit en route.

With all of its advantages and lifesaving capabilities, 9-1-1 service today covers approximately 75 percent of the U.S. population and 30 percent to 35 percent of the geographical area of the United States. Ninety to ninety-five percent of the coverage is via enhanced 9-1-1. As more cities establish 9-1-1 systems, response time of emergency personnel will continue to improve, resulting in more lives being saved.

SOURCES
National Emergency Number Association: *(Nine One One* 9-1-1 *What's it all about?).*
Stanton W, Executive Director National Emergency Number Association, Interview 2/13/90.

What happens when you call EMS

When your call is answered, you will talk to an emergency dispatcher who has had special training in dealing with crises over the phone. The dispatcher will ask you for your phone number and address and will ask other key questions to determine whether you need police, fire, or medical assistance.

It may seem that the dispatcher asks a lot of questions. The information you give helps the dispatcher to send the type of help needed, based on the severity of the emergency. Once the ambulance is on its way, the dispatcher may stay on the line and continue to talk with you. Many dispatchers today are also trained to give instructions before EMS personnel arrive (Fig. 2-7). These pre-arrival instructions, combined with your first aid training, help to ensure an effective emergency response.

Care for the Victim

Once you have checked the scene and the victim, you may need to provide care. Always care for life-threatening conditions before those that are not life threatening. For example, a breathing emergency would take priority over an injured leg. While you are waiting for more advanced medical help, watch for changes in the victim's breathing and consciousness. A change in the victim's level of consciousness—becoming less alert or awake—may be a sign of a seri-

Figure 2-7   Many dispatchers give instructions to citizen responders for what to do before EMS personnel arrive.

ous illness or injury. A condition that may not appear serious at first may become serious with time. Help the victim rest comfortably, and keep him or her from getting chilled or overheated. Reassure the victim.

SUMMARY

Emergency situations are often confusing and frightening. To take appropriate actions in any emergency, follow the three basic emergency action steps—*Check-Call-Care. Check* the scene and the victim. *Call* the local emergency number to activate the EMS system. Ask a conscious victim's permission to provide *care.* Then provide care until help arrives. You will learn how to check an ill or injured person in Chapter 4. Care for specific illnesses and injuries is discussed in later chapters.

Answers to Application Questions

1. The main danger in the garage could be the presence of carbon monoxide. Another could be fumes from a spilled toxic substance or an electrical hazard.

2. The presence of poisonous fumes would be the major factor that could cause you to decide to move your Dad immediately. Avoid breathing in poisonous fumes as you execute the move.

3. You would shout for help. If no one came, you would go to the phone and call EMS personnel. Presumably, you would know the location of the nearest phone in the house and be able to get to it very quickly. If the car is running, you would suspect carbon monoxide, so you would turn off the engine and move your father from the garage.

STUDY QUESTIONS

1. *You are driving along the Interstate. It is getting dark. Rain has been falling steadily, and now it is beginning to freeze. Suddenly the tractor-trailer in your lane ahead of you begins to sway and slide, then jackknifes and crashes onto its left side. Drivers put on their brakes and swerve, and by some miracle, everyone close by manages to avoid crashing into the fallen truck or each other. You pull onto the median and stop behind the truck. What questions do you want to have answered before you help the victim?*

2. List four possible dangers to be aware of at the scene of this emergency.

3. List four facts you should tell the EMS dispatcher when you call.

4. List the four conditions considered immediately life threatening in an emergency situation.

In questions 5 through 8, circle the letter of the correct answer.

5. To obtain a victim's consent to give care, you must tell the victim —

    a. Your level of training.
    b. Your age.
    c. What you think is wrong.
    d. Your job.

6. If you determine the scene is unsafe, you should —

    a. Call EMS personnel and go quickly to the victim.
    b. Retreat and call EMS personnel immediately.
    c. Do your best to make the scene safe so that you can approach the victim.
    d. Wait 5 minutes and try to approach the victim again.

7. If you are alone on the scene and the adult victim is unconscious, what should you do first?

    a. Go quickly to find someone nearby to help you.
    b. Find the nearest telephone and call EMS personnel.
    c. Stay with the victim and shout for help.
    d. Check the victim thoroughly to try to find out what is wrong.

8. Which of these conditions warrants calling EMS personnel?

    a. Suspected poisoning
    b. Injuries to the head, neck, or back
    c. Persistent abdominal pain
    d. All of the above

Write the answer in the blank.

9. When you care for a victim who is unconscious or too ill or injured to respond to your request for consent, you are acting on the principle of _____ _____ .

10. In any emergency, you should ___*check*___ the scene and the victim, ___*call*___ EMS personnel, and ___*care*___ for the victim.

Answers are listed in Appendix A.

ASSESSMENT

CHAPTER 3

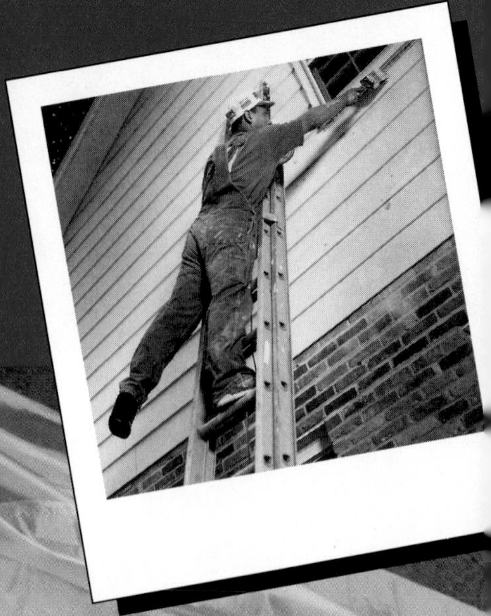

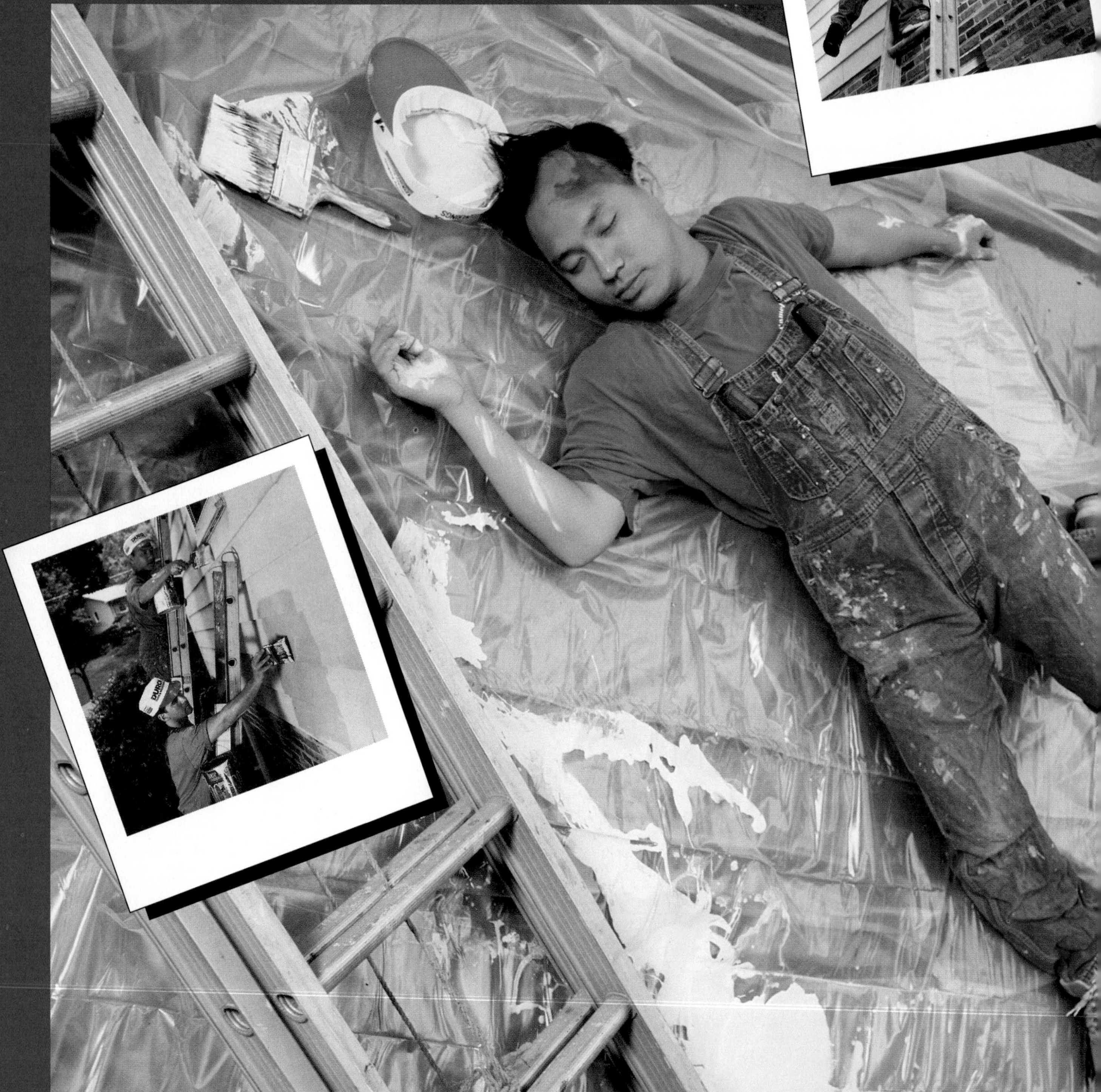

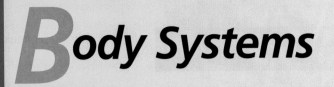

Body Systems

WHAT YOU SHOULD LEARN

After reading this chapter, you should be able to—

1. Identify the five body cavities and the major structures in each cavity.

2. Identify the eight body systems and the major structures in each system.

3. Describe the primary functions of each of the eight body systems.

4. Give one example of how body systems work together.

5. Describe the consequences of having a problem occur in one or more of the body systems.

6. Define the key terms for this chapter.

You and your friend Jim are painting the second floor trim on his house. Jim suddenly loses his balance, and both he and the ladder crash to the ground. When you reach Jim, he is unconscious, and blood is oozing from a cut on the left side of his head. No one responds to your shout for help. You race into the house, call 9-1-1, and tell the dispatcher what happened and that Jim's cut on the head is the only apparent sign of injury. The dispatcher tells you an ambulance is on the way and to stay with Jim and especially to watch his breathing until EMS personnel get there. The dispatcher also tells you to keep him warm and try to stop the bleeding. You put a blanket over Jim and a pad over the cut. Why watch his breathing, you wonder as you sit by Jim. He injured his head, as far as you can tell, not his chest. But as you watch him, you can tell that his breathing is changing, becoming faster, then slower. He looks pale, too, and when you touch his face, the skin feels cold. Why doesn't that ambulance get here?

Introduction

The human body is a miraculous machine. It performs many complex functions, each of which helps us live. You do not need to be an expert in human body structure and function to provide effective care. Neither should you need a medical dictionary to effectively describe an injury. By knowing a few key structures, their functions, and their location, you can recognize a serious illness or injury and accurately communicate with emergency care personnel about a victim's condition.

To remember the location of body structures, it helps to learn to visualize the structures that lie beneath the skin. The structures you can see or feel are reference points for locating the internal structures you cannot see or feel. For example, to locate the pulse on either side of the neck, you can use the Adam's apple on the front of the neck as a reference point. Using reference points will help you describe the location of injuries and other problems you may find. This chapter provides you with an overview of important reference points, terminology, and the structure and functions of eight body systems. Understanding the body systems and how they interact and depend on each other to keep the body functioning will help you give appropriate care to an ill or injured person.

BODY CAVITIES

A body cavity is a space in the body that contains organs, such as the heart, lungs, and liver. The five major cavities, illustrated in Figure 3-1, are the—

- **Cranial cavity,** located in the head. It contains the brain and is protected by the skull.
- **Spinal cavity,** extending from the bottom of the skull to the lower back. It contains the

Key Terms

Airway: The pathway for air from the mouth and nose to the lungs.

Arteries: Large blood vessels that carry blood away from the heart to all parts of the body.

Body system: A group of organs and other structures that work together to carry out specific functions.

Bone: A dense, hard tissue that forms the skeleton.

Brain: The center of the nervous system; controls all body functions.

Cells: The basic units of all living tissue.

Heart: A muscular organ that circulates blood throughout the body.

Lungs: A pair of light, spongy organs in the chest that provide the mechanism for taking oxygen in and removing carbon dioxide during breathing.

Muscle: A fibrous tissue that is able to contract, allowing and causing movement of organs and body parts.

Nerve: A part of the nervous system that sends impulses to and from the brain and all body parts.

Organ: A collection of similar tissues acting together to perform specific body functions.

Pulse: The expansion and contraction of the arteries caused by the ejection of blood from the heart into the arteries as it contracts.

Skin: The tough, supple membrane that covers much of the surface of the body.

Spinal cord: A bundle of nerves extending from the brain at the base of the skull to the lower back; protected by the spinal column.

Tissue: A collection of similar cells that act together to perform specific body functions.

Trunk: The part of the body containing the chest, abdomen, and pelvis.

Veins: Blood vessels that carry blood from all parts of the body to the heart.

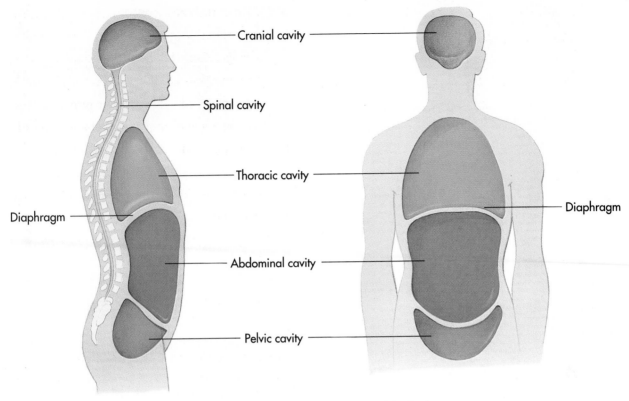

Figure 3-1   The five major cavities of the body.

spinal cord and is protected by the bones of the spine (vertebrae).

- **Thoracic cavity,** also called the chest cavity, located in the *trunk* above the **diaphragm,** a dome-shaped muscle used in breathing. The thoracic cavity contains the heart, lungs, and other important structures. It is protected by the rib cage and the upper spine.
- **Abdominal cavity,** located in the trunk between the diaphragm and the pelvis. It contains many organs, including the liver, gall bladder and pancreas, intestines, stomach, kidneys, and spleen. Because most of the abdominal cavity is not protected by any bones, the organs within it are especially vulnerable to injury.
- **Pelvic cavity,** located in the pelvis, the lowest part of the trunk. It contains the bladder, the rectum, and the reproductive organs. It is protected by the pelvic bones and the lower portion of the spine.

Knowing the general location and relative size of major organs in each cavity will help you assess a victim's injury or illness. The ma-

jor organs and their functions are more fully described in the next section of this chapter and in later chapters.

BODY SYSTEMS

The body is made up of billions of microscopic *cells,* the basic unit of all living tissue. There are many different types of cells. Each type contributes in a specific way to keep the body functioning normally. Collections of similar cells form *tissues,* which form organs (Fig. 3-2). An *organ* is a collection of similar tissues acting together to perform specific body functions. **Vital organs** perform functions that are essential for life. They include the brain, heart, and lungs.

A *body system* is a group of organs and other structures that are especially adapted to perform specific body functions. They work together to carry out a function needed for life. For example, the heart, blood, and blood vessels make up the circulatory system. The **circulatory system** keeps all parts of the body supplied with oxygen-rich blood.

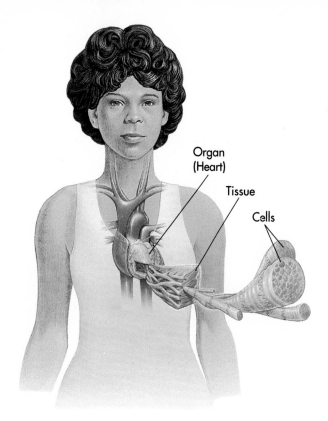

Figure 3-2   Cells and tissues make up organs.

For the body to work properly, all of the following systems must work well together:

- Respiratory
- Circulatory
- Nervous
- Musculoskeletal
- Integumentary
- Endocrine
- Digestive
- Genitourinary

The Respiratory System

The body must have a constant supply of oxygen to stay alive. The **respiratory system** supplies the body with oxygen through breathing. When you **inhale,** air fills the lungs, and the **oxygen** in the air is transferred to the blood. The blood carries oxygen to all parts of the body. This same system removes **carbon dioxide,** a waste gas. Carbon dioxide is transferred from the blood to the lungs. When you **exhale,** air is forced from the lungs, expelling carbon dioxide and other waste gases. This breathing process is called **respiration.**

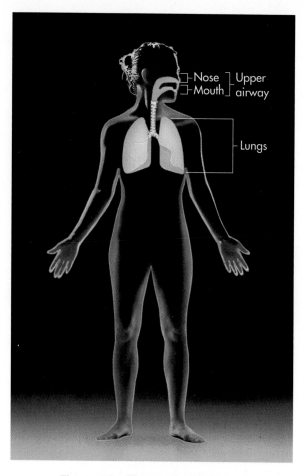

Figure 3-3   The respiratory system.

Structure and function

The respiratory system includes the airway and lungs. Figure 3-3 shows the parts of the respiratory system. The **airway,** the passage through which air travels to the lungs, begins at the nose and mouth. Air passes through the nose and mouth, through the **pharynx** (the throat), **larynx** (the voice box), and **trachea** (the windpipe), on its way to the lungs (Fig. 3-4). The **lungs** are a pair of light, spongy organs in the chest that provide the mechanism for taking in oxygen and removing carbon dioxide during breathing. Behind the trachea is the esophagus. The **esophagus** is a tube that carries food and liquids from the mouth to the stomach. A small flap of tissue, the **epiglottis,** covers the trachea when you swallow to keep food and liquids out of the lungs.

Air reaches the lungs through two tubes called **bronchi.** The bronchi branch into increasingly smaller tubes (Fig. 3-5, *A*) called **bronchioles.** These tubes eventually end in mil-

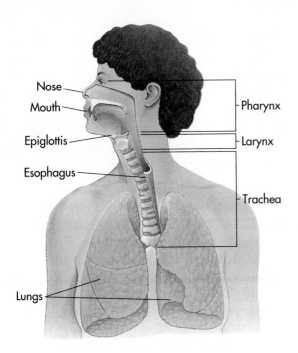

Figure 3-4 The respiratory system includes the pharynx, larynx, and trachea.

lions of microscopic air sacs called **alveoli** (Fig. 3-5, *B*). Oxygen and carbon dioxide pass into and out of the blood through the thin cell walls of the alveoli and microscopic blood vessels called **capillaries.**

Air enters the lungs when you inhale and leaves the lungs when you exhale. When the diaphragm and the chest muscles contract, you inhale. The chest expands, drawing air into the lungs. When the chest muscles and diaphragm relax, pushing air from the lungs, the chest cavity becomes smaller and you exhale (Fig. 3-6). (The average adult breathes about 12 to 20 times per minute, and a child or infant, depending on age, breathes between 20 to 40 times per minute.) This ongoing breathing process is involuntary—meaning you do not have to think about it—and is controlled by the brain.

Problems that require emergency care

Because of the body's constant need for oxygen, it is important to recognize breathing difficulties and to provide emergency care immediately. Some causes of breathing difficulties include airway obstructions, asthma, allergies, and injuries to the chest. Breathing difficulty is referred to as **respiratory distress.**

If a person has respiratory distress, you may hear or see noisy breathing or gasping. The victim may be conscious or unconscious. The conscious victim may be anxious or excited or may say that he or she feels short of breath. The victim's skin, particularly the lips and under the nails, may have a blue tint. This condition is called **cyanosis** and occurs when the blood and tissues do not get enough oxygen.

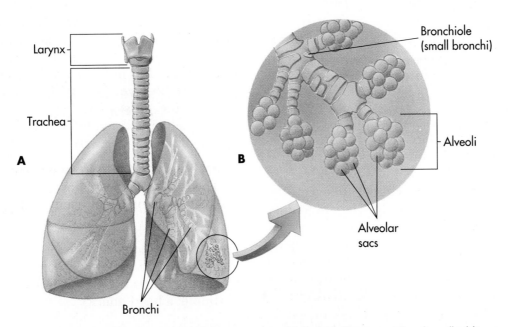

Figure 3-5 **A,** The bronchi branch into many small tubes. **B,** Oxygen and carbon dioxide pass into and out of blood through the walls of the alveoli and the capillaries.

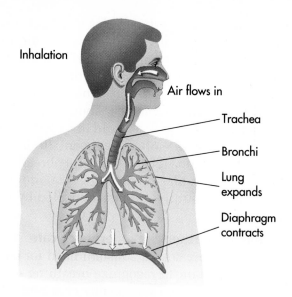

Inhalation

Air flows in

Trachea

Bronchi

Lung expands

Diaphragm contracts

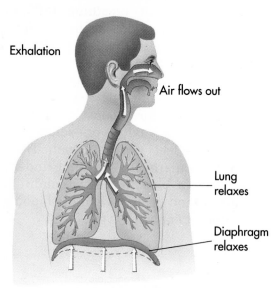

Exhalation

Air flows out

Lung relaxes

Diaphragm relaxes

Figure 3-6   The chest muscles and the diaphragm contract as you inhale and relax as you exhale.

If a person stops breathing, it is called **respiratory arrest.** Respiratory arrest is a life-threatening emergency. Without the oxygen obtained from breathing, other body systems cannot function. For example, without oxygen, the heart muscle stops functioning. The circulatory system will fail.

Respiratory problems require immediate attention. Making sure the airway is open and clear is critical. You may have to breathe for a nonbreathing victim or give abdominal thrusts **(Heimlich maneuver)** to someone who is choking. Breathing for the victim is called **rescue breathing.** These skills are discussed in detail in Chapter 5.

The Circulatory System

The circulatory system works with the respiratory system to carry oxygen-rich blood to every body cell. It also carries other nutrients throughout the body, removes waste, and returns oxygen-poor blood to the lungs. The circulatory system includes the heart, blood, and blood vessels. Figure 3-7 shows this system.

Structure and function

The **heart** is a muscular organ behind the **sternum,** or breastbone. The heart circulates blood throughout the body through veins and arteries. **Arteries** are large blood vessels that carry blood away from the heart to the rest of the body. The arteries subdivide into smaller blood vessels and ultimately become microscopic capillaries. The capillaries transport blood to all the cells of the body and nourish them with oxygen.

After the oxygen in the blood is transferred to the cells, **veins** carry the blood back to the heart. The heart circulates this blood to the lungs to pick up more oxygen before circulating it to other parts of the body. This cycle is called the **circulatory cycle.** The cross section of the heart in Figure 3-8 shows how blood moves through the heart to complete the circulatory cycle.

The pumping action of the heart is called a **contraction.** Contractions are controlled by the heart's electrical system, which makes the heart beat regularly. You can feel the evidence of the heart's contractions in the arteries that are close to the skin, for instance, at the neck or the wrist. The beat you feel with each contraction is called the **pulse.** The heart must beat regularly to deliver oxygen to body cells to keep the body functioning properly.

Problems that require emergency care

The following circulatory problems threaten the delivery of oxygen to body cells:

- Blood loss caused by severe bleeding (example: a severed artery)
- Impaired circulation (example: a blood clot)
- Failure of the heart to pump adequately (example: a heart attack)

Body tissues die when they do not receive oxygen. For example, when an artery supplying the brain with blood is blocked, brain tissue

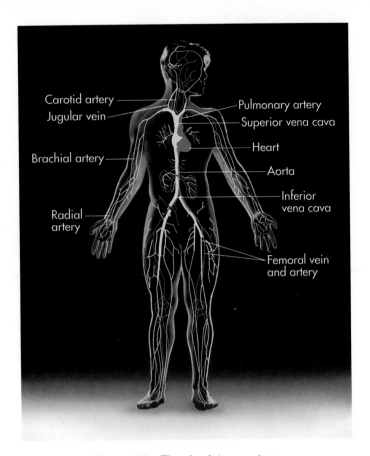

Figure 3-7   The circulatory system.

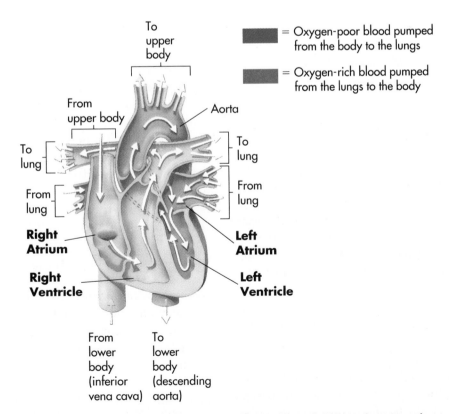

Figure 3-8   The heart is a two-sided pump made up of four chambers. A system of one-way valves keeps blood moving in the proper direction to complete the circulatory cycle.

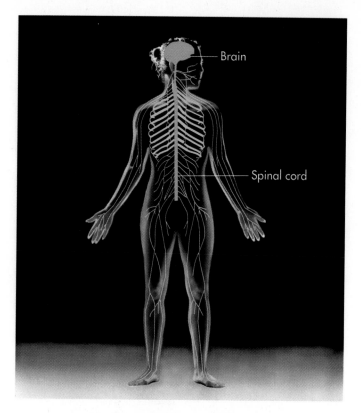

Figure 3-9   The nervous system.

dies. When an artery supplying the heart with blood is blocked, heart muscle tissue dies. This damage of heart muscle is a life-threatening emergency—heart attack.

When a person has a heart attack, the heart functions irregularly and may stop. If the heart stops, breathing will also stop. When the heart stops beating or beats too weakly to pump blood effectively, it is called **cardiac arrest.** Victims of either heart attack or cardiac arrest need immediate emergency care. Cardiac arrest victims need to have circulation maintained artificially by receiving chest compressions and rescue breathing. This combination of compressions and breaths is called **cardiopulmonary resuscitation** or **CPR.** You will learn more about the heart and how to perform CPR in Chapter 6.

The Nervous System

The **nervous system,** the most complex and delicate of all body systems, is one of the body's two major regulating and coordinating systems. (The other is the endocrine system, discussed later in this chapter.) The nervous system depends on a number of different sensory organs in the body to provide information about internal and external conditions that permit it to regulate and coordinate the body's activities.

Structure and function

The ***brain,*** the center of the nervous system, is the master organ of the body. It regulates all body functions, including the respiratory and circulatory systems. The primary functions of the brain are the sensory, motor, and integrated functions of consciousness, memory, emotions, and use of language.

The brain transmits and receives information through a network of nerves. Figure 3-9 shows the nervous system. The ***spinal cord,*** a large bundle of nerves, extends from the brain through a canal in the **spine,** or backbone. ***Nerves*** extend from the brain and spinal cord to every part of the body.

Nerves transmit information as electrical impulses from one area of the body to another. Some nerves conduct impulses from the body to the brain, allowing you to see, hear, smell, taste, and feel. These functions are the sensory functions. Other nerves conduct impulses from the brain to the muscles to control motor functions, or movement (Fig. 3-10).

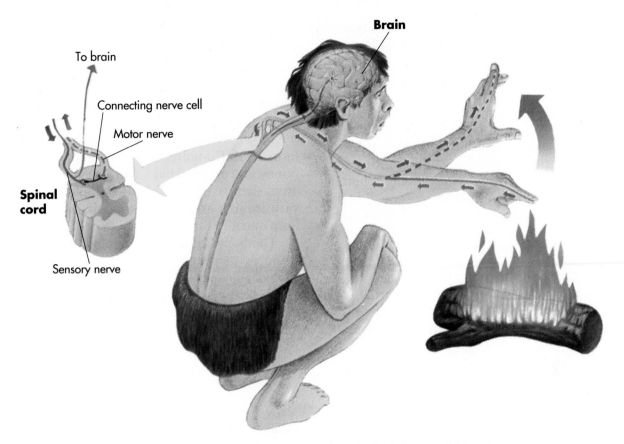

Figure 3-10   Messages are sent to and from the brain by way of the nerves.

The integrated functions of the brain are more complex. One of these functions is **consciousness.** Normally, when you are awake, you are fully conscious. In most cases, being conscious means that you know who you are, where you are, the approximate date and time, and what is happening around you. Your consciousness level can vary. For example, you can be highly aware in certain situations and less aware during periods of relaxation, sleep, illness, or injury.

Problems that require emergency care

Brain cells, unlike other body cells, cannot regenerate or grow back. Once brain cells die or are damaged, they are not replaced. Brain cells may die from disease or injury. When a particular part of the brain is diseased or injured, a person may lose the body functions controlled by that area of the brain. For example, if the part of the brain that regulates breathing is damaged, the person may stop breathing.

Illness or injury may change a person's level of consciousness. Consciousness may be affected by emotions, in which case the victim may be intensely aware of what is going on. At other times, the victim's mind may seem to be dull or cloudy. Illness or injury affecting the brain can also alter memory, emotions, and the ability to use language.

A head injury can cause a temporary loss of consciousness. Any head injury causing a loss of consciousness can also cause brain injury and must be considered serious. These injuries require evaluation by medical professionals because injury to the brain can cause blood to form pools in the skull. Pooling blood puts pressure on the brain and limits the supply of oxygen to the brain cells.

Injury to the spinal cord or a nerve can result in a permanent loss of feeling and movement below the injury. This condition is called **paralysis.** For example, a lower back injury can result in paralysis of the legs; a neck injury can result in paralysis of all four limbs. A broken bone or a deep wound can also cause nerve

MIND
AT
WORK

1. *Why did the dispatcher tell you to watch Jim's breathing?*

damage, resulting in a loss of sensation or movement. In Chapter 12, you will learn about techniques for caring for head, neck, and back injuries.

Musculoskeletal System

The **musculoskeletal system** is made up of the bones, muscles, ligaments, and tendons and comprises most of the body's weight. Together, these structures are primarily responsible for posture, locomotion, and other body movements but are also responsible for many other functions that are not as obvious.

Structure and function

The musculoskeletal system performs each of the following functions: supporting the body, protecting internal organs, allowing movement, storing minerals, producing blood cells, and producing heat.

Bones and ligaments

The body has over 200 bones. **Bone** is hard, dense tissue that forms the skeleton. The skeleton forms the framework that supports the body (Fig. 3-11). Where two or more bones join, they form a **joint.** Figure 3-12 shows a typical joint. Bones are usually held together at joints by fibrous bands of tissue called **ligaments.** Bones vary in size and shape, allowing them to perform specific functions.

The bones of the skull protect the brain. The spine is made of bones called **vertebrae** that protect the spinal cord. The **ribs** are bones that attach to the spine and to the breastbone, forming a protective shell for vital organs, such as the heart and lungs.

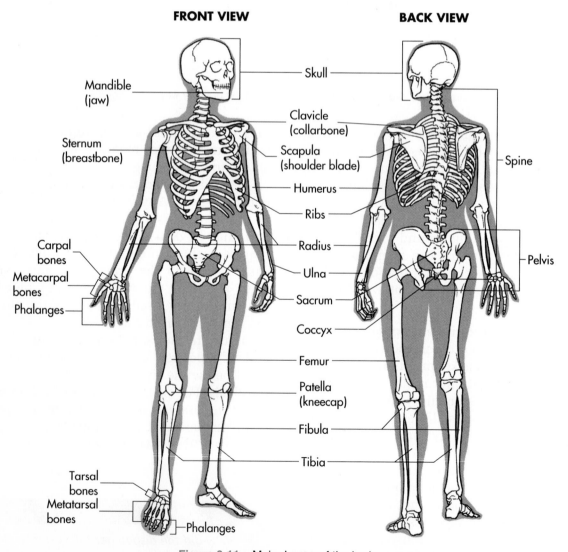

FRONT VIEW   **BACK VIEW**

Skull · Mandible (jaw) · Clavicle (collarbone) · Sternum (breastbone) · Scapula (shoulder blade) · Humerus · Ribs · Radius · Carpal bones · Ulna · Metacarpal bones · Sacrum · Phalanges · Coccyx · Femur · Patella (kneecap) · Fibula · Tibia · Tarsal bones · Metatarsal bones · Phalanges · Spine · Pelvis

Figure 3-11   Major bones of the body.

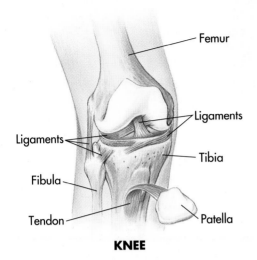

KNEE

Figure 3-12 A typical joint consists of two or more bones held together by ligaments.

In addition to supporting and protecting the body, bones aid movement. The bones of the arms and legs work like a system of levers and pulleys to position the hands and feet so that they can function. Bones of the wrist, hand, and fingers are progressively smaller to allow for fine movements like writing. The small bones of the feet enable you to walk smoothly. Together, the bones of the foot work as shock absorbers when you walk, run, or jump. Bones also store minerals and produce certain blood cells.

Muscles and tendons

Muscles are made of special tissue that can contract and relax, resulting in movement. Figure 3-13 shows the major muscles of the body. **Tendons** are tissues that attach muscles to bones. Muscles band together to form muscle

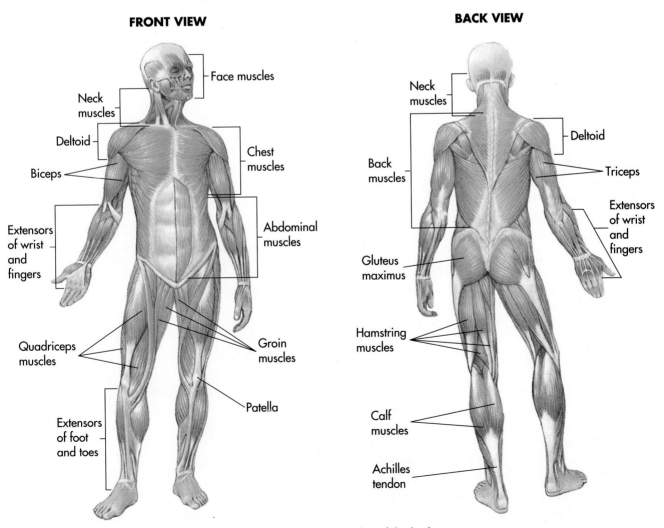

Figure 3-13 Major muscles of the body.

Figure 3-14   Muscle groups work together to produce movement.

groups. Muscles work together in groups to produce movement (Fig. 3-14). Working muscles produce heat. Muscles also protect underlying structures, such as bones, nerves, and blood vessels.

Muscle action is controlled by the nervous system. Nerves carry information from the muscles to the brain. The brain processes this information and directs the muscles through the nerves (Fig. 3-15).

Muscle actions are either voluntary or involuntary. Involuntary muscles, such as the heart, are automatically controlled by the brain. You don't have to think about involuntary muscles to make them work. Voluntary muscles, such as leg and arm muscles, are most often under your conscious control but often work automatically. You are sometimes aware of telling them to move, but you don't think about walking, for example; you just do it.

Figure 3-15   The brain controls muscle movement.

How Does a Person Catch a Frisbee®?

A Frisbee® slices the air as it spins in someone's direction. In a few seconds, it is in a person's hands and that person is tossing it back. But what really happens? How does a person catch a Frisbee®?

1. The left and the right eye each transmit the Frisbee's® image to the brain through electrical impulses that travel at a speed up to 300 feet per second.
2. The brain receives the image and then calculates the Frisbee's® path and the speed at which it is traveling.
3. The brain transmits electrical impulses to muscles in the arms and legs to reposition. As a person reaches for the Frisbee®, the pelvis and the vertebral column move to compensate for the change in balance. Tiny muscles and bones in the hand grasp the Frisbee® as it sails within reach.

Problems that require emergency care

Injuries to bones and muscles include fractures, dislocations, strains, and sprains. A fracture is a broken bone. Dislocations occur when bones of a joint are moved out of place, which is usually caused by physical trauma. Strains are injuries to muscles and tendons; sprains are injuries to ligaments. Although injuries to bones and muscles may not look serious, nearby nerves, blood vessels, and other organs may be damaged. Regardless of how they appear, these injuries may cause lifelong disabilities or become life-threatening emergencies. For example, torn ligaments in the knee can limit activity, and broken ribs can puncture the lungs and threaten breathing.

When you give emergency care, remember that injuries to muscles and bones often result in additional injuries. You will learn more about musculoskeletal injuries and how to care for them in later chapters.

The Integumentary System

The **integumentary system** consists of the skin, hair, and nails (Fig. 3-16). Most important among these structures is the skin. The skin protects the body and helps keep fluids within the body. It prevents **infection** by keeping out disease-producing **microorganisms,** or **pathogens.**

Structure and function

The *skin* is made of tough, elastic fibers that stretch without easily tearing, protecting it from injury. The skin also helps make vitamin D and stores minerals.

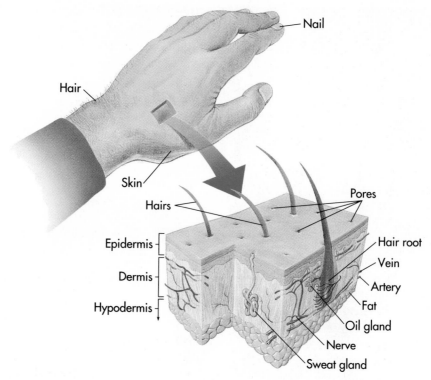

Figure 3-16 The skin, hair, and nails make up the integumentary system.

The outer surface of the skin consists of dead cells that are continually rubbed away and replaced by new cells. The skin contains the hair roots, oil glands, and sweat glands. Oil glands help to keep the skin soft, supple, and waterproof. Sweat glands and pores help regulate body temperature by releasing sweat. The nervous system monitors blood temperature and causes you to sweat if blood temperature rises even slightly. Although you may not see or feel it, sweat is released to the skin's surface.

Blood supplies the skin with nutrients and helps provide its color. When blood vessels dilate (become wider), the blood circulates close to the skin's surface. This dilation can make some people's skin appear flushed or red and makes the skin feel warm. The reddening may not appear with darker skin. When blood vessels constrict (become narrower), not as much blood is close to the skin's surface, causing the skin to look pale or ashen and feel cool. In people with darker skin, color changes may be most easily seen in the nail beds and the mucous membranes inside the mouth and inside the lower eyelids.

Nerves in the skin make it very sensitive to sensations such as touch, pain, and tempera-ture. Therefore, the skin is also an important part of the body's communication network and is a type of sensory organ.

Problems that require emergency care

Although the skin is tough, it can be injured. Sharp objects may puncture, cut, or tear the skin. Rough objects can scrape it, and extreme heat or cold may burn or freeze it. Burns and skin injuries that cause bleeding may result in the loss of vital fluids. Germs may enter the body through breaks in the skin, causing infection that can become a serious problem. In later chapters, you will learn how to care for skin injuries such as burns and cuts.

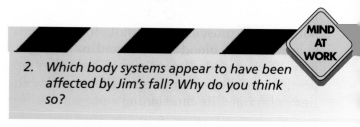

2. *Which body systems appear to have been affected by Jim's fall? Why do you think so?*

The Endocrine System

The **endocrine system** is the second of the two regulatory systems in the body. Together with

creted by small glands embedded in the pancreas. Without insulin, cells cannot use the sugar they need from food. Too much insulin forces blood sugar rapidly into the cells, lowering blood sugar levels and depriving the brain of the blood sugar it needs to function normally. Too little insulin results in too high a level of sugar in the blood. The condition in which the body does not produce enough insulin and blood sugar is abnormally high is called **diabetes.** Blood sugar levels that rise or fall abnormally can make a person ill, sometimes severely so. You will learn more about this kind of emergency in Chapter 14.

The Digestive System

The **digestive system,** also called the gastrointestinal system, consists of organs that work together to take in and break down food and eliminate waste. This digestive process provides the body with water, **electrolytes,** and other nutrients.

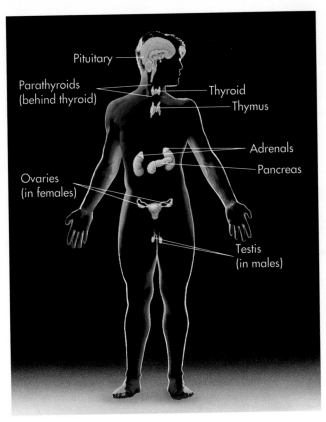

Figure 3-17   The endocrine system.

the nervous system, it coordinates the activities of other body systems.

Structure and function

The endocrine system consists of several glands (Fig. 3-17). **Glands** are organs that release substances into the blood or onto the skin. Some glands produce **hormones,** substances that enter the bloodstream and influence tissue activity in various parts of the body. For example, the thyroid gland makes a hormone that controls **metabolism,** the process by which all cells convert nutrients to energy. Other glands include the sweat and oil glands in the skin.

Problems that require emergency care

You do not need to know all the glands in the endocrine system or the hormones they produce. Problems in the endocrine system usually develop slowly and are seldom emergencies. Knowing how hormones work in general, however, helps you understand how some illnesses seem to develop suddenly.

For example, an emergency occurs when too much or too little of a hormone called insulin is secreted into the blood. Normally, insulin is se-

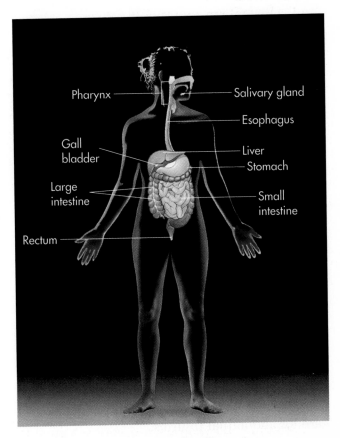

Figure 3-18   The digestive system.

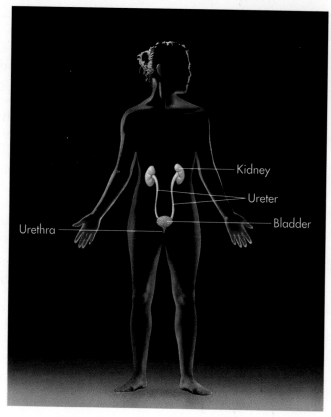

Figure 3-19   The urinary system.

Structure and function

The major organs of the digestive system include the esophagus, stomach, intestines, pancreas, gallbladder, and liver (Fig. 3-18). Food entering the system is broken down into a form the body can use. As food passes through the system, the body absorbs nutrients that can be converted to energy to be used by the cells. The unabsorbed portion continues through the system and is eliminated as waste.

Problems that require emergency care

Since most digestive system organs are in the unprotected abdominal cavity, they are very vulnerable to injury. Such an injury can occur, for example, if a body strikes a car's steering wheel in a collision. These organs can also be damaged by a penetrating injury, such as a stab or gunshot wound. Damaged organs may bleed internally, causing severe loss of blood, or spill waste products into the abdominal cavity. Such a spill can result in severe infection. Chapter 13 discusses in more detail how to recognize and care for abdominal injuries.

Genitourinary System

The **genitourinary system** is made up of two systems: the urinary system and the reproductive system. Although relatively close together in the body, they have very different functions. The urinary system plays a major role in managing body fluid and eliminating waste products; the reproductive system's primary purpose is to reproduce human life.

Structure and function

The **urinary system** consists of organs that eliminate waste products filtered from the blood (Fig. 3-19). The primary organs are the kidneys and the bladder. The **kidneys** are located behind the abdominal cavity just beneath the chest, one on each side. They filter wastes from the circulating blood to form urine. Urine is then stored in the **bladder,** a small muscular sac. The bladder stretches as it fills and then shrinks back after the urine is released.

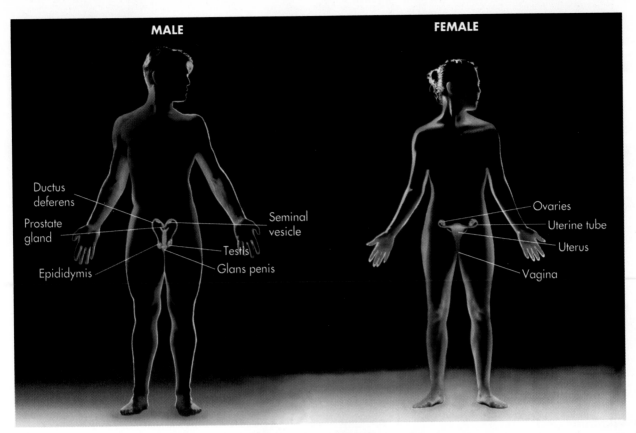

Figure 3-20 The male and female reproductive systems.

The female and male **reproductive systems** include the organs for sexual reproduction (Fig. 3-20). Injuries to the abdominal or pelvic area can damage organs in either system.

The female reproductive organs are smaller than many major organs and are protected by the pelvic bones. The soft tissue external structures are more susceptible to injury, although such injury is uncommon. The male reproductive organs are located outside of the pelvis and are more vulnerable to injury.

Problems that require emergency care

The frequency of injuries to the organs of the urinary system depends on their vulnerability. Unlike the abdominal organs, the kidneys are partially protected by the lower ribs, making them less vulnerable to injury. But the kidneys may be damaged by a significant blow to the back just below the rib cage or a penetrating wound, such as a stab or gunshot wound. Anyone with an injury to the back below the rib cage may have injured one or both kidneys. Because of the kidney's rich blood supply, such an injury often causes severe internal bleeding, often manifested by blood in the urine.

The bladder is injured less frequently than the kidneys, but injuries to the abdomen can rupture the bladder, particularly when it is full. Bone fragments from a fracture of the pelvis can also pierce the bladder or intestines.

Injuries to urinary system organs may not be obvious but should be suspected if there are significant injuries to the back just below the rib cage or to the abdomen. Chapter 13 discusses signs and symptoms to watch for and how to provide care.

The external reproductive organs, called **genitalia,** have a rich supply of blood and nerves. Injuries to these organs may cause bleeding but are rarely life threatening. Injuries to the genitalia are usually caused by a blow to the pelvic area but may result from sexual assault or rape. Although such injuries are rarely life threatening, they almost always cause the victim extreme distress. Such a victim may refuse care.

Did You Know?

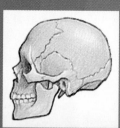

A baby is born with 350 bones. Adults have only 206 bones. Why do adults have fewer bones than babies?

Some bones that are separate at birth fuse together as a person grows. The skull is an excellent example.

We use 17 of our 30 facial muscles when we smile.

A nerve impulse can travel 360 feet per second, fast enough to cover the length of a football field in less than a second.

In a month, blood will have taken its fantastic journey around the body 43,000 times.

Blood vessels form a branching network of more than 60,000 miles, almost 3 times the distance around the earth.

The skin weighs about 7 pounds. If spread out flat, it would cover about 20 square feet.

An elephant's heart beats 25 times a minute and weighs 40 pounds. A human adult's heart beats about 70 times a minute and weighs 1 pound. A mouse's heart beats 700 times a minute and weighs approximately 1/2 gram (.0175 ounces).

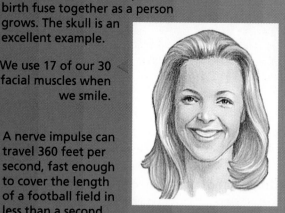

The stomach contains a corrosive acid called hydrochloric acid, which can eat a hole through a carpet. Why doesn't it eat a hole through your stomach? Certain cells that line the stomach produce a substance that neutralizes the acid.

The intestines are 28 feet long, the height of a two-story building. Food moves through the intestines at a rate of 1 inch per minute.

In a lifetime, the air you breathe could fill two dirigibles the size of the Hindenburg, which held 7 million cubic feet of gas.

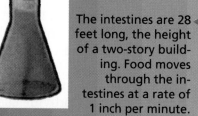

The brain receives about one eighth of the blood the heart pumps each minute. Whereas other body parts receive differing amounts of blood depending on the activity, the brain's portion remains the same.

TABLE 3-1

Body Systems

Systems	Major Structures	Primary Functions	How the System Works With Other Body Systems
Respiratory system	Airway and lungs	Supplies the body with oxygen and removes carbon dioxide through breathing	Works with the circulatory system to provide oxygen to cells; controlled by the nervous system
Circulatory system	Heart, blood, and blood vessels	Transports nutrients and oxygen to body cells and removes waste products	Works with the respiratory system to provide oxygen to cells; works in conjunction with the urinary and digestive systems to remove waste products; helps give skin color; controlled by the nervous system
Nervous system	Brain, spinal cord, and nerves	One of two primary regulatory systems in the body; transmits messages to and from the brain	Regulates all body systems through a network of nerves
Musculoskeletal system	Bones, ligaments, muscles, and tendons	Provides body's framework; protects internal organs and other underlying structures; allows movement; produces heat; manufactures blood components	Provides protection to organs and structures of other body systems; muscle action is controlled by the nervous system
Integumentary system	Skin, hair, and nails	An important part of the body's communication network; helps prevent infection and dehydration; assists with temperature regulation; aids in production of certain vitamins	Helps to protect the body from disease-producing organisms; together with the circulatory system helps to regulate body temperature; under control of the nervous system; communicates sensation to the brain through the nerves
Endocrine system	Glands	Secretes hormones and other substances into blood and onto skin	Together with the nervous system coordinates the activities of other systems
Digestive system	Mouth, esophagus, stomach, intestines, liver, pancreas, and gall bladder	Breaks down food into a usable form to supply the rest of the body with energy	Works with the circulatory system to transport nutrients to the body
Genitourinary system	Uterus and genitalia	Performs the processes of sexual reproduction	
	Kidneys and bladder	Removes wastes from the circulatory system and regulates water balance	

INTERRELATIONSHIPS OF BODY SYSTEMS

Each body system plays a vital role in survival (Table 3-1). Body systems work together to help the body maintain a constant healthy state. When the environment changes, body systems adapt to the new conditions. For example, because your musculoskeletal system works harder when you exercise, your respiratory and circulatory systems must also work harder to meet your body's increased oxygen demands. Your body systems also react to the stresses caused by illness or injury.

Body systems do not work independently of each other. The impact of an injury or illness is rarely restricted to one body system. For example, a stroke may result in brain damage that will impair movement and feeling. Injuries to the ribs can make breathing difficult. *If the heart stops beating for any reason, breathing will also stop.*

In any significant illness or injury, body systems may be seriously affected. The condition that results from a progressive failure of a body system or systems is called **shock.** Shock is the inability of the circulatory system to provide adequate oxygen to all parts of the body, especially the cells of the vital organs. Chapter 8 discusses shock in detail.

Generally, the more body systems involved in an emergency, the more serious the emergency. Body systems depend on each other for survival. In serious injury or illness, the body may not be able to keep functioning. In these cases, regardless of your best efforts, the victim may die.

SUMMARY

The body includes a number of systems, all of which must work together for the body to function properly. The brain, the center of the nervous system, controls all body functions including those of the other body systems. Knowing a few key structures, their functions, and their locations helps you to understand more about these body systems and how they relate to injuries and sudden illnesses.

Illness or injury that affects one body system can have a serious impact on other systems. Fortunately, basic care is usually all you need to give until EMS personnel arrive. By learning the basic principles of care described in later chapters, you may be able to make the difference between life and death.

Answers to Application Questions

1. His brain may have been injured by the blow to the head, and this damage to the nervous system could affect breathing and perhaps cause it to stop.

2. Respiratory—his breathing is changing, becoming faster, then slower.
   Nervous—he is unconscious.
   Integumentary—he has a cut on his head.

   Jim may have sustained damage to other systems, but these injuries are the most obvious.

STUDY QUESTIONS

1. Complete the table with the correct system, structures, or function(s).

Systems	Structures	Function(s)
a. *Resp*	b. *lungs, airway*	Supplies the body with the oxygen it needs through breathing
c. *Circ*	Heart, blood, blood vessels	d. *blood*
Integumentary	e. *skin, hair*	f. *protection, Vit E*
Musculoskeletal	g. *bones, ligs*	h. *structure*
i. *Nervous*	j. *brain, spinal cord*	Regulates all body functions; a communications network

2. Match each term with the correct definition.

   a. Arteries
   b. Cell
   c. Tissue
   d. Respiration

   e. Organ
   f. Endocrine system
   g. Spinal cord
   h. Veins

   D Process of breathing.

   G A large bundle of nerves extending from the brain through the spine.

   C A collection of similar cells that perform a specific function.

   F A body system that regulates and coordinates the activities of other body systems by producing chemicals that influence the activity of tissues.

   B The basic unit of living tissue.

   A Blood vessels that carry blood away from the heart to all parts of the body.

   H Blood vessels that carry blood to the heart.

   E A collection of similar tissues acting together to perform specific body functions.

In questions 3 through 9, circle the letter of the correct answer.

3. Which structure is not located in or part of the thoracic cavity?

    a. The liver
    b. The rib cage
    c. The heart
    d. The lungs

4. The two body systems that work together to provide oxygen to the body cells are—

    a. Musculoskeletal, integumentary.
    b. Circulatory, musculoskeletal.
    c. Respiratory, circulatory.
    d. Endocrine, nervous.

5. One of the main functions of the integumentary system is to—

    a. Transmit information to the brain.
    b. Produce blood cells.
    c. Prevent infection.
    d. Secrete hormones.

6. The function of the digestive system is to—

    a. Perform the process of reproduction.
    b. Transport nutrients and oxygen to body cells.
    c. Break down food into a form the body can use for energy.
    d. All of the above.

7. Which structure in the airway prevents food and liquid from entering the lungs?

    a. The trachea
    b. The epiglottis
    c. The esophagus
    d. The bronchi

8. If a person's use of language suddenly becomes impaired, which body system might be injured?

    a. The musculoskeletal system
    b. The nervous system
    c. The integumentary system
    d. The circulatory system

9. Which two body systems will react initially to alert a victim to a severe cut?

    a. Circulatory, respiratory
    b. Respiratory, musculoskeletal
    c. Nervous, respiratory
    d. Circulatory, nervous

Answers are listed in Appendix A.

CHAPTER 4

Checking the Victim

WHAT YOU SHOULD LEARN

After reading this chapter, you should be able to—

1. Identify the four life-threatening conditions.

2. Identify the five items you look for when checking for a life-threatening condition.

3. Describe how to perform the check for each life-threatening condition.

4. Identify the questions you would first ask the victim or bystanders in an interview.

5. Describe how to perform a check for nonlife-threatening conditions.

6. List six guidelines for preventing disease transmission.

7. Describe how to check infants and children for life-threatening and nonlife-threatening conditions.

8. Explain what influences your decision whether to transport a victim to a medical facility.

9. Define the key terms for this chapter.

After reading this chapter and completing the class activities, you should be able to demonstrate—

1. How to check for life-threatening emergencies.

2. How to make appropriate decisions when given an example of an emergency situation requiring you to check a victim.

As you ride along the bike trail on your way home, you are tired but relaxed. You must have ridden at least 10 miles. Then, as you round a sharp curve, you abruptly swerve. A person is sprawled facedown across the trail. You stop your bike. It is very quiet. The person lies motionless on the pavement.

Introduction

In earlier chapters you learned that as a citizen responder trained in first aid, you can make a difference in an emergency—you may even save a life. You learned how to recognize an emergency and that you would perform the three emergency action steps, *Check-Call-Care*, in any emergency. More important, you learned that your decision to act can be vital to the victim's survival. You can always do something to help.

In this chapter, you will learn how to check an ill or injured person for life-threatening conditions. You will also learn how to interview a conscious victim and any bystanders, check for nonlife-threatening conditions, and provide basic care in any emergency until EMS personnel arrive.

CHECK FOR LIFE-THREATENING CONDITIONS

An emergency situation is rarely clear cut. The exact order of the steps you take will vary depending on what you find when you reach the victim. If, when you check, the victim can speak or cry, then the victim is conscious, breathing, and has a heartbeat.

A conscious, breathing victim, however, may have a life-threatening condition. A victim may have difficulty breathing or persistent chest pain. He or she may drift in and out of consciousness. All these conditions are life-threatening. If the victim is conscious, you can introduce yourself, get the victim's **consent** to provide care, and attempt to find out what happened. You should look for **signs,** any observable evidence of injury or illness, and ask about **symptoms,** things the victim can tell you about his or her condition, such as dizziness or pain. Perhaps a bystander is available to help answer questions and to call EMS personnel if necessary.

If the victim is unconscious, the story is different. Unconsciousness is always a life-threatening condition. EMS personnel must be called immediately. Ideally, someone will be available to notify EMS personnel while you care for the victim, or you may be able to make the call yourself. If you are alone, however, when you call may depend on the circumstances. If an unconscious victim is bleeding so severely that you determine the bleeding is life threatening, for example, you may need to give care before you call. The steps that follow are the steps you take to find out if conditions exist that threaten the victim's life.

Key Terms

Brachial (BRA ke al) pulse: The pulse felt at the brachial artery on the inside of the upper arm.

Carotid (kah ROT id) arteries: Major blood vessels that supply blood to the head and neck.

Consent: Permission to give care, given by the victim to the rescuer.

Signs: Any observable evidence of an injury or illness, such as bleeding or unusually pale skin.

Symptoms: Things the victim tells you about his or her condition, such as, "My head hurts" or "I am dizzy."

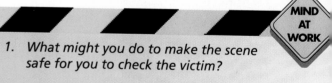

MIND AT WORK

1. *What might you do to make the scene safe for you to check the victim?*

CHECKING AN UNCONSCIOUS VICTIM

In the *Check* step, you check for life-threatening conditions first. Immediately life-threatening conditions include unconsciousness, no breathing, no heartbeat, and severe bleeding, or **hemorrhage.** You must check to find out if the victim is conscious, is breathing, and has signs of circulation, and whether the victim is bleeding severely.

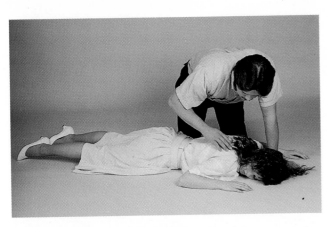

Figure 4-1   Determine if the person is conscious by gently tapping and asking, "Are you okay?"

Figure 4-2   If you are alone and must leave an unconscious victim, position the person on one side in case he or she vomits while you are gone.

Check for Consciousness

First, determine if the victim is conscious. You can leave the victim in the position in which you found him or her to check for consciousness. Gently tap him or her and ask, "Are you okay?" (Fig. 4-1). Do not jostle or move the victim. A victim who can respond to you is conscious, breathing, and has signs of circulation. A victim who is unable to respond may be unconscious. When someone is unconscious and lying on his or her back, the tongue may fall to the back of the throat and block the airway. This blockage may cause breathing to stop. Soon after, the heart will stop beating because of the lack of oxygen.

If an adult victim is unconscious, send someone to call EMS personnel. If you are alone, shout for help. If no one comes, carefully position the victim on one side in case he or she vomits while you go find a phone. Figure 4-2 shows this position, which is called the recovery position. Avoid twisting the neck and back as you do this. (Chapter 12 provides more information on protecting the neck and back.) If you leave the victim in this position for more than 30 minutes, or if you notice loss of circulation in the lower arms, turn the victim over to the other side. Find the nearest phone and call for help. Return to the victim, complete the check, and give the necessary care until EMS personnel arrive.

Check for Airway and Breathing

If you can, attempt to check the victim in whatever position you find him or her. Sometimes,

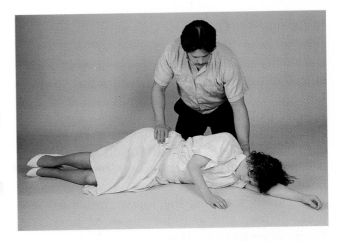

Figure 4-3   If the victim's position prevents you from checking the airway and breathing, roll the victim gently onto his or her back.

however, the victim's position may make checking for breathing impossible. In this case, you may roll the victim gently onto his or her back, but avoid twisting the spine (Fig. 4-3) (see Chapter 12).

To check for breathing, you must open the victim's airway. The airway is the passage for air from the nose and mouth to the lungs. An open airway allows enough air to enter the lungs for the victim to breathe. If the airway is blocked by vomit, blood, food, or an object, such as the tongue, a person cannot breathe. A person who can speak, cough, or cry has an open airway. It is more difficult to tell if an unconscious victim has an open airway. To open an unconscious victim's airway, push down on his or her forehead while pulling up on the bony part of the jaw with the other hand

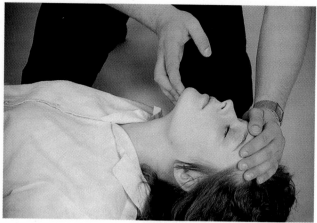

Figure 4-4 Tilt the head back and lift the chin to open the airway.

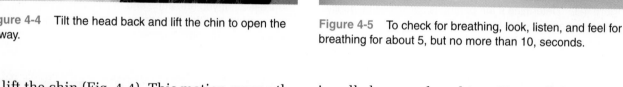

Figure 4-5 To check for breathing, look, listen, and feel for breathing for about 5, but no more than 10, seconds.

to lift the chin (Fig. 4-4). This motion moves the tongue away from the back of the throat, allowing air to enter the lungs. For someone with a suspected neck injury, this technique is modified slightly, as you will read in Chapter 5.

After opening the airway, check for breathing. An unconscious person must be checked carefully for signs of breathing. If the victim is breathing, the chest clearly rises and falls. Chest movement by itself, however, does not mean air is reaching the lungs. You must also look, listen, and feel for signs of breathing. Position yourself so that you can hear and feel air as it escapes from the nose and mouth. At the same time, watch the rise and fall of the chest. Take the time to look, listen, and feel for breathing for about 5 seconds but no more than 10 (Fig. 4-5).

If the victim is not breathing, you must give 2 slow, gentle breaths with the airway in the open position. Your breaths into the airway will get air into the victim's lungs. Sometimes, opening the airway does not result in a free passage of air, which may happen when a victim's airway is blocked by food, liquid, or other objects. In this case, you need to remove what is blocking the airway. First aid for an obstructed airway is described in Chapter 5. The longer a victim goes without oxygen, the more likely he or she is to die or suffer permanent brain damage. If the victim has signs of circulation, which include a pulse, normal breathing, coughing, or movement in response to rescue breaths, but is *not* breathing, you will need to breathe for him or her. This process of breathing for the victim

is called rescue breathing. You will learn how to give rescue breathing in Chapter 5.

Check for Signs of Circulation

The next step is checking for the circulation of blood. If the heart has stopped beating, blood no longer circulates throughout the body. Without adequate circulation, the victim will die in just a few minutes because the brain is not getting any oxygen.

If a person is breathing, his or her heart is beating and is circulating at least some blood. In the absence of breathing, you must determine if the victim's heart is beating by checking for signs of circulation for no more than 10 seconds, which include checking his or her pulse and observing whether there is coughing or movement in response to rescue breaths. For an adult or child, you feel for the pulse at either of the **carotid arteries** located in the neck (Fig. 4-6, *A* and *B*). For an infant, feel for the brachial pulse in the upper arm. To find the carotid pulse, feel for the Adam's apple and slide your fingers into the groove at the side of the neck. Sometimes the pulse may be difficult to find, since it may be slow or weak. If at first you do not find a pulse, relocate the Adam's apple and again slide your fingers into place. When you think you are in the right spot, take no more than 10 seconds to feel for the pulse. It is easier to feel for the pulse on the side of the victim's neck closer to you.

If the victim does not show signs of circulation, you need to give first aid to keep blood

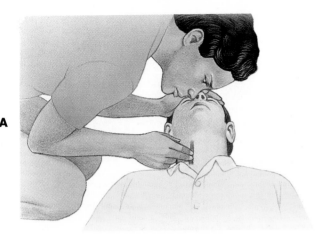
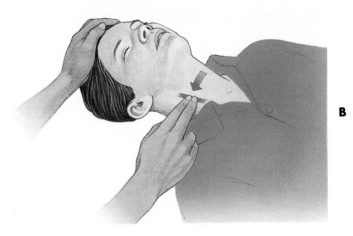

A

B

Figure 4-6   To find out if the heart is beating, check for signs of circulation. Check the pulse of an **A**, adult or **B**, child at the side of the neck.

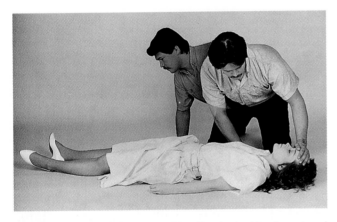

Figure 4-7   Check for severe bleeding by looking from head to toe.

containing oxygen circulating. This first aid involves giving chest compressions and rescue breaths and is called cardiopulmonary resuscitation (CPR). Chapter 6 describes how to do CPR.

Check for Severe Bleeding

After checking for signs of circulation, check for severe bleeding. Bleeding is severe when blood spurts from the wound or cannot be easily controlled. Check for bleeding by looking over the victim's body from head to toe for signs of bleeding, such as blood-soaked clothing (Fig. 4-7). Bleeding usually looks worse than it is. A small amount of blood on a slick surface or mixed with water almost always looks like a great deal of blood. It is not always easy to recognize severe bleeding. You must make a decision based on your best judg-

MIND AT WORK

2. What kinds of injuries or other problems might the victim on the bike trail have?

ment. Severe bleeding must be controlled as soon as possible. Make every effort to keep a barrier between you and the victim's blood. You will learn more about severe bleeding in Chapter 7.

Summary of the Check for Life-threatening Conditions

The check for life-threatening conditions lets you know about any conditions that need to be cared for immediately. Check for unconsciousness, no breathing, no signs of circulation, and severe bleeding. Call EMS personnel or send someone else to call as soon as you determine that the victim is unconscious. If the victim is conscious during your check of the victim, be alert to signs and symptoms that indicate a life-threatening condition.

The skill sheets at the end of this chapter detail the steps of the check for a conscious and unconscious victim.

MIND AT WORK

3. If the victim on the bike trail does not respond when you tap, what would your next step be? Why?

CHECKING A CONSCIOUS VICTIM

Once you have checked for immediately life-threatening conditions, you can begin to check for other conditions that may need care. Certain injuries or conditions are not immediately life threatening but could become so if not cared for. For example, you might find possible broken bones, minor bleeding, or a sudden illness with or without a known specific medical condition or learn of a specific medical condition, such as diabetes. Checking a conscious person has two basic steps:

1. Interview the victim and bystanders.
2. Check the victim head to toe.

It is a good idea to write down the information you find during the check for additional problems. If possible, have someone else write down the information or help you remember it. This information can be given to EMS personnel when they arrive. It may help to determine the type of medical care the victim will get later. Information might include such things as medications the victim is taking and any allergies the victim has.

Interview the Victim and Bystanders

Begin interviewing by asking the victim and bystanders simple questions to learn more about what happened and the victim's condition. The interview should not take much time. If you have not done so already, remember to identify yourself and to get consent to help. Begin by asking the victim's name. Using the victim's name will make him or her feel more comfortable. Gather additional information by asking the victim the following questions:

- What happened?
- Do you feel pain anywhere?
- Do you have any allergies?
- Do you have any medical conditions or are you taking any medication?

If the victim feels pain, ask where the pain is located and ask him or her to describe it. Ask when the pain started. Ask how bad the pain is. You can expect often to get descriptions such as burning, crushing, throbbing, aching, or sharp pain.

Figure 4-8 Parents or other adults may be able to give you helpful information or help you communicate with a sick or injured child.

Sometimes the victim will be unable to provide you with the proper information. Often, infants or children will not be able to respond helpfully. An adult may have momentarily lost consciousness and may not be able to recall what happened, or an elderly person may be confused. A victim may not speak your language. These victims may be frightened. Be calm and patient. Speak normally and in simple terms. Offer reassurance. Ask family members, friends, or bystanders what happened (Fig. 4-8). They may be able to give you helpful information or help you communicate with the victim.

Check Head to Toe

When you check a conscious victim, remember not to move him or her. Most injured people will find the most comfortable position for

Figure 4-9 Medical alert tags can provide important information about the victim.

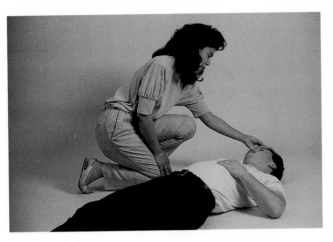

Figure 4-10   Feel the skin with your hand to determine the skin's temperature.

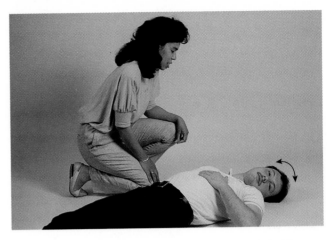

Figure 4-11   Ask the victim to gently move his head from side to side to check the neck.

themselves. For example, a person with a chest injury who is having trouble breathing may be in a sitting position and supporting the injured area. Let the victim stay this way. Do not ask him or her to change positions.

Before you begin to check the victim, tell him or her what you are going to do. Ask the victim to remain still. A victim may move around but will not usually move an injured or painful body part unless he or she is suffering from shock. (You will learn more about shock in Chapter 8.) Ask the victim to tell you if any areas hurt. *Avoid touching any painful area or having the victim move any area that is painful.* Use your senses— sight, sound, touch, and smell—to detect anything abnormal. For example, look around to determine how the incident might have occurred. Listen carefully to what the victim may tell you. Watch for facial expressions, and listen for a tone of voice that may reveal pain. Look for a medical alert tag on a necklace or bracelet (Fig. 4-9). This tag may tell you what might be wrong, who to call for help, and what care to give. As you examine the victim, remain constantly aware of his or her level of consciousness. If the victim becomes unconscious at any time, stop your check and call EMS personnel immediately if the call has not already been made. Remain at the victim's head, where it is easiest to check for breathing and signs of circulation. Check for breathing and signs of circulation and give any necessary care until EMS personnel arrive.

Begin your check at the victim's head, examining the scalp, face, ears, eyes, nose, and mouth. Look for cuts, bumps, bruises, and depressions. Look for signs that may indicate a serious problem. Watch for changes in consciousness. Notice if the victim is drowsy, not alert, or confused. Look for changes in or any difficulty breathing, A healthy person breathes regularly, quietly, and easily. Abnormal breathing includes noisy breathing, such as gasping for air or making gurgling or whistling sounds, breathing that is unusually fast or slow, and breathing that is painful.

Notice how the skin looks and feels. Avoid touching blood. The appearance of the skin and its temperature often indicate something about the victim's condition. For example, a victim with a flushed, pale, or **ashen** (gray) face may be ill. Note if the skin is reddish, bluish, pale, or ashen. Darker skin looks ashen instead of pale. The skin looks red when the body is forced to work harder because the heart pumps faster to get more blood to the tissues. This increased blood flow causes reddened skin and makes the skin feel warm. In contrast, the skin may look pale, ashen, or bluish and feel cool and moist if the blood flow is directed away from the skin's surface to increase the blood supply to vital organs. Determine the temperature of the skin by feeling it with the back of your hand (Fig. 4-10). In later chapters, you will learn more about what these changes may mean and what first aid to give.

As you do the head-to-toe examination, think about how the body normally looks. Be alert for any sign of injuries—anything that

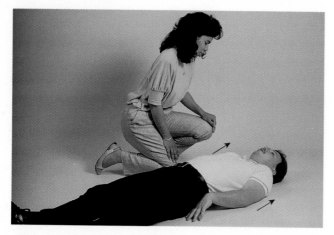

Figure 4-12 Ask the victim to shrug his shoulders to check the shoulders.

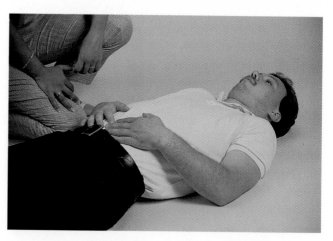

Figure 4-13 To check the chest and abdomen, ask the victim to breathe deeply and then blow the air out. Ask if he is experiencing pain.

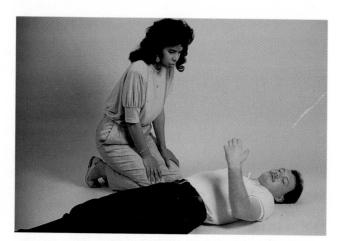

Figure 4-14 Check the arms by asking the victim to bend his arms one at a time.

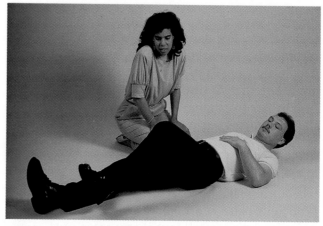

Figure 4-15 Check the legs by asking the victim to bend his legs one at a time.

Figure 4-16 If there are no signs of obvious injuries, help the victim into a sitting position.

looks or sounds unusual. If you are uncertain whether a finding is unusual, compare with the other side of the body.

If you do not suspect an injury to the head, neck, or back, determine if the victim has any specific injuries by asking the victim to try to move each body part in which he or she feels no pain or discomfort. To check the neck, ask if the injured person has neck pain. If he or she does not, ask if the person can slowly move his or her head from side to side (Fig. 4-11). Check the shoulders by asking the person to shrug them (Fig. 4-12). Check the chest and abdomen by asking the person to try to take a deep breath and then blow the air out (Fig. 4-13). Ask if he or she is experiencing pain during breathing. Check each arm by first asking the person if he or she can move the fingers and the hand. Next, ask if he or she can bend the arm (Fig. 4-14). In the same way, check the hips and legs by first asking if he or she can move the toes, foot, and

Figure 4-17   Help the victim slowly stand if no difficulties are found.

ankle. Then determine if the victim can bend the leg (Fig. 4-15). It is best to check only one **extremity** at a time.

If the victim can move all of the body parts without pain or discomfort and has no other apparent signs or symptoms of injury or illness, have him or her attempt to rest for a few minutes in a sitting position (Fig. 4-16). If no further difficulty develops, help the victim slowly stand when he or she is ready (Fig. 4-17).

If the person feels dizzy or is unable to move a body part or is experiencing pain with movement, help him or her rest in the most comfortable position. Keep the person from getting chilled or overheated, and reassure him or her. Determine what additional care is needed and whether to call EMS personnel.

As you do this examination, keep watching the victim's level of consciousness, breathing, and skin color. *If any problems develop, stop whatever you are doing and give first aid immediately.*

CHECKING INFANTS AND CHILDREN

Infants (age 0 to 1) and children (age 1 to 8) receive care that is slightly different from that provided for adult victims. When checking a child or infant for life-threatening conditions, follow the same steps as for an adult. However, if you are alone and find a child or an infant unconscious and not breathing, give rescue breathing for about 1 minute before calling the local emergency number. Rescue breathing will get oxygen into the child and may prevent the heart from stopping. To check the pulse on a child, check the carotid artery as with an adult. For an infant, age 1 year or younger, check the **brachial pulse** on the inside of the upper arm between the shoulder and the elbow (Fig. 4-18).

When checking a child for nonlife-threatening emergencies, observe the child before touching him or her. Look for signs that indicate changes in consciousness, any breathing difficulty, and any apparent injuries or conditions. All signs may change as soon as you touch the child because he or she may become anxious or upset. If a parent or adult guardian is present, ask him or her to help calm the infant or child. Parents can also tell you if the child has a medical condition that you should be aware of.

Communicate clearly with the parent or guardian and the child. Explain what you are going to do. Get at eye level with the child. Talk slowly and in a friendly manner. Use simple words. Ask questions that the child can answer easily. Often a parent or guardian will be holding a crying child. It is often best to check the child while the parent or guardian holds him or her. When you begin the examination, begin at the toes instead of the head. Checking in this order gives the child the opportunity to get

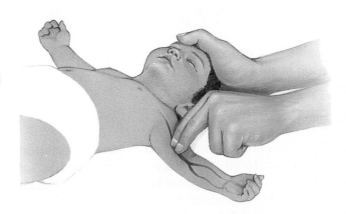

Figure 4-18   Check the pulse of an infant at the inside of the arm between the shoulder and the elbow.

From Horses . . . .
A History of Emergency Care

Emergency care originated during the French emperor Napoleon's campaigns in the late 1700s. The surgeon-in-chief for the Grand Army, Dominique Jean Larrey, became the first doctor to try to save the wounded during battles instead of waiting until the fighting was over (Major R). Using horse-drawn litters, Larrey and his men dashed onto the battlefield in what became known as "flying ambulances."

By the 1860s, the wartime principles of emergency care were applied to emergencies in some American cities. In 1878, a writer for *Harper's New Monthly Magazine* explained how accidents were reported to the police, who notified a local hospital by a telegraph signal. He described an early hospital ambulance ride in New York City (Rideing WH).

" *A well-kept horse was quickly harnessed to the ambulance; and as the surgeon took his seat behind, having first put on a jaunty uniform cap with gold lettering, the driver sprang to the box ... and with a sharp crack of the whip we rolled off the smooth asphalt of the courtyard and into the street .... As we swept around corners and dashed over crossings, both doctor and driver kept up a sharp cry of warning to pedestrians (Rideing WH).*"

While booming industrial cities developed emergency transport systems, rural populations had only rudimentary services. In most small towns, the mortician had the only vehicle large enough to handle the litters, so emergency victims were just as likely to ride in a hearse to the hospital as in an ambulance (Division of Medical Sciences).

Cars gave Americans a faster system of transport, but over the next 50 years, car collisions also created the need for more emergency vehicles. In 1966, a major report questioned the quality of emergency services (Division of Medical Sciences). Dismayed at the rising death toll on the nation's higways, Congress passed laws in 1966 and 1973 order-

---

used to the process and allows him or her to see what is going on.

PROVIDING CARE

Once you complete the head-to-toe examination for an adult, provide care for any specific injuries you find. To provide care for the victim until EMS personnel arrive, follow these general care guidelines:

- Do no harm.
- Monitor breathing and consciousness.

- Help the victim rest in the most comfortable position.
- Keep the victim from getting chilled or overheated.
- Reassure the victim.
- Provide any specific care needed.

Whenever possible, provide care in a manner that minimizes the risk of disease transmission between you and the victim. Following these basic guidelines will help reduce that risk:

- Avoid contact with the victim's body substances when possible.

to Helicopters

ing the improved training of ambulance workers and emergency department staffs, an improved communication network, and the development of regional units with specialized care.

Today, the telegraph signal has been replaced by the 9-1-1 telephone code, which, for over 75 percent of the United States' population, immediately connects a caller to a dispatcher who can send help. In some areas, a computer connected to the enhanced 9-1-1 system displays the caller's name, address, and phone number, even if the caller cannot speak. Ambulance workers have changed from coachmen to trained medical professionals who can provide lifesaving care at the scene. Horses have been replaced by ambulances and helicopters equipped to provide the most advanced prehospital care available.

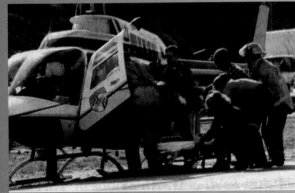

Craig C. Schleunes

The EMS system has expanded in sheer numbers and in services. Today, New York City has 15 times as many hospitals as it did in the 1870s. Hospitals have also vastly improved their emergency care and facilities. If patients suffer from critical conditions, such as heart attacks, burns, spinal cord injuries, or other traumatic injuries, or if the patients are children, the EMS system now has developed regional centers where specialists and specialized equipment are always available.

In two centuries, the EMS system has evolved from horses to helicopters. As technology continues to advance, it is difficult to imagine what changes the new century will bring.

SOURCES

Division of Medical Sciences, National Academy of Sciences—National Research Council: *Accidental death and disability: the neglected disease of modern society,* Washington, D.C., September 1966.

Major R, M.D.: *A history of medicine,* Springfield, Ill., Charles C. Thomas, 1954.

Rideing WH: Hospital life in New York, *Harper's New Monthly Magazine* 57(171), 1878.

- Place barriers, such as disposable gloves, plastic wrap, or a clean, dry, folded cloth, between the victim's body substances and yourself.
- Wear protective clothing, such as disposable gloves, to cover any cuts, scrapes, and skin conditions you may have (Fig. 4-19).
- Wash your hands with soap and water immediately after giving care (Fig. 4-20).
- Do not eat, drink, or touch your mouth, nose, or eyes when giving first aid.
- Do not touch objects that may be soiled with blood or other body substances.

- Always have a first aid kit handy, and make sure the items in it, such as disposable gloves, are replaced if you use them.

DECIDING TO TRANSPORT THE VICTIM

After completing your check of the victim, on a rare occasion, you might consider transporting the victim to the hospital yourself if the victim's condition is not severe. This decision is important. Do not transport a victim when the trip may aggravate the injury or illness or cause

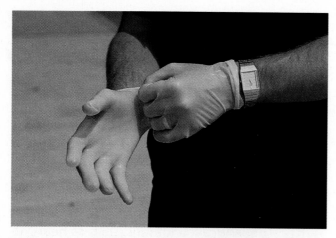

Figure 4-19 Wearing latex gloves is an effective way to decrease your risk of contracting or transmitting an infection.

Figure 4-20 Thorough handwashing after giving care helps protect you against disease.

additional injury, or when the victim has or may develop a life-threatening condition. In instances of a life-threatening condition or the possibility of further injury, call EMS personnel and wait for help.

If you do decide to transport the victim yourself, ask someone else to come with you to help keep the victim comfortable. Be sure you know the quickest route to the nearest medical facility with emergency-care capabilities. Pay close attention to the victim, and watch for any changes in his or her condition.

MIND AT WORK

4. *If you find that the victim on the trail is conscious, has no difficulty breathing, and has no severe bleeding, what should you do next? Why?*

Discourage a victim from driving himself or herself to the hospital. An injury may restrict movement, or the victim may become groggy or faint. A sudden onset of pain may be distracting. Also, an injured or ill person may drive faster than he or she normally would. Any of these conditions can make driving dangerous for the victim, passengers, pedestrians, and other drivers.

SUMMARY

When you respond to an emergency, check the scene. Make sure the scene is not dangerous to you, the victim, and bystanders. Check the victim for life-threatening conditions. Find out if the victim is conscious. Call EMS personnel if the victim is unconscious. Determine if the victim has any problems with breathing or circulation, and check for severe bleeding. Care for any life-threatening problems right away. Immediate care is essential for the victim's survival. Try to send a bystander to make the call to EMS personnel. Then you can continue to check breathing and circulation and provide care.

If you find no life-threatening conditions, interview the victim and any bystanders, and do a head-to-toe examination (toe-to-head for a child) to find and care for any other injuries. Nonlife-threatening problems could become serious if you do not give first aid.

Providing care is not an exact science. Because each emergency and each victim is unique, an emergency may not occur exactly as it was discussed and practiced in a classroom setting. Even within a single emergency, the care needed may change from one moment to the next. For example, the victim may be conscious, breathing, have signs of circulation, and have no severe bleeding. In this instance, you do not need to call EMS personnel immediately. However, during your head-to-toe examination, you may notice that the victim is beginning to experience breathing difficulty. At this point, someone should call EMS personnel.

Many variables exist when dealing with emergencies. You do not need to know exactly what is wrong with the victim to provide appropriate care. Ensure that you take care of life-threatening emergencies first.

Answers to Application Questions

1. In this particular emergency, you may not be able to do much to ensure scene safety, beyond guarding against the possibility that another biker might round the curve and hit you or the victim when you are giving care and making sure the scene is safe for you.

2. A head or spine injury is certainly a possibility, as is a medical emergency of some kind, such as an allergic reaction or a heart attack.

3. Shout for help. If no one responds and the victim is unconscious, position the victim on one side (recovery position) and find a telephone or someone to call EMS personnel. Once EMS personnel have been notified, return to the victim as soon as possible. If you cannot find a phone or someone to place the call, go get help.

4. Ask the victim what happened. Check for non-life-threatening conditions to find out if the victim has any problems that require you to call EMS personnel. If you find no problems, help the victim gradually to his or her feet.

STUDY QUESTIONS

1. Match each emergency action step with the actions it includes.

    a. Check the scene.
    b. Check for life-threatening emergencies.
    c. Call EMS personnel.
    d. Check for nonlife-threatening emergencies when appropriate.

    __B__ Open the airway.

    __A__ Look for bystanders who can help.

    __A__ Interview the victim and bystanders.

    __B__ Check for breathing.

    __D__ Do a head-to-toe examination.

    __C__ Call 9-1-1 or the local emergency number.

    __A__ Look for victims.

    __B__ Check for severe bleeding.

    __A__ Look for dangers.

    __B__ Check for signs of circulation.

    __A__ Look for clues to determine what happened.

    __D__ Ask for consent to give care.

2. List four immediately life-threatening conditions.

   Unconscious, No Breathing, No Circ, Severe Bleeding

3. *Several people are clustered in the middle of a street. A car is stopped in the right lane. As you approach the group, you can see a mangled bicycle lying on the pavement. You see your neighbor lying next to it. No one seems to be doing anything. You approach your neighbor and kneel next to him.*

   What steps would you take next?

4. Assuming the man has no life-threatening conditions, what would influence your decision whether to transport him to the hospital?

5. Describe when and why you would do a head-to-toe examination.

6. You walk into your boss's office for a meeting. You see a cup of coffee spilled on the desk. You find him lying on the floor, motionless. What should you do? Number the following actions in order:

   a. Call EMS personnel if no one responds to your call for help.
   b. Check for breathing.
   c. Check the scene.
   d. Check for signs of circulation and severe bleeding.
   e. Check for consciousness.
   f. Shout for help.

7. List six guidelines you can follow to prevent disease transmission.

In questions 8 through 12, circle the letter of the correct answer.

8. What is the purpose of your initial check of the victim?

   a. To check for minor injuries
   b. To determine if any life-threatening conditions exist that need immediate care
   c. To get consent from the victim before providing care
   d. To ask for information about the cause of the illness or injury

9. Once you determine the victim has no immediately life-threatening conditions, you should—

   a. Call EMS professionals for help.
   b. Transport the victim to the nearest hospital.
   c. Check for other injuries or conditions that could become life threatening if not cared for.
   d. Check for consciousness.

10. Before beginning a check for life-threatening conditions with an unconscious victim, you should first—

    a. Position the victim so that you can open the airway.
    b. Check the scene.
    c. Check for consciousness.
    d. Call EMS professionals for help.

11. After checking for consciousness, you determine that the victim is unconscious. What should you do next?

    a. Call EMS professionals for help.
    b. Give two slow, gentle breaths.
    c. Check for signs of circulation and severe bleeding.
    d. Begin a check for nonlife-threatening conditions.

12. Which of the following actions are performed during the check for a conscious victim?

    a. Gathering additional information about the victim's condition.
    b. Asking the victim to move body parts that are not painful.
    c. Checking for any breathing problems.
    d. All of the above.

Answers are listed in Appendix A.

SKILL SHEETS

👁 CHECK **the scene and the victim.**

1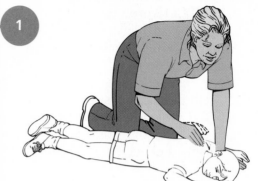

Check for consciousness

- Tap and gently shake person.
- Shout "Are you okay?"

If person responds . . .
- *Do check for conscious person.*

If person does not respond . . .

- Send someone to CALL 📞 *9-1-1 or local emergency number then . . .*

2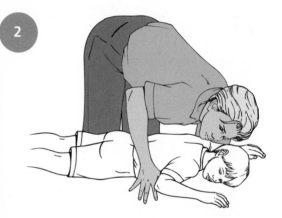

Check for breathing

- Look, listen, and feel for breathing for about 5 seconds.

If person is not breathing or you cannot tell . . .

3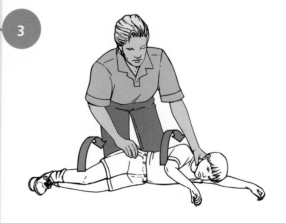

Roll the person onto the back

- Roll person toward you while supporting head and neck.

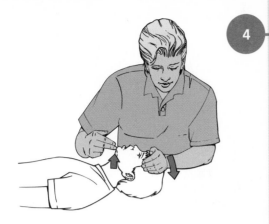

4

Open the airway

- Tilt head back and lift chin.

5

Recheck for breathing

- Look, listen, and feel for breathing for about 5 seconds.
- The total time for the breathing check should be no more than 10 seconds.

If person is not breathing . . .

6

Give 2 slow, gentle breaths

- Keep head tilted back.
- Pinch nose shut.
- Seal your lips tightly around person's mouth.
- Give 2 slow, gentle breaths, each lasting about 2 seconds for adults and about 1½ seconds for children and infants.
- Watch to see that your breaths go in and that the chest clearly rises.

Check for signs of circulation

- Locate Adam's apple.
- Slide your fingers down into groove of neck on side closer to you.
- Check for signs of circulation for no more than 10 seconds.

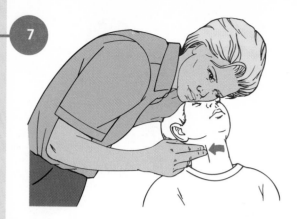

Check for severe bleeding

- Look from head to toe for severe bleeding.

CARE for the conditions you find.

If person has signs of circulation and is not breathing . . .

- *Do rescue breathing.*

If person does not have signs of circulation . . .

- *Do CPR.*

If person is bleeding severely . . .

- *Attempt to quickly control bleeding.*

SKILL SHEETS

Checking Someone Who Is Conscious

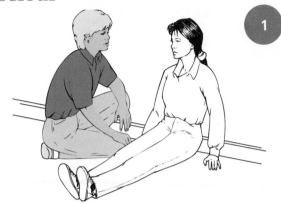

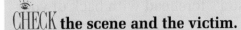 **CHECK the scene and the victim.**

1

Interview the person

- Introduce yourself, tell him or her your level of training, and get permission to give care.
- Ask—
  - His or her name?
  - What happened?
  - Do you feel pain anywhere?
  - Do you have any allergies?
  - Do you have any medical conditions or are you taking any medication?

Note: Send someone to CALL *9-1-1 or the local emergency number any time a life-threatening emergency becomes apparent.*

2

Check head to toe

- Visually inspect body.
- Before you begin, tell person what you are going to do.
- Look carefully for bleeding, cuts, bruises, and obvious deformities.
- Look for medical alert tag.

Note: Do not ask the person to move any areas in which he or she has discomfort or pain or if you suspect injury to the head or spine.

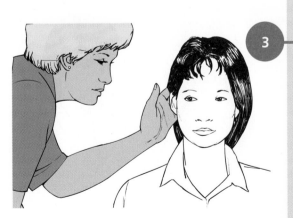

3

Check the head

- Look at scalp, face, ears, eyes, nose, and mouth for cuts, bumps, bruises, and depressions.
- Notice if victim is drowsy, not alert, or confused.

Check skin appearance and temperature

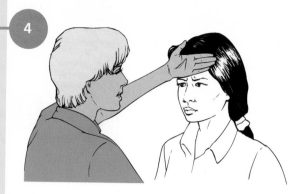

- Feel person's forehead with back of your hand.
- Look at person's face and lips.
- Ask yourself, is the skin—
  - Cold or hot?
  - Unusually wet or dry?
  - Pale, bluish, or flushed?

Check the neck

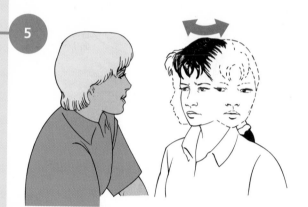

- If there is no discomfort and no suspected injury to neck, ask person to move head slowly from side to side.
- Note pain, discomfort, or inability to move.

Check the shoulders

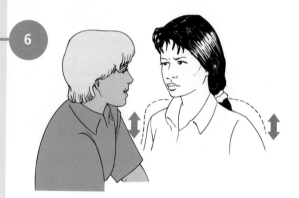

- Ask person to shrug shoulders.

Check the chest and abdomen

- Ask person to take a deep breath and blow air out.
- Ask if he or she is experiencing pain during breathing.

8

Check the arms

- Check one arm at a time.
- Ask person to—
  - Move hands and fingers.
  - Bend arm.

9

Check the hips and legs

- Check one leg at a time.
- Ask person to—
  - Move toes, foot, and ankle.
  - Bend leg.

CARE for any conditions you find.

If person can move all body parts without pain or discomfort and has no other apparent signs of injury or illness—

- *Have him or her rest for a few minutes in sitting position.*
- *Help person slowly stand when he or she is ready, if no further difficulty develops.*

If person is unable to move a body part or is experiencing pain on movement or dizziness—

- *Help him or her rest in most comfortable position.*
- *Keep person from getting chilled or overheated.*
- *Reassure him or her.*
- *Determine whether to call EMS personnel.*

LIFE-THREATENING EMERGENCIES

CHAPTER 5

It's a warm spring day. You and your friend, Kevin, are playing basketball on the public courts in the park. The ten-year-old next door, Steve, has tagged along. As you and Kevin attempt to play one-on-one, Steve tries to steal the ball. At one point, he is successful, and, dribbling the ball, he dashes to the far end of the court. You and Kevin become angry. You chase Steve. Suddenly, Steve stops in his tracks. He lets the ball go and brings his hands to his chest, gasping and making a strange wheezing sound. As you run to him, you see Steve is really having trouble breathing. As Steve struggles to catch his breath, you and Kevin try to decide what to do.

Breathing Emergencies

WHAT YOU SHOULD LEARN

After reading this chapter, you should be able to—

1. Describe the breathing process.

2. Identify ten signs and symptoms of respiratory distress.

3. Describe the care for a person experiencing respiratory distress.

4. Identify two common childhood illnesses that may cause respiratory distress.

5. Describe the purpose of rescue breathing.

6. Describe when and how to provide rescue breathing for an adult, child, and infant.

7. Describe when and how to use breathing devices.

8. Describe special considerations for rescue breathing.

9. Identify five causes of choking for adults, children, and infants.

10. Describe the care for conscious and unconscious choking for adult, child, and infant victims.

11. Define the key terms for this chapter.

After reading this chapter and completing the class activities, you should be able to demonstrate—

1. How to provide rescue breathing for adult, child, and infant victims.

2. How to care for conscious adult, child, and infant choking victims.

3. How to care for unconscious adult, child, and infant choking victims.

4. How to make appropriate decisions when given an example of an emergency situation in which a person may be experiencing respiratory distress or arrest.

Introduction

In previous chapters, you learned what you can do to help in an emergency. You learned three emergency action steps that guide your actions. Remember, these emergency action steps are—

- *Check* the scene and the victim.
- *Call* 9-1-1 or a local emergency number.
- *Care* for the victim until help arrives.

In this chapter, you will learn how to care for someone who is having trouble breathing or who has stopped breathing.

As you read in Chapter 4, once you have checked to ensure the scene is safe, you check the victim for life-threatening conditions. First you check to see if the victim is conscious. If the victim is unconscious and an adult, send someone to call EMS personnel immediately or make the call yourself. Then continue your check for other possible life-threatening emergencies as follows:

- *Check* for breathing.
- *Check* for signs of circulation.
- *Check* for severe bleeding.

If you find no apparent signs or symptoms of a life-threatening condition, check for non-life-threatening conditions that may need care.

If the victim is a child or an infant who is unconscious and no one is available to call EMS personnel, provide 1 minute of care before calling. Because oxygen is vital to life, you must always ensure that the victim has an open airway and is breathing. You should detect a breathing emergency during your check for life-threatening emergencies. A **breathing emergency** exists when someone's breathing is impaired and life is threatened. A breathing emergency can occur in two ways: breathing can become difficult, or breathing can stop. A person who is having difficulty breathing is in respiratory distress. A person who is not breathing is in respiratory arrest.

THE BREATHING PROCESS

Normal breathing requires the respiratory, circulatory, nervous, and musculoskeletal systems to work together. As you read in Chapter 3, injuries or illnesses that affect any of these systems may impair breathing and result in a breathing emergency. For example, if the heart stops beating, the victim will stop breathing.

Key Terms

Abdominal thrusts: A technique for unblocking a completely obstructed airway by compressing the abdomen; also called the Heimlich maneuver.

Airway obstruction: Complete or partial blockage of the airway that prevents air from reaching a person's lungs; the most common cause of respiratory emergencies.

Aspiration (as pĭ RA shun): Sucking or taking blood, vomit, saliva, or other foreign material into the lungs.

Breathing emergency: An emergency in which breathing is so impaired that life is threatened.

Head-tilt/chin-lift: A technique for opening the airway.

Rescue breathing: A technique of breathing for a nonbreathing victim.

Respiratory (re SPI rah to re *or* RES pah rah tor e) arrest: A condition in which breathing has stopped.

Respiratory distress: A condition in which breathing is difficult.

Stoma: An opening in the front of the neck through which a person whose larynx has been removed breathes.

Injury or disease in areas of the brain that control breathing may impair or stop breathing. Damage to muscles or bones of the chest and back can make breathing difficult or painful.

The human body requires a constant supply of oxygen for survival. When you breathe air into your lungs, the oxygen in the air is transferred to the blood. The blood transports the oxygen to the brain, other organs, muscles, and other parts of the body where it is used to provide energy. This energy allows the body to perform many functions, such as breathing, walking, talking, digesting food, and maintaining body temperature. Different functions require different levels of energy and, therefore, different amounts of oxygen. For example, sitting in a chair requires less energy than jogging around the block, so you do not usually breathe as rapidly or deeply when you sit as when you jog.

Without oxygen, brain cells can begin to die in 4 to 6 minutes (Fig. 5-1). Some tissues, such as the brain, are very sensitive to oxygen starvation. Unless the brain receives oxygen within minutes, permanent brain damage or death will result.

Breathing emergencies can be caused by any of the following:

- An obstructed airway (choking)
- Illness
- Certain respiratory conditions that can inhibit breathing (such as emphysema or asthma)
- Electrocution
- Shock
- Drowning
- Heart attack or heart disease
- Injury to the head, chest, or lungs
- Allergic reactions to foods, insect stings, or other **allergens**
- Drugs
- Inhaling or ingesting toxic substances

RESPIRATORY DISTRESS

Respiratory distress is the most common type of breathing emergency. It is a condition in which breathing becomes difficult. Respiratory

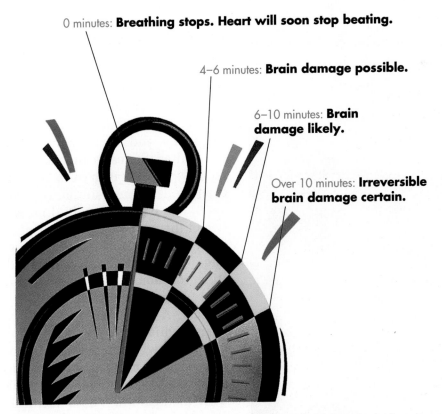

0 minutes: **Breathing stops. Heart will soon stop beating.**

4–6 minutes: **Brain damage possible.**

6–10 minutes: **Brain damage likely.**

Over 10 minutes: **Irreversible brain damage certain.**

Figure 5-1   Time is critical in life-threatening emergencies. Unless the brain gets oxygen within minutes of when breathing stops, brain damage or death will occur.

distress is not always caused by injuries, illnesses, or other problems such as those listed in the preceding paragraph. It may also result from excitement or anxiety. Learn to recognize the signs and symptoms of respiratory distress.

Signs and Symptoms of Respiratory Distress

A victim of respiratory distress may show various signs and symptoms. Victims may look as if they cannot catch their breath, or they may gasp for air. They may appear to breathe faster or slower than normal. Breaths may be unusually deep or shallow. They may make unusual noises, such as **wheezing** (hoarse whistling sounds), gurgling, or high-pitched sounds like crowing.

The victim's skin appearance and temperature can also indicate respiratory distress. At first, the victim's skin may be unusually moist and appear flushed. Later, it may appear pale, ashen, or **cyanotic** (bluish) and feel cool as the oxygen level in the blood falls.

Signs and Symptoms of Respiratory Distress
Abnormal breathing
Breathing is slow or rapid
Breaths are unusually deep or shallow
Victim is gasping for breath
Victim is wheezing, gurgling, or making high pitched noises such as crowing
Skin appearance
Victim's skin is unusually moist or cool.
Victim's skin has a flushed, pale, ashen, or bluish appearance
How the victim feels
Victim feels short of breath
Victim feels dizzy or lightheaded
Victim feels pain in the chest or tingling in hands, feet, or lips
Victim feels apprehensive or fearful

Victims may say they feel dizzy or lightheaded. They may feel pain in the chest or tingling in the hands, feet, or lips. Understandably, the victim may be apprehensive or fearful. Any of these symptoms is a clue that the victim may be in respiratory distress.

Specific Causes of Respiratory Distress

Although respiratory distress is sometimes caused by injury, other conditions, such as asthma, anaphylactic shock, and the childhood conditions croup and epiglottitis, can also cause respiratory distress. Hyperventilation is a form of respiratory distress that may also need immediate care.

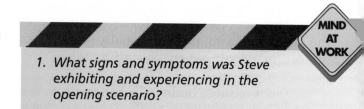

MIND AT WORK

1. *What signs and symptoms was Steve exhibiting and experiencing in the opening scenario?*

Asthma

Asthma is a condition that narrows the air passages and makes breathing difficult. During an asthma attack, the air passages become constricted, or narrowed, as a result of a spasm of the muscles lining the bronchi (the air passages that lead from the trachea to the alveoli) or swelling of the bronchi themselves.

Asthma is more common in children and young adults than in older adults, but the frequency and severity in all age groups in the United States is increasing. Asthma is the most frequent reason for hospitalization of children and young adults. Between 1979 and 1989, death rates for children with asthma between the ages of 10 and 14 increased 100 percent. Asthma attacks may be triggered by an allergic reaction to food, pollen, a drug, an insect sting, or emotional stress. For some people, cold air or physical activity may induce asthma. A characteristic sign of asthma is the hoarse whistling sounds made when exhaling, known as wheezing. Wheezing occurs because air becomes trapped in the lungs. Normally, people diagnosed with asthma control attacks with medication. These medications stop the muscle spasm, opening the airway and making breathing easier.

Emphysema

Emphysema is a disease in which the lungs and alveoli lose their ability to exchange carbon dioxide and oxygen effectively. Emphysema is often caused by smoking and usually develops over many years. Chronic (long-lasting or frequently recurring) emphysema will worsen over time. The most common symptom of emphysema is shortness of breath. Exhaling is extremely difficult. Victims may appear cyanotic. In advanced cases, the victim may feel restless, confused, and weak and may even go into respiratory or cardiac arrest.

Bronchitis

Bronchitis is a disease resulting in inflammation of the lining of the trachea, bronchi, and bronchioles. This inflammation causes a buildup of mucus that obstructs the passage of air and air exchange in the lungs. Chronic bronchitis is most commonly caused by long-term smoking; however, exposure to environmental irritants and pollutants may also lead to bronchitis. A person with bronchitis will typically have a persistent cough and may feel tightness in the chest and have trouble breathing. As with emphysema, the person may also feel restless, confused, and weak and may even go into respiratory or cardiac arrest.

Anaphylactic shock

Anaphylactic shock, also known as **anaphylaxis,** is a severe allergic reaction. Air passages may swell and restrict the victim's breathing. Anaphylaxis may be caused by insect stings, food, other allergens, or certain medications. Signs and symptoms of anaphylaxis include a rash, a feeling of tightness in the chest and throat, and swelling of the face, neck, and tongue. The person may also feel dizzy or confused. If not recognized early and cared for quickly, an allergic reaction can become a life-threatening emergency. Some people know that they are allergic to certain substances or to bee stings. They may have learned to avoid these substances or bees and may carry medication to reverse the allergic reaction (Fig. 5-2). People who have severe allergic reactions may wear a medical alert bracelet.

Childhood forms of respiratory distress

Infections of the respiratory system are more common in children and infants than adults. These can range from minor infections, such as

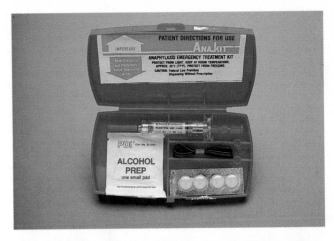

Figure 5-2 People who know they are allergic to certain substances or bee stings may carry an anaphylaxis kit with medication that reverses the allergic reaction.

the common cold, to life-threatening infections that block the airway.

Signs and symptoms of respiratory distress in children include—

- Agitation.
- Unusually fast or slow breathing.
- Drowsiness.
- Noisy breathing.
- Pale, ashen, flushed, bluish skin color.
- Increased difficulty breathing.
- Altered level of consciousness.
- Increased heart and breathing rates.

A common childhood illness that causes respiratory distress is croup. **Croup** is a viral infection that causes swelling of the tissues around the vocal cords. Besides the basic signs and symptoms of respiratory distress and a cough that sounds like the bark of a seal, croup is often preceded by 1 or 2 days of illness, sometimes with a fever. Croup occurs more often in the winter months, and the signs and symptoms of croup are more evident in the evening. It is not generally life threatening but can be very frightening for the child and the parents or caregiver.

Another childhood illness is **epiglottitis,** a bacterial infection that causes a severe inflammation of the epiglottis. You may recall from Chapter 3 that the epiglottis is a flap of tissue above the vocal cords that seals off the airway during swallowing. When the epiglottis becomes infected, it can swell and completely block the airway. A child with epiglottitis will appear ill and have a high fever and a sore

TOUR DE FRANCE

The portion of the Tour de France bicycle race that winds its way through the Alps is a legendary challenge. Each year, some 250,000 fans gather along the road of L'Alpe de Huez to watch professional cyclists attack the most difficult climb of the tour. The tortuous path twists 21 times and reaches a snowy summit of 5728 feet above sea level. Even athletes in superb condition find themselves struggling— legs wobble, shoulders begin to bob, and elbows stick out awkwardly. Many riders drop out.

A secret enemy of the riders is altitude. At higher elevations, the air pressure is lower, allowing oxygen molecules to spread farther apart in the atmosphere. Consequently, the cyclist gets less oxygen with each gulp of air and transports less oxygen to straining muscles. Oxygen is necessary for exercise because it helps release energy the muscles can use.

Endurance sports like bicycle racing are especially difficult at high altitudes. To equal oxygen intake at sea level, the cyclist must breathe faster and the heart must pump harder. The cyclist hyperventilates to meet his or her oxygen demands. Studies indicate that the athlete's aerobic capacity, which includes the heart's ability to pump oxygen to the muscles and the muscles' ability to use oxygen efficiently, can drop 5 to 10 percent when a person moves from sea level to 6500 feet.

To compensate for the change in altitude, the body makes adjustments within a few days. As the athlete becomes accustomed to the new climate, he or she begins to breathe in a greater volume of air with each breath. The body produces more red blood cells to carry oxygen more efficiently. These adjustments actually improve the aerobic capacity of athletes who train in the mountains or in low-pressure chambers.

Many U.S. Olympic team members live and train at high altitudes in places like Colorado Springs. U.S. Junior National Team cyclist Eric Harris, who is training for the Olympics, says he can feel a difference in his riding at high altitudes. He rides up to 110 miles a day during endurance training in January through April.

"Each of us has our own aerobic training level—your head pounds, your chest feels like knives are going into it with each breath. If you miss a breath by drinking or talking, it takes 10 to 20 more to make it up. Mountains are where cycling turns into an individual sport."

"You have to train in the mountains to be good in them. That's why I left Texas and moved to Utah and Colorado. No one from the low flatlands will be a great climber in the big mountains—maybe good, but never great."

Eric has accepted the challenge of the mountains, hoping to set cycling records to be listed among those of the Olympic greats.

throat. He or she will often be sitting up and straining to breathe. The child will be very frightened. Saliva will often be dripping from the mouth because swelling of the epiglottis prevents the child from swallowing.

You do not need to distinguish between croup and epiglottitis, since the care you provide will be the same. First aid for a child in respiratory distress includes allowing him or her to remain in the most comfortable position for breathing. At the first sign that the child's condition is worsening, call the local emergency number for an ambulance. Do not attempt to place any object in the child's mouth. Be aware that a child's airway may become completely blocked as a result of epiglottitis. A child in this condition needs immediate professional help.

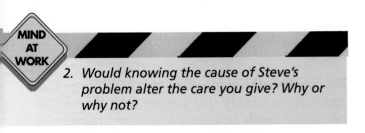

2. *Would knowing the cause of Steve's problem alter the care you give? Why or why not?*

Care for Respiratory Distress

Recognizing the signs and symptoms of respiratory distress and giving care are often keys to preventing other emergencies. Respiratory distress may signal the beginning of a life-threatening condition. For example, respiratory distress can be the first sign of a more serious breathing emergency or even a heart attack. Respiratory distress can lead to respiratory arrest. If not immediately cared for, respiratory arrest will result in death. Many of the signs and symptoms of different kinds of respiratory distress are similar. *You do not need to know the specific cause of a victim's respiratory distress to provide care effectively.* Remember to always check the scene to ensure your safety before you approach a victim. Respiratory distress can be caused by dangerous situations, such as the presence of toxic fumes.

If the victim is breathing, you know his or her heart is beating. Make sure the person is not bleeding severely. Help him or her rest in a comfortable position. Usually sitting is more

Figure 5-3 A person who is having trouble breathing may breathe more easily in a sitting position.

comfortable because breathing is easier in this position (Fig. 5-3). Provide fresh air by opening a door or window if you are indoors or by moving the victim to fresh air. Make sure someone has called the local emergency number for help.

If the victim is conscious, check for nonlife-threatening conditions. As you check, remember that a person experiencing breathing difficulty may have trouble talking. Therefore, talk to any bystanders who may know about the victim's condition. The victim can confirm answers or answer yes-or-no questions by nodding. If possible, try to reduce any anxiety that may contribute to the victim's breathing difficulty. Continue to look and listen for any changes in the victim's breathing and level of consciousness. Watch for additional signs and symptoms of respiratory distress. Calm and reassure the victim. Help maintain normal body temperature by preventing chilling on a cool day or by providing shade on a hot day. If it is available, assist the victim in taking his or her prescribed medication for the condition. Medications may be oxygen, an inhalant (bronchial dilator), or medication in an **anaphylaxis kit.**

Hyperventilation

Hyperventilation occurs when breathing is faster than normal. This rapid breathing can upset the body's balance of oxygen and carbon dioxide. Hyperventilation often results from fear or anxiety and is likely to occur in people who are tense and nervous. It can also be caused by head injuries, severe bleeding, or

Care for Respiratory Distress

Complete a check for life-threatening conditions.

Activate the EMS system.

Help the victim rest comfortably.

Check for any nonlife-threatening conditions.

Reassure the victim.

Assist with medication.

Keep the victim from getting chilled or overheated.

Monitor breathing and pulse.

illnesses such as high fever, heart failure, lung disease, or diabetic emergencies. It can also be triggered by asthma or exercise. A characteristic sign of hyperventilation is deep, rapid breathing. Despite their efforts to breathe, people who are hyperventilating feel that they cannot get enough air or that they are suffocating. Therefore, they are often fearful and apprehensive, or they may appear confused. They may say that they feel dizzy or that their fingers and toes or lips feel numb or tingly.

If the victim's breathing is rapid and he or she shows signs and symptoms of an injury or an underlying illness or condition, call EMS personnel immediately. This person needs advanced care right away. If, however, the victim's breathing is rapid and you are sure that it is caused by emotion, such as excitement, tell him or her to relax and breathe slowly. Reassurance is often enough to correct hyperventilation. If the victim's breathing still does not slow down, have the victim cup both hands around his or her mouth and nose and breathe into them. When the victim rebreathes exhaled air, the condition will usually correct itself. If the condition does not correct itself or if the victim becomes unconscious from hyperventilating, call EMS personnel immediately. Keep the victim's airway open and monitor breathing until EMS personnel arrive.

RESPIRATORY ARREST

In *respiratory arrest,* breathing stops. Causes of this condition may include illness, injury,

drowning, electrical shock, or an obstructed airway. The causes of respiratory distress can also lead to respiratory arrest. In respiratory arrest, the person gets no oxygen. The body can function without oxygen for only a few minutes before body systems begin to fail. Without oxygen, the heart muscle stops functioning, causing the circulatory system to fail. When the heart stops, other body systems start to fail. However, you can keep the person's respiratory system functioning artificially by giving rescue breathing.

MIND AT WORK

3. Could the cause of Steve's respiratory distress lead to respiratory arrest? Why or why not?

Rescue Breathing

Rescue breathing is a way of breathing air into someone to supply that person with the oxygen he or she needs to survive. Rescue breathing is given to victims who are not breathing but still have signs of circulation.

Rescue breathing works because the air you breathe into the victim contains more than enough oxygen to keep that person alive. The air you take in with every breath contains about 21 percent oxygen, but your body uses only 5 percent. The air you breathe out of your lungs and into the lungs of the victim contains about 16 percent oxygen, enough to keep someone alive.

Rescue breathing for adults

You will determine whether you need to give rescue breathing while checking for life-threatening emergencies. If you find that the person is not conscious, have someone call EMS personnel immediately or make the call yourself, if necessary. Continue to check for other life-threatening emergencies. If you cannot see, hear, or feel any signs of breathing, the victim is in respiratory arrest. Immediately give the victim 2 slow, gentle breaths to get air into his or her lungs. Then check circulation by feeling for the pulse and observing to see if normal breathing has resumed or if the victim coughs or moves in response to rescue breaths. Check for severe bleeding.

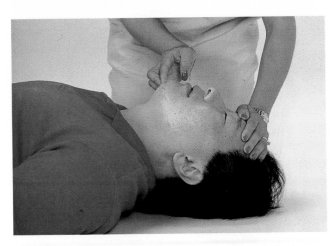

Figure 5-4 The head-tilt/chin-lift opens the victim's airway.

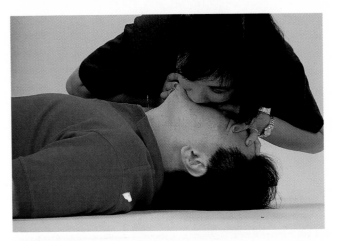

Figure 5-5 To give rescue breathing, tilt the head back, lift the chin, and pinch the nose shut. Breathe into the victim's mouth.

If the victim is not breathing but has signs of circulation, begin rescue breathing. To give breaths, keep the airway open with the ***head-tilt/chin-lift*** (Fig. 5-4). The head-tilt/chin-lift not only opens the airway by moving the tongue away from the back of the throat but also moves the epiglottis from the opening of the trachea. Put one hand on the victim's forehead and push down with the palm to tilt the head back. With the other hand, lift up on the bony part of the jaw near the chin. Avoid pressing on the soft tissue under the chin. Gently pinch the victim's nose shut with the thumb and index finger of your hand that is on the victim's forehead. Next, make a tight seal around his or her mouth with your mouth. Breathe slowly into the victim until you see his or her chest clearly rise (Fig. 5-5). Give two breaths. Each breath should last about 2 seconds for adults and 1½ seconds for children and infants, with a pause in between to let the air flow back out. Watch the victim's chest clearly rise each time you breathe into the victim to ensure that your breaths are going into the lungs.

If you do not see the victim's chest clearly rise as you give breaths, you may not have the head tilted far enough back to open the airway adequately. Retilt the victim's head and try again to give breaths. If your breaths still do not go in, assume the victim's airway is obstructed. You must now give care for an obstructed airway. (This technique is described later in this chapter.)

Check for signs of circulation after giving the 2 rescue breaths. If the victim has signs of circulation but is not breathing, continue rescue breathing by giving 1 breath every 5 seconds for adults. A good way to time the breaths is to count, "one one-thousand, two one-thousand, three one-thousand." Then take a breath yourself on "four one-thousand," and breathe into the victim on "five one-thousand." Counting this way ensures that you give 1 breath about every 5 seconds. Breathe slowly into the victim. Each breath should last about 2 seconds. After 1 minute of rescue breathing (about 12 breaths), recheck for signs of circulation to make sure the heart is still beating. Then check for breathing. If the victim still has signs of circulation but is not breathing, continue rescue breathing. Recheck for signs of circulation for no more than 10 seconds and breathing about every minute. Do not stop rescue breathing unless one of the following situations occurs:

- The victim begins to breathe on his or her own.
- The victim has no signs of circulation. Begin CPR as described in Chapter 6.
- Another trained person takes over for you.
- EMS personnel arrive on the scene and take over.
- You are too exhausted to continue.
- The scene becomes unsafe.

Practicing rescue breathing using the skill sheets at the end of this chapter will help you gain confidence in giving rescue breathing.

Rescue breathing for infants and children

If you discover that an infant or child is unconscious and no one is available to call EMS personnel, give 1 minute of care and then make

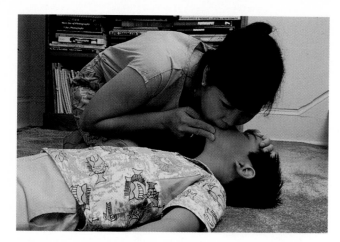

Figure 5-6   Tilt the head gently back only far enough to allow your breaths to go in.

the call yourself. Rescue breathing for infants and children is performed in much the same way as rescue breathing for adults. The minor differences take into account the infant's or child's less developed body and faster heartbeat and breathing rate. To provide rescue breathing for infants and children, use less air in each breath and deliver breaths at a slightly faster rate.

You do not need to tilt a child's or infant's head as far back as an adult's to open the airway. Tilt the head gently back only far enough to allow your breaths to go in (Fig. 5-6). Use the fingers and not the thumb to lift the lower jaw at the chin up and outward. Keep your fingers on the bony part of the jaw. Tipping the child's or infant's head back too far may obstruct the airway. Give 1 breath every 3 seconds for a child or infant. Figure 5-7, *A-C* shows rescue breathing for an adult, child, and infant.

When giving rescue breathing to an infant, it is easier to cover both the nose and mouth with your mouth rather than pinching the nose (Fig. 5-8). Remember to breathe slowly into the victim. Each breath should last about 1½ seconds. Be careful not to overinflate a child's or infant's lungs. Breathe only until you see the chest clearly rise. After 1 minute of rescue breathing (about 20 breaths in a child or in an infant), recheck for signs of circulation. Then check for

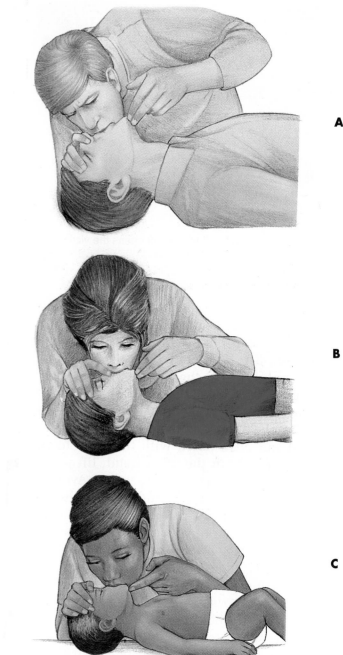

Figure 5-7   Rescue breathing for **A**, adults, **B**, children, and **C**, infants is basically the same.

breathing. If the infant still has signs of circulation but is not breathing, continue rescue breathing. Recheck for signs of circulation and breathing about every minute.

The Use of Breathing Devices

You may not feel comfortable with the thought of giving rescue breathing, especially to someone you do not know. Disease transmission is

MIND AT WORK

4. If Steve went into respiratory arrest, what would you do?

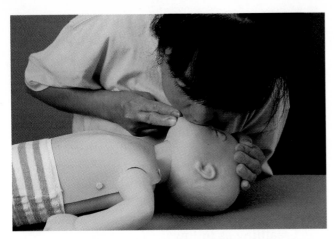

Figure 5-8   Cover both the nose and mouth of the infant with your mouth when giving rescue breathing to an infant.

an understandable concern, even though the chances of getting a disease from giving rescue breathing are extremely low. Breathing devices, such as resuscitation masks and face shields, create a barrier between your mouth and nose and the victim's. This barrier can help protect you from contact with blood and other body fluids. Some devices are small enough to fit in a pocket, first aid kit, or in the glove compartment of a car (Fig. 5-9, *A* and *B*). When using a breathing device during rescue breathing, follow the same procedures already described. Depending on the device, you may have to modify how you open the airway and maintain the correct airway position. Face shields, if available, should be used instead of mouth-to-mouth contact until a mask or bag-valve-mask is available. Do not delay rescue breathing while searching for a breathing barrier or learning how to use one.

A resuscitation mask has benefits over a face

shield. Its advantage is that it is equipped with a one-way valve that prevents the victim's exhaled air from entering the responder's mouth.

Special Considerations for Rescue Breathing

Rescue breathing is a very simple skill to perform. However, several situations exist that may require special attention. Being familiar with these situations will help you provide care for a person in respiratory arrest.

Air in the stomach

When you are giving rescue breathing, air normally enters the victim's lungs through the trachea. Sometimes, however, air may enter the victim's stomach through the esophagus. Several things may cause air to enter the victim's stomach. First, breathing into the victim longer than about 1-1½ seconds for children and infants may cause the extra air to fill the stomach. Do not overinflate the lungs. Stop the breath when the chest clearly rises. Second, if the victim's head is not tilted back far enough, the airway will not open completely. As a result, the chest may only rise slightly. Therefore, you may breathe more forcefully, causing air to enter the stomach. Retilt the head if your first breaths do not go in. Third, when breaths are given too quickly, increased pressure in the airway is created, causing air to enter the stomach. Give slow breaths to minimize pressure in the air passages.

Air in the stomach can cause gastric distention. **Gastric distention** can be serious because it can make the victim vomit. If an unconscious person vomits, he or she may be at risk

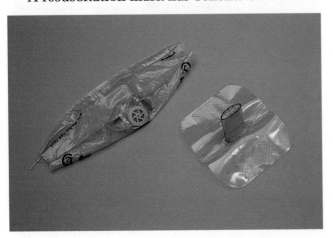

A

B

Figure 5-9   **A,** A face shield or, **B,** a mask, when placed between your mouth and nose and the victim's, can help prevent you from contacting a person's saliva or other body fluids.

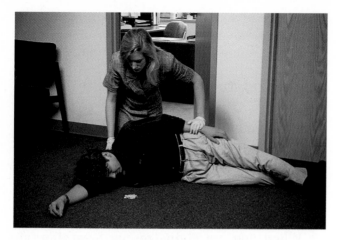

Figure 5-10   If vomiting occurs, roll the victim on the side and clear the mouth of any matter.

for aspiration. In **aspiration,** the stomach contents or other foreign material, such as saliva or blood, get into the lungs. Aspiration can hamper rescue breathing and may lead to fatal complications.

To avoid forcing air into the stomach, be sure to keep the victim's head tilted correctly for his or her size and age. Breathe slowly and gently into the victim, only enough to make the chest clearly rise. Breaths should not be given too quickly or too hard. Each breath should last about 2 seconds for adults. Pause between breaths long enough for the victim's lungs to empty and for you to take another breath.

Vomiting

When you give rescue breathing, the victim may vomit, whether or not gastric distention occurs. If the victim vomits, roll the victim onto one side (Fig. 5-10). Avoid twisting the neck

and back. This positioning helps to prevent vomit from entering the lungs. Quickly wipe the victim's mouth clean, reposition the victim on his or her back, reopen the airway, and continue with rescue breathing.

Mouth-to-nose breathing

Sometimes you may not be able to make an adequate seal over a victim's mouth to perform rescue breathing. For example, the person's jaw or mouth may be injured or shut too tightly to open or your mouth may be too small to cover the victim's. If so, provide mouth-to-nose rescue breathing as follows:

1. Maintain the head-tilt position with one hand on the forehead. Use your other hand to close the victim's mouth, making sure to push on the chin and not on the throat.
2. Open your mouth wide, take a deep breath, seal your mouth tightly around the victim's nose, and breathe into the victim's nose (Fig. 5-11). Open the victim's mouth between breaths, if possible, to let air out.

Mouth-to-stoma breathing

Some people have had an operation to remove all or part of the upper end of their airway. They breathe through an opening called a **stoma** in the front of the neck (Fig. 5-12). Air passes directly into the airway through the stoma instead of through the mouth and nose.

Most people with a stoma wear a medical alert bracelet or necklace or carry a card identifying this condition. You may not see the stoma immediately. You will probably notice the opening in the neck as you tilt the head back to

Figure 5-11   To give mouth-to-nose breathing, keep the head tilted back, close the victim's mouth, and seal your mouth around the victim's nose.

Hartman Films

Figure 5-12   You may need to perform rescue breathing on a victim with a stoma, which is an opening in the front of the neck.

Laryngectomies: *A Breath of Air*

Years ago a person diagnosed with cancer of the larynx had a small chance of survival. Today, advances in drugs, surgical techniques, and radiation therapy have led to increased survival rates. Laryngeal cancer is now one of the most curable cancers.

Cancer of the larynx may involve the vocal cords and surrounding tissue, giving rise to symptoms such as voice changes or difficulty breathing or swallowing. Surgical removal of the larynx, known as a total laryngectomy, is a common procedure for treating laryngeal cancer. The person who has this procedure is a "laryngectomee." When all of the larynx is removed, a connection no longer exists between the mouth, the nose, and the windpipe. A surgical opening, called a stoma, is made in the front of the neck, and the windpipe is attached to it. The patient breathes only through the stoma and not through the mouth or nose. This person is called a "total neck breather."

Some people have a condition that damages the effectiveness of their airway, such as growths or vocal cord paralysis. They can be assured of an adequate air supply by having an opening made from the outside of the neck into the windpipe. A tube is kept in this opening so that it cannot grow together again. This opening is also called a stoma. Since these individuals still have a larynx, they may be able to breathe to some degree through the nose and mouth. They are called "partial neck breathers."

Although someone who has had a total laryngectomy no longer has vocal cords, that person is still able to speak. The only aspect of speaking they no longer have is the ability to generate sound. Many laryngectomees communicate using an instrument called an artificial larynx, which generates sound electronically. The head of the instrument is held against the neck and the sound vibrates through the neck and into the mouth. The person shapes the word just as if the sound came from the vocal cords. Sometimes the resulting sound from neck placement is not satisfactory, in which case, a cap with a small straw-like tube is put on the head of the instrument, and the tube is placed into the corner of the mouth. In this way, the sound is delivered directly into the mouth, and the person uses more normal pronunciation to shape the sound into speech.

Another way to provide sound is to use the same sound source all of us use when we burp. The location of the sound is the upper end of the food tube or esophagus. The laryngectomee learns to move the air into the esophagus and make controlled sound as the air comes back out. With practice, the sound becomes refined and very effective for speech. This is known as esophageal speech. A variation of this form of communication is known as tracheoesophageal speech. A small surgical opening is created between the windpipe and esophagus. A valved tube is put in the opening. The tube allows air from the lungs to enter the esophagus, and the individual produces esophageal speech by exhaling rather than by injecting air into the esophagus.

The International Association of Laryngectomees (IAL) was formed in 1952 as an organization dedicated to the total rehabilitation of laryngectomees and their families. There are nearly 300 member clubs located throughout the United States and in several foreign countries. Supported by the American Cancer Society, the IAL is also a conduit for public information and education regarding laryngectomees. The IAL has been dedicated to helping educate emergency and public workers on the special needs of neck breathers in certain emergency situations such as respiratory arrest. Through their efforts, many lives have been saved.

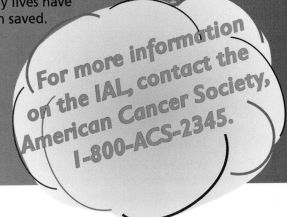

For more information on the IAL, contact the American Cancer Society, 1-800-ACS-2345.

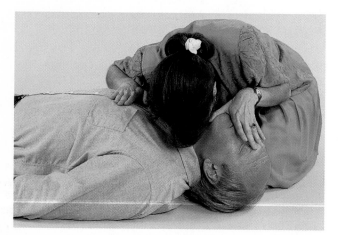

Figure 5-13 **A,** To check for breathing, look, listen, and feel for breaths with your ear over the stoma. **B,** To give rescue breathing, seal your mouth around the stoma and breathe into the victim.

check for breathing or move clothing to check signs of circulation. A stoma may be obscured by clothing, such as a turtleneck or scarf.

To give rescue breathing to someone with a stoma, you must give breaths through the stoma

instead of the mouth or nose. Follow the same basic steps as in mouth-to-mouth breathing, except—

1. Look, listen, and feel for breathing with your ear over the stoma (Fig. 5-13, *A*).
2. Give breaths into the stoma, breathing at the same rate as for mouth-to-mouth breathing (Fig. 5-13, *B*).
3. Remove your mouth from the stoma between breaths to let air flow back out.

If the chest does not clearly rise when you give rescue breaths, suspect that the victim may have had only part of the larynx removed. Some air thus continues to flow through the larynx to the lungs during normal breathing. When giving mouth-to-stoma breathing, air may leak through the nose and mouth, diminishing the amount of your rescue breaths that reach the lungs. If this occurs, you need to seal the nose and mouth with your hand to prevent air from escaping during rescue breathing (Fig. 5-14).

Victims with dentures
If you know or see that the victim is wearing dentures, do not automatically remove them. Dentures help rescue breathing by supporting the victim's mouth and cheeks during mouth-to-mouth breathing. If the dentures are loose, the head-tilt/chin-lift may help keep them in place. Remove the dentures only if they become so loose that they block the airway or make it difficult for you to give breaths.

Suspected head, neck, or back injuries
Head, neck, or back injuries should be sus-

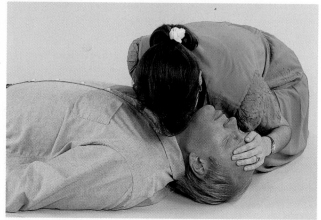

Figure 5-14 When performing rescue breathing on a person with a stoma, you may need to seal the victim's nose and mouth to prevent air from escaping.

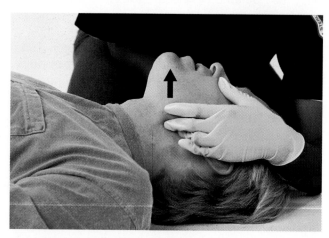

Figure 5-15 Use a two-handed jaw thrust when a chin-lift fails to open the airway of a victim with a suspected head or spine injury.

pected in victims who have sustained a violent force, such as from a motor vehicle crash, a fall, or a diving or other sports-related incident. If you suspect the victim may have a head, neck, or back injury, you should try to minimize movement of the head and neck when opening the airway. You can minimize movement by modifying your head-tilt/chin-lift technique.

First, try to open the victim's airway by lifting the chin without tilting the head back, which may be enough to allow air to pass into the lungs. If you attempt rescue breathing and your breaths are not going in, you may need to perform a two-handed jaw-thrust maneuver (see Fig. 5-15).

Open the airway by placing one hand on each side of the victim's head (you can rest your elbows on the surface on which the victim is lying) with your thumbs on the victim's cheeks and your fingers under the back of the lower jaw, next to the ears. Grab the back of the lower jaw, next to the ears, and lift with both hands. If the lips close, you can open the mouth with your thumb by pushing back the lower lip.

If mouth-to-mouth breathing is necessary while you maintain the jaw thrust, close the victim's nostrils by placing your cheek tightly against them. You may also use a breathing barrier to perform rescue breathing.

These techniques should allow you to open the victim's airway without moving the head or neck. But remember that a person who is not breathing needs oxygen. Opening the airway to allow oxygen is the primary concern for an unconscious victim.

CHOKING

Airway obstruction is the most common cause of respiratory emergencies. The two types of airway obstruction are anatomical and mechanical. A person suffering from a mechanical or anatomical airway obstruction is choking.

An **anatomical airway obstruction** occurs if the airway is blocked by the tongue or swollen tissues of the mouth and throat. This type of obstruction may result from injury to the neck or a medical emergency, such as anaphylaxis. The most common cause of obstruction in an unconscious person, especially if the person is lying on his or her back, is the tongue, which drops to the back of the throat and blocks the airway. This blockage occurs because muscles relax when deprived of oxygen, allowing the tongue and epiglottis to obstruct the airway. The head-tilt/chin-lift not only opens the airway by moving the tongue away from the back of the throat but also moves the epiglottis from the opening of the trachea.

A **mechanical airway obstruction** occurs when the airway is partially or completely blocked by a foreign object, such as a piece of food or a small toy, or by fluids, such as vomit, blood, mucus, or saliva.

Common causes of choking include—

* Trying to swallow large pieces of poorly chewed food.
* Drinking alcohol before or during meals. Alcohol dulls the nerves that aid swallowing, making choking on food more likely.
* Wearing dentures. Dentures make it difficult to sense whether food is fully chewed before swallowing.
* Eating while talking excitedly or laughing or eating too fast.
* Walking, playing, or running with food or objects in the mouth.

Signs of Choking

A person whose airway is blocked by a piece of food or other object can quickly stop breathing, lose consciousness, and die. You must be able to recognize that the airway is obstructed and give care immediately. If you mistake an obstructed airway for a heart attack or some other serious condition, you might be slow to give the right kind of care or you might give the wrong kind of care.

A person who is choking may have either a complete or partial airway obstruction. A person with a complete airway obstruction is not able to breathe at all. With a partial airway obstruction, the person's ability to breathe depends on how much air can get past the obstruction into the lungs.

MIND AT WORK

5. *Is it possible that Steve's condition may lead to an anatomical airway obstruction? Why?*

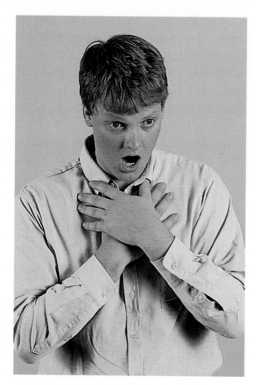

Figure 5-16 Clutching the throat with one or both hands is universally recognized as a distress signal for choking.

Figure 5-17 Abdominal thrusts simulate a cough, forcing trapped air in the lungs to push the object out of the airway.

Partial airway obstruction

A person with a partial airway obstruction can still move air to and from the lungs. This air allows the person to cough in an attempt to dislodge the object. The person may also be able to move air past the vocal cords to speak. The narrowed airway may cause a wheezing sound as air moves in and out of the lungs. The victim may clutch at his or her throat with one or both hands as a natural reaction to choking. This action is the universal distress signal for choking (Fig. 5-16). If the victim is coughing forcefully or wheezing, do not interfere with attempts to cough up the object. A person who is getting enough air to cough or speak also has enough air entering the lungs to breathe. Stay with the victim and encourage him or her to continue coughing to clear the obstruction. If coughing persists, call EMS personnel for help.

Complete airway obstruction

A partial airway obstruction can quickly become a complete airway obstruction. A person with a completely blocked airway is choking and is unable to speak, breathe, or cough. Sometimes the victim may cough weakly and

ineffectively or make high-pitched noises. All of these signs tell you the victim is not getting enough air to sustain life. Act immediately! If a bystander is available, have that person call EMS personnel while you begin to provide care. Give the following care.

Care for Choking

When someone is choking, your goal is to reestablish an open airway as quickly as possible. Give **abdominal thrusts,** also called the **Heimlich maneuver.** Abdominal thrusts compress the abdomen and create pressure that forces the diaphragm higher into the thoracic cavity, thus increasing pressure within the lungs and airway. This pressure simulates a cough, forcing air trapped in the lungs to push the object out of the airway, like a cork from a bottle of champagne (Fig. 5-17).

Care for a conscious choking adult or child

To give abdominal thrusts to a conscious choking adult or child, stand or kneel behind the victim and wrap your arms around his or her waist. Make a fist with one hand and place

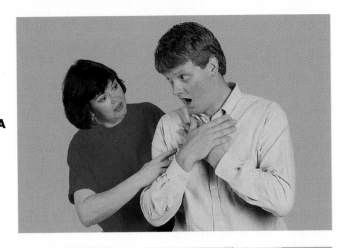

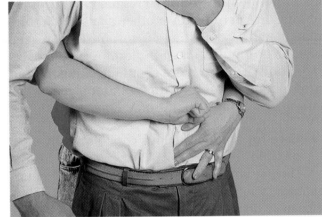

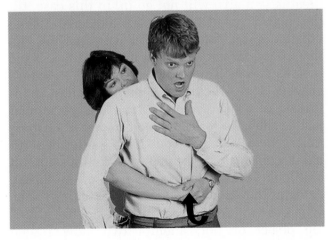

Figure 5-18 **A,** Stand behind the victim to give abdominal thrusts. **B,** Place the thumb side of your fist against the middle of the victim's abdomen. **C,** Grab your fist with your other hand and give quick, upward thrusts into the abdomen.

and distinct attempt to dislodge the obstruction. Repeat these thrusts until the object is dislodged or the victim becomes unconscious. The skill sheets at the end of this chapter show this technique in detail.

Care for a conscious choking adult or child who becomes unconscious

While giving abdominal thrusts to a conscious choking victim, you should anticipate that the victim will become unconscious if the obstruction is not removed. If unconsciousness occurs, carefully lower the victim to the floor on his or her back. Call EMS personnel if someone has not already called. Tilt the head back and open the mouth by grasping the lower jaw and tongue between the thumb and fingers and lifting the jaw. First look in the mouth. Look for an object in the back of the throat. Attempt to remove the object only if it is visible (Fig. 5-19 *A* and *B*). If you cannot see an object or if you

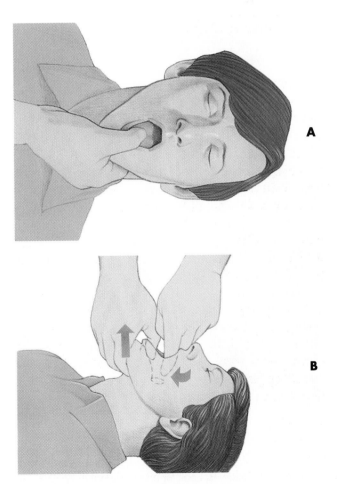

Figure 5-19 **A,** To do a finger sweep, first lift the lower jaw. **B,** Use a hooking action to sweep the object out of the airway.

the thumb side against the middle of the victim's abdomen, just above the navel and well below the lower tip of the breastbone (Fig. 5-18, *A* and *B*). Grab your fist with your other hand and give quick, upward thrusts into the abdomen (Fig. 5-18, *C*). Each thrust is a separate

are successful in removing an object, try to open the victims' airway using the head-tilt/chin-lift method and attempt 2 rescue breaths. Often the throat muscles relax enough after a person becomes unconscious to allow air past the obstruction and into the lungs. You will know air has made it successfully into the lungs if the victim's chest rises and falls with each rescue breath. If air does not go into the lungs (and the chest does not rise), perform chest compressions. Chest compressions are performed just as they are for CPR (see Chapter 6, *Cardiac Emergencies*) and are proven to be effective in dislodging an object in the throat. Further, many victims who have an obstructed airway will also not have circulation, thus chest compressions will not only be effective in relieving the obstruction, but will also provide necessary care for absence of circulation. After you have performed 15 chest compressions,

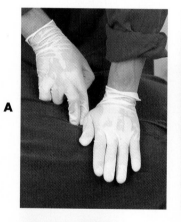

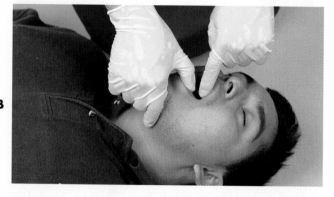

Figure 5-20 To perform chest compressions on an unconscious victim: **A,** find the hand position, position shoulders over the victim's chest, and compress the chest 15 times about 2 inches deep. **B,** Look for an object in the mouth by lifting the jaw. If you see it, sweep it out.

open the victim's mouth and look for an object in the back of the throat. Attempt to remove the object only if it is visible (Figure 5-19, *A* and *B*). Whether you are successful in removing a visible object or not, attempt two slow rescue breaths. Continue 15 chest compressions followed by an attempt to remove the object if you see it (Figure 5-20, *A* and *B*) followed by an attempt to give 2 slow rescue breaths until EMS arrives and takes over, another trained rescuer arrives and takes over, you are effective in removing the object **and** your two rescue breaths are successful, or the victim begins to cough on his or her own. If your two rescue breaths do go in and the victim shows other signs of circulation (such as coughing in response to rescue breaths or a pulse), then perform rescue breathing. You will learn more about checking for and providing care for a victim without signs of circulation in Chapter 6, *Cardiac Emergencies*.

Care for an unconscious choking adult or child

During your check for life-threatening emergencies, you may discover that an unconscious victim is not breathing and the two slow rescue breaths you give will not go in. In this case, tilt the victim's head further back and give 2 slow breaths again. You may not have tilted the victim's head far enough back the first time. If the breaths still will not go in, assume the victim's airway is obstructed and perform chest compressions. Chest compressions are performed just as they are for CPR (see Chapter 6, *Cardiac Emergencies*). After you have performed 15 chest compressions, open the victim's mouth and look for an object in the back of the throat. Attempt to remove the object only if it is visible. Whether you are successful in removing a visible object or not, attempt two slow rescue breaths. Continue this cycle of 15 chest compressions followed by an attempt to remove an object if you see it, followed by an attempt to give 2 slow rescue breaths until EMS arrives and takes over, another trained rescuer arrives and takes over, you are effective in removing the object and your two, effective rescue breaths go in, or the victim begins to cough on his or her own. You will learn more about checking for and providing care for victims with no signs of circulation in Chapter 6, *Cardiac Emergencies*.

Care for a conscious choking infant

Choking is a major cause of death and injury in infants. An infant starts to learn about the world by placing objects in his or her mouth. An infant can easily swallow small objects, such as pebbles, coins, beads, and parts of toys, which can then block the airway. Infants also often choke because it takes a long time to develop their eating skills. Infants can easily choke on foods such as nuts, hot dogs, grapes, and popcorn, which are often the perfect size to block their smaller airways.

If, while checking for life-threatening injuries, you determine that a conscious infant cannot breathe, cough, or cry, give first aid for a complete airway obstruction. Begin by giving 5 back blows followed by 5 chest thrusts.

Position the infant faceup on your forearm. Place your other hand on top of the infant, using your thumb and fingers to hold the infant's jaw while sandwiching the infant between your forearms. Turn the infant over so that he or she is face-down on your forearm (Fig. 5-21, *A*). Lower your arm onto your thigh so that the infant's head is lower than his or her chest. Give 5 firm back blows with the heel of your hand between the infant's shoulder blades (Fig. 5-21, *B*). Maintain support of the infant's head and neck by firmly holding the jaw between your thumb and forefinger.

To give chest thrusts, you will need to turn the infant back over. Start by placing your free hand and forearm along the infant's head and back so that the infant is sandwiched between your two hands and forearms. Continue to support the infant's head between your thumb and finger from the front while you cradle the back of the head with your other hand. Turn the infant onto his or her back. Lower your arm that is supporting the infant's back onto your thigh. The infant's head should be lower than his or her chest, which will assist in dislodging the object (Fig. 5-22, *A*). Give 5 chest thrusts (Fig. 5-22, *B*). To locate the correct place to give chest thrusts, imagine a line running across the infant's chest between the nipples. Place the pad of your ring finger on the breastbone, just under this imaginary line. Then place the pads of the two fingers next to the ring finger, one finger width below the nipple line. Raise the ring finger (Fig. 5-24). If you feel the notch at the end of

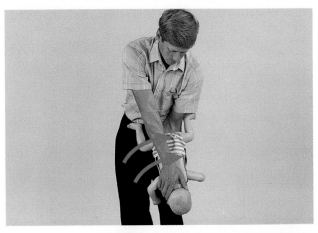

A

B

Figure 5-21   To give back blows, sandwich the infant between your forearms. Support the infant's head and neck by holding the jaw between your thumb and forefinger. **A,** Turn the infant over so that he or she is face-down on your forearm. **B,** Give 5 firm back blows with the heel of your hand while supporting your arm that is holding the infant on your thigh.

the infant's breastbone, move your fingers up a little bit.

Use the pads of the two fingers to compress the breastbone. Compress the breastbone ½ to 1 inch, then let the breastbone return to its normal position. Keep your fingers in contact with the infant's breastbone. Compress 5 times. You can give back blows and chest thrusts effectively whether you stand or sit, as long as the infant is supported on your thigh. If the infant is large or your hands are too small to adequately support the infant, you may prefer to sit. The infant's head must be lower than the chest.

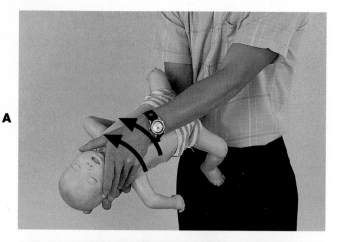

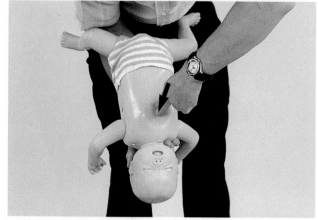

A

B

Figure 5-22   To give chest thrusts, sandwich the infant between your forearms. Continue to support the infant's head. **A,** Turn the infant onto his or her back and support your arm on your thigh. The infant's head should be lower than the chest. **B,** Give 5 chest thrusts.

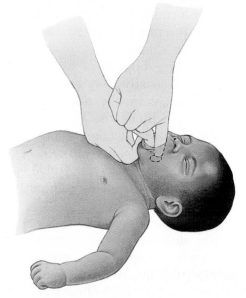

Figure 5-23   To do a foreign body check on an infant: Put your thumb into the infant's mouth and hold the tongue and lower jaw between the thumb and fingers. Lift the jaw upward. If you see an object, try to remove it with your little finger.

Care for a conscious choking infant who becomes unconscious

While giving chest thrusts (compressions) and back blows to a conscious choking infant, anticipate that the infant will become unconscious if the obstruction is not dislodged. If the infant becomes unconscious, lower the infant to a table or the floor and open the infant's airway. Open the infant's mouth, using your hand that is closer to the infant's feet. Put your thumb in the infant's mouth, and hold both the tongue and the lower jaw between the thumb and fingers. Lift the jaw upward and look in the mouth for an object. If you see an object, try to remove it with the little finger of your hand that is closer to the victim's head (Fig. 5-23). Then attempt two slow rescue breaths. If the breaths do not go in, reposition the airway and give breaths again (Fig. 5-24, _A_). If air still does not go in, position the infant for chest compressions (Fig. 5-24, _B_). Give 5 chest compressions followed by a visual check for an object if you see it. If you see an object, try to remove it with your little finger. If you do not see an object or after your attempt to remove it with your little finger, give one slow rescue breath. Continue the sequence of providing 5 chest compressions followed by an attempt to remove an object if you see it, followed by providing one slow rescue breath until you are able to get air in or EMS personnel arrive and take over. If you are able to get air into the infant, check for signs of circulation. You will learn more about caring for no signs of circulation in Chapter 6, _Cardiac Emergencies._

Care for an unconscious choking infant

The care for an unconscious infant with a complete airway obstruction begins when you check for life-threatening injuries. If you determine an infant is unconscious, not breathing, and you cannot get air into the lungs, retilt the head and attempt 2 more rescue breaths. If you still cannot get air into the infant, the airway is probably blocked. Proceed with the same care

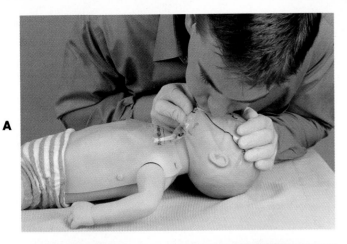

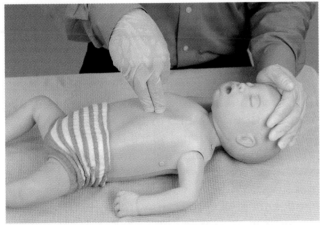

Figure 5-24 Then attempt two rescue breaths. **A,** If the breaths do not go in, reposition the airway and give breaths again. **B,** If air still does not go in, position the infant for chest compressions.

you would provide for an infant without signs of circulation, or no brachial pulse. Give 5 chest compressions followed by a visual check for an object if you see it. If you see an object, try to remove it with your little finger. If you do not see an object or after your attempt to remove it with your little finger, give one slow rescue breath. Continue the sequence of providing 5 chest compressions followed by an attempt to remove an object if you see it, followed by providing one slow rescue breath until you are able to get air in or EMS personnel arrive and take over. To perform a visual check for an object—

- Stand or kneel beside the infant's head.
- Open the infant's mouth and hold both the tongue and lower jaw between the thumb and fingers. Lift the jaw upwards.

- Look for an object. If you can see one, try to remove it with the little finger (see Fig. 5-23).

Whether you are successful in removing any piece or all of an object, open the infant's airway and attempt a rescue breath. If your first attempt to clear the airway is unsuccessful, do not stop. Position the infant and provide 5 chest compressions followed by a visual check for an object if you see it. If you see an object, try to remove it with your little finger. If you do not see an object or after your attempt to remove it with your little finger, give one slow rescue breath. Continue the sequence of providing 5 chest compressions followed by an attempt to remove an object if you see it, followed by providing one slow rescue breath until you are able to get air in or EMS personnel arrive and take over. If you are able to get air into the infant, check for signs of circulation. You will learn more about caring for victims with no signs of circulation in Chapter 6, *Cardiac Emergencies.*

When to Stop Care

If the victim begins to breathe or cough immediately, stop giving abdominal thrusts to a conscious adult or child or back blows and chest thrusts to a conscious infant. Make sure the object is cleared from the airway, and watch that the person is breathing freely again. Even after the object is dislodged, the person may still have breathing problems that you do not immediately see. Always call 9-1-1 or the local emergency number after providing care to anyone with breathing difficulty.

Special Considerations for Adult Choking Victims

In some instances, abdominal thrusts are not the best method of care for choking victims. Some choking victims need chest thrusts. For example, if you cannot reach far enough around the victim to give effective abdominal thrusts, you should give chest thrusts. You should also give chest thrusts instead of abdominal thrusts to choking victims who are in the late stages of pregnancy.

Chest thrusts for a conscious victim

To give chest thrusts to a conscious victim, stand behind the victim and place your arms under the victim's armpits and around the chest. As in abdominal thrusts, make a fist with one hand and place the thumb side against the center of the victim's breastbone. Be sure that your fist is centered on the breastbone, not on the ribs. Also make sure that your fist is not near the lower tip of the breastbone. Grab your fist with your other hand and thrust inward (Fig. 5-25). Repeat these thrusts until the victim can cough, speak, or breathe, or the victim becomes unconscious.

Figure 5-27 To give yourself abdominal thrusts, press your abdomen onto a firm object, such as the back of a chair.

Figure 5-25 Give chest thrusts if you cannot reach around the victim to give abdominal thrusts or if the victim is noticeably pregnant.

If you are alone and choking

If you are alone and choking and no one is around who can help, you can give yourself abdominal thrusts in one of two ways. (1) Make a fist with one hand and place the thumb side on the middle of your abdomen slightly above your navel and well below the tip of your breastbone. Grasp your fist with your other hand and give quick upward thrusts. (2) You can also lean forward and press your abdomen over any firm object, such as the back of a chair, a railing, or a sink (Fig. 5-27). Be careful not to lean over anything with a sharp edge or a corner that might injure you.

SPECIAL CONSIDERATIONS FOR CPR

When you are alone and need to provide care for an unconscious victim, **Call First**, that is, call 9-1-1 or the local emergency number before providing care for:

- An unconscious adult victim or child 8 years old or older; and
- An unconscious infant or child known to be at a high risk for heart problems.

When you are alone, provide 1 minute of care, then **Call Fast** for:

- An unconscious victim less than 8 years old;
- Any victim of submersion or near drowning;
- Any victim of arrest associated with trauma; and
- Any victim of drug overdoses.

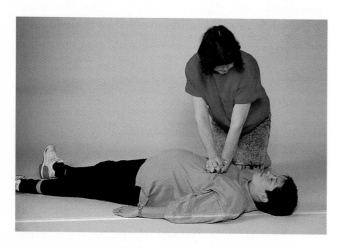

Figure 5-26 If the victim is unconscious, position her on her back.

The situations in **Call First** should be assumed to be cardiac emergencies such as sudden cardiac arrest, and the **time factor is critical**. The research shows that the shorter the time from collapse to first shock from an Automated External Defibrillator, the greater the chance of survival for an adult or child 8 years old or older. For an infant or child with a known risk for heart problems, early access to the EMS system and the advanced medical care that results increases that victim's chance of survival.

In the **Call Fast** situations, the conditions are most often related to breathing emergencies rather than sudden cardiac arrest. In these situations, providing support for airway, breathing and circulation through rescue breaths and/or chest compressions as appropriate is the most important initial step a trained responder should take.

SUMMARY

In this chapter, you have learned how to recognize and provide first aid for breathing emergencies. You now know to look for a breathing emergency because it can be life threatening. You have learned the signs and symptoms of respiratory distress and respiratory arrest and the appropriate care for each condition. You have also learned the basic techniques for rescue breathing and how to vary them for special situations. Finally, you have learned how to give care for a choking adult, child, and infant victim, both conscious and unconscious. By knowing how to care for breathing emergencies, you are now better prepared to care for cardiac and other emergencies. You will learn about cardiac emergencies in Chapter 6.

Answers to Application Questions

1. Steve had signs of respiratory distress. Signs of Steve's emergency were holding his throat, pale skin, and wheezing sounds when breathing.

2. No. Although the signs and symptoms of respiratory distress as a result of various causes are similar, the care is basically the same, regardless of the condition.

3. Yes. If the passages narrow as a result of swelling, preventing air exchange, Steve may suffer respiratory arrest. The possibility of respiratory arrest is the reason EMS personnel must be called right away.

4. Send Kevin to call 9-1-1 if someone has not already called. Your first step would be to open Steve's airway and check for breathing. If he is not breathing, give two rescue breaths and check for signs of circulation. If signs of circulation are present but Steve is not breathing, begin rescue breathing. If he is breathing, maintain an open airway.

5. Yes, if Steve's condition is asthma or a severe allergic reaction, an airway obstruction would occur. Also, if Steve became unconscious, his tongue could fall to the back of his throat and block the airway. In Steve's case, airway obstruction would be a serious emergency, since abdominal thrusts would not relieve this obstruction caused by swelling. Make sure EMS personnel are called immediately.

STUDY QUESTIONS

1. Match each term with the correct definition.

    a. Airway obstruction
    b. Aspiration
    c. Epiglottitis
    d. Check for object at the back of the throat
    e. Head-tilt/chin-lift
    f. Rescue breathing
    g. Respiratory arrest
    h. Respiratory distress

    B Sucking or taking blood, vomit, saliva, or other foreign material into the lungs; a danger when an unconscious victim vomits.

    F Technique of breathing for a nonbreathing victim.

    A Blockage of the airway that prevents air from reaching the victim's lungs.

    G Condition in which breathing stops.

    H Condition in which breathing becomes difficult.

    E Technique for opening the airway.

    D Technique used to see if there is foreign material blocking a victim's airway.

    C Condition in which the epiglottis swells.

2. Circle four signs and symptoms associated with respiratory distress that you find in the following scenario.

    When Rita walked into Mr. Boyd's office, she found him collapsed across his desk. His eyes were closed but she could hear him breathing, making a high whistling noise. He was flushed, sweating, and seemed to be trembling uncontrollably. When he heard Rita, he raised his head a little, "My chest hurts," he gasped, "and I feel dizzy and can't seem to catch my breath." He looked very frightened.

3. List three causes of choking.

4. Match each type of care with its purpose.

    a. Abdominal thrusts
    b. Recognizing and caring for respiratory distress
    c. Rescue breathing

    C Supply(ies) oxygen to the lungs when someone has stopped breathing.

    A Force(s) a foreign object out of the airway.

    B May prevent respiratory arrest from occurring.

In questions 5 through 16, circle the letter of the correct answer.

5. Which of the following is a sign of respiratory distress?

    a. Gasping for air
    b. Breathing that is slower than normal
    c. Wheezing
    d. All of the above

6. How are asthma, hyperventilation, and anaphylactic shock alike?

    a. They require rescue breathing.
    b. They are forms of respiratory distress.
    c. They are always life-threatening.
    d. They only occur in children and infants.

7. Care for victims of respiratory distress always includes which of the following?

    a. Helping the victim rest in a comfortable position
    b. Giving the victim water to drink
    c. Giving rescue breathing
    d. Delivering abdominal thrusts

8. Which of the following statements about rescue breathing is true?

    a. It supplies the body with oxygen necessary for survival.
    b. It always requires clearing the airway of foreign objects.
    c. It is given to victims who are breathing but do not have signs of circulation.
    d. It is only given when two rescuers are present.

9. For which condition would a victim need rescue breathing?

    a. Unconsciousness
    b. Unconsciousness and respiratory distress
    c. Unconsciousness, respiratory arrest, with signs of circulation
    d. Unconsciousness, respiratory distress, with no signs of circulation

10. When you give rescue breaths, how much air should you breathe into the victim?

   a. Enough to make the stomach clearly rise
   b. Enough to make the chest clearly rise
   c. Enough to feel resistance
   d. Enough to fill the victim's cheeks

11. Which action is a part of the care for an unconscious adult victim with an obstructed airway?

   a. Giving 2 rescue breaths
   b. Giving chest compressions
   c. Calling EMS personnel
   d. All of the above

12. What should you do for a conscious infant who is choking and cannot cry, cough, or breathe?

   a. Give back blows and chest thrusts.
   b. Give 1 rescue breath.
   c. Give abdominal thrusts.
   d. Lower the victim to the floor and open the airway.

13. After giving your first two rescue breaths to an unconscious adult victim with an obstructed airway, what should you do next?

   a. Reposition the head and give 2 rescue breaths.
   b. Look for an object in the back of the throat and attempt to remove it if it is visible.
   c. Check for signs of circulation, give 2 rescue breaths, and look for and remove an object at the back of the throat if it is visible.
   d. Check for and remove an object at the back of the throat if it is visible and then check for signs of circulation.

14. After 1 minute of rescue breathing, you check an adult victim for signs of circulation. The victim still has signs of circulation but still is not breathing. What should you do?

   a. Continue rescue breathing by giving 2 slow breaths.
   b. Continue rescue breathing by giving 1 breath every 5 seconds.
   c. Stop rescue breathing for 1 minute.
   d. Retilt the head.

15. While eating dinner, a friend suddenly starts to <u>cough weakly</u> and make <u>high-pitched</u> noises. What should you do?

    a. Lower him to the floor, check for and remove an object at the back of the throat if it is visible, give 2 slow breaths and up to 5 abdominal thrusts.
    b. Give abdominal thrusts until the object is dislodged or he becomes unconscious.
    c. Encourage him to continue coughing to try to dislodge the object.
    d. Open the airway using the head-tilt/chin-lift.

16. A woman is choking on a piece of candy but is <u>conscious and coughing forcefully</u>. What should you do?

    a. Slap her on the back until she coughs up the object.
    b. Give abdominal thrusts.
    c. Encourage her to continue coughing.
    d. Do a check at the back of the throat.

17. Number in order the following actions for performing rescue breathing, from the time you discover that an unconscious adult victim is not breathing.

    __2__ Check for signs of circulation and severe bleeding.

    __3__ Give 1 breath every 5 seconds.

    __1__ Give 2 slow, gentle breaths.

    __4__ Recheck for signs of circulation and breathing after 1 minute.

18. Number in order the following actions for providing care to an <u>unconscious choking infant</u>, from the time you first realize your breaths will not go in.

    _____ Give 5 chest compressions.

    _____ Check for an object.

    _____ Repeat 2 slow breaths.

    _____ Retilt the victim's head.

    _____ Remove an object if you see one.

Answers are listed in Appendix A.

SKILL SHEETS

Rescue Breathing For An Adult Or Child

CHECK - CALL - CARE

If person is not breathing . . .

Give rescue breathing

- Keep head tilted back.
- Pinch nose shut.
- Seal lips tightly around person's mouth.
- Give 1 slow, gentle breath every 5 seconds (1 slow breath about every 3 seconds for child).
- Watch to see that the chest clearly rises.
- Continue for 1 minute—about 12 breaths (adult); about 20 breaths (child).

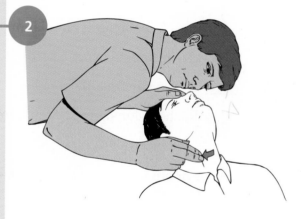

Recheck for signs of circulation and breathing about every minute

- Check for signs of circulation and look, listen, and feel for breathing for no more than 10 seconds.

If person has signs of circulation and is breathing . . .

- *Keep airway open.*
- *Monitor breathing.*
- *Wait for EMS personnel to arrive.*

If person has signs of circulation but is still not breathing . . .

- *Continue rescue breathing until EMS personnel arrive.*

If person does not have signs of circulation and is not breathing . . .

- *Begin CPR.*
- *Wait for EMS personnel to arrive.*

SKILL SHEETS

Rescue Breathing For An Infant

If infant is not breathing . . .

1

Give rescue breathing

- Keep head tilted back.
- Seal lips tightly around infant's mouth and nose.
- Give 1 slow, gentle breath about every 3 seconds.
- Watch to see that the chest clearly rises.
- Continue for 1 minute—about 20 breaths.

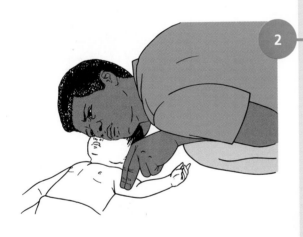

2

Recheck for signs of circulation and breathing every minute

- Check for signs of circulation and look, listen, and feel for breathing for no more than 10 seconds.

If infant has signs of circulation and is breathing . . .

- *Keep airway open.*
- *Monitor breathing.*
- *Wait for EMS personnel to arrive.*

If infant has signs of circulation but is still not breathing . . .

- *Continue rescue breathing until EMS personnel arrive.*

If infant does not have signs of circulation and is not breathing . . .

- *Begin CPR.*
- *Wait for EMS personnel to arrive.*

SKILL SHEETS

CHECK-CALL-CARE

If, when you check, the person is unable to speak, cough, cry, or breathe . . .

Care For A Conscious Choking Adult Or Child With An Obstructed Airway

1

Ask the person if you can provide care

2

Position hands

- Wrap your arms around person's waist.
- With one hand find navel. With other hand make fist.
- Place thumb side of fist against middle of person's abdomen just above navel and well below lower tip of breastbone.

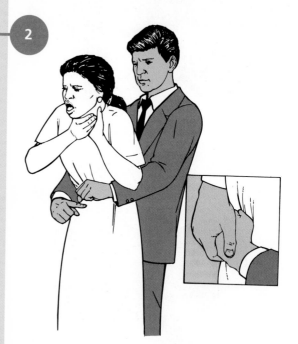

3

Give abdominal thrusts

- Press fist into person's abdomen with quick upward thrust.
- Each thrust should be separate and distinct attempt to dislodge object.

Repeat abdominal thrusts until . . .

- *Object is coughed up.*
- *Person starts to breathe or cough forcefully.*
- *Person becomes unconscious.*
- *EMS personnel arrive.*

SKILL SHEETS

Care For An Unconscious Choking Adult Or Child With An Airway Obstruction

 CHECK-CALL-CARE

If, when you check, person is not breathing and your breaths do not go in . . .

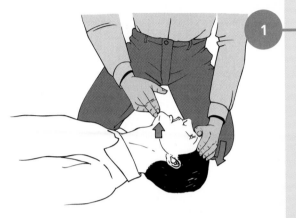

1

Reposition the person's airway

- Tilt person's head further back.

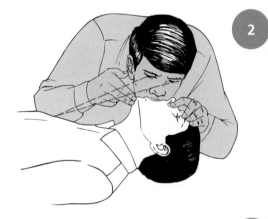

2

Reattempt 2 slow breaths

- Give 2 slow, gentle breaths, each lasting about 2 seconds for an adult and 1-1½ seconds for a child or infant.

If breaths still do not go in, make sure 9-1-1 or the local emergency number has been called and . . .

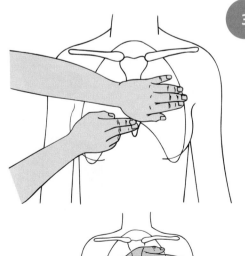

3

Find hand position

For an adult

- Locate notch at lower end of sternum.
- Place heel of other hand on sternum next to fingers.
- Keep fingers off chest.

For a child

- Maintain head tilt with hand on forehead
- Locate notch at lower end of sternum with other hand.
- Place heel of same hand on sternum immediately above where fingers were placed.

For an adult

Give 15 compressions

- Position shoulders over hands.
- Compress chest 1½ to 2 inches.
- Do 15 compressions in about 10 seconds.

For a child

- Position shoulders over hands.
- Compress chest 1-1½ inches.
- Do 5 compressions in about 3 seconds.
- Compress down and up smoothly, keeping hand contact with chest at all times.
- Maintain head-tilt with your hand on forehead.

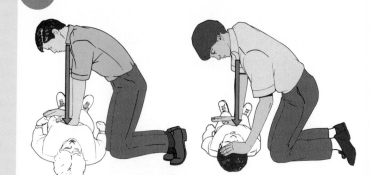

Check for foreign object (simulate attempt to remove)

- Grasp tongue and lower jaw and lift.
- Look for an object at the back of the throat. Attempt to remove it only if it is visible.

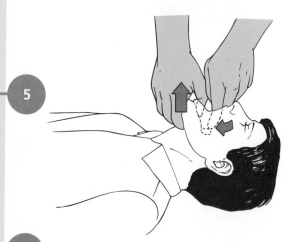

Open the airway and give 2 rescue breaths for an adult, 1 rescue breath for a child

If breaths go in . . .
- *Check for signs of circulation and breathing.*
- *If person has signs of circulation but is not breathing, do rescue breathing.*
- *If person does not have signs of circulation and is not breathing, do CPR.*
- *Check for and control severe bleeding.*
- *Wait for EMS personnel to arrive.*

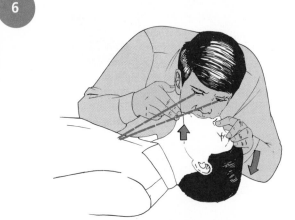

If breaths do not go in . . .
- *For an adult, give 15 compressions, followed by checking for a foreign object, and 2 rescue breaths, and for a child, give 5 compressions, followed by checking for a foreign object, and 1 rescue breath until . . .*
- *Obstruction is removed.*
- *Person starts to breathe or shows signs of circulation.*
- *EMS personnel arrive.*

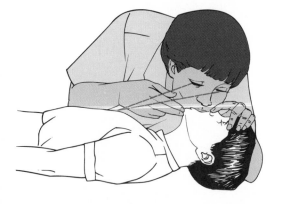

SKILL SHEETS

Care For A Conscious Choking Infant With An Obstructed Airway

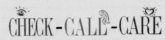

CHECK-CALL-CARE

If, when you check, the infant is unable to cough, cry, or breathe . . .

1

Position the infant face-down on your forearm

- Carefully support infant's head and neck.
- Lower forearm onto thigh.
- Infant's head should be lower than feet.

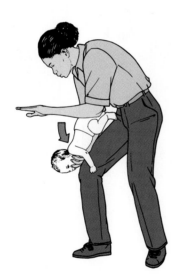

2

Give 5 back blows

- Using heel of your hand, give forceful back blows between infant's shoulder blades, 5 times.
- Each blow should be separate and distinct attempt to dislodge object.

Position the infant face-up on your forearm

- Carefully support the infant's head and neck.
- Lower your forearm onto thigh.
- Infant's head should be lower than feet.

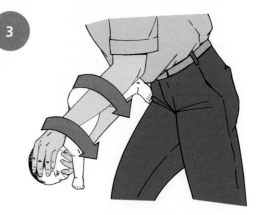

Give 5 chest thrusts

- Locate finger position for chest thrusts.
- Using pads of two fingers, smoothly compress breast bone ½ to 1 inch, 5 times.
- Each thrust should be separate and distinct attempt to dislodge object.

Repeat back blows and chest thrusts until . . .

- *Object is coughed up.*
- *Infant starts to breathe or cough forcefully.*
- *Infant becomes unconscious.*
- *EMS personnel arrive.*

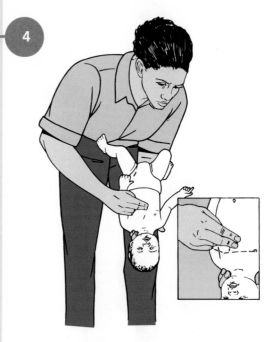

SKILL SHEETS

Care For An Unconscious Infant With An Airway Obstruction

CHECK - CALL - CARE

If, when you check, the infant is not breathing and your breaths do not go in . . .

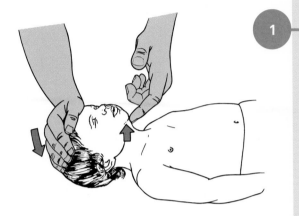

1

Reposition the infant's airway

- Tilt infant's head further back.

2

Reattempt 2 slow breaths

- Give 2 slow, gentle breaths, each lasting about 1½ seconds.

If breaths still do not go in . . .

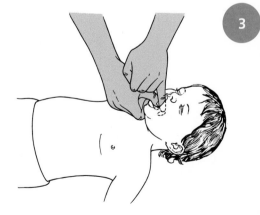

3

Lower the infant to a table or the floor

- Open the airway.
- Lift the jaw, and look in the mouth for a visible object.
- If you see it, attempt to remove it with your little finger.

Find finger position

- Maintain open airway with head-tilt.
- Pick up index finger.
- Adjust finger position as necessary.

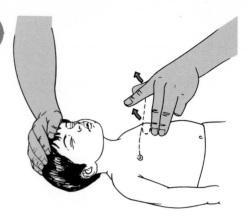

Give 5 compressions

- Compress chest ½ to 1 inch using pads of fingers.
- Do 5 compressions in 3 seconds.
- Press down and up smoothly keeping fingers in contact with chest.

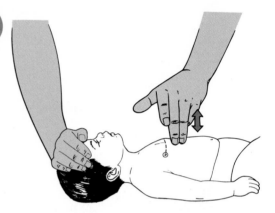

6

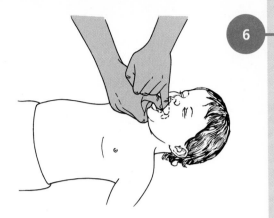

Do a foreign-body check

- Grasp tongue and lower jaw and lift.
- If object can be seen, remove it with your little finger.

7

Open the airway and give 1 rescue breath

- Tilt head back.
- Seal lips tightly around infant's mouth and nose and give breaths.

If breaths go in . . .

- *Check for signs of circulation and breathing.*
- *If infant has signs of circulation but is not breathing, do rescue breathing.*
- *If infant does not have signs of circulation and is not breathing, do CPR.*
- *Check for and control severe bleeding.*
- *Wait for EMS personnel to arrive.*

If breaths do not go in . . .

- *Give 5 chest compressions.*
- *Continue sequence of chest compressions, foreign body check, and 1 rescue breath until . . .*
  - *Obstruction is removed.*
  - *Infant starts to breathe or cry.*
  - *EMS personnel arrive and take over.*

CHAPTER 6

Cardiac Emergencies

WHAT YOU SHOULD LEARN

After reading this chapter, you should be able to—

1. Identify the common causes of heart attacks.

2. List the signs and symptoms of a heart attack.

3. Describe the care for a person suffering a heart attack.

4. Identify the primary sign of cardiac arrest.

5. Describe the purpose of CPR.

6. Explain how to give CPR to adults, children, and infants.

7. List the conditions in which a rescuer may stop CPR.

8. Identify the risk factors for cardiovascular disease that can be controlled.

9. Define the key terms for this chapter.

After reading this chapter and completing the class activities, you should be able to demonstrate—

1. How to give CPR to adults.

2. How to give CPR to children and infants.

3. How to make appropriate decisions in an emergency situation in which a person is experiencing persistent chest pain.

4. How to make appropriate decisions in an emergency situation in which a person has suffered a cardiac arrest.

As you come out of your house to run a quick errand, you see your neighbor, Mr. Getz, starting to mow his neglected lawn. "You picked a hot one for yard work," you shout across the driveway. Mr. Getz waves and motions, indicating the height of the grass. When you return, you look for your mail to find none. Looking out the window for the mailman a few minutes later, you are stunned to see Mr. Getz sprawled facedown on the grass.

Introduction

When checking for life-threatening emergencies, you identify and care for immediate threats to a victim's life. You check the victim's airway, breathing, and pulse and look for any severe bleeding. In Chapter 5, you learned how to open a victim's airway and how to provide rescue breathing for a victim who has signs of circulation but is not breathing.

In this chapter, you will learn how to recognize and provide care for sudden illnesses involving the heart. You will learn how to recognize and provide care for a victim having a heart attack and for a victim whose heart stops beating. The condition in which the heart stops, known as cardiac arrest, sometimes results from a heart attack. To provide care for a cardiac arrest victim, you need to learn how to perform cardiopulmonary resuscitation (CPR). Properly performed CPR can keep a victim's vital organs supplied with blood containing oxygen until EMS personnel arrive to provide advanced care.

This chapter also identifies the important risk factors for cardiovascular disease. People too often focus only on what to do after a cardiac arrest occurs. But you can do more to promote good cardiovascular health than just learning CPR. Learn to modify your behavior to prevent cardiovascular disease.

HEART ATTACK

The heart is a muscular organ that functions like a pump. It lies between the lungs, in the middle of the chest, behind the lower half of the **sternum** (breastbone). The heart is protected by the ribs and sternum in front and by the spine in back (Fig. 6-1). It is separated into right and left halves. Oxygen-poor blood enters the right side of the heart and is circulated to the lungs, where it picks up oxygen. The now oxygen-rich blood returns to the left side of the heart, from which it is circulated to all parts of the body. One-way valves direct the flow of blood as it moves through the heart (Fig. 6-2). For the circulatory system to be effective, the respiratory system must also be working so that the blood pumped by the heart can pick up oxygen in the lungs.

Like all living tissue, the cells of the heart need a continuous supply of oxygen. The ***coronary arteries*** supply the heart muscle with oxygen-rich blood (Fig. 6-3, *A*). If heart muscle is deprived of this blood, it dies. If enough of the muscle dies, the heart cannot circulate blood effectively, causing a ***heart attack.*** A heart attack interferes with the heart's electri-

---

Key Terms

Cardiac (KAR de ak) arrest: A condition in which the heart has stopped beating or beats too ineffectively to generate a pulse.

Cardiopulmonary (kar de o PUL mo ner e) resuscitation (re sus ǐ TA shun) (CPR): A technique that combines chest compressions and rescue breathing for a victim whose breathing and heart have stopped.

Cardiovascular (kar de o VAS ku lar) disease: Disease of the heart and blood vessels.

Cholesterol (ko LES ter ol): A fatty substance made by the body and found in certain foods; too much in the blood can cause fatty deposits on artery walls that may restrict or block blood flow.

Coronary (KOR ǒ ner e) arteries: Blood vessels that supply the heart muscle with oxygen-rich blood.

Heart attack: A sudden illness involving the death of heart muscle tissue when it does not receive oxygen-rich blood; also known as myocardial infarction.

Risk factors: Conditions or behaviors that increase the chance that a person will develop a disease.

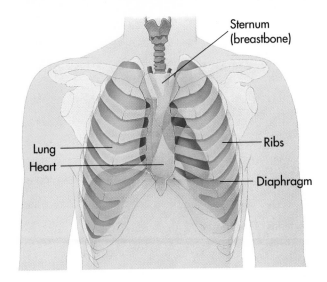

Figure 6-1 The heart is located in the middle of the chest, behind the lower half of the sternum.

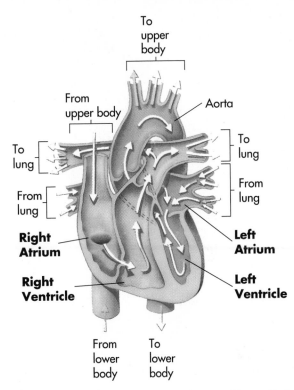

Figure 6-2 The heart has four chambers and is separated into right and left halves. The right side receives blood from the body and sends it to the lungs. The left side receives blood from the lungs and pumps it out through the body. One-way valves direct the flow of blood through the heart.

cal and mechanical systems. This interference may result in an irregular heartbeat, which may prevent blood from circulating effectively.

Common Cause of a Heart Attack

Heart attack is usually the result of cardiovascular disease. ***Cardiovascular disease***—disease of the heart and blood vessels—is the leading cause of death for adults over 44 years of age in the United States. It is estimated that 70 million Americans suffer from cardiovascular disease. Cardiovascular disease accounts for approximately 1 million deaths annually in the United States. Of these deaths, approximately 500,000 were due to heart attack, and most of these were **sudden deaths.**

Cardiovascular disease develops slowly. Fatty deposits of **cholesterol** and other material may gradually build up on the inner walls of the arteries. This condition, called **atherosclerosis,** causes progressive narrowing of these vessels. When coronary arteries narrow or are completely blocked, a heart attack may occur (Fig. 6-3, *B*). Atherosclerosis can also involve arteries in other parts of the body, such as the brain. Diseased arteries of the brain can lead to a stroke.

Because atherosclerosis develops gradually, it may go undetected for many years. Even with significantly reduced blood flow to the heart muscle, there may be no signals of heart trouble. Most people with atherosclerosis are un-

aware of it. As the narrowing progresses, some people experience early warning signs and symptoms when the heart does not receive enough blood. Others may suffer a heart attack or even cardiac arrest without any previous warning. Fortunately, atherosclerosis can be slowed or stopped by lifestyle changes, such as forming healthy eating habits. Later in this chapter and in Chapter 23, you will learn what you can do to keep your heart healthy.

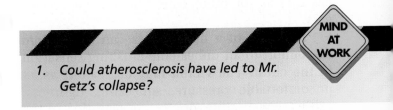

1. *Could atherosclerosis have led to Mr. Getz's collapse?*

Signs and Symptoms of a Heart Attack

The most prominent symptom of a heart attack is persistent chest pain or discomfort. However, distinguishing between the pain of a heart at-

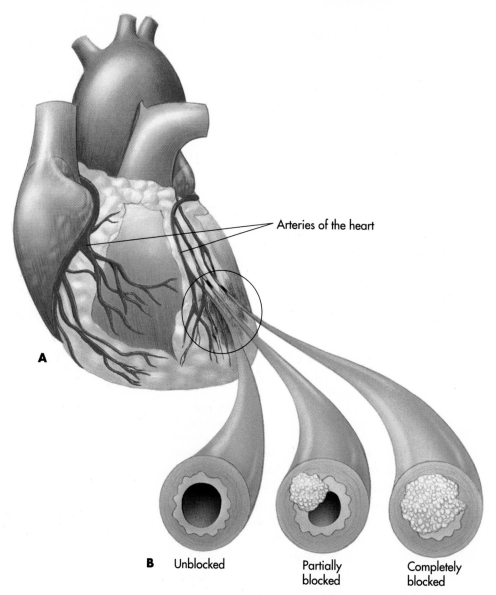

Figure 6-3 **A,** The coronary arteries supply the heart muscle with blood. **B,** Build-up of materials on the inner walls of these arteries reduces blood flow to the heart muscle and may cause a heart attack.

tack and chest pain caused by indigestion, muscle spasms, or other conditions is not always easy.

The pain of a heart attack can range from discomfort to an unbearable crushing sensation in the chest. The victim may describe it as an uncomfortable pressure, squeezing, tightness, aching, constricting, or a heavy sensation in the chest. Often, the pain is felt in the center of the chest behind the sternum. The pain may spread to the shoulder, arm, neck, or jaw (Fig. 6-4). The pain is constant and usually not relieved by resting, changing position, or taking medication. Any severe chest pain that lasts longer than 3-5 minutes or chest pain that is accompanied by other signs and symptoms of a heart attack should receive emergency medical care immediately.

Although a heart attack is often dramatic, heart attack victims can have relatively mild symptoms. The victim often mistakes the signs and symptoms for indigestion or gas. Some heart attack victims feel little or no chest pain or discomfort.

Some people with narrowed arteries may experience chest pain or pressure that comes and goes at different times. This type of pain is called **angina pectoris,** a medical term for pain

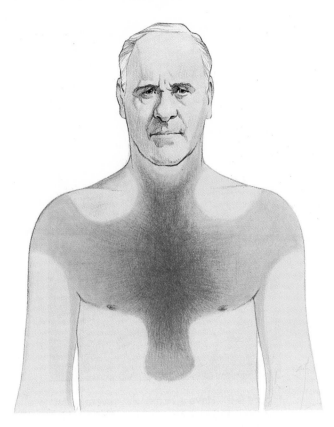

Figure 6-4 Heart attack pain is most often felt in the center of the chest, behind the breastbone. It may spread to the shoulder, arm, or jaw.

moist from perspiration. Some heart attack victims sweat profusely. The victim may also experience nausea and may vomit. The victim may feel short of breath or breathe noisily. These signs result from the stress the body experiences when the heart does not work effectively.

Since a heart attack may lead to cardiac arrest, it is important to recognize and act on these signs and symptoms. Prompt action may prevent cardiac arrest. A heart attack victim whose heart is still beating has a far better chance of living than a victim whose heart has stopped. Most people who die from a heart attack die within 1 to 2 hours after the first signs and symptoms appear. Many of these people could have been saved if bystanders or the victim had been aware of the signs and symptoms of a heart attack and acted promptly. Heart attacks are caused by obstructions in the coronary arteries. Since the obstruction may be a clot, early treatment with medication that dissolves clots can be helpful in minimizing damage to the heart.

in the chest. Angina pectoris develops when the heart needs more oxygen than it gets. When the coronary arteries are narrow and the heart needs more oxygen, such as during physical activity or emotional stress, heart muscle tissues may not get enough oxygen. This lack of oxygen can cause a constricting chest pain that may spread to the neck, jaw, and arms. Pain associated with angina usually lasts less than 10 minutes. A victim who knows that he or she has a history of angina may tell you he or she has prescribed medication that will temporarily widen the arteries and therefore help relieve the pain. Reducing the heart's demand for oxygen, such as by stopping physical activity and taking prescribed medication, often relieves angina symptoms.

Another prominent indicator of a heart attack is breathing difficulty. The victim may be breathing faster than normal because the body is trying to get much-needed oxygen to the heart. The victim's pulse may be faster or slower than normal, or irregular. The victim's skin may be pale, ashen, or bluish, particularly around the face. The face may also be

Signs and Symptoms of a Heart Attack

Persistent chest pain or discomfort

Victim has persistent pain or pressure in the chest that is not relieved by resting, changing position, or taking oral medication.

Victim has pain that may range from discomfort to an unbearable crushing sensation and may spread to neck, jaw, and arms.

Breathing difficulty

Victim breathes noisily.

Victim feels short of breath.

Victim breathes faster than normal.

Skin appearance

Victim's skin may be pale, ashen, or bluish in color.

Victim's face may be moist, or victim may sweat profusely.

Other

Victim may be nauseated and may vomit.

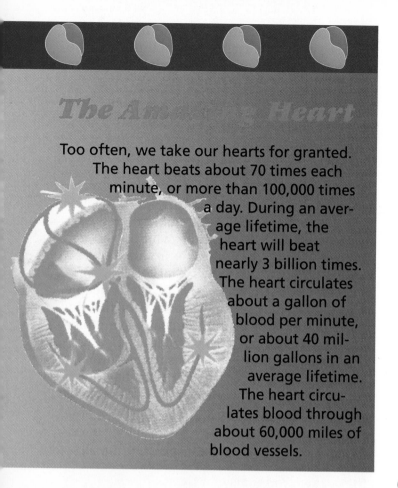

The Amazing Heart

Too often, we take our hearts for granted. The heart beats about 70 times each minute, or more than 100,000 times a day. During an average lifetime, the heart will beat nearly 3 billion times. The heart circulates about a gallon of blood per minute, or about 40 million gallons in an average lifetime. The heart circulates blood through about 60,000 miles of blood vessels.

Figure 6-5 Have a victim with severe chest pain stop and rest. Many victims find it easier to breathe while sitting.

Many heart attack victims delay seeking care. Nearly half of all heart attack victims wait 2 or more hours before going to the hospital. Victims often deny or do not realize they are having a heart attack. They may dismiss the signs and symptoms as indigestion or muscle soreness.

Remember, the key symptom of a heart attack is persistent chest pain. Call EMS personnel immediately and begin care for a heart attack.

Care for a Heart Attack

The most important first aid measure is to be able to recognize the signs and symptoms of a heart attack. You must take immediate action if any of these signs or symptoms appear. A heart attack victim may deny the seriousness of the symptoms he or she is experiencing. Do not let this denial influence you. If you think that he or she might be having a heart attack, you must act. Have the victim stop what he or she is doing and rest comfortably. Many heart attack victims find it easier to breathe while sitting (Fig.

6-5). Having the victim rest eases the heart's need for oxygen

If possible, talk to bystanders and the victim to get more information. Ask the victim if he or she has a history of heart disease. Some victims who have heart disease have prescribed medications for chest pain. You can help by getting the medication for the victim. A medication often prescribed for angina is nitroglycerin. **Nitroglycerin** is commonly prescribed as a small tablet that dissolves under the tongue. It is also available in a spray. Sometimes nitroglycerin patches are placed on the chest. Once absorbed into the body, nitroglycerin dilates the blood vessels to make it easier for blood to reach heart muscle tissue, thus relieving the chest pain.

Survival after a heart attack often depends on how soon the victim receives advanced medical care. Do not try to drive the victim to the hospital yourself, since cardiac arrest can occur at any time. Wait for EMS personnel.

Keep a calm and reassuring manner when providing first aid for a heart attack victim. Comforting the victim helps reduce anxiety and eases some of the discomfort. Watch the victim

Care for a Heart Attack

Recognize the signs and symptoms of a heart attack.

Call EMS personnel.

Convince the victim to stop activity and rest.

Help the victim rest comfortably.

Comfort the victim.

Assist the victim with medication, if prescribed.

Be prepared to give CPR if victim's heart stops beating.

closely until EMS personnel arrive. Continue to monitor the victim's breathing and signs of circulation. Watch for any changes in appearance or behavior. Since the heart attack victim's condition may deteriorate into cardiac arrest, be prepared to give CPR.

MIND AT WORK

2. If Mr. Getz had experienced chest pain, how might stopping and resting have prevented his collapse?

CARDIAC ARREST

Cardiac arrest occurs when the heart stops beating or beats too ineffectively to generate a pulse and blood cannot be circulated to the brain and other vital organs. Cardiac arrest is a life-threatening emergency because the vital organs of the body are no longer receiving oxygen-rich blood. Every year, more than 300,000 heart attack victims die of cardiac arrest before reaching a hospital.

Common Causes of Cardiac Arrest

Cardiovascular disease is the most common cause of cardiac arrest. Drowning, suffocation, and certain drugs can cause breathing to stop, which will soon lead to cardiac arrest. Severe injuries to the chest or severe blood loss can also cause the heart to stop. Electrocution dis-

rupts the heart's electrical activity and can cause the heart to stop. Stroke or other types of brain damage can also stop the heart.

Signs of Cardiac Arrest

A victim in cardiac arrest is not breathing and has no signs of circulation. The victim's heart has stopped beating. The absence of signs of circulation is the primary sign of cardiac arrest. No matter how hard you try, you will not be able to feel a pulse or find other signs of circulation. If you cannot feel a carotid pulse—the pulse at the artery on each side of the neck—no blood is reaching the brain. The victim will be unconscious and not breathing. The victim may not have shown the signs and symptoms of a heart attack before the cardiac arrest. Death resulting from sudden cardiac arrest is called **sudden death.**

MIND AT WORK

3. Is it possible that Mr. Getz may have suffered a cardiac arrest? Why or why not?

Care for Cardiac Arrest

A victim who is not breathing and has no signs of circulation is said to be **clinically dead.** However, the cells of the brain and other vital organs will continue to live for a short period of time until oxygen is depleted. This victim needs **cardiopulmonary resuscitation (CPR)**, which is a combination of chest compressions and rescue breathing. The term "cardio-" refers to the heart, and "pulmonary" refers to the lungs. Chest compressions are a method of making the blood flow when the heart is not beating. Given together, rescue breathing and chest compressions artificially take over the functions of the lungs and heart. CPR increases a cardiac arrest victim's chances of survival by keeping the brain supplied with oxygen until advanced medical care can be given. Without CPR, the brain will begin to die within 4 to 6 minutes. The irreversible damage caused by brain cell death is known as **biological death** (Fig. 6-6). Be aware, however, that even under the best of conditions, CPR only generates about one third of the normal blood flow to the

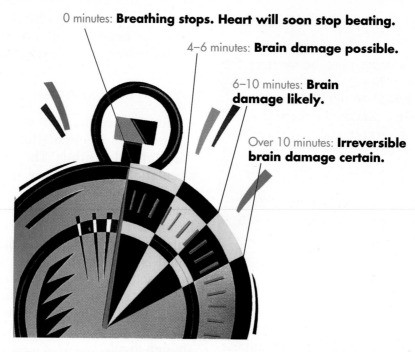

0 minutes: **Breathing stops. Heart will soon stop beating.**

4–6 minutes: **Brain damage possible.**

6–10 minutes: **Brain damage likely.**

Over 10 minutes: **Irreversible brain damage certain.**

Figure 6-6 Clinical death is a condition in which the heart and breathing stop. Without resuscitation, clinical death will result in biological death. Biological death is the irreversible death of brain cells.

brain. Specific techniques for giving CPR to adults, children, and infants are presented later in this chapter.

Despite the best efforts of the rescuer, CPR alone is not enough to help someone survive cardiac arrest. Advanced medical care is also needed. Call EMS personnel immediately if you determine that a victim is unconscious. If you are alone, provide 1 minute of care to a child 8 years of age or under or an infant. Trained emergency personnel can provide **advanced cardiac life support (ACLS).** EMS professionals act as an extension of hospital emergency departments. For example, some can administer medications or use a defibrillator (Fig. 6-7). A **defibrillator** is a device that sends an electric shock through the chest to the heart to enable the heart to resume its normal electrical activity and a functional heartbeat. **Defibrillation** given as soon as possible is the key to helping many victims survive cardiac arrest. Immediate CPR given by bystanders, combined with early defibrillation and advanced cardiac life support by EMS professionals, gives the victim of cardiac arrest the best chance for survival.

There are four steps in the cardiac chain of survival. Each step plays an important part in the victim's survival.

1. Early recognition and early access. The sooner you recognize the problem and call 9-1-1 or the local emergency number, the better.
2. Early CPR. Begin CPR immediately and continue until an AED arrives on the scene and is ready to use.
3. Early Defibrillation. Each minute that defibrillation is delayed reduces the chance of survival by about 10 percent.
4. Early Advanced Life Support. This is given by trained medical personnel who pro-

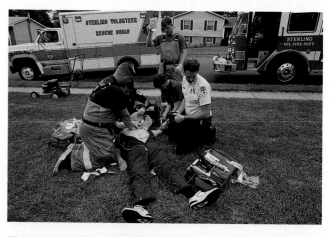

Figure 6-7 Use of a defibrillator and other advanced measures may restore a heartbeat in a victim of cardiac arrest.

vide further care and transport to medical facilities.

Some emergency professionals, such as fire fighters and police officers, and lay rescuers use **automated external defibrillators (AEDs).** AEDs, are now being placed in factories and other workplaces, stadiums, and other places where large numbers of people gather. AEDs are now more accessible to trained responders for use in an emergency.

For infants and children younger than 8 years old who are in cardiac arrest, the initial priorities continue to be calling EMS personnel and starting CPR promptly and continue to provide CPR until EMS personnel arrive. Effective chest compressions and rescue breaths can help keep the brain, heart, and other vital organs supplied with blood containing oxygen until the heart can be restarted. Any delay in starting CPR or advanced medical care reduces the victim's chance for survival. As someone trained in first aid, you are the first link in the victim's chain of survival.

Summary of care for cardiac arrest

As in any emergency, you provide care for cardiac arrest by following the emergency action steps. First aid for cardiac arrest victims always begins with a check for life-threatening conditions. Once you determine the victim is unconscious, send someone to call EMS personnel. Then check for breathing and signs of circulation. Take no more than 10 seconds to check for signs of circulation to be sure the heart is not beating. Unnecessary chest compressions may cause harm. If there are no signs of circulation, begin CPR immediately. Identify yourself to bystanders as someone trained in CPR.

If you are alone, find the nearest phone, call EMS personnel for help, and return and check breathing and signs of circulation. If you find no pulse, begin CPR. If the victim is a child or an infant, perform 1 minute of CPR before calling EMS personnel.

Even in the best of situations, when CPR is started promptly and EMS personnel arrive quickly, approximately 85 percent of cardiac arrest victims do not survive. Controlling your emotions and accepting death are not easy. Remember that any attempt to help is worthwhile. Since performing CPR and calling for help are only two of the many factors that de-

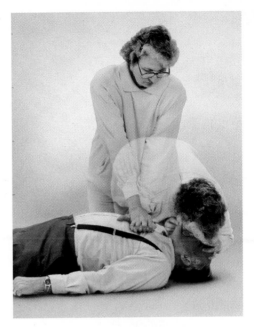

Figure 6-8 Position yourself so that you can give rescue breaths and chest compressions without having to move.

termine whether a cardiac arrest victim survives, you should feel assured that you did everything you could to help.

CPR FOR ADULTS

Chest compressions create pressure within the chest cavity that moves blood through the circulatory system. For CPR to be the most effective, the victim should be on his or her back on a firm, flat surface. The victim's head should be on the same level as the heart or lower. CPR is not effective if the victim is on a soft surface, like a sofa or mattress, or is sitting up in a chair.

Chest Compressions

To give chest compressions, kneel beside the victim. Position yourself midway between the chest and the head to be able to move easily between compressions and breaths (Fig. 6-8). Lean over the chest and place your hands in the correct position. Compress the chest by alternately pressing down and releasing. Ideally, chest compressions should be delivered straight down in a smooth, uniform pattern.

Finding the correct hand position

Using the correct hand position is important. It allows you to give the most effective

A Shocking Discovery

Every year, 250,000 Americans die from cardiac arrest in their homes and on the streets. However, the development of a simple, computerized electric-shocking device offers an opportunity to increase the likelihood of survival.

In many cardiac arrests, the heart flutters chaotically before it stops, a condition called ventricular fibrillation. The electrical impulses that cause the heart muscle to contract are no longer synchronized and fail to create the strong pumping action needed to circulate the blood.

Electric-shocking devices, or defibrillators, were introduced into mobile coronary units in 1966 (Pantridge JF, Geddes JS). The machines allow emergency personnel to monitor the heart's electrical rhythm. A doctor attaches electrodes to the victim and reviews the heart's rhythm. If necessary, an electric shock is delivered to the heart to try to restore its proper rhythm. Eventually, paramedics were trained to evaluate rhythms and administer electric shocks.

Fortunately, a new, easy-to-use Automated External Defibrillator (AED) allows emergency medical technicians, first responders, and even citizen responders to provide the lifesaving shocks. With the new defibrillators, a computer chip, rather than an advanced medical professional, analyzes the heart's rhythm. Typically, the responder places the two electrodes on the victim's chest and then presses two buttons—first "ANALYZE," then, if the condition warrants, "SHOCK." The machine does the rest.

AEDs monitor the heart's electrical activity through two electrodes placed on the chest. On a heart monitor, ventricular fibrillation looks like a chaotic, wavy line, whereas a normal heartbeat shows a pattern of evenly spaced, well-defined, spiked points. The computer chip determines the need for a shock by looking at the pattern, size, and frequency of the electrocardiogram waves.

If the rhythm indicates ventricular fibrillation, the machine readies an electrical charge. When the electrical charge disrupts the irregular heartbeat, this disruption is called defibrillation. This allows the heart's natural electrical system to begin to fire

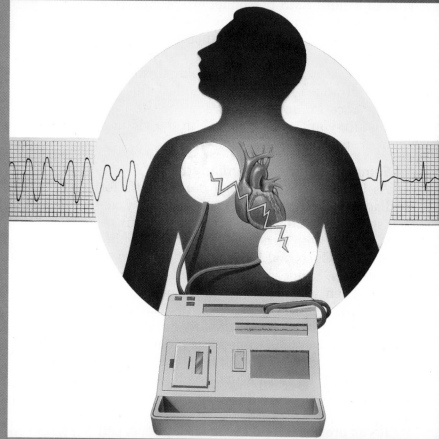

off electrical impulses correctly so that the heart can beat normally.

Researchers say rapid defibrillation is the most important single factor in determining whether someone survives a cardiac arrest (Cummins RO, et al.). When first responders are trained to use AEDs and AEDs are made available, the amount of time it takes to administer a shock in a cardiac emergency is greatly reduced. By extending training to first responders, communities should see an increase in survival rates. In Eugene and Springfield, Oregon, AEDs were placed on every fire truck and all fire

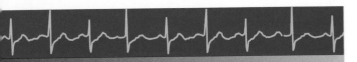

fighters were trained to use them. Researchers saw the survival rates for cardiac arrest in these communities increase by 18 percent in the first year (Graves JR, Austin D, Cummins RO). The International Association of Fire Chiefs has endorsed equipping every fire suppression unit in the United States with an AED (Murphy DM).

The ability to automatically defibrillate the heart within minutes of a cardiac arrest represents the single most significant advance in the treatment of cardiac arrest. AEDs also are being introduced in areas that hold large groups of people, such as convention centers, stadiums, large businesses, and industrial complexes. But not every community has been as aggressive in ensuring EMTs and first responders are AED trained or that AEDs are readily available. What about your community? If you or someone you know has suffered a cardiac arrest, will a first responder trained in defibrillation be dispatched to your aid?

SOURCES
1. Pantridge JF, Geddes JS: A mobile intensive care unit in the treatment of myocardial infarction, *Lancet* 2(1967): 271-273.
2. Cummins RO, Ornato JP, Theis WH, Pepe PE: Improving survival from sudden cardiac arrest: the "chain of survival" concept: a statement for health professionals from the Advanced Cardiac Life Support Subcommittee and the Emergency Cardiac Care Committee, American Heart Association, *Circulation* 1991(83): 1832-1847.
3. Graves JR, Austin D Jr, Cummins RO: *Rapid zap: automated defibrillation.* Englewood Cliffs, NJ, 1989, Prentice-Hall.
4. Murphy DM: Rapid defibrillation: fire service to lead the way, *JEMS* 1987 (12): 67–71.
5. American Heart Association. Guidelines 2000 for emergency cardiopulmonary resuscitation and emergency cardiovascular care. *Circulation*, 2000 (102).
6. National Center for Early Defibrillation. www.early-defib.org.

compressions without adding injury. The correct position for your hands is over the lower half of the sternum. At the lowest point of the sternum is an arrow-shaped piece of cartilage called the **xiphoid process.** You should avoid pressing directly on the xiphoid process, which can break and injure underlying tissues. The heel of your hand should be just above it.

To locate the correct hand position for chest compressions—

1. Find the lower edge of the victim's rib cage using the hand closer to the victim's feet. Slide your middle and index fingers up the edge of the rib cage to the notch where the ribs meet the sternum (Fig. 6-9, *A*). Place your middle finger on this notch. Place your index finger next to your middle finger.
2. Place the heel of your other hand on the sternum next to your index finger (Fig. 6-9, *B*). The heel of your hand should rest along the length of the sternum.
3. Once the heel of your hand is in position on the sternum, place your other hand directly on top of it (Fig. 6-9, *C*).
4. Use the heel of your hand to apply pressure on the sternum. Try to keep your fingers off the chest by interlacing them or holding them upward. Applying pressure with your fingers can lead to inefficient chest compressions or unnecessary damage to the chest.

The correct hand position provides the most effective compressions. It also decreases the chance of pushing the xiphoid process into the delicate organs beneath it, although this rarely occurs.

If you have arthritis or a similar condition, you may use an alternate hand position, grasping the wrist of the hand on the chest with the other hand (Fig. 6-10). You find the correct hand position in the same way.

The victim's clothing will not necessarily interfere with your ability to position your hands correctly to give chest compressions. If you can find the correct position without removing thin clothing, such as a T-shirt, do so. Sometimes a layer of thin clothing will help keep your hands from slipping, since the victim's chest may be moist with sweat. If you are not sure that you can find the correct

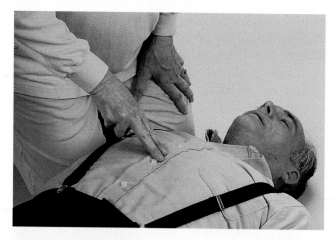

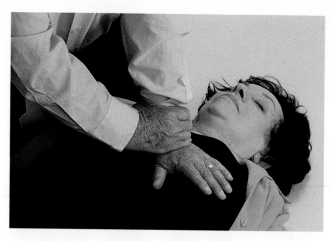

A

B

C

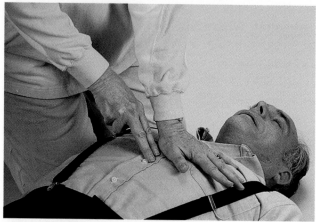

Figure 6-10   Grasping the wrist of the hand positioned on the chest is an alternate hand position for giving chest compressions.

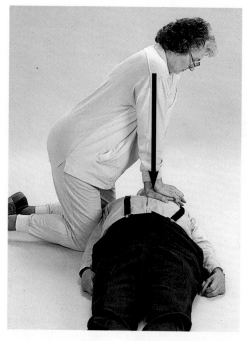

Figure 6-11   With your hands in place, position yourself so that your shoulders are directly over your hands, arms straight and elbows locked.

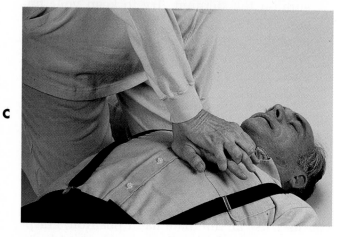

Figure 6-9   **A,** Find the notch where the lower ribs meet the sternum. **B,** Place the heel of your hand on the sternum, next to your finger. **C,** Place your other hand over the heel of the first. Use the heel of your bottom hand to apply pressure on the sternum.

Position of the rescuer

Your body position is important when giving chest compressions. Compressing the chest straight down provides the best blood flow. The correct body position is also less tiring for you.

Kneel beside the victim with your hands in the correct position. Straighten your arms and lock your elbows so that your shoulders are directly over your hands (Fig. 6-11). When you press down in this position, you will be push-

hand position, bare the victim's chest. You should not be overly concerned that you may not be able to find the correct hand position if the victim is obese, since fat does not accumulate as much over the sternum as it does elsewhere.

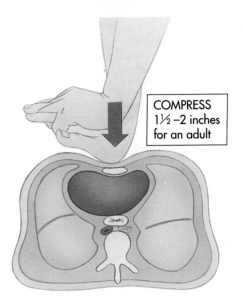 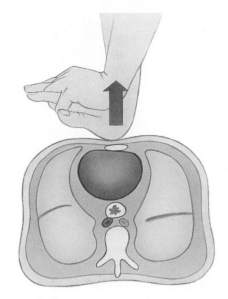

COMPRESS
1½ –2 inches
for an adult

Figure 6-12   Push straight down with the weight of your body, then release, allowing the chest to return to the normal position.

ing straight down onto the sternum. Locking your elbows keeps your arms straight and prevents you from tiring quickly.

Compressing the chest requires less effort in this position. When you press down, the weight of your upper body creates the force needed to compress the chest. Push with the weight of your upper body, not with the muscles of your arms. Push straight down. Do not rock back and forth. Rocking results in less effective compressions and unnecessarily uses much needed energy. If your arms and shoulders tire quickly, you are not using the correct body position. After each compression, release the pressure on the chest without removing your hands or changing hand position and allow the chest to return to its normal position before starting the next compression (Fig. 6-12).

Compression technique

Each compression should push the sternum down from 1½ to 2 inches (3.8 to 5.1 centimeters) (Fig. 6-12). The downward and upward movement should be smooth, not jerky. Maintain a steady down-and-up rhythm, and do not pause between compressions. Spend half of the time pushing down and half of the time coming up. When you press down, the chambers of the heart empty. When you come up, release all pressure on the chest. This release lets the chambers of the heart fill with blood between compressions. Keep your hands in their correct position on the sternum. If your hands slip, find the notch as you did before, and repo-

sition your hands correctly before continuing compressions.

Give compressions at the rate of about 100 per minute. As you do compressions, count aloud, "One and two and three and four and five and six and . . ." up to 15. Counting aloud will help you pace yourself. Push down as you say the number and come up as you say "and." You should be able to do the 15 compressions in about 9 to 10 seconds. Even though you are compressing the chest at a rate of about 100 times per minute, you will only actually perform about 60 compressions in a minute, because you must stop compressions and give 2 breaths between each group of 15 compressions.

Compression/Breathing Cycles

When you give CPR, do cycles of 15 compressions and 2 breaths. For each cycle, give 15 chest compressions, then open the airway with a head-tilt/chin-lift and give 2 rescue breaths (Fig. 6-13). This cycle should take about 15 seconds. For each new cycle of compressions and breaths, use the correct hand position by first finding the notch at the lower end of the sternum.

After doing 4 cycles of continuous CPR, check to see if the victim has signs of circulation. These 4 cycles should take about 1 minute. Check the carotid pulse after you have given the 2 breaths at the end of the fourth cycle (Fig. 6-14). Slide your fingers into position

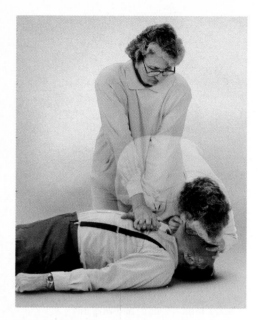

Figure 6-13   Give 15 compressions, then 2 breaths.

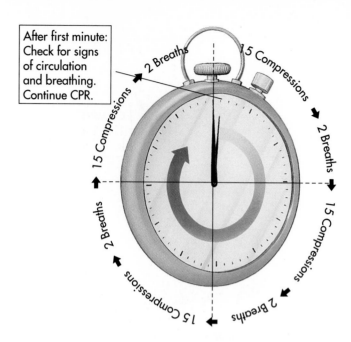

After first minute: Check for signs of circulation and breathing. Continue CPR.

15 Compressions   2 Breaths   15 Compressions   2 Breaths   15 Compressions   2 Breaths   15 Compressions   2 Breaths

Figure 6-14   Check for signs of circulation at the end of the fourth cycle of 15 compressions and 2 breaths and again every few minutes.

on the victim's neck. If there is no pulse or other signs of circulation, continue CPR, starting with 15 compressions. Check for signs of circulation again every few minutes. If you find signs of circulation, check for breathing. Give rescue breathing if necessary. If the victim is breathing, keep his or her airway open and monitor breathing and signs of circulation closely until EMS personnel arrive. The skill sheets at the end of this chapter provide step-by-step practice of CPR.

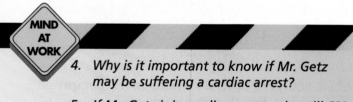

MIND AT WORK

> 4. *Why is it important to know if Mr. Getz may be suffering a cardiac arrest?*
>
> 5. *If Mr. Getz is in cardiac arrest, why will CPR alone not sustain his life?*

CARDIAC EMERGENCIES IN CHILDREN AND INFANTS

A child's heart is usually healthy. Unlike adults, children do not often initially suffer a **cardiac emergency.** Instead, what usually happens is that the child suffers a respiratory emergency; then a cardiac emergency develops. Common causes of respiratory emergency re-

sulting in a cardiac emergency for both infants and children include injuries from motor vehicle crashes, drowning, smoke inhalation, poisonings, airway obstruction, firearm injuries, and falls. A cardiac emergency can also result from an acute respiratory condition, such as an asthma attack and severe epiglottitis—a respiratory emergency that occurs mainly in children and infants. See Chapter 5 for other respiratory emergencies.

Most cardiac emergencies in children and infants are preventable. One way to prevent them in this age group is to prevent injuries. Another is to make sure that children and infants receive proper medical care. A third is to recognize the early signs of a respiratory emergency. These signs include—

- Agitation.
- Unusually fast or slow breathing.
- Drowsiness.
- Noisy breathing.
- Pale or ashen, flushed, or bluish skin color.
- Increased difficulty breathing.
- Altered level of consciousness.
- Increased heart and breathing rates.

If you recognize that an infant or child is in respiratory distress or respiratory arrest, provide the care you learned in Chapter 5 for those emergencies. If the infant or child is in cardiac

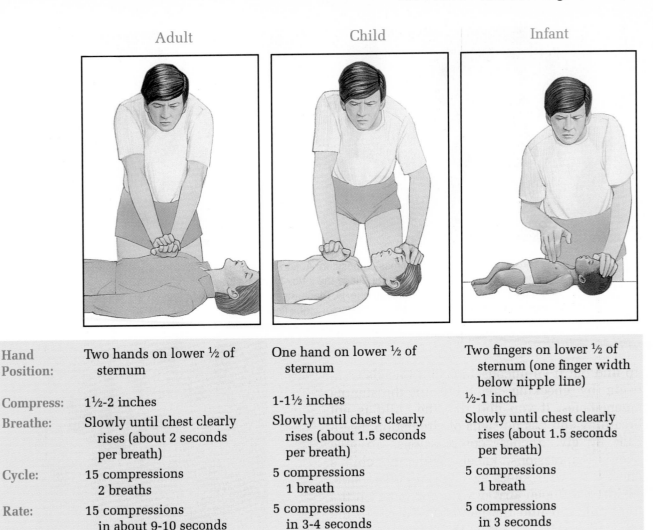

	Adult	Child	Infant
Hand Position:	Two hands on lower ½ of sternum	One hand on lower ½ of sternum	Two fingers on lower ½ of sternum (one finger width below nipple line)
Compress:	1½-2 inches	1-1½ inches	½-1 inch
Breathe:	Slowly until chest clearly rises (about 2 seconds per breath)	Slowly until chest clearly rises (about 1.5 seconds per breath)	Slowly until chest clearly rises (about 1.5 seconds per breath)
Cycle:	15 compressions 2 breaths	5 compressions 1 breath	5 compressions 1 breath
Rate:	15 compressions in about 9-10 seconds	5 compressions in 3-4 seconds	5 compressions in 3 seconds

Figure 6-15   The technique for chest compressions differs for adults, children, and infants.

arrest, start CPR immediately. In either event, send someone to call EMS personnel.

CPR FOR CHILDREN AND INFANTS

The technique of CPR for infants and children is similar to the technique for adults. Like CPR for adults, CPR for infants and children consists of a series of alternating compressions and breaths. Because of their smaller bodies and the fact that infants and children have faster heart and breathing rates, you must adjust your hand position, the rate of compressions, and the number of compressions and breaths in each cycle. Figure 6-15 compares these techniques for adults, children, and infants.

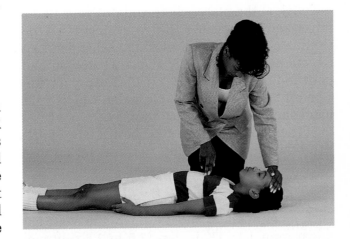

Figure 6-16   While kneeling beside the child, maintain an open airway with one hand and find the correct hand position with the other.

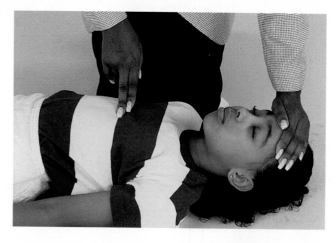
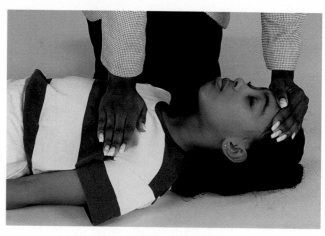

Figure 6-17   To locate compression position: **A,** find the notch where the lower rib meets the sternum with your middle finger. Place the index finger next to it so that both fingers rest on the lower end of the breastbone. **B,** Place the heel of the same hand on the breastbone immediately above where you had your index finger.

CPR for Children

To find out if an unconscious child needs CPR, begin by checking for other life-threatening emergencies. If you find that the child is not breathing and has no signs of circulation, begin CPR by giving chest compressions. To give chest compressions, kneel beside the child's chest with your knees against the child's side. Maintain an open airway with one hand on the forehead, and find the hand position with the other (Fig. 6-16). To locate the correct hand position on a child, slide your middle finger up the lower edge of the ribs until you locate the notch where the ribs meet the sternum. Place the index finger next to it. The two fingers should be resting on the lower end of the sternum (Fig. 6-17, *A*).

Look at the place where you put your index finger and remember it. Lift your fingers off the sternum, and put the heel of the same hand on the sternum immediately above where you had your index finger (Fig. 6-17, *B*). Keep your fingers off the child's chest. Only the heel of your hand should rest on the sternum.

When you compress the chest, use only the hand that is on the child's sternum. Do not use both hands to give chest compressions to a child. Push straight down, making sure your shoulder is directly over your hand (Fig. 6-18). Each compression should push the sternum down from 1 to 1½ inches (2.5 to 3.8 centimeters) (Fig. 6-19). The down-and-up movement should be smooth, not jerky. Release the pressure on the child's chest completely, but do not

Figure 6-18   When you compress the chest, use the heel of your hand. Push straight down, making sure your shoulder is directly over your hand.

lift your hand off the chest.

When you give CPR to a child, do cycles of 5 compressions and 1 breath at a rate of about 100 compressions per minute. While giving compressions with one hand, keep your other hand on the child's forehead to help maintain an open airway. After giving 5 compressions, remove your compression hand from the chest, lift the chin, and give 1 rescue breath. The breath should last about 1½ seconds. Use a chin-lift with a head-tilt to ensure that the

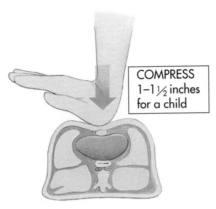

COMPRESS
1–1½ inches
for a child

Figure 6-19   Push straight down with the weight of your body and then release, allowing the chest to return to its normal position.

child's airway is open. Keeping one hand on the child's forehead reduces the time it takes to deliver each breath, allowing you to do more cycles per minute. After giving the breath, place your hand in the same position as before and continue compressions. You do not have to measure your hand position each time unless you lose your place.

Keep repeating the cycles of 5 compressions and 1 rescue breath (Fig. 6-20). After you do about 1 minute of continuous CPR, recheck the child for signs of circulation for no more than 10 seconds. If you do not find signs of circulation, continue CPR, beginning with compressions. Repeat the check for signs of circulation every few minutes.

If you find signs of circulation, then check breathing for no more than 10 seconds. If the child is breathing, keep the airway open and monitor breathing and pulse closely. Recheck signs of circulation every few minutes. If the child is not breathing, give rescue breathing

and keep checking for signs of circulation and breathing about every minute.

CPR for Infants

To find out if an infant needs CPR, begin by checking for life-threatening emergencies. Start by checking the infant's breathing and signs of circulation. To check the pulse in an infant, remember to locate the brachial pulse on the inside of the upper arm (Fig. 6-21). If the infant has no pulse or other signs of circulation, begin CPR.

Position the infant face-up on a firm, flat surface. The infant's head must be on the same level as the heart or lower. Stand or kneel facing the infant from the side. Bare the infant's chest. Keep the hand on the infant's head to maintain an open airway. Use the fingers of your other hand to give compressions.

To find the correct place to give compressions, imagine a line running across the chest

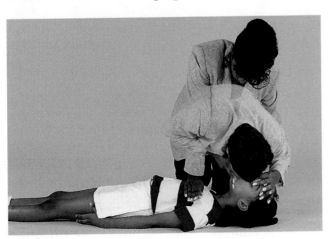

Figure 6-20   Give 5 compressions and then 1 breath.

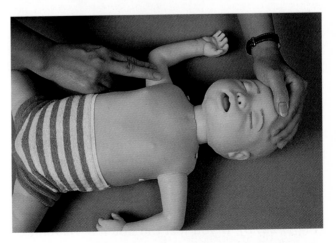

Figure 6-21   Feel for an infant's pulse on the inside of the upper arm, between the infant's elbow and shoulder.

A Matter of Choice

Your 75-year-old grandfather is living with your family. He has a terminal illness and is frequently in the hospital. He has no hope of regaining his health.

One afternoon, you go to his room to give him lunch. As you start to talk to him, you realize he has stopped breathing. You check for a pulse. He has none. You are suddenly faced with the fact that your grandfather is no longer alive . . . he's dead. You ask yourself . . . What would he want me to do?

No one can tell you what to do. No one can advise you. No one can predict the outcome. Since your grandfather hasn't made his wishes known to you, the decision to try to help your grandfather by giving CPR is a personal one you must make.

Your heart tells you to give CPR, yet your mind tells you not to. Various questions race through your mind. Can I face the fact I am losing someone I love? Shouldn't I always try to give CPR? What would the quality of his life be like after resuscitation? Again, what would grandfather want?

How would this situation have changed if your grandfather and family had planned for this possibility? For instance, what would have happened if your grandfather had given instructions in advance?

Often people who are terminally ill and feel there is no hope of regaining their health are prepared for the eventuality of death. Talking to your grandfather about preferences before a crisis occurs can help you with such decisions. Instructions that describe a person's wishes about medical treatment are called advance directives. These instructions are used when a person can no longer make his or her health care decisions. If your grandfather is able to make decisions, advance directives do not interfere with his right to do so.

As provided by the federal Patient Self-Determination Act, adults who are admitted to a hospital or a health care facility or who receive assistance from certain organizations that receive funds from Medicare or Medicaid have the right to make fundamental choices about their own care. They must be told about their right to make decisions about the level of life support that would be provided in an emergency situation. They would be offered the opportunity to make these choices at the time of admission.

Conversations with relatives, friends, or physicians, while the patient is still capable of making decisions, are the most common form of advance directives. However, because conversations may not be recalled accurately, the courts consider written directives more trustworthy.

Two examples of written advance directives are living wills and durable powers of attorney

between the infant's nipples (Fig. 6-22, *A*). Place your index finger of the hand closer to the infant's feet on the sternum (breastbone) just below this imaginary line. Then place the pads of the two fingers next to your index finger on the sternum. Raise the index finger (Fig. 6-22, *B*). If you feel the notch at the end of the infant's sternum, move your fingers up a bit.

Use the pads of two fingers to compress the chest (Fig. 6-22, *C*). Compress the chest ½ to 1 inch (1.3 to 2.5 cm), then let the sternum return to its normal position. When you compress, push straight down. The down-and-up movement of your compressions should be smooth, not jerky. Keep a steady rhythm. Do not pause between compressions except to give breaths. When you are coming up, release pressure on the infant's chest completely, but do not let

for health care. The types of health care decisions covered by these documents vary depending on where you live. Talking with a legal professional can help determine which advance directive options are recognized in your state and what they do and do not cover.

If your grandfather had established a living will, directions for health care would be in place before he became unable to communicate his wishes. The instructions that can be included in this document vary from state to state. A living will generally allows a person to refuse only medical care that "merely prolongs the process of dying," as in the case of a terminal illness.

If your grandfather had established a durable power of attorney for health care, the document would authorize someone to make medical decisions for him in any situation in which he could no longer make them for himself. This authorized person is called a health care surrogate or proxy. This surrogate, with the information given by the patient's physician, may consent to or refuse medical treatment on the patient's behalf. In this case, he or she would support the needs and wishes that affect the health care decisions and the advance directives of your grandfather.

A doctor could formalize your grandfather's preferences by writing "Do Not Resuscitate" (DNR) orders in your grandfather's medical records. Such orders would state that if your grandfather's heartbeat or breathing stops, he should not be resuscitated. The choice in deciding on DNR orders may be covered in a living will or in the durable power of attorney for health care.

Appointing someone to act as a health care surrogate, along with writing down your instructions, is the best way to formalize your wishes about medical care. Some of these documents can be obtained through a personal physician, attorney, or various state and health care organizations. A lawyer is not always needed to execute advance directives. However, if you have any questions concerning advance directives, it is wise to obtain legal advice.

Copies of advance directives should be provided to all personal physicians, family members, and the person chosen as the health care surrogate. Tell them what documents have been prepared and where the original and other copies are located. Discuss the document with all parties so that they understand the intent of all the requests. Keep these documents updated.

Keep in mind that advance directives are not limited to elderly people or people with terminal illnesses. Advance directives should be considered by anyone who has decided the care he or she would like to have provided. An unexpected illness or injury could create a need for decisions at any time.

Knowing about living wills, durable powers of attorneys for health care, and DNR orders can help you prepare for difficult decisions. If you are interested in learning more about your rights and the options available to you in your state, contact a legal professional.

SOURCES
1. Hospital Shared Services of Colorado, Stockard Inventory Program: *Your right to make health care decisions,* Denver, 1991.
2. Title 42 United States Code, Section 1395 cc(a)(1)(Q)(A) Patient Self-Determination Act.

your fingers lose contact with the chest (Fig. 6-23). Compress at a rate of at least 100 compressions per minute. That rate is slightly faster than the rate of compressions for a child. When you complete 5 compressions, give 1 rescue breath, covering the infant's nose and mouth with your mouth. The breath should take about 1½ seconds. Keep repeating cycles of 5 compressions and 1 breath.

Recheck for signs of circulation after about 1 minute of continuous CPR. Check the brachial pulse and for other signs of circulation for no more than 10 seconds. If there is no pulse or other signs of circulation, continue CPR, starting with compressions. Repeat the check for signs of circulation every few minutes.

If you do find signs of circulation, then check breathing for no more than 10 seconds. If

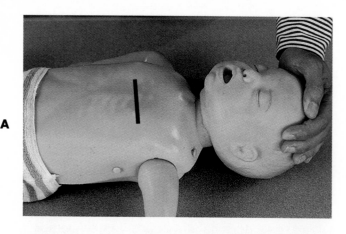

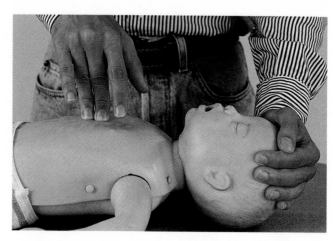

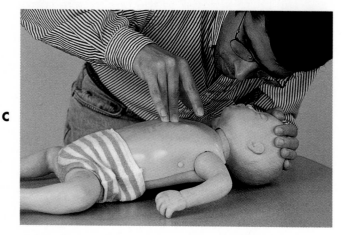

Figure 6-22   To locate compression position: **A,** Imagine a line running across the chest between the infant's nipples. **B,** Place the pads of the middle and ring fingers next to your index finger on the breastbone. Raise the index finger. **C,** Use the pads of the remaining two fingers to compress the chest.

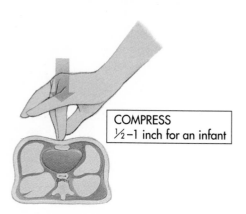

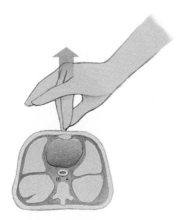

COMPRESS
½–1 inch for an infant

Figure 6-23   Push straight down with your fingers and then release the pressure on the chest completely.

the infant is breathing, keep the airway open and monitor breathing and signs of circulation closely. Recheck signs of circulation every few minutes. If the infant is not breathing, give rescue breathing and check signs of circulation and breathing about every minute.

MORE ABOUT ADULT CPR

Even when properly performed, CPR can be very strenuous. If another trained rescuer is on

the scene, he or she can help you perform CPR. You should also know when it may be appropriate to stop CPR.

If a Second Trained Rescuer Is at the Scene

If two rescuers trained in CPR are at the scene, you should both identify yourselves as CPR-trained rescuers. One of you should phone EMS personnel for help, if this has not been done, while the other provides CPR. Then one should

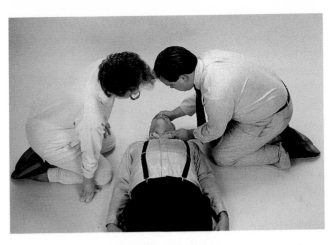

Figure 6-24 The second rescuer should again check the victim's pulse and other signs of circulation before resuming CPR.

take over CPR when the other is tired. If the first rescuer is tired and needs help, follow these steps:

1. The first rescuer stops CPR at the end of a cycle of 15 compressions and 2 breaths.
2. The second rescuer kneels next to the victim on the other side. The second rescuer tilts the head and feels for the carotid pulse (Fig. 6-24). If there is no pulse or other signs of circulation, the second rescuer continues CPR with 15 compressions.
3. The first rescuer then checks that the victim's chest is clearly rising during rescue breathing and feels the carotid pulse for an artificial pulse during chest compressions. This artificial pulse tells you that blood is being moved through the victim's body with each compression. A second rescuer could also do the 2 rescue breaths and the first rescuer could do the 15 chest compressions, or vice versa.

When to Stop CPR

Once you begin CPR, you should try not to interrupt the blood flow being created by your compressions. However, you can stop CPR—

- If another trained person takes over CPR for you.
- If EMS personnel arrive and take over care of the victim.
- If the scene suddenly becomes unsafe.
- If the person's heart starts beating.
- If you are too exhausted to continue.

If the victim's heartbeat returns but he or she is still not breathing, continue giving rescue breathing. If the victim is breathing and has a heartbeat, keep the airway open and monitor signs of circulation and breathing closely until EMS personnel arrive.

PREVENTING CARDIOVASCULAR DISEASE

Although a heart attack may seem to strike suddenly, the lifestyles of many Americans may gradually be endangering their hearts. An unhealthy lifestyle can eventually result in cardiovascular disease. Potentially harmful behaviors frequently begin early in life. For example, many children develop tastes for "junk" foods that are high in fat and have little or no nutritional value. Sometimes, children are not encouraged to exercise regularly.

Several studies have shown that cardiovascular disease actually begins in the teenage years, when most smoking begins. Teenagers are more likely to begin smoking if their parents smoke. Smoking contributes to cardiovascular disease, as well as to other diseases.

Risk Factors for Heart Disease

Scientists have identified numerous factors that increase the chances of a person developing heart disease. These are known as *risk factors.* Some risk factors for heart disease cannot be changed, for example, having a history of heart disease in your family. When one risk factor, such as **high blood pressure** (hypertension), is combined with other risk factors, such as obesity or cigarette smoking, the risk of heart attack or stroke is greatly increased.

Controlling risk factors

Controlling your risk factors involves adjusting your lifestyle to minimize the chance of future cardiovascular disease. Major risk factors you can change or modify include cigarette smoking, high blood pressure, lack of exercise, and high blood cholesterol levels.

Compared to nonsmokers, cigarette smokers are more than twice as likely to have a heart attack and 2 to 4 times as likely to suffer cardiac arrest. The earlier a person starts smoking or using other tobacco products, the greater the risk to his or her future health. Giving up smoking will rapidly reduce the risk of heart disease.

HEART HEALTHY IQ

The following statements represent a heart-healthy lifestyle that can reduce your chances of cardiovascular disease. Check each statement that reflects your lifestyle.

☐ I do not smoke and I try to avoid inhaling the smoke of others.

☐ I eat a balanced diet that limits my intake of saturated fat and cholesterol.

☐ I participate in continuous, vigorous physical activity for 20 to 30 minutes or more at least three times a week.

☐ I have my blood pressure checked regularly.

☐ I maintain an appropriate weight.

☐ I know my family history for heart disease.

If you only checked one or two statements, you should consider making changes in your lifestyle now.

After 10 to 15 years of not smoking, the risk becomes the same as if the person never smoked. If you do not smoke, do not start. If you do smoke, quit.

Uncontrolled high blood pressure can damage blood vessels in the heart and other organs. You can often control high blood pressure by losing excess weight and changing your diet. When these measures are not enough, medications can be prescribed. It is important to have regular checkups to guard against high blood pressure and its harmful effects.

Diets high in **saturated fats** and cholesterol increase the risk of heart disease. These diets raise the level of cholesterol in the blood and increase the chances that cholesterol and other fatty materials will be deposited on blood vessel walls and result in atherosclerosis.

Some cholesterol in the body is necessary. The amount of cholesterol in the blood is determined by how much your body produces and by the foods you eat. Foods high in cholesterol include egg yolks and organ meats, such as liver and kidneys.

An even greater contributor to an unhealthy blood cholesterol level is saturated fat. Saturated fats raise the blood cholesterol level by interfering with the body's ability to remove cholesterol from the blood. Saturated fats are found in beef, lamb, veal, pork, ham, coconut oil, palm oil, whole milk, and whole milk products, such as cheese, yogurt, and butter.

Rather than completely eliminating saturated fats and cholesterol from your diet, limit your intake. This is easier than you think. Moderation is the key. Make changes whenever you can by substituting low fat milk or skim milk for whole milk, substituting tub margarine for butter, trimming visible fat from meats, and broiling or baking rather than frying. Read labels carefully. A "cholesterol free" product may be high in unwanted saturated fat. For further information on a healthy diet, see Chapter 23.

Two additional ways to help prevent heart disease are to control your weight and to exercise regularly. In general, overweight people have a shorter life expectancy. Obese middle-aged men have nearly 3 times the risk of a fatal heart attack as normal-weight middle-aged men.

Regular exercise has many benefits, including increased muscle tone and weight control. Exercise may also help you survive a heart attack because the increased circulation of blood through the heart develops additional channels for blood flow. If the blood vessels that supply the heart are blocked in a heart attack, these additional channels can supply heart tissue with oxygen-rich blood.

Benefits of Managing Risk Factors

Managing your risk factors for cardiovascular disease really works. During the past 20 years, deaths from cardiovascular disease have decreased by 33 percent in the United States. As a result, as many as 250,000 lives may have been saved each year. Also, deaths from stroke have declined 50 percent.

Why did deaths from these causes decline? Probably, they declined as a result of improved detection and treatment, as well as significant lifestyle changes. People are becoming more aware of their risk factors for heart disease and are taking action to control them. If you take such action, you can improve your chances of living a long and healthy life.

SUMMARY

Recognizing signs and symptoms that may indicate a heart attack is important. If you think someone is suffering a heart attack or if you are unsure, call EMS personnel without delay. Then provide care by helping the victim rest in the most comfortable position until help arrives.

Cardiac arrest occurs when heartbeat and breathing stop. A person who suffers cardiac arrest is dying, since no oxygen is reaching body cells. Irreversible brain damage will occur from lack of oxygen. When brain cells die, it is called biological death.

Prompt action can help prevent biological death and increase the cardiac arrest victim's chances for survival. By calling EMS quickly, you activate a system that brings advanced cardiac life support (ACLS), including special medications and equipment, to the victim. By starting CPR immediately, you can help keep the brain supplied with oxygen until EMS personnel arrive.

If the victim is not breathing and does not have signs of circulation, start CPR using these simple guidelines:

1. Find the correct hand or finger position.
2. Give compressions. (Compress down and up smoothly.)
3. Give 2 rescue breaths (adult), 1 rescue breath (child or infant).
4. Repeat cycles of compressions and breaths.
5. Check for the return of signs of circulation after about a minute.
6. If there are no signs of circulation, continue CPR, starting with compressions.
7. Check for signs of circulation every few minutes.
8. If signs of circulation return, stop CPR and check to see if the person has started to breathe.
9. If the victim is still not breathing, begin rescue breathing.

Once you start CPR, do not stop unnecessarily. Continue CPR until the victim's heart starts beating, you are relieved by another trained person, the scene becomes unsafe, or EMS personnel arrive and take over.

Answers to Application Questions

1. Yes. The exertion of mowing grass in the heat can add an extra burden on the body, increasing its demand for oxygen. The heart works harder to keep up with the body's demand for oxygen, increasing its own oxygen needs. If the arteries are narrowed as a result of atherosclerosis, the delivery of oxygen-rich blood to the heart is severely restricted or completely cut off, causing the heart to beat irregularly or stop beating.

2. Resting lessens the oxygen needs of the heart, allowing it to recover from the strain placed on it.

3. Yes. If Mr. Getz suffered a heart attack, he may go into cardiac arrest. A heart attack becomes cardiac arrest when so much of the heart muscle is destroyed that the heart is unable to contract regularly and subsequently stops beating. There is no way to predict the extent of the damage sustained by the heart during a heart attack or to predict when a heart attack might become cardiac arrest. Therefore, it is very important to recognize and acknowledge signs and symptoms of a heart attack and to seek professional help quickly.

4. If Mr. Getz is suffering a cardiac arrest, he needs defibrillation as quickly as possible. Someone must call EMS personnel immediately and CPR must be started immediately.

5. CPR—the combination of chest compressions and rescue breathing—sustains the viability of vital organs such as the brain for a relatively short time. The possibility that CPR alone will result in a spontaneous return to life is very low. Usually, prompt CPR, early defibrillation, and other advanced cardiac life support measures in combination are needed to restore life.

STUDY QUESTIONS

1. Match each term with the correct definition.
   a. Cardiac arrest
   b. Cardiopulmonary resuscitation (CPR)
   c. Cholesterol
   d. Coronary arteries
   e. Heart
   f. Heart attack
   g. Cardiovascular disease
   h. Risk factors
   i. Angina pectoris

   _____ A muscular organ that circulates blood throughout the body.

   _____ A fatty substance that builds up on the inner walls of arteries.

   _____ The leading cause of death for adults over 44 years of age in the United States.

   _____ Temporary chest pain caused by a lack of oxygen to the heart.

   _____ Blood vessels that supply the heart with oxygen-rich blood.

   _____ A combination of chest compressions and rescue breaths.

   _____ Conditions or behaviors that increase the chance of developing disease.

   _____ Condition that results when the heart stops beating or beats too ineffectively to generate circulation.

   _____ A sudden illness involving the death of heart muscle tissue caused by insufficient oxygen-rich blood reaching the cells.

2. Name the primary sign of cardiac arrest.

3. List the situations in which a rescuer may stop CPR.

4. Describe the conditions that most often cause cardiac arrest in children and infants.

5. List four controllable risk factors for heart disease.

In questions 6 through 13, circle the letter of the correct answer.

6. Which is the most prominent indicator of a heart attack?
   a. Profuse sweating
   b. Pale skin
   c. Persistent chest pain
   d. Difficulty breathing

7. Which statement best describes the chest pain associated with heart attack?
   a. An uncomfortable pressure
   b. Persistent pain that may spread to the shoulder, arm, neck, or jaw
   c. Usually relieved by resting
   d. a and b

8. Which may happen as a result of a heart attack?
   a. The heart functions inadequately.
   b. Some heart muscle tissue may die from lack of oxygen.
   c. The heart may stop.
   d. All of the above.

9. Which should you do first to care effectively for a person having a heart attack?
   a. Position the victim for CPR.
   b. Call EMS personnel immediately.
   c. Begin rescue breathing.
   d. Call the person's physician.

10. How can you know if a person's heart is beating?
    a. The person has a pulse and other signs of circulation.
    b. The person is breathing.
    c. The person is conscious.
    d. Any or all of the above.

11. When is CPR needed?
    a. When the victim is not breathing
    b. When the victim has no carotid pulse or other signs of circulation
    c. For every heart attack victim
    d. When the heart attack victim loses consciousness

12. Which is the purpose of CPR?
    a. To keep a victim's airway open
    b. To identify any immediate threats to life
    c. To supply the vital organs with blood containing oxygen
    d. All of the above

13. CPR artificially takes over the functions of which two body systems?
    a. Nervous and respiratory systems
    b. Respiratory and circulatory systems
    c. Circulatory and nervous systems
    d. Circulatory and musculoskeletal systems

Use the following scenario to answer questions 14 through 16:

It is Saturday afternoon; you are at home with your parents. You and your mother start to watch a tennis match on television. At the commercial break, your mother mumbles something about indigestion and heads to the medicine cabinet to get an antacid. Twenty minutes later, you notice that your mom does not respond to a great play made by her favorite player. You ask what is wrong, and she complains that the antacid has not worked. She states that her chest and shoulder hurt. She is perspiring heavily. You notice that she is breathing fast and she looks ill.

14. List the signs and symptoms of a heart attack that you find in the scenario.

15. While waiting for EMS personnel to arrive, your mother loses consciousness. You discover that she is not breathing. You give 2 rescue breaths and check for signs of circulation. She has no signs of circulation. Number in order the following actions you would now take.

    _____ Give 15 compressions.

    _____ Give 2 rescue breaths.

    _____ Locate the compression position.

    _____ Repeat the cycle of 15 compressions and 2 breaths.

    _____ Recheck for signs of circulation after 1 minute.

16. After 1 minute of CPR, you recheck to see if your mother has signs of circulation. She does not. What should you do next?
    a. Give abdominal thrusts.
    b. Keep the airway open until EMS personnel arrive.
    c. Check for breathing, and begin rescue breathing if needed.
    d. Continue CPR.

Answers are listed in Appendix A.

SKILL SHEETS

CHECK - CALL - CARE

If, when you check, the person is not breathing and has no signs of circulation . . .

Find hand position

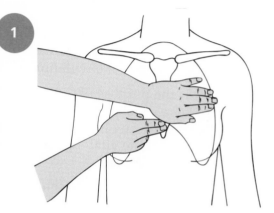

- Locate notch at lower end of sternum.
- Place heel of other hand on sternum next to fingers.
- Remove hand from notch and put it on top of other hand.
- Keep fingers off chest.

Give 15 compressions

- Position shoulders over hands.
- Compress chest 1½ to 2 inches.
- Do 15 compressions in about 10 seconds.
- Compress down and up smoothly, keeping hand contact with chest at all times.

Give 2 rescue breaths

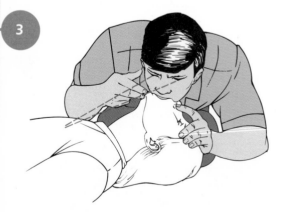

- Open airway with head-tilt/chin-lift.
- Pinch nose shut and seal your lips tightly around person's mouth.
- Give 2 rescue breaths, each lasting about 2 seconds.
- Watch chest clearly rise to be sure that your breaths go in.

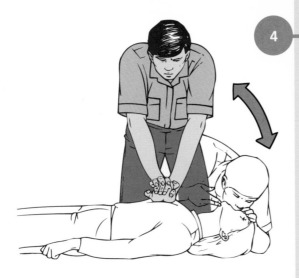

4

Repeat compression/breathing cycles

- Do 3 more sets of 15 compressions and 2 breaths.

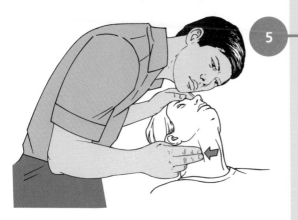

5

Recheck pulse and breathing

- After 1 minute, check for signs of circulation for no more than 10 seconds.
- Look, listen, and feel for breathing.

If person has signs of circulation and is breathing . . .

- *Keep airway open.*
- *Monitor breathing.*
- *Wait for EMS personnel to arrive.*

If person has signs of circulation but is still not breathing . . .

- *Do rescue breathing.*
- *Recheck signs of circulation about every minute.*
- *Wait for EMS personnel to arrive.*

If person does not have signs of circulation and is not breathing . . .

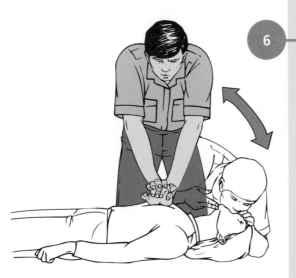

6

Continue compression/breathing cycles

- Locate correct hand position.
- Continue cycles of 15 compressions and 2 rescue breaths.
- Recheck signs of circulation every few minutes.
- Wait for EMS personnel to arrive.

SKILL SHEETS

CHECK-CALL-CARE

CPR For A Child

If, when you check, the person is not breathing and has no signs of circulation . . .

Find hand position

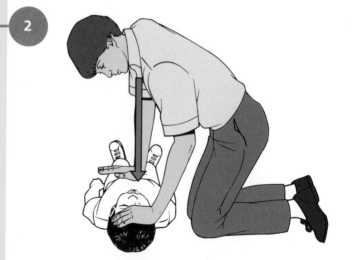

- Maintain head-tilt with hand on forehead.
- Locate notch at lower end of sternum with other hand.
- Place heel of same hand on sternum immediately above where fingers were placed.

Give 5 compressions

- Position shoulders over hands.
- Compress sternum 1 to 1½ inches.
- Do 5 compressions in about 3 seconds.
- Compress down and up smoothly, keeping hand contact with chest at all times.
- Maintain head-tilt with your hand on forehead.

Give 1 rescue breath

- Open airway with head-tilt/chin-lift.
- Pinch nose shut and seal lips tightly around child's mouth.
- Give 1 rescue breath lasting about 1½ seconds.
- Watch chest clearly rise to be sure that breath goes in.

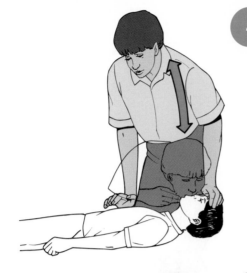

4

Repeat compression/breathing cycles

- Repeat cycles of 5 compressions and 1 breath for about 1 minute.

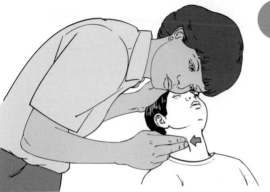

5

Recheck pulse and breathing

- After about 1 minute, check for signs of circulation for no more than 10 seconds.
- Look, listen, and feel for breathing.

If child has signs of circulation and is breathing . . .

- *Keep airway open.*
- *Monitor breathing.*
- *Wait for EMS personnel to arrive.*

If child has signs of circulation but is still not breathing . . .

- *Do rescue breathing.*
- *Recheck for signs of circulation about every minute.*
- *Wait for EMS personnel to arrive.*

If child does not have signs of circulation and is not breathing . . .

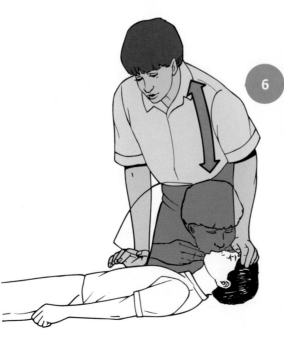

6

Continue cycles of 5 compressions and 1 rescue breath

- Locate correct hand position.
- Continue cycles of 5 compressions and 1 rescue breath.
- Recheck signs of circulation every few minutes.
- Wait for EMS personnel to arrive.

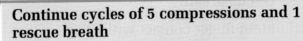

SKILL SHEETS

CHECK - CALL - CARE

If, when you check, the infant is not breathing and has no signs of circulation . . .

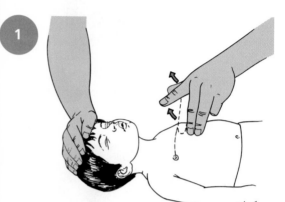

Find finger position

- Maintain head-tilt with hand on forehead.
- Place pads of fingers below imaginary line running across chest connecting nipples.
- Pick up your index finger.
- Adjust finger position if necessary.

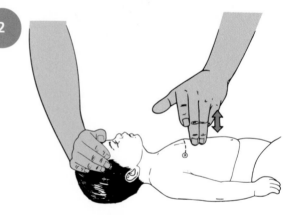

Give 5 compressions

- Compress sternum ½ to 1 inch using the pads of 2 fingers.
- Do 5 compressions in 3 seconds.
- Compress down and up smoothly, keeping finger in contact with chest at all times.
- Maintain head-tilt with hand on forehead.

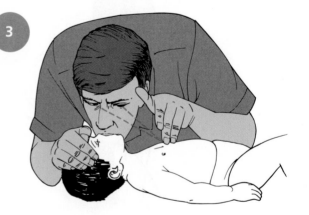

Give 1 rescue breath

- Maintain finger contact with chest.
- Seal lips tightly around infant's mouth and nose.
- Give 1 rescue breath lasting about 1-1½ seconds.
- Watch chest clearly rise to be sure that breath goes in.

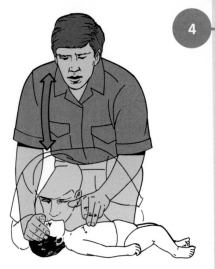

4

Repeat compression/breathing cycles

- Repeat cycles of 5 compressions and 1 breath for about 1 minute.

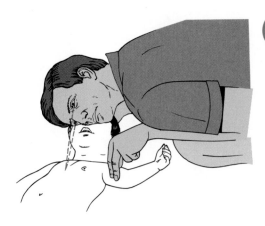

5

Recheck pulse and breathing

- After about 1 minute, check for signs of circulation for no more than 10 seconds.
- Look, listen, and feel for breathing.

If infant has signs of circulation and is breathing . . .

- *Keep airway open.*
- *Monitor breathing.*
- *Wait for EMS personnel to arrive.*

If infant has signs of circulation but is still not breathing . . .

- *Do rescue breathing.*
- *Recheck for signs of circulation about every minute.*
- *Wait for EMS personnel to arrive.*

If infant does not have signs of circulation and is not breathing . . .

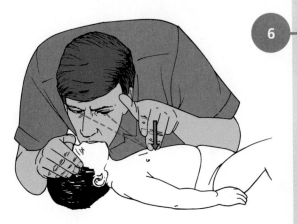

6

Continue compression/breathing cycles

- Locate correct hand position.
- Continue cycles of 5 compressions and 1 rescue breath.
- Recheck for signs of circulation every few minutes.
- Wait for EMS personnel to arrive.

CHAPTER 7

Bleeding

WHAT YOU SHOULD LEARN

After reading this chapter, you should be able to—

1. Explain why severe bleeding must be controlled immediately.

2. List three major functions of blood.

3. Identify two signs of life-threatening external bleeding.

4. Describe care for external bleeding.

5. Describe how to minimize the risk of disease transmission when providing care in a situation that involves visible blood.

6. Identify 12 signs and symptoms of internal bleeding.

7. Describe the care for internal bleeding.

8. Define the key terms for this chapter.

After reading this chapter and completing the class activities, you should be able to demonstrate—

1. How to control external bleeding.

2. How to make appropriate decisions in an emergency situation in which a person is bleeding externally.

3. How to make appropriate decisions in an emergency situation in which a person is bleeding internally.

Janelle and her friends are on a camping trip. Janelle caught half a dozen trout in the lake and begins to clean them for supper. Suddenly, the knife slips and cuts her hand deeply. Blood flows steadily, and Janelle cries out in pain. The cut continues to bleed and Janelle becomes upset. Breathing rapidly, she asks a friend to help her.

Introduction

Bleeding is the escape of blood from arteries, veins, or capillaries. A large amount of bleeding occurring in a short amount of time is called a **hemorrhage.** Bleeding is either external or internal. **External bleeding,** bleeding you can see coming from a wound, is usually obvious because it is visible. **Internal bleeding,** bleeding inside the body, is often difficult to recognize (Fig. 7-1). Uncontrolled bleeding, whether internal or external, is a life-threatening emergency. As you learned in the previous chapters, severe bleeding can result in death. You check for severe bleeding while checking for life-threatening emergencies. You may not identify internal bleeding, however, until you check for nonlife-threatening injuries. In this chapter, you will learn how to recognize and provide care for both internal and external bleeding.

BLOOD AND BLOOD VESSELS

Blood and blood vessels are the means by which oxygen and nutrients reach the vital organs of the body and waste products are carried away for disposal.

Blood Components

Blood consists of liquid and solid components and comprises approximately 7 percent of the body's total weight. The average adult has a blood volume of between 10 and 12 pints (5 and 6 liters). The liquid part of the blood is called **plasma.** The solid components are the red and white blood cells and cell fragments called **platelets.**

Plasma is a fluid that makes up about half of the total **blood volume.** Composed mostly of water, plasma maintains the blood volume needed for normal function of the circulatory system. Plasma also contains nutrients essential for energy production, growth, and cell maintenance, carries waste products for elimination, and transports the other blood components.

White blood cells are a key disease-fighting part of the immune system. They defend the body against invading microorganisms, or

Key Terms

Arteries: Large blood vessels that carry blood from the heart to all parts of the body.

Blood volume: The total amount of blood circulating within the body.

Capillaries (KAP i ler ez): Microscopic blood vessels linking arteries and veins that transfer oxygen and other nutrients from the blood to all body cells and remove waste products.

Clotting: The process by which blood thickens at a wound site to seal a hole or tear in a blood vessel and stop bleeding.

Direct pressure: The pressure applied on a wound to control bleeding, for example, by one's gloved hand.

External bleeding: Bleeding that can be seen coming from a wound.

Hemorrhage (HEM or ij): A loss of a large amount of blood in a short period of time.

Internal bleeding: Bleeding inside the body.

Pressure bandage: A bandage applied snugly to create pressure on a wound to aid in controlling bleeding.

Pressure points: Sites on the body where pressure can be applied to major arteries to slow the flow of blood to a body part.

Veins: Blood vessels that carry blood from all parts of the body to the heart.

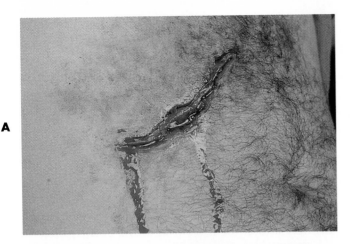

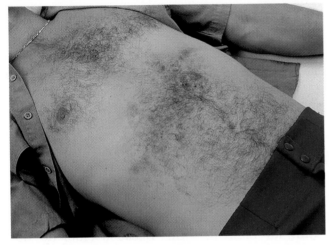

Figure 7-1   **A,** External bleeding is more easily recognized than **B,** internal bleeding.

pathogens. They also aid in producing antibodies that help the body resist infection.

Red blood cells account for most of the solid components of the blood. They are produced in the marrow in the hollow center of large bones, such as the large bone of the arm (humerus) and the thigh (femur). Red blood cells number nearly 260 million in each drop of blood. The red blood cells transport oxygen from the lungs to the body cells and carbon dioxide from the cells to the lungs. Red blood cells outnumber white blood cells about 1000 to 1.

Platelets are disk-shaped structures in the blood that are made up of cell fragments. Platelets are an essential part of the blood's *clotting* mechanism because of their tendency to bind together. Platelets help stop bleeding by forming blood clots at wound sites. Until blood clots form, bleeding must be controlled artificially.

Blood Functions

The blood has three major functions:

- Transporting oxygen, nutrients, and wastes
- Protecting against disease by producing antibodies and defending against pathogens
- Maintaining constant body temperature by circulating throughout the body

Blood Vessels

Blood is channeled through blood vessels. The three major types of blood vessels are arteries, capillaries, and veins (Fig. 7-2). **Arteries** carry blood away from the heart. Arteries vary in size. The smallest ones carry blood to the capillaries. **Capillaries** are microscopic blood vessels linking arteries and veins. They transfer oxygen and other nutrients from the blood into the cells. Capillaries pick up waste products, such as carbon dioxide, from the cells and move them into the veins. The **veins** carry blood back to the heart. The veins also carry waste products from the cells to the kidneys, intestines, and lungs, where waste products are eliminated.

Because the blood in the arteries is closer to the pumping action of the heart, blood in the arteries travels faster and under greater pressure than blood in the capillaries or veins. Blood flow in the arteries pulses with the heartbeat; blood in the veins flows more slowly and evenly.

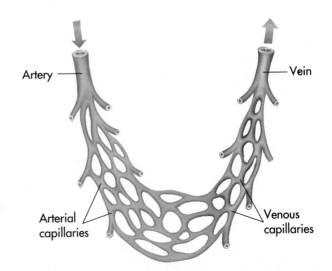

Figure 7-2   Blood flows through the three major types of blood vessels: arteries, capillaries, and veins.

MIND AT WORK

1. From the description, would you suspect that Janelle's bleeding is a result of an injury to an artery, a vein, or capillaries? Why?

WHEN BLEEDING OCCURS

When bleeding occurs, a complex chain of events is triggered in the body. The brain, heart, and lungs immediately attempt to compensate for blood loss to maintain the flow of oxygen-rich blood to the body tissues, particularly to the vital organs. The brain, recognizing a blood shortage, signals the heart to circulate more blood and constrict blood vessels in extremities. The brain signals the lungs to work harder, providing more oxygen.

Other important reactions to bleeding occur on a microscopic level. Platelets collect at the wound site in an effort to stop blood loss through clotting. White blood cells prevent infection by attacking microorganisms that enter through breaks in the skin. Over time, the body manufactures extra red blood cells to help transport more oxygen to the cells.

Blood volume is also affected by bleeding. Normally, excess fluid is absorbed from the bloodstream by the kidneys, lungs, intestines, and skin. However, when bleeding occurs, this excess fluid is reabsorbed into the bloodstream as plasma. This reabsorption helps to maintain the critical balance of fluids needed by the body to keep blood volume constant. Bleeding severe enough to critically reduce the blood volume is life threatening because tissues will die from lack of oxygen. Life-threatening bleeding can be either internal or external.

External Bleeding

External bleeding occurs when a blood vessel is opened externally, such as through a tear in the skin. You can see this type of bleeding. Most external bleeding you will encounter will be minor. The blood will not flow heavily or gush from the wound. You will be able to control it easily with pressure. Minor bleeding, such as a scraped knee, usually stops by itself within 10 minutes when the blood clots. Sometimes, however, the damaged blood vessel is too large or the blood is under too much pressure for effective clotting to occur. In these cases, bleeding can be life threatening, and you will need to recognize and control it promptly when you initially check for life-threatening conditions.

Signs and symptoms of life-threatening external bleeding

The signs of life-threatening external bleeding include—

- Blood spurting from a wound.
- Bleeding that fails to stop after all measures have been taken to control bleeding.

Each type of blood vessel bleeds differently. Arterial bleeding (bleeding from the artery) is often rapid and severe. It is life threatening. Because arterial blood is under more pressure, it usually spurts from the wound, making it difficult for clots to form. Because clots do not form as rapidly, arterial bleeding is harder to control. Its high concentration of oxygen gives arterial blood a bright red color.

Venous bleeding (bleeding from the veins) is generally easier to control than arterial bleeding. Veins are damaged more often because they are closer to the skin's surface. Venous blood is under less pressure than arterial blood and flows steadily from the wound without spurting. Only damage to veins deep in the body, such as those in the trunk or thigh, produces severe bleeding that is difficult to control. Because it is oxygen poor, venous blood is dark red or maroon.

Capillary bleeding, the most common type of bleeding, is usually slow because the vessels are small and the blood is under low pressure. It is often described as "oozing" from the wound. Clotting occurs easily with capillary bleeding. The blood is usually less red than arterial blood.

Care for external bleeding

External bleeding is usually easy to control. Generally, the pressure created by placing a sterile dressing and then a gloved hand, or even

MIND AT WORK

2. How could Janelle's situation become life threatening?

a gloved hand by itself, on a wound can control bleeding. This technique is called applying *di-rect pressure.* Pressure placed on a wound restricts the blood flow through the wound and allows normal clotting to occur. Elevating the injured area also slows the flow of blood and encourages clotting. Pressure on a wound can be maintained by applying a bandage snugly to the injured area. A bandage applied snugly to control bleeding is called a *pressure bandage.*

In some cases of severe bleeding, direct pressure on the wound and elevation of the wounded area may not control bleeding. In these cases, you will have to resort to other measures. In a further effort to slow bleeding, you can compress the artery supplying the area against an underlying bone at specific sites on the body. These sites are called *pressure points* (Fig. 7-3, *A*). The main pressure points used to control bleeding in the arms and legs are found at specific areas of the brachial and femoral arteries (Fig. 7-3, *B*). Pressure points in other areas of the body also control blood flow, but you are unlikely to need to use them. A tourniquet, a tight band placed around an arm or leg to help constrict blood flow to a wound, is no longer generally recommended for use by laypersons because it too often does more harm

than good. A tourniquet can cut off the blood supply to the limb below the tourniquet and can damage skin, nerves, and muscle by crushing the underlying tissue.

To give first aid for severe external bleeding, follow these general steps:

1. Place direct pressure on the wound with a sterile gauze pad or any clean cloth, such as a washcloth, towel, or handkerchief. Press hard. Using a pad or cloth will help keep the wound free from germs and aid clotting. Place your gloved hand over the pad and apply firm pressure (Fig. 7-4, *A*). If you do not have a pad or cloth available or an appropriate barrier, have the injured person apply pressure with his or her hand.
2. Elevate the injured area above the level of the heart if you do not suspect a broken bone (Fig. 7-4, *B*).
3. Apply a pressure bandage to hold the gauze pads or cloth in place (Fig. 7-4, *C*).
4. If blood soaks through the bandage, add more pads and bandages to help absorb the blood. Do not remove any blood-soaked pads because doing so can interfere with the blood-clotting process.
5. If bleeding continues, apply pressure at a

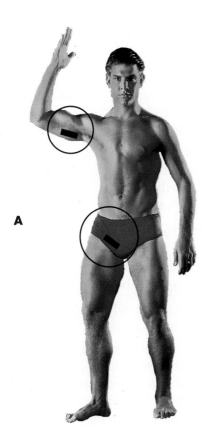

A

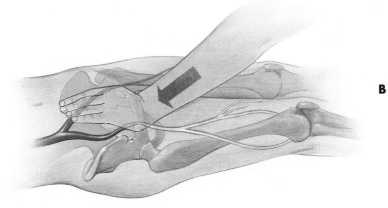

B

Figure 7-3 **A,** Pressure points are specific sites on the body where arteries lie close to the bone and the body's surface. **B,** Blood flow to an area can be controlled by applying pressure at one of these sites, compressing the artery against the bone.

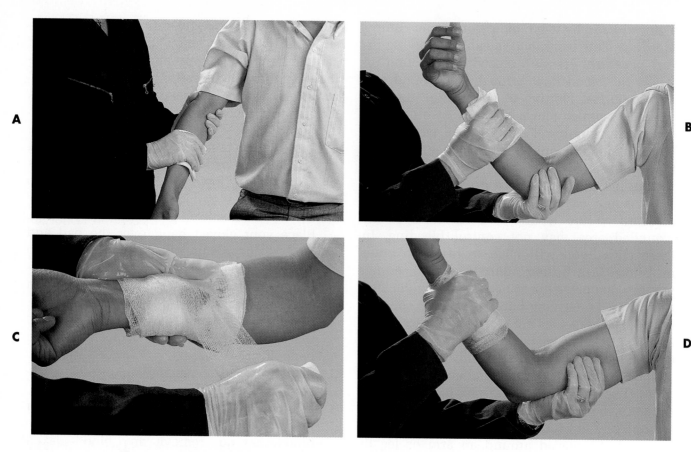

Figure 7-4   **A,** Apply direct pressure to the wound using a sterile gauze pad or clean cloth. **B,** Elevate the injured area above the level of the heart if there is no fracture. **C,** Apply a pressure bandage. The victim may be able to help you. **D,** If necessary, slow the flow of blood by applying pressure to the artery with your hand at the appropriate pressure point.

pressure point to slow the flow of blood (Fig. 7-4, *D*). Make sure that EMS personnel are called.

6. Continue to monitor airway and breathing. Observe the victim closely for signs and symptoms that may indicate that the victim's condition is worsening, such as breathing faster or slower, changes in skin color, and restlessness. If bleeding is not severe, provide additional care as needed.

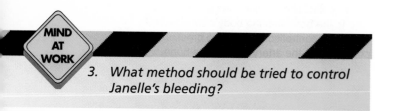

MIND AT WORK

3. *What method should be tried to control Janelle's bleeding?*

Preventing disease transmission

When a break or tear in the victim's skin causes bleeding, a potential risk for disease transmission exists for both the rescuer and the victim. Pathogens from the rescuer's skin can enter the victim's body, and any pathogens in the victim's blood can be transmitted to the rescuer. To reduce this risk, you should—

- Place an effective barrier between you and the victim's blood when you give first aid.
- If possible, wash your hands thoroughly with soap and water immediately after providing care, even if you wore gloves or used another barrier (Fig. 7-5). Use a utility or restroom sink, not one in a food-preparation area.
- Avoid eating, drinking, and touching your mouth, nose, or eyes while providing care or before washing your hands.

The most effective barrier in bleeding situations is latex or other rubber or plastic disposable gloves. Even a piece of plastic wrap, when carefully applied, may serve as an effective barrier. In some cases, a clean cloth or clothing

Figure 7-5 Thorough handwashing after giving care helps protect you against disease.

Figure 7-6 A clean, folded cloth folded several times may temporarily prevent you from touching blood.

folded several times may temporarily prevent you from touching blood (Fig. 7-6). When using folded cloth or clothing and an ungloved hand, watch closely for blood soaking through and add more cloth as necessary.

MIND AT WORK

4. *What barriers should Janelle's friend use to minimize the risk of disease transmission while providing care?*

Internal Bleeding

Internal bleeding is the escape of blood from arteries, veins, or capillaries into spaces in the body. Capillary bleeding, indicated by mild bruising, occurs beneath the skin and is not serious. However, deeper bleeding involves arteries and veins and can result in severe blood loss.

Severe internal bleeding usually occurs from injuries caused by a violent blunt force, such as a car crash when the driver is thrown against the steering wheel or when someone falls from a height. Internal bleeding may also occur when an object, such as a knife or bullet, penetrates the skin and damages internal structures. In any serious injury, suspect internal bleeding. For example, if you find a motorcycle rider thrown from a bike, you may not see any serious external bleeding, but you should consider that the violent forces involved indicate the likelihood of internal injuries. Internal bleeding could also occur from a fractured bone that ruptures an organ or blood vessels or tears surrounding tissues. The body's inability to adjust to severe internal bleeding will eventually produce signs and symptoms that indicate shock. Shock is discussed in more detail in Chapter 8.

Signs and symptoms of internal bleeding

Internal bleeding is more difficult to recognize than external bleeding because the signs and symptoms are less obvious and may take time to appear. These signs and symptoms include—

- Soft tissues, such as those in the abdomen, that are tender, swollen, or hard.
- Anxiety or restlessness.
- Rapid, weak pulse.
- Rapid breathing, shortness of breath.
- Skin that feels cool or moist or looks pale, ashen, or bluish.
- Discoloration of the skin (bruising) in the injured area.
- Nausea or vomiting, vomiting blood.
- Abdominal pain.

Blood: The Beat Goes On

The Ice Age—Prehistoric Man

3000 B.C.—The Fifth Dynasty

500 B.C.—Greek Civilization

Circa 200 A.D.—Late Roman Civilization

900–1400—The Middle Ages

1628—The Renaissance Period

1661

Primitive man draws a giant mammoth on a cave, with a red ochre marking resembling a heart in its chest.

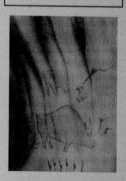

Ancient Greek physicians propound the theory of the humours, associating man's personality and health with four substances in the body—blood, black bile, yellow bile, and phlegm. An imbalance can cause diseases or emotional problems. A practice called bloodletting develops in which physicians open a patient's vein and let him or her bleed to fix an imbalance in the humours.

Dr. William Harvey cuts into live frogs and snakes to observe the heart. Through his studies, Harvey determines that blood circulates through the heart, the lungs, and the rest of the body.

Bloodletting flourishes during the Middle Ages. Astrology's influence grows, leading doctors to use astrological charts to determine when and where to open a vein. Medical schools sprout up in England, France, Belgium, and Italy.

Egyptians believe that blood is created in the stomach and that vessels running from the heart are filled with blood, air, feces, and tears.

The invention of the microscope allows Italian-born physician Malpighi to see the tiny capillaries that link veins and arteries.

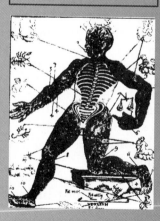

Galen, doctor of Roman Emperor Marcus Aurelius, theorizes that blood is continuously formed in the liver and then moves in two systems—one that combines with the air and a second that forms from food to nourish the body.

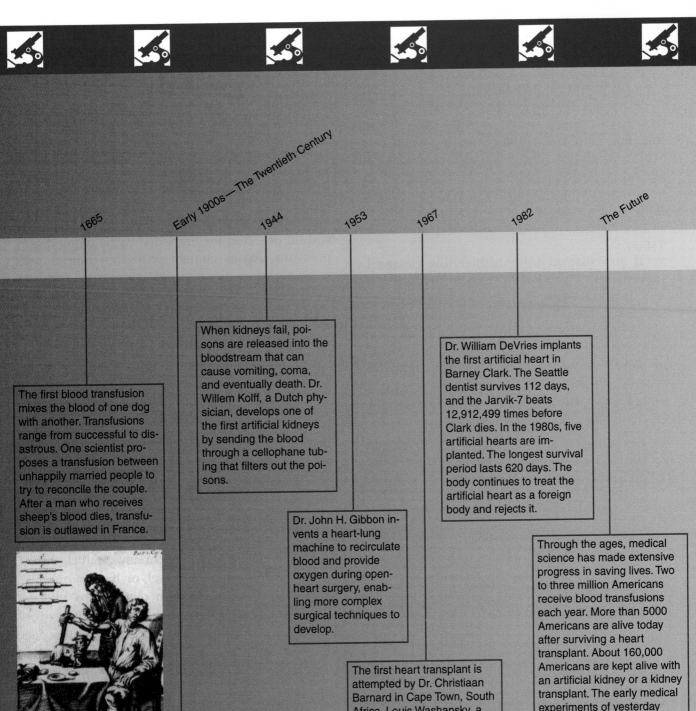

1665

Early 1900s—The Twentieth Century

1944

1953

1967

1982

The Future

The first blood transfusion mixes the blood of one dog with another. Transfusions range from successful to disastrous. One scientist proposes a transfusion between unhappily married people to try to reconcile the couple. After a man who receives sheep's blood dies, transfusion is outlawed in France.

When kidneys fail, poisons are released into the bloodstream that can cause vomiting, coma, and eventually death. Dr. Willem Kolff, a Dutch physician, develops one of the first artificial kidneys by sending the blood through a cellophane tubing that filters out the poisons.

Dr. William DeVries implants the first artificial heart in Barney Clark. The Seattle dentist survives 112 days, and the Jarvik-7 beats 12,912,499 times before Clark dies. In the 1980s, five artificial hearts are implanted. The longest survival period lasts 620 days. The body continues to treat the artificial heart as a foreign body and rejects it.

Dr. John H. Gibbon invents a heart-lung machine to recirculate blood and provide oxygen during open-heart surgery, enabling more complex surgical techniques to develop.

Through the ages, medical science has made extensive progress in saving lives. Two to three million Americans receive blood transfusions each year. More than 5000 Americans are alive today after surviving a heart transplant. About 160,000 Americans are kept alive with an artificial kidney or a kidney transplant. The early medical experiments of yesterday have become commonplace lifesaving procedures today.

The first heart transplant is attempted by Dr. Christiaan Barnard in Cape Town, South Africa. Louis Washansky, a 54-year-old grocer, receives the heart of a woman hit by a speeding car. Washansky survives 18 days.

Dr. Karl Landsteiner discovers that all human blood is not compatible and names the blood types. His work helps make blood transfusions commonplace.

Julie Harris/The George Washington University

- Excessive thirst.
- Decreased level of consciousness.
- A severe headache.

Care for internal bleeding

First aid for controlling internal bleeding depends on the severity and site of the bleeding. For minor internal bleeding, such as a bruise on an arm, apply ice or a chemical cold pack to the injured area to help reduce pain and swelling. Always remember to place something, such as a gauze pad or a towel, between the source of cold and the skin to prevent skin damage.

If you suspect internal bleeding caused by serious injury, call EMS personnel immediately. You can do little to control serious internal bleeding effectively. Activating the EMS system is the best help that you can provide. EMS personnel must transport the victim rapidly to the hospital. Usually, the victim needs immediate surgery. While waiting for EMS personnel to arrive, follow the general care steps you would follow for any emergency. These are—

1. Do no harm.
2. Monitor breathing and consciousness.
3. Help the victim rest in the most comfortable position.
4. Keep the victim from getting chilled or overheated.
5. Reassure the victim.
6. Provide any specific care needed.

SUMMARY

One of the most important things you can do in any emergency is to recognize and control life-threatening bleeding. Check for severe bleeding while checking for life-threatening emergencies. External bleeding is easily recognized and should be cared for immediately by using direct pressure. Avoid contact with the injured person's blood by using protective barriers, such as latex gloves. Wash your hands with soap and water immediately or as soon as possible after giving care.

Although internal bleeding is less obvious, it can also be life threatening. Recognize when a serious injury has occurred, and suspect the presence of internal bleeding. You may not identify internal bleeding until you check for nonlife-threatening conditions. When you identify or suspect life-threatening bleeding, activate the EMS system immediately, and provide care until EMS personnel arrive and take over.

Answers to Application Questions

1. The bleeding from Janelle's wound is probably from a vein. The blood is flowing rather than spurting. Spurting would indicate that the bleeding is from an artery.

2. Severe bleeding can reduce the blood volume in the body and become life threatening. An adequate amount of blood is needed to maintain the flow of oxygen-rich blood to the body, particularly to the vital organs.

3. Janelle's friend should first try to control the bleeding by applying direct pressure and elevating the wound. She should then apply a pressure bandage and determine if the wound needs further medical attention.

4. Janelle's friend should use a barrier, such as latex gloves or plastic wrap. If these items are not available, the friend could use a clean folded cloth or have Janelle use her hand to control the bleeding. The friend should wash her hands after providing care.

STUDY QUESTIONS

1. Match each term with the correct definition.

   a. Hemorrhage
   b. Arteries
   c. Capillaries
   d. Veins
   e. Internal bleeding

   f. External bleeding
   g. Direct pressure
   h. Pressure points
   i. Pressure bandage

   ___C___ Microscopic blood vessels that transfer oxygen and other nutrients to cells and remove waste products.

   ___G___ Using your gloved hand to apply pressure on the wound to control bleeding.

   ___A___ The loss of a large amount of blood in a short period of time.

   ___F___ Bleeding that can be seen coming from a wound.

   ___E___ The escape of blood from an artery, vein, or capillary into spaces inside the body.

   ___H___ Sites on the body where pressure can be applied to major arteries to control bleeding.

   ___D___ Blood vessels that carry blood from all parts of the body to the heart.

   ___B___ Vessels that transport blood to the capillaries for distribution to cells.

   ___I___ A bandage applied snugly to maintain pressure on the wound to control bleeding.

2. List two functions of blood.

3. List two signs and symptoms of life-threatening external bleeding.

4. Describe how to control external bleeding.

5. List five signs and symptoms of internal bleeding.

6. Describe how to control minor internal bleeding.

7. Match each step of care for controlling external bleeding with its specific task.

    a. Apply direct pressure   c. Apply pressure bandage
    b. Elevate   d. Apply pressure at a pressure point

    __B__ Uses gravity to slow blood flow to the injured area to help control bleeding.

    __D__ Places pressure on the major artery supplying the injured area against the bone, which limits blood flow.

    __C__ Maintains pressure on the wound and helps prevent infection.

    __A__ Places pressure on the wound, using a gloved hand, to slow blood flow and aid clotting.

Use the following scenario to answer questions 8 and 9:

> The usual Saturday morning baseball game is in progress. A few spectators are standing around on the sidelines. As Milo Stern takes a swing at a curve ball, he loses his grip on the bat, which flies several feet, hitting Chris Lawson hard on the thigh. Chris drops to the ground, clutching his leg. The skin where the leg was struck immediately becomes red and begins to swell.

8. What type of bleeding do you suspect Chris has? Internal

9. What steps would you take to care for Chris?

    elevate, ice

In question 10, circle the letter of the correct answer.

10. A child has fallen down a long flight of stairs. He says his arm hurts, and his face is moist and very pale. What would you do first?

   a. Call EMS personnel immediately.
   b. Apply pressure at the closest pressure point.
   c. Place an ice pack on the affected arm.
   d. Wrap a pressure bandage around the affected arm.

11. List three things you can do to reduce the risk of disease transmission when controlling bleeding.

Answers are listed in Appendix A.

SKILL SHEETS

CHECK - CALL - CARE

If, when you check, the person is bleeding . . .

Apply direct pressure

- Place sterile dressing or clean cloth over wound.
- Press firmly against wound with your gloved hand.

Elevate the body part

- Raise wound above level of heart.

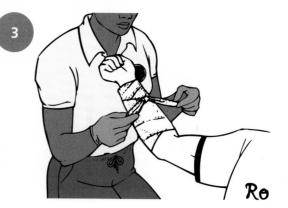

Apply a pressure bandage

- Using a roller bandage, cover dressing completely, using overlapping turns.
- Secure bandage.
- If blood soaks through bandage, place additional dressings and bandages over wound.

If bleeding stops . . .
• *Determine if further care is needed.*

If bleeding does not stop . . .
• *Send someone to call EMS personnel.*

Then . . .

4

Use a pressure point

• Maintain direct pressure and elevation.
• Locate brachial artery.
• Press brachial artery against underlying bone.

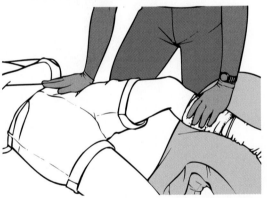

If bleeding is from leg, press with the heel of your hand where leg bends at hip.

5

Continue to take steps to minimize shock

• Maintain direct pressure, elevation, and pressure point.
• Position person on back.
• Monitor breathing and signs of circulation.
• Keep person from getting chilled or overheated.
• Apply additional dressings and/or bandages as necessary.

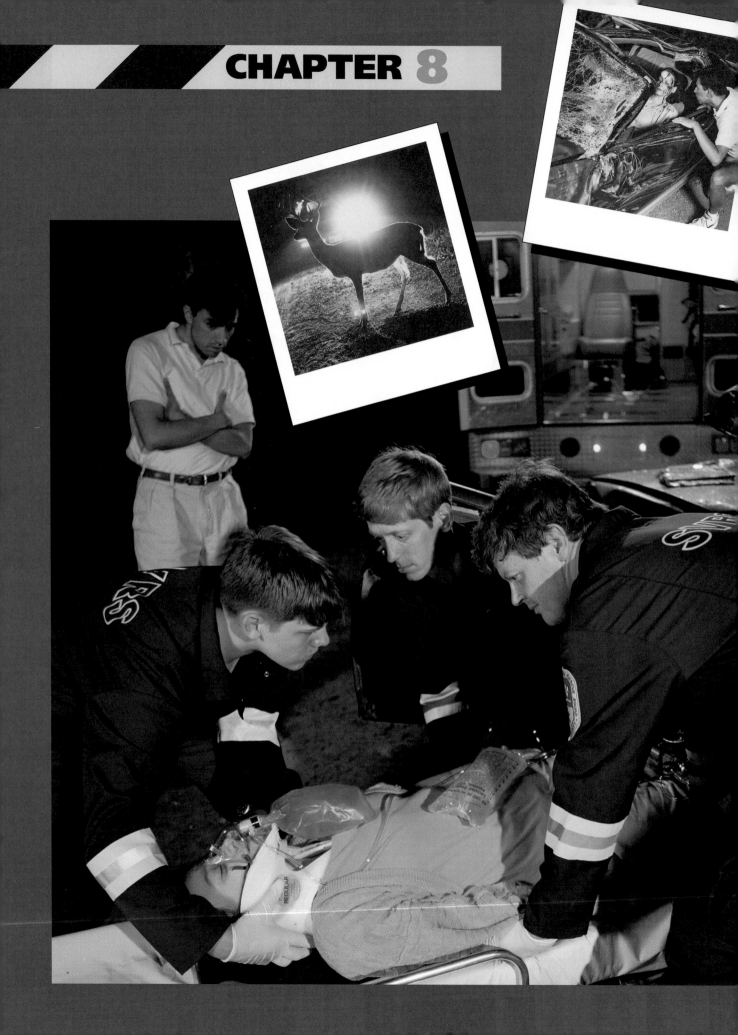

CHAPTER 8

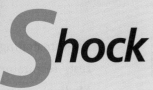hock

WHAT YOU SHOULD LEARN

After reading this chapter, you should be able to—

1. List two conditions that can result in shock.

2. List at least seven signs and symptoms of shock.

3. Explain what care can be given to minimize shock.

4. Define the key terms for this chapter.

10:55 P.M. *On an isolated road, a large deer leaps into the path of an on-coming car traveling 55 mph. The driver, a 21-year-old college student and track star, cannot avoid the collision. In the crash, both of her legs are crushed and are pinned in the wreckage.*

11:15 P.M. *Another car finally approaches. Seeing the crashed car, the driver stops and comes forward to help. He finds the woman conscious but restless and in obvious pain. He says he will go to call an ambulance at the nearest house about a mile down the road. He assures her he will return.*

11:25 P.M. *When the driver returns, he sees that the woman's condition has changed. She is now breathing faster, looks pale, and appears drowsy. He takes hold of her hand in an effort to comfort her and feels that her skin is cold and moist. Her pulse is fast but so weak he can hardly feel it.*

11:30 P.M. *The rescue squad arrives 10 minutes after receiving the phone call. The man explains that the woman became drowsy and is no longer conscious. Her breathing has become very irregular. The EMTs go to work immediately.*

11:40 P.M. *Finally, the rescuers free the victim's legs and remove her from the car. The man notices that she looks worse. He knows the hospital is still 10 minutes away.*

12:00 MIDNIGHT *Despite the best efforts of everyone involved, the woman is pronounced dead, slightly more than an hour after the crash. Her heart stopped beating en route to the hospital. Although the EMTs gave CPR and advanced life support measures, they were unable to save her. She was a victim of a progressively deteriorating condition called shock.*

Introduction

Emergencies fall into two general types: injuries and medical emergencies (Fig. 8-1). An *injury* is damage to the body caused by an external force, such as a blow, a fall, or a collision. Most injuries, such as cuts or minor bruises, are not emergencies. More violent forces, such as those that commonly occur in car crashes and other types of collisions, can damage internal organs, tissues, and bones, causing severe blood loss.

A *medical emergency,* on the other hand, is a sudden illness that results from problems that occur within the body. For instance, a heart attack, which is often caused by cardiovascular disease, is a medical emergency. Many medical problems can become emergencies. Those illnesses or injuries involving the circulatory, respiratory, or nervous systems are often life–threatening. Such problems can severely hamper the body's ability to circulate oxygen-rich blood to all parts of the body.

In preceding chapters, you learned that both medical emergencies and injuries can cause life-threatening conditions, such as cardiac arrest, respiratory arrest, and severe bleeding. Medical emergencies and injuries can also become life–threatening in another way—by leading to shock. When the body experiences injury or sudden illness, it responds in a number of ways. Survival depends on the body's ability to adapt to the physical stresses of illness or injury. When the body's measures to compensate fail, the victim can progress into a life-threatening condition called shock. Shock complicates the effects of injury or sudden illness. In this chapter, you will learn to recognize and give care to minimize shock.

SHOCK

Shock is a condition in which the circulatory system fails to circulate oxygen-rich blood to all parts of the body. When *vital organs,* such as the brain, heart, and lungs, do not receive oxygen-rich blood, they fail to function properly. Improperly functioning organs trigger a series of responses. These responses are the body's attempts to maintain adequate blood flow to the vital organs, preventing their failure.

When the body is healthy, three conditions are needed to maintain adequate blood flow:

- The heart must be working well.
- An adequate amount of oxygen-rich blood must be circulating in the body.
- The blood vessels must be intact and able to adjust blood flow.

When someone is injured or becomes suddenly ill, these normal body functions may be interrupted. In cases of minor injury or illness, this interruption is brief because the body is able to compensate quickly. With more severe injuries or illnesses, however, the body may be unable to adjust. When the body is unable to meet its demands for oxygen because blood fails to circulate adequately, shock occurs.

What Causes Shock?

You learned in Chapter 3 that the heart circulates blood by contracting and relaxing in a

Key Terms

Blood volume: The total amount of blood circulating within the body.

Injury: A condition that occurs when the body is subjected to an external force, such as a blow, a fall, or a collision.

Medical emergency: A sudden illness that results from problems that occur within the body.

Shock: The failure of the circulatory system to provide adequate oxygen-rich blood to all parts of the body.

Vital organs: Organs whose functions are essential to life, including the brain, heart, and lungs.

Figure 8-1 Emergencies result from both **A,** sudden illness and **B,** injury.

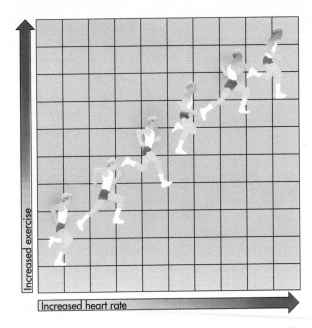

Figure 8-2 The heartbeat changes as necessary to adjust to the body's demands for oxygen.

consistent rhythmic pattern. The heart adjusts its speed and the force of its contractions to meet the body's changing demands for oxygen. For instance, when a person exercises, the heart beats faster and more forcefully to move more oxygen-rich blood to meet the working muscles' demand for more oxygen.

Similarly, when someone suffers a severe injury or sudden illness that affects the flow of blood, the heart beats faster and stronger at first to adjust to the increased demand for oxygen. Because the heart is beating faster, breathing must also speed up to meet the body's increased demand for oxygen (Fig. 8-2). You can detect these changes by feeling the pulse and listening to breathing when you check for non-life-threatening conditions.

For the heart to do its job properly, an adequate amount of blood must circulate within the body. As you learned in Chapter 7, this amount is referred to as *blood volume.* The body can compensate for some decrease in

blood volume. Consider what happens when you donate blood. You can lose 1 pint (about ½ liter) of blood over a 10- to 15-minute period without any significant stress to the body. Fluid is reabsorbed from the kidneys, lungs, and intestines to replace lost blood volume. In addition, the body immediately begins to manufacture the blood's solid components. However, with severe injuries involving greater or more rapid blood loss, the body may not be able to adjust adequately. Body cells do not receive enough oxygen, and shock occurs. Any significant fluid loss from the body, such as from severe bleeding or burns or even from diarrhea or vomiting, can precipitate shock.

Regardless of the cause, any significant decrease in body fluids affects the function of the heart. The heart will initially speed up to compensate for loss of body fluids and eventually will fail to beat rhythmically. The pulse may become irregular or be absent altogether.

The blood vessels act as pipelines, transporting oxygen and nutrients to all parts of the body and removing wastes. For the circulatory system to function properly, blood vessels must remain intact, preventing loss of blood volume. Normally, blood vessels decrease or increase the flow of blood to different areas of the body by constricting (decreasing their diameter) or dilating (increasing their diameter). This ability

*body could go into shock from being ill—dehydration

ensures that blood reaches the areas of the body that need it most, such as the vital organs. Injuries or illnesses, especially those that affect the brain and spinal cord, can cause blood vessels to lose this ability to change size. Blood vessels can also be affected if the nervous system is damaged by injury, infection, drugs, or poisons.

If the heart is damaged, it cannot circulate blood properly. If blood vessels are damaged, the body cannot adjust blood flow. Regardless of the cause, when body cells receive inadequate oxygen, the result is shock. Table 8-1 summarizes three common types of shock and their causes.

When shock occurs, the body attempts to prioritize its needs for blood by ensuring adequate flow to the vital organs, such as the heart, brain, lungs, and kidneys. The body reduces the amount of blood circulating to the less important tissues of the arms, legs, and skin. This reduction in blood circulation to the skin causes the skin of a person in shock to appear pale or ashen and feel cool. In later stages of shock, the skin, especially the lips and under the nails, may appear blue from a prolonged lack of oxygen. Increased sweating is also a natural reaction to stress caused by injury or illness, which makes the skin feel moist.

TABLE 8-1	
Common Types of Shock	
Type	**Cause**
Anaphylactic	Life-threatening allergic reaction to a substance, may cause airway to swell, affecting ability to breathe; can occur from insect stings or from foods and drugs
Cardiogenic	Failure of the heart to effectively circulate blood to all parts of the body; occurs with heart attack
Hypovolemic	Severe bleeding or loss of blood plasma; occurs with internal or external wounds or burns or with severe fluid loss as from vomiting and diarrhea

Signs and Symptoms of Shock

Although you may not always be able to determine the cause of shock, remember that shock is a life-threatening condition. You should learn to recognize the signs and symptoms of shock (Fig. 8-3).

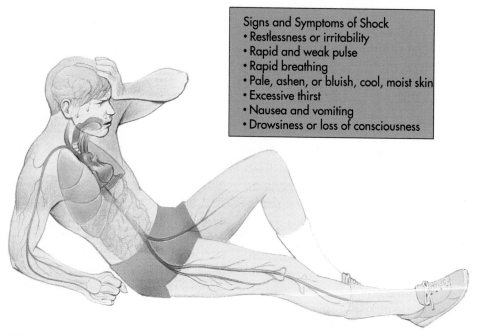

Signs and Symptoms of Shock
• Restlessness or irritability
• Rapid and weak pulse
• Rapid breathing
• Pale, ashen, or bluish, cool, moist skin
• Excessive thirst
• Nausea and vomiting
• Drowsiness or loss of consciousness

Figure 8-3 The signs and symptoms of shock may not be immediately obvious. Be alert for these signs and symptoms in cases of injury or sudden illness. Provide care at once to help reduce the effects of shock.

Shock victims usually show many of the same signs and symptoms. A common sign is restlessness or irritability. This behavior is often the first indicator that the body is experiencing a significant problem. Other clearly recognizable signs are pale or ashen, cool, moist skin; rapid breathing; and a rapid and weak pulse. If the victim does not show the telltale signs and symptoms of specific injury or illness, such as the persistent chest pain of heart attack, or obvious external bleeding, it can be difficult to know what is wrong. *Remember, you do not have to identify the specific nature of an illness or injury to provide care that may help save the victim's life.* If the signs and symptoms of shock are present, assume the victim has a potentially life-threatening injury or illness and proceed with giving care for shock.

Shock: The Domino Effect

- An injury causes severe bleeding.
- The heart attempts to compensate for the disruption of blood flow by beating faster. The victim first has a rapid pulse. More blood is lost. As blood volume drops, the pulse becomes weak or hard to find.
- The increased work load on the heart results in an increased oxygen demand. Therefore, breathing becomes faster.
- To maintain circulation of blood to the vital organs, blood vessels in the arms and legs and in the skin constrict. Therefore, the skin appears pale or ashen and feels cool. In response to the stress, the body perspires heavily and the skin feels moist.
- Since tissues of the arms and legs are now without oxygen, cells start to die. The brain now sends a signal to return blood to the arms and legs in an attempt to balance blood flow between these body parts and the vital organs.
- Vital organs are now not receiving adequate oxygen. The heart tries to compensate by beating even faster. More blood is lost and the victim's condition worsens.

- Without oxygen, the vital organs fail to function properly. As the brain is affected, the person becomes restless, drowsy, and eventually loses consciousness. As the heart is affected, it beats irregularly, resulting in an irregular pulse. The rhythm then becomes chaotic and the heart fails to circulate blood. There are no longer signs of circulation. When the heart stops, breathing stops.
- The body's continuous attempt to compensate for severe blood loss eventually results in death.

Signs and Symptoms of Shock

Restlessness or irritability

Rapid and weak pulse

Rapid breathing

Pale, or ashen, cool, moist skin

Excessive thirst

Nausea and vomiting

Drowsiness or loss of consciousness

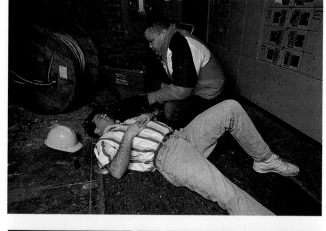

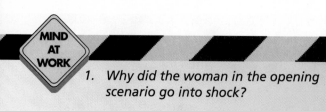

MIND AT WORK

1. *Why did the woman in the opening scenario go into shock?*

Care for Shock

First, check for life-threatening conditions. Any specific care you provide for life-threatening conditions will minimize the effects of shock. If you do not find any life-threatening conditions, check for nonlife-threatening conditions. During this check, the signs and symptoms of shock are most likely to become evident. Provide the general care you learned in Chapter 4:

- Do no harm.
- Monitor breathing and consciousness (Fig. 8-4, *A*).
- Make the victim as comfortable as possible. Helping the victim rest comfortably is important because pain can intensify the body's stress and accelerate the progression of shock. Helping the victim rest in a more comfortable position may minimize pain.
- Keep the victim from getting chilled or overheated (Fig. 8-4, *B*).
- Reassure the victim.
- Provide any specific care needed.

The general care you provide in an emergency will always help the body adjust to the stresses imposed by an injury or illness, thus reducing the effects of shock.

You can further help the victim manage the effects of shock if you—

Figure 8-4 **A,** Monitor the victim's airway and breathing. **B,** Keep the victim from getting chilled or overheated. **C,** Elevate the victim's legs to keep blood circulating to the vital organs.

- Control any external bleeding as soon as possible to minimize blood loss.
- Have the victim lie down.
- Elevate the legs about 12 inches (30.5 centimeters) to help blood circulate to the vital organs. Do not elevate the legs if the victim is nauseated or having trouble breathing, you

suspect head, neck, or back injuries or possible broken bones involving the hips or legs, or moving causes more pain (Fig. 8-4, *C*). If you are unsure of the victim's condition, or if it is painful for him or her to move, leave him or her lying flat.

- Do not give the victim anything to eat or drink, even though he or she is likely to be thirsty. The victim's condition may be severe enough to require surgery, in which case it is better that the stomach be empty.
- Call EMS personnel immediately. Shock cannot be managed effectively by first aid alone. A victim of shock requires advanced life support as soon as possible.

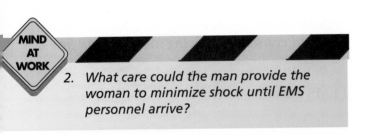

2. *What care could the man provide the woman to minimize shock until EMS personnel arrive?*

Shock in Children

Children have the same potential to develop shock as do adults. However, the signs and symptoms of shock may be harder to detect in children. Suspect that shock may develop with severe vomiting or diarrhea for the duration of a day. Replacing the fluids lost through vomiting or diarrhea is critical. Do not hesitate to call EMS personnel for a child who has developed severe vomiting or diarrhea.

SUMMARY

Do not wait for shock to develop before providing care to a victim of injury or sudden illness. Always follow the general care for any emergency to minimize the progressive stages of shock. Care for life-threatening conditions, such as breathing problems or severe external bleeding, before caring for lesser injuries. Remember that the key to managing shock effectively is calling EMS personnel and giving care as soon as possible.

Remember that shock is an inevitable development in serious injuries and illnesses, particularly if blood is lost or if the normal function of the heart is interrupted. With serious injuries or illnesses, shock is often the final stage before death. You cannot stop shock by administering first aid, but you can slow its progression. Call the local emergency number for an ambulance immediately if you notice signs of shock. Shock can be reversed only by advanced medical care and only if the victim is reached in time.

Answers to Application Questions

1. Her body could not compensate for her significant injuries that probably involved significant bleeding.

2. In this scenario, the man could minimize shock by keeping the woman from getting chilled and by providing reassurance. He could also control any external bleeding and provide any additional care that may be needed.

★ Keep checking for breathing & circulation — they can always change w/ shock & the injuries that caused it

STUDY QUESTIONS

1. Circle T if the statement is true, F if it is false.

   Shock is a condition resulting only from severe blood loss.   T (F)

2. From the scenario at the beginning of the chapter, list four signs and symptoms of shock.

3. List two conditions that frequently result in shock.

Use the following scenario to answer question 4.

> *Tara saw her brother Daren fall out of the tree he was climbing. When she reached him, he was lying on the ground, conscious, but in pain. One leg was strangely twisted. Tara ran into the house, called 9-1-1, and told the dispatcher what had happened. Then she ran back to Daren, who was pale, sweating, and constantly moving his head and arms. He seemed to be unable to lie still.*

4. What can Tara do to care for Daren until EMS personnel arrive?

In questions 5 through 9, circle the letter of the correct answer.

5. Which of the following can cause shock?

   a. Bleeding — hypovolemic
   b. Bee sting — anafylactic
   c. Heart attack — cardiogenic
   (d.) All of the above

6. When shock occurs, the body prioritizes its need for blood. Where does it send blood first?

   a. The arms and legs
   (b.) The brain, heart, and lungs
   c. The skin
   d. The spinal cord

7. Why does the skin appear pale during shock?

    a. Constriction of blood vessels near the skin's surface
    b. The majority of blood being sent to vital organs
    c. Profuse sweating
    d. a and b

8. Which of the following are included in the care for shock?

    a. Controlling bleeding when present
    b. Monitoring airway, breathing, and circulation
    c. Helping the victim rest comfortably
    d. All of the above

9. Which body systems are affected by shock?

    a. Circulatory and respiratory
    b. All body systems
    c. Circulatory, respiratory, and nervous
    d. Respiratory and nervous

10. Why is shock a life-threatening condition?

11. Why does elevating the victim's legs help to manage shock?

Answers are listed in Appendix A.

PART FOUR

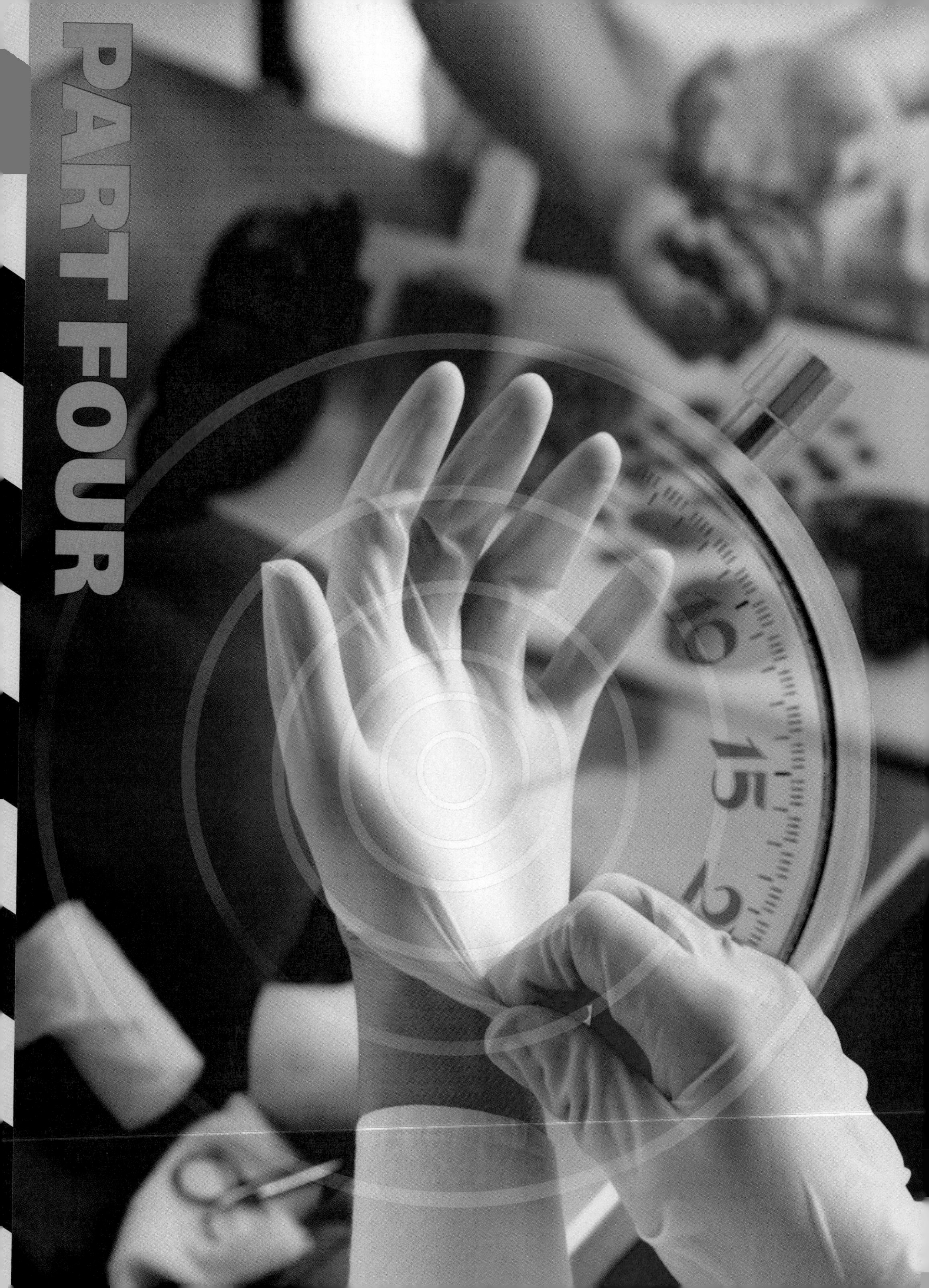

INJURIES

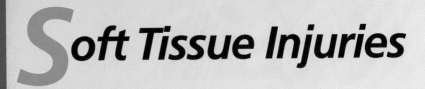

Soft Tissue Injuries

WHAT YOU SHOULD LEARN

After reading this chapter, you should be able to—

1. List two signs and symptoms of closed wounds.

2. Describe the best defense against infection of an open wound.

3. List four signs and symptoms of an infected wound.

4. Describe how to care for an infected wound.

5. List two purposes of bandaging.

6. Describe how to care for open and closed wounds and wounds with an impaled object.

7. List four sources of burns.

8. Describe two types of burns.

9. Explain when to call EMS personnel for a burn.

10. List the basic steps for burn care.

11. Describe how to care for thermal, chemical, electrical, and radiation burns.

12. Define the key terms for this chapter.

It is a hot, muggy day in May. The forecast of rain has not seemed to dampen the spirits of the four beachgoers headed for the coast. After a week of all-night studying and grueling exams, the soon-to-be graduates are anxious to join their friends.

As they approach the bridge, Joe, the driver, decides he can no longer ignore the car's continually climbing temperature gauge. He pulls over to the side of the road, explaining that at the end of the term, he had to decide between a new radiator or beach week. After a few minutes, Joe argues that he can safely open the radiator, since the fluid has had time to cool down.

Despite his friends' objections, Joe takes off his t-shirt and wraps it around the radiator cap. Slowly he releases the cap, a quarter turn at a time. Suddenly, on the last turn, the cap blows off, and scalding fluid and steam burst out of the radiator, burning his chest and arms. As he spins away from the steam, his back is also burned.

Introduction

An infant falls and bruises his arm while learning to walk; a toddler scrapes her knee while learning to run; a child needs stitches in his chin after he falls off the "monkey bars" on the playground; another child gets a black eye in a fist fight; a teenager suffers a sunburn after a weekend at the beach; and an adult cuts a hand while working in a woodshop. What do these injuries have in common? They are all soft tissue injuries.

SOFT TISSUE INJURIES

In the course of growing up and in our daily lives, soft tissue injuries occur often and in many different ways. The soft tissues of the skin have less resistance and are at greater risk for injury than the deeper, stronger tissues of muscle and bone. Organs, also composed of soft tissue, are vulnerable to damage from blunt trauma and penetrating forces. Some organs, however, such as the brain, heart, and lungs, are better protected by bones than other organs, such as the digestive or reproductive organs. Fortunately, most soft tissue injuries are minor, requiring little attention. Often only an adhesive bandage or ice and rest are needed. Some soft tissue injuries, however, are more severe and require immediate medical attention. In this chapter, you will learn how to recognize and care for types of soft tissue injuries.

WHAT ARE SOFT TISSUES?

The **soft tissues** include the layers of skin, fat, and muscles that protect the underlying body structures (Fig. 9-1). In Chapter 3, you learned that the skin is the largest single organ in the body and that without it the human body could not function. Skin provides a protective barrier for the body; it helps regulate the body's temperature; and it senses information about the environment by way of the nerves in the skin.

The skin is composed of layers. The outer layer of skin, the **epidermis,** provides a barrier to bacteria and other organisms that can cause infection. A deeper layer, called the **dermis,** contains the nerves, hair roots, sweat and oil glands, and blood vessels. Because the skin is well supplied with blood vessels and nerves, most soft tissue injuries are likely to bleed and be painful. The **hypodermis,** located beneath the epidermis and the dermis, contains fat, blood vessels, and connective tissues. This layer insulates the body to help maintain body temperature. The fat layer also stores energy. The amount of fat varies in different parts of the body and in each person.

The muscles lie beneath the fat layer and comprise the largest segment of the body's soft tissues. Most soft tissue injuries involve the

Key Terms

Bandage: Material used to wrap or cover a part of the body; commonly used to hold a dressing or splint in place.

Burn: An injury to the skin or other body tissues caused by heat, chemicals, electricity, or radiation.

Closed wound: An injury that does not break the skin and in which soft tissue damage occurs beneath the skin.

Critical burn: Any burn that is potentially life threatening, disabling, or disfiguring.

Deep burn: A burn that involves the two lower layers of skin, the dermis and the hy-

podermis, and may destroy underlying structures; it can be life threatening.

Dressing: A pad placed directly over a wound to absorb blood and other body fluids and to prevent infection.

Open wound: An injury resulting in a break in the skin's surface.

Soft tissues: Body structures that include the layers of skin, fat, and muscles.

Superficial burn: A burn involving only the top layer of skin, the epidermis, characterized by dry, red skin.

Wound: An injury to the soft tissues.

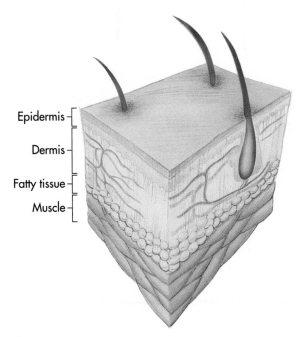

Epidermis

Dermis

Fatty tissue

Muscle

Figure 9-1   The soft tissues include the layers of skin, fat, and muscle.

outer layers of tissue. However, injuries from more violent forces, which can occur with sharp or penetrating objects or deep burns, can involve all the soft tissue layers. Although the muscles are considered soft tissues, muscle injuries are discussed more thoroughly in Chapter 10 with other musculoskeletal injuries.

TYPES OF SOFT TISSUE INJURIES

Any injury to the skin or soft tissues beneath threatens the body. Since the surface of the skin tends to collect microorganisms, injuries involving breaks in the skin can become infected unless properly cared for.

Some injuries to the soft tissues are called **wounds.** Wounds are typically classified as either closed or open. In a **closed wound,** the outer layer of skin is intact. The damage lies below the surface. A closed wound may bleed internally. With an **open wound,** the outer layer of skin is broken. Open wounds usually result in external bleeding.

Burns

Burns are a special kind of soft tissue injury. A burn occurs when intense or prolonged heat,

certain chemicals, electricity, or radiation contacts the skin or other body tissues. Exposure to any of these elements can result in burns to the skin and other body tissues. Burns account for about 25 percent of all soft tissue injuries. Thermal burns—burns caused by heat—are the most common. Sources of electricity, such as common household current or lightning, can penetrate the body, causing external and internal burn damage. Electrical current can also affect the heart's electrical system and the part of the brain that controls breathing and heartbeat. When certain chemicals contact the skin, they cause burns. Solar radiation from the sun's rays causes sunburn. The average citizen is rarely exposed to other forms of radiation.

Burns are classified as superficial or deep. **Superficial** (first degree) **burns** affect only the outer layer of skin. **Deep** (second and third degree) **burns** damage all the layers of skin and can affect other soft tissues and even bone. Burns are discussed in more detail later in this chapter.

Closed Wounds

The simplest closed wound is a bruise, also called a **contusion** (Fig. 9-2). Bruises result when the body is subjected to a force, such as when you bump your leg on a table or chair. This bump or blow usually results in damage to soft tissue layers and vessels beneath the skin, causing internal bleeding. When blood and other fluids seep into the surrounding tissues, the area discolors and swells. The amount of discoloration and swelling varies depending on the severity of the injury. At first, the area may only appear red. Over time, more blood and other fluids leak into the area, which turns dark red or purple. Violent forces can cause more severe soft tissue injuries involving larger blood vessels and the deeper layers of muscle tissue. These injuries can result in profuse bleeding beneath the skin.

Open Wounds

In an open wound, the break in the skin can be as minor as a scrape of the surface layers or as severe as a deep penetration. The amount of bleeding depends on the location and severity of the injury.

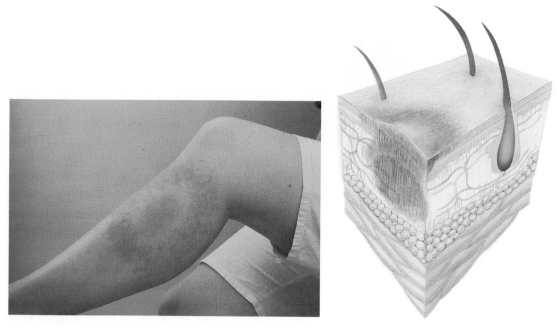

Figure 9-2   The simplest closed wound is a bruise.

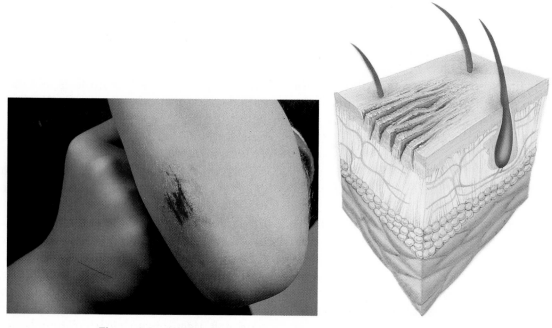

Figure 9-3   Abrasions can be painful, but bleeding is easily controlled.

The following are the four main types of open wounds:

- Abrasions
- Lacerations
- Avulsions
- Punctures

An **abrasion** is the most common type of open wound. It is characterized by skin that has been rubbed or scraped away (Fig. 9-3). This

type of skin damage often occurs when a child falls and scrapes his or her hands or knees. An abrasion is sometimes called a scrape, a rug burn, a road rash, or a strawberry. Because the scraping of the outer skin layers exposes sensitive nerve endings, an abrasion is usually painful. Bleeding is not severe and easily controlled, since only the small capillaries are damaged. Because of the way the injury occurs, dirt and other matter can easily become embed-

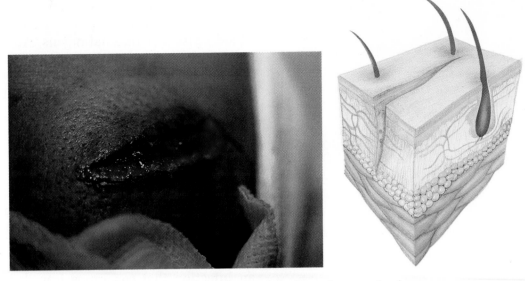

Figure 9-4   A laceration may have jagged or smooth edges.

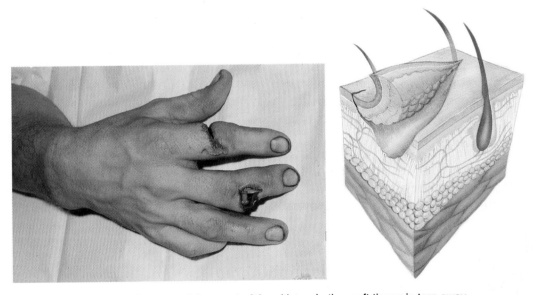

Figure 9-5   In an avulsion, part of the skin and other soft tissue is torn away.

ded in the skin, making it especially important to clean the wound to prevent infection and aid healing.

A **laceration** is a cut, usually from a sharp object. The cut may have either jagged or smooth edges (Fig. 9-4). Lacerations are commonly caused by sharp-edged objects, such as knives, scissors, or broken glass. A laceration can also result when a blunt force splits the skin. This splitting often occurs in areas where bone lies directly underneath the skin's surface, such as the chin bone or skull. Deep lacerations can also affect the layers of fat and muscle, damaging both nerves and blood vessels. Lacerations usually bleed freely and, depending on the structures involved, can bleed heavily. Because the nerves may also be injured, lacerations are not always painful. Severely damaged nerves cannot transmit pain signals to the brain. Lacerations can easily become infected if not cared for properly.

An **avulsion** is an injury in which a portion of the skin and sometimes other soft tissue is partially or completely torn away (Fig. 9-5). A partially avulsed piece of skin may remain attached but hangs like a flap. Bleeding is usually significant because avulsions often involve deeper soft tissue layers. Sometimes a body part, such as a finger, may be severed (Fig. 9-6). Such an injury is called an **amputation.**

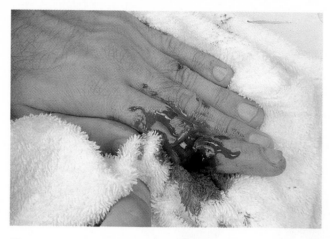

Figure 9-6   In a severe avulsion, a body part may be completely removed.

Although damage to the tissue is severe when a body part is severed, bleeding is usually not as bad as you might expect. The blood vessels usually constrict and retract (pull in) at the point of injury, slowing bleeding and making it relatively easy to control with direct pressure. In the past, a completely severed body part could not be successfully reattached. With today's medical technology, reattachment is often successful.

A **puncture wound** results when the skin is pierced with a pointed object, such as a nail, a piece of glass, a splinter, or a knife (Fig. 9-7). A gunshot wound is also a puncture wound. Because the skin usually closes around the penetrating object, external bleeding is generally

not severe. However, internal bleeding can be severe if the penetrating object damages major blood vessels or internal organs. An object that remains embedded in the open wound is called an **impaled object** (Fig. 9-8). An object may also pass completely through a body part, creating two open wounds—one at the entry point and one at the exit point.

INFECTION

Any break in the skin provides an entry point for disease-producing microorganisms. Even a small, seemingly unimportant laceration or abrasion has the potential to become the site of an infection that can range from being merely unpleasant to being life threatening.

Preventing Infection

When an injury breaks the skin, the best initial defense against infection is to cleanse the area thoroughly. For minor wounds, wash the area with plenty of soap and water. Most soaps are effective in removing harmful bacteria. Wounds that require medical attention because of more extensive tissue damage or bleeding need not be washed. These wounds will be cleaned thoroughly in the medical facility as a routine part of care. It is more important to control bleeding.

Although puncture wounds generally do not bleed profusely, they are potentially more dan-

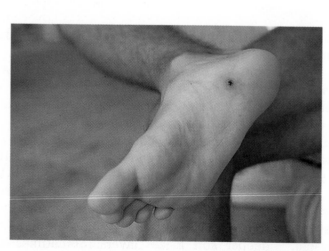

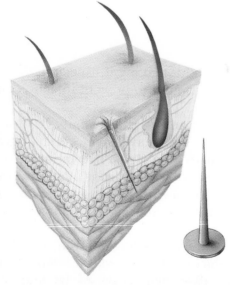

Figure 9-7   A puncture wound results when skin is pierced by a pointed object.

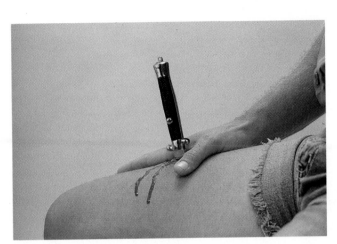

Figure 9-8 An object can become embedded in a wound.

gerous than wounds that do because they more readily become infected. Objects penetrating the soft tissues carry microorganisms that cause infections. Of particular danger is the microorganism that causes tetanus, a severe infection. **Tetanus** is a disease caused by a bacteria that produces a powerful poison in the body. This poison enters the nervous system and affects muscles. For example, jaw muscles will contract, causing "lockjaw." Once tetanus reaches the nervous system, its effects are highly dangerous and can be fatal. However, in many cases, tetanus can now be successfully treated with **antitoxins.**

One of the ways to prevent tetanus is through immunization. Like all immunizations, the tetanus immunization helps the immune system defend against the invading microorganisms that cause the disease. The immune system is the body system responsible for fighting off infection. Immunizations assist the natural function of the immune system by building up antibodies, disease-fighting proteins, which help protect the body against specific infections in the future. The tetanus immunization is given in infancy. However, the effect of the immunization eventually wears off. People must receive a booster shot at least every 10 years or whenever a wound is contaminated.

Signs and Symptoms of Infection

Sometimes, even the best care for a soft tissue injury is not enough to prevent infection. You can easily recognize infection's early signs and symptoms. The area around the wound becomes swollen and red. The area may feel warm or throb with pain. Some wounds have a pus discharge (Fig. 9-9). More serious infections may cause a person to develop a fever and feel ill. Red streaks may develop that progress from the wound in the direction of the heart. Those red streaks are caused by bacteria that are destroying tissue.

Caring for Infection

If you see these initial signs and symptoms of infection, care for the wound by keeping the area clean, elevating the area, and applying warm, wet compresses and an antibiotic ointment such as Neosporin®, Bacitracin®, or neomycin. For the few people who are sensitive to neomycin, Polysporin® is an effective

An Ounce of Prevention

A serious infection can cause severe medical problems. One such infection is tetanus, caused by the organism *Clostridium tetani*. This organism, commonly found in soil and feces of cows and horses, can infect many kinds of wounds. This probably explains why the cavalry in the American Civil War had higher rates of tetanus than the infantry. Worldwide, about 1 million people contract tetanus annually, with 20 to 50 percent of the cases resulting in death. In the United States, 36 cases were reported in 1994.

Tetanus is introduced into the body through a puncture wound, abrasion, laceration, or burn. Because the organism multiplies in an environment that is low in oxygen, puncture wounds and other deep wounds are at particular risk for tetanus infection. It produces a powerful toxin, one of the most lethal poisons known, that affects the central nervous system and specific muscles. People at increased risk for tetanus include people injecting themselves with drugs, burn victims, and people recovering from surgery. Newborn babies can be infected through the stump of the umbilical cord.

Signs and symptoms of tetanus include difficulty swallowing, irritability, headache, fever, and muscle spasms near the infected area. Later, as the infection progresses, it can affect other muscles, such as those in the jaw, causing the condition called "lockjaw." Once tetanus gets into the nervous system, its effects are irreversible.

The first line of defense against tetanus is to thoroughly clean an open wound. Major wounds should be cleaned and treated at a medical facility. Clean a minor wound with soap and water, and apply an antibiotic ointment and a clean or sterile dressing. If signs of wound infection develop, seek medical attention immediately. Infected wounds of the face, neck, and head should receive *immediate* medical care, since the tetanus toxin can travel rapidly to the brain. A health care provider will determine whether a tetanus shot is needed, depending on the victim's immunization status. Always contact your health care provider if you are unsure how long it has been since you received a tetanus immunization or booster.

The best way to prevent tetanus is to be immunized against it and then receive periodic booster shots. Immunizations assist the natural function of the immune system by building up antibodies, disease-fighting proteins that help protect the body against specific bacteria. Because the effects of immunization do not last a lifetime, booster shots help maintain the antibodies that protect against tetanus. Booster shots are recommended every 5 to 10 years or whenever a wound has been contaminated by dirt or an object, such as a rusty nail, causes a puncture wound. Most infants or young children in this country receive an immunization known as *DPT,* which includes the tetanus toxoid. About 70 percent of a sample of Americans 6 years or older were found to have antibodies in their systems that protect against tetanus. By age 60 to 69, however, the level of antibodies dropped to less than 50 percent and to about 30 percent by age 70. Fifty nine percent of tetanus cases and 75 percent of deaths from tetanus occur in people 60 years or older. All of us need to raise our awareness of the need for routine tetanus boosters.

SOURCE
Sanford JP: Tetanus—forgotten but not gone, *N Engl J Med* 332(12):812–813.

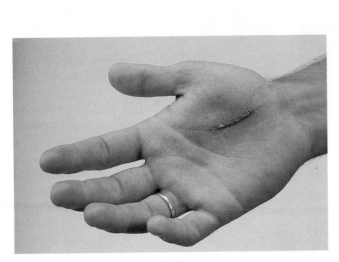

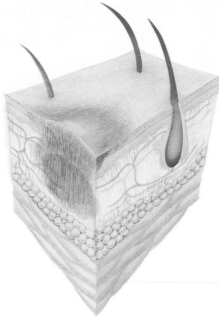

Figure 9-9   An infected wound may become swollen and may have a pus discharge.

substitute. Change coverings over the wound daily. If a fever or red streaks develop, the infection is worsening. Contact your local health care provider to determine what additional care is necessary.

DRESSINGS AND BANDAGES

All open wounds need some type of covering to help control bleeding and prevent infection. These coverings are commonly referred to as dressings and bandages. They exist in many varieties.

Dressings

Dressings are pads placed directly on the wound to absorb blood and other fluids and to prevent infection. To minimize the chance of infection, dressings should be sterile. Most dressings are porous, allowing air to circulate to the wound to promote healing. Standard dressings include varying sizes of cotton gauze, commonly ranging from 2 to 4 inches square. Much larger dressings called universal dressings are used to cover very large wounds and multiple wounds in one body area. Some dressings have nonstick surfaces to prevent the dressing from sticking to the wound (Fig. 9-10).

A special type of dressing, called an **occlusive dressing,** does not allow air to pass through. Examples of this kind of dressing are sterile aluminum foil, plastic wrap, and gauze soaked with petroleum jelly (Fig. 9-11). This type of dressing is used for certain chest and abdominal injuries discussed in Chapter 13.

Bandages

A **bandage** is any material that is used to wrap or cover any part of the body. Bandages are

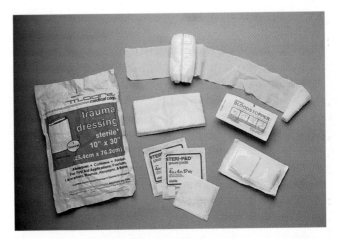

Figure 9-10   Dressings are pads placed directly on the wound. They come in various sizes. Some have surfaces that will not stick to a wound.

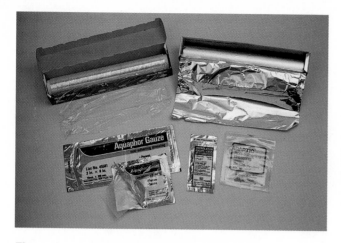

Figure 9-11 Airtight dressings are designed to prevent air from passing through.

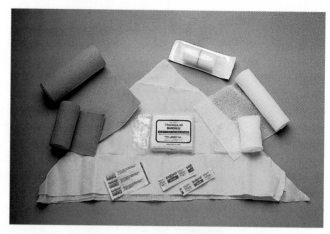

Figure 9-12 Different types of bandages are used to hold dressings in place, apply pressure to a wound, protect the wound from infection, and provide support to an injured area.

Figure 9-13 A common type of bandage is an adhesive compress.

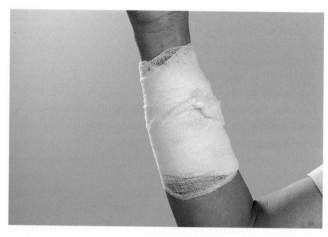

Figure 9-14 Roller bandages are usually made of gauze and are easy to apply.

used to hold dressings in place, to apply pressure to control bleeding, to protect a wound from dirt and infection, and to provide support to an injured limb or body part. Any bandage applied snugly to create pressure on a wound or an injury is called a **pressure bandage.** Many different types of bandages are available commercially (Fig. 9-12).

Types of bandages

A common type of bandage is a commercially made **adhesive compress** such as a Band-Aid® (Fig. 9-13). Available in assorted sizes, it consists of a small pad of nonstick gauze on a strip of adhesive tape that is applied directly to

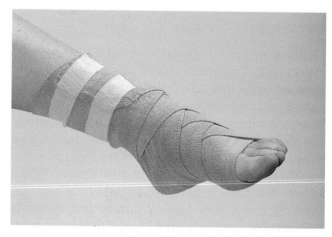

Figure 9-15 Elastic bandages can be applied to control swelling or support an injured limb.

A

B

Figure 9-16 **A,** A triangular bandage can be made by cutting a 40-inch square of cloth in half diagonally. **B,** A cravat is made by folding the triangular bandage.

small injuries. The **bandage compress** is a thick gauze dressing attached to a gauze bandage. This bandage can be tied in place. Bandage compresses, specially designed to help control severe bleeding, usually come in a sterile package.

A **roller bandage** is usually made of gauze or gauze-like material (Fig. 9-14). Roller bandages are available in assorted widths from $\frac{1}{2}$ to 12 inches (1.3 to 30.5 centimeters) and lengths from 5 to 10 yards (4.6 to 9.1 meters). A roller bandage is generally wrapped around the body part, over a dressing, using overlapping turns until the dressing is completely covered. It can be tied or taped in place. A roller bandage may also be used as a dressing. In Chapter 11, you will learn how to use roller bandages to hold splints in place.

Elastic roller bandages are designed to keep continuous pressure on a body part. When properly applied, they can effectively control swelling or support an injured limb (Fig. 9-15). Elastic bandages are available in 2-, 3-, 4-, and 6-inch (3.1, 7.6, 10.2, and 15.2 centimeters) widths. Because of their versatility, elastic bandages are used in athletic environments, where injuries to muscles, bones, and joints are common.

Another commonly used bandage is the **triangular bandage.** It can be made easily by cutting a 40-inch (101.6 centimeters) square of a cotton material such as muslin or similar cloth in half diagonally, making two triangular pieces (Fig. 9-16, *A*). Folded, it can hold a dressing or splint in place on most parts of

Figure 9-17 A triangular bandage is commonly used as a sling.

the body (Fig. 9-16, *B*). Used as a sling, the triangular bandage can support an injured shoulder, arm, or hand (Fig. 9-17).

Applying a roller bandage

To apply a roller bandage, follow these general guidelines:

- If possible, elevate the injured body part above the level of the heart (but not if doing so causes pain).
- Check warmth and color of the area below the injury site, especially fingers and toes.
- Secure the end of the bandage in place with a turn of the bandage. Wrap it around the body part until the dressing is completely covered and the bandage extends several inches beyond the dressing. Tie or tape the bandage in place (Fig. 9-18, *A-D*).

- Do not cover fingers or toes, if possible. By keeping these parts uncovered, you will be able to see if the bandage is too tight. If fingers or toes become cold or begin to turn pale, blue, or ashen, the bandage is too tight and should be loosened slightly.
- If blood soaks through the bandage, apply additional dressings and another bandage. *Do not remove the blood-soaked bandages and dressings.* Disturbing them may disrupt the formation of a clot and restart the bleeding.

Elastic roller bandages, sometimes called elastic wraps, can easily restrict blood flow if not applied properly. Restricted blood flow is not only painful but can cause tissue damage if not corrected. Figure 9-19, *A-D* shows some simple ways to ensure proper application of elastic roller bandages.

CARE FOR WOUNDS

As mentioned earlier, wounds may be classified as open or closed. In a closed wound, the skin is not broken. In an open wound, the skin is cut, punctured, scraped, or torn.

Care for Closed Wounds

Many closed wounds do not require special medical care. When the cause and signs and symptoms of the wound indicate it is not severe, you can use direct pressure on the area to decrease bleeding that occurs beneath the skin. Elevating the injured part helps reduce swelling. Applying cold can be effective early on in helping control both pain and swelling. When applying ice or a chemical cold pack, place a gauze pad, a towel, or other cloth

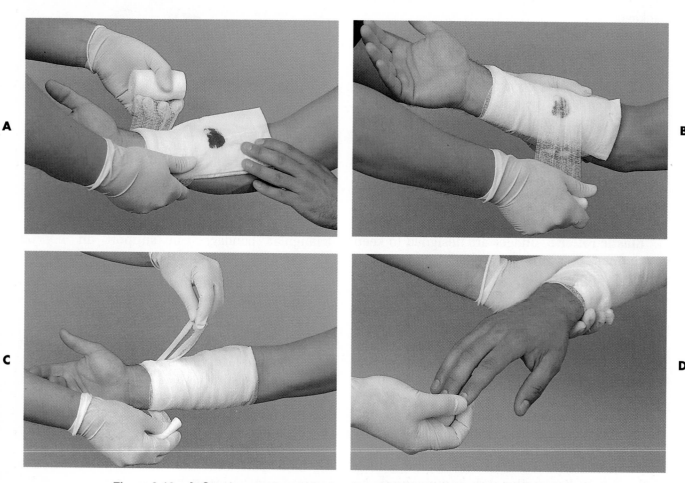

Figure 9-18   A, Start by securing a roller bandage over the dressing. **B,** Use overlapping turns to cover the dressing completely. **C,** Tie or tape the bandage in place. **D,** Check the fingers for warmth and color.

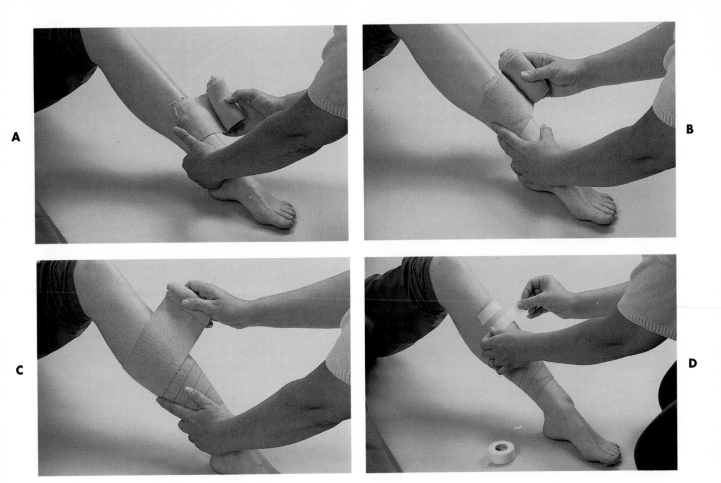

Figure 9-19   **A,** Start the elastic bandage at the point farthest from the heart. **B,** Anchor the bandage. **C,** Wrap the bandage using overlapping turns. **D,** Tape the end of the bandage in place.

between the source of the cold and the victim's skin (Fig. 9-20).

Do not dismiss a closed wound as "just a bruise," however. Be aware of possible serious injuries to internal organs or other underlying structures, such as the bones. Take the time to evaluate whether more serious injuries could be present. If a person complains of severe pain or cannot move a body part without pain, or if you think the force that caused the injury was great enough to cause serious damage, seek medical attention immediately. Care for musculoskeletal and internal injuries is described in later chapters.

Care for Major Open Wounds

A major open wound has severe bleeding, deep destruction of tissue, or a deeply embedded object. To care for a major open wound, follow these general guidelines:

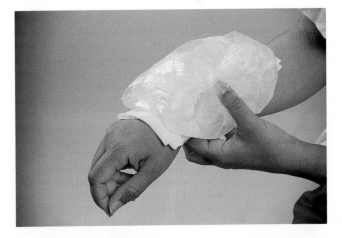

Figure 9-20   For a closed wound, apply ice to help control pain and swelling.

- *Do not waste time trying to wash the wound.*
- Ask someone to call EMS personnel, or make the call yourself.
- Put on disposable latex gloves if they are available.

- Quickly control bleeding using pressure and elevation as described in Chapter 7. Apply direct pressure by placing a sterile dressing over the wound. If nothing sterile is available, use any clean covering, such as plastic wrap or a towel, tie, handkerchief, sock, or disposable gloves. If you do not have a pad or cloth available, have the injured person use his or her hand. Do not contact the victim's blood, if possible.
- Apply a bandage over the dressings to maintain pressure on the wound.
- Wash your hands immediately after completing care, whether or not you wore gloves.
- Keep the victim from getting chilled or overheated.
- Have the victim rest comfortably and reassure him or her.
- Recommend to the victim that he or she get a tetanus booster shot if he or she has not had one within the last 10 years.

If the victim has an avulsion in which a body part has been completely severed, try to retrieve the severed body part. Wear gloves. Wrap the part in sterile gauze, if any is available, or in any clean material such as a washcloth. Place the wrapped part in a plastic bag. If possible, keep the part cool by placing the bag on ice (Fig. 9-21). Do not place the bag on dry ice or in ice water. Make sure the part is transported to the medical facility with the victim.

If the victim has an embedded object in the wound, follow these additional guidelines:

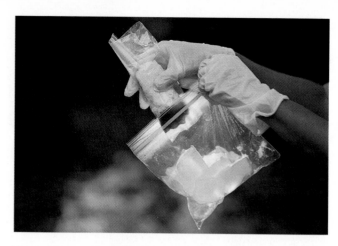

Figure 9-21   Wrap a severed body part in sterile gauze, put it in a plastic bag, and put the bag on ice.

- Do not remove the object.
- Use bulky dressings to stabilize it. Any movement of the object can result in further tissue damage (Fig. 9-22, *A*).
- Control bleeding by bandaging the dressings in place around the object (Fig. 9-22, *B*).

Care for Minor Open Wounds

In minor open wounds, such as abrasions, damage is only superficial and bleeding is minimal. To care for a minor open wound, follow these general guidelines:

- Put on disposable latex gloves, if possible.
- Wash the wound thoroughly with soap and water.
- Place a sterile dressing over the wound.
- Apply direct pressure for a few minutes to control any bleeding.

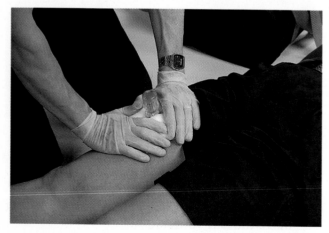

A

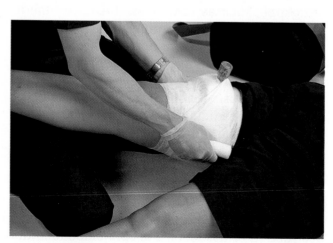

B

Figure 9-22   A, Use bulky dressings to support an embedded object. **B,** Use bandages over the dressing to control bleeding.

A Stitch in Time

It can be difficult to judge when a wound requires stitches. A general rule of thumb is that stitches are needed when the edges of skin do not fall together or when any wound is more than an inch long. Stitches speed the healing process, lessen the chances of infection, and improve the look of scars. They should be placed by a doctor within the first few hours after the injury. The following major injuries always require medical attention and often need stitches:

- Bleeding from an artery or bleeding that is difficult to control
- Deep cuts or avulsions that show the muscle or bone, involve joints such as the elbows, gape widely, or involve the hands, feet, or face
- Large punctures
- Large imbedded objects
- Some human and animal bites
- Wounds that, if left unattended, could leave a conspicuous scar, such as those that involve the lip or eyebrow

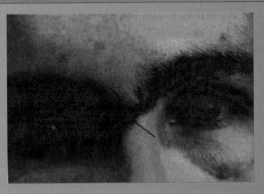

If you are caring for a wound and think it may need stitches, it probably does. If you are not sure, check with a doctor immediately. It can be dangerous to close a wound after a delay because of the probability of infection. Once applied, stitches are easily cared for by dabbing them with hydrogen peroxide once or twice a day. If the wound gets red or swollen or if pus begins to form, notify your health care provider.

Stitches in the face are often removed in less than a week. In the areas around the joints, they are often removed in 2 weeks. Stitches on most other body parts require removal within 6 to 10 days. Some stitches dissolve naturally and do not require removal.

- Once bleeding is controlled, remove the dressing and apply an antibiotic ointment.
- Apply a new sterile dressing. Hold the dressing in place with tape, an adhesive compress, or a roller bandage.
- Dispose of dressings and then gloves in a closed waste container.
- Wash your hands.

BURNS

In 1993, 4000 people in the United States died from fires and burns, making burns this country's fifth leading cause of unintentional death. Most of the burns occurred in the home. Over 1 million burn injuries in the United States a year require medical attention or result in restricted activity. About one third of those are treated at hospital emergency departments, and over 90,000 people are hospitalized for an average of 12 days. Fires cause over half of all deaths from burns. Hot liquids cause about a fourth, and electricity causes only a very small percentage of deaths from burns. The most common causes of nonfatal burns are scalds from hot liquids or foods and contact with hot surfaces. Burns can also occur when the body is exposed to certain chemicals or solar or other forms of radiation.

Burns first destroy the epidermis, the top layer of skin. If the burn progresses, the dermis, or second layer, is injured or destroyed. Burns break the skin and thus can cause infection, fluid loss, and loss of temperature control. The broken skin is then exposed to microorganisms, which can lead to infection. Deep burns can damage the underlying tissues of the hypodermis. Burns can also damage the respiratory system and the eyes.

The severity of a burn depends on—

- The temperature of the source of the burn.
- The length of exposure to the source.
- The location of the burn.
- The extent of the burn.
- The victim's age and medical condition.

In general, the skin of people over 60 becomes thinner and more susceptible to severe burn injuries as they age. Young children, whose skin is delicate, may also burn more severely. People with chronic medical problems also tend to have more complications from severe burns, especially if they are not well nourished, have heart or kidney problems, or may be exposed to the burn source for a prolonged period because they are unable to escape. People with nerve damage, for example from paralysis, may have no sensation, and therefore become burned more easily because they do not feel heat.

Types of Burns

Burns are classified by their source, such as heat, chemicals, electricity, or radiation. They are also classified by depth. The deeper the burn, the more severe it is. Generally, burns are classified into two depths: superficial (first degree) and deep (second and third degree).

Superficial burns

A superficial (first degree) burn involves only the top layer of skin (Fig. 9-23). The skin is red and dry, and the burn is usually painful. The area may swell. Most sunburns are superficial burns. Superficial burns generally heal in 5 to 6 days without permanent scarring. Sunburn may be severe enough, however, to require hospitalization.

Deep burns

A deep (second or third degree) burn involves both the epidermis and the dermis (Fig. 9-24). These injuries may also appear red and may have blisters that may open and weep clear fluid, making the skin appear wet. The burned skin may look mottled (blotched). These burns are usually painful, and the area often swells. The burn usually heals in 3 or 4 weeks. Scarring may occur.

A more severe deep burn can also destroy all the layers of skin, as well as any or all of the underlying structures—fat, muscles, bones, and nerves. These burns look brown or charred (black), with the tissues underneath some-

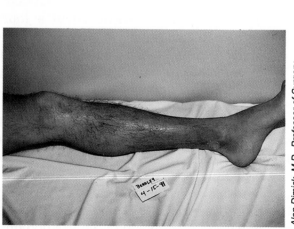

Alan Dimick, M.D., Professor of Surgery, Director of UAB Burn Center

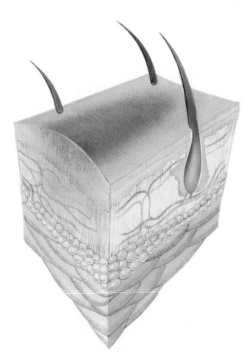

Figure 9-23   A superficial (first degree) burn.

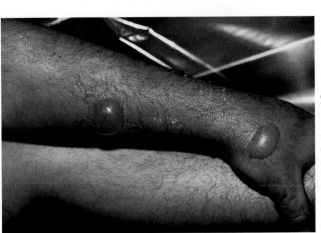

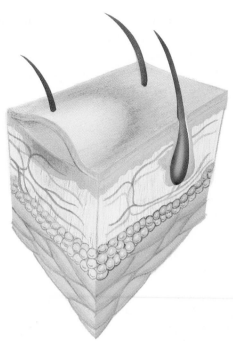

*Alan Dimick, M.D., Professor of Surgery,
Director of UAB Burn Center*

Figure 9-24 A deep (second degree) burn.

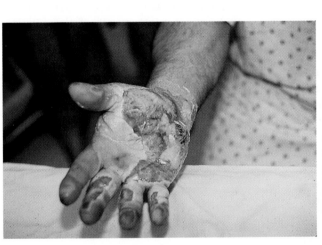

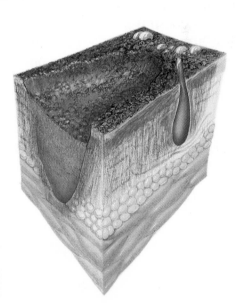

*Alan Dimick, M.D., Professor of Surgery,
Director of UAB Burn Center*

Figure 9-25 A deep (third degree) burn.

times appearing white (Fig. 9-25). They can be either extremely painful or relatively painless if the burn destroyed nerve endings in the skin. Deep burns are life threatening. Because such burns are open wounds, the body loses fluid, and shock is likely to occur. These burns also make the body highly prone to infection. Scarring occurs and may be severe. Many deep burn sites may require skin grafts.

Identifying Critical Burns

A **critical burn** requires the attention of medical professionals. Critical burns are potentially life threatening, disfiguring, or disabling. Knowing whether you should call EMS personnel for a burn is often difficult. It is not always easy or possible to assess the severity of a burn immediately after injury. Even superficial burns to large areas of the body or to certain body parts can be critical. You cannot judge severity by the pain the victim feels because nerve endings may be destroyed. Call 9-1-1 or the local emergency number immediately for assistance for the following burns:

- Burns whose victims are experiencing breathing difficulty
- Burns covering more than one body part or a large surface area
- Suspected burns to the airway
- Burns to the head, neck, hands, feet, or genitals
- Any deep burn to a person under age 5 or over age 60
- Burns resulting from chemicals, explosions, or electricity

If you have any question about the severity of a burn, call 9-1-1 or the local emergency number.

Expect that burns caused by flames or hot grease will require immediate medical attention, especially if the victim is under 5 or over 60 years of age. Call EMS personnel. Hot grease is slow to cool and difficult to remove from the skin. Steam can cause severe burns; steam contains more heat energy than boiling water. Burns that involve hot liquid, steam, or flames contacting clothing will also be serious, since the clothing traps the heat and prolongs its contact with the skin. Some synthetic fabrics melt and stick to the body. They may take longer to cool than the soft tissues.

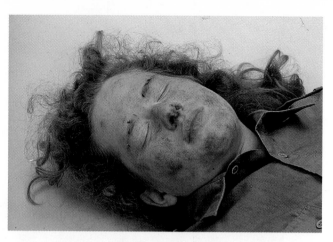

Figure 9-26   Facial burns may signal that air passages or lungs have been burned.

chemicals or radiation. If the scene is unsafe, call 9-1-1 or the local emergency number and wait for fire fighters or EMS personnel to arrive.

If the scene is safe, approach cautiously. Check for life-threatening conditions. Call EMS personnel if necessary. Pay close attention to the victim's airway. Note burns around the mouth or nose or the rest of the face that may signal that air passages or lungs have been burned (Fig. 9-26). If you suspect a burned airway or burned lungs, call 9-1-1 immediately and continue to monitor breathing. Air passages may swell, impairing or stopping breathing.

As you check for nonlife-threatening conditions, look for additional signs of burns. Look also for other injuries, especially if an explosion or electric shock occurred.

MIND AT WORK

1. *In the scenario at the beginning of the chapter, Joe is burned. Which type of burn has Joe sustained? Why do you think so?*

2. *Will Joe's burns require medical attention? Why or why not?*

CARE FOR BURNS

If burns are present, follow these four basic care steps:

- Cool the burned area to stop the burning.
- Cover the burned area.
- Prevent infection.
- Minimize shock by keeping the victim from getting chilled or overheated and by having the victim rest (see Chapter 8).

Even after the source of heat has been removed, soft tissue will continue to burn for minutes afterwards, causing more damage.

CHECKING FOR BURNS

As you approach the victim, decide if the scene is safe to enter. Look for fire, smoke, downed electrical wires, and warning signs for

Therefore, it is essential to cool any burned areas immediately with large amounts of cool water (Fig. 9-27, *A*). Do not use ice or ice water other than on small superficial burns. Ice causes loss of heat from the body and further damage to delicate tissues. Use whatever resources are available—a tub, shower, or garden hose. You can apply soaked towels, sheets, or other wet cloths to a burned face or other area that cannot be immersed. Be sure to keep these compresses cool and moist by adding more water. Otherwise, they will quickly absorb the heat from the skin's surface, dry out, and perhaps stick to the burned area. Remove any jewelry from the victim.

Allow several minutes for the burned area to cool. If pain continues when the area is removed from the water, continue cooling. When the burn is cool, remove all clothing from the area by carefully pulling or cutting material away (Fig. 9-27, *B*). Do not try to remove any clothing that is sticking to skin.

Burns often expose sensitive nerve endings. Cover the burned area to keep out air and help reduce pain (Fig. 9-27, *C*). Use dry, sterile dressings if possible, and loosely bandage them in place. The bandage should not put pressure on the burn surface. If the burn covers a large area of the body, cover it with clean, dry sheets or other cloth.

Covering the burn also helps to prevent infection. *Do not put ointments, butter, oil, or other commercial or home remedies on blisters or deep burns or on any burn that will receive medical attention.* Oils and ointments seal in heat, do not relieve pain well, and will have to be removed by medical personnel. Other home remedies can contaminate open skin areas, causing infection. Do not break blisters. Intact skin helps prevent infection.

For small superficial burns and burns with open blisters that are not sufficiently severe or extensive to require medical attention, care for the burned area as an open wound. Cool the area. Wash the area with soap and water, and keep the area clean. Apply an antibiotic ointment, and watch for signs of infection. A pharmacist or doctor may be able to recommend products that are effective in caring for superficial burns, such as sunburn.

Deep burns can cause shock as a result of pain and loss of body fluids. Lay the victim

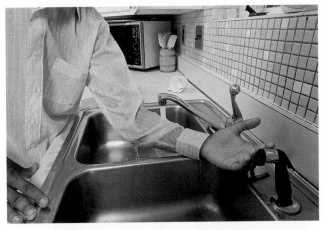

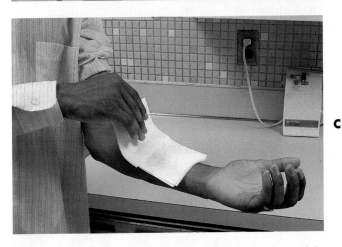

Figure 9-27   A, Large amounts of cool water are essential to cool burned areas. **B,** Remove any clothing covering the burned area. **C,** Cover the burned area.

down unless he or she is having difficulty breathing. Elevate burned areas above the level of the heart, if possible. Burn victims have a tendency to become chilled. Help the victim maintain normal body temperature by protecting him or her from drafts.

SPECIAL SITUATIONS

Burns can be caused by chemicals, electricity, and radiation. These burns have special requirements for care.

Chemical Burns

Chemical burns are common in industrial settings but also occur in the home. Typically, burns result from chemicals that are strong acids or alkalis. Cleaning solutions, such as household bleach, drain cleaners, toilet bowl cleaners; paint strippers; and lawn or garden chemicals are common sources of caustic chemicals, or chemicals that can eat away or destroy tissues. These substances can quickly injure the skin. As with heat burns, the stronger the chemical and the longer the contact, the more severe the burn. The chemical will continue to burn as long as it is on the skin. You must remove the chemical from the body as quickly as possible and call EMS personnel.

Flush the burn with large amounts of cool, running water (Fig. 9-28). Continue flushing until EMS personnel arrive. If the chemical is dry or a powdered form, brush the chemical from the skin with a gloved hand or a piece of cloth. Then flush the residue from the skin with water. Do not use a forceful flow of water from a hose; the force may further damage burned skin. Have the victim remove contaminated clothes, if possible, while you are continuing to flush the area. Do not forget the eyes. If an eye is burned by a chemical, flush the affected eye with water until EMS personnel arrive. Tip the head so that the affected eye is lower than the unaffected eye as you flush (Fig. 9-29). Doing so helps prevent the chemical from getting into the unharmed eye. Flush from the nose outward. If both eyes are affected, direct the flow to the bridge of the nose and flush both eyes from the inner corner outward. Be aware that chemicals can be inhaled, potentially damaging the airway or lungs. Call EMS personnel if you believe chemicals have been inhaled, and monitor breathing.

Electrical Burns

The human body is a good conductor of electricity. When someone comes in contact with an electrical source, such as a power line, a malfunctioning household appliance, or lightning, he or she conducts the electricity through the body. Electrical resistance of body parts produces heat, which can cause burn injuries (Fig. 9-30). The severity of an electrical burn depends on the type and amount of contact, the current's path through the body, and how long the contact lasted. Electrical burns are often deep. The victim may have an entrance wound and an exit wound where the current left the body. Although these wounds may look superficial, the tissues below may be severely damaged.

Electrical injuries cause problems in addition to burns. Electricity can make the heart beat erratically or even stop. Respiratory arrest may occur.

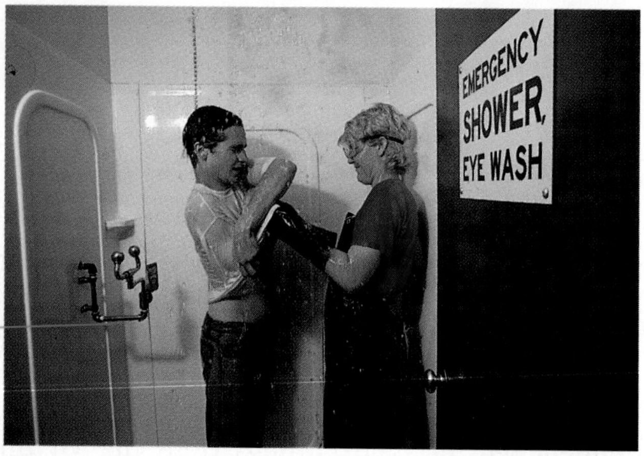

Figure 9-28 Flush a chemical burn with large amounts of cool running water.

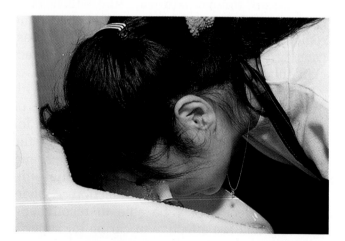

Figure 9-29 Flush the affected eye with cool water in the case of a chemical burn to the eye. Some facilities may have special eyewash stations.

STRIKING DISTANCE

In medieval times, people believed that ringing church bells would dissipate lightning during thunderstorms. It was an unfortunate superstition for the bell ringers. Over one period of 33 years, lightning struck 386 church steeples and 103 bell ringers died (Kessler E).

Church bell ringers have dropped off the list of people most likely to be struck during a thunderstorm, but lightning strikes remain extremely dangerous. On average, lightning causes more deaths annually in the United States than any other weather hazard, including blizzards, hurricanes, floods, tornadoes, earthquakes, and volcanic eruptions. The National Weather Service estimates that lightning kills nearly 100 people annually and injures about 300 others.

National Oceanic and Atmospheric Administration (NOAA)

Lightning occurs when particles of water, ice, and air moving inside storm clouds lose electrons. Eventually, the cloud becomes divided into layers of positive and negative particles. Most electrical currents run between the layers inside the cloud. However, occasionally, the negative charge flashes toward the ground, which has a positive charge. An electrical current snakes back and forth between the ground and the cloud many times in the seconds that we see a flash crackle down from the sky. Anything tall—a tower, a tree, or a person—becomes a path for the electrical current.

Traveling at speeds up to 300 miles per second, a lightning strike can hurl a person through the air, burn his or her clothes off, and sometimes cause the heart to stop beating. The most severe lightning strikes carry up to 50 million volts of electricity, enough to light 13,000 homes. Lightning can "flash" over a person's body, or, in its more dangerous path, it can travel through blood vessels and nerves to reach the ground.

Besides burns, lightning can also cause neurologic damage, fractures, and loss of hearing or eyesight. The victim sometimes acts confused and may describe the episode as getting hit on the head or hearing an explosion.

Use common sense around thunderstorms. If you see a storm approaching in the distance, do not wait until you are drenched to seek shelter. If a thunderstorm threatens, the National Weather Service advises you to—

- Go inside a large building or home.
- Get inside a car and roll up the windows.
- Stop swimming or boating as soon as you see or hear a storm. Water conducts electricity.
- Stay away from the telephone, except in an emergency. Telephone wires that are not properly grounded can conduct lightning into a building.
- Stay away from telephone poles and tall trees if you are caught outside.
- Stay off hilltops; try to crouch down in a ravine or valley.
- Stay away from farm equipment and small metal vehicles such as motorcycles, bicycles, and golf carts.
- Avoid wire fences, clotheslines, metal pipes and rails, and other conductors of electricity.
- Stay several yards apart from other people if you are in a group.

SOURCES

Kessler E: *The thunderstorm in human affairs,* Norman, Oklahoma, University of Oklahoma, 1983.

Randall T: "50 million volts may crash through a lightning victim," *The Chicago Tribune,* Section 2D, August 13, 1989, p.1.

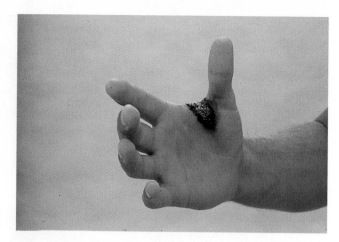

Figure 9-30   An electrical burn may severely damage underlying tissues.

Figure 9-31   Solar radiation burns can be painful.

The signs of electrical injury include—

*Smell

- Unconsciousness.
- Dazed, confused behavior.
- Obvious burns on the skin's surface.
- Breathing difficulty or no breathing.
- Burns both where the current entered and where it exited the body, often on the hand or foot.

Suspect a possible electrical injury if you hear a sudden loud pop or bang or see an unexpected flash.

Never approach a victim of an electrical injury until you are sure the power is turned off. *If a power line is down, call 9-1-1 or the local emergency number and wait for the fire department and the power company to arrive.* If people are in a car with a downed wire across it, tell them to stay in the vehicle and remain still.

To care for a victim of an electrical injury, make sure the scene is safe. The source of the electricity must be turned off. Check for other hazards. Call EMS personnel immediately. When the scene is safe, check and care for any life-threatening conditions. The victim may have breathing difficulties or be in cardiac arrest.

In your check for nonlife-threatening conditions, look for two burn sites, one where the current entered and one where it exited. Cover any burn injuries with a dry, sterile dressing, and give care for shock. Check for fractures.

With a victim of lightning, look for life-threatening conditions, such as respiratory or cardiac arrest. The victim may also have frac-

tures, including spinal fracture, so do not move him or her. Any burns are a lesser problem.

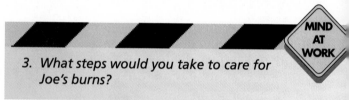

3. **What steps would you take to care for Joe's burns?**

Radiation Burns

Both the solar radiation of the sun and other types of radiation can cause burns. Solar burns are similar to heat burns. Usually they are mild but can be painful (Fig. 9-31). They may blister, involving more than one layer of skin. Care for sunburns as you would any other burn. Cool the burn and protect the burned area from further damage by staying out of the sun. (See Chapter 18 for more information on sunburn.) People are rarely exposed to other types of radiation unless working in special settings, such as certain medical, industrial, or research facilities. If you work in such settings, you will be informed and will be required to take precautions to prevent overexposure. Training is also provided to teach you how to prevent and respond to radiation emergencies.

SUMMARY

Caring for wounds involves a few simple steps. You need to control bleeding and minimize the risk of infection. Remember that with minor wounds, your primary concern is to cleanse the wound to prevent infection. With major wounds, you should control the bleeding quickly and seek medical attention. Wear gloves or use a barrier such as plastic wrap, dressings, or clean folded cloth to avoid contact with blood. Dressings and bandages, when correctly applied, help control bleeding, reduce pain, and can minimize the danger of infection.

Burns damage the layers of the skin and sometimes the internal structures as well. Heat, chemicals, electricity, and radiation all cause burns. When caring for a burn victim, always first ensure your personal safety. When the scene is safe, approach the victim, check for life-threatening conditions and for nonlife-threatening conditions, if necessary. Follow the steps for burn care. In addition, always check for inhalation injury if the person has a heat or chemical burn. With electrical burns and victims of lightning strike, check carefully for additional problems such as breathing difficulty, cardiac problems, and fractures.

In Chapter 10, you will learn how to provide care for injuries involving muscles and bones.

Answers to Application Questions

1. Joe's burn is probably a deep burn. The heat from steam and scalding fluid is likely to damage more than the first layer of skin.

2. Joe's burns will require medical attention. They cover more than one body part.

3. Call EMS personnel. Find a source of cool water and cool the burn. Remove any clothing from the burned areas. Cover the burned areas. Minimize shock by having Joe rest and keeping him from getting chilled or overheated. Consider the possibility of inhalation burns, so check for breathing difficulty.

STUDY QUESTIONS

1. Match each term with the correct definition.

   a. Soft tissue
   b. Critical burn
   c. Closed wound
   d. Open wound
   e. Bandages
   f. Deep burn

   __B__ Any burn that is potentially life threatening, disabling, or disfiguring.

   __F__ A burn that destroys skin and underlying tissues.

   __A__ The layers of the skin, fat, and muscles.

   __E__ Wrappings that hold dressings in place.

   __C__ Injury resulting in tissue damage beneath the skin's surface, while the skin remains intact.

   __D__ Injury resulting in a break in the skin's surface.

2. Match each type of injury to its example.

    a. Abrasion   c. Puncture
    b. Avulsion   d. Contusion

    __b__ Torn earlobe

    __d__ Black eye

    __a__ Scraped knee

    __c__ Gunshot wound

3. Match each type of wound with the appropriate care.

    a. A major open wound   c. A minor open wound
    b. A major open wound   d. A severed body part
        with an embedded object

    __A__ Cover with dressing and pressure bandage.

    __C__ Wash the wound thoroughly with soap and water.

    __D__ Wrap and place in plastic bag and then on ice.

    __B__ Use bulky dressings to stabilize.

4. List four signs and symptoms of infection.

5. List two purposes of bandaging.

6. List and describe four types of open wounds.

7. List four sources of burns.

8. List two types of burns.

In questions 9 through 24, circle the letter of the correct answer.

9. How would you protect a minor open wound from infection?

    a. Wash the area with soap and water.
    b. Apply a sterile dressing.
    c. Apply an antibiotic ointment.
    d. All of the above.

10. Which of the following is a sign of infection?

    a. Swelling or reddening around the wound
    b. Tingling in the injured area
    c. A cool sensation
    d. a and b

11. Which would you do to care for an infected wound?

    a. Keep the area clean.
    b. Apply warm, wet compresses and an antibiotic ointment.
    c. Elevate the injured area.
    d. All of the above.

12. Which statement applies to open wounds?

    a. They always bleed heavily.
    b. They are at risk for infection.
    c. They must always be cleaned immediately.
    d. All of the above.

13. Which distinguishes major open wounds from minor open wounds?

    a. The amount of dirt in the wound
    b. The depth of tissue damage
    c. The amount of pain that the victim is experiencing
    d. All of the above

14. Which should you do in caring for a major open wound?

    a. Apply a dressing and control bleeding.
    b. Wash the wound.
    c. Apply an occlusive dressing.
    d. All of the above.

15. Which should you do when caring for an injury in which the body part has been completely severed?

    a. Place the part directly on ice.
    b. Seek medical assistance and make sure the part is transported with the victim.
    c. Wash the body part thoroughly with soap and water.
    d. b and c.

16. Which states the value of immunizations?

    a. They provide lifetime protection against all threats of infection.
    b. They prepare your body to defend against certain infections.
    c. They stimulate the body to produce more blood.
    d. a and c.

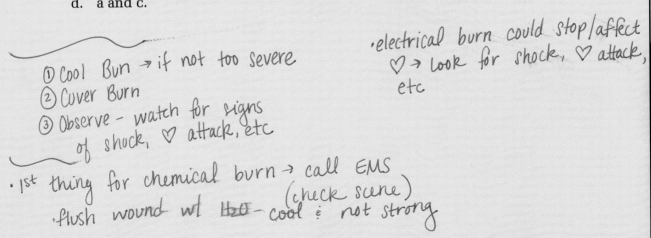

① Cool Burn → if not too severe
② Cover Burn
③ Observe - watch for signs of shock, ♡ attack, etc

•electrical burn could stop/affect ♡ → look for shock, ♡ attack, etc

•1st thing for chemical burn → call EMS (check scene)
•flush wound w/ H₂O - cool ̄c not strong

17. Six-year-old Laura falls on a sharp stick that stabs her leg and breaks off in the wound. What should her brother Alec do to care for the wound?

    a. Remove the object.
    b. Allow the area to bleed freely.
    c. Stabilize the object in the position in which he finds it.
    d. b and c.

18. Which should you do when applying bandages?

    a. Cover the dressing completely.
    b. Cover fingers or toes.
    c. Remove any blood-soaked bandages and apply new ones.
    d. All of the above.

19. Which could swelling and discoloration indicate?

    a. A closed wound
    b. Damage to underlying structures
    c. Internal bleeding
    d. All of the above

20. Which would you do in caring for a closed wound?

    a. Use a warm compress.
    b. Apply cold and elevate the injured area.
    c. Keep the injured area below the level of the heart.
    d. a and b.

21. Which would you do first in caring for an electrical burn injury?

    a. Remove the victim from the power source.
    b. Check for life-threatening conditions.
    c. Make sure the power source is turned off.
    d. Look for two burn sites.

22. Which burns require professional medical attention?

    a. Burns that cover more than one body part
    b. Burns resulting from electricity, explosions, or chemicals
    c. Burns whose victims are having difficulty breathing
    d. All of the above

23. The chemist at the lab table near you spills a liquid corrosive chemical on his arm. Which would you do first?

    a. Remove the chemical with a clean cloth.
    b. Put a sterile dressing over the burn site.
    c. Flush the burn with water.
    d. Have the victim remove contaminated clothes.

24. Luke's grandmother was burned on one leg and foot when a pan of boiling water tipped off the stove. Which should Luke have done first to care for her?

    a. Put ice on the burned area.
    b. Put a dry, sterile dressing on the burned area.
    c. Help her put her foot and leg in the bath tub and flood it with cool water.
    d. Wash the area and then apply a burn ointment.

Answers are listed in Appendix A.

CHAPTER 10

*M*usculoskeletal Injuries

WHAT YOU SHOULD LEARN

After reading this chapter, you should be able to—

1. Identify the four main structures of the musculoskeletal system.

2. List six common signs and symptoms of musculoskeletal injuries.

3. List three signs and symptoms that would cause you to suspect a serious musculoskeletal injury.

4. Describe the general care for musculoskeletal injuries.

5. Describe how to care for serious musculoskeletal injuries.

6. List the five purposes of immobilizing an injury.

7. List four principles of splinting.

8. Define the key terms for this chapter.

I never felt so helpless. Before I could even reach out to help her, my sister Rita picked up her suitcase and started down the front steps toward the street. She was talking to me, not looking down, and she missed the first step. They were stone steps, and I think her left shoulder hit all of them before she ended up in a heap at the bottom. By the time I reached her, I could see she was really hurt. She was conscious, but she didn't seem to be able to get up. She was lying down, holding her left shoulder, and moaning. The left arm just hung there. "Help me," she gasped. Not one other person was in sight.

Introduction

Injuries to the musculoskeletal system are common. Millions of people at home, at work, or at play injure their muscles, bones, or joints. No age group is exempt. A person may fall and bruise the muscles of the hip, making walking painful. Heavy machinery may fall on a worker and break ribs, making breathing difficult. A person who braces a hand against a dashboard in a car crash may injure the bones at the shoulder, disabling the arm. A person who falls while skiing may twist a leg, tearing the supportive tissues of a knee and making it impossible to stand or move.

Although musculoskeletal injuries are almost always painful, they are rarely life—threatening when cared for properly. However, when not recognized and taken care of properly, they can have serious consequences and even result in permanent disability or death. In this chapter, you will learn how to recognize and care for musculoskeletal injuries. Developing a better understanding of the structure and function of the body's framework will help you assess musculoskeletal injuries and give appropriate care.

THE MUSCULOSKELETAL SYSTEM

The musculoskeletal system is made up of muscles and bones that form the skeleton, as well as connective tissues, tendons, and ligaments. Together, these structures give the body shape, form, and stability. Bones and muscles connect to form various body segments. They work together to provide body movement.

Muscles

Muscles are soft tissues that are able to contract and relax. The body has over 600 muscles (Fig. 10-1). Most are **skeletal muscles,** which attach to the bones. Skeletal muscles account for most of your lean body weight (body weight without excess fat). All body movements result from skeletal muscles contracting and relaxing. Through a pathway of nerves, the brain directs muscles to contract, causing movement. Skeletal muscle actions are under your conscious control. Because you move them voluntarily, skeletal muscles are also called voluntary muscles. Skeletal muscles also protect the bones, nerves, and blood vessels.

Most skeletal muscles are anchored to bone at each end by strong, cordlike, fibrous tissues called **tendons.** Muscles and their adjoining tendons extend across joints. When the brain sends a command to move, nerve impulses travel through the spinal cord and nerve pathways to the individual muscles and stimulate the muscle fibers to contract. When the muscle fibers contract, pulling the ends of the muscle closer together, the muscles pull the bones, causing motion at the joint.

Key Terms

Bone: A dense, hard tissue that forms the skeleton.

Dislocation: The displacement of a bone from its normal position at a joint.

Fracture: A break or disruption in bone.

Immobilize: Using a splint or other method to keep an injured body part from moving.

Joint: A structure where two or more bones are joined.

Ligament: A fibrous band that holds bones together at a joint.

Muscle: A tissue that contracts and relaxes to create movement.

Skeletal muscles: Muscles that attach to bones.

Splint: A device used to immobilize body parts; to immobilize body parts with such a device.

Sprain: The stretching and tearing of ligaments and other soft tissue structures at a joint.

Strain: The stretching and tearing of muscles and tendons.

Tendon: A cordlike, fibrous band that attaches muscle to bone.

FRONT VIEW **BACK VIEW**

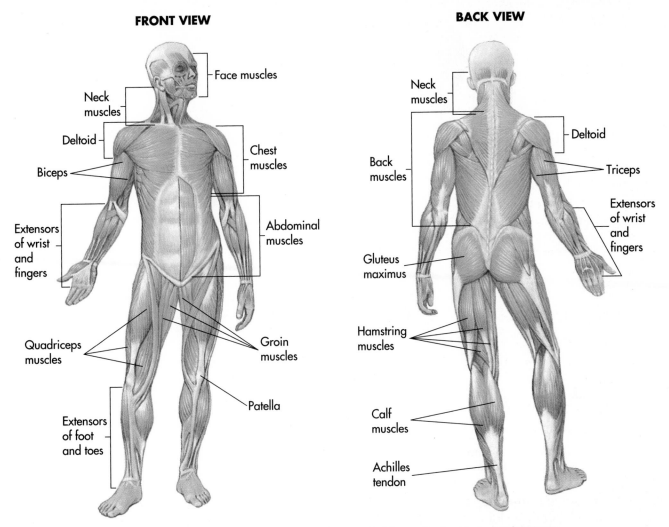

Figure 10-1   The body has over 600 muscles, most of them attached to bones by strong tissues called tendons. The shortening and lengthening of the muscles are what make the body move.

Muscles in a group often pull at the same time. For instance, the hamstring muscles are a group of muscles at the back of the thigh. When the hamstrings contract, the leg bends at the knee joint. The biceps are a group of muscles at the front of the arm. When the biceps contract, the arm bends at the elbow joint. Generally, when one group of muscles contracts, another group of muscles on the opposite side of the body part relaxes (Fig. 10-2). Even simple tasks, such as bending to pick up an object from the floor, involve a complex series of movements in which different muscle groups contract and relax.

Injuries to the brain, the spinal cord, or the nerves can affect muscle control. A loss of muscle movement is called **paralysis.** Less serious or isolated muscle injuries may only affect strength, because adjacent muscles can often do double duty and take over for the injured muscle.

The Skeleton

The skeleton is formed by over 200 bones of various sizes and shapes (Fig. 10-3). These bones shape the skeleton, giving each body part a characteristic form. The skeleton protects vital organs and other soft tissues. The skull protects the brain (Fig. 10-4, *A*). The ribs protect the heart and lungs (Fig. 10-4, *B*). The spinal cord is protected by the canal formed by the bones that form the spinal column (Fig. 10-4, *C*). Two or more bones come together

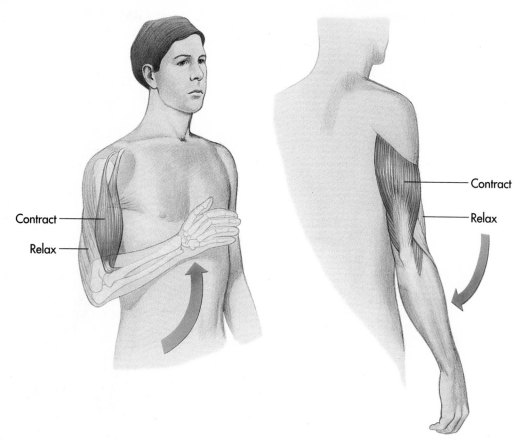

Figure 10-2   Movement occurs when one group of muscles contracts and an opposing group of muscles relaxes.

to form joints. ***Ligaments,*** fibrous bands that hold bones together at joints, give the skeleton stability and, with the muscles, help maintain posture.

Bones

Bones are hard, dense tissues. Their strong, rigid structure helps them to withstand stresses that cause injuries. The shape of bones depends on what the bones do and the stresses placed on them. For instance, although similar to the bones of the arms, the bones of the legs are much larger and stronger because they carry the body's weight (Fig. 10-5, p. 217).

Bones have a rich supply of blood and nerves. Some bones store and manufacture red blood cells and supply them to the circulating blood. Bone injuries can bleed and are usually painful. The bleeding can become life threatening if not properly cared for. Bones heal by forming new bone cells within a fibrous network of tissue that forms between the broken bone ends. Bone is the only body tissue that can regenerate in this way.

Bones weaken with age. Bones in young children are softer and more porous than adults' bones, so they bend and break more easily. At puberty, a child's bones become as hard as an adult's. As people age, their bones lose mass and density and are more likely to give way to even everyday stresses, which can cause significant injuries. For instance, an elderly person pivoting with the weight on one leg can break the strongest bone in the body, the femur (thigh bone). The gradual, progressive weakening of bone is called **osteoporosis.**

Bones are classified as long, short, flat, or irregular (Fig. 10-6, p. 218). Long bones are longer than they are wide. Long bones include the bones of the upper arm (humerus), the forearm (radius and ulna), the thigh (femur), and lower leg (tibia and fibula). Short bones are about as wide as they are long. Short bones include the small bones of the hand (metacarpals) and feet (metatarsals). Flat bones have a relatively thin, flat shape. Flat bones include the breastbone (sternum), the ribs, and the shoulder blade (scapula). Bones that do not fit in the

The Breaking Point

Osteoporosis, a degenerative bone disorder usually discovered after the age of 60, affects 30 percent of people over age 65. It will affect one out of four American women and occurs less frequently in men. Fair-skinned women with ancestors from northern Europe, the British Isles, Japan, or China are genetically predisposed to osteoporosis. Inactive people are more susceptible to osteoporosis.

Osteoporosis occurs when the calcium content of bones decreases. Normally, bones are hard, dense tissues that endure tremendous stresses. Bone-building cells constantly repair damage that occurs as a result of everyday stresses, keeping bones strong. Calcium is a key to bone growth, development, and repair. When the calcium content of bones decreases, bones become frail, less dense, and less able to repair the normal damage they incur.

This loss of density and strength leaves bones more susceptible to fractures. Where once tremendous force was necessary, fractures now may occur with little or no aggravation, especially to hips, vertebrae, and wrists. Spontaneous fractures are those that occur without trauma. The victim may be taking a walk or washing dishes when the fracture occurs. Some hip fractures thought to be caused by falls are actually spontaneous fractures that caused the victim's fall.

Osteoporosis can begin as early as age 30 to 35. The amount of calcium absorbed from the diet naturally declines with age, making calcium intake increasingly important. When calcium in the diet is inadequate, calcium in bones is withdrawn and used by the body to meet its other needs, leaving bones weakened.

Building strong bones before age 35 is the key to preventing osteoporosis. Calcium and exercise are necessary to bone building. The United States Recommended Daily Allowance (U.S. RDA) is currently 800 milligrams of calcium each day for adults. Many physicians recommend 1000 milligrams for women age 19 and over. Three to four daily servings of low-fat dairy products should provide adequate calcium. Vitamin D is also necessary because it aids in absorption of calcium. Exposure to sunshine enables the body to make vitamin D. Fifteen minutes of sunshine on the hands and face of a young, light-skinned individual are enough to supply the RDA of 5 to 10 micrograms of vitamin D per day. Dark-skinned people and people over age of 65 need more sun exposure. People who do not receive adequate sun exposure need to consume vitamin D. The best sources are vitamin-fortified milk and fatty fish such as tuna, salmon, and eel.

Calcium supplements combined with vitamin D are available for those who don't take in adequate calcium. However, before taking a calcium supplement, consult a physician. Many highly advertised calcium supplements are ineffective because they do not dissolve well in the body.

Exercise seems to increase bone density and the activity of bone-building cells. Regular exercise may reduce the rate of bone loss by promoting new bone formation and also stimulate the skeletal system to repair itself. An effective exercise program, such as aerobics, jogging, or walking, involves the weight-bearing muscles of the legs. If you have any questions regarding your health and osteoporosis, consult a physician or health care provider.

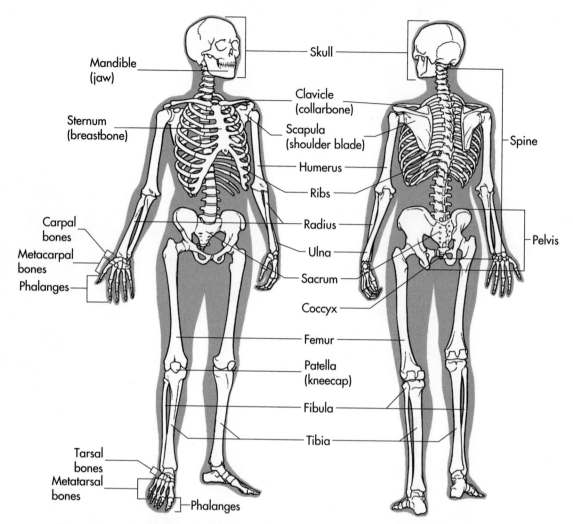

Mandible (jaw)

Sternum (breastbone)

Carpal bones

Metacarpal bones

Phalanges

Tarsal bones

Metatarsal bones

Phalanges

Skull

Clavicle (collarbone)

Scapula (shoulder blade)

Humerus

Ribs

Radius

Ulna

Sacrum

Coccyx

Femur

Patella (kneecap)

Fibula

Tibia

Spine

Pelvis

Figure 10-3 Over 200 bones in various sizes and shapes form the skeleton. The skeleton protects many of the organs inside the body.

other categories are called irregular bones, which include the vertebrae and the bones that make up the skull, including the bones of the face. Bones are weakest at the points where they change shape, and they usually fracture at these points. In children, the bones are weakest at the growth plates, located at the ends of long bones.

The bony structures that form the skeleton define the parts of the body. For example, the head is defined by the bones that form the skull, and the chest is defined by the bones that form the rib cage. Knowing the locations of the major bones in the body and the joints they form can help you locate a possible source of pain or recognize the general nature of an injury.

Joints

A *joint* is formed by the ends of two or more bones coming together at one place. Most joints allow motion. However, the ends of the bones at some joints are fused together, which restricts motion. Fused bones, such as the bones of the skull, form solid structures that protect their contents (Fig. 10-7).

Joints that allow movement are held together by tough, fibrous connective tissues called ligaments (Fig. 10-8). Ligaments resist joint movement. Joints surrounded by ligaments have restricted movement; joints that have few ligaments move more freely. For instance, the shoulder joint, with few ligaments, allows greater motion than the hip joint, although their structures are similar.

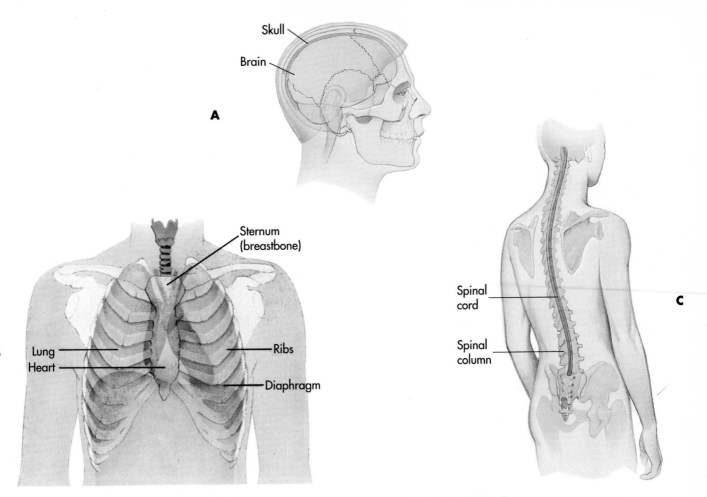

Figure 10-4   **A,** The immovable bones of the skull protect the brain. **B,** The rib cage protects the lungs and heart. **C,** The spinal cord is protected by the vertebrae.

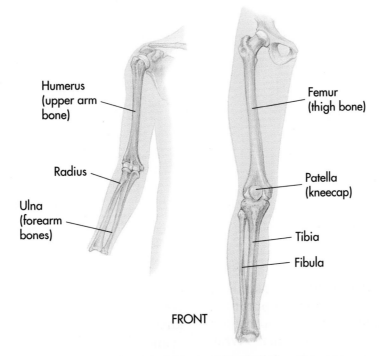

FRONT

Figure 10-5   Leg bones are larger and stronger than arm bones because they carry the body's weight.

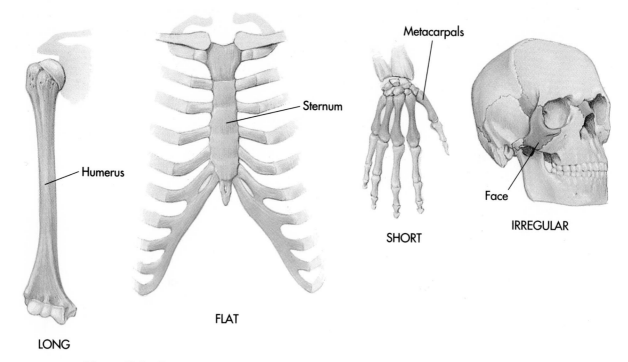

Figure 10-6   Bones vary in shape and size. Bones are weakest at the points where they change shape and usually fracture at these points.

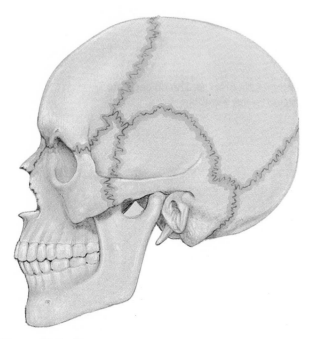

Figure 10-7   Fused bones, such as bones of the skull, form solid structures that protect their contents.

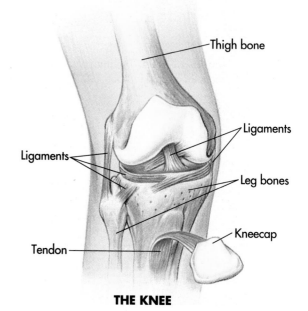

Figure 10-8   A typical joint consists of two or more bones held together by ligaments.

Joints that move more freely, such as the ankle and shoulder, have less natural support and are therefore more prone to injury. However, all joints have a normal range of movement. When a joint is forced beyond its normal range, ligaments stretch and tear, making the joint unsta-ble. Unstable joints can be disabling, particularly when they are weight bearing, such as the knee or ankle. Unstable joints are also prone to reinjury and often develop arthritis in later years.

INJURIES TO THE MUSCULOSKELETAL SYSTEM

Injuries to the musculoskeletal system are more commonly caused by mechanical forms of energy but can also occur from heat, chemical, or electrical energy, for example, when a person is deeply burned or struck by lightning. Mechanical energy produces direct, indirect, twisting, and contracting forces (Fig. 10-9). These forces can injure the structures of the musculoskeletal system. A direct force is the force of an object striking the body and causing injury at the point of impact. Direct forces can either be blunt or penetrating. For example, a fist striking the chin can break the jaw, or penetrating objects, such as bullets and knives, can injure structures beneath the skin at the point where they penetrate.

An indirect force travels through the body and causes injury to a body part away from the point of impact. For example, a fall on an outstretched hand may result in an injury to the shoulder or collarbone.

DIRECT

INDIRECT

TWISTING

CONTRACTING

Figure 10-9 Four forces—direct, indirect, twisting, and contracting—cause 76 percent of all injuries.

In twisting, one part of the body stays in one position while another part of the body turns. The twisting action can force body parts beyond their normal range of motion, causing injury. For example, if a ski and its binding keep the lower leg in one position while the body falls in another, the knee may be forced beyond its normal range of motion, causing injury. Twisting injuries are not always this complex. They more often occur as a result of simply stepping off a curb (ankle) or turning to reach for an out-of-the-way object (back).

Sudden or powerful muscle contractions can result in musculoskeletal injuries. These injuries commonly occur in sports activities, such as throwing a ball a long distance or hard without properly warming up or sprinting when out of shape. However, our daily routines also require sudden and powerful muscle contractions, for example, when we suddenly turn to catch a heavy object, such as a falling child. Although it happens rarely, sudden, powerful muscle contractions can even pull a piece of bone away from the point at which it is normally attached.

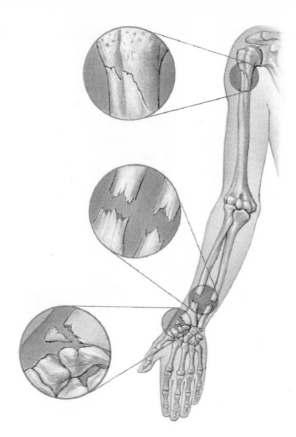

Figure 10-10   Fractures include chipped or cracked bones and bones broken all the way through.

Types of Musculoskeletal Injuries

The four basic types of musculoskeletal injuries are fracture, dislocation, sprain, and strain. Injuries to the musculoskeletal system can be classified according to the body structures that are damaged. Some injuries may involve damage to more than one structure. For example, a direct blow to the knee may injure both ligaments and bones. Injuries are also classified by the nature and extent of the damage.

Fracture

A *fracture* is a break or disruption in bone tissue. Fractures include chipped or cracked bones, as well as bones that are broken all the way through (Fig. 10-10). Fractures are commonly caused by direct and indirect forces. However, if strong enough, twisting forces and strong muscle contractions can cause a fracture.

Fractures are classified as open or closed. An **open fracture** involves an open wound. Open fractures often occur when the limb is severely angulated or bent, causing bone ends to tear the skin and surrounding soft tissues or when an object penetrates the skin and breaks the bone. Bone ends do not have to be visible for a fracture to be classified as open. **Closed fractures** leave the skin unbroken and are more common than open fractures. Open fractures are more serious than closed fractures because of the risks of infection and severe blood loss. Although fractures are rarely an immediate threat to life, any fracture involving a large bone, such as the femur or pelvis, can cause severe shock because bones and soft tissue may bleed heavily.

Fractures are not always obvious unless a telltale sign, such as an open wound with protruding bone ends or a severely deformed body part, is present. But the way in which the injury occurred is often enough to suggest a possible fracture.

Dislocation

A *dislocation* is a displacement or separation of a bone from its normal position at a joint (Fig. 10-11). Dislocations are usually caused by severe forces. A force violent enough to cause a dislocation can also cause a fracture and can damage nearby nerves and blood vessels. Some

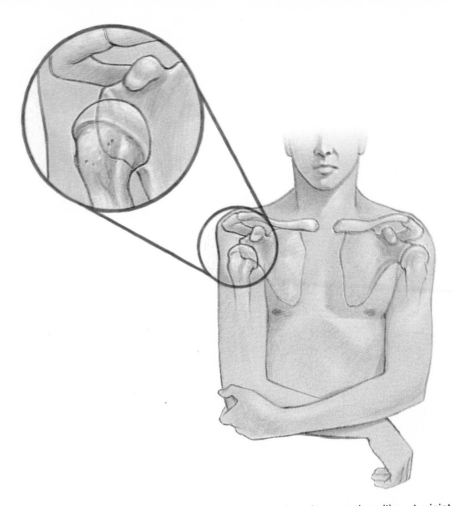

Figure 10-11   A dislocation is a separation of bone from its normal position at a joint.

joints, such as the shoulder's or finger's, dislocate easily because their bones and ligaments are small and fragile. Others, such as the joints of the elbow or the spine, are well protected because of the shape of the bones and the way they fit together and therefore dislocate less easily.

Dislocations are generally more obvious than fractures because the joint appears deformed (Fig. 10-12). The displaced bone end often causes an abnormal lump, ridge, or depression, sometimes making dislocations easier to identify than other musculoskeletal injuries. The person will not or cannot move the affected joint.

Sprain

A *sprain* is the partial or complete tearing of ligaments and other tissues at a joint (Fig.10-13, *A*). A sprain usually results when the bones that form a joint are forced beyond their normal range of motion. The more ligaments that are torn, the more severe the injury. The sudden,

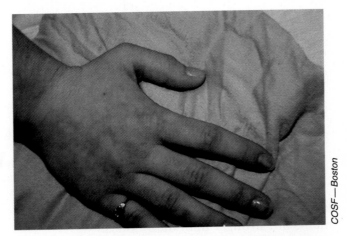

COSF—Boston

Figure 10-12   Because of deformity, dislocations are generally more obvious than fractures.

violent forcing of a joint beyond its limit can completely rupture ligaments and even dislocate the bones. Severe sprains may also involve a fracture of the bones that form the joint. Ligaments may pull bone away from its point of attachment. Young children are more likely to

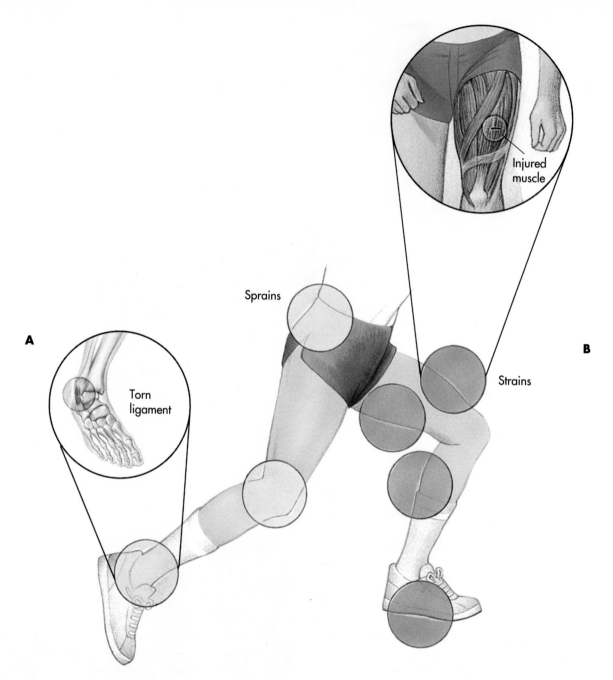

Figure 10-13   A, Injuries to joints are usually sprains. **B,** Injuries to the soft tissue between joints, the muscles and tendons, are strains.

have a fracture than a sprain because their ligaments are stronger than their bones.

Mild sprains, which stretch ligament fibers, generally heal quickly. The victim may have only a brief period of pain or discomfort and quickly return to activity with little or no soreness. For this reason, people often neglect sprains and the joint is often reinjured. Severe sprains or sprains that involve a fracture usually cause pain when the joint is moved or used. The weight-bearing joints of the ankle and knee and the joints of the

fingers and wrist are those most commonly sprained.

Surprisingly, a sprain can be more disabling than a fracture. When fractures heal, they usually leave the bone as strong as it was before, or stronger, decreasing the likelihood that a repeat break will occur at the same spot. On the other hand, ligaments cannot regenerate. If the stretched or torn ligaments are not repaired, they render the joint less stable and may restrict activity. The injured area may also be more susceptible to reinjury.

Strain

A *strain* is a stretching and tearing of muscle or tendon fibers. It is sometimes called a muscle pull or tear. Because tendons are tougher and stronger than muscles, tears usually occur in the muscle itself or where the muscle attaches to the tendon (Fig. 10-13, *B*). Strains are often the result of overexertion, such as lifting something too heavy or working a muscle too hard. They can also result from sudden or uncoordinated movement. Strains commonly involve the muscles in the neck or back, the front or back of the thigh, or the back of the lower leg. Strains of the neck and lower back can be particularly painful and therefore disabling.

Like sprains, strains are often neglected, which commonly leads to reinjury. Strains sometimes recur chronically, especially to the muscles of the neck, lower back, and the back of the thigh. Neck and back problems are two of the leading causes of absenteeism from work, accounting for billions of dollars in worker's compensation claims and lost productivity annually.

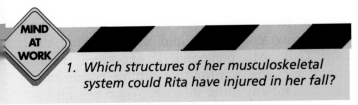

MIND AT WORK

1. Which structures of her musculoskeletal system could Rita have injured in her fall?

Checking for Musculoskeletal Injuries

You identify and care for injuries to the musculoskeletal system during the check for nonlife-threatening conditions. Because the injuries appear similar, it may be difficult for you to determine exactly what type of injury has occurred. As you do the check, think about how the body normally looks and feels. Ask how the injury happened and if there are any areas that are painful. Visually inspect the entire body, beginning with the head. Compare the two sides of the body. Then, carefully check each body part. Do not ask the victim to move any areas in which he or she has pain or discomfort or if you suspect injury to the head or spine. Start with the neck, followed by the shoulders, the chest, and so on. As you conduct the check, look and listen for clues that may indicate a musculoskeletal injury.

Common signs and symptoms of musculoskeletal injuries

Six common signs and symptoms associated with musculoskeletal injuries are—

- Pain.
- Swelling.
- Deformity.
- Discoloration of the skin.
- Inability to use the affected part normally.
- Loss of sensation in the affected part.

Not every injury will have all of these signs and symptoms.

Pain, swelling, and discoloration of the skin commonly occur with any significant injury. Irritation to nerve endings that supply the injured area causes pain. Pain is the body's signal that something is wrong. The injured area may be painful to touch and to move. Swelling is caused by bleeding from damaged blood vessels and tissues in the injured area. However, swelling is often deceiving. It may appear rapidly at the site of injury, develop gradually, or not appear at all. Swelling by itself, therefore, is not a reliable sign of the severity of an injury or of which structures are involved. Bleeding may discolor the skin in surrounding tissues. At first, the skin may only look red. As blood seeps to the skin's surface, the area begins to look bruised.

Deformity is also a sign of significant injury. Abnormal lumps, ridges, depressions, or unusual bends or angles in body parts are types of deformities. Obvious deformity is often a sign of fracture or dislocation (Fig. 10-14). Comparing the injured part to an uninjured part may help you detect deformity.

A victim's inability to move or use an injured part may also indicate a significant injury. The victim may tell you he or she is unable to move or that it is simply too painful to move. Do not assume, however, that a wrist or ankle is not broken just because the victim can move it. Moving or using injured parts can disturb tissues, further irritating nerve endings, which causes or increases pain. Often, the muscles of an affected area contract in an attempt to hold the injured part in place. This muscle contraction helps to reduce pain and prevent additional damage. Similarly, a victim often supports the injured part in the most comfortable position. To manage musculoskeletal injuries,

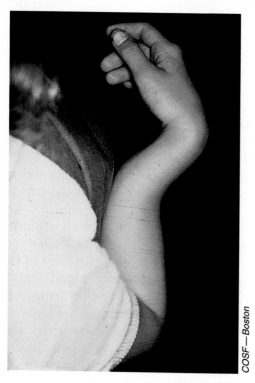

COSF—Boston

Figure 10-14   Serious bone or joint injuries may appear deformed.

- Deformity
- Moderate or severe swelling and discoloration
- Inability to move or use the affected body part
- Bone fragments protruding from a wound
- Victim feels bones grating or felt or heard a snap or pop at the time of injury
- Loss of circulation or sensation in an **extremity** (the shoulders to the fingers; the hips to the toes), or tingling, cold, or bluish color
- Cause of the injury, such as a fall or vehicle crash, suggests the injury may be severe

MIND AT WORK

2. **What would indicate that Rita's injury is severe?**

avoid any motion or use of an injured body part that causes pain. As well as pain, lack of sensation in the affected part can also be a symptom of serious injury or may indicate injury in another area. Fingers or toes, for example, can lose sensation if the leg or arm is injured.

Specific signs and symptoms of musculoskeletal injuries

In the check for nonlife-threatening conditions, you may notice certain telltale signs that can help you determine the type of injury. Often, what the victim feels or can recall from the moment of injury provides important clues.

Sprains and strains are fairly easy to tell apart. Because a sprain involves the soft tissues at a joint, pain, swelling, and deformity are generally confined to the joint area. Strains involve the soft tissue structures that, for the most part, stretch between joints. Therefore, in most strains, pain, swelling, and any deformity are generally in the areas between the joints.

However, it is not always easy to determine if an injury involves a fracture or dislocation or both. Sometimes, the only reliable way to determine the nature of the injury is by X-ray. Always suspect a serious injury when any of the following signs and symptoms are present:

Care for Musculoskeletal Injuries

Some musculoskeletal injuries are obvious because they involve severe deformities, such as protruding bones, or bleeding. The victim may also be in extreme pain. Check for any life-threatening conditions and give appropriate care. Call EMS personnel if necessary. Then check for any nonlife-threatening conditions and care for any other injuries. When you find a musculoskeletal injury, call EMS personnel immediately if—

- The injury involves the head or spine.
- The injury impairs walking or breathing.
- You see or suspect a fracture or dislocation.
- You see or suspect multiple musculoskeletal injuries.

General care

The general care for all musculoskeletal injuries is similar. Just remember rest, ice, and elevation (Fig. 10-15).

Rest. Avoid any movements or activities that cause pain. Help the victim find the most comfortable position. If you suspect head or spine injuries, leave the victim lying flat.

Ice. Regardless of whether you believe the injury is a closed fracture, dislocation, sprain, or strain, apply ice or a cold pack. Cold helps reduce swelling and eases pain and discomfort.

Heat or Cold

Spring is the season of flowers, trees, strains, and sprains. Almost as soon as armchair athletes come out of hibernation to become intramural heroes, emergency departments see an increase in sprained ankles, twisted knees, and strained backs. So what do you do when you attempt the first slide of the softball season and wind up injured? Should you apply heat or apply cold?

The answer is both. First cold, then heat. And it does not matter whether it is a strain or a sprain.

How cold helps initially

When a person twists an ankle or strains his or her back, the tissues underneath the skin are injured. Blood and fluids seep out from the torn blood vessels and cause swelling to occur at the site of the injury. Your initial first aid objective is to keep the in-jured area cool to help control internal bleeding and reduce pain. Cold causes the broken blood vessels to constrict, limiting the blood and fluid that seep out. Cold also reduces muscle spasms and numbs the nerve endings.

How heat helps repair the tissue

A physician will most likely advise applying ice to the injury periodically for about 72 hours or until the swelling goes away. After that, applying heat is often the more appropriate care. Heat speeds up chemical reactions needed to repair the tissue. White blood cells move in to rid the body of infections, and other cells begin the repair process, expediting proper healing of the injury. Applying heat too early, however, can cause swelling to increase, delaying healing. If you are unsure whether to use cold or heat on an injured area, always apply cold until you can consult a physician or health care provider.

STRAIN

SPRAIN

An injury causes damage to blood vessels, causing bleeding in the injured area. Injury irritates nerve endings, causing pain.

Applying ice or a cold pack constricts blood vessels, showing bleeding that causes the injury to swell. Cold deadens nerve endings relieving pain.

Applying heat dilates blood vessels, increasing blood flow to the injured area. Nerve endings become more sensitive.

Figure 10-15   General care for all musculoskeletal injuries is similar. Remember rest, ice, and elevation.

Place a layer of gauze or cloth between the source of cold and the skin to prevent damage to the skin. You can make an ice pack by placing ice in a plastic bag and wrapping it with a towel or cloth or by using a large bag of frozen vegetables, such as peas. Leave an ice or a cold pack on the victim for no longer than 30 minutes. Then remove it for 10 to 15 minutes, and replace it. Do not apply a cold pack to an open fracture because doing so would require you to put pressure on the open fracture site, which could cause discomfort to the victim.

Elevation. Elevating the injured area helps slow the flow of blood, reducing swelling. If possible, elevate the injured area above the level of the heart. *Do not attempt to elevate a part you suspect is fractured or dislocated un-*

less it has been immobilized using a technique called splinting.

Immobilization

If you suspect a serious musculoskeletal injury, you must **immobilize** the injured part (keep it from moving) before giving additional care, such as applying ice or elevating it.

The purposes of immobilizing an injury are to—

* Lessen pain.
* Prevent further damage to soft tissues, which also reduces the possibility of paralysis.
* Reduce the risk of serious bleeding.
* Reduce the possibility of loss of circulation to the injured part.
* Prevent closed fractures from becoming open fractures.

You can immobilize an injured part by applying a splint, sling, or bandages to keep the injured body part from moving. A **splint** is a device that maintains an injured part in place. An effective splint must extend above and below the injury site (Fig. 10-16, *A* and *B*). For instance, to immobilize a fractured bone, the splint must include the joints above and below the fracture. To immobilize a sprain or dislocation, the splint must include the bones above and below the injured joint.

When using a splint, follow these four basic principles:

* Splint only if you can do it without causing more pain and discomfort to the victim.

A 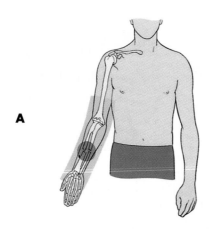   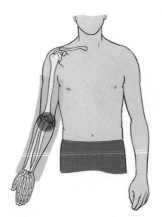 **B**

Figure 10-16   **A,** To immobilize a bone, a splint must include the joints above and below the fracture. **B,** To immobilize a joint, a splint must include the bones above and below the injured joint.

- Splint an injury in the position in which you find it. Do not move, straighten, or bend the injured part.
- Splint the injured area and the joints above and below the injury site.
- Check for proper circulation (feeling, warmth, and color) before and after splinting.

Keep the victim as comfortable as possible, and avoid overheating or chilling. Monitor breathing and signs of circulation. Chapter 11 describes splinting in detail.

3. **What can Rita's sister do to make her more comfortable?**

4. **Should her sister call EMS personnel before providing care for Rita? Why or why not?**

CONSIDERATIONS FOR TRANSPORTING A VICTIM

Some musculoskeletal injuries are obviously minor and do not require professional medical care. Others are not minor and may require you to call EMS personnel. If you discover a life-threatening emergency or think it likely one might develop, call EMS personnel and wait for help. Always call EMS personnel for any injury involving severe bleeding; suspected injuries to the head or spine; and possible serious injuries that may be difficult to transport properly, such as to the back, hips, and legs, or that you are unable to adequately immobilize. Remember that fractures of large bones and severe sprains can bleed severely and are likely to cause shock.

Some injuries are not serious enough for you to call EMS personnel but still require professional medical care. If you decide to transport the victim yourself to a medical facility, follow the general rule: "When in doubt, splint." Always splint the injury before moving the victim. If possible, have someone drive you so that you can continue to provide care. (See Chapter 2 for information on transporting a victim.)

SUMMARY

Sometimes it is difficult to tell whether an injury is a fracture, dislocation, sprain, or strain. Since you cannot be sure which type of injury a victim might have, always care for the injury as if it is serious. If EMS personnel are on the way, do not move the victim. Control any bleeding first, wearing gloves or using appropriate barriers. Take steps to minimize shock and monitor breathing and signs of circulation. If you are going to transport the victim to a medical facility, be sure to immobilize the injury before moving the victim.

Answers to Application Questions

1. Rita could have a serious shoulder injury, possibly injuring the bones, muscles, ligaments, and tendons. She might also have injured her neck and back.

2. Rita is obviously in pain—moaning and holding her shoulder. She repeatedly hit her shoulder while falling. She seems unable to get up. She appears unable to move her left arm.

3. Help her find the most comfortable position; keep from moving her head, neck, and back as much as possible; immobilize her upper extremity and apply ice to the injured area; prevent her from becoming chilled or overheated to delay the onset of shock and keep her comfortable until EMS personnel arrive.

4. Although the injury does not appear to be life-threatening—the victim is conscious, breathing, has signs of circulation, and is not bleeding severely—Rita may well have a fracture or dislocation and could also have injured her head, neck, or back. Call EMS personnel immediately. Then make Rita as comfortable as possible, taking care not to move her head, neck, and back. Watch for signs and symptoms of shock.

STUDY QUESTIONS

1. Match each item with the correct definition.

a. Bone
b. Dislocation
c. Fracture
d. Joint
e. Ligaments
f. Muscle

g. Skeletal muscles
h. Splint
i. Sprain
j. Strain
k. Tendon

H Device used to keep body parts from moving.

B Displacement of a bone from its normal position at a joint.

F Tissue that contracts and relaxes to create movement.

C Broken bone.

A Dense, hard tissue that forms the skeleton.

I Injury that stretches and tears ligaments and other soft tissues at joints.

K Fibrous band attaching muscle to bone.

D Structure formed where two or more bones meet.

J Injury that stretches and tears muscles and tendons.

G Muscles that attach to bones.

E Fibrous bands holding bones together at joints.

2. List three common signs and symptoms of musculoskeletal injuries.

3. List four principles of splinting.

[handwritten notes:]

Injuries to muscles:
1. Ice   2. Immobilize

Muscle to Bone → Tendon
Bone to Bone → Ligament

• joints are on extremeties

In questions 4 through 8, circle the letter of the correct answer.

4. Which should you do when caring for an injured joint?

    a. Take the victim to a place where he or she can lie down.
    b. Straighten the injured area before splinting.
    c. Immobilize the injured area in the position found.
    d. All of the above.

5. Which would lead you to suspect a serious musculoskeletal injury?

    a. You saw severe swelling and discoloration.
    b. The area was significantly deformed.
    c. The victim heard a snap at the time of the injury.
    d. All of the above.

6. You find a person lying at the foot of a steep cliff. Her right leg is twisted at an unusual angle and you can see protruding bones and blood. Which do you do first?

    a. Straighten the leg.
    b. Check for life-threatening conditions.
    c. Use direct pressure to stop the bleeding.
    d. Look for material to use to immobilize the injured area.

7. Why should you immobilize a musculoskeletal injury?

    a. To prevent further soft tissue damage
    b. To lessen pain
    c. To reduce the risk of serious bleeding
    d. All of the above

8. Which step would you take before and after splinting an injury?

    a. Move the splinted area to ensure the victim is not in pain.
    b. Check for feeling, warmth, and color.
    c. Slide the splint down to extend below the injured area.
    d. All of the above.

Answers are listed in Appendix A.

CHAPTER 11

Injuries to the Extremities

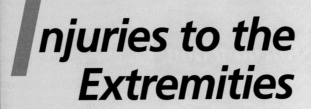

WHAT YOU SHOULD LEARN

After reading this chapter, you should be able to—

1. List seven signs and symptoms that suggest a serious extremity injury.

2. Describe how to care for injuries to the shoulder, upper arm, and elbow.

3. Describe how to care for injuries to the forearm, wrist, and hand.

4. List three specific signs and symptoms of a fractured thigh bone.

5. Describe how to care for injuries to the thigh, lower leg, and knee.

6. Describe how to care for injuries to the ankle and foot.

7. Define the key terms for this chapter.

After reading this chapter and completing the class activities, you should be able to demonstrate—

1. How to make appropriate decisions in an emergency situation involving injuries to the extremities.

2. How to effectively immobilize an injured body part.

They were just getting into their regular morning run, heading down the slope where the path went beside the creek for about 150 yards and then swung up toward the road. The rain earlier must have made the path slippery. Sam was in back, so Mario didn't see him fall, but he certainly heard it. Sam let out a yell. Mario turned around and jogged back to Sam. "It's my knee," Sam moaned. "I don't think I can stand up." His face was twisted with pain. Mario looked at the knee. It looked swollen.

Introduction

njuries to the *extremities,* the shoulder to the fingers and the hip to the toes, are quite common. They range from a simple bruise to an injury with severe serious bleeding, such as a fracture of the femur, or thigh bone. With any injury to the extremities, the prompt care you give can help prevent further pain and damage and a life-long disability.

As you will learn in this chapter, first aid care for soft tissue and musculoskeletal injuries involving the extremities is like care for other parts of the body. In general, control severe bleeding first, wearing gloves or using another barrier. Then rest the injured body part, apply ice or a cold pack, and elevate the area if it does not cause pain and if you do not suspect a fracture or injury to the head, neck, or back. If you suspect a serious injury or need to transport the victim, immobilize the injured body part first and determine what further care is needed. Call EMS personnel and continue to monitor the victim's condition until medical professionals arrive. To minimize shock, keep the victim from getting chilled or overheated, and help the victim rest in the most comfortable position.

IMMOBILIZING EXTREMITY INJURIES

To immobilize an extremity injury, you can use a splint. Splints, whether commercially made or improvised, are of three types—soft, rigid, and anatomic. Commercial splints also include the traction splint, used by trained professional rescuers for fractures of the femur. Soft splints include folded blankets, towels, pillows, and a sling or cravats (Fig. 11-1). A sling is a triangular bandage tied to support an arm, forearm, wrist, or hand (Fig. 11-2). A cravat is a folded triangular bandage used to hold dressings or splints in place. Bandages and a wad of cloth can serve as effective splints for small body parts such as the hands or fingers (Fig. 11-3).

Rigid splints include boards, metal strips, and folded magazines or newspapers (Fig. 11-4). Anatomic splints refer to the use of the body as a splint. You may not ordinarily think of the body as a splint, but it works very well. For example, an arm can be splinted to the chest. An injured leg can be splinted to the uninjured leg (Fig. 11-5).

As a citizen responder, you are more likely to have access to triangular bandages, or other materials you can use in fashioning a soft or anatomic splint. Although you are unlikely to have commercial splints immediately available to you, when they are available, you should become familiar with them before you have to use them. Commercial splints include padded board splints, air splints, and specially designed flexible splints (Fig. 11-6).

To splint an injured body part—

1. Support the injured part in the position you find it. If possible, have the victim or a bystander help you (Fig. 11-7, *A*).
2. Cover any open wounds with a dressing and bandage to help control bleeding and prevent infection. Wear gloves or use a protective barrier.

Key Terms

Arm: The part of the upper extremity from the shoulder to the hand.

Extremities: The shoulder to the fingers; the hip to the toes.

Forearm: The part of the upper extremity from the elbow to the wrist.

Leg: The part of the lower extremity from the pelvis to the ankle.

Lower extremities: The parts of the body from the hip to the toes.

Lower leg: The part of the lower extremity from the knee to the ankle.

Thigh: The part of the lower extremity from the pelvis to the knee.

Upper arm: The part of the upper extremity from the shoulder to the elbow.

Upper extremities: The parts of the body from the shoulder to the fingers.

Figure 11-1 Soft splints include folded blankets, towels, pillows, and a sling or cravat.

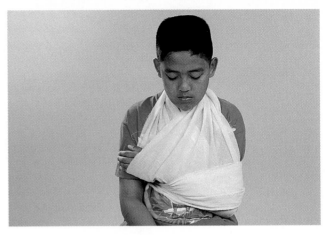

Figure 11-2 A sling supports the arm.

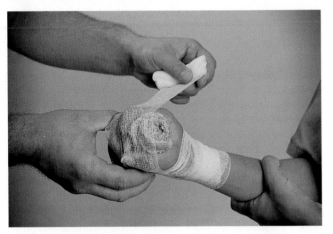

Figure 11-3 A wad of cloth and bandages can effectively splint small body parts.

Figure 11-4 Rigid splints include boards, metal strips, and folded magazines or newspapers.

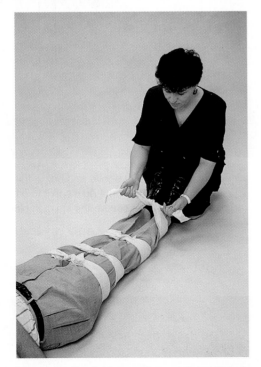

Figure 11-5 An injured leg can be splinted to the uninjured leg.

3. Check the area below the injury site for color, warmth, and sensation.
4. Apply the splint to immobilize the joints above and below an injured area. If you are using a rigid splint, pad the splint so that it is shaped to the injured part (Fig. 11-7, *B*). This padding will help prevent further injury.
5. Secure the splint in place with folded triangular bandages (cravats), roller bandages, or other wide strips of cloth (Fig. 11-7, *C*). Avoid securing the splint directly over an open wound.
6. Check the fingers or toes to ensure that circulation has not been restricted by applying the splint too tightly. Loosen the splint if the victim complains of numbness or if the fingers or toes discolor (turn blue) or become cold.
7. Elevate the splinted part, if possible.

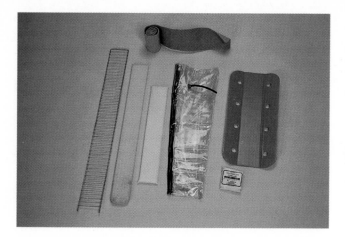

Figure 11-6 Commercial splints.

After the injury has been immobilized, help the victim rest in the most comfortable position, apply ice or a cold pack to the injured area, prevent the victim from becoming chilled or overheated, and reassure him or her. Determine what additional care is needed. Whether you are waiting for EMS personnel to arrive or have decided to transport the injured person to a medical facility yourself, continue to monitor the victim's level of consciousness, breathing, and skin color and temperature. Be alert for signs and symptoms, such as those of shock, that may indicate the victim's condition is worsening.

SIGNS AND SYMPTOMS OF SERIOUS EXTREMITY INJURIES

The extremities consist of bones, soft tissues, blood vessels, and nerves. They are subject to various kinds of injury. Injury can affect the soft tissues, resulting in open or closed wounds. Injury can also affect the musculoskeletal system, resulting in sprains, strains, fractures, or dislocations. Signs and symptoms of a serious extremity injury include—

- Pain or tenderness.
- Swelling.
- Discoloration.
- Deformity of the limb.
- Inability to use the limb.
- Severe external bleeding.
- Loss of feeling or sensation.

Figure 11-7 **A,** Support the arm above and below the injury site. The victim can help you. **B,** Pad a rigid splint to conform to the injured body part. **C,** Then secure the splint in place.

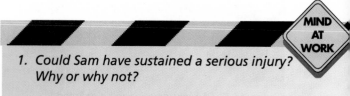

1. Could Sam have sustained a serious injury? Why or why not?

MIND AT WORK

UPPER EXTREMITY INJURIES

The **upper extremities** are the parts of the body from the shoulders to the fingers. The bones of each upper extremity include the collarbone (clavicle), shoulder blade (scapula), bones of the arm (humerus) from the shoulder to the elbow, and **forearm** (radius and ulna) from the elbow to the wrist **(carpals),** and bones of the hand **(metacarpals)** and fingers **(phalanges).** Figure 11-8 shows the major structures of the upper extremities. In addition to damaging bones and muscles, injuries to the upper extremities may damage blood vessels, nerves, and other soft tissues.

The upper extremities are the most commonly injured parts of the body. These injuries may occur in many different ways. The most frequent cause is falling on the hand of an outstretched arm. Since the hands are rarely protected, abrasions occur easily. Because a falling person instinctively tries to break the fall by extending the arms and hands, these areas receive the force of the body's weight. This force can cause a serious injury, such as a severe sprain, fracture, or dislocation of the

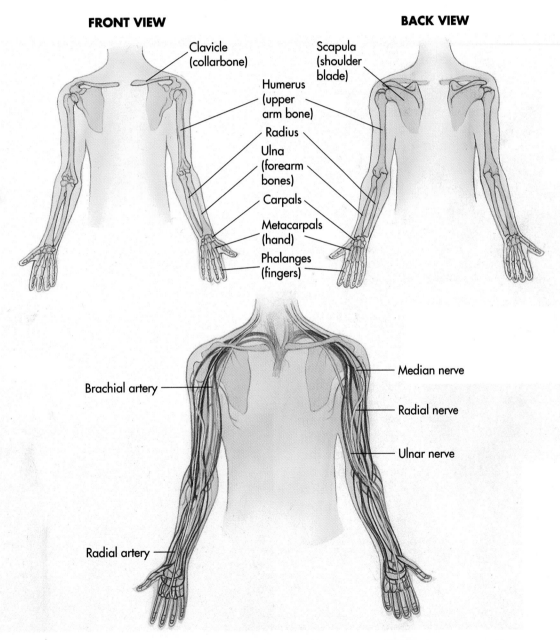

FRONT VIEW   **BACK VIEW**

Clavicle (collarbone)
Scapula (shoulder blade)
Humerus (upper arm bone)
Radius
Ulna (forearm bones)
Carpals
Metacarpals (hand)
Phalanges (fingers)

Brachial artery
Median nerve
Radial nerve
Ulnar nerve

Radial artery

Figure 11-8   The upper extremities include the bones of the arms and hands, nerves, and blood vessels.

hand, the wrist, the forearm, the elbow, the upper arm, or the shoulder.

When caring for upper extremity injuries, minimize any movement of the injured part. If an injured person is holding the forearm securely against the chest, do not change the position. Holding the arm against the chest is an effective method of immobilization. Caring for a victim with an upper extremity injury does not require specialized equipment. Help the person support the extremity by binding it to the chest with a folded triangular bandage or strips of cloth.

Shoulder Injuries

The shoulder consists of three bones that meet to form the shoulder joint. These bones are the clavicle, scapula, and humerus. The most common shoulder injuries are sprains. However, injuries to the shoulder may also involve a fracture or dislocation of one or more of these bones.

Types of shoulder injuries

The most frequently injured bone of the shoulder is the **clavicle,** or collarbone, more commonly injured in children than adults. Typically, the clavicle is fractured or separates from its normal position at its inner or outer end as a result of a fall (Fig. 11-9). A shoulder **separation** commonly occurs from a fall on the point of the shoulder that forces the outer end of the clavicle to separate from the joint where it touches the scapula. The victim usually feels pain in the shoulder area, which may radiate down the upper extremity. A person with a clavicle injury usually attempts to ease the pain by holding the forearm against the chest (Fig. 11-10). Since the clavicle lies directly over major blood vessels and nerves to the upper extremity, it is especially important to immobilize a fractured clavicle promptly to prevent injury to these structures.

Scapula, or shoulder blade, fractures are not common. A fracture of the scapula typically results from a violent force such as a fall from a height or being hit by a car. The signs and symptoms of a fractured scapula are the same as for any other extremity fracture, although you are less likely to see deformity of the scapula. The most significant symptoms are ex-

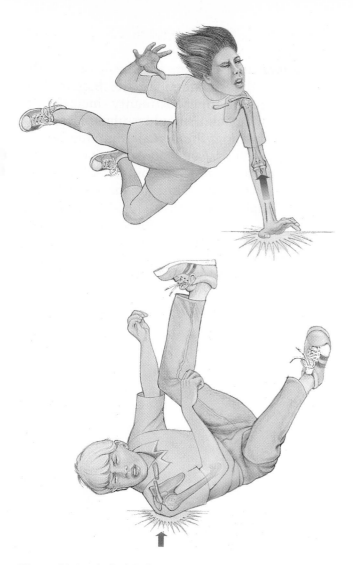

Figure 11-9   A clavicle fracture is commonly caused by a fall.

Figure 11-10   Someone with a fractured clavicle will usually support the arm on the injured side.

treme pain and the inability to move the upper extremity.

Because it takes great force to break the scapula, the force may have been great enough also to injure the chest cavity or head or spine. If the chest cavity is injured, the person with a fractured scapula may have difficulty breathing.

A dislocation of the shoulder joint is another common type of shoulder injury. Like fractures, dislocations often result from falls or direct blows when the arm is in the throwing position. Such dislocations happen frequently in sports, such as football and rugby, when a player attempts to break a fall with an out-stretched arm or gets tackled with the arm positioned away from the body (Fig. 11-11). This movement can result in ligaments tearing, displacing bones. Shoulder dislocations are painful and can often be identified by the deformity present. As with other shoulder injuries, the victim often tries to minimize the pain by holding the upper extremity in the most comfortable position.

Care for shoulder injuries

To care for shoulder injuries, first control any external bleeding with direct pressure. Allow the person to continue to support the upper extremity in the position in which he or she

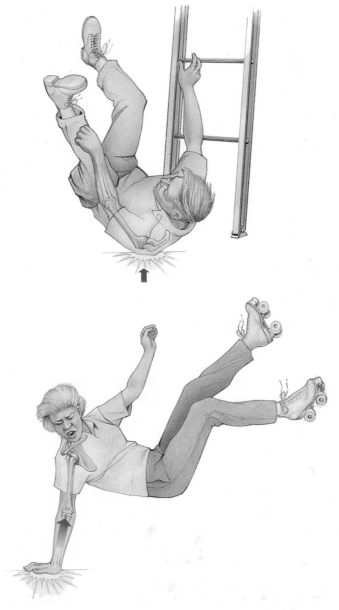

Figure 11-11 Dislocations are usually the result of a fall.

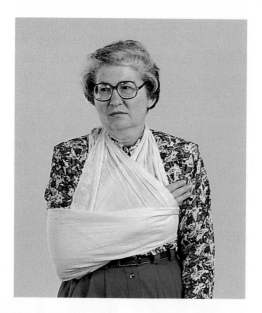

Figure 11-12   Splint the arm against the chest in the position the victim is holding it, using a sling, cravats, and a small pillow or a rolled blanket when necessary.

is holding it, usually the most comfortable position. If the person is holding the upper extremity away from the body, use a pillow, rolled blanket, or similar object to fill the gap between the upper extremity and chest to provide support for the injured area. Splint the upper extremity in place (Fig. 11-12). Apply cold to the injured area to help minimize pain and reduce swelling. Be sure to place gauze or cloth between the source of cold and the skin.

Arm Injuries

The **arm** is the upper extremity from the shoulder to the hand. The bones of the arm are the **humerus,** the **radius,** and the **ulna.** The humerus is the largest bone in the arm.

Types of upper arm injuries

The humerus can be fractured at any point, although it is usually fractured at the upper end near the shoulder or in the middle of the bone. The upper end of the humerus often fractures in the elderly and in young children as a result of a fall. Breaks in the middle of the bone mostly occur in young adults. When the humerus is fractured, the blood vessels and nerves supplying the entire upper extremity may be damaged. Most humerus fractures are very painful and do not permit the victim to use the arm. A humerus fracture can also cause considerable arm deformity.

Care for upper arm injuries

To care for a serious **upper arm** injury, immobilize the arm from the shoulder to the elbow. Care for the upper arm in the same way as for shoulder injuries. First control any external bleeding. Use direct pressure unless the bleeding is located directly over the suspected break. Wear gloves or use a barrier. Place the upper extremity in a sling and bind it to the chest with **cravats,** folded triangular bandages used to hold dressings or splints in place. Apply ice or a cold pack. You can use a short splint, if one is available, to give more support to the arm (Fig. 11-13). Remember to check for feeling, warmth, and color before and after applying the splint.

Elbow Injuries

The elbow is a joint formed by the humerus and the two bones of the forearm, the radius and the ulna. Injuries to the elbow can cause permanent disability, since all the nerves and blood vessels to the forearm and hand go through the elbow. Therefore, take elbow injuries seriously.

Types of elbow injuries

Like other joints, the elbow can be sprained, fractured, or dislocated. Injuries to a joint like the elbow can be made worse by movement because movement can easily damage the nerves and blood vessels located in the elbow. An injured elbow may be in a bent or straight position.

Care for elbow injuries

If the victim says he or she cannot move the elbow or you cannot find a pulse at the wrist, do not try to move the elbow. Call 9-1-1 or the local emergency number immediately. To provide care, first control any external bleeding with direct pressure. Next, immobilize the arm from the shoulder to the wrist in the best way possible. The simplest way is to place the arm in a sling and secure it to the chest. If placing the arm in a sling is not possible, immobilize the elbow with a splint and two cravats. If the elbow is bent, apply the splint diagonally across the underside of the arm (Fig. 11-14, *A*). The splint should extend several inches beyond the elbow and the wrist.

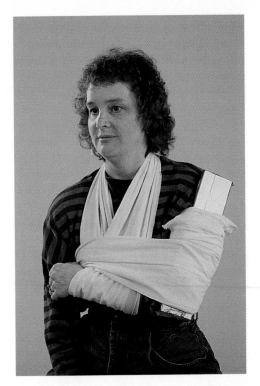

Figure 11-13   A short, padded splint can provide additional support for an injury to the upper arm.

If the elbow is straight, apply the splint along the arm. Secure the splint at the wrist and upper arm with cravats or roller bandages (Fig. 11-14, *B*). If a splint is not available, secure the arm to the body using two cravats (Fig. 11-14, *C*). Always be sure the knots are tied against the splint and not directly on the arm. Apply ice or a cold pack.

Forearm, Wrist, and Hand Injuries

The forearm is the area between the elbow and the wrist. Fractures of the wrist may involve one or both of the two forearm bones, the radius and ulna. If a person falls on an outstretched upper extremity, both forearm bones may break, but not always in the same place.

Types of forearm, wrist, and hand injuries

When both bones fracture, the arm may look s-shaped (Fig. 11-15). Because the radial artery and nerve are near the bones, a fracture may cause severe bleeding or a loss of movement in the wrist and hand. The wrist is a common site of sprains and fractures. It is often difficult to tell the extent of the injury. Care for wrist injuries in the same way as forearm injuries.

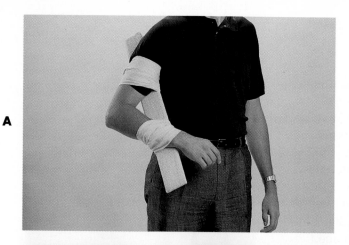

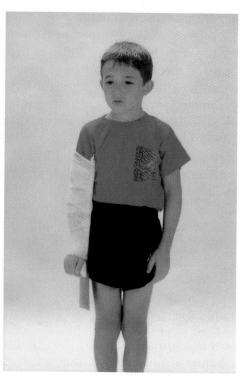

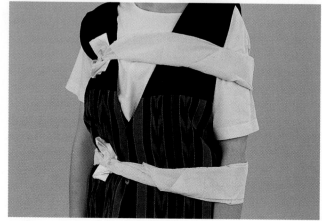

Figure 11-14   A, If the elbow is bent, apply the splint diagonally across the underside of the arm. **B,** If the arm is straight, apply the splint along the underside of the arm. **C,** If a splint is not available, secure the arm to the body using two cravats.

*Victim has to help you by bracing injury

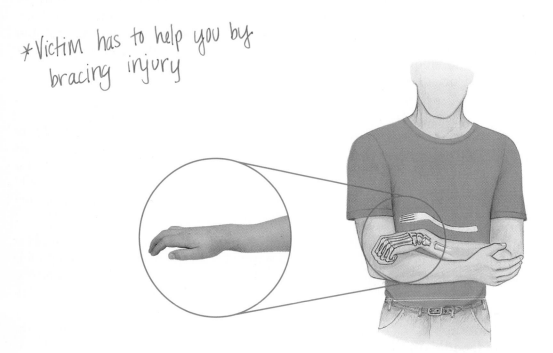

Figure 11-15   Fractures of both forearm bones often have a characteristic s-shaped deformity.

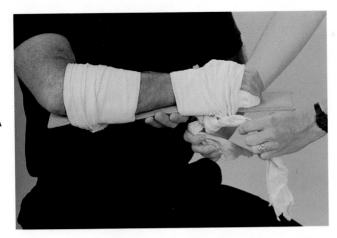
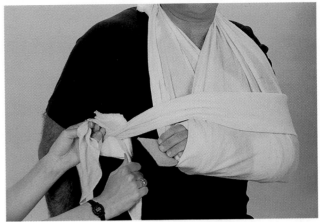

Figure 11-16   **A,** If the forearm is fractured, place a splint under the forearm and secure it with two cravats. **B,** Put the arm in a sling and secure it to the chest with cravats.

↑ immobilizes shoulder as well

Because the hands are used in so many daily activities, they are susceptible to injury. Most injuries to the hands and fingers involve only minor soft tissue damage. However, a serious injury may damage nerves, blood vessels, and bones. Home, recreational, and industrial mishaps often produce lacerations, avulsions, burns, and fractures of the hands.

Care for forearm, wrist, and hand injuries

First control any external bleeding, wearing gloves or using a barrier. Then care for the injured forearm, wrist, or hand by immobilizing the injured part. Support the injured part by placing a soft or rigid splint underneath the forearm, extending it to both the hand and elbow. If the splint is rigid, place a roll of gauze or a similar object in the palm to keep the palm and fingers in a normal position and pad the splint. Check the fingers for feeling, warmth, and color. Then secure the splint with cravats or a roller bandage (Fig. 11-16, *A*). Put the arm in a sling and secure it to the chest with cravats (Fig. 11-16, *B*). Recheck the fingers. For a hand or finger injury, a bulky dressing is effective (Fig. 11-17). For a possible fractured or dislocated finger, fasten a small splint, such as an ice cream stick, to the finger with tape (Fig. 11-18). You can also tape the injured finger to the finger next to it. Do not attempt to put the bones back into place if you suspect a finger or thumb dislocation. Always apply ice and elevate injuries to the forearm, wrist, and hand.

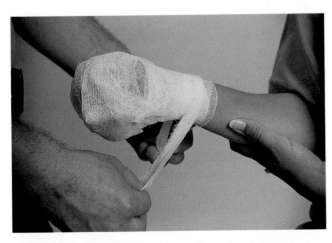

Figure 11-17   A bulky dressing is an effective splint for a hand or finger injury.

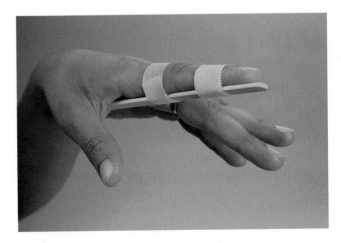

Figure 11-18   An ice cream stick can be used to splint a finger injury.

Carpal Tunnel Syndrome

Elaine W. was a 14-year-old violin student when she first noticed troubling symptoms. After long practice sessions, she felt a strange tingling sensation in the fingers of her left hand. Soon, she was experiencing pain so severe that it woke her up at night. Then, she states, "I woke up one November morning and I couldn't move my left hand at all." Frightened, she consulted her doctor, who diagnosed her with carpal tunnel syndrome. When rest and splinting did not alleviate her symptoms, Elaine had surgery to correct the problem. Although the surgery eliminated the pain and tingling, she still—some years later—has trouble holding things. "Wet dishes are the worst," she says. And at work, she uses a pencil to tap out words on her word processor.

Elaine is just one of 5 million Americans who suffer from carpal tunnel syndrome, a painful and debilitating irritation of the nerves and tendons in the wrist. The area for which the syndrome is named—the carpal tunnel—is the passageway formed by tendons and bones through which the nerves that supply the hand travel. When a person performs repetitive hand motion for long periods of time without rest, such as long typing sessions, assembly-line tasks, or in Elaine's case, practicing the violin, the nerves can become irritated, resulting in pain and numbness. Carpal tunnel syndrome is now the most commonly re-ported on-the-job injury. If untreated, it can cause permanent disability.

The first symptoms of carpal tunnel syndrome include hand and wrist pain and numbness. People with the syndrome describe the pain as an "electric" sensation that may radiate to the arm, shoulder, and back. Over 90 percent of carpal tunnel syndrome sufferers report that the pain is worse at night and so severe that it wakes them up from a sound sleep. In time, the sufferer may lose grip strength in the hand, making even everyday tasks awkward or impossible.

Although carpal tunnel syndrome is not a new condition (it was first described in 1854), it has only recently become a serious occupational hazard. One U.S. legislator describes carpal tunnel syndrome as "the industrial disease of the Information Age." If employers do not do something about it, some experts foresee that half of every dollar earned by companies may go to treat carpal tunnel syndrome and its related disorders.

Many of today's occupations involve constant repetitive motions of the hand and wrist and at faster and faster speeds. Technical innovations—from grocery store scanners to computer keyboards—also contribute to the increase in carpal tunnel syndrome. For instance, typing on a typewriter requires the typist to take frequent breaks to insert paper and manually return the type-

LOWER EXTREMITY INJURIES

Injuries to the *lower extremity,* the part of the body from the hip to the toes, can involve both soft tissue and musculoskeletal damage. The major bones of the thigh and leg are large and strong to carry the body's weight. Bones of the lower extremity include the thigh bone (femur), the kneecap (patella), the two bones in the lower **leg** (tibia and fibula), and the bones of the ankle **(tarsals),** foot **(metatarsals),** and toes **(phalanges).** Because of the size and strength of the bones in the thigh and lower leg, a significant amount of force is required to cause a fracture. The **femoral arteries** are the major suppliers of blood to the lower extremities. If a femoral artery is damaged, which may happen with a fracture of the femur, the blood loss can be life threatening.

Figure 11-19 shows the major structures of the lower extremities. When caring for lower extremity injuries, follow the same general principles of care described in Chapter 10. Serious injury to the lower extremities can result in an inability to bear weight. Contact EMS personnel to transport the victim to a medical facility.

writer carriage at the end of each line. With to-day's computers, all these tasks are built in, with the result that computer typists spend long hours with their hands extended over a keyboard. Without frequent breaks, these typists are at risk for carpal tunnel syndrome.

What can be done to treat carpal tunnel syndrome? Individuals with the syndrome are treated with physical therapy and elaborate wrist splints that immobilize the affected area. Sometimes surgery is needed to correct the nerve damage. These treatments are often not effective in alleviating all the symptoms, and sufferers must learn to live with their disability.

Because of the surge in carpal tunnel syndrome cases, the Occupational Safety and Health Administration (OSHA) has drawn up guidelines for certain occupations, such as meatpacking, designed to prevent the onset of the syndrome. Specially designed desks, chairs, and other office equipment for typists and

data entry clerks take some of the stress off wrists and hands, and in some companies, typists are required to take rest breaks.

These guidelines make sense for those who find themselves stuck at a keyboard for long hours or who perform the same task over and over. Identify early signs and symptoms and take steps to prevent wrist strain. Take frequent breaks, and for the marathon typist, make sure your chair is comfortable and that you can reach the keyboard without straining. Your wrists will thank you.

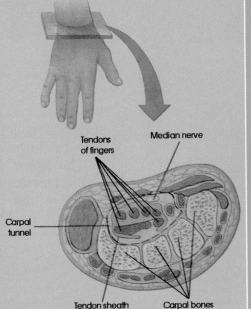

Tendons of fingers

Median nerve

Carpal tunnel

Tendon sheath

Carpal bones

SOURCES
CTS: Relief at hand, *The University of California Berkeley Wellness Letter* 11(4): 7, 1995.
Gabor A: On-the-job-straining: repetitive motion is the Information Age's hottest hazard, *US News and World Report* 108(20): 51-53, 1990.
Katz RT: Carpal tunnel syndrome: a practical review, *American Family Physician* 49(6): 1371-1382, 1994.
Treating for carpal tunnel syndrome, *Lancet* 338 (8765): 479-481, 1991.

Thigh and Lower Leg Injuries

The **thigh** is the lower extremity from the pelvis to the knee. The **femur,** or thigh bone, is the largest bone in the body. Because it bears most of the weight of the body, it is very important to the ability to walk and run. The lower leg is the part of the lower extremity from the knee to the ankle.

Types of thigh and lower leg injuries

Thigh injuries range from bruises and torn muscles to severe injuries such as fractures or dislocations. The upper end of the femur meets the pelvis at the hip joint (Fig. 11-20). Most fe-

mur fractures involve the upper end of the bone. Even though the hip joint itself is not involved, such injuries are often called hip fractures.

A fracture of the femur usually produces a characteristic deformity. When the fracture occurs, the thigh muscles contract. Because the thigh muscles are so strong, they pull the broken bone ends together, causing them to overlap. This pulling may cause the injured lower extremity to be noticeably shorter than the other lower extremity. The injured lower extremity may also be turned outward (Fig. 11-21, p. 245). Other signs and symptoms of a frac-

FRONT VIEW **BACK VIEW**

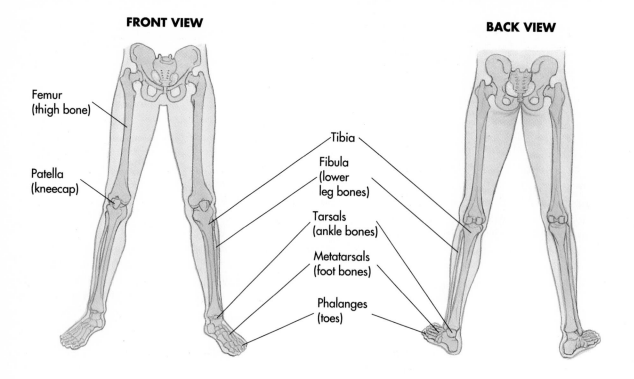

Femur
(thigh bone)

Patella
(kneecap)

Tibia

Fibula
(lower
leg bones)

Tarsals
(ankle bones)

Metatarsals
(foot bones)

Phalanges
(toes)

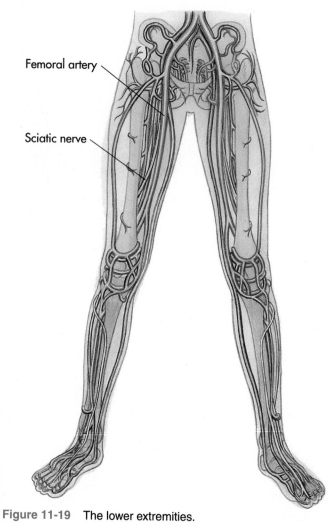

Femoral artery

Sciatic nerve

Figure 11-19 The lower extremities.

tured femur include severe pain and inability to move the lower extremity.

The **lower leg** is the lower extremity between the knee and the ankle. A fracture in the lower leg may involve one or both bones, the **tibia** and the **fibula.** Sometimes both are frac-

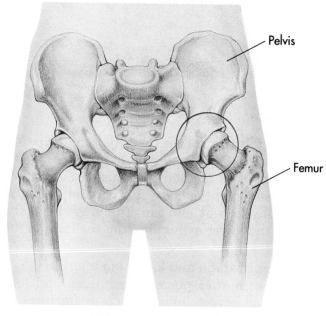

Pelvis

Femur

Figure 11-20 The upper end of the femur meets the pelvis at the hip joint.

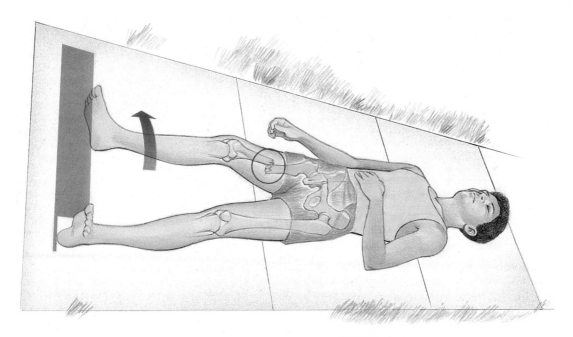

Figure 11-21   A fractured femur often produces a characteristic deformity. The injured leg is shorter than the uninjured leg and may be turned outward.

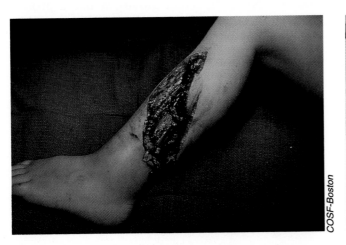

Figure 11-22   A fracture of the lower leg can be an open fracture.   ↑·*if not bleeding, put nothing on it → you'd get gauze stuck in wound*

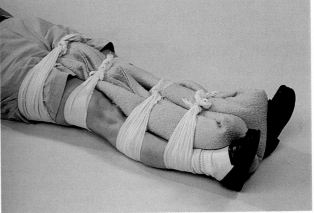

COSF–Boston

Figure 11-23   To splint an injured leg, secure the injured leg to the uninjured leg with cravats. A pillow or rolled blanket can be placed between the legs.

tured simultaneously. However, a blow to the outside of the lower leg can cause an isolated fracture of the smaller bone (fibula). Because these two bones lie just beneath the skin, open fractures are common (Fig. 11-22). Lower leg fractures may cause a severe deformity in which the lower leg is bent at an unusual angle (angulated), as well as pain and inability to move the leg.

Care for thigh and lower leg injuries

Initial care for the victim with a serious injury to the thigh or lower leg is to stop any ex-

ternal bleeding and call EMS personnel immediately. Wear gloves or use a barrier if you have to touch the victim's blood. EMS personnel are much better prepared than a layperson to care for and transport a victim with a serious lower extremity injury. While waiting for EMS personnel to arrive, immobilize the injured area and help the victim rest in the most comfortable position. Do not forget that the ground acts as an excellent splint. If the victim's lower extremity is supported by the ground, do not move it. Rather, used rolled towels or blankets to support the leg in the position in which you found it. In other situations, such as when you must transport the person, you can secure the injured lower extremity to the uninjured lower extremity with several wide cravats placed above and below the site of the injury. If one is available, place a pillow or rolled blanket between the lower extremities and bind them together above and below the site of the injury (Fig. 11-23). Apply ice or a cold pack to reduce pain and swelling. Do not be surprised if EMS personnel later undo the splint and apply a more rigid splint or a mechanical device called a traction splint. This device reduces the deformity of the lower extremity by applying traction to overcome the pull of the thigh muscles that are causing the bone ends to overlap.

A fractured femur can result in serious internal bleeding. The likelihood of shock is considerable. Therefore, take steps to minimize shock. Keep the person lying down and try to keep him or her calm. Keep the person from becoming overheated or chilled, and make sure that EMS personnel have been called. Monitor breathing. Notice how the skin looks and feels, and watch for changes in the victim's level of consciousness. See Chapter 8 for more detailed information on shock.

Knee Injuries

The knee joint is very vulnerable to injury. The knee comprises the lower end of the femur, the upper ends of the tibia and fibula, and the patella or kneecap. The **patella** is a free-floating bone that moves on the lower front surface of the thigh bone.

Types of knee injuries

Knee injuries range from cuts and bruises to sprains, fractures, and dislocations. Deep lacerations in the area of the knee can cause severe joint infections. Sprains, fractures, and dislocations of the knee are common in athletic activities that involve quick movements or exert unusual force on the knee.

The patella is unprotected in that it lies directly beneath the skin. This part of the knee is very vulnerable to bruises and lacerations, as well as dislocations. Violent forces to the front of the knee, such as those caused by hitting the dashboard of a motor vehicle or falling

Figure 11-24   Support a knee injury in the bent position if the victim cannot straighten the knee.

and landing on bent knees, can fracture the kneecap.

Care for knee injuries

To care for an injured knee, first control any external bleeding. Wear gloves or use a protective barrier. If the knee is bent and cannot be straightened without pain, you can support it on a pillow or folded blanket in the bent position (Fig. 11-24). If the knee is on the ground, the ground will provide adequate support. Apply ice or a cold pack. Call EMS personnel to have the victim transported to a medical facility for examination. Help the victim to rest in the most comfortable position until EMS personnel arrive. If you decide to splint the injured area and the knee is straight, you can secure it to the uninjured leg as you might do for an injury of the thigh or lower leg.

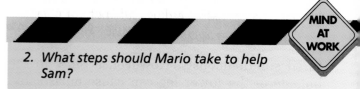

2. What steps should Mario take to help Sam?

MIND AT WORK

Ankle and Foot Injuries

Ankle and foot injuries are commonly caused by twisting forces. Injuries range from minor sprains with little swelling and pain, which heal with a few days' rest, to fractures and dislocations. As with other joint injuries, you cannot always distinguish between minor and severe injuries. You should initially care for all

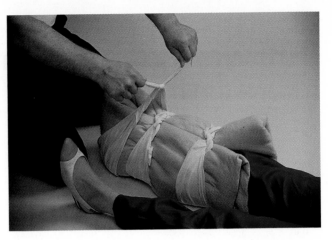

Figure 11-26   An injured ankle can be immobilized with a pillow or rolled blanket secured with two or three cravats.

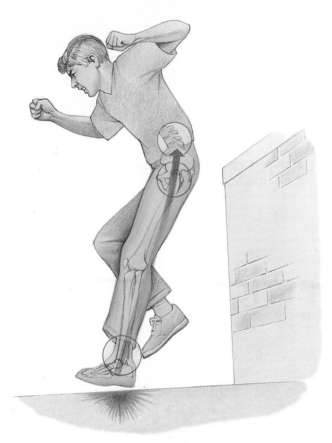

Figure 11-25   In a jump or fall from a height, the impact can be transmitted up the legs, causing injuries to the thighs, hips, or spine.

ankle and foot injuries as if they are serious. If the ankle or foot is painful to move, if it cannot bear weight, or if the foot or ankle is swollen, a physician should evaluate the injury. Foot injuries may also involve the toes. Although toe injuries are painful, they are rarely serious.

Types of ankle and foot injuries

Most commonly, ankle and foot injuries are caused by severe twisting forces that occur when the foot turns in or out at the ankle, such as in stepping off the curb or landing from a jump. Fractures of the feet and ankles can occur from forcefully landing on the heel. With any great force, such as falling from a height and landing on the feet, fractures are possible. The force of the impact may also be transmitted up the lower extremities. This transmitted force can result in an injury elsewhere in the body,

such as the thigh, pelvis, or even the spine (Fig. 11-25).

Care for ankle and foot injuries

Care for ankle and foot injuries by controlling any external bleeding while wearing gloves or using another barrier. Next, immobilize the ankle and foot by using a soft splint such as a pillow or rolled blanket. Check the toes for feeling, warmth, and color. Wrap the injured area with the soft splint, and secure it with two or three cravats (Fig. 11-26). Recheck the toes. Then elevate the injured ankle or foot to help reduce the swelling. Apply ice or a cold pack. Suspect that any victim who has fallen or jumped from a height may also have injuries elsewhere. Call EMS personnel and keep the victim from moving until EMS personnel arrive and evaluate his or her condition.

SUMMARY

You can care for musculoskeletal and soft tissue injuries to the extremities by providing care that focuses on minimizing pain, shock, and further damage to the injured area. Immobilize the injured area and apply ice or a cold pack. Control any external bleeding. Reassure the victim. Care for any life-threatening problems and seek advanced medical help if necessary.

Answers to Application Questions

1. Yes; Sam's knee hurts, he cannot use it, and it is swelling.

2. He should make Sam as comfortable as possible and go find a phone to call EMS personnel. If he is able to use a phone in a private house or place of business, he could ask for ice or a cold pack and a blanket or pillow to use to immobilize Sam's knee.

STUDY QUESTIONS

1. Match each term with the correct definition.

   a. Upper arm   c. Thigh
   b. Forearm   d. Lower leg

   __C__ The part of the lower extremity from the pelvis to the knee.

   __B__ The part of the upper extremity from the elbow to the wrist.

   __D__ The part of the lower extremity from the knee to the ankle.

   __A__ The part of the upper extremity from the shoulder to the elbow.

2. Name the most frequent cause of upper extremity injuries.

3. What signs and symptoms of an extremity injury do you find in the scenario that follows? Circle the signs and symptoms in the passage below.

   A person attempting to leap a 4-foot gate catches one foot on the gatetop and falls hard on the other side. He appears to be unable to get up. He says his left leg and arm both hurt. When you check him, you find that he is unable to move the leg, which is beginning to swell. The left arm looks deformed at the shoulder, and he has no sensation in the fingers of that arm. The arm is beginning to look bruised and is painful. He says he feels a little nauseated and dizzy, and he has a scrape on his hand.

4. Describe the care you would give for the person in the scenario above.

5. List two specific signs and symptoms of a fractured femur.

   shock, disfiguration

6. List three types of splints.

In questions 7 through 9, circle the letter of the correct answer.

7. A man who has fallen down a steep flight of stairs is clutching his right forearm to his chest. He says his shoulder hurts and he cannot move his arm. How would you care for him?

a. Allow him to continue supporting the forearm.
b. Splint the upper extremity to the chest in a comfortable position.
c. Have him move the upper extremity into its normal position.
d. a and b.

8. A child has fallen from a bicycle onto the pavement and landed on her elbow. The elbow is bent and the girl says she cannot move it. What do you do after calling EMS personnel?

a. Straighten the elbow and splint it.
b. Drive her to the hospital.
c. Immobilize the elbow in the bent position.
d. Ask her to continue to try to move the elbow.

9. A person with an open fracture of the femur is lying on the ground. Which should you do first?

a. Call EMS personnel.
b. Raise the injured lower extremity to splint it.
c. Apply ice or a cold pack.
d. Control external bleeding.

10. An elderly woman has tripped and fallen over some gardening tools. She is lying on the ground, conscious and breathing. Her lower leg is bleeding profusely from a gash and seems to be bent at an odd angle. List the steps of care you would provide.

Answers are listed in Appendix A.

Tie off ABOVE & BELOW the injury

SKILL SHEETS

Applying An Anatomic Splint

CHECK - CALL - CARE

When you check for nonlife-threatening conditions, you suspect the person may have a serious injury. If you decide to use an anatomic splint to immobilize the injury . . .

Support the injured area

* Support injured area above and below injury site.
* Let ground support leg whenever possible, or have victim or bystander help you.

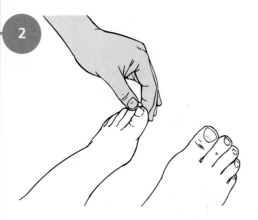

Check for feeling, warmth, and color

* Check for feeling, warmth, and color below injury.

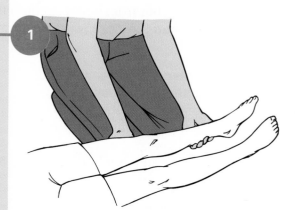

Position the bandages (ties)

* Thread several folded triangular bandages above and below injured area.
* Do not thread bandage at injury site.

4

Position the splint

- Carefully move uninjured limb next to injured limb.

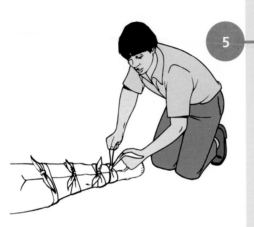

5

Secure the splint in place

- Tie ends of each triangular bandage together with knots.
- Check to see that triangular bandages are snug but not too tight.
- If more than 1 finger fits under bandages, tighten bandages.

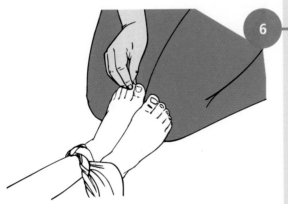

6

Recheck for feeling, warmth, and color

- Check for feeling, warmth, and color below injury.
- Splint should fit snugly but not so tightly that blood flow is impaired.
- If area below injury is bluish or cool, loosen splint.

If you are not able to check warmth and color because sock or shoe is in place, check for feeling.

SKILL SHEETS

CHECK- CALL- CARE

When you check for nonlife-threatening conditions, you suspect the person may have a serious injury. If you decide to use a soft splint to immobilize the injury . . .

1

Support the injured area

- Support injured area above and below injury site.
- Let ground support leg whenever possible, or have victim or bystander help you.

2

Check for feeling, warmth, and color*

- Check for feeling, warmth, and color below injury.*

3

Position the bandages (ties)

- Thread several folded triangular bandages above and below injured area.

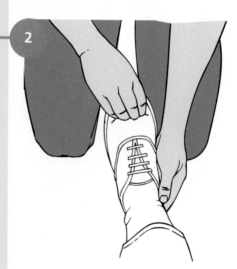

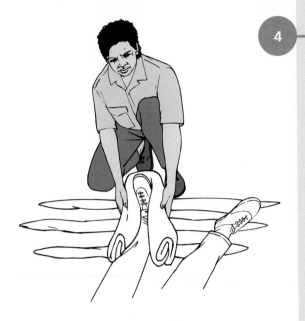

4

Position the splint

- Carefully fold or wrap soft object (folded blanket or pillow) around injured area.

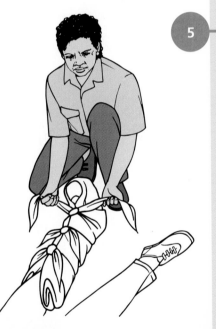

5

Secure the splint in place

- Tie ends of each triangular bandage together, with knots.
- For injury to ankle, tie bandages around foot, from heel to front of ankle.
- Check to see that triangular bandages are snug but not too tight.
- If more than 1 finger fits under bandages, tighten bandages.

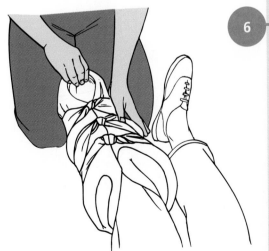

6

Recheck for feeling, warmth, and color*

- Check for feeling, warmth, and color below injury.
- Splint should fit snugly but not so tightly that blood flow is impaired.
- If area below injury is bluish or cool, loosen splint.

*If you are not able to check warmth and color because a sock or shoe is in place, check for feeling.

SKILL SHEETS

CHECK- CALL -CARE

When you check for nonlife-threatening conditions, you suspect the person may have a serious injury. If you decide to use a rigid splint to immobilize the injury . . .

Support the injured area

- Support injured area above and below injury site.
- Let ground support limb whenever possible, or have victim or bystander help you.

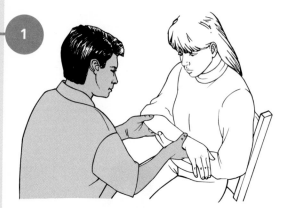

Check for feeling, warmth, and color

- Check for feeling, warmth, and color below the injury.

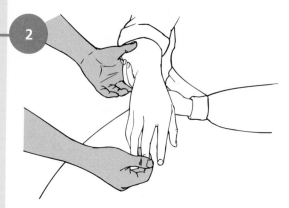

Position the splint

- Have victim or bystander hold splint in place.
- Pad splint to keep injured area in natural position.

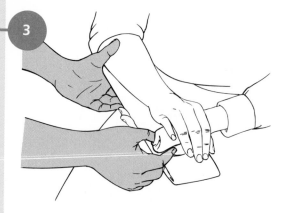

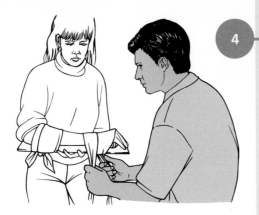

④

Secure the splint

- Secure splint above and below injury with folded triangular bandages or roller bandages.
- If triangular bandages are used, leave injured area uncovered.
- Check to see that bandages are snug but not too tight.
- If more than 1 finger fits under bandages, tighten bandages.

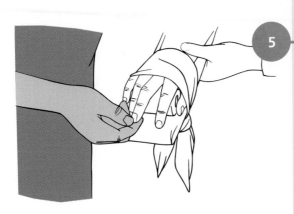

⑤

Recheck for feeling, warmth, and color

- Check for feeling, warmth, and color below injury.
- Splint should fit snugly but not so tightly that blood flow is impaired.
- If area below injury is bluish or cool, loosen splint.

If a rigid splint is used on a forearm you must also immobilize the elbow. Bind the arm to the chest using folded triangular bandages or apply a sling.

SKILL SHEETS

CHECK- CALL- CARE

When you check for nonlife-threatening conditions, you suspect the person may have a serious injury. If you decide to use a sling and binder to immobilize the injury . . .

Applying A Sling And Binder

Support the injured area

- Support injured area above and below injury site.
- Have victim or bystander help you.

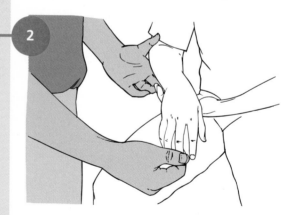

Check for feeling, warmth, and color

- Check hand and fingers for feeling, warmth, and color.

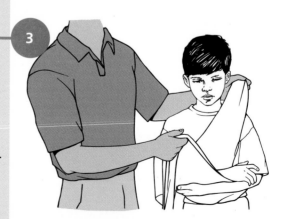

Position the splint

- Place triangular bandage under injured arm, across chest, and over uninjured shoulder to form sling.
- Position point of bandage at elbow.
- Bring other end across chest and over opposite shoulder.

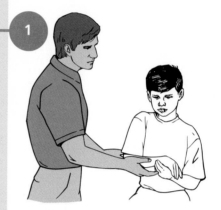

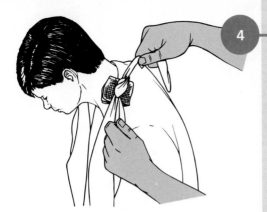

4

Secure the splint

- Tie ends of sling at side of neck opposite injury.
- Placing pad of gauze under knot will make knot more comfortable.

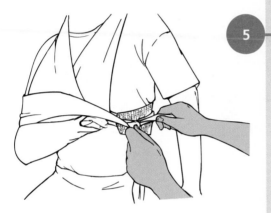

5

Secure the arm to the chest

- Bind injured arm to chest using folded triangular bandage.
- Tie ends of binder on opposite side.
- Place pad under knot.

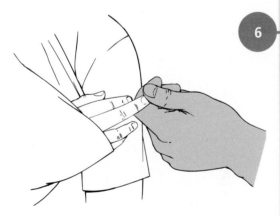

6

Recheck for feeling, warmth, and color

- Check for feeling, warmth, and color below injury.
- Splint should fit snugly but not so tightly that blood flow is impaired.
- If area below injury is bluish or cool, loosen splint.

CHAPTER 12

Injuries to the Head, Neck, and Back

WHAT YOU SHOULD LEARN

After reading this chapter, you should be able to—

1. *Name the most common cause of head, neck, and back injuries.*

2. *List nine situations that might indicate serious head, neck, and back injuries.*

3. *List 14 signs and symptoms of head, neck, and back injuries.*

4. *Describe how to effectively minimize movement of the victim's head and spine.*

5. *List three circumstances in which you do not move the victim's head in line with the body.*

6. *Describe how to care for specific injuries to the head, face, neck, and low back.*

7. *Define the key terms for this chapter.*

Spring break at the beach. High school and college students are having fun in the sun. The weather is great, the water refreshing. The day is perfect for a game of touch football on the beach. Later in the day, the tide comes in, and the game becomes more aggressive. Players lunge into the surf to catch passes and tag runners. As the game is about to end, the quarterback throws a long pass. The receiver has the chance to score the winning touchdown, or the defender can deflect the pass to guarantee victory. They both run into the surf and dive headfirst at the ball. As they strike the water, a wave crashes over them, forcing them underwater. Both players strike their heads on the sandy bottom. The result? Both are pulled from the surf by their friends. One player stands up and walks out of the water. The other cannot move.

Introduction

Although injuries to the head, neck, and back account for a small percentage of all injuries annually, they cause more than half the fatalities from injuries. Each year, nearly 2 million Americans suffer an injury to the head or to the most vulnerable part of the neck and back, the spine. Most of these victims are males between ages 15 and 30.

Motor vehicle collisions account for about half of all head and spine injuries. Other causes include falls, injuries from sports and recreational activities, and violent acts such as assault. Figure 12-1 shows the most common causes of spinal injuries.

In addition to the victims who die each year in the United States from head or spine injuries, nearly 80,000 victims are permanently disabled. Today, hundreds of thousands of permanently disabled victims of head or spine injury live in the United States. These survivors have a wide range of physical and mental impairments, including paralysis, speech and memory problems, and behavioral disorders.

Fortunately, prompt appropriate care can often prevent head, neck, and back injuries from resulting in death or disability. In this chapter, you will learn how to recognize when a head, neck, or back injury may be serious. You will also learn how to provide appropriate care to minimize the effects of these injuries.

RECOGNIZING SERIOUS HEAD, NECK, AND BACK INJURIES

Injuries to the head, neck, or back often damage both bone and soft tissue, including brain tissue and the spinal cord. It is usually difficult to determine the extent of damage in head, neck, and back injuries. In most cases, the only way to assess the damage is by being examined by a trained health care professional and having X-ray films taken in an emergency department. Since you cannot always know how severe an injury is, provide initial care as if the injury is serious.

THE HEAD

The head contains the brain, special sense organs, the mouth and nose, and related structures. It is formed by the skull and the face. The broad, flat bones of the skull are fused together to form a hollow shell. This hollow shell, the cranial cavity, contains the brain. The face is on the front of the skull. The bones of the face include the bones of the cheek, forehead, nose, and jaw.

The Brain

Injuries to the head can affect the brain. The brain can be bruised or lacerated when extreme force causes it to move in the skull, stretching and tearing tissue or bumping against the skull.

Key Terms

Concussion (kon KUSH un): An injury to the brain caused by a violent blow to the head, followed by a temporary impairment of brain function, usually without permanent damage to the brain.

In-line stabilization: A technique used to minimize movement of the victim's head and neck and keep them in line with the body to protect the spine while providing care.

Spinal cord: A bundle of nerves extending from the base of the skull to the lower back, protected by the spine.

Spine: A strong, flexible column of vertebrae, extending from the base of the skull to the tip of the tailbone (coccyx), that supports the head and the trunk and encases and protects the spinal cord; also called the spinal column or the vertebral column.

Vertebrae (VER te bra): The 33 bones of the spine.

SPINAL CORD INJURIES

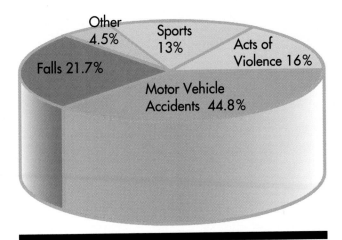

Spinal Cord Injuries: The Facts and Figures, 1993, University of Alabama, Birmingham, Spinal Cord Injury Care Systems, part of the National S.C.I. Data Base

Figure 12-1   Sports-related injuries account for 13 percent of all spinal injuries.

Extreme force, or trauma, can fracture the thick bones of the skull. The major concern with skull fractures is damage to the brain. Blood from a ruptured vessel in the brain can accumulate within the skull (Fig. 12-2). Because the skull contains very little free space, bleeding can build up pressure that can further damage brain tissue.

Bleeding within the skull can occur rapidly or slowly over a period of days. This bleeding will affect the brain, resulting in changes in consciousness. Unconsciousness, semiconsciousness, or drifting in and out of consciousness is often the first and most important sign of a serious head injury.

The Face

The face contains both bones and soft tissue. Although some injuries to the face are minor, many can be life threatening. With a facial injury, consider that the force that caused it may have been sufficiently strong to fracture facial bones and damage the brain or the spine. Facial injuries can also affect the airway and the victim's ability to breathe.

THE NECK

The neck, which contains the larynx and part of the trachea, also contains major blood vessels, muscles and tendons, and cervical bones of the spine. Any injury to the neck must be considered serious. The neck can be injured by crushing or penetrating forces and by sharp-edged objects that can lacerate tissues and blood vessels or by forces that cause the neck to stretch or bend too far. Injuries to muscles, bones, and nerves can result in severe pain and headaches.

THE BACK

The back is made up of soft tissue, bones, cartilage, nerves, muscles, tendons, and ligaments. It supports the skull, shoulder bones, ribs, and pelvis and protects the spinal cord and other vital organs. The part of the back that is most susceptible to severe injury is the spine.

THE SPINE

The **spine** is a strong, flexible column of vertebrae, extending from the base of the skull to the tip of the tailbone, that supports the head and the trunk and encases and protects the spinal

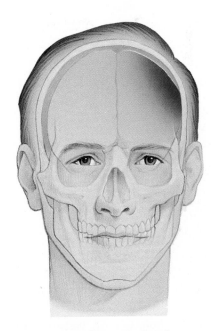

Figure 12-2   Injuries to the head can rupture blood vessels in the brain. Pressure builds within the skull as blood accumulates, causing brain injury.

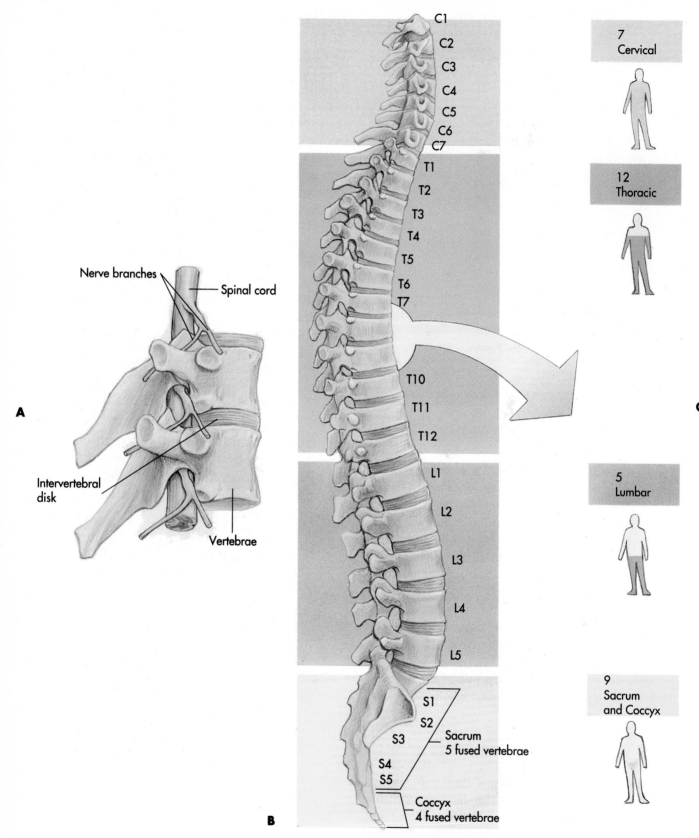

A

Nerve branches

Spinal cord

Intervertebral disk

Vertebrae

B

C1
C2
C3
C4
C5
C6
C7
T1
T2
T3
T4
T5
T6
T7
T10
T11
T12
L1
L2
L3
L4
L5
S1
S2
S3
Sacrum
5 fused vertebrae
S4
S5
Coccyx
4 fused vertebrae

C

7
Cervical

12
Thoracic

5
Lumbar

9
Sacrum
and Coccyx

Figure 12-3   A, Vertebrae are separated by cushions of cartilage called disks. **B** and **C,**
The spine is divided into five regions. Traumatic injury to a region of the spine can paralyze
specific body areas.

cord. The spine is also called the **spinal column** or **vertebral column.** The spine consists of small bones, *vertebrae*, with circular openings. The vertebrae are separated from each other by cushions of cartilage called disks (Fig. 12-3, *A*). This cartilage acts as a shock absorber when a person walks, runs, or jumps. The **spinal cord,** a bundle of nerves, runs through the hollow part of the vertebrae. Nerve branches extend to various parts of the body through openings on the sides of the vertebrae.

The spine is divided into five regions: the cervical (neck) region, the thoracic (midback) region, the lumbar (lower back) region, the sacrum (the lower part of the spine), and the coccyx (tailbone), the small triangular bone at the lower end of the spinal column (Fig. 12-3, *B*). Injuries to the spinal column include fractures and dislocations of the vertebrae, sprained ligaments, and compression or displacement of the disks between the vertebrae.

Injuries to the spine often fracture the vertebrae and sprain the ligaments. These injuries usually heal without problems. With severe injuries, however, the vertebrae may shift and compress or sever the spinal cord. Both can cause temporary or permanent paralysis, even death. Which parts of the body are paralyzed depends on which area of the spinal cord is damaged (Fig. 12-3, *C*).

EVALUATING CAUSES AND INDICATIONS OF HEAD, NECK, AND BACK INJURY

Consider the cause of the injury to help you determine when a head, neck, or back injury may be serious. The cause often is the best initial measure of an injury's severity. Check the scene and think about the forces involved in the injury. Strong forces are likely to cause severe injury to the head and spine. For example, a driver whose head breaks a car windshield in a crash may have a potentially serious head and spine injury. Similarly, a diver who hits his or her head on the bottom of a swimming pool may have a serious injury. Evaluate the scene for clues as to whether a head, neck, or back injury is potentially serious.

Injury Situations

Head, neck, and back injuries are often minor. However, you should consider the possibility of a serious head, neck, or back injury in several situations. These include—

- A fall from a height greater than the victim's height.
- Any diving mishap in which the possibility exists that the person has struck or otherwise injured the head, neck, or back.
- A person found unconscious for unknown reasons.
- Any injury involving a severe blunt force to the head or trunk, such as from a car or baseball bat.
- Any injury that penetrates the head or trunk, such as a knife or gunshot wound.
- A motor vehicle crash involving a driver or passengers not wearing safety belts.
- Any person thrown from a vehicle.
- Any injury in which a victim's helmet is broken or cracked, including a bicycle, motorcycle, football, or industrial helmet.
- Anytime a person is struck by lightning.

Signs and Symptoms of Serious Head, Neck, or Back Injuries

You may also find certain signs and symptoms that indicate a serious head, neck, or back injury. These signs and symptoms may be obvious at first or may develop later. These include—

- Changes in the level of consciousness.
- Severe pain or pressure in the head, neck, or back.
- Tingling or loss of sensation in the extremities.
- Partial or complete loss of movement of any body part.
- Unusual bumps or depressions on the head or neck.
- Sudden loss of memory.
- Blood or other fluids in the ears or nose.
- Profuse external bleeding of the head, neck, or back.
- Seizures in a person who does not have a seizure disorder.
- Impaired breathing or impaired vision as a result of injury.

• break to face → you'll see it b/c bone is so close to surface ; keep it still - hard to immobilize

- Nausea or vomiting.
- Persistent headache.
- Loss of balance.
- Bruising of the head, especially around the eyes or behind the ears.

These signs and symptoms alone do not always suggest a serious head or spine injury, but they may when combined with the cause of the injury. Regardless of the situation, always call 9-1-1 or the local emergency number when you suspect a serious head, neck, or back injury.

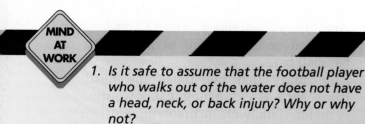

MIND AT WORK

1. Is it safe to assume that the football player who walks out of the water does not have a head, neck, or back injury? Why or why not?

GENERAL CARE FOR HEAD, NECK, AND BACK INJURIES

Head, neck, and back injuries can become life-threatening emergencies. A serious injury to the head or neck can cause a victim to stop breathing. Providing care for serious head, neck, and back injuries involves supporting the respiratory, circulatory, and nervous systems. Always give the following care while waiting for EMS personnel to arrive:

- Minimize movement of any body part.
- Minimize movement of the head, neck, and back, specifically.
- Maintain an open airway.
- Monitor consciousness and breathing.
- Control any external bleeding. Wear gloves or use another protective barrier.
- Keep the person from getting chilled or overheated.

Caring for a head, neck, or back injury is similar to caring for any soft tissue or musculoskeletal injury. You should immobilize the injured area and control any bleeding. Because excessive movement of the head, neck, or back can damage the spinal cord irreversibly, keep the victim as still as possible until you can obtain advanced care. To minimize movement of the head and neck to protect the spine, use the technique called ***in-line stabilization.***

In-line Stabilization

To perform in-line stabilization, place your hands on both sides of the victim's head, position it gently, if necessary, in line with the body, and support it in that position until EMS personnel arrive. Try to keep the person from moving the lower body, since this movement will change the position of the head and neck. You can do this in various ways, depending on how you find the victim (Fig. 12-4). This skill is simple to perform, but it is crucial to preventing further serious injury to the victim. Keeping the head in this anatomical position helps prevent further damage to the spinal column.

However, some circumstances require that you do not move the victim's head in line with the body. These include—

- When the victim's head is severely angled to one side.
- When the victim complains of pain, pressure, or muscle spasms on initial movement of the head.
- When you feel resistance when attempting to move the head.

In these circumstances, support the victim's head in the position in which it was found.

Maintain an Open Airway

As you learned in Chapter 4, you do not always have to roll the victim onto his or her back to check breathing. A cry of pain, chest movement as a result of inhaling and exhaling, or the sound of breathing tells you the victim is breathing, in which case you would not have to move him or her to check. If the victim is breathing, support the victim in the position in which you found him or her. If the victim is not breathing, or you cannot tell, roll the victim gently onto his or her back, but avoid twisting the spine. To open the airway and give rescue breathing if necessary, use the jaw-thrust maneuver described in Chapter 5 to avoid moving the head or neck.

If the victim begins to vomit, position the victim onto one side to keep the airway clear. This positioning is more easily done by two people to minimize movement of the victim's head, neck, and back. Ask another rescuer to

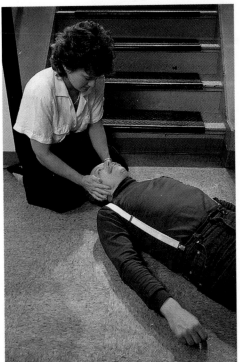

Figure 12-4 Support the victim's head in line with the body in the position in which you find the victim, using in-line stabilization.

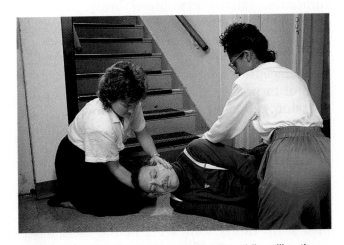

Figure 12-5 Maintain in-line stabilization while rolling the victim's body.

help move the victim's body while you maintain in-line stabilization (Fig. 12-5).

Monitor Consciousness and Breathing

While stabilizing the head and neck, observe the victim's level of consciousness and breathing. A serious injury can result in changes in consciousness. The victim may give inappropriate responses to name, time, place, or what happened. He or she may speak incoherently (in a way that cannot be understood). The victim may be drowsy, appear to lapse into sleep, and then suddenly awaken or lose consciousness completely. Breathing may become rapid or ir-

signs of concussion: · nausea · tired · disoriented · glossy eyed

regular. Because injury to the head or neck can paralyze chest nerves and muscles, breathing can stop. If breathing stops, perform rescue breathing.

Control External Bleeding

Some head and neck injuries include soft tissue damage. Because many blood vessels are located in the head and two major arteries (the carotid arteries) and the jugular veins are located in the neck, the victim can lose significant blood quickly. If the victim is bleeding externally, control it promptly with dressings, direct pressure, and bandages. Do not apply pressure to both carotid arteries simultaneously, and do not put a bandage around the neck. Doing so could cut off or seriously diminish the oxygen supply to the brain.

Maintain Normal Body Temperature

A serious injury to the head or spine can disrupt the body's normal heating or cooling mechanism. When this disruption occurs, the person is more susceptible to shock. For example, a person suffering a serious head, neck, or back injury while outside on a cold day will be more likely to succumb to hypothermia because the normal shivering response to rewarm the body may not work. For this reason, it is important to minimize shock by keeping the victim from becoming chilled or overheated.

Care for Specific Head and Neck Injuries

The head is easily injured because it lacks the padding of muscle and fat found in other areas of the body. You can feel bone just beneath the surface of the skin over most of the head, including the chin, cheekbones, and scalp (Fig. 12-6). When you are checking a victim with a suspected head injury, look for any swollen or bruised areas, but do not put direct

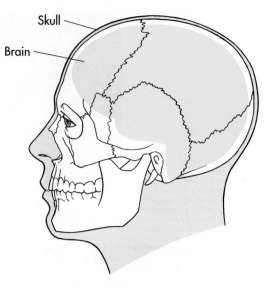

Figure 12-6 The head is easily injured because it lacks the padding of muscle and fat found in other areas of the body.

pressure on any area that is swollen, depressed, or soft.

Concussion

Any significant force to the head can cause a ***concussion.*** A concussion is a temporary impairment of brain function. It usually does not result in permanent physical damage to brain tissue. In most cases, the victim loses consciousness for only an instant and may say that he or she "blacked out" or "saw stars." A concussion sometimes results in a loss of consciousness for longer periods of time. Other times, a victim may be confused or have **amnesia** (loss of memory). Anyone suspected of having a concussion should be examined by a physician.

Scalp injury

Scalp bleeding can be minor or severe. Even minor lacerations can bleed heavily because the scalp contains many blood vessels. The bleeding is usually easily controlled with direct pressure. Wear gloves or use another barrier. Because the skull may be fractured, be careful to press gently at first. If you feel a depression, a spongy area, or bone fragments, do not put direct pressure on the wound. Call EMS personnel. Attempt to control bleeding with pressure on the area around the wound (Fig. 12-7). Examine the injured area carefully because the victim's hair may hide part of the wound. If you are unsure about the extent of a scalp injury, call 9-1-1 or the local emergency number. EMS personnel will be better able to evaluate the injury.

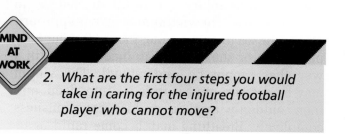

MIND AT WORK

2. *What are the first four steps you would take in caring for the injured football player who cannot move?*

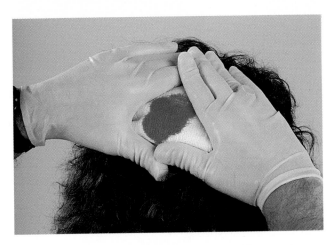

Figure 12-7 To avoid putting pressure on a deep scalp wound, apply pressure around the wound.

If the victim has only an open wound, control the bleeding with direct pressure. Apply several dressings and hold them in place with your gloved hand. If gloves are not available,

use a protective barrier. Secure the dressings with a roller bandage or triangular bandage (Fig. 12-8, *A* and *B*).

Cheek injury

Injury to the cheek usually involves only soft tissue. Control bleeding from the cheek in the same manner as other soft tissue bleeding. The only difference is that you may have to control bleeding on either the outside or the inside of the cheek or both. Begin by examining both the outside and inside of the cheek. Bleeding inside the cheek may result from a blow that caused the teeth to cut the cheek inside or from a laceration or puncture wound outside the cheek. To control bleeding, place several dressings, folded or rolled, inside the mouth, against the cheek. If possible, have the victim hold them in place. If the victim cannot hold the dressing, wear gloves or use another

A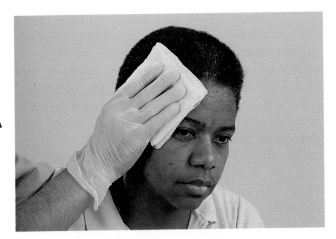

B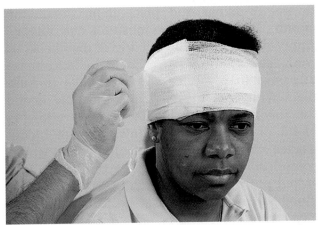

Figure 12-8 **A,** Apply pressure to control bleeding from a scalp wound. **B,** Then secure dressings with a bandage.

A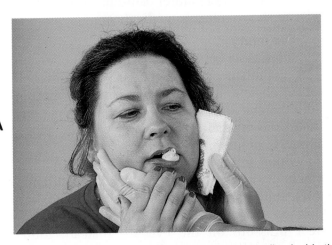

B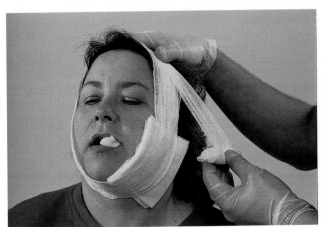

Figure 12-9 **A,** To control bleeding inside the cheek, place folded dressings inside the mouth against the wound. **B,** To control bleeding on the outside, use dressings to apply pressure directly to the wound. Bandage so as not to restrict breathing.

What's the best pressure angle?

barrier. If external bleeding is also present, place dressings on the outside of the cheek and apply direct pressure (Fig. 12-9, *A* and *B*).

If an object passes completely through the cheek and becomes embedded and you cannot control bleeding with the object in place, the object should be removed so that you can control the bleeding and keep the airway clear. *This circumstance is the only exception to the general rule not to remove impaled objects from the body.* An embedded object in the cheek cannot be easily stabilized, makes control of bleeding more difficult, and may become dislodged and obstruct the airway. You can remove the object by pulling it out the same direction it entered. If doing so is difficult, stabilize the object with bulky dressings and leave it in place. Position the victim on the back or one side to keep the airway clear and call EMS personnel. Wear gloves or use another barrier.

Once the object is removed, fold or roll several dressings and place them inside the mouth. Be sure not to obstruct the airway. Apply dressings to the outside of the cheek, as well. The victim may be able to hold these dressings in place, or you may have to hold them with your gloved hand. Bleeding inside the cheek can result in the victim swallowing blood. If the victim swallows enough blood, nausea or vomiting can result, which would complicate the situation. Place the victim in a seated position leaning slightly forward so that blood will not drain into the throat. As with any serious bleeding or embedded object, call EMS personnel.

Nose injury

Nose injuries are usually caused by a blow from a blunt object. The result is often a nosebleed. High blood pressure or changes in altitude can also cause nosebleeds. In most cases, you can control bleeding by having the victim sit with the head slightly forward while pinching the nostrils together (Fig. 12-10). Apply this pressure for at least 10 minutes. Other methods of controlling bleeding include applying an ice pack to the bridge of the nose or putting pressure on the upper lip just beneath the nose. Keep the victim leaning slightly forward so that blood does not drain into the throat and cause the victim to vomit.

Once you have controlled the bleeding, tell the victim to avoid rubbing, blowing, or picking

Figure 12-10   To control a nosebleed, have the victim lean forward and pinch the nostrils together until bleeding stops.

the nose, since these actions could restart the bleeding. You may suggest applying a little petroleum jelly inside the nostril later to help keep the mucous membranes in the nostril moist.

You should seek additional medical care if the nosebleed continues after you use the techniques described, if bleeding recurs, or if the victim says the bleeding is the result of high blood pressure. If the victim loses consciousness, place the victim on his or her side to allow blood to drain from the nose. Contact EMS personnel immediately.

If you think an object is in the nostril, look into the nostril. If you see the object and can easily grasp it, then do so. Wear gloves. However, do not probe the nostril with your finger. Doing so may push the object farther into the nose and cause bleeding, block the airway, or make it more difficult to remove later. If the object cannot be removed easily, the victim should receive medical care.

Eye injury

Injuries to the eye can involve the bone and soft tissue surrounding the eye or the eyeball. Blunt objects, like a fist or a baseball, may injure the eye area, or a smaller object may penetrate the eyeball. Care for open or closed wounds around the eyeball as you would for any other soft tissue injury.

Injury to the eyeball itself requires different care. Injuries that penetrate the eyeball are very serious and can cause blindness. Never put direct pressure on the eyeball. Instead, follow these guidelines when providing care for an eye which has been impaled by an object.

1. Place the victim on his or her back.
2. Do not attempt to remove any object embedded in the eye.
3. Place a sterile dressing around the object (Fig. 12-11, *A*).
4. Stabilize any embedded object as best you can. You can stabilize the object by placing

Figure 12-12   If chemicals enter the eye, flush the eye continuously with water.

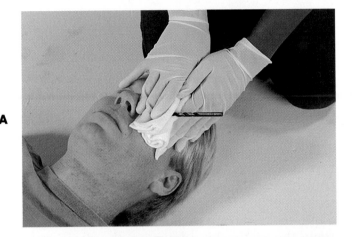

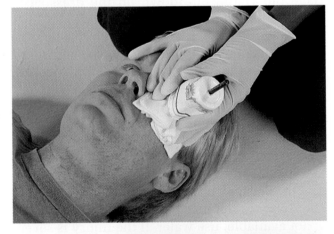

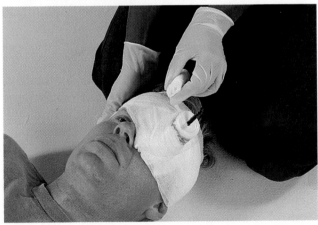

Figure 12-11   **A,** Place sterile dressings around an object embedded in the eye. **B,** Support the object with a paper cup. **C,** Carefully bandage the cup in place.

a paper cup to support the object (Fig. 12-11, *B*).
5. Apply a bandage (Fig. 12-11, *C*).

Foreign bodies that get in the eye, such as dirt, sand, or slivers of wood or metal, are irritating and can cause significant damage. The eye produces tears immediately in an attempt to flush out such objects. Pain from the irritation is often severe. The victim may have difficulty opening the eye because light further irritates it.

First, try to remove the foreign body by telling the victim to blink several times. Then try gently flushing the eye with water. If the object remains, the victim should receive professional medical attention. Flushing the eye with water is also appropriate if the victim has any chemical in his or her eye (Fig. 12-12). The eye should be continuously flushed until EMS personnel arrive.

Ear injury

Ear injuries are common. Either the soft tissue of the ear or the eardrum within the ear may be injured. Open wounds, such as lacerations or abrasions, can result from recreational injuries, for example, being struck by a racquetball or falling off a bike. An avulsion of the ear may occur when a pierced earring catches on something and tears away from the ear. You can control bleeding from the soft tissues of the ear by applying direct pressure with a gloved hand or other barrier to the affected area.

If the victim has a serious head injury, blood or other fluid may be in the ear canal or be draining from the ear. *Do not attempt to stop this drainage with direct pressure.* Instead, just cover the ear lightly with a sterile dressing. Call EMS personnel.

The ear can also be injured internally. A direct blow to the head may rupture the eardrum. Sudden pressure changes, such as those caused by an explosion or a deep-water dive, can also injure the ear internally. The victim may lose hearing or balance or experience inner ear pain. These injuries require professional medical care.

A foreign object, such as dirt, an insect, or cotton, can easily become lodged in the ear canal. If you can easily see and grasp the object, remove it. Do not try to remove any object by using a pin, toothpick, or a similar sharp item. You could force the object farther back or puncture the eardrum. Sometimes you can remove the object if you pull down on the earlobe, tilt the head to the side, and shake or gently strike the head on the affected side. If you cannot easily remove the object, the victim should seek professional medical care.

Mouth, jaw, and neck injuries

Your primary concern for any injury to the mouth, jaw, or neck is to ensure an open airway. Injuries in these areas may cause breathing problems if blood or loose teeth obstruct the airway. A swollen or crushed trachea may also obstruct breathing. With any blow to the head that is strong enough to fracture bone or result in heavy bleeding, suspect possible spinal injury.

If you do not suspect a serious head, neck, or back injury, place the victim in a seated position with the head tilted slightly forward to allow any blood to drain. If this position is not possible, place the victim on his or her side to allow blood to drain from the mouth.

For injuries that penetrate the lip, place a rolled dressing between the lip and the gum. You can place another dressing on the outer surface of the lip. If the tongue is bleeding, apply a dressing and direct pressure with a gloved hand. Applying ice or a cold pack to the lips or tongue can help reduce swelling and ease pain. Place gauze between the source of cold and the tongue. If the bleeding cannot be controlled easily, the victim should seek medical attention.

If the injury knocked out one or more of the victim's teeth, control the bleeding and

Figure 12-13   If a tooth is knocked out, place a sterile dressing directly in the space left by the tooth. Tell the victim to bite down.

save the tooth or teeth for replantation. To control the bleeding, roll a sterile dressing and insert it into the space left by the missing tooth or teeth. Wear gloves or use a barrier. Have the victim bite down on the dressing to maintain pressure (Fig. 12-13).

Opinions vary as to how the tooth should be saved. One thought is to place the dislodged tooth or teeth in the injured person's mouth. This method, however, is not always the best approach, since a crying child could aspirate the tooth or the tooth could otherwise become an airway obstruction. The tooth could also be swallowed with blood or saliva. In addition, you may need to control serious bleeding in the mouth. Because of these concerns, it is best to simply place the tooth in a cup of milk. If milk is not available, use water. If the injury is severe enough to call EMS personnel, give the tooth to them when they arrive. If the injury is not severe enough to contact EMS personnel, the victim should immediately seek a dentist who can replant the tooth. *For the tooth to be successfully replanted, time is critical.* Ideally, the tooth should be replanted within an hour after the injury.

Injuries serious enough to fracture or dislocate the jaw can also cause other head or neck injuries. Be sure to maintain an open airway. Check inside the mouth for bleeding. Control bleeding as you would for other head injuries. Minimize movement of the head and neck. Call EMS personnel for an injury of this type.

A soft tissue injury of the neck can produce severe bleeding and swelling that may result in airway obstruction. Because the spine may also be involved, care for a serious neck injury as you would a possible spinal injury. If the victim has struck his or her neck on a steering wheel or run into a clothesline, the injury can be devastating. The trachea may be crushed or collapsed, causing an airway obstruction that requires immediate medical attention. While waiting for EMS personnel, try to keep the victim from moving, and encourage him or her to breathe slowly. Control any external bleeding with direct pressure, wearing a glove or using another barrier. Be careful not to apply pressure that constricts both carotid arteries. For a large laceration to the neck, apply an occlusive dressing to avoid the possibility of air getting into a vein.

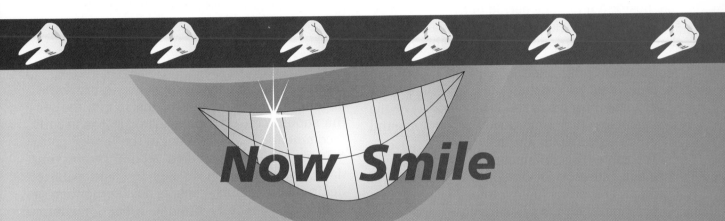

Now Smile

Knocked-out teeth no longer spell doom for pearly whites. Most dentists can successfully replant a knocked-out tooth if they can do so quickly and if the tooth is properly handled.

Replanting a tooth is similar to replanting a tree. On each tooth, tiny root fibers called periodontal fibers attach to the jawbone to hold the tooth in place. Inside the tooth, a canal filled with bundles of blood vessels and nerves runs from the tooth into the jawbone and surrounding tissues.

"When these fibers and tissues are torn from the socket, it is important that they be replaced within an hour," says American Academy of Pediatric Dentists expert, Dr. J. Bogart. Generally, the sooner the tooth is replanted, the greater the chance it will survive. The knocked-out tooth must be handled carefully to protect the fragile tissues. Be careful to pick up the tooth by the chewing edge (crown), not the root. Do not rub or handle the root part of the tooth. It is best to preserve the tooth by placing it in a closed container of cool, fresh milk until it reaches the dentist. Because milk is not always available at an injury scene, water may be substituted.

A dentist or emergency physician will clean the tooth, taking care not to damage the root fibers. The tooth is then placed back into the socket and secured with special splinting devices. The devices keep the tooth stable for 2 to 3 weeks while the fibers reattach to the jawbone. The bundles of blood vessels and nerves grow back within 6 weeks.

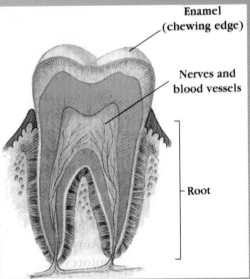

Enamel (chewing edge)

Nerves and blood vessels

Root

SOURCES

Bogart J, DDS: Executive Director, American Academy of Pediatric Dentists. Interview April 1990.
Medford H, DDS: Acute care of an avulsed tooth, *Ann Emerg Med* 11:559-61, 1982

LOWER BACK INJURY

Certain injuries to the neck and back are not life threatening but can be extremely painful and temporarily disabling and may occur without warning. These injuries usually occur from forcing the back beyond its limits in strength or flexibility. Using improper lifting techniques when lifting or moving heavy objects is one way to injure the back. Working in a cramped space in a bent-over or awkward position may cause back pain, as can sitting or standing in one position for a long period of time.

Often acute back pain that develops suddenly is a result of one of the following causes:

- Ligament pulls and muscle strains—violent movement or unaccustomed effort stretches or tears muscles in the back or neck, or the ligaments that bind together or surround each section of the spine.
- Vertebrae displacement—twisting movement causes two vertebrae to slip out of place, and facets (bony projections) lock in a position that puts pressure on a nerve or irritates the joint, often causing muscles to go into spasm.
- Slipped (prolapsed) disk—pressure and wear and tear on one of the cartilage disks that separate the vertebrae cause the soft center of the disk to protrude through the disk's outer layer. This center part presses on a nerve often causing muscles to spasm.

Signs and Symptoms of Lower Back Injury

Signs and symptoms of lower back injury include—

- Shooting pain in the lower back; sharp pain in one leg.
- Sharp pain and tightness across the lower back.
- A sudden, sharp pain in the back and a feeling that something snapped.
- Inability to bend over.

Regardless of the possible cause of back pain, call EMS personnel immediately if the victim has any of the following signs or symptoms:

- Numbness or tingling in any extremity

- Difficulty moving
- Loss of bladder or bowel control

These signs and symptoms indicate possible damage to the spinal cord. Wait for medical help and keep the victim warm and quiet.

A person with pain in one side of the small of the back who also has a fever or feels ill should call a physician. The victim may have a kidney infection. Older adults with back pain may have a life-threatening emergency—an aortic **aneurysm.** Older adults with severe back pain should be brought to an emergency department immediately.

Care for Lower Back Injury

Because the care for lower back injury varies depending on the nature of the injury, the victim should consult a physician. Heat is usually recommended for strains of the lower back; cold is usually recommended for sprains initially, followed by heat. Bed rest and pain-relieving medications, such as acetaminophen or ibuprofen, generally provide relief for strains and muscle spasms. Exercises are frequently recommended to strengthen the back and abdominal muscles after the pain has gone and should only be done at the direction of a physician or physical therapist.

PREVENTING HEAD AND SPINE INJURIES

Injuries to the head and spine are a major cause of death, disability, and disfigurement. However, many such injuries can be prevented. By using safety practices in all areas of your life, you can help reduce risks to yourself and to others around you.

Safety practices that can help prevent injuries to the head and spine include—

- Wearing safety belts (lap and shoulder restraints) and placing children in car safety seats.
- When appropriate, wearing approved helmets, eyewear, faceguards, and mouthguards (Fig. 12-14).
- Taking steps to prevent falls.
- Obeying rules in sports and recreational activities.

Figure 12-14   Wearing a helmet helps protect against head and spine injuries.

- Avoiding inappropriate use of alcohol and other drugs.
- Inspecting work and recreational equipment periodically.
- Thinking and talking about safety.

Further information on preventing head and spine injuries is presented in Chapter 23.

SUMMARY

In this chapter, you have learned how to recognize and care for serious head and spine injuries, specific injuries to the head and neck, and problems with the lower back. Often the cause is the best indicator of whether an injury to the head, neck, and back should be considered serious. If you have any doubts about the seriousness of an injury, call EMS personnel.

Like injuries elsewhere on the body, injuries to the head, neck, and back often involve both soft tissues and bone. Control bleeding as necessary, usually with direct pressure with a gloved hand on the wound. With scalp injuries, be careful not to apply pressure to a possible skull fracture. Similarly, with eye injuries, remember not to apply pressure on the eyeball. If you suspect that the victim may have a fracture of the skull or spine, minimize movement of the injured area when providing care. This minimizing of movement is best accomplished by using in-line stabilization.

As you read the next chapter about how to care for injuries to the chest and abdomen, remember the principles of care for head, neck, and back injuries. Serious injuries of the chest and abdomen often also affect the spine.

Answers to Application Questions

1. No. Signs and symptoms could develop later. He did strike his head and could have injured his neck or back in doing so.

2. Have someone call EMS personnel; stabilize the victim's head; check for breathing and open the airway if necessary. Watch closely for other signs of serious head, neck, or back injury.

STUDY QUESTIONS

1. Match each term with the correct definition.

   a. Concussion
   b. In-line stabilization
   c. Spinal column
   d. Spinal cord
   e. Vertebrae

   __B__ Technique used to minimize movement of the victim's head and neck while providing care.

   __A__ Head injury that usually does not permanently damage the brain.

   __C__ Column of vertebrae extending from the base of the skull to the tip of the tailbone.

   __E__ The 33 bones of the spinal column.

   __D__ A bundle of nerves extending from the base of the skull to the lower back, protected by the spinal column.

2. List five situations that might result in serious head, neck, or back injuries.

3. List six signals of head, neck, or back injuries.

4. List five ways to prevent head and spine injuries.

5. List the steps of care for an eye injury in which the eyeball has been penetrated.

In questions 6 through 13, circle the letter of the correct answer.

6. Which are the most common causes of serious head, neck, and back injury?

    a. Diving mishaps
    b. Motor vehicle collisions
    c. Falls
    d. Assaults

7. Serious injuries to the head, neck, or back can damage—

    a. Soft tissues.
    b. Nerve tissues.
    c. Bones.
    d. All of the above.

8. Which should you consider when determining the severity of a head, neck, or back injury?

    a. The cause of the injury
    b. The physical signs and symptoms present
    c. What bystanders who saw the injury occur can tell you
    d. All of the above

9. Which should you do when caring for a victim of head injury?

    a. Stabilize the head and spine
    b. Stop the flow of fluids from the ears
    c. Remove any embedded object
    d. Apply direct pressure to control all scalp bleeding

10. At the scene of a car crash, a victim has blood seeping from his ears. Which should you do?

    a. Loosely cover the ears with a sterile dressing.
    b. Do nothing; this is a normal finding in a head injury.
    c. Collect the fluid in a sterile container for analysis.
    d. Pack the ears with sterile dressings to prevent further fluid loss.

11. Which is your primary concern when caring for an injury to the mouth or neck?

    a. Infection
    b. Airway obstruction
    c. Swelling
    d. None of the above

12. Caring for a penetrating injury to the eyeball includes—

    a. Not putting direct pressure on the eyeball.
    b. Removing objects penetrating the eye.
    c. Washing the affected eye.
    d. a and c.

13. Which is a sign or symptom of an injured ear?

    a. Hearing loss
    b. Loss of balance
    c. Inner ear pain
    d. All of the above

14. As you begin to apply direct pressure to control bleeding for a scalp injury, you notice a depression of the skull in the area of the bleeding. How should you alter care?

15. What should you do for a victim of suspected head and spine injury whom you find lying on his side, moaning in pain?

16. What care would you give to a person who suddenly experienced a sharp pain in the back followed by numbness in one leg?

Answers are listed in Appendix A.

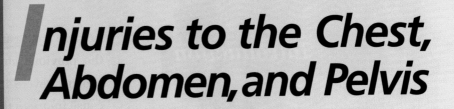

CHAPTER 13

Injuries to the Chest, Abdomen, and Pelvis

WHAT YOU SHOULD LEARN

After reading this chapter, you should be able to—

1. Explain why injuries to the chest, abdomen, and pelvis can be fatal.

2. List the five general steps of care for these injuries.

3. List the seven signs and symptoms of chest injury.

4. Describe how to care for rib fractures.

5. Describe how to care for a sucking chest wound.

6. List 13 signs and symptoms of serious abdominal and pelvic injuries.

7. Describe the care for open and closed abdominal and pelvic injuries.

8. Describe how to care for injuries to the genitals.

9. Define the key terms for this chapter.

It wasn't anyone's fault exactly. Mr. McGuffy should have known better than to walk out from between two parked cars like a little kid, but he was in a hurry to mail off his rent money. Cora Markowitz was taking her daughter, Lila, to day care and was distracted trying to explain what clouds were made of. In any case, her car struck Mr. McGuffy a glancing blow on one side just as he stepped into the street and sent him sprawling. Cora put on the brakes, jumped out of the car, and ran over to Mr. McGuffy, who was already sitting up and starting to clamber to his feet. "I'm OK," he said, in a shaky voice, but Cora wasn't so sure. He looked sick, weak, and as if he was in pain.

Introduction

Many injuries to the chest and abdomen involve only soft tissues. Often these injuries, like those that occur elsewhere on the body, are only minor cuts, scrapes, burns, and bruises. Occasionally, severe injuries occur, such as fractures or injuries to organs, that cause severe bleeding or impair breathing. Fractures and lacerations often occur in motor vehicle collisions to occupants not wearing safety belts. Falls, sports mishaps, and other forms of **trauma,** the violent force or mechanism that can cause injury, may also cause such injuries.

Injuries to the pelvis may be minor soft tissue injuries or serious injuries to bone and internal structures. The pelvis is the lower part of the trunk, containing part of the intestines, bladder, and reproductive organs. It includes a group of large bones that forms a protective girdle around the organs inside. A great force is required to cause serious injury to the pelvic bones.

Because the chest, abdomen, and pelvis contain many organs important to life, injury to these areas can be fatal. You may recall from the previous chapter that a force capable of causing severe injury in these areas may also cause injury to the spine.

General care for these injuries includes—

- Calling EMS personnel.
- Limiting movement.
- Monitoring breathing and signs of circulation.
- Controlling bleeding.
- Minimizing shock.

This chapter describes the signs and symptoms of different injuries to the chest, abdomen, and pelvis and the care for them. In all cases, follow the Emergency Action Steps. *Check* the scene and the victim. *Call* EMS personnel. *Care* for the victim. *Care* for all life-threatening injuries first. *All injuries described in the following sections of this chapter are serious enough that you should always call EMS personnel immediately.*

INJURIES TO THE CHEST

The **chest** is the upper part of the trunk. It is shaped by 12 pairs of ribs. Ten of the pairs attach to the **sternum** (breastbone) in front and to the spine in back. Two pairs, the floating ribs, attach only to the spine. The **rib cage,** the cage of bones formed by the ribs, the sternum, and the spine, protects vital organs, such as the heart, major blood vessels, and the lungs (Fig. 13-1). Also in the chest are the esophagus, the trachea, and the muscles of respiration.

Chest injuries are the second leading cause of trauma deaths each year. Approximately 35 percent of all traffic fatalities in the United States involve chest injuries. Injuries to the chest may result from a wide variety of other causes, such as falls, sports mishaps, and crushing or penetrating forces (Fig. 13-2).

Chest wounds are either open or closed. Open chest wounds occur when an object, such as a knife or bullet, penetrates the chest wall. Fractured ribs may break through the skin to

Key Terms

Abdomen: The middle part of the trunk, containing the stomach, liver, intestines, and spleen.
Chest: The upper part of the trunk, containing the heart, major blood vessels, and lungs.
Genitals: The external reproductive organs.
Pelvis: The lower part of the trunk, containing the intestines, bladder, and internal reproductive organs.
Rib cage: The cage of bones formed by the 12 pairs of ribs, the sternum, and the spine.
Sternum: The long, flat bone in the middle of the front of the rib cage; also called the breastbone.

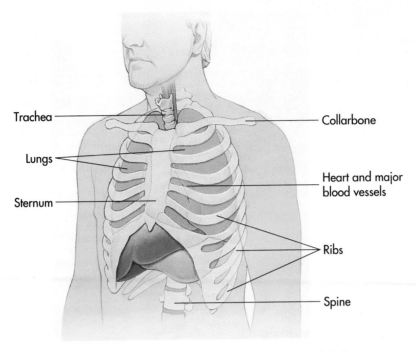

Trachea

Lungs

Sternum

Collarbone

Heart and major
blood vessels

Ribs

Spine

Figure 13-1   The rib cage surrounds and protects several vital organs.

Figure 13-2   About one third of the deaths from motor vehicle collisions involve chest injuries. Crushing forces, falls, and sports mishaps can also lead to chest injuries.

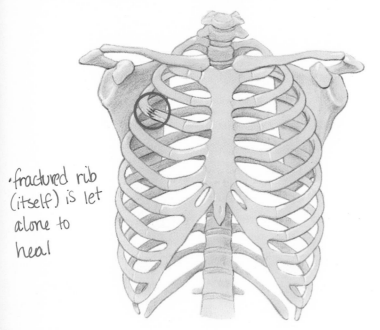

*fractured rib
(itself) is let
alone to
heal*

Figure 13-3   A simple rib fracture is painful but rarely life threatening.

Figure 13-4   When a rib fracture occurs, use a pillow or folded blanket to support and immobilize the injured area.

*stays sitting for
pressure*

cause an open chest injury. A chest wound is closed if the skin is not broken. Closed chest wounds are generally caused by blunt objects, such as steering wheels.

Signs and Symptoms of Chest Injuries

You should know the signs and symptoms of serious chest injuries. These injuries may occur with both open and closed wounds. You will recognize some of these signs and symptoms from Chapter 5. They include—

- Difficulty breathing.
- Severe pain at the site of the injury.
- Flushed, pale, ashen, or bluish discoloration of the skin.
- Obvious deformity, such as that caused by a fracture.
- Coughing up blood.
- Bruising at the site of a blunt injury, such as that caused by a shoulder harness.
- A sucking noise when the victim breathes.

Care for Specific Types of Chest Injuries

Chest injuries may involve the bones that form the chest cavity or they may involve the organs or other structures in the cavity itself.

Rib fractures

Rib fractures are usually caused by direct force to the chest. Although painful, a simple rib fracture is rarely life threatening (Fig. 13-3). A victim with a fractured rib generally remains calm, but his or her breathing is shallow because normal or deep breathing is painful. The victim will usually attempt to ease the pain by supporting the injured area with a hand or arm. Therefore, shallow breathing and holding the area are both signs of possible rib fracture. If you suspect a fractured rib, have the victim rest in a position that will make breathing easier. Do not move the victim if you suspect a spinal injury. Call EMS personnel. Binding the victim's arm to the chest on the injured side will help support the injured area and make breathing more comfortable. You can use an object such as a pillow or rolled blanket to support and immobilize the area (Fig. 13-4). Monitor breathing and how the skin looks and feels, and take steps to minimize shock.

Rib fractures are less common in children because children's ribs are so flexible that they bend rather than break. However, the forces

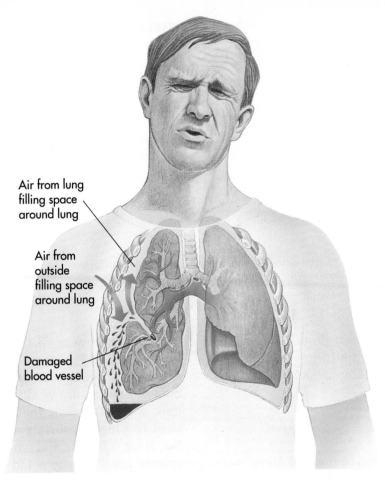

Air from lung filling space around lung

Air from outside filling space around lung

Damaged blood vessel

Figure 13-5   A puncture wound that penetrates the lung or the chest cavity surrounding the lung allows air to go in and out of the cavity.

than can cause a rib fracture in adults severely bruise the lung tissue of children—a life-threatening injury. You must suspect such an injury in a child from the cause of the injury, bruising on the chest, and difficulty breathing.

Puncture injuries

Puncture wounds to the chest range from minor to life threatening. Stab and gunshot wounds are examples of puncture injuries. A forceful puncture may penetrate the rib cage and allow air to enter the chest through the wound (Fig. 13-5). Air in the chest cavity does not allow the lungs to function normally. The penetrating object can injure any structure within the chest, including the lungs.

Puncture wounds cause varying degrees of internal or external bleeding. A puncture wound to the chest is a life-threatening injury. If the injury penetrates the rib cage, air can pass freely in and out of the chest cavity, and the victim cannot breathe normally. With each breath the victim takes, you hear a sucking sound coming from the wound. This sound is the primary sign of a penetrating chest injury called a **sucking chest wound.**

Without proper care, the victim's condition will worsen. The affected lung or lungs will fail to function, and breathing will become more difficult. Call EMS personnel. Your main concern is the breathing problem. To care for a sucking chest wound, cover the wound with an **occlusive dressing,** a dressing that does not allow air to pass through it. A piece of plastic wrap, a plastic bag, or aluminum foil folded several times and placed over the wound makes an effective occlusive dressing. Tape the dressing in place, except for one side or corner that is to remain loose. A taped-down dressing keeps air from entering the wound during inhalation, but having an open corner allows air

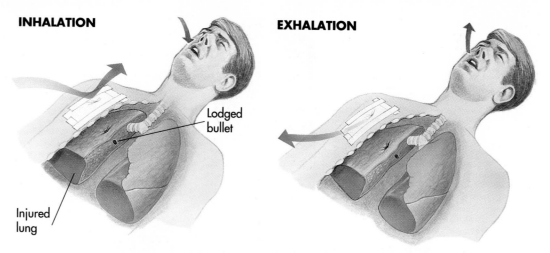

INHALATION

EXHALATION

Lodged bullet

Injured lung

Figure 13-6 A special dressing with one loose corner keeps air from entering the wound during inhalation and allows air to escape during exhalation. This helps keep the injured lung from collapsing.

to escape during exhalation (Fig. 13-6). If these materials are not available to use as dressings, use a folded cloth. Take steps to minimize shock.

INJURIES TO THE ABDOMEN

The **abdomen** is the area immediately under the chest and above the pelvis. It is easily injured because it is not surrounded by bones. The upper abdomen is partially protected in front by the lower ribs. It is protected in back by the spine. The muscles of the back and abdomen also help protect the internal organs, many of which are vital (Fig. 13-7). Most important are the organs that are easily injured or tend to bleed profusely when injured, such as the liver, spleen, and stomach. The liver and spleen are less protected in children because the major part of the organ is positioned below the rib cage and the abdominal muscles are less strong than those of adults.

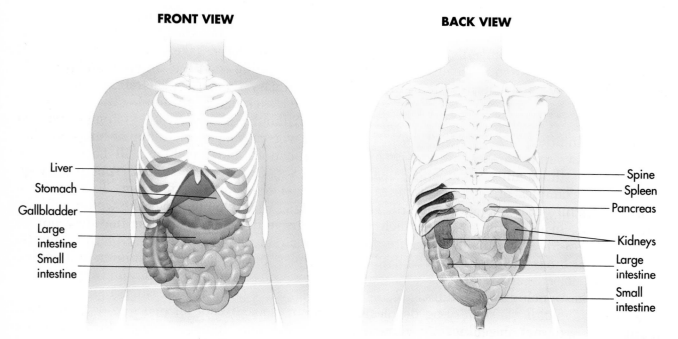

FRONT VIEW

BACK VIEW

Liver
Stomach
Gallbladder
Large intestine
Small intestine

Spine
Spleen
Pancreas
Kidneys
Large intestine
Small intestine

Figure 13-7 Unlike the organs of the chest or pelvis, organs in the abdominal cavity are relatively unprotected by bones.

The liver is rich in blood. Located in the upper right part of the abdomen, this organ is protected somewhat by the lower ribs. However, it is delicate and can be torn by blows from blunt objects or penetrated by a fractured rib. The resulting bleeding can be severe and can quickly be fatal. A liver, when injured, can also leak bile into the abdomen, which can cause severe irritation and infection.

The spleen is behind the stomach and is protected somewhat by the lower left ribs. Like the liver, this organ is easily damaged. The spleen may rupture when the abdomen is struck forcefully by a blunt object. Since the spleen stores blood, an injury to the spleen can cause a severe loss of blood in a short time and can be life threatening.

The stomach is one of the main digestive organs. The upper part of the stomach changes shape depending on its contents, the stage of digestion, and the size and strength of the stomach muscles. It is lined with many blood vessels and nerves. It can bleed severely when injured, and food contents may leak into the abdominal cavity and possibly cause infection.

Signs and Symptoms of Abdominal Injury

The signs and symptoms of serious abdominal injury include—

- Severe pain.
- Bruising.
- External bleeding.
- Nausea.
- Vomiting (sometimes vomit containing blood).
- Weakness.
- Thirst.
- Pain, tenderness, or a tight feeling in the abdomen.
- Organs protruding from the abdomen.
- Rigid abdominal muscles.
- Other signs and symptoms of shock.

Care for Abdominal Injuries

Like a chest injury, an injury to the abdomen is either open or closed. Even with a closed wound, the rupture of an organ can cause serious internal bleeding that results in shock. Injuries to the abdomen can be very painful. It is especially difficult to determine if a person has an abdominal injury if he or she is unconscious. With people who have multiple injuries, you should ensure the possibility of abdominal injury is not overlooked. Serious reactions can occur if organs leak blood or other contents into the abdomen.

With a severe open injury, abdominal organs sometimes protrude through the wound (Fig. 13-8, *A*). To care for an open wound to the abdomen, follow these steps (Fig. 13-8, *B-D*):

- Call EMS personnel.
- Put on disposable latex gloves or use another barrier.
- Carefully position the victim on the back.
- Do not apply direct pressure.
- Do not push any protruding organs back in.
- Remove clothing from around the wound.
- Apply moist, sterile dressings loosely over the wound. (Warm tap water can be used.) *has to be moist or will stick to organs*
- Cover dressings loosely with plastic wrap, if available.
- Cover dressings lightly with a folded towel to maintain warmth.

Shock is likely to occur with a serious abdominal injury. Call EMS personnel immediately, and take steps to minimize shock. Keep the victim from becoming chilled or overheated, and monitor breathing and how the skin looks and feels until EMS personnel arrive.

To care for a closed abdominal injury—

- Call EMS personnel.
- Carefully position the victim on the back unless you suspect spinal injury.
- Bend the victim's knees slightly. This position allows the muscles of the abdomen to relax. If moving the victim's legs causes pain, leave them straight.
- Place rolled-up blankets or pillows under the victim's knees.
- Take steps to minimize shock. Keep the victim from becoming chilled or overheated, and monitor breathing and how the skin looks and feels until EMS personnel arrive.

INJURIES TO THE PELVIS

The **pelvis** is the lower part of the trunk and contains the bladder, reproductive organs, and

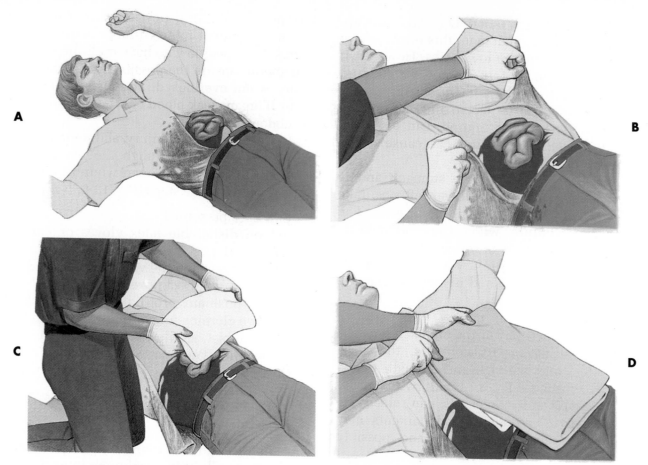

Figure 13-8 **A,** Severe injuries to the abdominal cavity can result in protruding organs. **B,** Carefully remove clothing from around the wound. **C,** Apply a large, moist, sterile dressing over the wound and cover it with plastic wrap. **D,** Place a folded towel or other cloth over the dressing to maintain warmth.

part of the large intestine, including the rectum. Major arteries (the femoral arteries) and nerves pass through the pelvis. The organs within the pelvis are well protected on the sides and back but not in front (Fig. 13-9). Injuries to the pelvis may include fractures to the pelvic bone and damage to structures within. Fractured bones may puncture or lacerate these structures, or they can be injured when struck forceful blows by blunt or penetrating objects.

Signs and Symptoms of Pelvic Injury

Signs and symptoms of pelvic injury are the same as those for an abdominal injury. Certain pelvic injuries may also cause loss of sensation in the legs or inability to move them. This loss of sensation or movement may indicate an injury to the lower spine.

Care for Pelvic Injuries

Care for pelvic injuries is similar to that for abdominal injuries. Do not move the victim unless necessary. If possible, try to keep the victim lying flat. Otherwise, help him or her into a comfortable position. Control any external bleeding, and cover any protruding organs. Wear gloves or use another barrier. Always call EMS personnel and take steps to minimize shock. Major bleeding can occur with pelvic injuries.

An injury to the pelvis sometimes involves the *genitals,* the external reproductive organs. Genital injuries are either closed wounds, such as a bruise, or open wounds, such as an avulsion or laceration. Any injury to the genitals is extremely painful. Care for a closed wound to the genitals as you would for any closed

FRONT VIEW

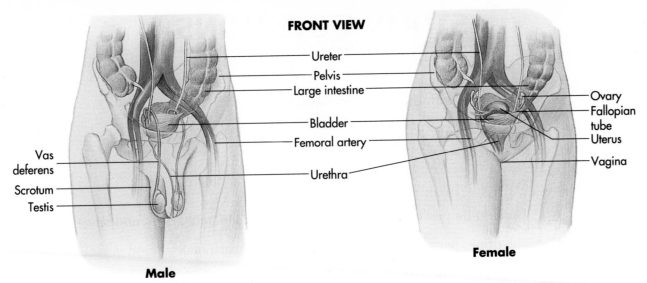

Figure 13-9   The internal structures of the pelvis are well protected on the sides and back, but not in front.

wound. If the injury is an open wound, apply a sterile dressing and direct pressure with your gloved hand or the victim's hand or use a barrier. If any parts are completely avulsed, wrap them as described in Chapter 9, and make sure they are transported with the victim. Injuries to the genital area can be embarrassing for both the victim and the rescuer. Explain briefly what you are going to do, then do it. Do not act in a timid or hesitant manner. Hesitation or shyness will only make the situation more difficult for you and the victim.

SUMMARY

Injuries to the chest, abdomen, or pelvis can be serious. They can damage soft tissues, bones, and internal organs. Although many injuries are immediately obvious, some may be detected only as the victim's condition worsens over time. Watch for the signs and symptoms of serious injuries that require medical attention.

Care for any life-threatening conditions, then give any additional care needed for specific injuries. For open wounds to the chest, abdomen, or pelvis, control bleeding. Wear gloves or use a barrier. If you suspect a fracture, immobilize the injured part. Use special dressings for sucking chest wounds and open abdominal wounds when these materials are available. Always call EMS personnel as soon as possible. Professional medical care gives the victim of a serious injury the best chance for survival and full recovery.

MIND AT WORK

1. *What steps should Cora take to care for Mr. McGuffy?*

Answer to Application Question

1. She should have Mr. McGuffy lie down and she should call EMS personnel or have another person call, if possible. She should keep Mr. McGuffy lying down and try to keep him from moving. Because the injury was the result of trauma, she should apply in-line stabilization to Mr. McGuffy's head and neck, monitor his breathing and signs of circulation while waiting for EMS personnel to arrive, and try to keep Mr. McGuffy from getting chilled or overheated.

STUDY QUESTIONS

1. Match each term with the correct definition.
    a. Abdomen
    b. Chest
    c. Genitals
    d. Pelvis
    e. Sternum

    __C__ External reproductive organs.

    __A__ The middle part of the trunk, containing the stomach, liver, and spleen.

    __B__ The upper part of the trunk, containing the heart, major blood vessels, and lungs.

    __E__ Long, flat bone in the middle of the front of the rib cage, also called the breast-bone.

    __D__ The lower part of the trunk, containing the intestines, bladder, and reproductive organs.

2. List five general steps of care for injuries to the chest, abdomen, and pelvis.

3. List four signs and symptoms of chest injury.

4. A horse being loaded into a trailer kicks a man in the chest. He is clutching the left side of his chest and says it hurts to breathe. What type of injury could you suspect he has, and what care would you give?

5. Name the primary sign of a sucking chest wound.

6. List four signs and symptoms of abdominal and pelvic injury.

In question 7, circle the letter of the correct answer.

7. Care for injuries to the chest, abdomen, and pelvis includes—
    a. Monitoring breathing and signs of circulation and limiting movement.
    b. Controlling external bleeding.
    c. Taking steps to minimize shock.
    d. All of the above.

8. What signs and symptoms of chest injury do you find in the scenario that follows? Circle the signs and symptoms in the passage below.

   You arrive at the local convenience store late Saturday night to satisfy your frozen yogurt craving. As you enter, you notice drops of blood on the floor. A robbery has just occurred — the store clerk appears to have been beaten and stabbed. He is conscious but in considerable pain and having difficulty breathing. You hear a sucking sound when he breathes.

9. List four things you can do to care for the store clerk.

10. What two steps of care would you take for any serious injury to the chest, abdomen, or pelvis?

Answers are listed in Appendix A.

MEDICAL EMERGENCIES

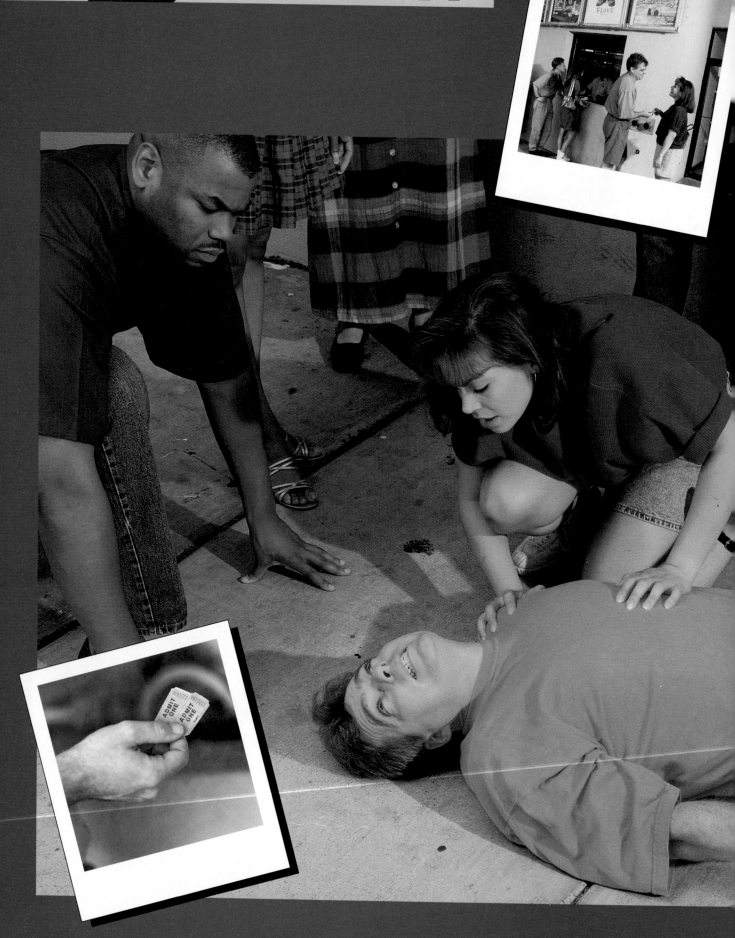

Sudden Illnesses

WHAT YOU SHOULD LEARN

After reading this chapter, you should be able to—

1. Identify the signs and symptoms of four specific sudden illnesses.

2. List six general guidelines of care for someone who suddenly becomes ill.

3. Describe the care for a person who faints.

4. Describe the care for a person who you suspect is having a diabetic emergency.

5. Describe the care for a person having a seizure.

6. List nine instances when you should call EMS personnel for a seizure victim.

7. Describe the care for a person who you suspect is having a stroke.

8. List six ways to reduce the risk of stroke or transient ischemic attack (TIA).

9. Define the key terms for this chapter.

Julio and Michelle were walking to the neighborhood theater to catch an evening movie. "I hope this show's as good as Tony said it is," Julio said. "I spent all day helping my dad paint the trim on some windows, and it must have been 95 degrees out in the sun. I'm really beat." Suddenly, Michelle thought Julio missed a step. He sort of stumbled or tripped or something, then he stopped altogether. He made a funny little noise. "What's the matter?" Michelle started to ask, but before she could say it all, Julio collapsed on the ground. His eyes rolled back, his body went rigid, and his arms and legs began to jerk uncontrollably. Michelle looked frantically around for somebody, anybody, who could help.

Introduction

While some illnesses develop over time, others can strike without a moment's notice. However, if you look closely, you may see the signs of a developing sudden illness. You may hear the person describe his or her symptoms or you may notice a change in the person's appearance. By knowing the signs and symptoms of sudden illness and paying careful attention to details at the emergency scene, you can determine how best to help a victim of sudden illness.

Sudden illnesses become evident in a variety of ways. Many different conditions, such as a diabetic emergency, stroke, epilepsy, poisoning, heart attack, and shock, can all cause a change in a person's level of consciousness. A victim of sudden illness may faint or complain of feeling lightheaded, dizzy, or weak. He or she may feel nauseated or may vomit. Breathing, pulse, body temperature, and skin color may change. A person who looks or feels ill generally is ill.

Sudden illness may result from a condition that has a rapid and intense onset then subsides quickly (acute), or it may result from a persistent condition that continues over a long period of time (chronic). In an emergency, you may not know what caused the illness. However, you do not need to know the exact cause to provide appropriate care for the victim. In this chapter, you will learn that knowing and following the emergency action steps—the basic principles of *Check-Call-Care*—are all you need to give first aid to a victim of sudden illness.

Faced with a person who has an unknown illness, you may not be sure whether to call for emergency medical help. Sometimes, as with simple fainting, the condition is momentary

Key Terms

Diabetes (di ə BE tez) mellitus (mel I tus): A condition in which the body does not produce enough insulin, or does not use insulin effectively enough, to regulate the amount of sugar (glucose) in the bloodstream; often referred to simply as diabetes.

Diabetic emergency: A situation in which a person becomes ill because of an imbalance of sugar (glucose) and insulin in the bloodstream.

Epilepsy (EP i lep se): A chronic condition characterized by seizures that may vary in type and duration; can usually be controlled by medication.

Fainting: A partial or complete loss of consciousness resulting from a temporary reduction of blood flow to the brain.

Glucose: A simple sugar found in certain foods, especially fruits, and a major source of energy occurring in human and animal body fluids.

Hyperglycemia (hi per gli SE me ə): A condition in which too much sugar (glucose) is in the bloodstream and the insulin level in the body is too low.

Hypoglycemia (hi po gli SE me ə): A condition in which too little sugar (glucose) is in the bloodstream and the insulin level in the body is too high.

Insulin (IN su lin): A hormone produced in the pancreas that enables the body to use sugar (glucose) for energy; frequently used to treat diabetes.

Seizure (SE zhur): An irregularity in the brain's electrical activity, often marked by loss of consciousness and uncontrollable muscle movement; also called a convulsion.

Stroke: A disruption of blood flow to a part of the brain, which causes permanent damage to brain tissue; also called a cerebrovascular accident (CVA).

Transient (TRANZ e ent) ischemic (is KE mik) attack (TIA): A temporary episode that, like a stroke, is caused by a disruption of blood flow to the brain; sometimes called a mini-stroke.

and the person immediately recovers. In this case, EMS personnel may not be needed. However, if the problem is not resolved quickly, or if you have any doubts about its severity, always call 9-1-1 or the local emergency number for help. It is better to err on the side of caution. Refer to Chapter 2 for conditions and situations in which you should call EMS personnel.

SPECIFIC SUDDEN ILLNESSES

Some of the sudden illnesses you may encounter include fainting, diabetic emergencies, seizures, and stroke. You will see that the basic care for these illnesses follows the general guidelines for care:

- Do no harm.
- Monitor breathing and consciousness.
- Help the victim rest in the most comfortable position.
- Keep the victim from getting chilled or overheated.
- Reassure the victim.
- Provide any specific care needed.

Depending on the condition in which you find the victim, you may be able to do little more than help him or her rest comfortably until professional help arrives. However, knowing enough about sudden illness to recognize when to call 9-1-1 or the local emergency number is your top priority as a citizen responder.

Fainting

One of the most common sudden illnesses is fainting. **Fainting** (also known as **syncope**) is a partial or complete loss of consciousness. It is caused by a temporary reduction of blood flow to the brain, such as when blood pools in the legs and lower body. When the brain is suddenly deprived of its normal blood flow, it momentarily shuts down and the person faints.

Fainting can be triggered by an emotionally stressful event, such as the sight of blood. It may be caused by pain, specific medical conditions such as heart disease, standing for long

Figure 14-1 A sudden change in positions can sometimes trigger fainting.

periods of time, or overexertion. Some people, such as pregnant women or the elderly, are more likely than others to faint when suddenly changing positions, such as moving from sitting or lying down to standing (Fig. 14-1). Anytime changes inside the body momentarily reduce the blood flow to the brain, fainting may occur.

Signs and symptoms of fainting

Fainting may occur with or without warning. Often, the change in level of consciousness may initially make the victim feel lightheaded or dizzy. Because fainting is a form of shock, he or she may show signs of shock, such as pale, cool, or moist skin (see Chapter 8). The victim may feel nauseated and complain of numbness or tingling in the fingers and toes. Other signs and symptoms that precede fainting include sweating, vomiting, distortion or dimming of vision, and head or abdominal pain. Some victims feel as though everything is going dark just before they lose consciousness.

Care for fainting

Usually, fainting is a self-correcting condition. When the victim collapses, normal circulation to the brain resumes. The victim typically regains consciousness within a minute. Fainting itself does not usually harm the victim, but related injuries, such as from falling, may occur. If you can reach the person as he or she is starting to collapse, lower him or her to the ground or other flat surface. Position the victim on his or her back. Unless the victim is nauseated; is having trouble breathing; you suspect head, neck, or back injuries or possible broken bones involving the hips or legs; or

after having someone rest after fainting, check ABCs

Figure 14-2 To care for fainting, place the victim on his back, elevate the feet, and loosen any restrictive clothing, such as a tie or collar.

moving causes more pain, elevate the legs about 12 inches (30.5 centimeters) to keep the blood circulating to the vital organs. If you are unsure of the victim's condition, or if it is painful for him or her to move, leave him or her lying flat. Loosen any restrictive clothing, such as a tie or collar (Fig. 14-2). Check for any other life-threatening and nonlife-threatening conditions. Do not give the victim anything to eat or drink. Also, do not slap the victim or splash water on his or her face. Splashing water could cause the victim to **aspirate** the water.

As long as the victim of fainting recovers quickly and has no lasting symptoms, it is not necessary to call EMS personnel. However, it may be appropriate to have a bystander or family member take the victim to a physician or

emergency department to determine if the fainting episode is linked to a more serious condition.

Diabetic Emergencies

Diabetes mellitus is one of the leading causes of death and disability in the United States today. Consider the following facts and figures on diabetes:

- An estimated 14 million Americans currently have diabetes, and more than 600,000 additional cases are diagnosed each year.
- Diabetes contributes to other conditions, such as blindness; kidney, heart, and periodontal (tooth) disease; and stroke.
- Direct costs associated with diabetes were $85 billion in 1992. For the same year, an additional $47 billion in indirect costs was attributed to disability, work loss, and premature mortality.

To function normally, body cells need sugar as a source of energy. Through the digestive process, the body breaks down food into simple sugars such as **glucose**, which are absorbed into the bloodstream. However, sugar cannot pass freely from the blood into the body cells. **Insulin,** a hormone produced in the pancreas, is needed for sugar to pass into the cells. Without a proper balance of sugar and insulin, the cells will starve and the body will not function properly (Fig. 14-3). The condition in which the body does not produce enough insulin or does not use insulin effectively is called **diabetes mellitus,** commonly known as diabetes. A situ-

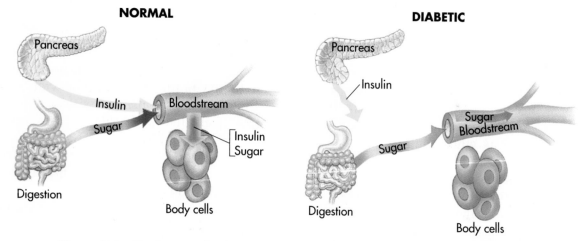

Figure 14-3 The hormone insulin is needed to take sugar from the blood into the body cells.

ation in which a person becomes ill because of an imbalance of insulin and sugar in the bloodstream is called a ***diabetic emergency.***

There are two major types of diabetes. In Type I diabetes (also known as insulin-dependent diabetes), the body produces little or no insulin. Since Type I diabetes tends to develop in childhood, it is commonly called juvenile diabetes. Most people who have Type I diabetes have to inject insulin into their bodies daily. In Type II diabetes (also called noninsulin-dependent diabetes), the body produces insulin, but either the cells do not use the insulin effectively or not enough insulin is produced. Type II diabetes, which is much more common than Type I diabetes, is also known as adult onset diabetes because it usually occurs in adults. Most people who have Type II diabetes can regulate their blood glucose levels sufficiently through diet and do not require insulin injections.

Anyone who has diabetes must carefully monitor his or her diet and amount of exercise. People who have insulin-dependent diabetes (and occasionally those who have noninsulin-dependent diabetes) must also regulate their use of insulin (Fig. 14-4). When diet and exercise are not controlled, either of two problems can occur—too much or too little sugar in the body. This imbalance of sugar and insulin in the blood causes illness.

When the insulin level in the body is too low, the sugar level in the blood is high. This condition is called ***hyperglycemia*** (Fig.

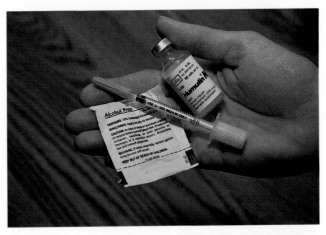

Figure 14-4   People who have insulin-dependent diabetes inject insulin to regulate the amount in the body.

14-5, *A*). Sugar is present in the blood, but it cannot be transported from the blood into the cells without insulin. In this condition, body cells become starved for sugar. The body attempts to meet its need for energy by using other stored food and energy sources, such as fats. However, converting fat to energy is less efficient, produces waste products, and increases the acidity level in the blood, causing a condition called **diabetic ketoacidosis.** A person with diabetic ketoacidosis becomes ill. He or she may have flushed, hot, dry skin and a sweet, fruity breath odor that can be mistaken for the smell of alcohol. The victim also may appear restless or agitated. If the condition is not treated promptly, **diabetic coma,** a life-threatening emergency, can occur.

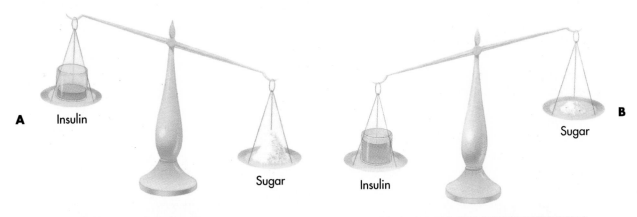

A   Insulin

Sugar

B

Insulin

Sugar

DIABETIC COMA (HYPERGLYCEMIA)   **INSULIN REACTION (HYPOGLYCEMIA)**

Figure 14-5   **A,** Hyperglycemia occurs when there is insufficient insulin in the body, causing a high level of sugar in the blood. **B,** Hypoglycemia occurs when the insulin level in the body is high, causing a low level of sugar in the blood.

Innovations in the Treatment of Diabetes

In an effort to save lives and reduce medical costs, many doctors and researchers have devoted their resources to developing innovative ways to treat diabetes. The following information highlights the technological breakthroughs that have resulted from these endeavors.

New Oral Medication

Metformin, the first new diabetes medication to be approved in the United States for nearly 30 years, was approved by the Food and Drug Administration in December 1994 and became available by prescription in May 1995. Metformin is an oral medication designed to treat Type II diabetes. Metformin will be sold under the trade name of Glucophage and is estimated to cost about $30 for a month's treatment. Metformin is one of a class of drugs called biguanides. Biguanides improve insulin sensitivity by boosting the effectiveness of insulin already found in the body.

Doctors and patients alike are excited about the approval of Metformin because it is affordable, works with the body's natural supply of insulin, can be used in patients who do not respond well to diet and exercise programs, can be prescribed alone or in combination with other diabetes medications, may replace or forestall the need for some insulin injections, and gives patients much better blood sugar control. Metformin is expected to be widely used among those who have Type II diabetes.

Noninvasive Glucose Monitors

Many patients who have diabetes find it inconvenient or difficult to puncture their fingers several times a day to monitor their blood glucose levels. To overcome resistance to this monitoring process, several companies are attempting to create a noninvasive device that would eliminate the need to puncture the skin.

The most promising device of this kind now in development monitors blood glucose levels by sending a near-infrared laser light beam through a fold in the skin. A patient would put his or her finger or other body part on the monitor, and the blood glucose level would be measured by analyz-ing the scattering of light passing through the skin. Doctors and researchers are hopeful that some versions of noninvasive glucose monitors will be ready for review by the FDA in the near future.

New Insulin Analog

Although insulin therapy has come a long way since it was first made commercially available in 1923, present-day therapy still has major shortcomings. Perhaps the greatest difficulty is the inability of insulin injections to accurately mimic the natural concentrations of insulin the body produces in response to diet. When patients inject themselves 30 minutes before a meal, the insulin level peaks between 30 minutes and 2 to 3 hours after the injection and lasts 4 to 6 hours. The result is a risk of high blood glucose levels after a meal and low levels several hours later when food is digested and the insulin is still working.

Scientists are attempting to overcome this problem by creating a faster, short-acting insulin analog. An analog is a drug that resembles another drug in structure and components but produces different effects. The most promising analog created to date is called Lispro. Lispro works more like natural insulin by going to work quickly, then disappearing rapidly from circulation. Lispro, which can be injected within 5 minutes of eating, peaks in 45 to 50 minutes and stays in the system for about 3 hours. This analog not only provides better glucose control but makes the patient less likely to forget an injection.

Worldwide testing of Lispro has begun, involving more than 3000 people in 25 countries who have Type I and Type II diabetes. Lispro may be available commercially within the next few years.

Internal Programmable Pump

Some people who have diabetes wear an external insulin pump, about the size of a beeper, which can be programmed to deliver insulin on demand. Although many patients are pleased with this method of treatment, most of those who have Type I diabetes continue to choose the multiple-injection approach. Dissatisfaction with the external pumps

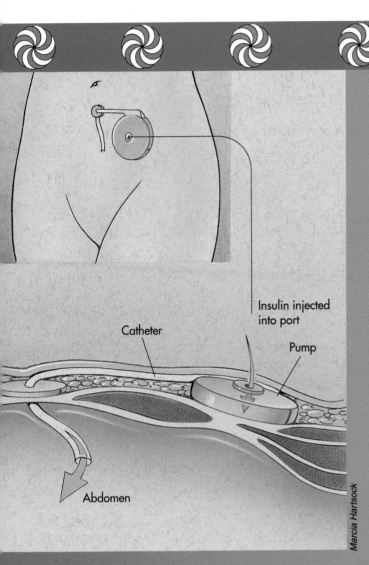

Catheter

Insulin injected
into port

Pump

Abdomen

Marcia Hartsock

Islets of Langerhans (pronounced I letz of LAN gur hanz)—the sections of the pancreas responsible for insulin production—and transplanting them into insulin-dependent diabetes patients. In preliminary tests, the transplanted cells appear to function normally, allowing recipients to become insulin independent with normal blood sugar levels.

Experimentation of this kind has been under way for decades. However, the ongoing challenge has been to identify encapsulating substances that prevent or reduce the chances of having the recipient's body reject the cells as foreign material. The most promising encapsulating techniques to date involve the use of a seaweed-derived polymer known as alginate. The encapsulated cells are simply poured into the patient's abdominal cavity through a funnel. Once inside the recipient's abdominal cavity, the encapsulated cells respond to increased levels of glucose just as pancreatic islet cells normally would—by secreting insulin.

Islet transplantation research has been quite successful in recent years. Transplanted cells have been found to function normally in mice for at least a year, and the same procedure is expected to be studied widely in dogs in the near future. To date, the procedure has been attempted in only two humans.

Although these innovations are still being developed and tested, some may not be far from being perfected. Such technologies, once they become widely available, would provide a much greater range of treatment options for both major types of diabetes.

may be from their expense, extensive maintenance, and inconvenience to wear. Now scientists are hoping to spare patients the aggravation of external pumps. On the horizon, however, is a device that will simulate natural insulin delivery through a closed-loop system implanted in the wall of the abdomen, where insulin can be absorbed rapidly.

The closed-loop insulin-delivery machine would incorporate a sensor to measure plasma or tissue glucose levels continuously, then transfer that information to a pump that would deliver insulin as needed. The pump produces a slight bulge under the skin, much like a pacemaker, but a French study of internal programmable pumps showed excellent results with a minimum of inconvenience. Two American companies are now testing their versions.

Islet Cell Transplantation

A research team at the Islet Transplantation Center at St. Vincent Medical Center in Los Angeles is perfecting a technique of encapsulating cells from the

SOURCES
Baum R: Diabetes treatment: encapsulated cells make insulin in patient, *Chemical and Emergency News*, March 21, 1994.
National Diabetes Information Clearinghouse: *Diabetes statistics*, September 1994.
Squires S: "New Drug Approved for Type II Diabetics," *Washington Post Health*, May 16, 1995.
Weir GS: What lies ahead in diabetes care, *Patient Care* February 15, 1995.

On the other hand, when the insulin level in the body is too high, the person has a low blood sugar level. This condition is known as *hypoglycemia* (Fig. 14-5, *B*). The blood sugar level can become too low if the diabetic—

- Takes too much insulin.
- Fails to eat adequately.
- Overexercises and burns off sugar faster than normal.
- Experiences great emotional stress.

In this situation, sugar is used up rapidly, so not enough sugar is available for the brain to function properly. If left untreated, hypoglycemia may result in a life-threatening condition called **insulin shock.**

Many people who have diabetes have blood glucose monitors that can be used to check their blood sugar level if they are conscious. Many hypoglycemic and hyperglycemic episodes are now managed at home because of the rapid information these monitors provide.

Signs and symptoms of diabetic emergencies

Although hyperglycemia and hypoglycemia are different conditions, their major signs and symptoms are similar. These include—

- Changes in level of consciousness, including dizziness, drowsiness, and confusion.
- Irregular breathing.
- Abnormal pulse (rapid or weak).
- Feeling or looking ill.

It is not important for you to differentiate between insulin shock and diabetic coma because the basic care for both of these diabetic emergencies is the same.

Care for diabetic emergencies

First, check and care for any life-threatening conditions. If the person is conscious, check for nonlife-threatening conditions by looking for anything visibly wrong. Ask if he or she has diabetes, or look for a medical alert tag. If the person tells you that he or she has diabetes and exhibits the signs or symptoms above, then suspect a diabetic emergency. If the conscious victim can take food or fluids, give him or her sugar (Fig. 14-6). Most candy, fruit juices, and nondiet soft drinks contain enough sugar to begin to reverse hypoglycemia. Common table sugar, either dry or dissolved in a glass of water, also works well to return the victim's blood sugar to an acceptable level. If the person's

*small doses of sugar

Figure 14-6   If a victim of a diabetic emergency is conscious, give him or her food or fluids containing sugar.

problem is low blood sugar (hypoglycemia), the sugar you give will help quickly. If the person's blood sugar level is already too high (hyperglycemia), the additional sugar will do no further harm. Often, a person who has diabetes will know what is wrong and will ask for something with sugar in it. He or she may carry a readily available source of sugar for such situations. If the victim is conscious but does not feel better approximately 5 minutes after taking sugar, EMS personnel should be called immediately.

If the person is unconscious, call EMS personnel immediately. Do not give the victim anything by mouth. Instead, monitor signs of circulation and breathing and keep him or her from getting overheated or chilled.

Seizures

When the normal functions of the brain are disrupted by injury, disease, fever, poisoning, or infection, the electrical activity of the brain becomes irregular. This irregularity can cause a loss of body control known as a *seizure.*

Seizures may be caused by an acute or chronic condition. The chronic condition is known as *epilepsy.* More than 2 million Americans currently have epilepsy and 125,000 new cases are diagnosed annually. Epilepsy is usually controlled with medication. Approximately 70 percent of people who have epilepsy can be expected to enter remission, defined as 5 years without seizures. Most people who are seizure-free for 2 to 5 years can be taken off medication. The most clearly established risk factors for epilepsy are severe head trauma, central nervous system infections, having a family member who has epilepsy, and stroke. A large proportion of new cases of epilepsy among the elderly is due to stroke. Stroke is discussed later in this chapter.

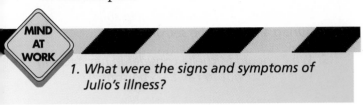

MIND AT WORK

1. What were the signs and symptoms of Julio's illness?

Signs and symptoms of seizures

Before a seizure occurs, the person may experience an aura. An **aura** is an unusual sensation or feeling, such as a visual hallucination; a strange sound, taste, or smell; or an urgent need to get to safety. If the person recognizes the aura, he or she may have time to tell bystanders and sit down before the seizure occurs.

Seizures generally last 1 to 3 minutes and can produce a wide range of signs and symptoms. When a person has a seizure, breathing may become irregular and even stop temporarily. The person may drool, the eyes may roll upward, and the body may become rigid. The person may also urinate or defecate. Seizures that cause the victim to experience mild blackouts that others may mistake for daydreaming are commonly known as nonconvulsive seizures because the body remains relatively still during the episode. More severe seizures, known as convulsive seizures, may cause the victim to experience sudden, uncontrolled muscular contractions (convulsions), lasting several minutes.

Infants and young children may be at risk for epilepsy, as well as for seizures brought on by a rapid increase in body temperature, known as **febrile seizures.** Febrile seizures usually affect young people under the age of 18 and are most common in children under the age of 5. Febrile seizures are typically triggered by infections of the ear, throat, or digestive system and are most likely to occur when the infant or child runs a fever of over 102° F (38.9° C). A person experiencing a febrile seizure may experience some or all of the following signs and symptoms:

- A sudden rise of body temperature
- A change in level of consciousness
- Rhythmic jerking of the head and limbs
- Urinating or defecating
- Confusion
- Drowsiness
- Crying out
- Becoming rigid
- Holding the breath
- Upward rolling of the eyes

Febrile seizures occur in 2 percent to 3 percent of children between the ages of 3 months and 5 years. Although febrile seizures do not cause epilepsy, victims of febrile seizures have a 15 percent to 20 percent risk that they will develop epilepsy later in life.

Care for seizures

Although it may be frightening to see someone having a seizure, you can easily help care for the person. Remember that he or she cannot control the seizure and the violent muscular contractions that may occur, so do not try to stop the seizure. Do not hold or restrain the person, since doing so can cause musculoskeletal injuries. As always, stay calm so that you can provide the most appropriate care.

Your objectives for care are to protect the victim from injury and maintain an open airway. First, move nearby objects, such as furniture, that might cause injury. Protect the person's head by placing a thin cushion, such as folded clothing, beneath it. If possible, loosen any clothing that may restrict breathing.

Do not try to place anything in the person's mouth or between his or her teeth. Contrary to the myth, people having seizures do not swallow their tongues. Seizure victims rarely bite their tongues or cheeks with enough force to cause any significant bleeding. However, some blood may be present. Position the person on his or her side as soon as the seizure ends, which will help blood or other fluids drain out of the mouth. Avoid direct contact with any blood by using an appropriate barrier, such as latex gloves.

When the seizure is over, the person will probably be drowsy and disoriented and will need to rest. If breathing becomes abnormal during the seizure, it usually returns to normal soon afterwards. Look for nonlife-threatening conditions, checking to see if the person was injured during the seizure. Be reassuring and comforting. If the seizure occurred in public, the person may be embarrassed and self-conscious. Try to provide a measure of privacy for the person. Ask bystanders not to crowd around the person. If possible, take the person to a nearby place, away from bystanders, to rest. If it is not possible to move the person to a more secluded location, use your body or an object, such as a blanket, to shield the person from onlookers. Stay with the person until he or she is fully conscious and aware of the surroundings.

Care for an infant or child who experiences a febrile seizure is much the same as for any other seizure victim. However, immediately after a febrile seizure, it is important to cool the body. Cooling can be accomplished by removing all of the victim's excess clothing and giving him or her a sponge bath in lukewarm water. Be careful not to cool the infant or child too much, since this could bring on another seizure. Contact your doctor before using a medication, such as acetaminophen, to control fever. Giving aspirin to a feverish infant has been linked to **Reye's syndrome,** an illness that affects the brain and other internal organs.

Most febrile seizures last less than 5 minutes and are not life threatening. It is not essential to call EMS personnel every time an infant or child has a febrile seizure; however, it would be appropriate to call EMS personnel the first time one occurs. If the child has a febrile seizure at a later date that ends quickly and is associated with another illness, the child should be taken to a doctor or an emergency department as soon as possible to be checked.

Although most victims of seizure recover within a few minutes after the seizure ends, actual recovery time depends on the type and severity of the seizure. If the victim is known to have periodic seizures, you do not need to call EMS personnel immediately. However, EMS personnel should be called if—

- The seizure lasts more than 5 minutes.
- The victim has repeated seizures, one after another.
- The victim appears to be injured.
- The victim is not known to have a predisposing condition, such as epilepsy, that could have brought on the seizure.
- The victim is pregnant.
- The victim is an infant or child who is experiencing an initial febrile seizure.
- The victim is known to have diabetes.
- The seizure takes place in water.

- The victim fails to regain consciousness after the seizure.

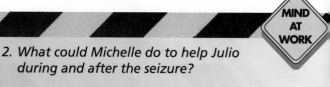

2. **What could Michelle do to help Julio during and after the seizure?**

3. **What should Michelle consider in her decision whether or not to call EMS personnel?**

Stroke

A **stroke,** also called a cerebrovascular accident (CVA), is a disruption of blood flow to a part of the brain, causing permanent damage to brain tissue. Most commonly, a stroke is caused by a blood clot, called a **thrombus** or **embolus,** that forms or lodges in the arteries that supply blood to the brain. Another common cause of stroke is bleeding from a ruptured artery in the brain caused by a head injury, high blood pressure, or an **aneurysm**—a weak area in an artery wall that balloons out and can rupture. Fat deposits lining an artery **(atherosclerosis)** may also cause stroke (Fig. 14-7). Less commonly, a tumor or swelling from a head injury may compress an artery and cause a stroke.

A **transient ischemic attack (TIA),** often referred to as a "mini-stroke," is a temporary episode that, like a stroke, is caused by a disruption in blood flow to a part of the brain. However, unlike a stroke, the signs and symptoms of TIA disappear within a few minutes or hours of its onset. Although the indicators of TIA disappear quickly, the person is not out of danger at that point. In fact, someone who experiences TIA has a nearly 10 times greater chance of having a stroke in the future than someone who has not experienced TIA. Since you cannot tell a stroke from TIA, you need only remember that any strokelike signs or symptoms require an immediate call to EMS personnel.

Signs and symptoms of stroke

As with other sudden illnesses, the primary signs and symptoms of stroke or TIA are looking or feeling ill or displaying abnormal behavior. Other symptoms include sudden weakness and numbness of the face, arm, or leg. Usually, weakness or numbness occurs only on one side of the body. The victim may have difficulty

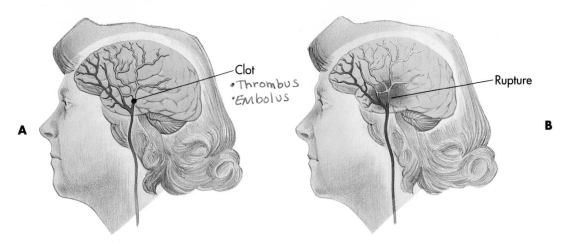

Clot
• Thrombus
• Embolus

Rupture

A

B

Figure 14-7   A stroke can be caused by **A,** a blood clot or **B,** bleeding from a ruptured artery in the brain.

talking or being understood when speaking. Vision may be blurred or dimmed; the pupils of the eyes may be of unequal size. The person may also experience a sudden, severe headache; dizziness, confusion, or change in mood; or ringing in the ears. The victim may drool, become unconscious, or defecate or urinate.

Care for stroke

If the victim is unconscious, make sure he or she has an open airway and care for any life-threatening conditions that may occur. If fluid or vomit is in the victim's mouth, position him or her on one side to allow any fluids to drain out of the mouth (Fig. 14-8). When possible, position the victim's affected or paralyzed side down. Doing so will prevent further injury and aid breathing. You may have to use a finger sweep to remove some of the material from the mouth. Call EMS personnel immediately, stay with the victim, and monitor his or her breathing and signs of circulation.

If the victim is conscious, check for nonlife-threatening conditions. If you see signs or hear the victim complain of symptoms of a stroke, call EMS personnel. A stroke can make the victim fearful and anxious. Offer comfort and reassurance. Often he or she does not understand what has happened. Have the victim rest in a comfortable position. Do not give him or her anything to eat or drink. Although a stroke may cause the victim to experience difficulty speaking, he or she can usually understand what you say. If the victims is unable to speak, you may have to develop a nonverbal system, such as hand squeezing or eye blinking, to communicate.

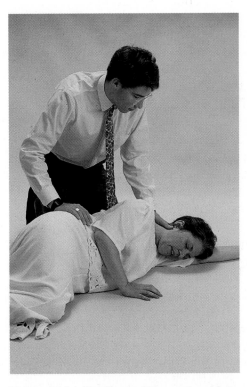

Figure 14-8   Position a victim on the side to help fluids or vomitus drain from the victim's mouth.

In the past, a stroke almost always caused irreversible brain damage. Today, new drugs and medical procedures can limit or, in some cases, reduce the damage caused by stroke. *Many of these new treatments are time-sensitive; therefore, you should quickly activate the EMS system to get the best care for the victim.*

Preventing stroke

The risk factors for stroke and TIA are similar to those for heart disease (see Chapter 6).

Some risk factors are beyond your control, such as age, sex, or family history of stroke, TIA, diabetes, or heart disease.

However, you can help prevent stroke if you—

- Control your blood pressure.
- Do not smoke.
- Eat a healthy diet.
- Exercise regularly.
- Control diabetes.

- Promptly report any signs or symptoms of stroke to your doctor.

Hypertension (high blood pressure) increases your risk of stroke by approximately seven times over someone who does not have hypertension. It is important to have your blood pressure checked regularly and, if it is high, to follow your doctor's advice on how to lower it. High blood pressure puts pressure on arteries and makes them more likely to burst. Even mild

The Brain Makes A Comeback

Neuroscientists have been mystified for years by the random effects of stroke. For many stroke survivors, talking becomes a tangle of words, a word like "piddlypop" spilling out instead of "hello." One man spoke normally unless he was asked to name fruits and vegetables. Each stroke survivor seemed to have a unique, perplexing set of problems, and doctors found recovery equally unpredictable.

Research into brain function after a stroke has shed new light on the way the brain works. Many strokes are caused when blood flow to the brain is cut off by a blood clot or hemorrhage. The oxygen-deprived brain cells rupture and die. Neuroscientists once believed that the cells died from lack of oxygen. However, their conclusion did not explain why stroke survivors sometimes got worse over a period of several hours.

Researchers have found that when oxygen-deprived brain cells rupture, they release huge quantities of the amino acid glutamate. Glutamate gushes into surviving brain cells and destroys them. Normally, small amounts of glutamate act as transmitters between the cells, but large amounts are damaging to these cells. Researchers believe that if they could inhibit the reaction of glutamate within the cell, they could prevent the most severe brain damage and, perhaps, the death of stroke victims.

Researchers are developing several drugs to try to block the flood of glutamate that occurs after a stroke. They have found that drugs similar to phencyclidine, a potent animal tranquilizer and street drug known as PCP, have proven the most effective. Like PCP, the drugs cause temporary hallucinations. However, doctors say the promising results outweigh the side effects.

Another drug that is now being tested as a possible treatment for the damage caused by stroke is omega-conotoxin. Omega-conotoxin is derived from the venom of the cone snail, which can instantly paralyze a fish and can even kill a human. Recent research shows that when omega-conotoxin is administered after a stroke, it temporarily blocks the channels that deliver the damaging flood of glutamate to the brain cells. When rats were given a synthesized version of omega-conotoxin, the death of neurons in the brain was slowed down or even halted.

Strokes still present many mysteries, but scientists are learning more about stroke every day. With more than 3 million stroke survivors in the United States today, doctors are hopeful that new drugs may eventually eliminate the long-term effects.

SOURCES
American Heart Association: *1993 Heart and stroke facts statistics.*
Blakeslee S: "Pervasive Chemical Crucial to the Body is Indicted as an Agent in Brain Damage," *The New York Times,* November 29, 1988.
Killer snails, healer snails, *Discover,* May 1994, p. 32.

hypertension can increase your risk of stroke. You can often control high blood pressure by losing weight, changing your diet, exercising routinely, and managing stress. If those measures are not sufficient, your physician may prescribe medication.

Cigarette smoking is another major risk factor of stroke. Smoking is linked to heart disease and cancer, as well as to stroke. It increases blood pressure and makes blood more likely to clot. If you smoke and would like to quit, many techniques and support systems are available to help you do so. Your doctor or local health department can help you find assistance. No matter how difficult or painful quitting may be, it is well worth it. The benefits of not smoking begin as soon as you stop, and some of smoking's damage may actually be reversible. Approximately 10 years after a person has stopped smoking, his or her risk of stroke is the same as the risk for a person who never smoked. Even if you do not smoke, be aware that inhaling second-hand smoke (smoke from others) is detrimental to your health. Avoid long-term exposure to smoke and protect children from this danger.

Diets that are high in saturated fats and cholesterol can increase your risk of stroke by causing fatty materials to build up on the walls of your blood vessels. Foods high in cholesterol include egg yolks and organ meats, such as liver and kidneys. Saturated fats are found in beef, lamb, veal, pork, ham, whole milk, and whole-milk products. Moderating your intake of these foods can help prevent stroke.

Regular exercise reduces your chances of stroke by strengthening the heart and increasing blood circulation, which develops more channels for blood flow. These additional channels provide alternate routes for blood if the primary channels become blocked. Exercise also helps in weight control. Being overweight increases the chance of developing high blood pressure, heart disease, and atherosclerosis.

Having diabetes is another major risk factor for stroke. If you have been diagnosed with diabetes, follow your doctor's advice about how to control it. If untreated, diabetes can cause destructive changes in the blood vessels throughout the body.

By paying attention to the symptoms of stroke and reporting them to your doctor, you can prevent damage before it occurs. Experiencing TIA is the clearest warning that a stroke may occur. Do not ignore the strokelike symptoms, even if they disappear completely within minutes or hours.

SUMMARY

Sudden illness can strike anyone at any time. Even if you do not know the cause of the illness, you can still provide proper care. Following the general guidelines for care will help prevent the condition from becoming worse.

Diabetic emergencies, seizures, fainting, and stroke are all sudden illnesses. Recognizing the general signs and symptoms of sudden illness, such as changes in consciousness, profuse sweating, confusion, and weakness, will help you determine the necessary care to give the victim until EMS personnel arrive to take over.

Answers to Application Questions

1. The signs and symptoms of Julio's illness include his body collapsing to the ground and becoming rigid, his eyes rolling back, and his arms and legs jerking uncontrollably.

2. During the seizure, Michelle could protect Julio's head, loosen any clothing that might restrict breathing, and move any nearby objects that could cause injury. After the seizure, Michelle could ensure Julio's airway is open, position Julio on his side so that any fluids could drain; look and care for nonlife-threatening conditions that may have occurred during the seizure; provide reassurance, maintain crowd control, or find Julio a more secluded place to rest; stay with Julio until he is fully conscious and aware of his surroundings; and call 9-1-1 or the local emergency number, if necessary.

3. Michelle should call EMS personnel if Julio was injured when he fell or during the seizure, another seizure follows the end of the first one, the seizure lasted more than 5 minutes, Julio is not known to have epilepsy, Julio is a known diabetic, or Julio fails to regain consciousness after the seizure.

STUDY QUESTIONS

1. Match each term with the correct definition.
   a. Epilepsy
   b. Fainting
   c. Hyperglycemia
   d. Hypoglycemia
   e. Insulin
   f. Seizure
   g. Stroke
   h. Diabetic emergency
   i. Transient ischemic attack (TIA)

   __E__ A hormone that enables the cells to use sugar.

   __B__ A temporary reduction of blood flow to the brain, resulting in loss of consciousness.

   __G__ A disruption of blood flow to the brain that causes brain tissue damage.

   __E__ A disruption of the brain's electrical activity, which may cause loss of consciousness and body control.

   __D__ A condition in which too little sugar is in the bloodstream.

   __C__ A condition in which too much sugar is in the bloodstream.

   __A__ A chronic condition characterized by seizures and usually controlled by medication.

   __I__ A temporary disruption of blood flow to the brain; sometimes called a mini-stroke.

   __H__ A situation in which a person becomes ill because of an imbalance of sugar (glucose) and insulin in the bloodstream.

2. List four general signs or symptoms of a sudden illness.

3. List four general guidelines of care that should be applied in any sudden illness.

4. List six instances in which you should call EMS personnel for a seizure victim.

5. List six ways to decrease the risk of stroke or TIA.

6. Describe how to care for a seizure victim once the seizure is over.

7. What signs and symptoms of sudden illness do you find in the scenario that follows? Circle the signs and symptoms in the passage below.

   I was at the grocery store with my grandmother. As the butcher reached over the counter to hand her a package of steaks, my grandmother stumbled toward a nearby chair. She sat in the chair, looking confused. I noticed that she was sweating profusely and her pupils were different sizes. I stood beside her and asked if I could help. At first, she didn't seem to recognize me. Then she mumbled something to me. I could not understand her very well, but I think she was telling me that she felt weak and wanted me to let her rest for a few minutes.

8. What care would you give for the grandmother in the scenario?

In questions 9 through 16, circle the letter of the correct answer.

9. If you were caring for someone who looked pale, was unconscious, and was breathing irregularly, what would you do?
    a. Call 9-1-1 or the local emergency number.
    b. Inject the victim with insulin.
    c. Give sugar to the victim.
    d. Let the victim rest for a while.

10. A friend who has diabetes is drowsy and seems confused. He is not sure if he took his insulin today. What should you do?
    a. Suggest he rest for an hour or so.
    b. Tell him to take his insulin.
    c. Tell him to eat or drink something with sugar in it.
    d. Check his breathing and signs of circulation.

11. Your father has diabetes. He also suffered a stroke a year ago. You find him lying on the floor, unconscious. What should you do after calling EMS personnel?
    a. Phone his doctor.
    b. Lift his head up and try to give him a sugary drink.
    c. Check for breathing, signs of circulation, and severe bleeding.
    d. Inject him with insulin yourself, while waiting for EMS personnel to arrive.

12. In caring for the victim of a seizure, you should—
    a. Move any objects that might cause injury.
    b. Try to hold the person still.
    c. Place a spoon between the person's teeth.
    d. Splash the person's face with water.

13. To reduce the risk of aspiration of blood or other fluids in a seizure victim—
    a. Place an object between the victim's teeth.
    b. Position the victim on his or her side after the seizure ends.
    c. Place a thick object, such as a rolled blanket, under the victim's head.
    d. Move the victim into a sitting position.

14. Controlling high blood pressure reduces your risk of—
    a. Heart disease, stroke, and TIA.   c. Diabetes.
    b. Seizure.   d. Epilepsy.

15. At the office, your boss complains that she has had a severe headache for several hours. Her speech suddenly becomes slurred. She loses her balance and falls to the floor. What would you do?
    a. Give her two aspirin.
    b. Help her find and take her high blood pressure medication.
    c. Call 9-1-1 or the local emergency number.
    d. Tell her to rest for a while.

16. Which of the following is (are) included in the care you give for fainting?
    a. If possible, help to lower the victim to the floor or other flat surface.
    b. If possible, elevate the legs.
    c. Give the victim something to eat or drink.
    d. a and b.

Answers are listed in Appendix A.

CHAPTER 15

Poisoning

WHAT YOU SHOULD LEARN

After reading this chapter, you should be able to—

1. List the four ways poisons enter the body.

2. Identify 15 signs and symptoms of poisoning.

3. Describe the role of a poison control center (PCC).

4. Identify the general guidelines of care for any poisoning emergency.

5. Describe how to care for a victim of ingested, inhaled, and absorbed poison.

6. Identify the signs and symptoms of anaphylaxis.

7. List seven ways to prevent ingested, inhaled, and absorbed poisoning.

8. Define the key terms for this chapter.

Ashley never realized what a handful her little sister Kristen was to watch until she had to babysit her. How did someone who wasn't two yet move so fast and so quietly? When she wasn't grabbing an electric cord, she was busy emptying out her toy box. Luckily, Ashley was able to interest Kristen in her favorite TV show, so Ashley had some time to herself. It was only a minute or two–no more than five–that she left her there, but now Kristen was gone. Ashley checked Kristen's room and the closet where she liked to hide. It was when Ashley reached the kitchen that she knew there was trouble. There was Kristen, sitting on the kitchen table surprised by Ashley's entry. The chair she'd used to climb up had been knocked over. A bottle which had been filled with brightly colored vitamin and mineral tablets was on the table...empty.

Introduction

Chapter 14 described sudden illnesses caused by conditions inside the body. Poisoning is also considered a sudden illness. However, unlike those conditions that have an internal cause, such as fainting and stroke, poisoning results when external substances enter the body. The substance could be a food that is swallowed, a pesticide that is absorbed through the skin, or a venom that enters the body through a bite or sting. Even certain plants and foods can be poisonous. In this chapter and in Chapters 16 and 17, you will learn how to recognize and care for various kinds of poisoning emergencies.

Between 1 and 2 million poisonings occur each year in the United States. More than 90 percent of all poisonings take place in the home. Unintentional poisonings far outnumber intentional ones, and most unintentional poisonings occur in children under age 5. Although the death rate from poisoning in children under age 5 has dropped in the last 30 years, poisoning fatalities still pose a serious risk. In fact, among adults 18 and older, poisoning fatalities have markedly increased during the same period.

This increase in poisoning fatalities among adults can be linked to two factors: (1) increases in intentional poisonings (suicides) and (2) increases in drug-related poisonings. Although illegal street drugs like cocaine attract more attention, the misuse and abuse of prescription medications are actually more prevalent. About two thirds of all unintentional poisonings involve drugs and medications. Half of all drug overdoses are caused by misused or abused prescribed medication. Drug misuse and abuse are discussed in detail in Chapter 17.

HOW POISONS ENTER THE BODY

A **poison** is any substance that can cause injury, illness, or death when introduced into the body in relatively small amounts. Poisons include solids, liquids, and fumes (gases and vapors). A poison can enter the body in four ways: inhalation, ingestion, absorption, and injection (Fig. 15-1, *A* to *D*).

Poisoning by inhalation occurs when a person breathes in toxic fumes. **Inhaled poisons** include—

- Gases, such as carbon monoxide, from an engine, kerosene heater, or other source of combustion.
- Gases, such as carbon dioxide, that can occur naturally from decomposition.
- Gases, such as nitrous oxide, used for medical purposes.
- Gases, such as chlorine, found in some commercial swimming facilities.
- Fumes from household products, such as glues and paints.
- Fumes from drugs, such as crack cocaine.

Ingestion means swallowing. **Ingested poisons** include foods, such as certain mushrooms and shellfish; drugs, such as alcohol; medica-

Key Terms

Absorbed poison: A poison that enters the body after it comes in contact with the skin.

Anaphylaxis (an ə fi LAK sis): A severe allergic reaction; a form of shock.

Ingested poison: A poison that is swallowed.

Inhaled poison: A poison breathed into the lungs.

Injected poison: A poison that enters the body through the skin through a bite, sting, or as drugs or misused medications through a hypodermic needle.

Poison: Any substance that can cause injury, illness, or death when introduced into the body in relatively small amounts.

Poison control center (PCC): A specialized health care center that provides information in cases of poisoning or suspected poisoning emergencies.

tions, such as aspirin; and household and garden items, such as cleaning products, pesticides, and plants (Fig. 15-2). Many substances not poisonous in small amounts are poisonous in larger amounts. Medications (prescription or over-the-counter) can be poisonous if they are not taken as prescribed or directed.

An **absorbed poison** enters the body after it comes in contact with the skin. Absorbed poisons come from plants such as poison ivy, poison oak, and poison sumac, as well as from fertilizers and pesticides used in lawn and plant care.

Injected poisons enter the body through the bites or stings of certain insects, spiders, ticks, marine life, animals, and snakes or as drugs or misused medications injected with a hypodermic needle. Poisoning from bites and stings is covered in Chapter 16.

SIGNS AND SYMPTOMS OF POISONING

The most important thing is to recognize that a poisoning may have occurred. As with other serious emergencies, such as shock; a heart attack; or a head, neck, and spine injury, check the scene and the condition of the victim, then get any possible information from the victim or bystanders. If you then have even a slight suspicion that the victim has been poisoned, seek medical assistance immediately.

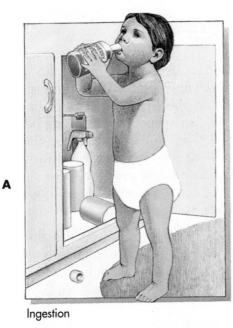

Ingestion

Inhalation

Absorption

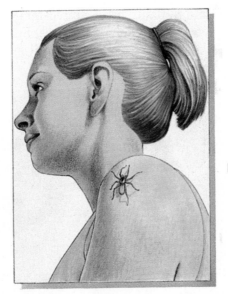

Injection

Figure 15-1   A poison can enter the body in four ways: **A**, ingestion, **B**, inhalation, **C**, absorption, and **D**, injection.

Common Causes of Poisoning (by age group)

Under 6	6-19	Over 19
Analgesic medications	Analgesic medications	Analgesic medications
Cleaning substances	Bites and stings	Antidepressant drugs
Cosmetics and personal care products	Cleaning substances	Bites and stings
Cough and cold remedies	Cosmetics	Chemicals
Gastrointestinal medications	Cough and cold remedies	Cleaning substances
Plants	Food products/food poisoning	Food products/food poisoning
Topical medications	Plants	Fumes and vapors
Vitamins	Stimulants and street drugs	Insecticides
		Sedatives and hallucinogenic drugs

As you approach the victim, check the scene to make sure it is safe to enter. Be aware of any unusual odors, flames, smoke, open or spilled containers, an open medicine cabinet, an overturned or damaged plant, or other signals of possible poisoning.

When you reach the victim, check for life-threatening and nonlife-threatening conditions. The victim of poisoning generally looks ill and displays signs and symptoms common to other sudden illnesses. The signs and symptoms of poisoning include nausea, vomiting, diarrhea, chest or abdominal pain, breathing difficulty, sweating, loss of consciousness, seizures, headache, dizziness, weakness, irregular pupil size, burning or tearing eyes, and abnormal skin color. Other signs of poisoning are burn injuries around the lips or tongue or on the skin. You may also suspect a poisoning based on any information you have from or about the victim. Look also for any **drug paraphernalia** or empty containers at or near the scene.

If you suspect a poisoning, try to get answers to the following questions:

- What type of poison did the victim ingest, inhale, inject, or come into contact with?
- How much poison did the victim ingest, inhale, inject, or come into contact with?
- When did the poisoning take place (approximate time)?

This information will help ensure the most appropriate care.

MIND AT WORK

1. What clues did Ashley find at the scene to alert her that Kristen may have been poisoned?

Figure 15-2   Many common household plants are poisonous.

POISON CONTROL CENTERS

Poison control centers (PCCs) are specialized health care centers that provide information in cases of poisoning or suspected poisoning

Common Signs and Symptoms of Poisoning

Nausea

Vomiting

Diarrhea

Chest or abdominal pain

Breathing difficulty

Sweating

Loss of consciousness

Seizures

Burn injuries around the lips or tongue or on the skin

Headache

Dizziness

Weakness

Irregular pupil size

Burning or tearing eyes

Abnormal skin color

Figure 15-3 The local poison control center phone number should be posted by your phone.

emergencies. A network of PCCs exists throughout the United States, as well as abroad. Some PCCs are located in the emergency departments of large hospitals. Medical professionals in these centers have access to information about virtually all poisonous substances and can tell you how to care for someone who has been poisoned. You should have your local PCC number posted by your phone (Fig. 15-3). You can obtain the phone number from your telephone directory, your doctor, a local hospital, or your local EMS system.

PCCs answer over 2 million poisoning calls each year. Since many poisonings can be cared for without the help of EMS professionals, PCCs help prevent overburdening of the EMS system. If the victim is conscious, call your local PCC first. The center will tell you what care to give and whether EMS personnel are needed.

If the victim is unconscious or if you do not know your PCC number, call 9-1-1 or your local emergency number. Often the dispatcher will link you with the PCC. The dispatcher may also monitor your conversation with the PCC and send an ambulance if needed, which saves

time by eliminating the need for a second call (Fig. 15-4).

CARE FOR POISONING

The severity of a poisoning depends on the type and amount of the substance; how and where it entered the body; the time elapsed since the poison entered the body; and the victim's size, weight, and age. Some poisons act quickly and produce characteristic signs and symptoms. Others act slowly and cannot be easily identified. Sometimes you will be able to identify the specific poison, sometimes not. The important thing is to learn and follow the general guidelines of care for any poisoning emergency. These include—

- Check the scene to make sure it is safe to approach and to gather clues about what happened.
- Remove the victim from the source of the poison, if necessary and possible.
- Check for life-threatening conditions.
- If the victim is conscious, ask questions to get more information.

Figure 15-4 When you call your emergency number, a dispatcher can link you with the Poison Control Center and send an ambulance if needed.

- Look for any drug or product containers, and take them with you to the telephone.
- Call your PCC or the local emergency number.
- Give care according to the directions of PCC personnel or the EMS dispatcher.

Do not give the victim anything to drink or eat unless so advised by medical professionals. If the poison is unknown and the victim vomits, save some of the vomit, which the hospital may analyze to identify the poison. Use any clean container to collect vomit. Although vomit is rarely infectious or harmful, is it a good idea to wear latex gloves while collecting a vomit sample. If the victim goes to the hospital, bottles of all ingested poisons or drugs should also accompany him or her.

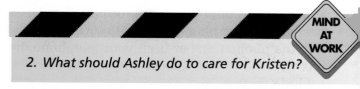

2. What should Ashley do to care for Kristen?

Inhaled Poisons

When you provide care for a victim of poisoning, you need to follow precautions to ensure that you do not become poisoned as well. This is particularly true with inhaled poisons. **Toxic fumes** come from a variety of sources and may or may not have an odor. If you notice clues at the scene of an emergency that might lead you to suspect that toxic fumes are present, such as a strong smell of fuel or a hissing sound like gas escaping from a pipe or valve, you may not be able to reach the victim without risking your safety. In cases like this, be prepared to call 9-1-1 or the local emergency number instead of entering the scene. Let the EMS professional know what you have discovered, and only enter the scene if he or she tells you it is safe to do so.

A commonly inhaled poison is **carbon monoxide (CO),** which is present in substances such as car exhaust and tobacco smoke. CO can also be produced by fires, defective cooking equipment, defective furnaces, and kerosene heaters. CO is also found in indoor skating rinks and when charcoal is used indoors. CO is a colorless, odorless gas that causes more than half of all poisoning deaths in the United States each year. Nearly 4000 people die each year from CO poisoning, and at least 10,000 others become ill. Carbon monoxide detectors, which work much like smoke detectors, are now available for use in homes.

A pale or bluish skin color, which indicates a lack of oxygen, may signal CO poisoning. For years, people were taught that carbon monoxide poisoning was indicated by a cherry-red color of the skin and lips. However, new evidence shows that such redness only occurs after most victims have died. CO is highly lethal and can cause death after only a few minutes of exposure.

All victims of inhaled poison need oxygen as soon as possible. First and foremost, however, remember to *Check-Call-Care.* Check the scene to determine if it is safe for you to help. If you can remove the person from the source of the poison without endangering yourself, then do so. You can help a conscious victim by getting him or her to fresh air and then calling EMS personnel. If you find the victim unconscious, remove him or her from the environment if it is safe to do so and call EMS personnel immediately. After the call to EMS personnel has been made, you can provide care for any other life-threatening conditions.

Ingested Poisons

In some cases of ingested poisoning, the PCC may instruct you to induce vomiting. Vomiting may prevent the poison from moving from the stomach to the small intestine, where most absorption takes place. *However, vomiting*

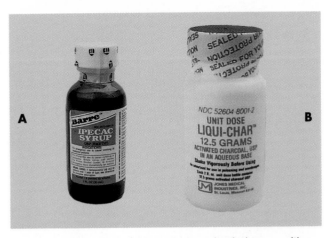

Figure 15-5 **A,** Syrup of ipecac is used to induce vomiting in victims who have swallowed certain kinds of poisons. **B,** Activated charcoal is used to absorb and neutralize ingested poisons.

should only be induced if advised by a medical professional.

To induce vomiting, you may be asked to give the victim **syrup of ipecac,** which is inexpensive and available at a pharmacy. It usually comes in a 30-ml bottle (about 2 tablespoons) (Fig. 15-5, *A*). Two tablespoons, followed by a glass of water, is the usual dose for a person over 12 years of age. For children ages 1 to 12, the usual dose is 1 tablespoon followed by half a glass of water. Vomiting usually occurs within 20 minutes. Make sure you read and follow the directions on the syrup of ipecac container.

In some instances, vomiting should not be induced. These include when the victim—

- Is unconscious.
- Is having a seizure.
- Is pregnant (in the last trimester).
- Has ingested a corrosive substance (such as drain or oven cleaner) or a petroleum product (such as kerosene or gasoline).
- Is known to have heart disease.

Since vomiting often removes less than half of the poison, you may be directed by a medical professional to counteract the remaining poison. **Activated charcoal,** which comes in powder or liquid form, is used to absorb and neutralize ingested poison (Fig. 15-5, *B*). Before use, powdered activated charcoal should be mixed with water to form a solution with the consistency of a thin milkshake. Always follow the directions on the bottle for proper usage.

Like syrup of ipecac, activated charcoal is inexpensive and can be purchased at a phar-

Safe Food Tips

Wash hands thoroughly with soap and water before preparing or handling food, between handling raw and cooked foods, and whenever handling food preparation surfaces, dishes, and utensils.

Thaw all frozen meats, poultry, or fish in the refrigerator, not at room temperature.

Never put cooked meats back onto a surface used to hold or store the meat before cooking unless the surface has been washed thoroughly.

Rinse all raw fruits and vegetables thoroughly before use.

Wash and dry tops of canned goods before opening.

Keep cold foods in the refrigerator at or below 40° F (4° C).

Be sure hot foods are heated to and kept at or above 140° F (60° C).

Throw out all perishable foods not kept at safe hot or cold temperatures. Dispose of all perishable foods left out at room temperature for 2 hours or more.

Store dry foods such as flour, sugar, and cereal in glass, plastic, or metal containers with tight lids.

Store all foods in containers that are clean, have tight-fitting covers, and are insect- and rodent-resistant.

Store food items away from nonfood items.

Use an inventory system to rotate and use up all food items.

sues. Vomiting these corrosives could burn the esophagus, throat, and mouth. Diluting the corrosive substance decreases the potential for burning and damaging tissues.

Foods can be another type of ingested poison. Approximately 33 million Americans are affected by food poisoning each year. Two of the most common categories of food poisoning are bacterial food poisoning and chemical food poisoning (also known as environmental food poisoning). Bacterial food poisoning typically occurs when bacteria grow on food that is allowed to stand at room temperature after it is cooked. The bacteria release **toxins** into the food. Even when the food is reheated, the toxins may not be destroyed. Foods most responsible for this type of poisoning are ham, tongue, sausage, dried meat, fish products, and dairy and dairy-based products. Chemical food poisoning typically occurs when foods with high acid content, such as fruit juices or sauerkraut, are stored in containers lined with zinc, cadmium, or copper, or in enameled metal pans. Another primary source of chemical food poisoning is lead, which may be found in pipes that supply water for drinking and cooking.

One of the most common causes of food poisoning is the *Salmonella* bacteria, most often found in poultry and raw eggs. Proper handling and cooking of food can help prevent *Salmonella* poisoning. The most deadly type of food poisoning is botulism, which is caused by a bacterial toxin associated with home canning. Before opening a canned or bottled food, inspect the can or lid to see if it is swollen or if the "safety button" in the center of the lid has

macy. However, activated charcoal is not as readily available as syrup of ipecac, so you may have to ask a pharmacist to order some. Syrup of ipecac and activated charcoal should be part of your home first aid supplies, in case you are directed to use one or both of them. Be aware that these medications should not be given at the same time. Activated charcoal is only to be used after vomiting has been successfully induced, and only if indicated by a medical professional.

You can dilute some ingested poisons by giving the victim water to drink. Examples of such poisons are caustic or corrosive chemicals, such as acids, that can eat away or destroy tis-

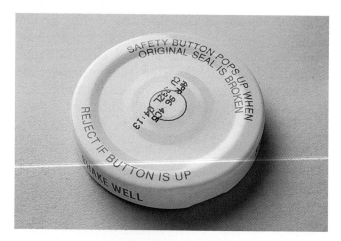

Figure 15-6 Inspect the safety button of the lid before opening a canned or bottled food.

A

John Shaw/Tom Stack & Associates

B

John Shaw/Tom Stack & Associates

C

Walt Anderson/Tom Stack & Associates

Figure 15-7   **A,** Poison ivy. **B,** Poison sumac. **C,** Poison oak.

popped up (Fig. 15-6). If either has occurred, throw the food away.

The signs and symptoms of food poisoning, which can begin between 1 and 48 hours after eating contaminated food, include nausea, vomiting, abdominal pain, diarrhea, fever, and dehydration. Severe cases of food poisoning can result in shock or death, particularly in children, the elderly, and those with an impaired immune system. Some victims of food poisoning may require antibiotic or antitoxin therapy. Fortunately, most food poisoning can be prevented by proper cooking, refrigeration, and sanitation.

Absorbed Poisons

People often come into contact with poisonous substances that can be absorbed into the body. Millions of people each year suffer irritating effects after touching or brushing against poisonous plants such as poison ivy, poison oak, and poison sumac (Fig. 15-7, *A* to *C*). Other poisons absorbed through the skin include dry and wet chemicals, such as those used in yard and garden maintenance, which may also burn the surface of the skin.

To care for the effects of poison plant contact, immediately rinse the affected area thoroughly with water (Fig. 15-8, *A*). Using soap cannot hurt, but soap may not do much to remove the poisonous plant oil that causes the allergic reaction. Before washing the affected area, you may need to have the victim remove any jewelry. This is only necessary if the jewelry is contaminated or if it constricts circulation due to swelling. If a rash or weeping lesion (an oozing sore) develops, seek advice from a pharmacist or doctor about possible treatment. Medicated lotions, such as Calamine®, may help soothe the area. **Antihistamines,** such as Benadryl®, may also help dry up the lesions and help alleviate itching. These over-the-counter products are available at a pharmacy. If the condition worsens and large areas of the body or the face are affected, the person should see a doctor, who may administer **antiinflammatory drugs,** such as **corticosteroids,** or other medications to relieve discomfort.

If other poisons, such as dry or wet chemicals, contact the skin, flush the affected area continuously with large amounts of water (Fig.

Figure 15-8 **A,** To care for skin contact with a poisonous plant, immediately rinse the affected area thoroughly with water. **B,** Whenever chemical poisons come in contact with the skin or eyes, flush the affected area continuously with large amounts of water.

15-8, *B*). Garden hoses and showers suit this purpose well. Activate the EMS system immediately, then continue to flush the area until EMS personnel arrive.

If running water is not available, brush off dry chemicals, such as lime. Take care not to get any of the dry chemicals in your eyes or the eyes of the victim or any bystanders. Many dry chemicals are activated by contact with water, but if continuous running water is available, it will flush the chemical from the skin before the activated chemical can do harm. Running water reduces the threat to you and quickly and easily removes the substance from the victim.

Injected Poisons

Insect and animal stings and bites are among the most common sources of injected poisons. Chapter 16 describes the general signs and symptoms of stings and bites of insects, spiders, ticks, marine life, snakes, scorpions, animals, and humans, as well as the appropriate care for each. Chapter 17 provides information about another common source of injected poisons—the use of injected drugs.

ANAPHYLAXIS

Severe allergic reactions to poisons are rare. But when one occurs, it is truly a life-threatening medical emergency. This reaction is called ***anaphylaxis*** and was discussed in Chapter 5. Anaphylaxis is a form of shock. It can be caused by an insect bite or sting or contact with certain drugs, medications, foods, and chemicals. Anaphylaxis can result from any of the four modes of poisoning described in this chapter.

Signs and Symptoms of Anaphylaxis

Anaphylaxis usually occurs suddenly, within seconds or minutes after the victim comes into contact with the poisonous substance. The skin or area of the body that came in contact with the substance usually swells and turns red (Fig. 15-9). Other signs and symptoms include hives (reddish bumps on the skin), rash, itching and burning skin and eyes, weakness, nausea, vomiting, restlessness, dizziness, dilated pu-

Figure 15-9 In anaphylaxis, the skin or area of the body usually swells and turns red.

pils, slurred speech, chest discomfort or pain, weak or rapid pulse, and rapid or difficult breathing that includes coughing and wheezing. This breathing difficulty can progress to an obstructed airway as the tongue, throat, and bronchial passageways swell. Death from anaphylaxis usually occurs because the victim's breathing is severely impaired.

Care for Anaphylaxis

If an unusual inflammation or rash is noticeable immediately after contact with a possible source of poison, it could be an allergic reaction. Observe the victim carefully, because any allergic reaction can develop into anaphylaxis. Check the victim's airway and breathing. If the victim has any breathing difficulty or complains that his or her throat is closing, call EMS personnel immediately. Help the victim into the most comfortable position for breathing, continue to monitor his or her breathing, and offer reassurance.

People who know they are extremely allergic to certain substances usually try to avoid them, although this avoidance is sometimes impossible. These people may carry an anaphylaxis kit in case they have a severe allergic reaction. Such kits are available by prescription only. The kit contains a dose of the drug epinephrine (adrenaline) that can be injected into the body to counteract the anaphylactic reaction (Fig. 15-10). If you are allergic to a substance, contact a doctor to discuss whether you need such a kit. You can assist the victim in using his or her kit, if necessary.

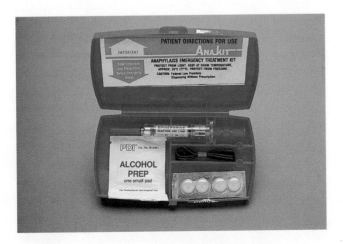

Figure 15-10 The contents of an anaphylaxis kit.

PREVENTING POISONING

The best approach to poisoning emergencies is to prevent them from occurring in the first place. Prevention is a simple principle, but often people do not take enough precautions. Of all the child poisoning cases reported, the vast majority occurred when the child was under the direct supervision of a parent or guardian. It takes only a brief lapse of supervision for a child to get into trouble. Children are naturally curious and can get into things in ways adults might not consider possible. Many substances commonly found in or around the house are poisonous. Children are especially vulnerable to these substances because of their tendency to put everything in their mouths. Extra care may be needed in monitoring the actions of children in homes that are not childproof. For example, in such homes, medications may not be stored in childproof containers.

When giving medication to a child, do so carefully. Medicine is not candy and should never be called candy to entice a child to take it. Cough syrup looks like a soft drink to children, and many coated medicine tablets look like candy. Some children's medicine has a pleasant candy flavor so that children will take it more easily. When giving any of these substances, make it clear to the child that it is medicine. Take care also to keep the medication out of reach of children.

By following these general guidelines, you will be able to prevent most ingested, absorbed, and inhaled poisoning emergencies:

- Keep all medications and household products well out of the reach of children. Special latches and clamps are available to keep children from opening cabinets. Use these or other methods to keep children from reaching any substances that may be poisonous. Consider all household or drugstore products to be potentially harmful.
- Use childproof safety caps on containers of medication and other potentially dangerous products.
- Keep products in their original containers, with the labels in place.
- Use poison symbols to identify dangerous substances, and teach children what the symbols mean.

Poisonous Plants

By the time we are adults, most of us are aware that eating an unidentified mushroom can be a one-way ticket to the local hospital. We are rarely aware, however, of the many poisonous plants that inhabit our homes and gardens. Actually, of the approximately 30,000 known species of plants, only about 700 are poisonous. But a number of these plants are not located in the rain forest or on some tropical island; they are quietly sitting in pots or vases in our living rooms.

Many poisonous household products now have some sort of warning label, but we are rarely warned about the dangers of a seemingly innocuous houseplant or shrub. Take, for example, lily of the valley, with its delicate, sweet-scented, little white bells, which is a mainstay of bridal bouquets. If you were to nibble the stem, flowers, leaves, or red berries of the plant, you would regret it. The effects of the poison in this plant include burning of the mouth and throat, vomiting, irregular heartbeat, coma, and circulatory failure. In Africa, lily of the valley plants have been used to poison the tips of arrows.

Be aware of certain plants associated with the holiday season. Holly berries, if eaten, are sufficiently toxic to cause illness, especially in a child. Eating mistletoe berries can result in vomiting, diarrhea, delirium, cardiovascular collapse, and death. Skin contact with the sap of a poinsettia causes blistering. In fact, the sap of "snow on the mountain," a relative of the poinsettia, is so powerful it has been used in place of a hot iron to brand cattle.

Several common houseplants are highly toxic. The philodendron is a popular plant for home and office because it flourishes without direct sunlight and needs little care. The philodendron and other plants in the same family have leaves of various sizes, shapes, and colors. But the plants in this family all have one aspect in common: some parts contain needlelike crystals of a chemical—calcium oxalate—that become embedded in the mouth and tongue when plant parts are chewed, causing intense burning and severe swelling. The dieffenbachia, a large, handsome houseplant related to the philodendron, has large bright green leaves striped with white. It is also known as "dumb cane" because chewing the leaves can make the mouth and tongue so swollen that speaking is impossible. Another houseplant to be aware of is the Jerusalem cherry, whose red or orange fruit look like cherry tomatoes and are somewhat poisonous.

The most dangerous plant grown in the home or garden is the oleander. In the United States, oleanders are grown as houseplants in the north and as outdoor shrubs in California, Florida, and other warm areas. The leaves are stiff, narrow, dark green, and shiny, and the flowers are pink, white, or red. Drinking the water from a vase that has held oleander flowers can make a person violently ill, as will eating the leaves, stems, or flowers. People have been poisoned from eating hot dogs roasted on sticks from an oleander bush as well as from inhaling from the smoke from the burning foliage.

A number of the plants we commonly grow in gardens are poisonous if eaten, for example, the bulbs and other parts of the narcissus, hyacinth, and snowdrop. The berries of English ivy and yew can cause vomiting, stomach pains, headache, diarrhea, and convulsions. Foxglove plants can cause heart failure. Eating the flowers of the lavender plant or the bulb of the autumn crocus can result in kidney damage, dehydration, abdominal pains, and shock. The castor plant is grown mainly for the oil produced from its pleasant-tasting, shiny, black-and-brown seeds. It only takes one or two of those seeds, chewed and swallowed, to kill.

Treat certain products of the orchard and vegetable garden with caution. The seeds inside the

pits of peaches, apricots, cherries, and other fruit contain potentially lethal cyanide. So do apple seeds. The leaves of rhubarb can damage the kidneys. Eating the raw shoots and berries of asparagus can result in unpleasant skin rashes and blisters. Even the potato plant isn't entirely safe; all the green parts of the plant are poisonous, and so are green areas on potatoes themselves. Always cut away the green spots and sprouts on a potato before cooking, and do not expose uncooked potatoes to sunlight. The leaves and stems of the tomato plant, which is related to the potato, are poisonous also.

Other poisonous relatives of the potato include tobacco, jasmine, and jimsonweed. Eating them can result in respiratory failure, headache, abdominal pain, delirium, and weakness. Skin contact can cause severe skin irritation. Jimsonweed was named after the Jamestown, Virginia settlement where, in 1676, some soldiers sent to put down an uprising were poisoned by cooked jimsonweed greens and fruit. A tall plant with thick stems, toothed leaves, trumpet-shaped white or lavendar flowers, and a fruit encased in a green, spiny husk, jimsonweed grows wild in fields, along roadsides, and sometimes in back yards and gardens. If eaten, it can cause convulsions, hallucinations, coma, and death. Other poisonous plants common in woods, fields, vacant lots, or gardens include mountain laurel, deadly nightshade, and Japanese honeysuckle.

The most violently toxic plant that grows wild in the northern hemisphere is the water hemlock. Its poison acts on the central nervous system in about 1/2 hour. Children have been poisoned by just using its hollow stems for peashooters. The ancient Greeks used an extract from another hemlock plant, the poison hemlock, for executions, the most famous victim being the philosopher Socrates.

What precautions can you take to ensure against plant poisoning? First of all, learn about the plants you have in your home, office, and garden. Nurseries and other places that sell house and garden plants rarely provide warnings about the possibilities of poisoning. Many poison control centers state that their most frequent calls concern children who have eaten plants. Keep plants you know are toxic out of reach of infants and small children (or better yet, keep toxic plants out of homes with children altogether), remove berries and leaves from the floor, and if you don't know whether a plant can be poisonous, consult a poison control center. Keep the number of the poison control center with your emergency phone numbers.

Do not store bulbs where they can be mistaken for onions. Clean up any clippings and leaves from garden work, but don't burn them, because poisonous plants, when burned, can produce poisonous smoke that is dangerous if inhaled. Don't bite into an unfamiliar seed, no matter where you find it. One plant in the pea family, the rosary pea, which grows in the tropics, produces a black and red seed that has been used in costume jewelry. People have died from chewing or swallowing only one rosary pea. Learn about the weeds and wild plants that grow in your neighborhood, and never eat any part of a plant you cannot positively identify. Poison hemlock is also known as fool's parsley. If you have a yen to forage for wild plant foods, take a field identification course taught by someone credentialed in the subject. Do not rely on field guidebooks. Even the clearest photograph is no proof against mistaking a "safe" plant for an unsafe one, and that first bite of a water hemlock root that you mistook for a wild carrot could be your last.

SOURCES

Coil SM: *Poisonous plants*, New York, 1991, Franklin Watts.

Lerner C: *Dumb cane and daffodils: poisonous plants in the house and garden*, New York, 1990, William Morrow.

Westbrooks RG, Preacher JW: *Poisonous plants of eastern North America*, Columbia, South Carolina, 1986, University of South Carolina Press.

Woodward L: *Poisonous plants: a colorful field guide*, New York, 1985, Hippocrene Books.

Figure 15-11   Wear proper clothing for any activities that may put you in contact with a poisonous substance.

- Dispose of outdated medications and household products properly and in a timely manner.
- Use potentially dangerous chemicals only in well-ventilated areas.
- Wear proper clothing when work or recreation may put you in contact with a poisonous substance (Fig. 15-11). Your employer must follow strict guidelines to protect you from coming into contact with poisonous substances in the workplace.
- Immediately wash those areas of the body that you suspect may have come into contact with a poisonous plant.

One of the best ways to prevent poisonings is to be aware of which common household items can be poisonous. These include acetaminophen, acids, ammonia, aspirin, bleach, cosmetics, detergents, drain cleaner, heating fuel, iodine, lye, lighter fluid, oven cleaner, paint, pesticides, toilet bowl cleaner, turpentine, and weed killer. Some common household plants and garden shrubs are also poisonous.

SUMMARY

Poisoning can occur in any one of four ways: inhalation, ingestion, absorption, and injection. For suspected poisonings, call the local poison control center or emergency number. Beyond providing general care information for a suspected poisoning or for administering a substance to counteract the remaining poison, PCC personnel may advise you to provide some specific care, such as inducing vomiting. Carefully following the directions of professionals and keeping your household first aid kit fully supplied can help you respond appropriately to a poisoning emergency. However, the best way to avoid poisoning is by taking steps to prevent it.

Answers to Application Questions

1. Ashley sees the chair used to climb up to the table and an empty vitamin container on the table next to Kristen.

2. Ashley should take the empty container to the phone, call the local poison control center, and follow the directions of its personnel.

STUDY QUESTIONS

1. Match each term with the correct definition.

   a. Absorbed poison
   b. Anaphylaxis
   c. Ingested poison
   d. Inhaled poison
   e. Injected poison
   f. Poison control center (PCC)

   ___E___ A poison introduced into the body through bites, stings, or a hypodermic needle.

   ___B___ A life-threatening allergic reaction.

   ___F___ A center staffed by professionals who can tell you how to provide care in a poisoning emergency.

   ___C___ A poison that is swallowed.

   ___A___ A poison that enters the body through contact with the skin.

   ___D___ A poison that enters the body through breathing.

2. List at least six common signs and symptoms of poisoning.

3. List four factors that determine the severity of poisoning.

4. Describe how to care for a person who has spilled a poisonous substance on his or her skin or has touched a poisonous plant, such as poison ivy.

5. Describe seven steps you can take to prevent poisoning emergencies in your home.

6. Circle the signs and symptoms associated with poisoning in the following scenario.

I was mowing my lawn when I looked down and saw a strange plant that appeared to be a weed. I leaned down and plucked the plant out of the ground with my bare hands. A little while later, my hands started itching and burning. My fingers became swollen, and red bumps began to appear all over my body.

7.   What kind of care would you give to the person in the scenario above?

In questions 8 through 12, circle the letter of the correct answer.

8.   You suspect a conscious man has swallowed poison. What should you do?

   a.   Give him something to drink.
   b.   Induce vomiting.
   c.   Call your local PCC.
   d.   Have him lie down.

9.   You suspect an unconscious child has swallowed poison. What should you do?

   a.   Call 9-1-1 or the local emergency number.
   b.   Give rescue breathing.
   c.   Dilute the poison by giving him or her something to drink.
   d.   Check the airway.

10. In caring for the victim of an inhaled poison, what should you do?

   a.   Be sure the scene is safe for you to enter.
   b.   Remove the victim from the source of the poison if possible.
   c.   Call the PCC, 9-1-1, or the local emergency number.
   d.   All of the above.

11. Which of the following are potential sources for carbon monoxide (CO) poisoning?

    a. Car exhaust
    b. A kerosene heater
    c. A defective furnace
    d. All of the above

12. Which of the following are included in the general guidelines of care for any poisoning emergency?

    a. Check the scene to make sure it is safe to approach and to gather clues about what happened.
    b. Remove the victim from the source of poison if necessary and possible.
    c. Give care according to the directions of PCC personnel or the EMS dispatcher.
    d. All of the above.

Answers are listed in Appendix A.

CHAPTER 16

Bites and Stings

WHAT YOU SHOULD LEARN

After reading this chapter, you should be able to—

1. Identify five signs and symptoms of the most common types of bites and stings.

2. Describe how to care for an insect, spider, and scorpion sting.

3. Describe how to care for a tick bite.

4. Describe how to care for snakebites.

5. Describe how to care for marine life bites or stings.

6. Describe how to care for domestic or wild animal bites.

7. Describe how to care for human bites.

8. List 11 ways to protect yourself from insect and tick bites.

9. Define the key terms for this chapter.

"I'm exhausted," Tonya moaned. "Look at the view," Darrell said, trying to take her mind off her aching feet. From where they stood on a cliff in the state park, the river flowed gracefully through the canyon and around the next bend. "I'm too tired to enjoy the view," Tonya said. She slumped to the ground and pulled off her hiking boots and socks. "This breeze feels great," she sighed. Then Tonya screamed. "My ankle!" she cried, scrambling to her feet. It took him only a few seconds to get to her. Even though she was clutching her ankle, he could still see a puncture wound and that the area was swelling. Tonya was obviously in a lot of pain.

Introduction

*C*hapter 15 described the four ways that poisons enter the body: absorption, inhalation, ingestion, and injection. **Injected poisons** enter the body through a bite, sting, or hypodermic needle. Bites and stings are among the most common forms of injected poisonings. In this chapter, you will learn how to recognize, care for, and prevent some of the most common types of bites and stings—those of insects, ticks, spiders and scorpions, marine life, snakes, domestic and wild animals, and humans. Chapter 17 provides information on another common form of injected poisoning: injected drug misuse and abuse.

SIGNS AND SYMPTOMS OF COMMON BITES AND STINGS

As with other kinds of poisoning, poisons that are injected through bites and stings may produce various signs and symptoms. Specific signs and symptoms depend on factors such as the type and location of the bite or sting; the amount of poison injected; the time elapsed since the poisoning; and the victim's size, weight, and age. Less severe reactions to bites and stings may trigger signs and symptoms including—

Key Terms

Antivenin: A substance used to counteract the poisonous effects of snake, spider, or insect venom.

Lyme disease: An illness transmitted by a certain kind of infected tick; victims may or may not develop a rash.

Rabies: A disease caused by a virus transmitted through the saliva of infected mammals.

Rocky Mountain spotted fever (RMSF): A disease transmitted by a certain kind of infected tick; victims develop a spotted rash.

- A bite or sting mark at the point of injection (entry site).
- A stinger, tentacle, or venom sac remaining in or near the entry site.
- Redness at and around the entry site.
- Swelling at and around the entry site.
- Pain or tenderness at and around the entry site.

Severe allergic reactions to bites and stings may bring on a life-threatening condition, a form of shock known as **anaphylaxis.** The signs and symptoms of and care for anaphylaxis are described in Chapters 5 and 15.

CARE FOR SPECIFIC BITES AND STINGS

The following sections provide detailed instructions on how to care for specific kinds of bites and stings. Table 16-1 highlights this information.

Insects

Between 1 and 2 million Americans are severely allergic to substances in the venom of bees, wasps, hornets, and yellow jackets. For these people, even one sting can result in anaphylaxis. Such highly allergic reactions account for the nearly 100 reported deaths that occur from insect stings each year. When highly allergic people are stung, they need immediate medical care for anaphylaxis. However, for most people, insect stings may be painful or uncomfortable but are not life threatening. To give care for an insect sting, first examine the sting site to see if the stinger is in the skin. If it is, remove it to prevent any further poisoning. Scrape the stinger away from the skin with your fingernail, the edge of a knife blade, or a plastic card, such as a credit card (Fig. 16-1). Often the venom sac will still be attached to the stinger. Do not remove the stinger with tweezers, since squeezing the stinger may put pressure on the venom sac and cause further poisoning.

Next, wash the site with soap and water. Cover it to keep it clean. Apply a cold pack to the area to reduce the pain and swelling. Place a layer of gauze or cloth between the source of cold and the skin to prevent skin damage. Observe the victim periodically for signs of an

Figure 16-1 If someone is stung and a stinger is present, scrape it away from the skin with your fingernail or a plastic card, such as a credit card.

allergic reaction. Be sure to ask the victim if he or she has had any prior allergic reactions to insect bites or stings.

Ticks

Ticks can contract disease, carry disease, and transmit it to humans. ***Rocky Mountain spotted fever (RMSF)*** is a serious tick-borne disease. RMSF is caused by the transmission of microscopic bacteria from the wood tick or dog tick host to other warm-blooded animals, including humans. The disease gets part of its name from the spotted rash that appears after a victim becomes infected. The rash may first appear on wrists or ankles but spreads rapidly to most other parts of the body. Other signs and symptoms of RSMF include fever and chills, severe headache, and joint and muscle aches.

Early treatment by medical professionals is important because more than 20 percent of untreated patients die from shock or kidney failure. Although the disease was first diagnosed in the western United States, cases of RMSF continue to be reported throughout North and South America today. RMSF is sometimes known by various regional names, such as black fever, mountain fever, tick fever, spotted fever, or pinta fever.

Another disease transmitted by ticks is known as ***Lyme disease.*** Lyme disease, or Lyme borreliosis, is an illness that affects a growing number of people in the United States. Cases of Lyme disease have been reported in more than

40 states, so everyone should take appropriate precautions to protect against it.

Not all ticks carry Lyme disease. Lyme disease is spread primarily by a type of tick that commonly attaches itself to field mice and deer. It is sometimes called a deer tick. This tick is found around beaches and in wooded and grassy areas. Like all ticks, it attaches itself to any warm-blooded animal that brushes by it, including humans.

Deer ticks are very tiny and difficult to see, especially in the late spring and summer. They are much smaller than the common dog tick or wood tick. They can be as small as a poppy seed, the period at the end of this sentence, or the head of a pin (Fig. 16-2). Even in the adult stage, they are only as large as a grape seed. A deer tick can attach to you without you knowing it is there. Many people who develop Lyme disease cannot recall having been bitten.

You can get Lyme disease from the bite of an infected tick at any time of the year. However, the risk is greatest between May and July, when ticks are most active and outdoor activities are at their peak.

The first sign of infection may appear a few days or a few weeks after a tick bite. Typically, a rash starts as a small red area at the site of the bite. It may spread up to 6 to 8 inches (15 to 20 centimeters) across (Fig. 16-3). In fair-skinned people, the center of the rash is lighter in color and the outer edges are red and raised, sometimes giving the rash a bull's-eye appearance. In dark-skinned people, the rash area may look

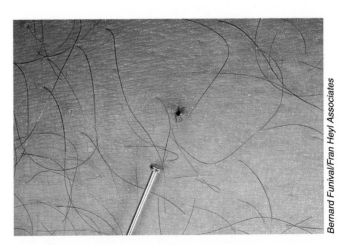

Bernard Funival/Fran Heyl Associates

Figure 16-2 A deer tick can be as small as the head of a pin.

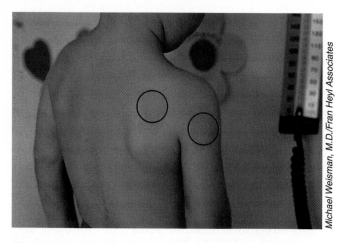

Michael Weisman, M.D./Fran Heyl Associates

Figure 16-3   A person with Lyme disease may develop a rash.

black and blue, like a bruise. A rash can appear anywhere on the body, and more than one rash may appear on various body parts. You can even have Lyme disease without developing a rash.

Most other signs and symptoms of Lyme disease are similar to those of RMSF and include fever and chills, headache, weakness or fatigue, and flulike joint and muscle aches. These signs and symptoms may develop slowly and may not occur at the same time as a rash. The more severe symptoms of Lyme disease may appear weeks, months, or even years after a tick bite.

Lyme disease can get worse if it is not treated. In its advanced stages, Lyme disease may cause arthritis, numbness, memory loss, problems with vision or hearing, high fever, and stiff neck. Some of these signs and symp-

toms could indicate brain or nervous system problems. An irregular or rapid heartbeat could indicate heart problems.

If you find an embedded tick, grasp the tick with fine-tipped tweezers as close to the skin as possible and pull slowly, steadily, and firmly (Fig. 16-4). If you do not have tweezers, use a glove, plastic wrap, a piece of paper, or a leaf to protect your fingers. It is not a good idea to use your bare hands to remove a tick; however, if you do, wash your hands immediately afterwards to avoid becoming infected. Do not try to burn a tick off with a hot match or a burning cigarette. Do not use other home remedies, like coating the tick with Vaseline or nail polish or pricking it with a pin. These remedies are not always effective in removing the tick and can promote further harm to the victim.

If you cannot remove the tick, obtain medical care. Even if you can remove the tick, you may want to let your physician know that you have been bitten by a tick in case you become ill within the following month or two. Mouthparts of adult ticks may sometimes remain in your skin, but these will not cause disease. Once the tick is removed, apply an **antiseptic,** such as alcohol, to the site of the bite. If an **antibiotic** ointment is available, apply it to help prevent wound infection as well. Observe the site periodically thereafter. If a rash or flulike symptoms develop, seek medical help. Redness at the site of a tick bite does not mean you are infected with a disease.

A physician will usually use antibiotics to treat Lyme disease and RMSF. Antibiotics work best and most quickly when taken early. Clinical trials are now under way on a Lyme disease vaccine that, if effective, may be available by 1996. If you suspect you may have been infected with Lyme disease or RMSF, do not delay seeking treatment. Treatment is slower and less effective in advanced stages.

Additional information on Lyme disease and RMSF may be available from your state or local health department. You can also contact the American Lyme Disease Foundation, Inc. by calling 1-800-876-LYME.

Spiders and Scorpions

Few spiders in the United States have venom that causes death. However, the bites of the

Figure 16-4   Remove a tick by pulling slowly, steadily, and firmly with fine-tipped tweezers.

black widow and brown recluse spiders can make you seriously ill and are occasionally fatal. These spiders live in most parts of the United States. You can identify them by the unique designs on their bodies (Fig. 16-5, *A* and *B*). The black widow spider is black with a reddish hourglass shape on its underbody. The brown recluse spider is light brown with a darker brown, violin-shaped marking on the top of its body.

A

Rob Planck/Tom Stack & Associates

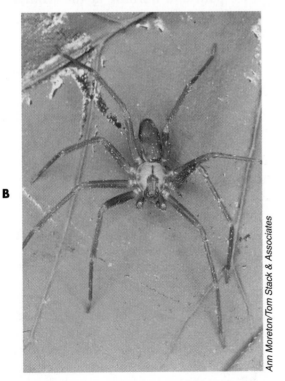

B

Ann Moreton/Tom Stack & Associates

Figure 16-5 **A,** The black widow spider and, **B,** brown recluse spider have characteristic markings.

Both spiders prefer dark, out-of-the-way places where they are seldom disturbed. Bites usually occur on the hands and arms of people reaching into places such as wood, rock, and brush piles or rummaging in dark garages and attics. Often, the victim will not know that he or she has been bitten until signs or symptoms develop.

The bite of the black widow spider is the more painful and often the more deadly of the two, especially in very young and elderly victims. Its venom is even deadlier than that of a rattlesnake, although the smaller amount of venom injected by the spider usually produces less of a reaction than that of a snakebite.

The bite of a black widow spider usually causes a sharp pinprick pain, followed by a dull pain in the area of the bite. Signs and symptoms of this bite include muscular rigidity in the shoulders, back, and abdomen, as well as restlessness, anxiety, sweating, weakness, and drooping eyelids.

A brown recluse spider bite may produce little or no pain initially, but localized pain develops an hour or more later. A blood-filled blister forms under the surface of the skin, sometimes in a target or bull's-eye pattern. The blister increases in size and eventually ruptures, leaving a black scar.

If the victim recognizes the spider as either a black widow or brown recluse, he or she should seek professional help at a medical facility as soon as possible. Professionals will clean the wound and give medication to reduce the pain and inflammation. An **antivenin,** a substance used to counteract the poisonous effects of the venom, is available for black widow bites. Antivenin is used mostly for children and the elderly and is rarely necessary when bites occur in healthy adults.

Scorpions live in dry regions of the southwestern United States and Mexico. They are usually about 3 inches (8 centimeters) long and have 8 legs and a pair of crab-like pincers. At the end of the tail is a stinger, used to inject venom. Scorpions live in cool, damp places, such as basements, junk piles, wood piles, and under the bark of living or fallen trees. They are most active in the evening and at night, which is when most stings occur. Like spiders, only a few species of scorpions have a poten-

Rob Planck/Tom Stack & Associates

Figure 16-6   The bites of only a few species of scorpions found in the United States can be fatal.

tially fatal sting (Fig. 16-6). *However, because it is difficult to distinguish the highly poisonous scorpions from the nonpoisonous scorpions, all scorpion bites should be treated as medical emergencies.*

Signs and symptoms of spider bites and scorpion stings may include—

- A mark indicating a possible bite or sting.
- Severe pain in the sting or bite area.
- A blister, lesion, or swelling at the entry site.
- Nausea and vomiting.
- Difficulty breathing or swallowing.
- Sweating and salivating profusely.
- Irregular heart rhythms.
- Muscle cramping or abdominal pain.

In the event of a scorpion sting, call 9-1-1 or the local emergency number. The victim may need to go to a medical facility where he or she can receive an antivenin. While waiting for EMS personnel, wash the wound and apply a cold pack to the site to reduce swelling. Remember to place a layer of gauze or cloth between the source of cold and the skin to prevent skin damage.

Snakes

Few areas of medicine have provoked more controversy about care for an injury than snakebites. Snakebite care issues, such as whether to use a tourniquet, cut the wound, ap-

ply ice, when to apply suction, use electric shocks, or capture the snake, have been discussed at length over the years. All this controversy is rather amazing since, of the 8000 people reported bitten annually in the United States, fewer than 12 die. Figure 16-7 shows the four kinds of poisonous snakes found in the United States. Rattlesnakes account for most snakebites and nearly all deaths from snakebites. Most deaths occur because the victim has an allergic reaction or is in poor health, or because too much time passes before the victim receives medical care. Although advice to citizen responders has varied greatly over the years, elaborate care is usually unnecessary because, in most cases, the victim can reach professional medical care within 30 minutes. Often care can be reached much faster, since most bites occur near the home, not in the wild.

Signs and symptoms that indicate a poisonous snakebite include—

- One or two distinct puncture wounds, which may or may not bleed. The exception is the coral snake, whose teeth leave a semicircular mark.
- Severe pain and burning at the wound site immediately after or within 4 hours of the incident.
- Swelling and discoloration at the wound site immediately after or within 4 hours of the incident.

Follow these guidelines to care for someone bitten by a snake:

- Wash the wound, if possible.
- Immobilize the affected part.
- Keep the affected area lower than the heart, if possible.
- Call 9-1-1 or the local emergency number.
- Minimize the victim's movement. If possible, carry a victim who must be transported or have him or her walk slowly.

If you know the victim cannot get professional medical care within 30 minutes, consider suctioning the wound using an appropriate snakebite kit. People at high risk of being bitten by a snake in the wild (away from medical care) should consider carrying a snakebite kit and know how to use its contents.

Figure 16-7   There are four kinds of poisonous snakes found in the United States: **A,** Rattlesnake. **B,** Copperhead. **C,** Water moccasin. **D,** Coral snake.

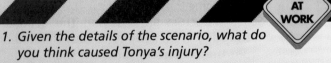

MIND AT WORK

1. *Given the details of the scenario, what do you think caused Tonya's injury?*

2. *How should Darrell care for Tonya's injury?*

3. *What should Darrell consider when deciding how to get professional medical help for Tonya?*

Regardless of what you may have otherwise heard or read—

- *Do not apply ice.* Snake venom, unlike other kinds of venom, gets drawn further into the body as the cold constricts the blood vessels around the wound.
- *Do not cut the wound.* Cutting the wound can further injure the victim and has not been shown to remove any significant amount of venom.
- *Do not apply a tourniquet.* A tourniquet severely restricts blood flow to the limb, which could result in the loss of the limb.

- *Do not use electric shock.* This technique has not been conclusively shown to affect the poison and can be dangerous. It is inappropriate in the majority of snakebite cases in the United States, since professional help is usually readily attainable.

Spiders and Snakes

Some scientists believe the venoms of these feared creatures may unlock the mysteries of some neurological disorders and cancers. Researchers are studying the venom of different spiders and snakes to isolate the powerful chemicals that allow the animals to kill and eat their prey.

In Cambridge, Massachusetts, scientists are focusing on the protein chemicals the spider uses to paralyze its prey. They believe that certain compounds in the venom, called glutamate blockers, may offer help for stroke and other neurological disorders.

The compound glutamate is vital to communication between nerve cells in both humans and insects. It serves as a transmitter between cells. With too little glutamate, the cells cannot transmit information through the nerve network, causing paralysis. Too much glutamate damages the cells.

Brain damage from cerebral palsy, epilepsy, and stroke is caused in part by excess glutamate. Damaged cells release excess quantities of glutamate when they rupture, causing the undamaged cells to rupture in a chain reaction. Researchers think the spider venom contains glutamate blockers that may prevent this chain reaction. Researchers are currently studying the reactions in test tubes and hope to begin testing on rodents in the years to come.

In Seattle, doctors are studying the actions of chemicals found in snake venom. They isolated proteins from the venoms of different snake varieties and mixed them with human cancer cells to see if the proteins could destroy the tumors. After experimenting with venoms from many different kinds of snakes and scorpions, they have narrowed their experiments to the Western Diamondback rattlesnake.

The cancer cells are killed by a small protein that comes from the snake's digestive juices. Unfortunately, the protein kills normal cells as well. To combat this problem, researchers are linking the protein with an antibody that attaches only to certain cancer cells. They hope that the antibody, with its bound toxin, can attach itself to the outside of the cancer cell, inject the poison, and destroy it. This procedure would spare the normal cells.

After studying the reactions in test tubes, doctors have begun injecting the venom/antibody in mice that have tumors. If they are sucessful in this first stage of testing, further testing will continue.

SOURCES
Goldin, Stan: Director of Biochemistry, Cambridge NeuroScience Research Inc., 1 Kendall Square, Cambridge, Massachusetts 02139. Interview, April 1990.
Twardzik, Daniel: PhD. Affiliate Professor of Medicine, University of Washington School of Medicine. Research Fellow, Oncogen/Bristol Meyers/Squibb in Seattle, Washington. Interview, April 1990.

Marine Life

The stings of some forms of marine life are not only painful but can also make you sick (Fig. 16-8). The side effects include allergic reactions that can cause breathing and heart problems and paralysis. If the sting occurs in water, move the person from the water to dry land as soon as possible. Call 9-1-1 or your local emergency phone number if the victim doesn't know what stung him or her, has a history of allergic reactions to marine life stings, is stung on the face or neck, or starts to have difficulty breathing.

If you know the sting is from a jellyfish, sea anemone, or Portuguese man-of-war, soak the injured part in vinegar as soon as possible. Vinegar often works best to offset the toxin and reduce pain. Rubbing alcohol or a baking

Figure 16-8   The painful sting of some marine animals can cause serious injury and illness.

soda paste may also be used. Do not rub the wound or apply fresh water or ammonia, since these substances will increase pain. Meat tenderizer is no longer recommended, because the active ingredient once used to reduce pain is no longer contained in most meat tenderizers.

If you know the sting is from a sting ray, sea urchin, or spiny fish, flush the wound with tap water. Ocean water may also be used. Immobilize the injured part, usually the foot, and soak the affected area in nonscalding hot water (as hot as the person can stand) for about 30 minutes or until the pain goes away. Toxins from these animals are heat-sensitive, and dramatic relief of local pain often occurs from one application of hot fluid. If hot water is not available, packing the area in hot sand may have a similar effect if the sand is hot enough. Then carefully clean the wound and apply a bandage. Watch for signs of infection, and check with a health care provider to determine if a tetanus shot is needed. (Tetanus is discussed later in this chapter.)

Domestic and Wild Animals

The bite of a domestic or wild animal carries the risk of infection, as well as soft tissue injury. One of the most serious possible results is rabies. **Rabies** is a disease caused by a virus transmitted through the saliva of diseased mammals, such as skunks, bats, raccoons, cats, dogs, cattle, and foxes. Dog bites are the most common of all bites from domestic or wild animals.

Animals with rabies may act in unusual ways. For example, nocturnal animals, such as raccoons, may be active in the daytime. A wild animal that usually tries to avoid humans may not run away when you approach. Rabid animals may salivate, appear partially paralyzed, or act irritable, aggressive, or strangely quiet. To reduce your risk of becoming infected with rabies, do not pet or feed wild animals and do not touch the body of a dead wild animal.

If not treated, rabies is fatal. *Anyone bitten by a wild or domestic animal must get professional medical attention as soon as possible.* To prevent rabies from developing, the victim receives a series of vaccine injections to build up immunity. In the past, caring for rabies meant a lengthy series of painful injections that had many unpleasant side effects. The vaccines used now require fewer and less painful injections and have fewer side effects.

Tetanus is another potentially fatal infection. Tetanus is caused by the transmission of bacteria that produce a toxin, which can occur in wounds created by animal and human bites. The toxin associated with tetanus, which attacks the central nervous system, is one of the most lethal (deadly) poisons known. More than 50,000 people worldwide die annually from tetanus infection. Wounds to the face, head, and neck are the most likely to be fatal because those areas are close to the brain.

Signs and symptoms of tetanus are irritability, headache, fever, and painful muscular spasms. One of the most common symptoms of tetanus is muscular stiffness in the jaw, which is why tetanus is sometimes known as "lockjaw." It can take anywhere from 3 days to 5 weeks before these signs and symptoms occur. Eventually, if the condition is not treated, every muscle in the body goes into spasms. Care for tetanus includes prompt and thorough cleansing of the wound by a medical professional, followed by a series of immunization injections. Care for tetanus is discussed further in Chapter 9.

If someone is bitten by a wild or domestic animal, try to get him or her away from the animal without endangering yourself. Do not try to restrain or capture the animal. If the wound is minor, wash it with soap and water, control any bleeding, apply a dressing, and take the victim to a doctor or medical facility. If the wound is bleeding heavily, control the bleeding but do not clean the wound. Seek medical attention immediately. The wound will be properly cleaned at a medical facility.

If possible, try to remember what the animal looks like and the area in which it was last seen. Call 9-1-1 or the local emergency number. The dispatcher will get the proper authorities, such as animal control, to the scene.

Humans

Human bites are quite common. They account for up to 23 percent of all bites cared for by urban physicians. Human bites differ from other bites in that they may be more contaminated, tend to occur in higher-risk areas of the body (especially on the hands), and often receive delayed care. At least 42 different species of bacteria have been reported in human saliva, so it is not surprising that serious infection often follows the occurrence of a human bite. *However, according to the Centers for Disease Control and Prevention (CDC), human bites are not considered to carry a risk of transmitting the human immunodeficiency virus (HIV), the virus that causes the acquired immunodeficiency syndrome (AIDS).* Children are often the inflictors and the recipients of human bite wounds.

As with animal bites, it is important to get the victim of a human bite to professional medical care as soon as possible so that antibiotic therapy can be prescribed if necessary. If the wound is not severe, wash it with soap and water, control any bleeding, apply a dressing, and take the victim to a doctor or medical facility. If the bite is severe, control bleeding and call EMS personnel. The wound will be properly cleaned at a medical facility.

TABLE 16-1

Caring for Bites and Stings

Insect Bites and Stings	Tick Bites	Spider Bites	Scorpion Stings	Snakebites	Marine Life Stings	Domestic and Wild Animal Bites	Human Bites
Signs and Symptoms:	**Signs and Symptoms:**	**Signs and Symptoms:**	**Signs and Symptoms:**	**Signs and Symptoms:**	**Signs and Symptoms:**	**Signs and Symptoms:**	**Signs and Symptoms:**
Stinger may be present Pain Local swelling Hives or rash Nausea and vomiting Breathing difficulty	Bull's eye, spotted, or black and blue rash around bite or on other body parts Fever and chills Flulike aches	Bite mark or blister Pain or cramping Nausea and vomiting Difficulty breathing and swallowing Profuse sweating or salivation Irregular heartbeat	Bite mark Local swelling Pain or cramping Nausea and vomiting Difficulty breathing or swallowing Profuse sweating or salivation Irregular heartbeat	Bite mark Severe pain and burning Local swelling and discoloration	Possible marks Pain Local swelling	Bite mark Bleeding Pain	Bite mark Bleeding Pain
Care:	**Care:**	**Care:**	**Care:**	**Care:**	**Care:**	**Care:**	**Care:**
Remove stinger; scrape it away with card or knife Wash wound Cover wound Apply a cold pack Watch for signs and symptoms of allergic reactions; take steps to minimize shock if they occur	Remove tick with tweezers Apply antiseptic and antibiotic ointment to wound Watch for signs of infection Get medical attention if necessary	If black widow or brown recluse—call EMS personnel immediately to receive antivenin and have wound cleaned	Wash wound Apply a cold pack Get medical care to receive antivenin Call EMS personnel or local emergency number	Wash wound Immobilize bitten part and keep it lower than the heart Call EMS personnel or local emergency number Minimize victim's movement	If jellyfish—soak area in either vinegar, alcohol, or baking soda paste If stingray—immobilize and soak area in nonscalding hot water until pain goes away. Clean and bandage wound Call EMS personnel or local emergency number, if necessary	If wound is minor—wash wound, control bleeding, apply a dressing, and get medical attention as soon as possible If wound is severe—call EMS personnel or local emergency number, control bleeding, and do not wash wound	If wound is minor—wash wound, control bleeding, apply a dressing, and get medical attention as soon as possible If wound is severe—call EMS personnel or local emergency number, control bleeding, and do not wash wound

PREVENTING BITES AND STINGS

Preventing bites and stings from insects, spiders, ticks, snakes, and scorpions is the best protection against the transmission of injected poisons. When in wooded or grassy areas, follow these general guidelines to prevent bites and stings:

- Apply insect or tick repellent to yourself (as directed below).
- Wear long-sleeved shirts and long pants.
- Tuck your pant legs into your socks or boots. Tuck your shirt into your pants.
- Wear light-colored clothing to make it easier to see tiny insects or ticks.
- Use a rubber band or tape the area where pants and socks meet to prevent ticks or other insects from getting under clothing.
- Inspect yourself carefully for insects or ticks after being outdoors or have someone else do it. If you are outdoors for a long period of time, check yourself several times during the day.
- Check especially in moist, hairy areas of the body (including the back of the neck and the scalp line).
- Shower immediately after coming indoors, using a washcloth to scrub off any unembedded insects or ticks. Carefully inspect yourself for embedded ticks and remove them appropriately.
- Keep an eye out for and avoid the nests of wasps, bees, and hornets.
- If you have pets that go outdoors, spray them with repellent made for your type of pet. Apply the repellent according to the label, and check your pet for ticks often.
- When hiking in woods and fields, stay in the middle of trails. Avoid underbrush, fallen trees, and tall grass.
- Wear sturdy hiking boots.
- Avoid walking in areas known to be populated with snakes.

- Make noise as you walk through areas that may be populated with snakes, since many snakes will leave if they hear you coming.
- If you encounter a snake, look around, because other snakes may be nearby. Turn around and walk away on the same path you came on.

If you will be in a grassy or wooded area for a length of time or if you know the area is highly infested with insects or ticks, you may want to use a repellent. Diethyltoluamide (DEET) is an active ingredient in many skin-applied repellents that are effective against ticks and other insects. Repellents containing DEET can be applied on exposed areas of skin and clothing. However, repellents containing permethrin, another common repellent, should be used only on clothing.

If you use a repellent, follow these general rules:

- Keep all repellents out of the reach of children.
- To apply repellent to the face, first spray it on your hands and then apply it from your hands to your face. Avoid sensitive areas, such as the lips and the eyes.
- Never spray repellents containing permethrin on your skin or a child's skin.
- Never use repellents on a wound or on irritated skin.
- Never put repellents on children's hands. They may put them in their eyes or mouth.
- Use repellents sparingly and according to label instructions. One application will last 4 to 8 hours. Heavier or more frequent applications will not increase effectiveness and may be toxic.
- Wash treated skin with soap and water and remove treated clothing after you come indoors.
- If you suspect you are having an allergic reaction to a repellent, wash the treated skin immediately and call a physician.

To prevent stings from marine animals, you might consider wearing a wet suit or dry suit or protective footwear in the water—especially at times when or in areas where there is a high risk of such occurrences.

MIND AT WORK

4. *What could Tonya have done to help prevent her injury?*

To prevent dog bites, the Humane Society of the United States offers the following guidelines:

- Don't run past a dog. The dog's natural instinct is to chase and catch prey.
- If a dog threatens you, don't scream. Avoid eye contact, try to remain motionless until the dog leaves, then back away slowly until the dog is out of sight.
- Don't approach a strange dog, especially one that is tied or confined.
- Always let a dog see and sniff you before you pet the animal.

Many of the 2 million dog bites that are reported in the United States each year could have been prevented by taking these precautions.

SUMMARY

Bites and stings are one of the most common types of injected poisonings. For suspected injected poisonings, call the local poison control center or local emergency number. Remember, the best way to avoid any kind of poisoning is to take steps to prevent it. In the next chapter, you will learn how misuse and abuse of substances, such as drugs and medications, can poison the body.

Answers to Application Questions

1. The sounds of hissing and dry leaves crackling, as well as pain and bleeding at or near Tonya's ankle, indicate that she was probably bitten by a snake.

2. Darrell should find a phone or contact a park ranger to call 9-1-1 or the local emergency number immediately. Then, if possible, Darrell should wash the wound, immobilize Tonya's leg, keep her leg lower than her heart, and minimize her movement.

3. Darrell should consider how to access a phone, the distance to professional help, whether he can get Tonya to help before help can get to her, and whether he has a way to transport her to a medical facility.

4. To prevent her injury, Tonya could have made noise to scare away the snake, kept her socks and boots on, and not used the log as a footrest.

STUDY QUESTIONS

1. Match each term with the correct definition.

   a. Injected poison
   b. Lyme disease
   c. Antivenin
   d. Rabies
   e. Rocky Mountain spotted fever

   __B__ An illness people get from the bite of a specific type of infected tick; victims may or may not develop a rash.

   __A__ A poison introduced into the body through bites, stings, or a hypodermic needle.

   __C__ A substance used to counteract the poisonous effects of snake, spider, or insect venom.

   __E__ A disease transmitted by a certain kind of tick; victims develop a spotted rash.

   __D__ A disease caused by a virus transmitted through the saliva of infected mammals.

2. List the steps of care for a tick bite.

3. Describe at least four ways to prevent bites and stings.

4. List three signs or symptoms of common types of bites and stings.

5. List the steps of care for a snakebite.

6. *You are playing with your 5-year-old sister at a neighborhood park. Suddenly, a dog runs out of the bushes, jumps on your sister, and bites her on the cheek. The wound is deep and bleeding heavily.*

   What should you do? Write your answer on the lines below the scenario.

   _____

   _____

In questions 7 through 12, circle the letter of the correct answer.

7. In caring for a bee sting, what should you do?

   a. Remove the remaining stinger by scraping it from the skin.
   b. Remove the remaining stinger using tweezers.
   c. Pull the stinger out with your bare hands.
   d. Rub over the stinger with an alcohol swab.

8. When spending time outdoors in woods or tall grass, what should you do to prevent bites and stings?

    a. Wear light-colored clothing.
    b. Use insect or tick repellent.
    c. Tuck pant legs into boots or socks.
    d. All of the above.

9. Which of the following are signs and symptoms of Lyme disease?

    a. Breathing difficulty
    b. Headache, fever, weakness, joint and muscle pain
    c. Paralysis
    d. Sneezing

10. Which of the following should you do to care for a scorpion sting?

    a. Apply suction to the wound.
    b. Wash the wound and apply a cold pack.
    c. Call 9-1-1 or the local emergency number.
    d. b and c.

11. Which of the following should you apply to a jellyfish, sea anemone, or Portuguese man-of-war sting?

    a. Vinegar
    b. Meat tenderizer
    c. A baking soda paste
    d. a or c

12. Which of the following should you do to care for a severe human bite?

    a. Wash the wound with an antiseptic.
    b. Control bleeding and follow precautions to prevent disease transmission.
    c. Contact EMS personnel immediately.
    d. b and c.

Answers are listed in Appendix A.

CHAPTER 17

Substance Misuse and Abuse

WHAT YOU SHOULD LEARN

After reading this chapter, you should be able to—

1. Identify the six main categories of commonly misused or abused substances.

2. Identify the signs and symptoms that may indicate substance misuse or abuse.

3. Describe how to care for someone who you suspect or know is misusing or abusing a substance.

4. Explain how you can help prevent unintentional drug misuse.

5. Define the key terms for this chapter.

As she entered the room, Susan felt nervous. In fact, she'd felt too nervous to eat much all day. This was her first off-campus party. Luckily, she knew a few people, and one of them, Alicia, spotted her and shoved a cold beer into her hand. Susan gulped it gratefully and began to feel less nervous almost at once. The next drink was something a little more exotic, but it tasted just fine. So did the next one and the beer after that. Then— "I've got to go somewhere," she muttered to the group she was standing with. The room had begun to spin. Susan just made it to the bathroom in time to vomit and then collapse onto the floor, where she passed out cold. Two of her friends found her and tried to rouse her, but Susan was totally limp and unresponsive. "She looks pale," Wanda said, "I think she's really in bad shape." "What should we do?" sobbed Alicia.

Introduction

When you hear the term substance abuse, what thoughts flash through your mind? Narcotics? Cocaine? Marijuana? Because of the publicity they receive, we tend to think of illegal (also known as illicit or controlled) drugs when we hear of substance abuse. In the United States today, however, legal (also called licit or noncontrolled) substances are among those most often misused or abused. Such legal substances include nicotine (found in tobacco products); alcohol (found in beer, wine, and liquor); and over-the-counter medications, such as aspirin, sleeping pills, and diet pills.

The term substance abuse refers to a broad range of improperly used medical and nonmedical substances. Substance abuse costs the United States tens of billions of dollars each year in medical care, insurance, and lost productivity. Even more important, however, are the lives lost or permanently impaired each year from injuries or medical emergencies related to substance abuse or misuse.

This chapter will teach you about common forms of substance misuse and abuse, how to recognize these problems, and how to care for its victims. In an emergency caused by substance abuse or misuse, the immediate care you give can save a life.

Key Terms

Addiction: The compulsive need to use a substance. Stopping use would cause the user to suffer mental, physical, and emotional distress.

Cannabis products: Substances, such as marijuana and hashish, that are derived from the *Cannabis sativa* plant; can produce feelings of elation, distorted perceptions of time and space, and impaired motor coordination and judgment.

Dependency: The desire or need to continually use a substance.

Depressants: Substances that affect the central nervous system to slow down physical and mental activity, such as tranquilizers and sleeping pills.

Drug: Any substance, other than food, intended to affect the functions of the body.

Hallucinogens (hǝ LOO sin ǝ genz): Substances that affect mood, sensation, thought, emotion, and self-awareness; alter perceptions of time and space; and produce hallucinations and delusions. Also known as psychedelics.

Inhalants: Substances inhaled to produce a mood-altering effect, such as glue and paint thinners.

Medication: A drug given therapeutically to prevent or treat the effects of a disease or condition or otherwise enhance mental or physical well-being.

Narcotics: Drugs prescribed to relieve pain.

Overdose: An excess use of a drug, resulting in adverse reactions ranging from and including mania and hysteria to coma and death; specific reactions include changes in blood pressure and heartbeat, sweating, vomiting, and liver failure.

Stimulants: Substances that affect the central nervous system and increase physical and mental activity.

Substance abuse: The deliberate, persistent, excessive use of a substance without regard to health concerns or accepted medical practices.

Substance misuse: The use of a substance for unintended purposes or for intended purposes but in improper amounts or doses.

Tolerance: Condition in which the effects of a substance on the body decrease as a result of continual use.

Withdrawal: The condition produced when a person stops using or abusing a substance to which he or she is addicted.

EFFECTS OF MISUSE AND ABUSE

Substance abuse and misuse pose a very serious threat to the health of millions of Americans. According to the Drug Abuse Warning Network (DAWN), drug-related emergency department admissions are at an all-time high. The number of emergency department patients who say that they have used illegal substances has risen dramatically. The greatest increase is in the number of people who admit to using cocaine and crack.

More than 100,000 Americans die annually as a result of substance abuse. Experts estimate that as many as two thirds of all homicides and serious assaults occurring annually involve alcohol alone. Other problems directly or indirectly related to substance abuse include dropping out of school, adolescent pregnancy, suicide, involvement in crime, and transmission of the human immunodeficiency virus (HIV), the virus that causes acquired immunodeficiency syndrome (AIDS).

FORMS OF SUBSTANCE MISUSE AND ABUSE

Substance misuse is the use of a substance for unintended purposes or for appropriate purposes but in improper amounts or doses. *Substance abuse* is the deliberate, persistent, and excessive use of a substance without regard to health concerns or accepted medical practices. Many substances that are abused or misused are not illegal. Other substances are legal only when prescribed by a physician. Some are illegal only for those under age (for example, alcohol). Figure 17-1 shows some commonly misused and abused substances that are legal.

A *drug* is any substance other than food taken to affect body functions. A drug given

Figure 17-1 Substance abuse and misuse involve a broad range of improperly used medical and nonmedical substances.

therapeutically to prevent or correct a disease or otherwise enhance mental or physical well-being is a **medication.** Any drug can cause **dependency,** the desire to continually use the substance. The victim feels that he or she needs the drug to function normally. Those with a compulsive need for a substance and who would suffer mental, physical, and emotional distress if they stopped taking it are said to have an **addiction** to that substance.

When one continually uses a substance, its effects on the body decrease—a condition called **tolerance.** The person then has to increase the dose and frequency of the substance use to obtain the desired effect.

An **overdose** occurs when someone uses an excessive amount of a drug, resulting in adverse reactions ranging from and including mania and hysteria to coma and death. Specific reactions include changes in blood pressure and heartbeat, sweating, vomiting, and liver failure. An overdose may occur unintentionally if a person takes too much medication at one time, for example, when someone forgets that he or she took one dose of a medication and takes an additional dose (Fig. 17-2).

An overdose may also be intentional, such as in suicide attempts. Sometimes the victim takes a sufficiently high dose of a substance to be certain to cause death. Other times, to gain attention or help, the victim takes enough of a substance to need medical attention but not enough to cause death.

The term **withdrawal** describes the condition produced when a person stops using or abusing a drug to which he or she is addicted. Stopping the use of a substance may occur as a deliberate decision or because the person is unable to obtain the specific drug. Withdrawal from certain substances, such as alcohol, can cause severe mental and physical discomfort. Because withdrawal may become a serious medical condition, medical professionals often oversee the process.

MISUSED AND ABUSED SUBSTANCES

Substances are categorized according to their effects on the body. The six major categories are stimulants, depressants, hallucinogens, narcotics, inhalants, and cannabis products. The category to which a substance belongs depends mostly on the way the substance is taken or the effects it has on the central nervous system. Some substances depress the nervous system, whereas others speed up its activity. Some are not easily categorized because they have various effects or may be taken in a variety of ways. Figure 17-3 shows a variety of legal and illegal substances that are commonly misused and abused. A heightened or exaggerated effect may be produced when two or more substances are used at the same time. This is called a synergistic effect and can be deadly. Table 17-1 on page 346 identifies commonly misused and abused substances.

Stimulants

Stimulants are drugs that affect the central nervous system by increasing physical and mental activity. They produce temporary feelings of alertness and prevent fatigue. They are sometimes used for weight reduction because they also suppress appetite.

Many stimulants are ingested as pills, but some can be absorbed or inhaled. Amphetamines, dextroamphetamines, and methamphetamines are stimulants. Their slang names include uppers, bennies, black beauties, speed, crystal, meth, and crank. One dangerous stimulant is called "ice." Ice is an extremely addictive smokeable form of methamphetamine.

Cocaine is one of the most publicized and powerful stimulants. Cocaine can be taken into the body in different ways. The most common way is sniffing it in powder form, known as

Figure 17-2 Misuse of a medication can occur when a person unintentionally takes an extra dose.

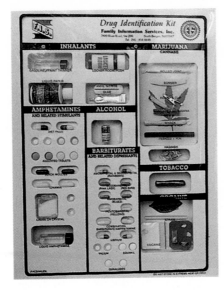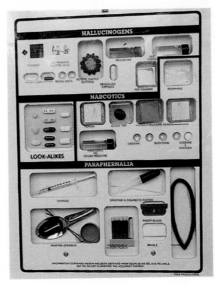

Figure 17-3   Misused and abused substances.

"snorting." In this method, the drug is absorbed into the blood through capillaries in the nose. Slang names for cocaine include coke, snow, blow, flake, foot, and nose candy. A purer and more potent form of cocaine is crack. Crack is smoked. The vapors that are inhaled into the lungs reach the brain and cause almost immediate effects. Crack is highly addictive. Slang names for crack include rock and freebase rocks.

Interestingly, the most common stimulants in America are legal. Leading the list is caffeine, present in coffee, tea, many kinds of sodas, chocolate, diet pills, and pills used to combat fatigue. The next most common stimulant is nicotine, found in tobacco products. Other stimulants used for medical purposes are asthma medications or decongestants that can be taken by mouth or inhaled (Fig. 17-4).

Hallucinogens

Hallucinogens, also known as psychedelics, are substances that cause changes in mood, sensation, thought, emotion, and self-awareness. They alter one's perception of time and space and produce visual, auditory, and tactile delusions.

Among the most widely abused hallucinogens are lysergic acid diethylamide (LSD), called acid; psilocybin, called mushrooms; phencyclidine (PCP), called angel dust; and mescaline, called peyote, buttons, or mesc.

These substances are usually ingested, but PCP is also often inhaled.

Hallucinogens often have physical effects similar to stimulants but are classified differently because of the other effects they produce. Hallucinogens sometimes cause what is called a "bad trip." A bad trip can involve intense fear, panic, paranoid delusions, vivid hallucinations, profound depression, tension, and anxiety. The victim may be irrational and feel threatened by any attempt others make to help.

Depressants

Depressants are substances that affect the central nervous system by decreasing physical and mental activity. Depressants are commonly

Figure 17-4   Medication used to treat asthma is a common legal stimulant.

TABLE 17-1

Commonly Misused and Abused Substances

Category	Substances	Possible Effects
Stimulants	Caffeine Cocaine, crack cocaine Methamphetamines Amphetamines Dextroamphetamines Nicotine Over-the-counter diet aids Asthma treatments	Increase mental and physical activity, produce temporary feelings of alertness, prevent fatigue, suppress appetite.
Hallucinogens	LSD (lysergic acid diethylamide) PCP (phencyclidine) Mescaline Peyote Psilocybin	Cause changes in mood, sensation, thought, emotion, and self-awareness; alter perceptions of time and space; and may produce profound depression, tension, and anxiety, as well as visual, auditory, or tactile hallucinations.
Depressants	Barbiturates Narcotics Alcohol Antihistamines Sedatives Tranquilizers Over-the-counter sleep aids	Decrease mental and physical activity, alter consciousness, relieve anxiety and pain, promote sleep, depress respiration, relax muscles, and impair coordination and judgment.
Narcotics	Morphine Codeine Heroin Methadone Opium	Relieve pain, may produce stupor or euphoria, may cause coma or death, and are highly addictive.
Inhalants	Medical anesthetics Gasoline and kerosene Glues in organic cements Lighter fluid Paint and varnish thinners Aerosol propellants	Alter moods; may produce a partial or complete loss of feeling; may produce effects similar to drunkenness, such as slurred speech, lack of inhibitions, and impaired motor coordination. Can also cause damage to the heart, lungs, brain, and liver.

used for medical purposes. Common depressants are barbiturates, benzodiazepines, narcotics, and alcohol. Most depressants are ingested or injected. Their slang names include downers, rainbows, barbs, goofballs, yellow jackets, purple hearts, nemmies, tooies, reds, quaaludes, or ludes.

Alcohol is the most widely used and abused substance in the United States (Fig. 17-5). In small amounts, its effects may be fairly mild. In higher doses, its effects can be toxic. Slang names for alcoholic beverages include booze, juice, brew, vino, and hooch.

Alcohol is like other depressants in its ef-

fects and risks for overdose. Frequent drinkers may become dependent on the effects of alcohol and increasingly tolerant of those effects. Drinking alcohol in large or frequent amounts causes many unhealthy consequences. Alcohol poisoning can occur when a large amount of alcohol is consumed in a short period of time. Alcohol poisoning can result in unconsciousness and, if untreated, death.

The digestive system may also be irritated by heavy or chronic drinking. Alcohol can cause the esophagus to rupture, or it can injure the stomach lining. Chronic drinking can also affect the brain and cause a lack of coor-

TABLE 17-1

Commonly Misused and Abused Substances (Continued)

Category	Substances	Possible Effects
Cannabis products	Hashish Marijuana THC (tetrahydrocannabinol)	Produce feelings of elation, increase appetite, distort perceptions of time and space, and impair motor coordination and judgment. May irritate throat, redden eyes, increase pulse, and cause dizziness.
Other	MDMA (methylenedioxymethamphetamine or ecstasy)	Elevates blood pressure and produces euphoria or irratic mood swings, rapid heartbeat, profuse sweating, agitation, and sensory distortions.
	Anabolic steroids	Enhance physical performance, increase muscle mass, and stimulate appetite and weight gain. Chronic use can cause sterility, disruption of normal growth, liver cancer, personality changes, and aggressive behavior.
	Aspirin	Relieves minor pain and reduces fever. Can impair normal blood clotting and cause inflammation of the stomach and small intestine.
	Laxatives	Relieve constipation. Can cause uncontrolled diarrhea and dehydration.
	Decongestant nasal sprays	Relieve congestion and swelling of nasal passages. Chronic use can cause nosebleeds and changes in the lining of the nose, making it difficult to breathe without sprays.

Figure 17-5   Alcohol is the most widely used and abused substance in the United States.

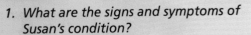

MIND AT WORK

1. **What are the signs and symptoms of Susan's condition?**

2. **What do you think is the cause of Susan's condition? Can you be sure?**

3. **Should Susan's friends call for assistance from EMS personnel? Why or why not?**

dination, memory loss, and apathy. Other problems include liver disease, such as cirrhosis (Fig. 17-6, *A* and *B*). In addition, many psychological, family, social, and work problems are related to chronic drinking.

All depressants alter consciousness to some degree. They relieve anxiety, promote sleep, depress respiration, relieve pain, relax muscles, and impair coordination and judgment. Like other substances, the larger the dose or the stronger the substance, the greater its effects.

The Incalculable Cost of Alcohol Abuse

The hospital morgue is full: a teenager who drowned while boating, an elderly man who died of a chronic liver disease, and a woman who was shot by her boyfriend. The group seems to share no connection other than that each body lies in the same morgue.

But there is a connection: alcohol.

Public health officials are seeing a growing number of injuries, illnesses, and other social problems in which alcohol plays a role. More than 100,000 people die each year from alcohol-related causes. Currently in the United States, an estimated 10 million adults and 3 million adolescents under the age of 18 are alcoholics. From the child abused by her alcoholic parent to the driver who drinks and causes a six-car pileup, our country feels the influence of alcohol abuse.

Because alcohol impairs judgment and coordination, even a first-time drinker who overindulges can become a death statistic. Each year, alcohol-related motor vehicle crashes result in approximately 17,500 deaths in the United States. In addition, impaired driving is a leading cause of death among persons under 25 years of age. Nearly one third of all drownings and about half of all deaths caused by fire also involve alcohol. Researchers say strength, judgment, stamina, motor skills, speed, and intellect are all factors in injury prevention. Alcohol impairs many of these abilities. Subsequently, alcohol is a major risk factor for every type of injury.

Tragically, drinking alcohol is a risk often taken by young people. In 1989, a 25-year-old Olympic diving champion drove into a group of teenagers at the end of a country road, killing two people and injuring four others. His blood alcohol concentration was 0.20 percent, twice the legal limit. In one night, both his life and the lives of many others were destroyed.

Reckless and violent behavior has been linked to alcohol abuse in study after study. Nearly one half of all homicides, a third of all suicides, and two thirds of all assaults involve alcohol. One of the best predictors of violence is alcohol abuse. Crime and other social problems are also linked to alcohol. Social workers find alcohol abuse a factor in nearly 50 percent of child abuse cases. Prevalence of alcohol abuse among the homeless ranges from 20 percent to 45 percent.

These personal and social consequences create a tremendous economic burden. According to the National Institute on Drug Abuse, the cost of alcohol addiction runs an estimated $118 billion annually. This cost is associated with time missed

A

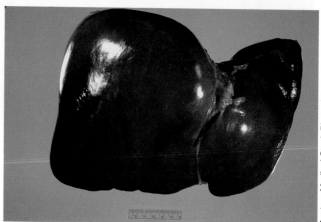

B

The George Washington University

Custom Medical Stock Photo, Inc.

Figure 17-6   A, Chronic drinking can result in cirrhosis, a disease of the liver.
B, A healthy liver.

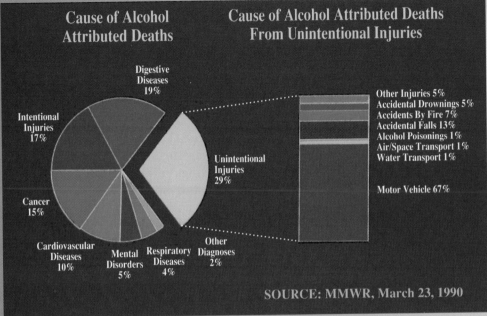

Cause of Alcohol Attributed Deaths

Cause of Alcohol Attributed Deaths From Unintentional Injuries

Digestive Diseases 19%

Intentional Injuries 17%

Cancer 15%

Cardiovascular Diseases 10%

Mental Disorders 5%

Respiratory Diseases 4%

Other Diagnoses 2%

Unintentional Injuries 29%

Other Injuries 5%
Accidental Drownings 5%
Accidents By Fire 7%
Accidental Falls 13%
Alcohol Poisonings 1%
Air/Space Transport 1%
Water Transport 1%

Motor Vehicle 67%

SOURCE: MMWR, March 23, 1990

from work, reduced job productivity, medical bills, support for families, and property damage.

Health care costs account for $15 to $20 billion of alcohol costs, and research documenting the detrimental health effects of alcohol is growing. Doctors now say that even moderate drinking increases risks of high blood pressure, cirrhosis of the liver, and decreased motor development for children whose mothers drink while pregnant. Prolonged or heavy drinking causes more serious long-term effects on your health, including risk of heart attack, many cancers, stroke, gastrointestinal bleeding, kidney failure, and problems of the nervous system, such as tremors and dementia.

Our morgues are filling up with people ravaged by a drug they could and did not control. In terms of economic cost, lives, and productivity, alcohol abuse outdistances cocaine, heroin, and all other drugs. Avoid alcohol or drink moderately so that you will not end up an unfortunate statistic.

SOURCES
Associated Press: *The New York Times,* January 31, 1989, p. 87.
Centers for Disease Control: Alcohol-related mortality and years of potential life lost—United States, 1987, *Morbidity and Mortality Weekly Report,* 39(11):173, 1990.
Morbidity and Mortality Weekly Report, March 23, 1990.
Morbidity and Mortality Weekly Report, December 2, 1994.
National Clearinghouse for Alcohol and Drug Information: *The fact is . . . OSAP responds to national crisis,* Rockville, MD, Summer 1990, p. 2.

Narcotics

Narcotics, derived from opium, are drugs used mainly to relieve pain. Narcotics are so powerful and highly addictive that all are illegal without a prescription, and some are not prescribed at all. When taken in large doses, narcotics can produce euphoria, stupor, coma, or death. The most common natural narcotics are morphine and codeine. Most other narcotics, including heroin, are synthetic or semisynthetic.

Inhalants

Substances inhaled to produce mood-altering effects are called **inhalants.** Inhalants also depress the central nervous system. In addition, inhalant use can damage the heart, lungs, brain, and liver. Inhalants include medical anesthetics, such as amyl nitrite and nitrous oxide (also known as "laughing gas"), as well as hydrocarbons, known as solvents. Solvents' effects are similar to those of alcohol. People who use solvents may appear to be drunk. Solvents include toluene, found in glues; butane, found in lighter fluids; acetone, found in nail polish removers; fuels, such as gasoline and kerosene; and propellants, found in aerosol sprays.

Cannabis Products

Cannabis products, including marijuana, tetrahydrocannabinol or THC, and hashish, are all derived from the plant *Cannabis sativa.* Slang names for marijuana include pot, grass, weed, reefer, ganja, tea, and dope. Marijuana is the most widely used illicit drug in the United States. It is typically smoked in cigarette form or in a pipe. The effects include feelings of elation, distorted perceptions of time and space, and impaired judgment and motor coordination. Marijuana irritates the throat, reddens the eyes, and causes a rapid pulse, dizziness, and often an increased appetite. Depending on the dose, the person, and many other factors, cannabis products can produce effects similar to those of substances in any of the other major substance categories.

Marijuana, although illicit, has been used for some medicinal purposes. Marijuana or its legal synthetic versions are used as an antinausea medication for people who are undergoing chemotherapy for cancer, for treating glaucoma, for treating muscular weakness caused by multiple sclerosis, and to combat the weight loss caused by cancer and AIDS.

Other Substances

Some other substances do not fit neatly into these categories. These include designer drugs, steroids, and over-the-counter substances that can be purchased without a prescription.

Designer drugs

In the early 1980s, the spread of designer drugs was a frightening possibility. Today, it is a reality. **Designer drugs** are variations of other substances, such as narcotics and amphetamines. Through simple and inexpensive methods, the molecular structure of substances produced for medicinal purposes can be modified by chemists into extremely potent and dangerous street drugs; hence the term "designer drug." When the chemical makeup

Figure 17-7 Steroids are drugs sometimes used by athletes to enhance performance and increase muscle mass.

of a drug is altered, the user can experience a variety of unpredictable and dangerous effects. The chemist may have no knowledge of the effects a new designer drug might produce. One designer drug, a form of the commonly used surgical anesthetic fentanyl, can be made 2000 to 6000 times stronger than its original form.

One of the more commonly used designer drugs is methylenedioxymethamphetamine (MDMA), often called "ecstasy." Although ecstasy is structurally related to stimulants and hallucinogens, its effects are somewhat different from either category. Ecstasy can evoke a euphoric high that makes it popular. Other signs and symptoms of ecstasy use range from the stimulant-like effects of high blood pressure, rapid heartbeat, profuse sweating, and agitation to the hallucinogenic-like effects of paranoia, sensory distortion, and erratic mood swings.

Anabolic steroids

Anabolic steroids are drugs sometimes used by athletes to enhance performance and increase muscle mass (Fig. 17-7). Their medical uses include stimulating weight gain for persons unable to gain weight naturally. They should not be confused with corticosteroids, which are used to counteract the toxic effects of and allergic reactions to absorbed poisons, such as poison ivy. Chronic use of anabolic steroids can lead to sterility, liver cancer, and personality changes, such as aggressive behavior. Steroid use by younger people may also disrupt normal growth. Slang names for anabolic

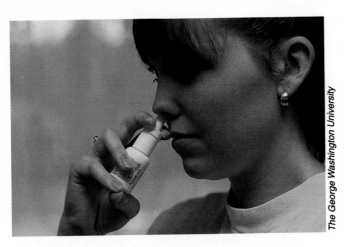

The George Washington University

Figure 17-8 Antihistamines, such as nasal sprays, are used to relieve the congestion of colds and allergies but, if misused, can cause dependency.

steroids include androgens, hormones, juice, roids, and vitamins.

Over-the-counter substances

Aspirin, laxatives, and nasal sprays are among the most commonly misused or abused over-the-counter substances. Aspirin is an effective minor pain reliever and fever reducer, which is found in a variety of medicines. People use aspirin for many reasons and conditions. In recent years, cardiologists have praised the benefits of aspirin for the treatment of heart disease. As useful as aspirin is, misuse can have toxic effects on the body. Typically, aspirin can cause inflammation of the stomach and small intestine that results in bleeding ulcers. Aspirin can also impair normal blood clotting.

Laxatives are used to relieve constipation. They come in a variety of forms and strengths. If used improperly, laxatives can cause uncontrolled diarrhea that may result in dehydration. The very young and the elderly are particularly susceptible to dehydration.

The abuse of laxatives is frequently associated with attempted weight loss and eating disorders, such as anorexia nervosa or bulimia. **Anorexia nervosa** is a disorder that typically affects young women and is characterized by a long-term refusal to eat food with sufficient nutrients and calories. Anorexics typically use laxatives to keep from gaining weight. **Bulimia** is a condition in which victims gorge themselves with food, then purge by vomiting or using laxatives. For this reason, the behavior associated with bulimia is often referred to as "binging and purging." Anorexia nervosa and bulimia both have underlying psychological factors that contribute to their onset. The effect of both of these eating disorders is severe malnutrition, which can result in death.

Decongestant nasal sprays can help relieve the congestion of colds or hay fever (Fig. 17-8). If misused, they can cause physical dependency. Using the spray over a long period can cause nosebleeds and changes in the lining of the nose that make it difficult to breathe without the spray.

SIGNS AND SYMPTOMS OF SUBSTANCE MISUSE AND ABUSE

Many of the signs and symptoms of substance misuse and abuse are similar to those of other medical emergencies. You should not necessarily assume that someone who is stumbling, is disoriented, or has a fruity, alcohol-like odor on the breath is intoxicated by alcohol or other drugs, since he or she may be a victim of a diabetic emergency (see Chapter 14).

The misuse or abuse of stimulants can have many unhealthy effects on the body, which mimic other conditions. For example, a stimulant overdose can cause moist or flushed skin, sweating, chills, nausea, vomiting, fever, headache, dizziness, rapid pulse, rapid breathing, high blood pressure, and chest pain. In some instances, it can cause respiratory distress, disrupt normal heart rhythms, or cause death. The victim may appear very excited, restless, talkative, or irritable or suddenly lose consciousness. Stimulant abuse can lead to addiction and can cause heart attack or stroke.

Specific signs and symptoms of hallucinogen abuse may include sudden mood changes and a flushed face. The victim may claim to see or hear something not present. He or she may be anxious and frightened.

Specific signs and symptoms of depressant abuse may include drowsiness, confusion, slurred speech, slow heart and breathing rates, and poor coordination. A person who abuses alcohol may smell of alcohol. A person who has consumed a great deal of alcohol in a short time

Steroids: Body Meltdown

If you think using steroids is the way to get those sculpted, muscular bodies that are typical of body-builders and many professional athletes, think again. These drugs may build up bodies on the out-side, but they can cause a body meltdown on the inside. Doctors and other public health officials warn of the dangers of steroid abuse and are parti-cularly concerned about the long-term effects of high doses.

Anabolic steroids are synthetic chemicals that mimic the hormone testosterone. Testosterone gives the male his masculine characteristics—deep-er voice, beard and mustache, and other sex char-acteristics. Anabolic steroids have several legiti-mate, legal uses. They are prescribed by doctors to treat skeletal and growth disorders, certain types of anemia, some kinds of breast cancer, and to off-set the negative effects of irradiation and chemo-therapy.

Steroids are also used illegally to create proteins and other substances that build muscle tissue, which is why they are popular with some athletes and bodybuilders. In recent years, several profes-sional athletes have made the headlines because of their abuse of steroids. Doctors are now getting a better idea of the devastating effects that illegal steroid use can have on the body. The problem is that some young athletes and bodybuilders are lis-tening to their gym buddies rather than their doc-tors. Steroids are being used in greater doses than ever before and at earlier ages. Although both young males and females abuse steroids, the abuse of steroids among young males is becoming as prevalent as eating disorders in young females.

Before you listen to another person's opinion of steroids, consider these effects:

- **Stunted growth.** In children, steroids cause the growth plates in the bones to close prematurely. As a teenager, you may have been destined to be six-foot-four, but taking steroids can permanently stunt your growth.
- **Heart disease and stroke.** Steroids cause dan-gerous changes in cholesterol levels. One study found dramatic drops in the amount of good cho-lesterol (HDL), which helps remove the fatty de-posits on the artery walls, in steroid users. The re-search also shows dramatic increases in bad cholesterol (LDL), which clogs the arteries and causes heart problems. Your steroid-doped body may look fine on the outside, but inside, it may look like the body of a man in his fifties whose ar-teries are so clogged that he needs heart surgery.
- **Aggressive personality and psychological disorders.** Some people who take anabolic ster-oids become unnaturally aggressive. A few have developed documentable mental disorders. In a *Sports Illustrated* article, a South Carolina football player described his nightmare with steroids. He described pulling a gun on a pizza delivery boy in his dorm and how his family intervened when he

may be unconscious or hard to arouse. The per-son may vomit violently.

Specific signs and symptoms of alcohol withdrawal, a potentially dangerous condition, include confusion and restlessness, trembling, hallucinations, and seizures. Always call EMS personnel if you suspect a person is suffering from alcohol withdrawal or from any form of substance abuse.

Remember that, as in other medical emer-gencies, you do not have to diagnose substance misuse or abuse to provide care. However, you may be able to find clues that suggest the nature of the problem. Such clues may help you pro-vide more complete information to EMS per-sonnel so that they can provide prompt and ap-propriate care. Often these clues will come from the victim, bystanders, or the scene itself. Look for containers, pill bottles, drug parapher-nalia, and signs of other medical problems. If the victim is incoherent or unconscious, try to get information from any bystanders or family members. Since many of the physical signs of substance abuse mimic other conditions, you may not be able to determine that a person has overdosed on a substance. To provide care for

began threatening suicide. Many doctors feel the psychiatric effects of steroids may be the most threatening side effect.

- **Lowered white blood cell count.** Taking steroids also affects the number of white blood cells in your body. With fewer white blood cells, your body has fewer antibodies to fight off infections, including cancers and other diseases.
- **Sexual dysfunction and disorders.** Synthetic steroids cause your body to cut off its own natural production of steroids, resulting in shrinking testicles in men. If you are a woman, you may grow facial hair, your breast size may decrease, and your voice may get permanently deeper. In both sexes, steroids may cause sterility and reduce sexual interest.
- **Impaired liver function and liver disease.** Steroids seriously affect the liver's ability to function. They irritate the liver, causing tissue damage and an inability to clear bile. Doctors also have found blood-filled benign tumors in the livers of steroid users.

Steroids pose dangers beyond these physiological side effects. Because steroids are often sold on the black market, they are increasingly sold by drug traffickers who obtain their wares from unsanitary laboratories. Yet another danger comes from the fact that sharing needles to inject steroids increases the transmission of viruses such as HIV, which causes AIDS, and hepatitis.

SOURCES

Altman L: New breakfast of champions: a recipe for victory or disaster?, *The New York Times*, November 20, 1988.

Chaikin T, Telander R: The nightmare of steroids, *Sports Illustrated*, 69:18 1988.

National Institute on Drug Abuse. "Anabolic steroids: a threat to body and mind." National Institutes of Health, No. 94-3721, 1991.

USA Today, Vol. 121, No. 2573, February 1993.

the victim, you need only recognize abnormalities in breathing, skin color and moisture, body temperature, and behavior, any of which may indicate a condition requiring professional help.

CARE FOR SUBSTANCE MISUSE AND ABUSE

Since substance abuse and misuse are forms of poisoning, care follows the same general principles. However, as in other medical emergencies, people who misuse or abuse substances may become aggressive or uncooperative when you try to help. If the person becomes agitated or makes the scene unsafe in any way, retreat and call EMS personnel and the police. *Provide care only if you feel the person is not a danger to you and others.*

Your initial care for substance misuse or abuse does not require that you know the specific substance taken. Follow these general principles as you would for any poisoning:

Sources of Help for Victims of Substance Abuse

Al-Anon Family Group Headquarters
1372 Broadway
7th Floor
New York, NY 10018
(800) 356-9996

Alcohol and Drug Treatment Information Service
(800) 477-3447

Alcohol Hotline
(800) ALCOHOL

Alcoholics Anonymous
P.O. Box 459
Grand Central Station
New York, NY 10163
Treatment Hotline (212) 870-3400

Mothers Against Drunk Driving (MADD)
511 E. John Carpenter Freeway,
Suite 700
Irving, TX 75062
(214) 744-6233
(800) 438-6233 (victims only)

Narcotics Anonymous
P.O. Box 9999
Van Nuys, CA 91409
(818) 773-9999

National Clearinghouse for Alcohol and Drug Information
P.O. Box 2345
Rockville, MD 20852
(301) 468-2600

National Cocaine Hotline
(800) 622-2255

National Council on Alcoholism and Drug Dependence Helpline
(800) 622-2255

National Institute on Drug Abuse
Drug Information/Treatment Hotline
12280 Wilkins Avenue
1st Floor
Rockville, MD 20852
(800) 622-HELP

Remove Intoxicated Drivers (RID)
P.O. Box 520
Schenectady, NY 12301
(518) 372-0034

Students Against Driving Drunk (SADD)
P.O. Box 800
Marlboro, MA 01752
(508) 481-3568

- Check the scene to be sure it is safe to help the person.
- Check for any life-threatening conditions.
- Call 9-1-1, the local emergency number, or poison control center (PCC) personnel and follow their directions. Also call the police if the victim seems dangerous.
- Care for any conditions.
- Question the victim or bystanders to try to find out what substance was taken, how much was taken, and when it was taken.
- Calm and reassure the victim.
- Prevent the victim from getting chilled or overheated.

Withdraw from the area if the victim becomes violent or threatening. If you suspect that someone has used a designer drug, tell EMS or PCC personnel. Telling EMS or PCC personnel is important because a person who has overdosed on a designer drug frequently may not respond to usual medical treatment.

Once the victim is past the immediate danger of a substance abuse emergency, he or she will need further assistance. If you know the victim, you may be able to help him or her contact one of the many agencies and organizations that offer ongoing assistance to victims of substance abuse. Community-based programs through schools and religious institutions provide access to hot lines and local support groups. Some of the resources listed above may have facilities or contacts in your area. Look in the advertising pages of the phone book under Counseling, Drug Abuse and Addiction Information, Social Service Organizations, Clinics, and Health Services for additional resources.

PREVENTING SUBSTANCE ABUSE

Experts in the field of substance abuse generally agree that prevention efforts are far more cost effective than treatment. Yet, preventing substance abuse is a complex process that involves many underlying factors. Various approaches, including educating people about substances and their effects on health and attempting to instill fear of penalties, have not by themselves proved particularly effective. It is becoming clearer that, to be effective, prevention efforts must address the various underlying issues of and approaches to substance abuse.

The following factors may contribute to substance abuse:

- A lack of parental supervision.
- The breakdown of traditional family structures.
- A wish to escape unpleasant surroundings and stressful situations.
- The widespread availability of substances.
- Peer pressure and the basic need to belong.
- Low self-esteem, including feelings of guilt or shame.
- Media glamorization, especially of alcohol and tobacco, promoting the idea that using substances enhances fun and popularity.
- A history of substance abuse in the home or community environments.

Recognizing and understanding these factors may help prevent and treat substance abuse.

PREVENTING SUBSTANCE MISUSE

Some poisonings from medicinal substances occur when the victims knowingly increase the dosage beyond what is directed. The best way to prevent such misuse is to take medications only as directed. On the other hand, many poisonings from medicinal substances are not intentional. The following guidelines can help prevent unintentional misuse or overdose:

- Read the product information and use only as directed.
- Ask your doctor or pharmacist about the intended use and side effects of prescription and over-the-counter medication. If you are taking more than one medication, check for possible interaction effects.
- Never use another person's prescribed medications; what is right for one person is seldom right for another.
- Always keep medications in their appropriate, marked containers.
- Destroy all out-of-date medications. Time can alter the chemical composition of medications, causing them to be less effective and possibly even toxic.
- Always keep medications out of reach of children.

SUMMARY

There are six major categories of substances which, when abused or misused, can produce a variety of signs and symptoms, some of which are indistinguishable from those of other medical emergencies. Remember, you do not have to diagnose the condition to provide care. If you suspect that the victim's condition is caused by substance misuse or abuse, provide care for a poisoning emergency. Call your local EMS or PCC personnel and follow their directions. Also call the police if necessary. If the victim becomes violent or threatening, retreat to safety and wait for EMS personnel and police to arrive.

Answers to Application Questions

1. The signs and symptoms of Susan's condition are dizziness, nausea, vomiting, unconsciousness, and unusually pale skin.

2. The signs and symptoms of Susan's condition, along with the fact that she has been drinking, seem to indicate a case of alcohol poisoning. Although you cannot be sure of the cause of Susan's condition, the fact that she is unconscious means that she needs immediate care.

3. Yes, Susan's friends must call 9-1-1 or the local emergency number because EMS personnel should always be called in cases of unconsciousness.

STUDY QUESTIONS

1. Match each term with its definition.

   a. Addiction
   b. Dependency
   c. Medication
   d. Drug

   e. Overdose
   f. Substance abuse
   g. Tolerance
   h. Withdrawal

   __F__ Deliberate, persistent, excessive use of a substance.

   __C__ A drug given to prevent or correct a disease or otherwise enhance mental or physical well-being.

   __D__ Any substance other than food intended to affect the functions of the body.

   __E__ An excess use of a drug, resulting in adverse reactions ranging from and including mania and hysteria to coma and death; specific reactions include changes in blood pressure and heartbeat, sweating, vomiting, and liver failure.

   __A__ The compulsive desire or need to use a substance.

   __H__ The condition produced when a person stops using or abusing a substance to which he or she is addicted.

   __B__ A desire to continually use a substance, feeling that it is needed to function normally.

   __G__ A condition that occurs when a substance user has to increase the dose and frequency of use of a substance to obtain the desired effect.

2. List four signs or symptoms that might indicate substance abuse or misuse.

3. List four commonly misused or abused legal substances.

   Caffeine   Nicotine

4. List four things you can do to prevent unintentional substance misuse.

5. Describe the care for a victim of suspected substance misuse or abuse.

6. Match each type of substance with the effects it has on the body.

   a. Depressants
   b. Hallucinogens
   c. Inhalants

   d. Stimulants
   e. Narcotics
   f. Cannabis products

_B_ Affect mood, sensation, thought, emotion, and self-awareness; alter perception of time and space; and produce hallucinations and delusions.

_C_ Produce mood-altering effects similar to those of alcohol. Found in glues and solvents.

_A_ Slow down the physical activities of the brain, producing temporary feelings of relaxation.

_D_ Speed up the physical and mental activity of the brain, producing temporary feelings of alertness and improved task performance.

_E_ Relieve pain.

_F_ Produce feelings of elation, disoriented perceptions of time and space, and impaired judgment.

7. List two clues at the scene of an emergency that might indicate substance abuse or misuse.

In questions 8 through 10, circle the letter of the correct answer.

8. Which of the following is true of substance abuse?

   a. It occurs only among the elderly who are forgetful and may have poor eyesight.
   b. It is the use of a substance for intended purposes but in improper amounts or doses.
   c. It is the use of a substance without regard to health concerns or accepted medical practices.
   d. Its effects are minor and rarely result in medical complications.

9. The effects of designer drugs are—

   a. Well-known.
   b. Unpredictable.
   c. Harmless.
   d. Easily controlled.

10. Which of the following guidelines can help prevent unintentional substance misuse?

    a. Read the product information and use only as directed.
    b. Check for possible interaction effects if you are taking more than one medication.
    c. Destroy all out-of-date medication.
    d. All of the above.

Answers are listed in Appendix A.

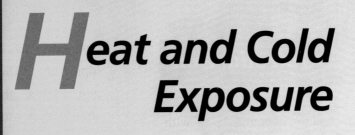

CHAPTER 18

Heat and Cold Exposure

WHAT YOU SHOULD LEARN

After reading this chapter, you should be able to—

1. Identify three conditions that can result from over-exposure to heat.

2. List six signs and symptoms of heat exhaustion.

3. List five signs and symptoms of heat stroke.

4. Describe the care for heat-related illness.

5. List four signs and symptoms of frostbite.

6. Describe the care for frostbite.

7. List five signs and symptoms of hypothermia.

8. Describe the care for hypothermia.

9. Describe five ways to help prevent heat- and cold-related illness.

10. Define the key terms for this chapter.

"Why did Mom decide the garden needed weeding today?" Cynthia wondered to herself. "It must be in the 90s already and the humidity's awful!" She looks over at her mother, Lou, who has been serenely pulling up unwanted plants for an hour. "Here I am, sweating buckets in shorts and a tank top while Mom manages to look cool even when she's covered head to toe in a white shirt and pants, and a floppy, wide-brimmed hat." Oddly, as Cynthia ponders the thought, she suddenly feels a chill. "Oh well," thinks Cynthia, "I'll help out here as long as Mom needs me." Then the phone rings and Lou goes indoors to answer it. Still weeding, Cynthia begins to feel a little dizzy. "Maybe I'll just sit down for a minute," thinks Cynthia, resting her head down on her knees. Lou returns to the garden to find Cynthia looking very pale. "Here, honey," Lou holds out her water bottle. "Take a little drink of water," she advises. Cynthia takes a sip. "It makes me feel sick," she says.

Introduction

The human body is equipped to withstand extremes in temperature. Usually, its mechanisms for regulating body temperature work very well. However, when the body is overwhelmed by extremes of heat and cold, illness may occur.

Extreme temperatures can occur anywhere, both indoors and outdoors, but a person can develop a heat- or cold-related illness even if temperatures are not extreme. The effects of humidity, wind, clothing, living and working environments, physical activity, age, and an individual's health are all factors in heat- and cold-related illness.

Illnesses caused by exposure to temperature extremes are progressive and can quickly become life threatening. Once the signs and symptoms of a heat- or cold-related illness begin to appear, a victim's condition can rapidly deteriorate and lead to death. If the victim exhibits any of the signs and symptoms of sudden illness, the environmental conditions should alert you to look for the presence of a heat- or cold-related illness and give the appropriate care. Immediate care can prevent the illness from becoming life threatening. In this chapter, you will learn how extremes of heat and cold affect the body, how to recognize temperature-related emergencies, and how to provide care.

HOW BODY TEMPERATURE IS CONTROLLED

Body temperature must remain constant for the body to work efficiently. Normal body temperature is 98.6 degrees F (37 degrees C). Body heat is generated primarily through the conversion of food to energy. Heat is also produced by muscle contractions, as in exercise or shivering.

Heat always moves from warm areas to cooler ones. Since the body is usually warmer than the surrounding air, it tends to lose heat to the air. The body maintains its temperature by constantly balancing heat loss with heat production (Fig. 18-1). The heat produced in routine activities is usually enough to balance normal heat loss.

When body heat increases, the body removes heat through the skin. Blood vessels near the skin dilate, or widen, to bring more warm blood to the surface. Heat then escapes and the body cools (Fig. 18-2, *A*).

The body is also cooled by the evaporation of sweat. When the air temperature is very warm, the blood vessels dilate and sweating increases. But when the humidity is high, sweat cannot evaporate as quickly. It stays longer on the skin and has little or no cooling effect.

When the body reacts to cold, blood vessels near the skin constrict (narrow) and move warm blood to the center of the body. Thus less heat escapes through the skin, and the body stays warm (Fig. 18-2, *B*). When constriction of blood vessels fails to keep the body warm, the body shivers to produce heat through muscle action.

Key Terms

Frostbite: A condition in which body tissues freeze; most commonly occurs in the fingers, toes, ears, and nose.

Heat cramps: Painful spasms of skeletal muscles after exercise or work in warm or moderate temperatures; usually involve the calf and abdominal muscles.

Heat exhaustion: The early stage and most common form of heat-related illness; often results from strenuous work or exercise in a hot environment.

Heat stroke: A life-threatening condition that develops when the body's cooling mechanisms are overwhelmed and body systems begin to fail.

Hypothermia: A life-threatening condition in which the body's warming mechanisms fail to maintain normal body temperature and the entire body cools.

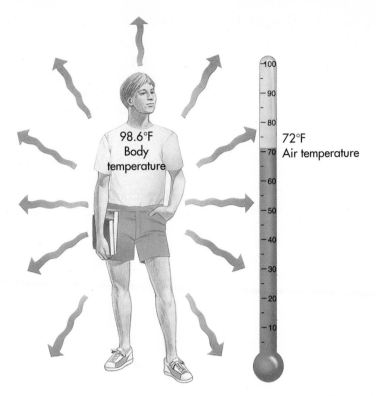

Figure 18-1   Since the body is usually warmer than the surrounding air, it tends to lose heat to the air.

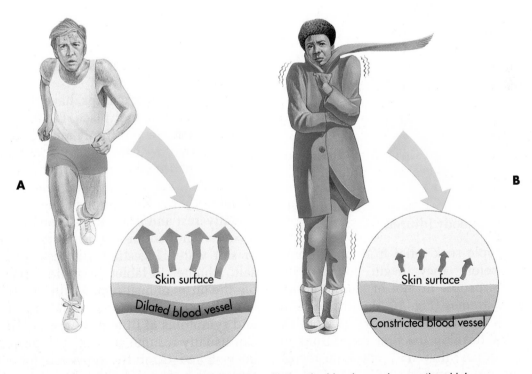

Figure 18-2   **A,** Your body removes heat by dilating the blood vessels near the skin's surface. **B,** The body conserves heat by constricting the blood vessels near the skin.

Environmental Factors that Affect the Body's Ability to Regulate Temperature

Three main factors can affect how well the body maintains its temperature: air temperature, humidity, and wind. Extreme heat or cold accompanied by high humidity hampers the body's ability to maintain temperature effectively (Fig. 18-3). A low temperature combined with a strong wind rapidly cools exposed body parts. The combination of temperature and wind speed form what is called the **wind chill factor.**

Other factors, such as the clothing you wear, how often you take breaks from exposure to extreme temperature, how much and how often you drink water, and how intense your activity is, also affect how well your body manages temperature extremes. These are all factors you can control to prevent heat- or cold-related illness.

People at Increased Risk for Heat- or Cold-Related Illness

Although anyone can be at risk for heat- and cold-related illness, some people are at greater risk than others. People at increased risk for heat- or cold-related illness include—

- Those who work or exercise strenuously.
- Elderly people.
- Young children.
- Those with predisposing health problems, such as diabetes or heart disease.
- Those who have had a heat- or cold-related illness in the past.
- Those who have cardiovascular disease or other conditions that cause poor circulation.
- Those who take medications to eliminate water from the body (diuretics).

Usually people seek relief from an extreme temperature before they begin to feel ill. However, some people do not or cannot easily escape these extremes (Fig. 18-4). Athletes and those who work outdoors often keep working even after they develop the first indications of illness. Many times, they may not even recognize the signs and symptoms.

Heat- and cold-related illness occurs more frequently among the elderly, especially those living in poorly ventilated or poorly insulated buildings or buildings with poor heating or cooling systems. Young children and people with health problems are also at risk because their bodies do not respond as effectively to temperature extremes.

HEAT EMERGENCIES

Heat cramps, heat exhaustion, and heat stroke are conditions caused by overexposure to heat. Heat cramps are the least severe but, if not cared for, may be followed by heat exhaustion and heat stroke. Heat exhaustion and heat stroke are heat-related illnesses.

Heat Cramps

Heat cramps are painful spasms of skeletal muscles. The exact cause of heat cramps is not known, although it is believed to be a combination of loss of fluid and salt from heavy sweating. Heat cramps develop fairly rapidly and usually occur after heavy exercise or work in warm or even moderate temperatures. Heat cramps are severe muscle contractions, usually in the legs and the abdomen, but can occur in any voluntary muscle. Body temperature is usually normal and the skin moist. However, heat cramps may also indicate that a person is in the early stages of a more severe heat-related emergency.

To care for heat cramps, have the victim rest comfortably in a cool place. Lightly stretch the muscle, then grasp it firmly and squeeze it (Fig. 18-5). Provide cool water or a commercial sports drink that contains nutrients such as carbohydrates, electrolytes, and simple sugars to replace those lost through heavy sweating. Usually, rest and fluids are all the body needs to recover. The victim should not take salt tablets or salt water. Ingesting high concentrations of salt, whether in tablet or liquid form, can hasten the onset of heat-related illness.

When the cramps stop and no other signs and symptoms of illness are present, the person can usually resume activity. The person should be watched carefully, however, for signs and symptoms of developing heat-related illness. He or she should continue to drink plenty of fluids during and after activity.

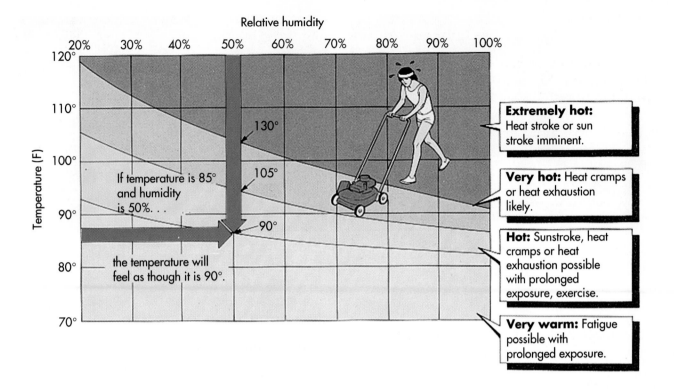

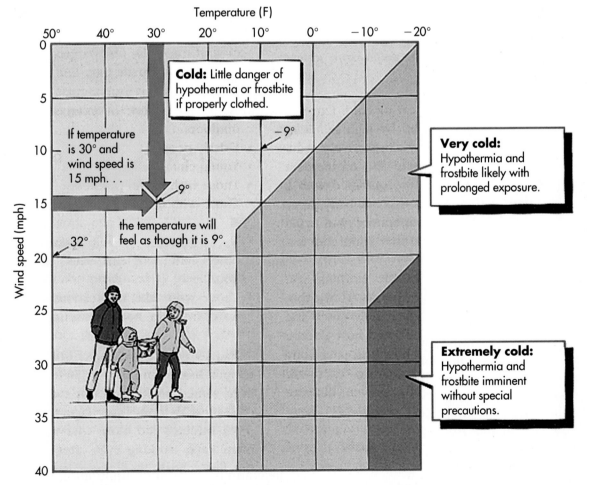

Figure 18-3 Temperature, humidity, and wind are the three main factors affecting body temperature.

Figure 18-4 In certain situations, it is difficult to escape temperature extremes.

Figure 18-5 Resting, lightly stretching the affected muscle, and replenishing fluids are usually enough for the body to recover from heat cramps.

Heat-Related Illness

Heat-related illness, if not cared for promptly, can get progressively worse in a very short period of time. By recognizing the signs and symptoms of the early stages of heat-related illness and responding appropriately, you may be able to prevent the condition from becoming life threatening.

Early stages of heat-related illness

Heat exhaustion is the early stage and the most common form of heat-related illness. It typically occurs after long periods of strenuous exercise or work in a hot environment. Although heat exhaustion is commonly associated with athletes, it also affects fire fighters, construction workers, factory workers, and others who are very active and wear heavy clothing in a hot, humid environment. However, strenuous activity is not a prerequisite for heat exhaustion—it can happen when a person is relaxing or standing still in the heat.

Heat exhaustion is an early indication that the body's temperature-regulating mechanism is becoming overwhelmed. It is not always preceded by heat cramps. Over time, the victim loses fluid through sweating, which decreases the blood volume. Blood flow to the skin increases, reducing blood flow to the vital organs. Because the circulatory system is affected, the person goes into a form of shock (see Chapter 8).

The signs and symptoms of heat exhaustion include—

• Normal or below normal body temperature.

• Cool, moist, pale skin.
• Headache.
• Nausea.
• Dizziness and weakness.
• Exhaustion.

Heat exhaustion in its early stage can usually be reversed with prompt care. Often the victim feels better when he or she rests in a cool place and drinks cool water. If heat exhaustion progresses, however, the victim's condition worsens. Body temperature climbs. A victim may vomit and begin to show changes in his or her level of consciousness. Without prompt care, heat exhaustion can quickly advance to a more serious, life-threatening stage of heat-related illness—heat stroke.

MIND AT WORK

1. Why does Cynthia feel dizzy?

Late stages of heat-related illness

Heat stroke is the least common and most severe heat emergency. Heat stroke most often occurs when people ignore the signs and symptoms of heat exhaustion or do not act quickly enough to provide care. Heat stroke develops when the body systems are overwhelmed by heat and begin to stop functioning. Sweating often stops because body fluid levels are low. When sweating stops, the body cannot cool

TOO MUCH OF A GOOD THING

Contrary to some beliefs, tan is not in. Although brief exposure to the sun causes your skin to produce the vitamin D necessary for the healthy formation of bones, long exposure can cause problems, such as sunburn, skin cancer, and early aging—a classic case of too much of a good thing being bad.

Two kinds of ultraviolet (UV) light rays cause problems. Ultraviolet beta (UVB) rays are the burn-producing rays that more commonly cause skin cancer. These are rays that damage the skin's surface and cause you to blister and peel. The other rays, ultraviolet alpha (UVA) rays, have been heralded by tanning salons as "safe rays." Tanning salons claim to use lights that only emit UVA rays. Although UVA rays may not appear as harmful to the skin's surface as UVB rays, they more readily penetrate the deeper layers of the skin, increasing the risk of skin cancer, skin aging, eye damage, and changes that may alter the skin's ability to fight disease.

How do you get enough sun without getting too much? First, avoid exposure to the sun between 10:00 a.m. and 4:00 p.m., when UV rays are most harmful. Second, pay attention to the daily UV Index. Third, wear proper clothing. Fourth, if you are going to be exposed to the sun, protect your skin and eyes.

In addition to knowing what hours are the most dangerous for sun exposure, you can also become aware of which days are the most hazardous. To help you do this, the Environmental Protection Agency (EPA) and the National Weather Service (NWS) have developed the UV Index. The UV Index provides a forecast of the expected risk of overexposure to the sun and indicates the degree of caution you should take when working, playing, or exercising outdoors. The UV Index predicts exposure levels as a number on a scale of 0 to 10+, where 0 indicates a low risk of overexposure and 10+ indicates a very high risk of overexposure. This index takes various factors into account, such as cloud cover and local conditions, and is available on a next-day basis in cities across the United States. Many televised and radio weather reports provide UV Index information for a daily or multi-day period. Some local weather phone lines also carry this information.

Using a sunscreen is another important way to protect yourself. Commercial sunscreens come in various strengths. The American Academy of Dermatology recommends year-round sun protection, including use of a high Sun Protection Factor (SPF) sunscreen for everyone but particularly for people who are fair-skinned and burn easily. The Food and Drug Administration (FDA) has evaluated SPF readings and recognizes values between 2 and 15. An SPF of 15 means that the sunscreen provides 15 times the protection of unprotected skin. The FDA has not determined whether sunscreens with ratings over 15 offer additional protection.

You should apply sunscreen 15 to 30 minutes before exposure to the sun and reapply it often (every 60 to 90 minutes). Swimmers should use sunscreens labeled as water-resistant and reapply them as described on the label. Your best bet is to use a sunscreen that claims to protect against both UVB and UVA rays. Carefully check the label to determine the protection a product offers. Some products only offer protection against UVB rays.

It is equally important to protect your eyes from sun damage. Sunglasses are a sunscreen for your eyes and provide important protection from UV rays. Be sure to wear sunglasses that have UV-absorbing ability (usually labeled). Ophthalmologists recommend sunglasses that have a UV absorption of at least 90 percent. The EPA suggests using sunglasses with 99 to 100 percent UVA and UVB protection to reduce the harmful effects of sun exposure that can lead to cataracts and other eye damage.

The next time the sun beckons, be smart about how you venture out. Get as much information as possible in advance, then protect yourself accordingly.

itself effectively through evaporation and body temperature rapidly rises. Body temperature soon reaches a level at which the brain and other vital organs, such as the heart and kidneys, begin to fail. If the body is not cooled, convulsions, coma, and death will result. Heat stroke is a serious medical emergency. You must recognize the signs and symptoms of this later stage of heat-related illness and provide care immediately.

The signs and symptoms of heat stroke include—

- High body temperature, often as high as 106 degrees F (41 degrees C).
- Red, hot skin, which may be either dry or moist.
- Change in level of consciousness.
- Rapid, weak pulse.
- Rapid, shallow breathing.

Someone in heat stroke may at first have a strong, rapid pulse, while the heart works hard to rid the body of heat by dilating blood vessels and sending more blood to the skin. As consciousness deteriorates, the circulatory system begins to fail also, and the pulse becomes weak and irregular. *Without prompt care, the victim will die.*

Care for Heat-Related Illness

Time is of the essence when caring for heat-related illness. The longer a heat-related illness goes untreated, the worse the condition becomes. Specific steps for care depend on whether you find a victim in the early or late stages of a heat-related illness.

Care in early stages

When you recognize heat-related illness in its early stages, you can usually reverse it. When any signs and symptoms of sudden illness develop and you suspect the illness is caused by overexposure to heat, follow these general care steps immediately:

- Cool the body.
- Give fluids if the victim is conscious.
- Minimize shock.

Remove the victim from the hot environment and give him or her cool water to drink. Moving the victim out of the sun or away from

Figure 18-6   For early stages of heat-related illness, apply cool, wet cloths and fan the victim to increase evaporation. Give cool water to drink.

the heat allows the body's own temperature-regulating mechanism to recover, cooling the body more quickly. Loosen any tight clothing and remove clothing soaked with perspiration. Apply cool, wet cloths, such as towels or sheets, to the wrists, ankles, armpits, groin, and back of the neck, and fan the victim to increase evaporation.

If the victim is conscious, slowly drinking cool water will help replenish the vital fluids lost through sweating (Fig. 18-6). The victim is likely to be nauseated, and water is less likely than other fluids to cause vomiting and is more quickly absorbed into the body from the stomach. Do not let the victim drink too quickly. Give one half glass (4 ounces or 118.3 milliliters) about every 15 minutes. Let the victim rest in a comfortable position, and watch carefully for changes in his or her condition. A victim of heat-related illness should not resume normal activities the same day.

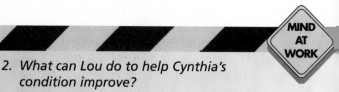

2. What can Lou do to help Cynthia's condition improve?

MIND AT WORK

Care in late stages

Refusing water, vomiting, and changes in the victim's level of consciousness are indications that the victim's condition is worsening. Call EMS personnel immediately if you have

Figure 18-7   To cool the body of the victim of heat-related illness, cover it with cool, wet towels and apply ice packs.

not already done so. If the person feels nauseated or vomits, stop giving fluids and position the victim on the side. Make sure the airway is clear. Monitor breathing and consciousness. Keep the victim lying down, and continue to cool the body.

If you observe changes in the victim's level of consciousness, call EMS personnel and cool the body quickly by any means available. Soak towels or sheets and apply them to the victim's body. Use a water hose, if one is available, to cool the victim. If you have ice or cold packs, place them on each of the victim's wrists and ankles, on the groin, in each armpit, and on the neck to cool the large blood vessels (Fig. 18-7). Do not apply rubbing (isopropyl) alcohol to the victim's skin. Alcohol closes the skin's pores and prevents heat loss. Immersing the victim in a tub of cool water is not a good idea unless professional medical care is delayed because doing so may make it difficult to maintain an open airway. A person in heat stroke may experience respiratory or cardiac arrest. Be prepared to do rescue breathing or CPR.

COLD EMERGENCIES

Frostbite and hypothermia are two types of cold emergencies. Frostbite occurs in body parts exposed to the cold. Hypothermia develops when the body can no longer generate sufficient heat to maintain normal body temperature.

Frostbite

Frostbite is the freezing of body tissues. It usually occurs in exposed areas of the body, depending on the air temperature, length of exposure, and the wind. Frostbite can be superficial or deep. In superficial frostbite, the skin is frozen but the tissues below are not. In deep frostbite, both the skin and underlying tissues are frozen. Both types of frostbite are serious. The water in and between the body's cells freezes and swells. The ice crystals and swelling damage or destroy the cells. Frostbite can cause the eventual loss of fingers, hands, arms, toes, feet, and legs.

The signs and symptoms of frostbite include—

- Lack of feeling in the affected area.
- Skin that appears waxy.
- Skin that is cold to the touch.
- Skin that is discolored (flushed, white, yellow, blue).

When caring for frostbite, handle the affected area gently. Never rub an affected area. Rubbing causes further damage because of the sharp ice crystals in the skin. If there is no chance that the frostbitten part will refreeze, you may begin rewarming the affected area gently by soaking the affected part in water no warmer than 100 to 105 degrees F (38 to 41 degrees C). Use a thermometer to check the water, if possible. If not, test the water temperature yourself. If the temperature is uncomfortable to your touch, the water is too warm. To minimize further tissue damage, do not let the affected part touch the bottom or sides of the container holding the warm water (Fig. 18-8, *A*, p. 370). Keep the frostbitten part in the water until it appears red and feels warm. Bandage the area with a dry, clean dressing. If fingers or toes are frostbitten, place cotton or gauze between them (Fig. 18-8, *B*, p. 370). Avoid breaking any blisters. Do not allow the affected area to refreeze. Do not allow the victim to walk on feet that have been thawed until all feeling has returned to the affected area. Seek professional medical attention as soon as possible.

Hypothermia

In **hypothermia,** the entire body cools when its warming mechanisms fail. The victim will die

High-Tech War Against Cold

In the past, humans depended entirely on nature for clothing. Animal skins, furs, and feathers protected us from freezing temperatures. As long as seasonal changes and cold climates exist, preventing cold-related illness, such as hypothermia, remains important when we work or play outside. Although natural fibers, such as wool and down, are still very useful, a whole family of synthetic fibers is now used to make clothing. Being outdoors has become a lot more comfortable than in the past.

The best way to use outdoor fabrics is to layer them. Layering creates warmth by trapping warm air between the layers to insulate the body. Layering is an old concept. It enables you to regulate your body temperature and deal with changes in the environment. By wearing several layers of clothing, you can take clothes off when warm and put them back on if you get cold.

Start off with an underwear layer. Commonly called long underwear, it includes thin, snug-fitting pants and a long-sleeved shirt. Underwear should supply you with basic insulation and pull moisture away from your skin—damp, sweaty skin can chill you when you slow down or stop moving. Natural fibers, such as cotton, wool, and silk, can be quite warm and are okay for light activity. For heavier exercise, however, synthetic fabrics absorb less moisture and actually carry water droplets away from your skin. Polypropylene and Capalene are two popular synthetic fabrics for underwear.

Next, to provide additional warmth, add one or more insulating layers. The weight of insulating clothing should be considered in relation to planned activities, weather conditions, and how efficiently the garment compresses to pack when you are not wearing it. Depending on the temperature, a wool sweater or a down jacket may provide an insulating layer for the upper body. But, don't forget your legs. Wool pants are a better choice than jeans or corduroys. Synthetic materials used in jackets and pants include Thinsulate™, Quallofil®, Polartec®, and pile (a plush, nonpiling polyester fiber). Although down is an excellent, lightweight insulator, it becomes useless when wet, so a water-repellent or quick-drying fabric like pile may keep you warmer in a damp climate.

Finish with a windproof, and preferably waterproof, shell layer. Synthetic, high-tech fabrics make a strong showing here. Windproof fabrics have names like Supplex, Silmond, Captiva, or rip-stop nylon. Coatings, such as Hypalon, applied to jackets and pants are completely water repellent. However, the newest waterproof fabrics are "breathable." They repel wind and rain but allow your perspiration to pass through the fabric so that you stay dry and warmer. Gore-Tex®, Thintech, Ultrex, and Super Microft are some of the names given to these fabrics. Pay close attention to vents and closures in garments, which should seal tightly and open freely to adapt to changing activities and weather conditions. It is also important to make sure your outer garments are big enough to fit over several layers of clothing.

A hat is vital to staying truly warm. Gloves, insulating socks, neck "gaiters," and headbands all protect you from the cold. Visit your local outdoor store for more information about the best clothing for your specific work or recreational activities.

Sources

1. Recreation Equipment Incorporated: *Layering for comfort: FYI, an informational brochure from REI,* Seattle, 1991.
2. Recreation Equipment Incorporated: *Understanding outdoor fabrics: FYI, An informational brochure from REI,* Seattle, 1991.
3. Recreation Equipment Incorporated: *Outerwear product information guide,* Seattle, 1995.

Inner Layer

Recreational Equipment Inc.

Capalene   Lightweight, synthetic fabric that doesn't absorb moisture. Designed to pull moisture away from skin where it can evaporate.

Cotton   Soft, natural fibers that absorb moisture and allow air to circulate.

Insulating Layer

Quallofil ® Exceptionally warm, wet or dry.

Pile   Soft, polyester fabric that is warmer per pound than wool. Insulates when wet and is quick drying.

Shell Layer

Ripstop Nylon Windproof, resistant to moisture, and has some breathability. Protects against fog, light rain, snow.

Hypalon   Versatile, synthetic rubber applied to lightweight nylon is completely water-repellent. Unaffected by saltwater and highly resistant to abrasion.

Supplex   Lightweight nylon that is cotton-soft yet strong. Windproof, breathable, some water repellancy, quick drying.

Gore-Tex ® Is used in combination with water-repellent exterior fabric. Allows perspiration to escape while preventing water and wind from seeping in.

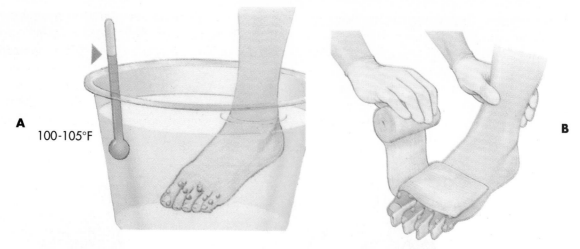

Figure 18-8   A, Warm the frostbitten area gently by soaking it in water. Do not allow the frostbitten area to touch the container. **B,** After rewarming, bandage the area with a dry, sterile dressing. If fingers or toes are frostbitten, place gauze between them.

if not given care. In hypothermia, body temperature drops below 95 degrees F (35 degrees C). Most thermometers used to measure body temperature do not measure below 94 degrees F (34 degrees C). As the body cools, an abnormal heart rhythm (ventricular fibrillation) may develop and the heart eventually stops. Death then occurs.

The signs and symptoms of hypothermia include—

- Shivering (may be absent in later stages).
- Slow, irregular pulse.
- Numbness.
- Glassy stare.
- Apathy or change in level of consciousness.

The air temperature does not have to be below freezing for people to develop hypothermia. Elderly people in poorly heated homes, particularly people with poor nutrition and who get little exercise, can develop hypothermia at higher temperatures. The homeless and the ill are also at risk. Certain substances, such as alcohol and barbiturates, can also interfere with the body's normal response to cold, causing hypothermia to occur more easily. Medical conditions, such as infection, insulin reaction, stroke, and brain tumor, also make a person more susceptible. Anyone remaining in cold water or wet clothing for a prolonged time may also easily develop hypothermia.

Hypothermia is a medical emergency that requires prompt care. Check and care for any life-threatening conditions. Call EMS personnel. Carefully remove any wet clothing and dry

the victim. Warm the body gradually by wrapping the victim in blankets or putting on dry clothing and moving him or her to a warm environment (Fig. 18-9). If they are available, apply hot water bottles, heating pads (if the victim is dry), chemical heat packs, or other heat sources to the body. Keep a barrier, such as a blanket, towel, or clothing, between the heat source and the victim to avoid burning him or her. If the

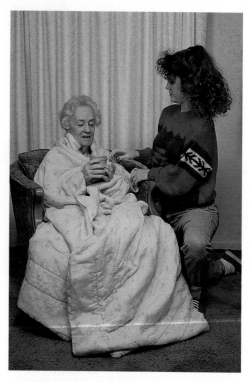

Figure 18-9   For a hypothermia victim, rewarm the body gradually.

victim is alert, give him or her warm nonalcoholic and decaffeinated liquids to drink. Do not warm the victim too quickly, such as by immersing the victim in warm water. Rapid rewarming can cause dangerous heart rhythms. Be extremely gentle in handling the victim.

In cases of severe hypothermia, the victim may be unconscious. Breathing may have slowed or stopped. The pulse may be slow and irregular. The body may feel stiff as the muscles become rigid. Monitor breathing and signs of circulation, give rescue breathing if necessary, and continue to warm the victim until EMS personnel arrive. Be prepared to start CPR.

Care for Heat and Cold Emergencies

COLD EMERGENCIES

FROSTBITE
Cover affected area.

Handle gently, never rub.

Soak affected part in water 100 to 105 degrees F (38 to 41 degrees C).

Do not let affected part touch bottom or sides of container.

Keep in water until red and warm.

Avoid breaking blisters.

Bandage with dry, clean dressing.

Do not allow affected area to refreeze.

Do not allow victim to walk on thawed feet until all feeling has returned to affected area.

Call EMS personnel or transport the victim to a medical facility.

HYPOTHERMIA
Call EMS personnel.

Move victim to a warm place, if possible.

Warm body gradually by wrapping in blankets or putting on dry clothing.

Apply heat sources (hot water bottle, chemical heat pack, or heating pad if victim is dry), if available.

Give warm liquids to conscious victim.

Do not rewarm too quickly.

Handle gently.

Be prepared to do rescue breathing or CPR.

HEAT EMERGENCIES

HEAT CRAMPS
Have victim rest in cool place.

Give cool water or sports drink.

Stretch and squeeze the muscle.

HEAT-RELATED ILLNESS
Have victim rest in cool place.

If victim is conscious, give small amounts of cool water to drink.

Monitor victim's breathing and signs of circulation; watch for signs and symptoms of worsening condition.

Loosen tight clothing.

Remove perspiration-soaked clothing.

Cool the body by any means available, such as—

- Wet towels or sheets.
- Ice packs.
- Water hose.
- Fanning victim.

Be prepared to do rescue breathing or CPR.

Call EMS personnel immediately if victim refuses water, vomits, or begins to have changes in level of consciousness.

An Icy Rescue

Rescuers who pulled Michelle Funk from an icy creek near her home thought she was dead. The child's eyes stared dully ahead, her body was chilled and blue, and her heart had stopped beating. The 2½-year-old had been under the icy water for more than an hour. By all basic measurements of life, she was dead.

Years ago, Michelle's family would have prepared for her funeral. Instead, paramedics performed CPR on Michelle's still body as they rushed her to a children's medical center, where Dr. Robert G. Bolte took over care. Bolte had been reading about a rewarming technique used on adult hypothermia victims and thought it would work on Michelle. Surgeons sometimes intentionally cool a patient when preparing for surgery and use heart-lung machines to rewarm the patient's blood after surgery. This cooling helps keep oxygen in the blood longer. Bolte attached Michelle to the heart-lung machine, which provided oxygen and removed carbon dioxide, in addition to warming the blood. When Michelle's temperature reached 77 degrees F (25 degrees C), the unconscious child gasped. Soon, her heart was pumping on its own.

Doctors once believed the brain could not survive more than 5 to 7 minutes without oxygen, but survivals like Michelle's have changed opinions. Ironically, freezing water actually helps to protect the body from drowning.

In icy water, a person's body temperature begins to drop almost as soon as the body hits the water. The body loses heat in water 25 to 30 times faster than it does in the air. As the body's core temperature drops, the metabolic rate drops. Activity in the cells comes almost to a standstill, and the cells require very little oxygen. Any oxygen left in the blood is diverted from other parts of the body to the brain and heart.

This state of suspended animation allows humans to survive under water at least four times as long as doctors once believed possible. Nearly 20 cases of miraculous survivals have been documented in medical journals, although unsuccessful cases are rarely described. Most cases involve children who spent 15 minutes or longer in water temperatures of 41 degrees F (5 degrees C) or less. Children survive better because their bodies cool faster than do adults'.

Researchers once theorized that the physiological responses were caused by a "mammalian dive reflex" similar to a response found in whales and seals. They believed the same dive mechanism that allowed whales and seals to stay under water for long periods of time was triggered in drowning humans. Experiments have failed to support the idea. Many researchers now say the best explanation for the slowdown is simply the body's response to extreme cold.

After being attached to the heart-lung machine for nearly an hour, Michelle was moved into an intensive care unit. She stayed in a coma for more than a week. She was blind for a short period, and doctors weren't sure she would recover. But slowly she began to respond. First she smiled when her parents came into the room, and soon she was talking like a 2½-year-old again. After she left the hospital, she suffered a tremor from nerve damage. But Michelle was one of the lucky ones—eventually she regained her full sight, balance, and coordination.

Although breakthroughs have saved many lives, parents still must be vigilant around their children and others near water. Most near-drowning victims are not as lucky as Michelle. One out of every three survivors suffers neurological damage. There is no replacement for close supervision.

PREVENTING HEAT AND COLD EMERGENCIES

Generally, illnesses caused by overexposure to extreme temperatures are preventable. To prevent heat or cold emergencies from happening to you or anyone you know, follow these guidelines:

- Avoid being outdoors in the hottest or coldest part of the day.
- Change your activity level according to the temperature.
- Take frequent breaks.
- Dress appropriately for the environment.
- Drink large amounts of fluids before, during, and after activity.

The easiest way to prevent illness caused by temperature extremes is to avoid being outside during the part of the day when temperatures are most extreme. For instance, if you plan to work outdoors in hot weather, plan your activity for the early morning and evening hours when the sun is not as strong. Likewise, if you must be outdoors on cold days, plan your activities for the warmest part of the day.

However, not everyone can avoid temperature extremes. Often work or other situations require exposure to extreme conditions. But you can take additional precautions, such as changing your activity level and taking frequent breaks. For instance, in very hot conditions, exercise only for brief periods, then rest in a cool, shaded area. Frequent breaks allow your body to readjust to normal body temperature, enabling it to better withstand brief periods of exposure to temperature extremes (Fig. 18-10). Avoid heavy exercise during the hottest or coldest part of the day. Extremes of temperature promote fatigue, which hampers the body's ability to adjust.

Always wear clothing appropriate to the environmental conditions and your activity level. When possible, wear light-colored cotton clothing in the heat. Cotton absorbs perspiration and lets air circulate through the material, which lets heat escape and perspiration evaporate, cooling the body. Light-colored clothing reflects the sun's rays.

When you are in the cold, wear layers of clothing made of tightly woven fibers, such as wool, that trap warm air against your body.

Figure 18-10 Taking frequent breaks when exercising in extreme temperatures allows your body to readjust to normal body temperature.

Wear a head covering in both heat and cold. A hat protects the head from the sun's rays in the summer and prevents heat from escaping in the winter. Also, protect other areas of the body, such as the fingers, toes, ears, and nose, from cold exposure by wearing protective coverings.

Whether in heat or cold, always drink enough fluids. Drinking at least six 8-ounce (236.6 milliliters) glasses of fluids is the most important thing you can do to prevent heat- or cold-related illness. Plan to drink fluids when you take a break. Just as you would drink cool fluids in the summer, drink warm fluids in the winter. Cool and warm fluids help the body maintain a normal temperature. If cold or hot drinks are not available, drink plenty of plain water. Do not drink beverages containing caffeine or alcohol. Caffeine and alcohol hinder the body's temperature-regulating mechanism.

MIND AT WORK

3. *What could Cynthia have done to prevent heat exhaustion?*

SUMMARY

Overexposure to extreme heat and cold may cause a person to become ill. The likelihood of illness also depends on factors such as physical activity, clothing, wind, humidity, working and living conditions, and a person's age and physical condition.

Heat cramps are an early indication that the body's normal temperature-regulating mechanism is not working efficiently. They may signal that the person is in the early stage of a heat-related illness. For heat-related illness, it is important to stop physical activity, cool the victim, and call EMS personnel. Heat stroke can rapidly lead to death if it is left untreated.

Frostbite and hypothermia are both serious cold-related conditions, and the victim of either needs professional medical care. Hypothermia can be life threatening. For both hypothermia and frostbite, it is important to warm the victim gradually and handle him or her with care.

Answers to Application Questions

1. Cynthia feels dizzy because, in an effort to cool the body, blood flow to the skin is increased, bringing warm blood to the surface and allowing heat to escape. As more blood flows to the skin, blood flow to vital organs, such as the brain, is reduced. This reduction of blood flow causes a lack of oxygen-rich blood in the brain, creating a temporary decline in the level of consciousness and making the person feel weak and dizzy or faint.

2. Lou should get Cynthia out of the sun immediately, then make sure that she rests in a cool place and sips cool water.

3. Cynthia could have worn a hat, taken frequent breaks, and kept drinking liquids throughout her activity.

STUDY QUESTIONS

1. Match each term with the correct definition.

    a. Frostbite   c. Heat exhaustion   e. Hypothermia
    b. Heat cramps   d. Heat stroke

    _____ The early stage and most common form of heat-related illness.

    _____ A life-threatening condition that develops when the body's warming mechanisms fail to maintain normal body temperature.

    _____ A life-threatening condition that develops when the body's cooling mechanism fails.

    _____ The freezing of body tissues caused by overexposure to the cold.

    _____ Painful spasms of skeletal muscles that develop after heavy exercise or work outdoors in warm or moderate temperatures.

2. List four factors that affect body temperature.

3. List three conditions that can result from overexposure to heat.

4. List four signs and symptoms of heat-related illness.

5. List two signs and symptoms of a heat-related illness for which EMS personnel should be called.

6. List two ways to cool a victim of a suspected heat-related illness.

7. List two conditions that result from overexposure to the cold.

8. List four ways to prevent heat and cold emergencies.

In questions 9 and 10, circle the letter of the correct answer.

9. To care for heat cramps—

   a. Have the victim rest comfortably in a cool place.
   b. Call EMS personnel.
   c. Give salt tablets.
   d. All of the above.

10. What should you do if the victim of a suspected heat-related illness begins to lose consciousness?

   a. Cool the body using wet sheets, towels, or cold packs.
   b. Cool the body by applying rubbing alcohol.
   c. Call EMS personnel.
   d. a and c.

Use the following scenario to answer questions 11 and 12.

You and a friend have been skiing all morning. The snow is great, but it is really cold. Your buddy has complained for the last half hour or so that his hands and feet are freezing. Now he says he can't feel his fingers and toes. You decide to return to the ski lodge. Once inside, your friend has trouble removing his mittens and ski boots. You help him take them off and notice that his fingers look waxy and white and feel cold. Your friend says he still can't feel them.

11. Circle the signs and symptoms of frostbite you find in the scenario above.

12. How would you care for your friend's hands and feet?

Use the following scenario to answer questions 13 and 14.

You are working on a community service project delivering meals to elderly, home-bound individuals. It is a blustery winter day that has you running from the van to each front door. As you enter the last home, you notice that it is not much warmer inside the house than it is outside. An elderly woman, bundled in blankets, is sitting as close as possible to a small space heater. You speak to her, introducing yourself and asking how things are, but you get no response. The woman's eyes are glassy as she makes an effort to look at you. She seems weak and exhausted, barely able to keep her head up. You touch her arm, but she does not seem to feel it.

13. Circle the signs and symptoms in the scenario above that would lead you to suspect a cold-related illness.

14. Describe the actions you would take to care for the woman in the scenario.

Answers are listed in Appendix A.

SPECIAL SITUATIONS

CHAPTER 19

Reaching and Moving Victims

WHAT YOU SHOULD LEARN

After reading this chapter, you should be able to—

1. List four situations in which an emergency move of a victim is necessary.

2. List five limitations you should be aware of before you attempt to move someone.

3. Describe eight guidelines you should follow when moving someone.

4. Describe how to perform four emergency moves.

5. Identify the most appropriate emergency move for a victim of suspected head or spine injury.

6. Describe two out-of-water assists that you can use to help someone who is in trouble in the water.

7. Describe three in-water assists that you can use to help someone who is in trouble in the water.

8. List the five general guidelines for caring for an injured person in the water who you suspect may have a spinal injury.

9. Describe two methods to support or stabilize a victim's head and neck in the water.

10. Define the key terms for this chapter.

You arrive at your boss's house a little concerned about being late. "Bad traffic," you explain nervously as he takes you to the poolside patio. There you find a group of your co-workers and other people from the office enjoying themselves. Eric, from Accounts, wobbles over to the pool edge and falls in the deep end. Although he tries to swim to the side, he makes no progress because the weight of his wet clothes pulls him down. Eric starts to struggle and yell for help. The crowd that gathers by the pool is pointing, laughing, and shouting.

Introduction

*I*n earlier chapters, you learned how to care for victims of injury and illness when it is safe to do so. Sometimes, however, the victim is in a dangerous situation and must be rescued before you can give care. In this chapter, you will learn how to safely move victims on land and rescue victims from water without endangering or injuring yourself.

REACHING AND MOVING VICTIMS ON LAND

Usually, when you give first aid, you will not face hazards that require moving the victim immediately. In most cases, you can follow the emergency action steps by checking the scene and the victim, calling 9-1-1 or the local emergency number, and giving care for the victim where you find him or her. Moving a victim needlessly can lead to further injury. For example, if the victim has a fracture of the leg, movement could result in the end of the bone tearing the skin. Soft tissue damage, damage to nerves, blood loss, and infection all could result unnecessarily.

You should move a victim only when you can do so safely and when there is immediate danger, such as fire, lack of oxygen, presence of toxic gas, risk of drowning, risk of explosion, a

Key Terms

Active drowning victim: A person exhibiting universal behavior that includes struggling at the surface for 20 to 60 seconds before submerging.

Distressed swimmer: A person capable of staying afloat but likely to need assistance to get to safety.

Passive drowning victim: An unconscious victim facedown, submerged or at the surface.

collapsing structure, or uncontrollable traffic hazards (Fig. 19-1).

Before you act, consider the following limitations to ensure moving one or more victims quickly and safely:

- Dangerous conditions at the scene
- The size of the victim
- Your physical ability
- Whether others can help you
- The victim's condition

Considering these limitations will help you decide how to proceed. For example, if you are injured, you may be unable to move the person and will only risk making the situation worse. If you become part of the problem, EMS personnel will have one more person to rescue.

To protect yourself and the victim, follow these guidelines when moving a victim:

- Only attempt to move a person you are sure you can comfortably handle.
- Bend your body at the knees and hips.
- Lift with your legs, not your back.
- Walk carefully, using short steps.
- When possible, move forward rather than backward.
- Always look where you are going.
- Support the victim's head and spine, if necessary.
- Avoid bending or twisting a victim with possible head or spine injury.

Gaining Access

Sometimes providing care is not possible because the victim is inaccessible. One example is a situation in which someone is able to call 9-1-1 or the local emergency number for help but is unable to unlock the door of the home or office to let in anyone. Victims may also be inaccessible in many motor vehicle collisions. Vehicle doors are sometimes locked or crushed, windows may be tightly rolled up, or the vehicle may be unstable. In other instances, fire, water, or other obstacles may prevent you from reaching the victim safely.

In these cases, you must immediately begin to think of how to safely gain access to the victim. If you cannot reach the victim, you cannot check him or her or provide care. But remember, when attempting to reach a victim, your

Figure 19-1   You should move a victim only if he is in immediate danger, such as from a collapsing structure.

safety is the most important consideration. Protect yourself and the victim by doing only what you are trained to do and by using equipment appropriate for the situation. In traffic, items such as reflective markers or flares and flashlights may help keep you safe as you attempt to gain access to a trapped victim.

Emergency Moves

You can move a person to safety in many different ways, but no one way is best for every situation. The object is to move a person to safety without injuring yourself or causing further injury to the victim. The following are four common types of emergency moves:

- Walking assist
- Pack-strap carry
- Two-person seat carry
- Clothes drag

All of these emergency moves can be done by one or two people and without any equipment, which is important because with most rescues, limited resources are available.

Walking assist

The most basic emergency move is the walking assist. Either one or two rescuers can use this method with a conscious victim. To perform a walking assist, place the victim's arm across your shoulders and hold it in place with one hand. Support the victim with your other hand around the victim's waist (Fig. 19-2, *A*). In this way, your body acts as a "crutch," supporting the victim's weight while you both walk. A second rescuer, if present, can support the victim in the same way on the other side (Fig. 19-2, *B*). This assist is not appropriate to use if you suspect that the victim has a spinal injury.

Pack-strap carry

The pack-strap carry can be used with both conscious and unconscious victims. To use it with an unconscious victim requires a second person to help position the victim on your back. To perform the pack-strap carry, have the victim stand or have a second person support the victim. Position yourself with your back to the victim, back straight, knees bent, so that your shoulders fit into the victim's armpits. Cross the victim's arms in front of you,

Figure 19-2   The most basic emergency move is the walking assist. **A,** The rescuer's body supports the victim's weight. **B,** A second rescuer can support the victim from the other side.

Figure 19-3   **A,** To perform the pack-strap carry, position yourself with your back to the victim. Cross the victim's arms in front of you and grasp the victim's wrists. **B,** Lean forward slightly and pull the victim onto your back.

and grasp the victim's wrists (Fig. 19-3, *A*). Lean forward slightly and pull the victim up and onto your back (Fig. 19-3, *B*). Stand up and walk to safety. Depending on the size of your victim, you may be able to hold both of the victim's wrists with one hand, leaving your other hand free to help maintain balance, open doors, and remove obstructions. This assist is not appropriate to use if you suspect that the victim has a spinal injury.

A

B

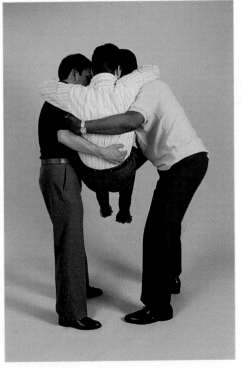

C

Figure 19-4   The two-person seat carry can be used for anyone who is conscious or not seriously injured. **A** and **B,** Lock arms under the victim's legs. **C,** Lift the victim in the seat formed by the rescuer's arms.

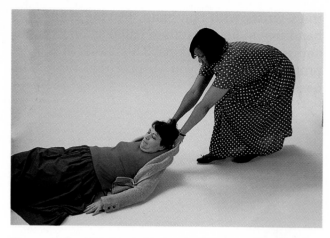

Figure 19-5 Use the clothes drag to move a person suspected of having a head or spine injury.

Two-person seat carry

The two-person seat carry requires a second rescuer. This carry can be used for any victim who is conscious or not otherwise seriously injured. Put one arm behind the victim's thighs and the other across the victim's back. Interlock your arms with those of a second rescuer behind the victim's legs and across the victim's back. Lift the victim in the "seat" formed by the rescuers' arms (Fig. 19-4, *A-C*).

Clothes drag

The clothes drag can be used to move a person suspected of having a head or spine injury. This move helps keep the victim's head and neck stabilized. Grasp the victim's clothing behind the neck, gathering enough to secure a firm grip. Using the clothing, pull the victim headfirst to safety. During the move, the victim's head is cradled by both clothing and the rescuer's arms (Fig. 19-5). This emergency move is exhausting and may cause back strain for the rescuer, even when done properly.

REACHING AND MOVING VICTIMS IN THE WATER

Drownings are the fourth most common cause of death from unintentional injury in the United States. Every year approximately 5000 Americans drown. Drownings may occur during activities such as swimming, boating, hunting, fishing, and even taking a bath. People may drown who never intended to be in the water. They may simply have been near the water,

fallen or slipped in, and not known what to do. Small children can even drown in a bucket of water.

Children under 5 years old and young adults from ages 15 to 24 have the highest rates of drowning. Children with seizure disorders are four times more likely to drown than those without such disorders. Most young children who drown, do so in home pools. In Los Angeles, half of all drownings occur in home pools and almost 90 percent of these drownings involve toddlers. Drowning rates are highest in the western and southern United States, in part because of the number of home pools in those regions. But children can also drown in many other kinds of water. In rural areas, for example, drainage canals and irrigation ditches have been the sites of many drownings.

If someone is in trouble in the water, some basic skills you can learn can help. Always remember to stay safe. If there is any chance that you cannot safely and easily help the person in trouble, call for professional assistance.

Recognizing an Emergency

An emergency can happen to anyone in or around the water, regardless of how good a swimmer the person is or what he or she is doing at the time. A strong swimmer can get into trouble in the water because of sudden illness. A nonswimmer playing in shallow water can be swept into deep water by a wave. The key to recognizing an emergency is staying alert and knowing the signals that indicate an emergency is happening.

Use all of your senses when observing others in and around the water. You may see that a swimmer is acting oddly, or you may hear a scream or sudden splash. Pay attention to anything that seems unusual.

Being able to recognize a person who is having trouble in the water may help save that person's life. Most drowning people cannot or do not call for help. They spend their energy just trying to keep their head above water. They might slip underwater quickly and never resurface. There are two kinds of water emergency situations—a swimmer in distress and a drowning person. Each kind poses a different danger and can be recognized by different behaviors.

Figure 19-6 A distressed swimmer can stay afloat and usually call for help.

Figure 19-7 An active drowning victim struggles to stay afloat and is unable to call out for help.

Figure 19-8 A passive drowning victim can be found floating near the surface or submerged on the bottom of the pool.

A ***distressed swimmer*** may be too tired to get to shore or the side of the pool but is able to stay afloat and breathe and may be calling for help. The person may be floating, treading water, or clinging to a line for support. Someone who is trying to swim but making little or no forward progress may be in distress (Fig. 19-6). If not helped, a person in distress may lose the ability to float and become a drowning victim.

An ***active drowning victim*** is vertical in the water but has no supporting kick and is unable to move forward or tread water. The victim's arms are at the side pressing down in an instinctive attempt to keep the head above water

to breathe (Fig. 19-7). All energy is going into the struggle to breathe, and the person cannot call out for help. A ***passive drowning victim*** is not moving and will be floating facedown on the bottom or near the surface of the water (Fig. 19-8). Table 19-1 shows characteristics of drowning persons.

Once you recognize that there is an emergency, you need to decide to act—and how to act. This is not always as simple as it sounds. Often people are slow to act in an emergency because they are not sure exactly what to do or they think someone else will do whatever is needed. What if no one else is there or is taking

TABLE 19-1

Characteristics of Distressed Swimmers and Drowning Victims as Compared to Swimmers

	Swimmer	Distressed Swimmer	Active Drowning Victim	Passive Drowning Victim
Breathing	Rhythmic breathing	Can continue breathing and call for help	Struggles to breathe; cannot call out for help	Not breathing
Arm and leg action	Relatively coordinated movement	Floating, sculling, or treading water; can wave for help	Arms to sides, pressing down; no supporting kick	None
Body position	Horizontal	Horizontal, vertical, or diagonal, depending on means of support	Vertical	Facedown; submerged or near surface
Locomotion	Recognizable progress	Little or no forward progress; less and less able to support self	None; has only 20-60 seconds before submerging	None

action? If you decide to act, you may save a person's life. To prepare yourself for this moment of decision, think now about emergency situations and what you might do.

As in any emergency situation, proceed safely once you have decided to act. Make sure the scene is safe—don't go rushing into a dangerous situation where you too may become a victim. If the person is in the water, decide first whether he or she needs help getting out, and then act based on your training. Look for any other victims. Look for bystanders who can help you give first aid or call for help.

If the victim is in the water, your first goal is to stay safe. Rushing into the water to help a victim may cause you to become a victim, too. Once you ensure your own safety, your goal is to help get the person out of the water. If the person is unconscious, send someone else to call EMS personnel while you start the rescue. If the person is conscious, you can first act to get the person out of the water and then determine whether EMS personnel are needed.

Out-of-Water Assists

You can help a person in trouble in the water by using reaching assists or throwing assists. Whenever possible, start the rescue by talking to the person. Let the person know help is coming. If noise is a problem or if the person is too far away to hear you, use gestures. Tell the per-

son what you want him or her to do to help with the rescue, such as grasping a line, rescue buoy, or any other object that floats. Ask the person to move toward you by kicking or stroking. Some people have reached safety by themselves with the calm and encouraging assistance of someone calling to them.

Reaching assists

If the person is close enough, you can use a reaching assist to help him or her out of the water. Firmly brace yourself on a pool deck or pier and reach out to the person with any object that will extend your reach, such as a pole, an oar or paddle, a tree branch, a shirt, a belt, or a towel (Fig. 19-9). Community pools and recreational

Figure 19-9 With a reaching assist, you remain safe while reaching out to the victim.

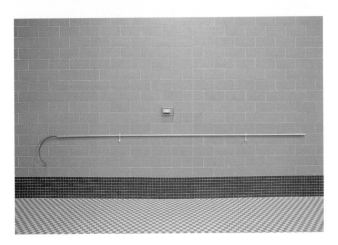

Figure 19-10 A shepherd's crook can be found at most public swimming facilities.

areas, as well as hotel and motel pools, often have reaching equipment beside the water, such as a **shepherd's crook** (an aluminum or fiberglass pole with a large hook on one end) (Fig. 19-10). When the person grasps the object, slowly and carefully pull him or her to safety. To prevent yourself from being pulled into the water, keep your body low and lean back as you pull the victim.

If you are using a shepherd's crook and the person cannot grasp it, use the hook to encircle the person's body. Keep yourself firmly braced, put the hook around the person's chest under the armpits, and carefully pull him or her to safety. Be careful not to injure the person with the point of the hook as you do this. For a person on the bottom of a pool, try to reach him or her with the hook. Try to encircle the person's body and pull the person to the surface. Then

bring the person to the edge and turn him or her face-up.

If you have no object for reaching, lie flat on the pool deck or pier and reach with your arm. If you are already in the water, hold onto the pool ladder, overflow trough, piling, or other secure object with one hand and extend your free hand or one of your legs to the victim (Fig. 19-11, *A* and *B*). Do not release your grasp at the edge, and do not swim out into the water.

Throwing assists

An effective way to rescue someone beyond your reach is to throw to the victim a floating object with a line attached. The person can grasp the object so that you can pull him or her to safety. Objects you can throw include a heaving line, ring buoy, throw bag, rescue tube, or homemade device (Fig. 19-12). You can use any object at hand that will float, such as a picnic jug or tire. Safety equipment for throwing may be in plain view in swimming areas at community pools, hotel and motel pools, and public waterfronts. Recreation and aquatic supply stores sell this equipment for residential pools. You can use certain types of equipment for throwing assists.

You can make your own **heaving jug** for throwing to a victim. Put a half-inch of water in a gallon plastic container, seal it, and attach 50 to 75 feet of floating line to the handle. Throw it by holding the handle and using an underhand swinging motion. The weight of the water in the jug helps direct the throw (Fig. 19-13). Aim the device beyond the victim but within reach

A

 B

Figure 19-11 When no object is available to extend to the victim, try to extend your **A**, hand or **B**, foot to the victim.

Figure 19-12   Throwing devices.

Figure 19-13   A heaving jug is a simple homemade device that can be thrown to a victim.

Figure 19-14   A ring buoy is another piece of rescue equipment that is commonly found at public swimming facilities.

Figure 19-15   A throw bag is a compact rescue device that can be thrown to a victim.

of the attached line, and instruct the victim to grab hold.

A **heaving line** should float. It should be white, yellow, or some other highly visible color. A buoyant, weighted object on the end will make throwing easier and more accurate. Hang about half of the coiled line on the open palm of your nonthrowing arm, and throw the other half underhand to the victim.

A **ring buoy** is made of buoyant cork, **kapok,** cellular foam, or plastic-covered material and weighs about 2 pounds. It should have a towline or lightweight line with an object or knot at the end to keep the line from slipping out from under your foot when you throw it. The buoy and coiled line should be kept on a post where anyone can quickly grasp it to throw to someone in trouble. Hold the under-

side of the ring with your fingers and throw it underhand (Fig. 19-14).

The **throw bag** is a small but useful rescue device. It is a nylon bag containing 50 to 75 feet of coiled floating line. A foam disk in the bag gives it shape and keeps it from sinking. Throw bags are often used in canoes and other boats. Hold the end of the line with one hand and throw the bag with your other hand, using an underhand swing (Fig. 19-15).

To perform a throwing assist, follow these guidelines:

1. Get into a stride position (with the leg opposite that of your throwing arm in front of the other leg). This position lets you keep your balance when you throw the equipment.
2. Bend your knees.

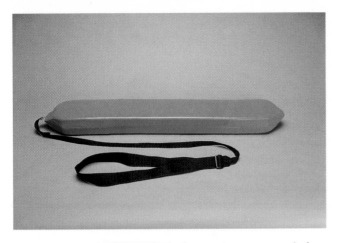

Figure 19-16   A rescue tube is the most common and effective piece of equipment lifeguards use.

3. Step on your end of the line with your forward foot.
4. Try to throw the device just beyond the victim but within reach.
5. Throw the device so that any wind or current will bring it back to the victim.
6. When the victim has grasped the device, slowly pull him or her to safety. Lean back away from the victim as you pull.

The **rescue tube** is a vinyl, foam-filled floating support about 45 to 54 inches long (Fig. 19-16). It is an extremely effective and versatile piece of lifeguarding equipment. It is popular because it is easy to use and can support three to five people, depending on its size. Attached to the rescue tube is a tow line and shoulder strap with a total length of 6 to 12 feet.

If the throwing assist does not work and the water is shallow enough for wading, try a wading assist with equipment.

In-Water Assists

If you know the water is shallow enough that you can stand with your head out of the water, wade into the water to assist the person.

Wading assist with equipment

Take a buoyant object and extend it to the victim. Use a rescue tube, a ring buoy, a buoyant cushion, a kickboard, or a life jacket. You may also reach with a ring buoy, tree branch, pole, air mattress, plastic cooler, or paddle (Fig. 19-17, *A* and *B*). If a current or soft bottom makes wading dangerous, do not enter the water.

Once the person grasps the object, either pull the person to safety or, if it is a buoyant object, let it go and tell the person to kick toward safety using it for support. Always keep the object between you and the person to help prevent the person from grasping you and putting you in danger.

A victim who has been lying motionless and face-down in the water for several seconds is probably unconscious. If the water is not over your head, wade into the water carefully with some kind of flotation equipment and turn the person face-up. Bring the victim to the side of the pool or to the shoreline, and then remove him or her from the water.

A

B

Figure 19-17   If you can enter the water without endangering yourself, wade in and reach to the victim. If possible, extend your reach with a **A**, ring buoy, **B**, tree branch, or similar object.

Figure 19-18 When performing a walking assist, maintain a firm grasp on the victim while walking out of the water.

Figure 19-19 When performing a beach drag, walk backward slowly while dragging the victim toward shore.

Figure 19-20 If another person is available, have him or her help you.

Walking assist

If the person is in shallow water where he or she can stand, he or she may be able to walk with some support. Follow these guidelines to perform a walking assist:

1. Place one of the person's arms around your neck and across your shoulder.
2. Grasp the wrist of the arm that is across your shoulder, and wrap your free arm around the person's back or waist.
3. Maintain a firm grasp, and help the person walk out of the water (Fig. 19-18).

Beach drag

You may use the beach drag with a person in shallow water on a sloping shore or beach. This method works well with a heavy or unconscious person.

MIND AT WORK

1. What can you do to help Eric once he has fallen into your boss's pool?

1. Stand behind the person, and grasp him or her under the armpits, supporting the person's head with your forearms.
2. While walking backward slowly, drag the person toward the shore (Fig. 19-19).
3. Remove the person completely from the water or at least to a point where the head and shoulders are out of the water.

You may use a two-person drag if another person is present to help you (Fig. 19-20).

Spinal Injury

Along with the risk of drowning, some water activities also involve the risk of spinal injury (see Chapter 12). Each year in the United States, about 1000 disabling neck and back injuries occur as a result of water activities, such as head-first entry into shallow water. When the injury damages the spinal cord, severe disability is likely, including permanent paralysis. The person may never be able to move his or her arms or legs again.

Most spinal injuries occur in shallow water. These injuries may result from diving into above-ground pools or the shallow end of in-ground pools and striking objects when diving.

It Only Takes a Second

Each year in the United States, approximately 1000 people suffer permanent damage to their spinal cord. Most of these injuries occur from diving mishaps. Statisticians describe the typical accident victim with grim accuracy. He is a single, white male between the ages of 15 and 30, an active person who loves sports and the outdoors.

Bill Brooks fits this description. The 29-year-old from Davidsonville, Maryland, tried to dive through an inner tube into a pool, but his neck hit the tube. As he floated in the water, he was aware of everything, yet powerless to move.

At the hospital, doctors told Brooks he was a "C5" quadriplegic, which described the area of the neck that he had damaged. In college, Brooks had played baseball, and after college, he had taken up slow-pitch softball. In one afternoon, Brooks had lost control of his legs, chest, and arms. He lost the ability to dress himself, feed himself, go to the bathroom by himself, or even hold a softball in his hand.

Months of rehabilitation have improved Brooks' life. Although his right hand remains paralyzed, with his left hand, Brooks can grasp a telephone and control a computer mouse. With the computer mouse, he is learning to design the sprinkler systems he once installed as the foreman for a sprinkler company. Brooks is learning to survive with his injury, but his spinal nerves will never regenerate, so there is little hope that he will ever walk again.

Many states and private organizations have begun education and prevention campaigns to reduce the high rate of diving injuries. The American Red Cross offers the following tips to prevent head and spine injuries:

- Check for adequate water depth. When you first enter the water, enter feet first.
- For diving off a 1-meter diving board, the water should be at least 10 feet deep. This depth should extend 16 feet in front of the diver. The higher the board, the deeper the water should be. Pools at homes, motels, or hotels often do not have an adequate area for safe diving.
- Never dive into an above-ground pool.
- Starting blocks should be used only by trained swimmers under the supervision of a qualified coach.
- Never drink alcohol and dive or swim.
- Never dive in water where you cannot see the bottom. Objects, such as logs or pilings, may be hidden below the surface.
- Running into the water and then diving headfirst into the waves is dangerous.
- If you are bodysurfing, always keep your arms out in front of you to protect your head and neck.

Figure 19-21   The hip/shoulder support helps limit movement of the spine for a victim, while keeping the face clear of water.

Unsupervised use of **starting blocks** may also lead to serious injury. Injuries can also result from headfirst entry into the surf at a beach, off a dock at a lake, or from a cliff into a water-filled **quarry.** In this section, you will learn how to recognize a potential spinal injury in the water and what to do to prevent further injury.

Recognizing a spinal injury

Usually a spinal injury is caused by hitting the bottom or an object in the water. Your major concern is to keep the person's face out of the water to let him or her breathe and to prevent the person's head and back from moving further. Movement can cause more injury and increase the risk of the person's being paralyzed.

If you think the person may have a spinal injury, give care assuming the spine is injured. If the person is in the water, your goal is to prevent any further movement of the head or neck and move the person to safety. *Always check first whether a lifeguard or other trained professional is present before touching or moving a person who may have a spinal injury.* This section describes what you can do by yourself or with the assistance of bystanders to care for a victim of spinal injury.

General guidelines for care

You can stabilize a person's spine in several ways while the person is still in the water. These methods are described in the next sections. Follow these general guidelines for a person with a suspected spinal injury in shallow water:

1. Be sure someone has called 9-1-1 or the local emergency number. If other people are available, ask someone else in your group or a bystander to help you.
2. Minimize movement of the victim's head, neck, and back. First, try to keep the victim's head in line with the body. Do not pull on the head. Use your hands, arms, or body, depending on which technique you use. The two methods described in the next sections can be used.
3. Position the victim face-up at the surface of the water. You may have to bring a submerged victim to the surface and to a face-up position. Keep the victim's face out of the water to let the victim breathe.
4. Check for consciousness and breathing once you have stabilized the victim's spine.
5. Support the victim in the water with his or her head and spine stabilized until help arrives.

In-line stabilization techniques

The following section describes two methods for stabilizing the victim's spine in the water. These methods will enable you to provide care for the victim whether he or she is face-up or face-down.

Hip/shoulder support. This method helps limit movement of the spine. Use it for a victim who is face-up. Support the victim at the hips and shoulders to keep the face out of the water.

Figure 19-22 When performing the head splint technique, **A,** squeeze the victim's arms against his head, **B,** move the victim slowly forward and rotate the victim toward you until he is face-up, and **C,** position the victim's head in the crook of your arm with the head in line with the body.

1. Approach the victim from the side, and lower yourself to chest depth.
2. Slide one arm under the victim's shoulders and the other under the hip bones. Support the victim's body horizontally, keeping the face clear of the water (Fig. 19-21).
3. Do not lift the victim but support him or her in the water until help arrives.

Head splint. The head splint is used to limit movement of the spine for a person face-down at or near the surface of the water. This victim must be turned face-up to breathe.

1. Approach the victim from the side.
2. Gently move the victim's arms up alongside the head by grasping the victim's arms midway between the shoulder and elbow. Grasp the victim's right arm with your right hand. Grasp the victim's left arm with your left hand.
3. Squeeze the victim's arms against his or her head. This maneuver helps keep the head in line with the body (Fig. 19-22, *A*).
4. With your body at about shoulder depth in the water, glide the victim slowly forward.
5. Continue moving slowly and rotate the victim toward you until he or she is face-up. This rotation is done by pushing the victim's arm that is closer to you under water,

Figure 19-23   Use an object, such as a tree branch, to reach a victim who has fallen through the ice.

while pulling the victim's other arm across the surface (Fig. 19-22, *B*).

6. Position the victim's head in the crook of your arm with the head in line with the body (Fig. 19-22, *C*).

7. Maintain this position in the water until help arrives.

Ice Rescues

If a person falls through ice, never go out onto the ice yourself to attempt a rescue. A person who has fallen through ice presents a very dangerous situation, and you are likely to become a victim. Instead, follow these guidelines:

• Send someone to call 9-1-1 or the local emergency number immediately. Trained rescuers may be needed to get the person out of the ice, and even if you succeed in rescuing the person, he or she will probably need medical care.

• From a secure place on land, try a reaching or throwing assist. Use anything at hand that the person can grasp for support, such as a tree branch, a pole, a life jacket, a weighted rope, or a ladder (Fig. 19-23). Act quickly, because within minutes the person's hands may become too numb to grasp the object.

• If you can do it safely, pull the victim to shore. If you cannot, talk to the victim and make sure he or she is secure as possible with the object until help arrives.

• If you get the victim to shore before EMS personnel arrive, provide care for hypothermia.

SUMMARY

Do not make the mistake of moving an ill or injured person unnecessarily. Remember to take the time to survey the scene for life-threatening or potentially life-threatening situations. If it is necessary to move a victim, remember the variety of emergency moves you can use. Use the safest and easiest method to rapidly move the victim without injuring yourself or the victim.

In water emergencies, use the basic methods of reaching, throwing, or wading to rescue someone without endangering yourself. Many drownings could be prevented by following simple precautions when around water. Further training in water safety and lifeguarding is available through your local American Red Cross unit.

Answer to Application Question

1. You can make a reaching assist by using rescue equipment that should be near the pool, such as a shepherd's crook. Other equipment available may include a leaf skimmer attached to a pole or a pole used to vacuum the pool. You may also firmly brace yourself on the pool deck and reach out to Eric, or you can extend your reach by using a towel or a shirt. You can also throw items that float out to him, such as a picnic jug, an air mattress, or an inflatable toy. Remember that your first goal is to stay safe. Rushing into the water to help a victim may cause you to become a victim too.

STUDY QUESTIONS

1. List four situations in which it may be necessary to move a victim.

2. List four limitations you should consider before attempting to move a victim.

3. List four guidelines to follow when moving a victim.

4. Name four common types of emergency moves.

5. List three methods of rescuing a distressed swimmer.

6. List four characteristics of an active drowning victim.

In questions 7 through 11, circle the letter of the correct answer.

7. Which would you use to move a victim with a suspected head or spine injury?

   a. Pack-strap carry
   b. Walking assist
   c. Clothes drag
   d. Two-person seat carry

8. In which of the following situations would a wading assist be appropriate?

   a. You can reach the victim by extending a branch from the shore.
   b. You suspect or see strong currents.
   c. The bottom is not firm.
   d. The water is shallow and you can stand with your head out of the water.

9. You see a man struggling in the rushing waters of a flooded creek. Which is the best way to try to rescue him without endangering yourself?

   a. Plunge into the water and grab him.
   b. Wade in and reach out to him with an object.
   c. From the bank, extend an object for him to reach.
   d. Yell to him to kick forcefully.

10. If a person is unconscious and too heavy for you to carry, which method could you use to get the person out of the water?

   a. A walking assist
   b. A wading assist
   c. The two-person seat carry
   d. The beach drag

11. Which two techniques can be used for stabilizing the head and spine of a person with a suspected spinal injury?

   a. Head and back support and the head splint
   b. Hip/shoulder support and the head splint
   c. Head splint and the head/back immobilization technique
   d. Head and chin support and the head and back support

Answers are listed in Appendix A.

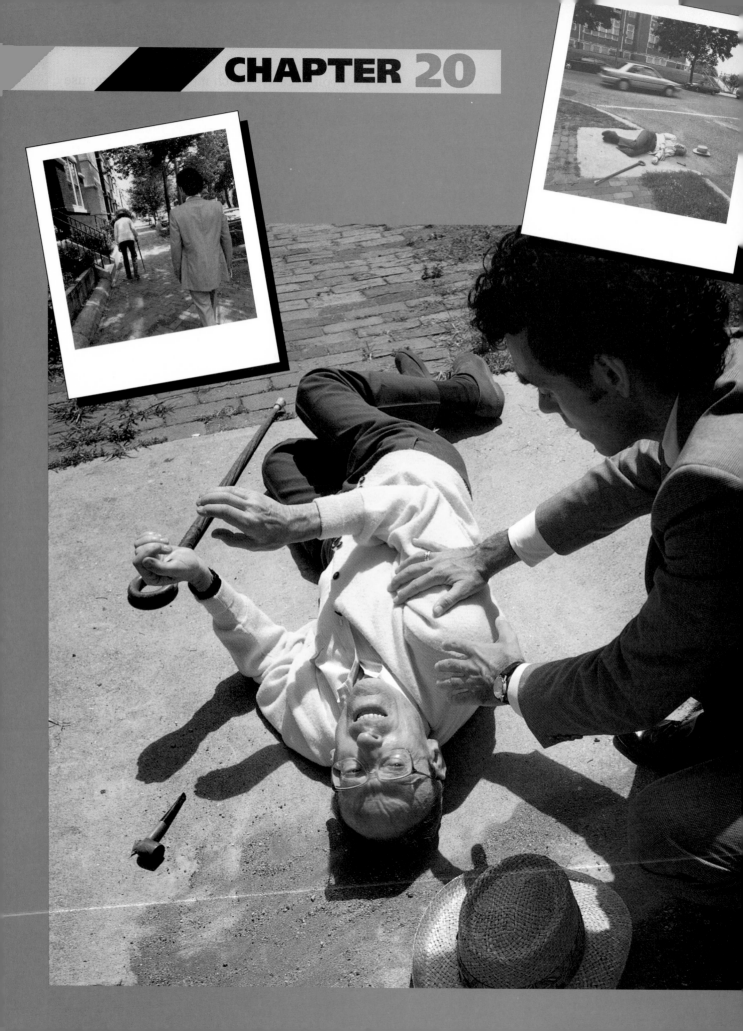

CHAPTER 20

People with Special Needs

WHAT YOU SHOULD LEARN

After reading this chapter, you should be able to—

1. Describe considerations for checking an infant, a toddler, a preschooler, a school-age child, and an adolescent.

2. Explain how to observe an ill or injured child and how to communicate with the parents or caregiver.

3. Describe how to check an older adult.

4. Describe four problems that can affect older adults and the implications for care.

5. Explain ways of communicating with victims who are hearing impaired.

6. Explain your options when trying to communicate with a victim with whom you have a language barrier.

7. Explain what you should do if you come across a crime scene or hostile victim.

8. Define the key terms for this chapter.

I can't believe it! One minute, this man is walking down the sidewalk about 15 feet ahead of me, and suddenly he sort of lurches off the curb and collapses. Cars are passing in all directions, but not one even slows down. When I reach him, I can see he's elderly. His hat has fallen off, and there's blood staining his hair. His eyes are open, but they don't look very focused. He looks dazed and frightened. I ask him if he's okay. He looks up at me, but I can't tell if he knows what I said. Maybe he can't hear me. Perhaps he's confused. I'm not sure what I should do next.

Introduction

*I*n an emergency, you should be aware of the special needs and considerations of children, older adults, people with disabilities, and people who do not speak the same language you speak. Knowing these needs and considerations will help you better understand the nature of the emergency and give appropriate care. A young child may be terrified. An elderly adult may be confused. A disabled person may be unable to hear or see you. A victim may not speak the language(s) you speak. Being able to communicate with and reassure people with special needs can be crucial to your ability to care for them effectively.

Key Terms

Alzheimer's disease: A progressive, degenerative disease that affects the brain, resulting in impaired memory, thinking, and behavior.

Child abuse: The physical, psychological, or sexual assault of a child, resulting in injury and emotional trauma.

Disability: The absence or impairment of motor, sensory, or mental function.

Hearing impairment: Partial or total loss of hearing.

Impairment: Damage or reduction in quality, quantity, value, or strength.

Mental (cognitive) function: The brain's capacity to reason and process information.

Motor function: The ability to move the body or a body part.

Motor impairment: The total or partial inability to move or to use a body part.

Sensory function: The ability to see, hear, touch, taste, and smell.

Sudden infant death syndrome (SIDS): The sudden death of a seemingly normal, healthy infant that occurs during the infant's sleep without evidence of disease.

Vision impairment: Partial or total loss of sight.

INFANTS AND CHILDREN

Infants and children have unique needs and require special care. Assessing a conscious infant's or child's condition can be difficult, especially if he or she does not know you. At certain ages, infants and children do not readily accept strangers. Furthermore, infants and very young children cannot tell you what is wrong.

Communicating With an Ill or Injured Child

We tend to react more strongly and emotionally to a child who is in pain or terror. You will need to try exceptionally hard to control your emotions and your facial expressions. Doing so will be helpful to both the child and any concerned adults. To help an ill or injured child, you also need to try to imagine how the child feels. A child is afraid of the unknown. He or she is afraid of being ill or hurt, being touched by strangers, and being separated from his or her parents or other caregiving adults.

How you interact with an ill or injured infant or child is very important. You need to reduce the child's anxiety and panic and gain the child's trust and cooperation, if possible. Move in slowly. The sudden appearance of a stranger may upset the child. Get as close to the infant's or child's eye level as you can, and keep your voice calm (Fig. 20-1). Smile at the child. Ask the child's name, and use it when you talk to him or her. Talk slowly and distinctly, and use words and terms the child will easily understand. Ask questions the child will be able to answer easily. Explain to the child and the parents or caregiver what you are going to do. Reassure a child that you are there to help and will not leave him or her.

Checking Infants and Children

To be able to effectively check infants and children, it is useful to be aware of certain characteristics of children in specific age groups.

Characteristics of infants and children

Children up to 1 year of age are commonly referred to as infants. Infants less than 6 months old are relatively easy to approach and are unlikely to be afraid of you. Older infants, however, often exhibit "stranger anxiety." They may

Figure 20-1 To communicate with a child, get as close to eye level as you can.

Figure 20-2 Allow a parent to hold the child while you check him or her.

Figure 20-3 Demonstrating first aid steps on a stuffed animal or doll helps a toddler understand how you will care for him or her.

turn away from you and cry and cling to their parent or caregiver. If a family member or the caregiver is calm and cooperative, ask that person to help you. Try to check the infant in the parent's or caregiver's lap or arms.

Children ages 1 and 2 years are often referred to as toddlers. Toddlers may not cooperate with your attempts to check them. They are usually very concerned about being separated from a parent or caregiver. If you reassure the toddler that he or she will not be separated from a parent or caregiver, the toddler may be comforted. If possible, give the toddler a few minutes to get used to you before attempting to check him or her and check the toddler in the parent's or caregiver's lap (Fig. 20-2). A toddler may also respond to praise or be comforted by holding a special toy or blanket.

Children ages 3, 4, and 5 are commonly referred to as preschoolers. Children in this age group are usually easy to check if you use their natural curiosity. Allow them to inspect items such as bandages. Opportunities to explore can allay many fears and be a helpful distraction. Reassure the child that you are going to help and will not leave him or her. Sometimes you can demonstrate what you are going to do on a stuffed animal or a doll (Fig. 20-3). The child may be upset by seeing his or her cut or other injury, so cover it with a dressing as soon as possible.

School-age children are between 6 and 12 years of age. They are usually cooperative and can be a good source of information about what happened. You can usually talk readily with school-age children. Do not let the child's general chronological age, however, influence you to expect an injured or ill child to behave in a way consistent with that age. An injured 11-year-old, for example, may behave more like a 7-year-old. Be especially careful not to talk down to these children. Let them know if you are going to do anything that may be painful. Children in this age group are becoming conscious of their bodies and may not like exposure. Respect their modesty.

Adolescents are between 13 and 18 years of age and are typically more adult than child. Direct your questions to an adolescent victim rather than to a parent or guardian. Allow input from a parent or guardian, however. Occasionally, if a parent or guardian is present, you may not be able to get an accurate idea of what happened or what is wrong. Adolescents are modest and often respond better to a rescuer of the same gender.

Interacting with parents and caregivers

If the family is excited or agitated, the child is likely to be too. When you can calm the family, the child will often calm down as well. Remember to get consent from any adult responsible for the child when possible. Any concerned adults need your support, so behave as calmly as possible.

Observing an infant or child

You can obtain a lot of information by observing the infant or child before actually touching him or her. Look for signs that indicate changes in the level of consciousness, any breathing difficulty, and any apparent injuries and conditions. Realize that the situation may change as soon as you touch the child because he or she may become anxious or upset. Do not separate the infant or child from loved ones. Often a parent, guardian, or caregiver will be holding a crying infant or child. In this case, you can check the child while the adult continues to hold him or her. Unlike some ill or injured adults, an infant or child is unlikely to try to cover up or deny how he or she feels. An infant or child in pain, for example, will generally let you know that he or she hurts and the source of the pain as well as he or she can.

Whenever possible, begin your check of a conscious child at the toe rather than the head. Checking this way is less threatening to the child and allows him or her to watch what is going on and take part in it. Ask a young child to point to any place that hurts. An older child can tell you the location of painful areas. If you need to hold an infant, always support the head when you pick him or her up (Fig. 20-4).

Special Problems

Certain problems are unique to children, such as specific kinds of injury and illness. The following sections discuss some of these concerns.

Figure 20-4 Support the head of an infant when picking up him or her.

Injury

Injury is the number one cause of death for children in the United States. Many of these deaths are the result of motor vehicle crashes. The greatest dangers to a child involved in a motor vehicle incident are airway obstruction and bleeding. Severe bleeding must be controlled as quickly as possible. A relatively small amount of blood lost by an adult is a large amount for an infant or child. Because a child's head is large and heavy in proportion to the rest of its body, the head is the most often injured part of the child's body. A child injured as the result of force or a blow may also have damage to the organs in the abdominal and chest cavities. Such damage can cause severe internal bleeding. A child secured only by a lap belt may have serious abdominal or spinal injuries in a car crash. Try to find out what happened, because a severely injured child may not immediately show signs of injury.

To avoid some of the needless deaths of children associated with motor vehicle crashes, laws have been enacted requiring that children ride in safety seats or wear safety belts. As a result, more children's lives are saved. You may have to check and care for an injured child

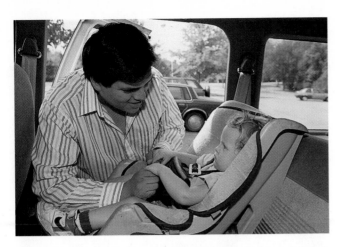

Figure 20-5 You may have to check and care for an injured child while he or she is in a safety seat.

while he or she is in a safety seat (Fig. 20-5). A safety seat does not normally pose any problems while you are checking a child. Leave the child in the seat if the seat has not been damaged. If the child is to be transported to a medical facility for examination, he or she can often be safely secured in the safety seat for transport.

Illness

Certain signs and symptoms in an infant or child can indicate specific problems. Often these problems are not life threatening, but some can be. A high fever in a child often indicates some form of infection. In a young child, even a minor infection can result in a rather high fever, which is often defined as a temperature above 103 degrees F (40 degrees C). Prolonged or excessively high fever can result in seizures (see Chapter 14). Your initial care for a child with a high fever is to gently cool the child. Remove excessive clothing or blankets, and sponge the child with lukewarm water. Call a physician at once. *Do not give the child aspirin.* For a child, taking aspirin can result in an extremely serious medical condition called Reye's syndrome. See Chapter 5 for details on respiratory problems in infants and children.

Poisoning

Poisoning is the fifth largest cause of unintentional death in the United States for people ages 1 to 24. For the younger of these victims, mainly children under 5 years of age, poisoning often occurs from ingesting household products or medications. Care for poisoning is discussed in Chapter 15, and how to help prevent poison-

ing of children in the home is discussed in Chapters 15 and 23.

Child abuse

At some point, you may encounter a situation involving an injured child in which you have reason to suspect child abuse. *Child abuse* is the physical, psychological, or sexual assault of a child resulting in injury and emotional trauma. Child abuse involves an injury or a pattern of injuries that do not result from a mishap. The child's injuries cannot be logically explained, or a caregiver or parent gives an inconsistent or suspicious account of how the injuries occurred.

The signs of child abuse include—

- An injury that does not fit the description of what caused the injury.
- Obvious or suspected fractures in a child less than 2 years of age; any unexplained fractures.
- Injuries in various stages of healing, especially bruises and burns.
- Bruises and burns in unusual shapes, such as bruises shaped like belt buckles or burns the size of a cigarette tip.
- Unexplained lacerations or abrasions, especially to the mouth, lips, and eyes.
- Injuries to the genitalia; pain when the child sits down.
- More injuries than are common for a child of the same age.

When caring for a child who may have been abused, your first priority is to care for the child's injuries or illness. An abused child may be frightened, hysterical, or withdrawn. He or she may be unwilling to talk about the incident in an attempt to protect the abuser. If you suspect abuse, explain your concerns to responding police officers or EMTs, if possible.

If you think you have reasonable cause to believe that abuse has occurred, you can report your suspicions to a community or state agency, such as the Department of Social Services, the Department of Children and Family Services, or Child Protective Services. You may be afraid to report suspected child abuse because you do not wish to get involved or are afraid of getting sued. However, in most states, when you make a report in good faith, you are immune from any civil or criminal liability or penalty, even if you made a mistake. In this instance,

SIDS

"For the first few months, I would lie awake in bed at night and wonder if she was still breathing. I mean you just never know. I couldn't get to sleep until I checked on her at least once." This is how one mother described her first experience with parenting.

Sudden Infant Death Syndrome (SIDS) is the sudden, unexpected, and unexplained death of apparently healthy babies. It is the major cause of death for infants between the ages of 1 month and 1 year. In the United States, SIDS, sometimes called crib death, is responsible for the death of about 7000 infants each year.

Because it cannot be predicted or prevented, SIDS causes many new parents to feel anxious. With no warning signs or symptoms, a sleeping infant can stop breathing and never wake up again. Parents and other family members of SIDS victims often have trouble dealing with this traumatic event. Along with the stress of mourning their loss, they endure tremendous feelings of guilt, believing that they should have been able to prevent the child's death.

Researchers are working to find the cause(s) of SIDS. At this time, several risk factors—characteristics that occur more often in SIDS victims than in normal babies—have been discovered. Yet these risk factors are not causes and cannot be used to predict which infants will die. For example, 95 percent of SIDS deaths occur in infants between 2 and 4 months of age, so being in this age group is a risk factor. Other risk factors for SIDS include smoking during pregnancy, first pregnancy under 20 years of age, several children already born to the mother, a baby with a low birth weight, and a baby with a low growth rate during the mother's pregnancy.

The best prevention for SIDS, as well as many other infant diseases, is for pregnant women to practice healthy behaviors while pregnant. They should get proper prenatal care, eat a balanced diet, not smoke or drink alcoholic beverages, and get adequate rest and exercise.

Some basic facts about SIDS:

- 90 percent of SIDS deaths occur while the infant is asleep.
- SIDS deaths can occur between the ages of 2 weeks and 18 months. Ninety-five percent of SIDS deaths occur between 2 and 4 months of age.
- The majority of SIDS deaths occur in fall and winter.
- Between 30 and 50 percent of SIDS victims have minor respiratory or gastrointestinal infections at the time of death.
- SIDS occurs slightly more often in boys than in girls.

For more information, call the National SIDS Resource Center at (703) 821-8955, ext. 249 or 474.

Sources

National SIDS Resources Center (formerly National SIDS Clearinghouse): *Fact sheets: SIDS information for the EMT,* McLean, VA, 1990.

Department of Health and Human Services, Health Resources and Services Administration, Maternal and Child Health Bureau: *Information exchange: newsletter of the national SIDS clearinghouse,* IE32, July 1991.

"good faith" means that you honestly believe that abuse has occurred or the potential for abuse exists and a prudent and reasonable person in the same position would also honestly believe abuse has occurred or the potential for abuse exists. You do not need to identify yourself when you report child abuse, although your report will have more credibility if you do.

Sudden infant death syndrome (SIDS)

Sudden infant death syndrome (SIDS) is a disorder that causes seemingly healthy infants to stop breathing while they sleep. SIDS is a leading cause of death for infants between 1 month and 1 year of age. By the time the infant's condition has been discovered, he or she will be in cardiac arrest. Make sure someone has called EMS personnel or call yourself. Give the infant CPR until EMS personnel arrive.

An incident involving a severely ill or injured infant or child or one who has died can be emotionally upsetting. After such an episode, find someone you trust with whom you can talk about the experience and express your feelings. If you continue to be distressed, seek some professional counseling. The feelings engendered by such incidents need to be dealt with and understood or they can result in serious stress reactions. For more information on stress, see Chapter 23.

OLDER ADULTS

Older adults, or the elderly, are generally considered those people over 65 years of age. They are quickly becoming the fastest growing age group in the United States. A major reason is an increase in life expectancy because of medical advancements and improvements in health care and knowledge. Since 1900, life expectancy has increased by 57 percent. For example, in 1900, the average life expectancy was 49 years. Today, the average life expectancy is over 75 years.

Normal aging brings about some changes. People age at different rates, however, and so do their organs and body parts. A person may have a "young" heart but "old" skin, for example, and someone with wrinkled, fragile skin may have strong bones or excellent respiratory function.

Figure 20-6   Speak to an elderly victim at eye level so that he or she can see or hear you more clearly.

Overall, however, body function generally declines as we age, with some changes beginning as early as age 30. The lungs become less efficient, so older people are at high risk of developing pneumonia and other lung diseases. The amount of blood pumped by the heart with each beat decreases, and the heart rate slows. The blood vessels harden, causing increased work for the heart. Hearing and vision usually decline, often causing some degree of sight and hearing loss. Reflexes become slower, and arthritis may affect joints, causing movement to become painful. Four out of five older adults develop some sort of chronic condition or disease.

Checking an Older Adult

To check an ill or injured older adult, attempt to learn the person's name and use it when you speak to him or her. Consider using Mrs., Mr., or Ms. as a sign of respect. Get at the person's eye level so that he or she can see and hear you more clearly (Fig. 20-6). If the person seems confused at first, the confusion may be the result of impaired vision or hearing. If he or she usually wears eyeglasses and cannot find them, try to locate them. Speak slowly and clearly and look at the person's face while you talk. Notice if he or she has a hearing aid. Someone who is dependent on glasses to see is likely to be very anxious without them. If the person is truly confused, try to find out if the confusion is the result of the injury or a condition he or she already has. Information from family members or bystanders is frequently helpful. The person may be afraid of falling, so if he or she is standing, offer an arm or hand. Remember that an older person may need to move very slowly.

Try to find out what medications the person is taking and if he or she has any medical conditions so that you can tell EMS personnel. Look for a medical alert bracelet that will give you the victim's name and address and information about any specific condition the victim has. Be aware that an elderly person may not recognize the signs and symptoms of a serious condition. An elderly person may also minimize any signs and symptoms for fear of losing his or her independence or being placed in a nursing home.

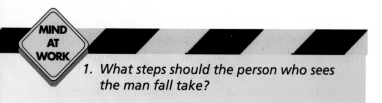

MIND AT WORK

1. *What steps should the person who sees the man fall take?*

Special Situations

Physical and mental changes can occur as a result of aging. As a result of these changes, many older adults are particularly susceptible to certain problems. These problems may require you to adapt your way of communicating and be aware of certain potential conditions.

Falls

Falls are the sixth leading cause of death for people over 65 years of age. As a result of slower reflexes, failing eyesight and hearing, arthritis, and problems such as unsteady balance and movement, older adults are at increased risk of falls. Falls frequently result in fractures because the bones become weaker and more brittle with age.

Head injuries

An older adult is also at greater risk of serious head injuries. As we age, the size of the brain decreases. This decrease results in more space between the surface of the brain and the inside of the skull. This space allows more movement of the brain within the skull, which can increase the likelihood of serious head injury. Occasionally, an older adult may not develop the signs and symptoms of a head injury until days after a fall. Therefore, unless you know the cause of a behavior change, you

should always suspect a head injury as a possible cause of unusual behavior in an elderly person, especially if the victim has had a fall or a blow to the head.

Confusion

The elderly are at increased risk of altered thinking patterns and confusion. Some of this change is the result of aging. Certain diseases, such as ***Alzheimer's disease,*** affect the brain, resulting in impaired memory and thinking and altered behavior. Confusion that comes on suddenly, however, may be the result of medication, even a medication the person has been taking regularly. An ill or injured person who has problems seeing or hearing may also become confused when ill or injured. This problem increases when the person is in an unfamiliar environment. A head injury can also result in confusion.

Confusion can be a sign of a medical emergency. An elderly person with pneumonia, for example, may not run a fever, have chest pain, or be coughing, but because sufficient oxygen is not reaching the brain, the person may be confused. An elderly person can have a serious infection without fever, pain, or nausea. An elderly person having a heart attack may not have chest pain, pale or ashen skin, or other classic signs and symptoms, but may be restless, short of breath, and confused.

Depression is common in older adults. A depressed older adult may seem confused at first. A depressed person may also have symptoms, such as sudden shortness of breath or chest pains, with no apparent cause. Whatever the reason for any confusion, do not talk down to the victim or treat the victim like a child.

Problems with heat and cold

An elderly person is more susceptible to heat and cold. The person may be unable to feel temperature extremes because his or her body may no longer regulate temperature effectively. Body temperature may change rapidly to a dangerously high or low level.

The body of an elderly person retains heat because of a decreased ability to sweat and the impaired ability of the circulatory system to adjust to heat. If an elderly person shows signs of heat-related illness, take his or her temperature, and if it is above normal, call 9-1-1 or the local emergency number. Slowly cool the person off with a lukewarm sponge bath, and provide care as described in Chapter 18. If you find an elderly person hot to the touch, unable to speak, and unconscious or semi-conscious, call EMS personnel immediately. Put the person in a cooler location if possible, but do not try to quickly cool the person with cold water or put him or her in front of a fan or air conditioner.

An elderly person may become chilled and suffer hypothermia simply by sitting in a draft or in front of a fan or air conditioner. Hypothermia can occur at any time of the year in temperature that is 65 degrees F (18 degrees C) or less. People can go on for several days suffering from mild hypothermia that they do not recognize. The older person with mild hypothermia will want to lie down frequently, which will lower the body temperature even further. If you suspect hypothermia, feel the person's skin to see if it is cold. Take the person's temperature. If his or her temperature is below 98.6 degrees F (37 degrees C), put the person in a warm room, wrap him or her in one or two blankets, give the person warm, decaffeinated, and non-alcoholic liquid to drink, and call a physician for advice. However, if the body temperature is below 95 degrees F (35 degrees C), call EMS personnel. This condition is life-threatening. Do not apply any direct heat, such as a heating pad, electric blanket turned high, or a hot bath. Doing so will cause blood flow to increase to the area being heated and take blood away from the vital organs.

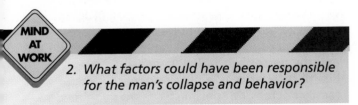

MIND AT WORK

2. *What factors could have been responsible for the man's collapse and behavior?*

PEOPLE WITH DISABILITIES

The absence or impairment of motor, sensory, or mental function is called a **disability. Impairment** is damage or reduction in quality, quantity, value, or strength. People who have a disability may be impaired in one or more functions. The United States Department of Health and Human Services estimates that over 36 million people in the United States have disabili-

ties. With many disabled people, communication can be a major challenge in finding out what has happened and what might be wrong in an emergency situation.

Physical Disability

Physical disability includes impairment of **motor function,** or movement, and of **sensory function,** impairment of one or more of the senses, including sight, hearing, taste, smell, and touch. People may be impaired in one or both of these functions.

General hints for approaching an ill or injured person who you have reason to believe is in some way disabled include the following:

- Speak to the person before touching him or her.
- Ask "How can I help?" or "Do you need help?"
- Ask for assistance and information from the person who has the disability—he or she has been living with the disability and best understands it. If the person is not able to communicate, ask any of his or her available family members, friends, or companions.
- Do not remove any braces, canes, other physical support, eyeglasses, or hearing aids. Removal of these items puts the person at a disadvantage of losing necessary physical support for the body.
- Look for medical alert jewelry at the person's wrist or neck.
- A person with a disability may have an animal assistant, such as a guide dog or hearing dog. Be aware that this animal may be protective of the person in an emergency situation. Someone may need to calm and restrain the animal. Allow the animal to stay with the person if possible, which will help reassure them both.

Hearing impairment

Hearing impairment is a partial or total loss of hearing. Some people are born with impaired hearing. Hearing impairment can also result from an injury or illness affecting the ear, the nerves leading from the brain to the ear, or the brain itself. You may not initially be aware that the ill or injured person is hearing impaired. Often the victim will tell you, either in speech or by pointing to the ear and shaking the head, "No." Some people carry a card stating

Memories

"Joe, I'm really beginning to worry about your dad. At first it was just little things—like forgetting where he put his glasses and what day it was and how to work the VCR, but now it's worse. Last week he went out and Mrs. Chung found him wandering the street and brought him home. He couldn't remember where he lived or who he was! Yesterday he just walked out while we were talking. Later, he didn't remember anything about it. It's not safe for him to be out by himself anymore. Maybe there's something that will make him better. I just don't know what I'm going to do!"

Joe's dad needs several medical examinations to try to determine the reasons for his memory decline. Perhaps he has a condition that can be reversed or helped. But the chances are high that he has a condition known as Alzheimer's disease. At one time considered a rare disorder, today Alzheimer's disease is the most common cause of dementia. Dementia is the severe enough loss of intellectual functions, such as thinking, remembering, and reasoning, to interfere with a person's daily activities.

Alzheimer's disease affects an estimated 4 million American adults and results in 100,000 deaths annually. Most victims are over 65; however, Alzheimer's disease can strike people in their 40s and 50s. Men and women are affected almost equally (*Alzheimer's disease fact sheet*). At this time, scientists are still looking for the cause of Alzheimer's disease. A confirmed diagnosis of the disease can only be made by examining the victim's brain tissue after death. While there are no treatments to stop or reverse the mental decline from Alzheimer's disease, several drugs are available now to help manage some of the symptoms.

Signals of Alzheimer's disease develop gradually. They include confusion, progressive memory loss, and changes in personality, behavior, and the ability to think and communicate. Eventually, victims of Alzheimer's disease become totally unable to care for themselves (*If you think someone you know has Alzheimer's disease*).

There are a number of disorders that have symptoms similar to those of Alzheimer's disease. Some of them can be treated. Therefore, it is very important that anyone who is experiencing memory loss or confusion have a thorough medical examination.

Most people with illnesses such as Alzheimer's disease are cared for by their families for much of their illness. Providing care at home requires careful planning. The home has to be made safe, and routines must be set up for daily activities, such as mealtimes, personal care, and leisure.

Services That Help

It is important for anyone caring for a person with Alzheimer's disease, or a related problem, to realize that they are not alone. There are people and organizations that can help both you and the person with Alzheimer's disease. For health care services, a physician, perhaps your family doctor or a specialist, can give you medical advice, including help with difficult behavior and personality changes.

that they are hearing impaired. You may see a hearing aid in a person's ear.

The biggest obstacle you must overcome in caring for a person with a hearing impairment is communication. You will need to figure out how to get that person's consent to give care, and you need to find out what the problem may be. Often the ill or injured person can read lips. Position yourself where the victim can see your face clearly. Look straight at the victim while you speak, and speak slowly. Do not modify the way you form words. Do not turn your face

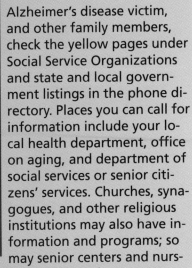

If you are caring for an Alzheimer's disease victim living at home, you may need help with some basic services such as nutrition and transportation. A visiting nurse or nutritionist can help you, and a volunteer program like Meals on Wheels may be helpful. Volunteer or paid transportation services may also be available to take Alzheimer's disease victims to and from health facilities, adult day care, and other programs.

Visiting nurses, home health aides, and homemakers can come to your home and provide help with health care, bathing and dressing, shopping, and cooking. Many adult day care centers provide recreational activities designed for people with Alzheimer's disease. Some hospitals, nursing homes, and other facilities may take in Alzheimer's disease victims for short stays. For Alzheimer's disease victims who can no longer live at home, group homes or foster homes may be available. Nursing homes offer more skilled nursing, and some specialize in the care of victims of Alzheimer's disease or similar diseases. A few hospice programs accept Alzheimer's disease victims who are nearing the end of their lives. Explore to find out which, if any, services are covered by Medicare, Medicaid, Social Security disability, or veterans' benefits in your state. A lawyer or a social worker may be able to help you.

To locate services that can help you, the Alzheimer's disease victim, and other family members, check the yellow pages under Social Service Organizations and state and local government listings in the phone directory. Places you can call for information include your local health department, office on aging, and department of social services or senior citizens' services. Churches, synagogues, and other religious institutions may also have information and programs; so may senior centers and nursing home staffs, hospital geriatric departments, doctors, nurses, social workers, and counselors. Your location may have a chapter of the Alzheimer's Association nearby. To locate a chapter near you, call the Association's 24-hour, toll-free number: 1-800-272-3900. This organization has chapters and support groups across the country from which you can get information and guidance.

Sources
Alzheimer's Disease and Related Disorders Association, Inc: *Alzheimer's disease fact sheet*, 1990.
Alzheimer's Disease and Related Disorders Association, Inc: *If you think someone you know has Alzheimer's disease*, 1990.
Alzheimer's Disease and Related Disorders Association, Inc: *Alzheimer's disease: services you may need*, 1990.

away while you speak. Many people with a hearing impairment, however, do not read lips. Using gestures and writing messages on paper may be the most effective way you can communicate in an emergency. If you know sign language, use it. Some people who are hearing impaired have a machine called a Telecommunications Device for the Deaf (TDD). You can use this device to type messages and questions to the victim, and the victim can type replies to you (Fig. 20-7, *A-D*). Many people who have hearing impairments can speak, some dis-

Figure 20-7   Communicate with a hearing-impaired victim in the best way possible:
A, signing; **B,** lip reading; **C,** writing; **D,** TDD.

tinctly, some not so clearly. If you have trouble understanding, ask the person to repeat what he or she said. Do not pretend to understand. If the person cannot speak, use written messages.

Vision impairment

Vision impairment is a partial or total loss of sight. Vision impairment can occur from many causes. Some people are born visually impaired. Others become visually impaired as a result of disease or injury. Vision impairment is not necessarily a problem with the eyes. It can occur from problems with the vision centers in the brain.

People with vision impairment are generally not embarrassed by their condition. It is no more difficult to communicate verbally with a person who has a partial or total loss of sight than with someone who can see. You do not need to speak loudly or in overly simple terms. Checking a person who has a vision impairment is like checking a victim who has good vi-

sion. The victim may not be able to tell you certain things about how an injury occurred but can usually give you a generally accurate account based on his or her interpretation of sound and touch.

When caring for a person with a vision impairment, help to reassure him or her by explaining what is going on and what you are doing. If you must move a visually impaired person who can walk, stand beside the person and have him or her hold on to your arm (Fig. 20-8). Walk at a normal pace, and alert the person to any obstacles in the way, such as stairs, identifying whether to step up or down. If the person has a seeing eye dog, try to keep them together. Ask the person to tell you how to handle the dog or ask him or her to do it.

Motor impairment

The person with ***motor impairment*** is unable to move normally. He or she may be missing a body part or have a problem with the

Figure 20-8 If a person with a vision impairment can walk, stand beside the person and have him hold your arm.

bones or muscles or the nerves controlling them. Causes of motor impairment include stroke, **muscular dystrophy, multiple sclerosis,** paralysis, **cerebral palsy,** or loss of a limb. In caring for an ill or injured person with motor impairment, be aware that the person may view accepting help as failure and may refuse your help to prove that he or she does not need it.

Determining which problems are preexisting and which are the result of immediate injury or illness can be difficult. If you care for all problems you detect as if they are new, you can hardly go wrong. Checking one side of the body against the other in your check for nonlife-threatening conditions may not be effective with a person with motor impairment, since body parts may not look normal as a result of a specific condition.

Mental impairment

Mental, or *cognitive, function* includes the brain's capacity to reason and process information. A person with mental impairment has problems performing these operations. Some types of mental impairment are genetic, or, such as **Down syndrome,** are genetic alter-

ations. Others result from injuries or infections that occur during pregnancy, shortly after birth, or later in life. Some causes are never determined.

You may not be able to determine if a victim is mentally impaired, or it may be obvious. Approach the person as you would any other person in his or her age group. When you speak, try to determine the other person's level of understanding. If the person appears not to understand you, rephrase what you were saying in simpler terms. Listen carefully to what the person says. People who are mentally impaired often lead very orderly and structured lives. A sudden illness or injury can disrupt the order in a person's life and cause a great deal of anxiety and fear. Take time to explain who you are and what you are going to do. Offer reassurance. Try to gain the victim's trust. If a parent, guardian, or caregiver is present, ask that person to help you care for the person.

LANGUAGE BARRIERS

Another reason for an uncomprehending look when you speak to a victim is that the person may not understand English or another language you may speak. Getting the consent of a victim with whom you have a language barrier can be a problem. Find out if any bystanders speak the victim's language and can help translate. Do your best to communicate nonverbally. Use gestures and facial expressions. If the person is in pain, he or she will probably be anxious to let you know where that pain is. Watch his or her gestures and facial expressions carefully. When you speak to the victim, speak slowly and avoid the inclination to yell or speak very loudly. The victim probably has no trouble hearing you. When you call EMS personnel, explain that you are having difficulty communicating with the victim and say what nationality you believe the victim is or what language you believe the victim speaks. EMS may have someone available, such as a dispatcher, who can help with communication. If the victim has a life-threatening condition, such as severe bleeding, consent is implied. The victim will most likely be willing for you to give care in such case, anyhow.

SPECIAL SITUATIONS

Situations may arise that you should handle with extreme caution. In certain instances, your first reaction may be to go to the aid of a victim. Instead, you should call 9-1-1 and stay at a safe distance until the scene is secured. Do not enter the scene of a suicide. If you happen to be on the scene when an unarmed person threatens suicide, call EMS personnel and the police. If the scene is safe, listen to the person and try to keep him or her talking until help arrives. Do not argue with the person. Leave or do not enter any scene where there is a weapon or where a crime has been committed. Do not approach the scene of a physical or sexual assault. These are crime scenes. Phone 9-1-1 and stay at a safe distance.

Sometimes a victim may be hostile or angry. A victim's rage or hostility may be caused by the injury, pain, or fear. Some victims are afraid of losing control, which causes them to act resentful and suspicious. Hostile behavior may also result from the use of alcohol or other drugs, lack of oxygen, or a medical condition. Once a victim realizes that you are there to help and are not a threat, the hostility usually goes away. If a victim refuses your care or threatens you, withdraw. Never try to argue with or restrain a victim. Call EMS personnel if someone has not already done so.

Uninjured family members may also display anger. They may pressure you to do something immediately. Often this anger stems from panic, anxiety, or guilt. Try to remain calm, and be sympathetic but firm. Explain what you are going to do. If possible, find a way that family members can help, such as by comforting the victim.

SUMMARY

No two emergency situations are alike. Situations involving people with special needs, problems, and characteristics require your awareness and understanding. To give effective care to an older adult, an infant or child, a person with a disability, or anyone with whom communication is a challenge. You may need to adapt your approach and your attitude. Situations may also occur in which you should not intervene. If a situation is in any way unsafe, do not approach the victim and if you have already approached, withdraw. If the situation is a crime scene, stay away and phone for appropriate help.

Answers to Application Questions

1. He should check the scene for safety. If traffic is very threatening, he might have to help the man move onto the sidewalk. He should ask a bystander to call EMS personnel; he should try to reassure the man and try to control the bleeding if it is severe, keeping a barrier between himself and the victim's blood, if possible. Try to keep the man from moving, as much as possible.

2. Depending on the weather, he could have been affected by heat or cold. He could have a sudden illness, such as a heart attack, stroke, or a seizure. He could have fainted. He could be confused, mentally impaired, unable to hear, or have poor vision.

STUDY QUESTIONS

1. Match each term with the correct definition.
   - a. Sensory function
   - b. Child abuse
   - c. Alzheimer's disease
   - d. Disability
   - e. Impairment
   - f. Motor impairment

   _____ The absence or impairment of motor, sensory, or mental function.

   _____ A progressive, degenerative disease that affects the brain, resulting in impaired memory, thinking, and behavior.

   _____ The total or partial inability to move or to use a body part.

   _____ The physical, psychological, or sexual assault of a child, resulting in injury and emotional trauma.

   _____ Damage or reduction in quality, quantity, value, or strength.

   _____ The ability to see, hear, touch, taste, and smell.

2. You are walking to the mailbox. A child on a skateboard suddenly rolls into the street from between two parked cars. A car, fortunately moving very slowly, strikes the child, knocking him to the pavement. Three people in the vicinity run to the scene. The driver gets out of the car, looking shocked and stunned. Describe in order the steps you would take.

3. A neighbor phones saying her grandmother has fallen and is lying on the bathroom floor. She asks you to come help. When you get there, the grandmother is conscious but unable to get up. She does not recognize her granddaughter. She says her left leg and hip hurt. What steps would you take?

In questions 4 through 8, circle the letter of the correct answer.

4. In which of the following ways should you move a person with vision impairment who can walk?

   a. Grasp the victim's arm or belt, and support the victim as you walk.
   b. Walk in front of the victim, and have him or her keep a hand on your shoulder.
   c. Walk behind the person with a hand on the person's back.
   d. Walk beside the person, and let him or her grasp your arm while you are walking.

5. The best position you can take in talking to an ill or injured young child is—

   a. Holding the child in your arms or lap.
   b. At eye level with the child.
   c. Standing up looking down at the child.
   d. Behind the child out of direct sight.

6. Which should you do if an ill or injured elderly person appears to be confused?

   a. Assume the person is in a permanent state of confusion.
   b. Inquire about any medications the person is taking.
   c. Assume the person has fallen and injured his or her head.
   d. All of the above.

7. What should you do if you become aware that a physical assault has taken place?

   a. Call EMS personnel and then approach the victim.
   b. Call EMS personnel and do not enter the scene.
   c. Approach the victim and have someone call EMS personnel.
   d. Assess the victim for life-threatening conditions.

8. A small child in a car seat is in an automobile collision. How would you check the child?

   a. Remove the child from the car seat.
   b. Ask any relative of the child who is on the scene to remove the child from the seat.
   c. Check the child while the child is in the car seat.
   d. Wait until EMS personnel arrive.

In questions 9 through 11, write the correct answer on the line.

9. You enter the apartment of an elderly person and find him lying down and semi-conscious. His skin is hot to the touch. The room is very warm and stuffy. This person could be suffering from _____.

10. If an elderly person's body temperature is below 95 degrees F (35 degrees C), you should immediately _____.

11. A conscious person who does not appear to hear or understand what you say may be _____, _____, or may _____.

12. List four possible causes of confusion in an elderly person.

Answers are listed in Appendix A.

CHAPTER 21

Childbirth

WHAT YOU SHOULD LEARN

After reading this chapter, you should be able to—

1. Describe the four stages of labor.

2. Identify six factors you need to know to determine the mother's condition before the birth.

3. Identify equipment and supplies needed to assist with the delivery of a baby.

4. Describe two techniques the expectant mother can use to cope with labor pain and discomfort.

5. Describe how to assist with the delivery of a baby.

6. Identify the two priorities of care for a newborn.

7. Describe three steps to take in caring for the mother after delivery.

8. Identify four possible complications of childbirth that require EMS care.

9. Define the key terms for this chapter.

As you promised, you head out to check up on the wife of your best friend, Gus. Sadie is expecting their first child in a couple of weeks. They live a ways out of town, and Gus had to go away for a day or two. You've been trying to call Sadie for hours, but all you get is a busy signal. Getting there takes a little longer than usual because a heavy thunderstorm a few hours before had not improved the dirt road. As you approach the house, you notice that the front door is partly open. "Sadie," you yell, "It's Jim."

"Jim," Sadie calls, "I'm in here." You go into the bedroom and there's Sadie on the bed. You can see some bloody fluid on the bedspread. Sadie grimaces with the beginning of the next contraction. "I'm sure glad to see you, Jim," she gasps. "I guess this baby's not waiting for her daddy to get home and the phone isn't working."

Introduction

Someday you may be faced with having to assist with childbirth. If you have never seen or experienced childbirth, your expectations probably consist of what others have told you.

Terms such as exhausting, stressful, exciting, fulfilling, painful, and scary are sometimes used to describe a planned childbirth, one that occurs in the hospital or at home under the supervision of a health care provider. If you find yourself assisting with the delivery of a baby, however, it is probably not happening in a planned situation. Therefore, your feelings, as well as those of the expectant mother, may be intensified by fear of the unexpected or the possibility that something might go wrong.

Take comfort in knowing that things rarely go wrong. Childbirth is a natural process. Thousands of children all over the world are born each day, without complications, in areas where no medical assistance is available.

By following a few simple steps, you can effectively assist in the birth process. This chapter will help you better understand the birth process, how to assist with the delivery of a baby, how to provide care for both the mother and newborn after the delivery, as well as how to recognize complications requiring care from EMS personnel.

PREGNANCY

Pregnancy begins when an egg (ovum) is fertilized by a sperm, forming an **embryo.** The embryo implants itself within the mother's **uterus,** a pear-shaped organ that lies at the top center of the pelvis. The embryo is surrounded by the **amniotic sac.** This fluid-filled sac is also called the "bag of waters." The fluid helps protect the baby from injury and infection.

As the embryo grows, its organs and body parts develop. After about 8 weeks, the embryo is called a **fetus.** To continue to develop properly, the fetus must receive nutrients. The fetus receives these nutrients from the mother through a specialized organ attached to the lining of the uterus called the **placenta.** The placenta is attached to the fetus by a flexible structure called the **umbilical cord.** The fetus will continue to develop for approximately 40 weeks (about 9 months), at which time the birth process will begin (Fig. 21-1).

Key Terms

Amniotic sac: A fluid-filled sac that encloses, bathes, and protects the developing baby; commonly called the bag of waters.

Birth canal: The passageway from the uterus to the vaginal opening through which a baby passes during birth.

Cervix: A short tube at the upper end of the birth canal; the opening of the uterus.

Contraction: The rhythmic tightening of muscles in the uterus during labor.

Crowning: The point in labor when the baby's head is visible at the opening of the vagina.

Labor: The birth process; beginning with the contraction of the uterus and dilation of the cervix and ending with the stabilization and recovery of the mother.

Placenta: An organ attached to the uterus and unborn child through which nutrients are delivered to the baby; expelled after the baby is delivered.

Umbilical cord: A flexible structure that attaches the placenta to the unborn child, allowing for the passage of blood, nutrients, and waste.

Uterus: A pear-shaped organ in a woman's pelvis in which an embryo forms and develops into a baby.

Vagina: *See* Birth canal.

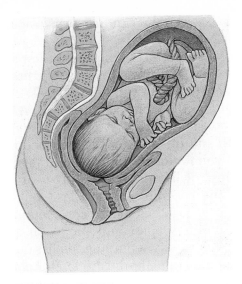

Figure 21-1   Mother and fetus at 40 weeks.

THE BIRTH PROCESS

The birth process begins with the onset of labor. **Labor** is the final phase of pregnancy. It is a process in which many systems work together to bring about birth. Labor begins with a rhythmic contraction of the uterus. As these contractions continue, they dilate the **cervix**—a short tube at the upper end of the **birth canal,** or **vagina.** The birth canal is the passageway from the uterus to the vaginal opening. As soon as the cervix is sufficiently dilated, the baby travels from the uterus through the birth canal. The baby emerges from the vaginal opening at the lower end of the canal. For first-time mothers, this process normally takes between 12 and 24 hours. Subsequent babies are usually delivered more quickly.

Labor

Labor has four distinct stages. The length and intensity of each stage vary.

Stage one—preparation

In the first stage, the mother's body prepares for the birth. This stage covers the period of time from the first contraction until the cervix is fully dilated. Most of the hours of labor are spent in stage one. A **contraction** is a rhythmic tightening of the muscles in the uterus. It is like a wave. It begins gently, rises to a peak of intensity, then drops off and subsides. The muscles then relax, and there is a break before the next contraction starts. As the time for delivery approaches, the contractions become closer together, last longer, and feel stronger. Normally, when contractions are less than 3 minutes apart, childbirth is near.

Stage two—delivery of the baby

The second stage of labor involves the delivery of the baby. It begins once the cervix is completely dilated and ends from 15 minutes to 3 hours after the baby moves into the birth canal with the birth. The mother makes pushing efforts by tightening the muscles to assist the baby's progress. The baby's head becomes visible as it emerges from the vagina. The moment in labor when the top of the head begins to emerge is called **crowning** (Fig. 21-2). When

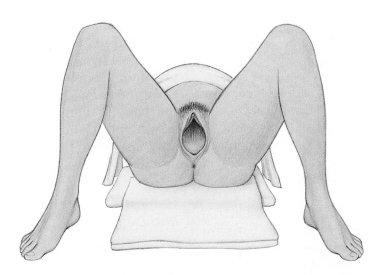

Figure 21-2   When crowning begins, birth is imminent.

crowning occurs, birth is imminent and you must be prepared to receive the baby.

Stage three—delivery of the placenta

The third stage of labor begins once the baby's body emerges. During this stage, the placenta usually separates from the wall of the uterus and is expelled from the birth canal. This process normally occurs within 30 minutes of the delivery of the baby.

Stage four—recovery

The final stage of labor involves the initial recovery and monitoring of the mother following childbirth. Normally, this stage lasts for approximately 1 hour. During this time, the uterus contracts to control bleeding and the mother begins to recover from the physical and emotional stress that occurred during childbirth.

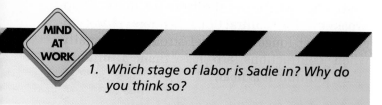

MIND AT WORK

1. Which stage of labor is Sadie in? Why do you think so?

Assessing Labor

In the event you must provide care for a pregnant woman, you will want to determine whether she is in labor. If she is in labor, you should determine in what stage of labor she may be and whether she expects any complications. You should find out if anyone has called EMS personnel and if not, make the call immediately. You can determine these and other factors by asking a few key questions and making some observations. Ask about the following factors:

- Have EMS personnel been called? If so, how long ago and what was the response?
- Is there a bloody discharge? This pink or light red, thick discharge from the vagina is the mucous plug that falls from the cervix as it begins to dilate, also signaling the onset of labor.
- Has the amniotic sac ruptured? When the sac ruptures, fluid flows from the vagina in a sudden gush or a trickle. Some women think they have lost control of their bladder. The breaking of the sac usually signals the beginning of labor, but not always. People

often describe the rupture of the sac as "the water breaking."

- Is this the first pregnancy? The first stage of labor normally takes longer with first pregnancies than with subsequent ones.
- What are the contractions like? Are they very close together? Are they strong? The length and intensity of the contractions will give you valuable information about the progress of labor. As labor progresses, contractions become stronger, last longer, and are closer together. When contractions are 2 to 5 minutes apart and 45 to 60 seconds long, the baby is beginning to pass out of the uterus and into the birth canal. Labor may continue from 15 minutes to 3 hours.
- Does she expect any complications?
- Does she have the urge to bear down, or push? If the expectant mother expresses a strong urge to push, this signals that labor is far along.
- Is the baby crowning? If the baby's head is visible, the baby is about to be born.

PREPARING FOR DELIVERY

Preparing for delivery involves both preparing yourself and helping the mother cope with labor and delivery.

Preparing Yourself

Although childbirth can be exciting, it can also be frightening to witness. Childbirth is messy. It involves a discharge of watery, sometimes bloody, fluid at stages one and two of labor and what appears to be a rather large loss of blood after stage two. Try not to be alarmed at the loss of blood. It is a normal part of the birth process. Only bleeding that cannot be controlled after the baby is born is a problem. Take a deep breath and try to relax. Remember that you are only assisting in the process; the expectant mother is doing all the work.

Helping the Mother Cope With Labor and Delivery

Explain to the expectant mother that the baby is about to be born. Be calm and reassuring. A woman having her first child often feels fear and apprehension about the pain and the condition of the baby. Labor pain ranges from discomfort similar to menstrual cramps to intense pressure or pain. Many women experience something in between. Factors that can increase pain and discomfort during the first stage of labor include—

- Irregular breathing.
- Tensing up because of fear.
- Not knowing what to expect.
- Feeling alone and unsupported.

You can help the expectant mother cope with the discomfort and pain of labor. Begin by reassuring her that you are there to help. If necessary and possible, explain what to expect as labor progresses. Suggest specific physical activities that she can do to relax, such as regulating her breathing. Ask her to breathe in slowly and deeply through the nose and out through the mouth. Ask her to try to focus on one object in the room while regulating her breathing. By staying calm, firm, and confident and offering encouragement, you can help reduce fear and apprehension. Reducing fear will aid in reducing pain and discomfort.

Breathing slowly and deeply in through the nose and out through the mouth during labor can help the expectant mother in several ways:

- It aids muscle relaxation.
- It offers a distraction from the pain of strong contractions as labor progresses.
- It ensures adequate oxygen to both the mother and the baby during labor.

Taking childbirth classes, such as those offered at local hospitals, helps people become more competent in techniques used to help an expectant mother relax. Many expectant mothers also participate in such training, which could greatly simplify your role of assisting with the birth process. Many books and videos on the subject of childbirth are available.

ASSISTING WITH DELIVERY

It is difficult to predict how much time you have before the baby is delivered. However, if the expectant mother says that she feels the need to push or feels as if she has to have a bowel movement, delivery is near.

You should time the expectant mother's contractions from the beginning of one contraction to the beginning of the next. If they are less than 3 minutes apart and last for 45 to 60 seconds, prepare to assist with the delivery of the baby.

Assisting with the delivery of the baby is often a simple process. The expectant mother is doing all the work. She will be pushing down, using certain muscles. Your job is to create a clean environment and to help guide the baby from the birth canal, minimizing injury to the mother and baby. Begin by positioning the mother. She should be lying on her back, with her head and upper back raised, not lying flat. Her legs should be bent, with the knees drawn up and apart (Fig. 21-3, *A*). Positioning the mother in this way will make her more comfortable.

Next, establish a clean environment for delivery. Since it is unlikely that you will have sterile supplies, use items such as clean sheets, blankets, towels, or even clothes. Newspapers, which are very absorbent, can be used if nothing else is available. To make the area around the mother as sanitary as possible, place these items over the mother's abdomen and under her buttocks and legs (Fig. 21-3, *B*). Keep a clean, warm towel or blanket handy to wrap the newborn. Because you will be coming in contact with the mother's and baby's body fluids, be sure to wear disposable latex gloves. If gloves are not available, try to find some other item to use as a barrier, for example, a plastic bag or plastic wrap may be secured around your hands. Put something on over your clothing, if possible, to protect yourself from splashing fluids.

Other items that can be helpful include a bulb syringe to suction secretions from the infant's nose and mouth immediately after birth, gauze pads or sanitary pads to help absorb secretions and vaginal bleeding, and a large plastic bag or towel to hold the placenta after delivery.

As crowning occurs, place a hand on the top of the baby's head and apply light pressure (Fig.

2. What information can Sadie give that will help you to assist with the delivery?

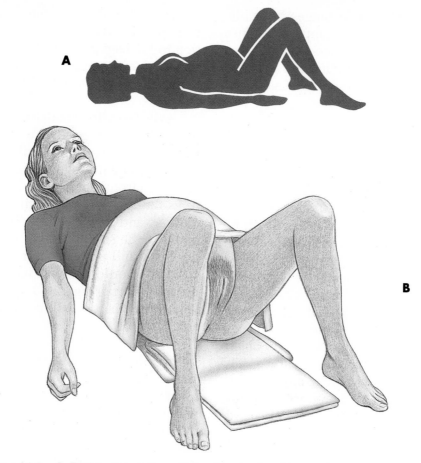

Figure 21-3 **A,** Position the mother with her legs bent and knees drawn up and apart. **B,** Place clean sheets, blankets, towels, or even clothes under the mother.

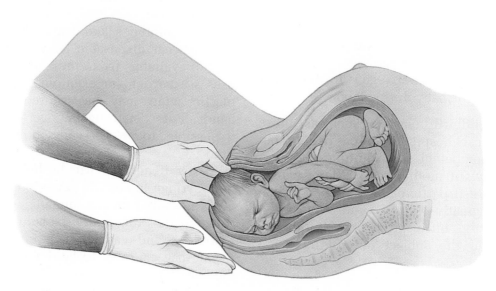

Figure 21-4 Place your hand on top of the baby's head and apply light pressure.

21-4). In this way, you allow the head to emerge slowly, not forcefully. This will help prevent tearing of the vagina and injury to the baby. At this point, the expectant mother should stop pushing. Instruct the mother to concentrate on her breathing techniques. Ask her to pant. This technique will help her stop pushing and help prevent a forceful birth.

Once the head is out, the baby and shoulders should rotate with another push. Support

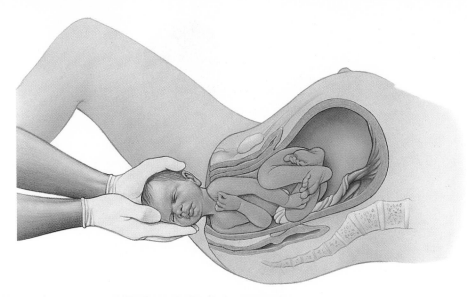

Figure 21-5 As the infant emerges, support the head.

the head (Fig. 21-5). This will enable the shoulders and the rest of the body to pass through the birth canal. Check to see if the umbilical cord is looped around the baby's neck. If it is, gently slip it over the baby's head. If this cannot be done, slip it over the baby's shoulders as they emerge. The baby can slide through the loop.

Guide one shoulder out at a time. Do not pull the baby. As the baby emerges, he or she will be wet and slippery. Use a clean towel to catch the baby. Place the baby on its side, between the mother and you so that you can provide care without fear of dropping the newborn. If possible, note the time the baby was born.

CARING FOR THE NEWBORN AND MOTHER

Your first priority of care when the baby arrives is to take some initial steps of care for him or her. Once these steps are accomplished, you can care for the mother.

Caring for the Newborn

The first few minutes of the baby's life are a difficult transition from life inside the mother's uterus to life outside. You have two priorities at this point. Your first is to see that the baby's airway is open and clear. Since a newborn baby breathes primarily through the nose, it is important to immediately clear the nasal passages and mouth thoroughly. You can do this by using your finger, a gauze pad, or a bulb syringe (Fig. 21-6).

Most babies begin crying and breathing spontaneously. If the baby does not make any sound, stimulate the baby to elicit the crying response by flicking your fingers on the soles of the baby's feet. Crying helps clear the baby's airways of fluids and promotes breathing. If the baby does not begin breathing on his or her own within the first minute after birth, begin rescue breathing. If the baby does not have signs of circulation, begin CPR. You can review these techniques in Chapters 5 and 6.

Your second responsibility to the baby is to maintain normal body temperature. Newborns lose heat quickly; therefore, it is important to keep him or her warm. Dry the newborn and wrap him or her in a clean, warm towel or blanket. Continue to monitor breathing, circulation, and skin color. You may place the child on the mother's abdomen.

Caring for the Mother

You can continue to meet the needs of the newborn while caring for the mother. Help the mother to begin nursing the newborn if possible. This will stimulate the uterus to contract and help slow bleeding. The placenta will still be in the uterus, attached to the baby by the umbilical cord. Contractions of the uterus will usually expel the placenta within 30 minutes. Do not pull on the umbilical cord. Do not worry if the placenta is not expelled soon. Catch the placenta in a clean towel or container. It is not

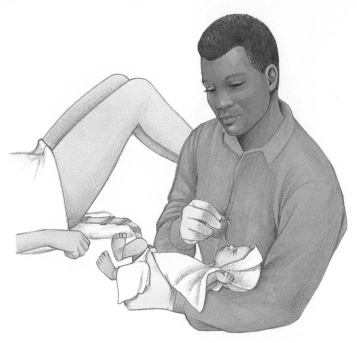

Figure 21-6 A bulb syringe can be used to clear a newborn baby's mouth and nose of any secretions.

necessary to separate the placenta from the newborn by tying and cutting the umbilical cord. In the event that you or another citizen responder must transport the mother and child to the hospital, leave the placenta attached to the newborn and place the placenta in a plastic bag or wrap it in a towel.

Expect some additional vaginal bleeding when the placenta is delivered. Using gauze pads or clean towels, gently clean the mother. Place a sanitary pad or a towel over the vagina. Do not insert anything inside the vagina. Have the mother place her legs together. Feel for a grapefruit-sized mass in the lower abdomen. This is the uterus. Gently massage the lower portion of the abdomen. Massage will cause the uterus to contract and slow bleeding.

Many new mothers experience shock-like signs or symptoms, such as cool, pale, moist skin, shivering, and slight dizziness. Keep the mother positioned on her back. Keep her from getting chilled or overheated, and continue to monitor her condition.

SPECIAL SITUATIONS

Most deliveries are fairly routine with few, if any, surprises or problems. However, you should be aware of certain complications or special situations that can occur.

Complications During Pregnancy

Complications during pregnancy are rare; however, they do occur. One such complication is a **miscarriage,** or **spontaneous abortion.** Since the nature and extent of most complications can only be determined by medical professionals during or following a more complete examination, you should not be concerned with trying to "diagnose" a particular problem. Instead, concern yourself with recognizing signs and symptoms that suggest a serious complication during pregnancy. Two important signs and symptoms you should be concerned about are vaginal bleeding and abdominal pain. Any persistent or profuse vaginal bleeding, or bleeding in which tissue passes through the vagina during pregnancy, is abnormal, as is any abdominal pain.

An expectant mother exhibiting these signs and symptoms needs to receive advanced medical care quickly. While waiting for an ambulance, take steps to minimize shock. These include—

- Helping the woman into the most comfortable position.
- Absorbing bleeding.
- Keeping the woman from becoming chilled or overheated.

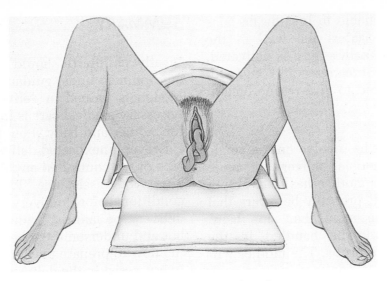

Figure 21-7   Prolapsed cord.

Complications During Childbirth

The vast majority of all births occur without complication. However, this fact is reassuring only if the one you are assisting with is not complicated. For the few that do have complications, delivery can be stressful and even life threatening for the expectant mother and the baby. More common complications include persistent vaginal bleeding, prolapsed cord, breech birth, and multiple births. Learn to recognize the signs of a complicated birth and provide the appropriate care. Call 9-1-1 or the local emergency number immediately if you have not already done so. All of these conditions require the help of more advanced medical personnel.

Persistent bleeding

The most common complication of childbirth is persistent vaginal bleeding. While waiting for the ambulance to arrive, you should take steps to absorb the blood. Do not pack the vagina with dressings. Try to keep the mother calm and take steps to minimize shock, as explained in Chapter 8.

Prolapsed umbilical cord

A **prolapsed umbilical cord** occurs when a loop of the umbilical cord protrudes from the vagina while the baby is still in the birth canal (Fig. 21-7). If this condition occurs, it can threaten the baby's life. As the baby moves through the birth canal, the cord will be compressed between the unborn child and the birth canal, and blood flow to the baby will stop. Without this blood flow, the baby will die within a few minutes because of lack of oxygen. If you notice a prolapsed cord, have the expectant mother assume a knee-chest position (Fig. 21-8). This will help take pressure off the cord.

Breech birth

Most babies are born head first. However, on rare occasions, the baby is delivered feet or buttocks first. This condition is commonly called **breech birth.** If you encounter a breech delivery, support the baby's body as it exits from the birth canal while you are waiting for the head to deliver. Do not pull on the baby's body. Pulling will not help deliver the head.

Because the weight of the baby's head lodged in the birth canal will reduce or stop blood flow by compressing the cord, the baby will be unable to get any oxygen. Should the baby try to take a spontaneous breath, he

Figure 21-8   The knee-chest position will take pressure off the cord.

or she will also be unable to breathe because the face is pressed against the wall of the birth canal. When the baby's head is delivered, check the infant for breathing and signs of circulation. Be prepared to give rescue breathing or CPR as necessary.

Multiple births

Although most births involve only a single baby, a few will involve delivery of more than one baby. If the mother has had proper prenatal care, she will probably be aware that she is going to have more than one baby. Multiple births should be handled in the same manner as single births. The mother will have a separate set of contractions for each child being born. There may also be a separate placenta for each child, although this is not always the case.

SUMMARY

Ideally, childbirth should occur in a controlled environment under guidance of health care professionals trained in delivery. In this way, the necessary medical care is immediately available for mother and baby should any problem arise. However, unexpected deliveries may occur outside of the controlled environment that may require your assistance. To assess the mother's condition before delivery and to assist in the delivery, be familiar with the four stages of labor and understand the birth process. By knowing how to prepare the expectant mother for delivery, assist in the delivery, and provide proper care for the mother and baby, you will be able to successfully assist in bringing a new child into the world.

Answers to Application Questions

1. She is probably still in stage one, but getting close to stage two. The bloody fluid on the bed is probably from the mucous plug, and possibly the amniotic sac has broken.

2. Sadie can tell you how close the contractions are, when she began to have them, if the water broke, where the clean sheets and towels are, and where to find gloves.

STUDY QUESTIONS

1. Match each term with the correct definition.
    a. Amniotic sac
    b. Birth canal
    c. Placenta
    d. Umbilical cord
    e. Crowning
    f. Cervix
    g. Contraction
    h. Uterus

    _____ A pear-shaped organ in a woman's pelvis in which a fertilized egg develops into a baby.

    _____ A rhythmic tightening of certain muscles during delivery.

    _____ An organ attached to the uterus that supplies nutrients to the fetus.

    _____ The appearance of the baby's head at the vaginal opening.

    _____ The upper part of the birth canal.

    _____ A fluid-filled structure that protects the developing fetus.

_____ A flexible structure that attaches the placenta to the fetus; carries blood, nutrients, and waste.

_____ The passageway from the uterus to the vaginal opening through which the baby passes during birth.

2. Name and briefly describe the four stages of labor.

3. List the two priorities of care for a newborn.

4. List six factors in determining a mother's condition before the birth.

In questions 5 through 10, circle the letter of the correct answer. Read the scenario to answer questions 5 through 9.

> *You happen upon a small gathering of people only to discover a woman has gone into labor. The woman is lying on the floor in pain. She says this is her first child. She tells you that her labor pains started about an hour ago, but she thought it was only gas. She says also that the baby is not due for another 3 weeks.*

5. You are reassured that there is enough time for the ambulance to arrive because labor for a first baby usually lasts—
   a. 4 to 8 hours.   c. 12 to 24 hours.
   b. 8 to 12 hours.   d. 24 to 36 hours.

6. When the baby's head is crowning at the vaginal opening, you should—
   a. Maintain firm finger pressure against the center of the skull.
   b. Place your hand lightly on the top of the baby's head.
   c. Place the palm of your hand firmly against the baby's skull.
   d. Place one hand on either side of the baby's head.

7. If a mother has a breech delivery, what part of the baby will be seen first?
   a. Head   c. Foot/feet or buttocks
   b. Arms   d. b or c

8. If the baby is not crying or does not appear to be breathing, you should first—
   a. Hold the baby up by its ankles and spank its buttocks.
   b. Suction the baby's throat with the bulb syringe.
   c. Flick the soles of the baby's feet with your fingers.
   d. Begin rescue breathing.

9. To assist with delivery of a baby, what preparations should you make?
   a. Have someone start a large pan of water boiling on the stove.
   b. Place clean sheets, blankets, or towels under the mother's buttocks.
   c. Have the mother lie flat on her back with legs extended.
   d. All of the above.

10. Which can a woman do to help cope with the pain and discomfort of labor?
    a. Focus on an object in the room while regulating her breathing.
    b. Assume a knee-chest position.
    c. Hold her breath then suddenly release it.
    d. Alternately tense and relax all muscles in her body.

Answers are listed in Appendix A.

CHAPTER 22

When Help Is Delayed

WHAT YOU SHOULD LEARN

After reading this chapter, you should be able to—

1. List three types of problems that could create a delayed-help situation.

2. Describe the information you should gather in a delayed-help situation before making a plan to get help.

3. List four ways to get help in a delayed-help situation.

4. Describe the four options to consider in getting help in a delayed-help situation.

5. List the steps to take before leaving a victim alone for an extended period of time.

6. Describe how to protect a victim from heat or cold.

7. Describe four types of shelters you can use or construct.

8. List three general types of preparation for venturing into an environment where help may be delayed.

9. Define the key terms for this chapter.

You and your buddies Frank and Jeff are out enjoying a day of rock climbing in the Evergreen Mountains. The sky is clear and the temperature is warm. Dropping temperatures and rain are predicted for the night, but by then you will be relaxing at home. Frank comments how good it feels every time the three of you are out in the mountains. Suddenly Jeff screams "Help!" He loses his balance, slips and falls, and lands on a ridge about 5 feet down. When you and Frank make your way down to him, you can see that Jeff is in excruciating pain.

Introduction

*I*n previous chapters, you learned how to apply the emergency action steps *Check-Call-Care* to many emergency situations. You also learned how to determine when advanced medical care is needed and when you should call EMS personnel. In some situations, however, advanced medical care is not easy to contact or close. Situations in which medical care is delayed for 30 minutes or more are called **delayed-help situations.**

Delayed-help situations include rural areas, such as farms and wilderness or back-country environments. Often, people living or working in these areas may be able to call EMS personnel but, because of distance or adverse travel conditions, may wait a long time before EMS personnel arrive. Difficulties in communication may also exist.

In delayed-help environments, as in all emergency situations, use the emergency action steps *Check-Call-Care* as your basic plan of action to help the victim and keep yourself safe.

Special considerations, however, may change how you check the scene and the victim, call for help, and care for the victim. For instance, you may need to decide whether to transport a victim or leave a victim alone while you get help. You may also need to improvise or modify the care you provide, depending on the environment and the circumstances.

This chapter provides information to help you execute *Check-Call-Care* in delayed-help situations. You will also learn how to prepare for emergencies in this environment. If you live, work, or recreate in delayed-help environments, it is important that you understand the limitations of obtaining emergency care.

TYPES OF DELAYED-HELP SITUATIONS

A delayed-help situation is one in which emergency medical care is delayed for more than 30 minutes. This delay exists because there may be no easy way—

- To call for help.
- For emergency personnel to reach the victim.
- To transport the victim to medical care.

Rural Areas

Rural areas include country and farm areas, which are less settled and populated than cities and where neighbors often live far away. Although it is usually easy to communicate with emergency medical personnel, response time is often delayed because of long distances and adverse road conditions. Temporary events, such as power outages and rising water, may cut off communication and access to EMS personnel.

Emergencies that occur in a rural environment usually involve equipment, animals, electricity, falls, fires, overturned vehicles, chemicals or pesticides, and agricultural machinery mishaps, such as those resulting from tractors, combines, and augurs. It is important to be aware of situations and circumstances that may put you or someone else in danger.

Key Terms

Delayed-help situation: A situation in which emergency assistance is delayed for more than 30 minutes.

Tourniquet: A wide band that is wrapped tightly around an extremity to control severe bleeding; used as a last resort measure.

Wilderness: An area that is uninhabited by human beings, uncultivated, and left in its natural condition.

In rural areas, people are usually aware that help may be delayed. If telephone service is available, it may be possible to communicate with an emergency dispatcher who can tell you how to care for the victim until more advanced care is available.

Wilderness

A **wilderness** is an area that is not settled, uncultivated, and left in its natural condition. A phone and emergency personnel may be miles away. Some people are required to work in wilderness areas. Others are drawn to wilderness activities because of the challenge, the adventure, and the opportunity to reach out into the unknown. However, what attracts people to the wilderness often presents barriers to getting help in an emergency.

If an emergency occurs in the wilderness, you need to consider how you are going to get help and what care you will give. If the victim cannot move and you have no means of transport, you may need to send someone to get help or go yourself. If the victim is able to move or be moved, you need to decide how to safely transport him or her. If he or she cannot be moved, you will have to shelter the victim from the elements to prevent his or her condition from deteriorating until you return.

Other Delayed-help Environments

Disasters, such as hurricanes, earthquakes, or terrorist acts, may also create delayed-help situations. Phone and electrical services may be cut off or restricted. Roads may be damaged. Medical facilities may be crowded or destroyed by the disaster. If you live, work, or plan to travel in an area in which natural disasters occur, it is important to plan ahead for such occurrences.

Boating activities may also involve delayed-help situations. On the water, communication with medical personnel may be possible, but transportation to a medical facility may be limited or delayed.

APPLYING THE EMERGENCY ACTION STEPS

In a delayed-help environment, you may have to modify the emergency action steps *Check-Call-Care*. As you learned in Chapter 3, the *Check* step involves noting unusual noises, sights, odors, appearance, and behavior that may indicate an emergency. The *Check* step in a delayed-help environment may need to be more detailed. The information you collect will be needed to develop a plan for getting help, securing resources, and for caring for the victim.

The *Call* step may also be modified. In some instances, a phone may be only 2 miles away; in other situations the nearest road may be 10 miles away. Unlike an urban or rural setting, where you can usually call EMS personnel immediately, in the wilderness you must decide how to get help. Depending on how difficult it is to summon help, the *Call* step may be delayed for a few minutes or a few hours. You may even decide to take the victim to help.

As in any situation, the *Care* step in a delayed-help environment involves periodically rechecking the victim's condition while providing care until help arrives. The primary change in a delayed-help environment is that you monitor the victim for a longer period of time because you have to wait longer for help.

CHECK

In a delayed-help situation, the *Check* step of the emergency action steps includes checking the scene, checking the victim, and checking for available resources.

Check the Scene

Begin by checking the scene. Check the whole scene to get a general idea of what happened. Look for dangers that could threaten your safety or the safety of the victim, such as falling rocks or tree limbs (Fig. 22-1). If you see any dangers,

1. Are you, Frank, and Jeff in a delayed-help situation? If so, what factors make it a delayed-help situation?

Figure 22-1 Check the scene for dangers that could threaten your safety or the safety of the victim.

do not approach the victim until you have carefully planned how you will avoid or eliminate the danger. Note any impending problems, such as a threatening storm.

Check the Victim

When you are sure it is safe, approach the victim carefully and continue the *Check* step by checking first for life-threatening conditions.

Check for a loss of consciousness, no breathing or breathing difficulty, no signs of circulation, and severe bleeding (Fig. 22-2). If the victim has fallen or if you don't know how the injury occurred, assume that he or she has a head, neck, or back injury. Care for any conditions you find in the same way you have learned in this course.

Next, check the victim for any other problems that are not immediately life threatening, but may become so over time. In delayed-help

situations, this check may need to occur before getting help. This ensures that you have all the information about the victim's condition you need to make a plan for getting help. Whenever possible, perform a head-to-toe check even if the victim is unconscious or has life-threatening conditions. If you have other people to assist, do the check while someone else gives rescue breathing. Write down the information that you gather (Fig. 22-3) so that you remember it. If you have nothing to write with, try to remember the most important or unusual observations.

MIND AT WORK

2. *What dangers should you look for at the scene of Jeff's fall? What immediately life-threatening conditions might Jeff have, and what conditions might shortly become life threatening?*

Figure 22-2 Check the victim for life-threatening injuries.

Check for Resources

After checking the victim, start gathering information you will need for planning how and when to get help. Check the surrounding environment for conditions or developing conditions that could endanger you or the victim during the time it will take to get help. Also, note any conditions that would make it difficult for you to go get help. Consider whether you may have to move the victim.

Think about resources you have available for calling for help, caring for the victim, and sustaining you and others. Resources include people available to help, communication or signaling devices, food and water, shelter, first aid supplies, and means of transportation.

CALL

In a delayed-help situation, the *Call* step can be divided into two phases: making a plan for getting help and executing the plan.

Making a Plan

In a delayed-help situation, you have four options for getting help—

- Stay where you are and call, radio, or signal for help.
- Send someone to go get help or leave the victim alone to get help.
- Transport the victim to help.

Figure 22-3 Write down the information you gather while interviewing the victim.

- Care for the victim where you are until the victim has recovered enough to travel on his or her own.

Consider all the information you have gathered during the *Check* step about the conditions at the scene, the victim's condition, the resources available where you are, and the available means for summoning help. Discuss your options with others, including the victim, if appropriate. To help decide on the best approach, ask yourself and others these questions:

- **Is advanced medical care needed and if so, how soon?** If you discovered any conditions for which you would normally call 9-1-1, or if any such conditions seem likely to develop, you should plan to get help immediately.
- **Is there a way to call from the scene for help or advice?** If communication is possible, contact EMS personnel as soon as you have enough information about the victim's condition and the victim is safe from dangers at the scene. Emergency medical personnel can tell you how to care for the victim and advise you about getting help.

The Unreckoned Cost

Rippling grain; cattle grazing by a stream; apple orchards in the spring; dark green fields of soy beans stretching as far as the eye can see—to many, a farm or ranch may not seem a particularly dangerous place. Yet historically, farming has been one of the most hazardous occupations in the United States. The death rate for agricultural workers is five times the national average for all industries.

The very nature of farming puts workers at risk. Crops must be planted and harvested under pressure from weather and time. Money isn't always available to make needed equipment repairs or hire necessary labor. Equipment tends to be large and heavy, and much farm machinery is designed to chop, crush, cut, or compress. Although newer equipment usually includes some safety features, such as rollover protection structures on tractors, older equipment provides little, if any, built-in safety protection.

The possibilities for injury are many. Equipment turns over, crushing the driver or passenger. Machinery traps arms and legs, mangling or amputating them. Gas generated by stored silage causes serious lung damage or death. Shifting grain buries people alive. The list goes on and on. The greatest number of deaths are caused by tractor overturns and runovers, followed by other machinery injuries, drowning, firearms, falls, fires, electric current, animals, poisoning, suffocation, and lightning. In 1993, farm injuries in the United States caused 1000 deaths and disabled 130, 000 people.

Children up to age 16 make up a disproportionate number of these farm fatalities and injuries. Nationally, one in five agricultural fatality victims is under age 18. Approximately 300 children anually die farm-related death, and thousands are injured, many permanently disabled. Too often, these children lack adequate supervision or are doing a task beyond their capabilities. Farm children tend to take on adult work at an early age. Children only eight years old drive tractors. Five-year-olds feed farm animals, including those with young who therefore may be extremely aggressive and protective. Children also play around machinery, tools, wire, gasoline pumps, and other potential hazards in barns and other areas.

Nowhere is the need for training to deal with delayed-help emergency situations greater than in the farming community. Farms are often isolated, far from neighbors, towns, or easily traveled roads. Many roads have no identifying signs. Injuries may occur in isolated areas of the farm where vehicle access is problematic. Weather may make reaching the injured person difficult or even immediately impossible. Emergency medical service is generally more limited than in urban areas. Responders are often volunteers who have other duties and may be far from the scene of the emergency. The first person on the scene, often a family member, is generally the person who gives the initial care and whose actions often determine whether the victim lives or dies.

Various individuals, groups, and organizations have developed resources to address the farm injury situation. First Care is a program developed by Allen L. Van Beek, M.D., a microsurgeon and plastic surgeon. Raised on a farm, at age 13, he had a first-hand experience with farm injuries when a

- **If phone or radio communication is not possible, is there a way to signal for help?** The advantages of signaling are that it is faster and safer than going for help. The disadvantages include that you may not know whether your signal has been received and that the receivers may not know what type of help you need.

- **If there is no way to call for help, is it possible to go get help?** Consider whether you can get help safely while not jeopardizing the safety of the victim. Carefully weigh the decision if going to get help means leaving the victim alone.

- **Is there a way to transport the victim to help?** Consider whether you have a safe and practical way to transport the victim. Ask whether the victim's injuries allow for safe transport. If the victim cannot walk, it will be extremely difficult to carry him or her any distance, even if you have a large number of people to assist. Unless a vehicle or

tractor ran over both his legs. In 1968, as an army flight surgeon stationed in Vietnam, he worked with Col. George Omer, M.D., a hand surgeon who told him about microsurgery, a new form of surgery that had the potential to save severed limbs. After Vietnam, Dr. Van Beek studied reconstructive and plastic surgery. Perfoming surgery with the aid of a microscope and microscopic needles, he has repaired or reattached countless fingers, hands, arms, and legs mangled or severed in farm injuries. Many of the victims are children.

Dr. Van Beek developed First Care to fill what he felt was a huge void in the rural health care system. First Care is designed to teach the person who first comes upon a victim how to cope in those first minutes after an emergency and provide care until advanced medical help can arrive. The program includes color slides of farm injury victims to familiarize those who will find the victims with the sight of mangled limbs so that they will not panic. The program is sponsored by the Minnesota Farm Bureau Federation and The North Memorial Medical Center. It is taught by volunteers and includes a manual, a video, and a first aid kit designed expressly for farm injuries and is packaged in an oil- and water-resistant box that fits in the cab of a tractor or combine. For more information about this program, contact the Minnesota Farm Bureau Federation, 1976 Wooddale Drive, P.O. Box 84370, St. Paul, MN 55164-0370; phone: (612) 739-7300; fax: (612) 578-2159.

Other organizations include Farm Safety 4 Just Kids, an organization located in Earlham, Iowa, that works to prevent farm-related childhood injuries, health risks, and fatalities. It puts out a variety of resource materials and activity ideas , including a catalogue of items to teach farm safety. One of its efforts is to raise the awareness of farm families about the developmental stages of children and how parents can apply that knowledge to tailor farm tasks to a child's skills, judgment, and maturity. To learn more about this program, contact Farm Safety 4 Just Kids, P.O. Box 458, Earlham, IA 50072-0458; phone: (515) 758-2827 or 1-800-423-KIDS; fax: (515) 758-2517.

FARMEDIC Training, Inc. is a nonprofit corporation that has been training EMS professionals in farm emergencies. It is currently working also to train farm families and workers who are the first people on the scene of an emergency to respond appropriately. FARMEDIC is in the process of developing a curriculum for a "First on The Scene" program for farm family members, farm workers, agricultural business people, and agricultural students. For more information, contact FARMEDIC, Alfred State College, National Training Center, Alfred, NY 14802; phone: (607) 587-4734 or 800-437-6010; fax: (607) 587-4737.

other means of transportation is available, you probably will not be able to transport the victim to help without great difficulty.

- **Is it possible to provide care where you are until the victim can travel?** Think about the risks of caring for the victim without medical assistance and the possibility that serious complications may develop. On the other hand, consider how quickly the victim may be able to recover, enabling you to safely transport him or her to medical care.

- **Is it safe to wait for help where you are?** Environmental hazards, such as a threatening storm or falling temperatures, may make it unsafe to wait for help.

You may discover that there is no "best" plan for getting help. You may have to compromise, reducing overall risk by accepting certain risks.

For example, consider a situation in which you are hiking in a remote area on a cold but sunny day. Late in the afternoon, one of your

Figure 22-4 When calling for help, describe all important aspects of the victim's condition, your location, and other information rescuers will need.

companions injures an ankle. Generally, the safest thing to do for the ankle would be to immobilize it, send someone for help, and wait with the victim until emergency transportation arrives. However, you know that it will take until nightfall for someone to summon help and many more hours for help to arrive. No one in your party is dressed to survive the low temperatures overnight. Because of the danger from the cold, you may decide that the plan with the lowest overall risk is to immobilize the ankle and then assist the victim in walking to shelter, even though following this plan may cause further injury to the ankle.

Getting Help

Once you have a plan, you need to execute it. Getting help may mean calling or signaling for help, sending for help, taking the victim to help, or even going without additional help until the victim has recovered enough to travel.

Calling

If you have some means of quickly calling for help, such as a telephone or two-way radio, make sure you have gathered all the necessary information about the victim's condition and your location that EMS or rescue personnel will need to plan their response (Fig. 22-4). Having essential information when you call reduces confusion and improves the likelihood that correct help will be sent to the right location. In addition, if you include all essential information in your first communication, emergency

personnel will be able to respond even if later communication attempts fail.

It is important to give the rescuers specific information about your location. Identifying prominent landmarks and marking your area can help rescuers find your location. Consider that some landmarks are clearly visible during the day but are not visible at night. Flares are one way of marking your location. Do not use flares in heavily wooded or dry areas that could ignite. You may need to send someone to meet EMS personnel at a main road or easy to identify location and have them guide EMS personnel to the victim. Do not give mileage approximations to the EMS dispatcher unless you are sure of the distance.

Improvised distress signals

If you have no way to call for help and it is dangerous or impractical to use flares or send someone for help, you may have to improvise. Two of the most widely used general distress signals are—

- **Signals in Threes.** A series or set of three can be used to signal "Help!" Three shots, three flashes of light, three shouts, three whistles, or three smoky fires are all examples (Fig. 22-5). Use extreme caution when building fires. Always stay near the fire, and have water or dirt close by to extinguish sparks. Do not use fires in dry areas. A small fire can easily get out of control. Build your fires in a triangle at least 50 yards (45 meters) apart so that they are visible as separate fires.
- **Ground-to-Air Signals.** To signal an aircraft, use either signals in threes (three fires or three flashes of light) or else mark a large "X" on the ground. The X ground-to-air signal is a general distress signal meaning "unable to proceed" or "need immediate help." If constructing an X signal, make sure that you choose a large, open area and that the X you construct stands out against its background. The X signal should be at least 20 feet (6 meters) across.

In addition, smoke, mirrors, flare guns, and whistles create a visual or auditory attraction (Fig. 22-6). Smoke signals can be effective because they can be seen for many miles. If you are on a boat, making an urgent "pan-pan" call over marine radio indicates that you have an emergency. You should be familiar with various

Figure 22-5   A set of three or an "X" is used to signal "Help."

Figure 22-6   A mirror can be used to summon help.

ways of signaling that are appropriate for your location and environment.

Sending for help

When you send someone to get help, the person should not leave without certain information. This information will help rescue personnel determine what resources they need for the rescue and should include a note indicating the victim's condition, a map indicating the location of the victim, and a list of other members in the group and available resources. Record weather, terrain, and access routes. This information must be carried in writing in the event that something happens to the person or if he or she gets lost.

The safety of the messenger seeking help is extremely important. Make sure you send enough people to ensure the messenger's safety and success in delivering the message. If going for help involves hazards or challenges, do not send people who are not prepared to overcome these problems.

Another consideration in going for help is making sure you can lead rescuers back to the victim. When in the wilderness or on the water, the most accurate way to describe your location is to use compass readings. You should be trained in map and chart reading and the use of a compass if you travel or work in delayed-help environments.

In many areas hikers frequent, paths may be

Figure 22-7   A compass, surveyor's tape, or ropes can help you mark your path.

Figure 22-8   If you must leave an unconscious victim to go get help, position the person on one side in case he or she vomits while you are gone.

marked. Sometimes, however, you may have to mark your own path and the victim's location. When going for help, always mark your way so that you can find your way back. You can use ropes and surveyor's tape to track your path (Fig. 22-7). It is also important to regularly look back at the area you just traveled, which can assist you on your return trip. What you see may look different from the area you are facing.

When sending for help, make sure that you leave enough people to care for the victim while waiting for help. Those remaining with the victim should be those in your party best equipped to care for the victim.

Finally, before sending anyone for help, consider whether tasks at the scene require everyone's help. For instance, moving a victim a short distance to a shelter is easier to do when everyone helps.

Leaving a victim alone

Generally, it is not a good idea to leave a victim alone. Sometimes, however, it may be necessary. If you are alone with the victim, have no way to call or signal for help, and are reasonably sure that no one will happen by, then you may decide as a last resort that it is best to leave the victim and go get help.

If you decide to leave the victim alone, plan the route you will follow to go for help. Follow the guidelines under "Sending for Help" that explain the importance of making sure you know how to lead rescuers back to the victim. Write down the route, the time you are leaving, and when you expect to arrive. Leave this information with the victim.

Before you go, do what you can to provide for the victim's needs while you are gone. If possible, make sure that food and water are available and provide a container for the victim to use as a urinal or bedpan. If the victim cannot move, make sure that these things are within reach.

Make certain that the victim has adequate clothing and shelter and that he or she is protected from the ground, if necessary. See "Protection from the Elements" in this chapter for more information. Recheck any splints or bandages, and adjust them if necessary so that they are not too tight. If the victim is unconscious or completely unable to move, place him or her in the recovery position, lying on one side with the face angled toward the ground, to protect the airway in case of vomiting (Fig. 22-8).

Before you go, make sure that a conscious victim understands that you are going to get help. Give the victim an idea of when to expect a response. Be as reassuring and positive as the situation allows.

Transporting a victim to help

In situations involving injury or sudden illness, it is usually best to have help come to you. Consider transporting a victim to help only if a vehicle or other means of transportation is available beyond simply carrying the victim. Even if you have a large number of people to take turns, carrying a victim any significant distance is very difficult and can be hazardous, especially if the terrain is not smooth and flat.

Factors to consider when deciding to move the victim include the extent of the injuries, distance to be traveled, and available help. Remember that excessive movement may aggravate or worsen the victim's condition. You should not attempt to move or transport a victim who you suspect has a spinal injury unless you have special training and equipment. However, if the scene is not safe or a potential for danger exists, you may have to move the victim.

If you decide to transport a victim to help, plan the route you will follow. Remember that you may need to travel more slowly to avoid further injury to the victim. It is better to have a person besides the driver who will care for the victim during transport. Know what you should do if you must interrupt the transport so that you can care for the victim if his or her condition worsens. If possible, inform someone else of your route and alternate plans.

Moving an injured victim into a vehicle is likely to cause pain, which may be unavoidable. Plan and rehearse how you will move the victim into the vehicle. Immobilize any possible bone or joint injuries before moving the victim to the vehicle. Select a place in the vehicle for the victim that will be as comfortable as possible and that will allow care to be provided during transport. Bring the vehicle as close to the victim as possible. Before placing the victim in the vehicle, make sure he or she will fit in the location you have selected. Use an uninjured person as a "test victim" to make sure the space is adequate. Provide padding to make the victim as comfortable as possible.

Transport the victim at a safe speed following the route you have planned. The attendant should constantly monitor the victim's condition and work with the driver to make any necessary changes in transport conditions. If a vehicle is unavailable, you may have to use other methods.

CARE

In a delayed-help situation, you may need to care for the victim for a long time. It is important that you remain calm so that you can provide the best care possible, whether for a few minutes or a few hours. Provide support and reassurance to the victim until EMS personnel arrive and take over care.

Monitoring the Victim

After you complete your initial check of the victim and provide care for the conditions found, regularly monitor the victim's condition while waiting for help. Monitoring is especially important in a delayed-help situation because the longer help is delayed, the more time there is for the victim's condition to change.

Continuously monitor the breathing victim who is unconscious or has an altered level of consciousness. Listen to and observe the victim's breathing. If the victim stops breathing or vomits, you will need to give care. Otherwise, the victim should be rechecked about every 15 minutes. If the victim can answer questions, rechecking can consist mainly of asking the victim if his or her condition has changed. You should also watch for changes in skin appearance and temperature and level of consciousness. Changes in these conditions may indicate developing problems, such as heat or cold emergencies and shock. Recheck any splints or bandages, and adjust them if they are too tight.

Keep a written record, and note any changes you find and the time the changes occur. Also note the care you provide.

Fractures and Dislocations

If you are not certain how serious an injury is, care for it as if it is a more serious injury. For example, if you suspect a bone or joint injury, care for it as if it were serious.

In Chapters 10 and 11, you learned how to recognize and provide care for musculoskeletal injuries. In the wilderness, you may have to be creative in improvising materials with which to immobilize an injury (Fig. 22-9, *A* and *B*). You should not attempt to move a person with a possible fracture unless it is absolutely neces-

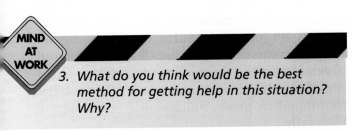

MIND AT WORK

3. What do you think would be the best method for getting help in this situation? Why?

Figure 22-9   **A,** Tree branches can be used to make an improvised arm splint. **B,** An ankle can be splinted using clothing.

sary or the injury does not affect the person's ability to walk. As a rule, do not attempt to move a person or have the person move without splinting the injured part unless necessary. If you splint an injured limb, loosen the splint and recheck the limb about every 15 minutes.

Bleeding

In delayed-help situations, the appropriate care for severe bleeding is the same as you learned in Chapter 7—apply direct pressure, first with your gloved hand and then with a pressure bandage, elevate the wound if possible, and, if necessary, apply pressure at a pressure point.

Most external bleeding can be easily controlled. Direct pressure should be maintained for a full 10 minutes to allow for a blood clot to form.

If bleeding cannot be controlled, consider applying a tourniquet in addition to maintaining direct pressure. A ***tourniquet*** is a wide band of cloth or other material placed tightly just above a wound to stop all flow of blood beyond the point of application. Do not use a narrow band, rope, or wire. Application of a tourniquet can control severe bleeding from an open wound of the arm or leg, but it is rarely needed and should not be used except in situations where other measures fail. *The use of a tourniquet is dangerous.* When left in place for an extended period, uninjured tissues may die from lack of blood and oxygen. Releasing the tourniquet increases the danger of shock, and bleeding may resume. If a tourniquet is applied too loosely, it will not stop arterial blood flow

to the affected limb and will only slow or stop venous blood flow from the limb. Applying a tourniquet means risking a limb in order to save a life.

To apply a tourniquet, place it just above the wound. Do not allow it to touch the wound edges. If the wound is in a joint area or just below, place the tourniquet immediately above the joint.

- Wrap the tourniquet band twice tightly around the limb, and tie an overhand knot (Fig. 22-10, *A*).
- Place a short, strong stick or similar object that will not break on the overhand knot; tie two overhand knots on top of the stick (Fig. 22-10, *B*).
- Twist the stick to tighten the tourniquet until bleeding stops (Fig. 22-10, *C*).
- Secure the stick in place with the loose ends of the tourniquet, a strip of cloth, or other material (Fig. 22-10, *D* and *E*).
- Make a written note of the location of the tourniquet and the time it was applied, and attach the note to the victim's clothing.
- Treat the victim for shock, and give necessary first aid for other injuries.
- Do not cover a tourniquet.

Note the time the tourniquet was applied. Loosen it after 5 minutes to determine if bleeding has stopped. If bleeding continues, tighten the tourniquet for another 5-minute period. Then, loosen the tourniquet and recheck bleeding. If bleeding has stopped, leave the loosened tourniquet in place. Follow-up medical care is imperative.

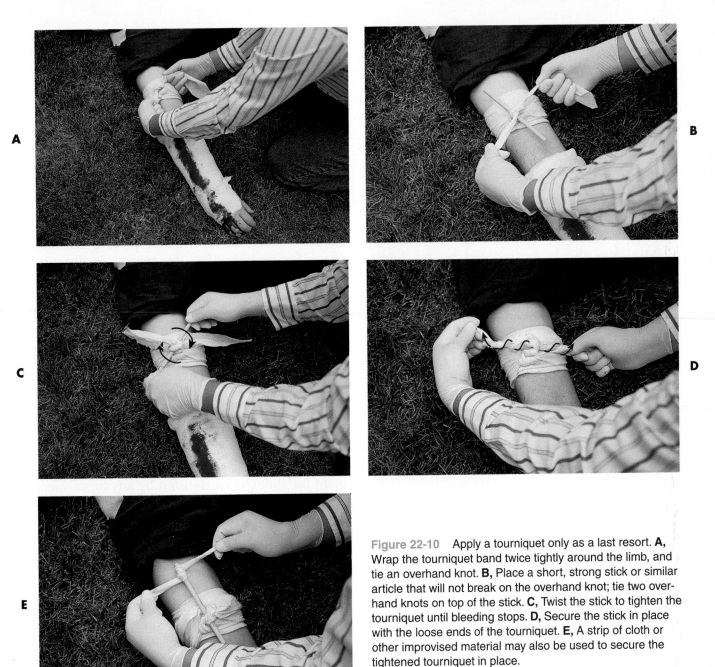

Figure 22-10 Apply a tourniquet only as a last resort. **A,** Wrap the tourniquet band twice tightly around the limb, and tie an overhand knot. **B,** Place a short, strong stick or similar article that will not break on the overhand knot; tie two overhand knots on top of the stick. **C,** Twist the stick to tighten the tourniquet until bleeding stops. **D,** Secure the stick in place with the loose ends of the tourniquet. **E,** A strip of cloth or other improvised material may also be used to secure the tightened tourniquet in place.

Burns

General steps for caring for a burn in a delayed-help environment are the same as in other settings:

- **Cool the burned area to stop the burning.** Immerse the burned area in cool water. Smother flames with blankets or other material if water is not available. Using cool water on serious burns increases the possibility of hypothermia and shock, especially in a cold environment. Be careful not to use more water than necessary and to immerse only the burned area.

- **Cover the burned area.** Once the burn has been cooled, your main concern is keeping the area clean. Use a clean, dry cloth or a sterile burn dressing (such as one with a water-based gel coating) to cover the burn. Be sure that the gel on the dressing can easily be washed away with water.

- **Prevent infection.** Since the danger of infection is greater in delayed-help environments, apply a thin layer of antibiotic ointment to the cooled burn. Keep a dressing over the burn as mentioned. If an emergency facility is more than a day away, you must redress the burn daily. Redressing includes taking old dressings off, cleaning the burned area with sterile water and mild soap, re-applying a thin layer of antibiotic ointment, and covering with a clean dressing. If none of these materials are available, leave the burn alone; it will form a scab.
- **Minimize shock.** Partial- and full-thickness burns, or burns covering more than one body part, can cause serious loss of body fluids. Give fully conscious victims water or clear juices to drink. Adults should receive 4 ounces (1/2 cup) over a 20 minute period, sipping slowly. A child should receive half that amount, 2 ounces (1/4 cup) and an infant half of that, 1 ounce (1/8 cup) over the 20-minute period. Elevate burned areas above the level of the heart and keep the burned victim from becoming chilled. Always monitor breathing and consciousness. The victim of serious burns requires transport to a medical facility as soon as possible.

Sudden Illness

If you are a diabetic or responsible for someone who is a diabetic, you should become familiar with the signs and symptoms of low blood sugar. If you are a diabetic, training someone you will be with in a delayed-help environment as to how to give you your insulin is also a good idea. This may include measuring the dosage and giving the shot.

When caring for a victim of sudden illness, such as someone experiencing a diabetic emergency or a seizure, follow the same procedures as if you were not in a delayed-help situation. However, there are a few extra things to think about if you are far from help or transportation. Be sure victims recovering from an episode of low blood sugar rest after eating/drinking something sweet. In addition, if the victim does not show signs of improvement within 5 minutes after ingesting a sweet substance, you need to give the person swater in the amounts described in the Shock section below. Transport that person to a medical facility. Some wilderness first aid experts recommend rubbing small amounts of a sugar and water mixture (or some other sweet liquid such as fruit juice of a sports drink) on the gums of an unconscious person. Remember, victims of diabetic emergencies need to get a sugary substance into their system immediately. However, never give an unconscious person anything to eat or drink.

The care for someone who has experienced a seizure in a delayed-help environment is the same as the care given in other environments. Do no further harm and complete a detailed check for injuries after the seizure is over. Be sure to maintain the victim's body temperature to help to prevent shock, such as by putting some form of insulation between the victim and the ground and covering the victim with a blanket or coat if necessary. Consider ending the trip if you suspect any injuries or possible recurrence of the seizure.

Shock

In a delayed-help situation, it is likely you will have to provide care for shock. Although treatment for shock is carried out by advanced medical personnel, it is possible to minimize or delay its onset.

Remember that shock is not always initially present. It may develop while you are waiting for help. Check for signs and symptoms of shock every time you recheck the victim's condition. Be alert for conditions that may cause shock to develop over time, such as slow bleeding, vomiting, diarrhea, or heat loss.

If you or someone you are with is susceptible to a severe form of anaphylaxis or anaphylactic shock as a result of an insect bite or bee or wasp sting, be sure someone knows the location of necessary medication, such as oral antihistimines or injectible epinephrine, and how to use it. Anaphylactic shock can be life threatening if the victim does not receive care immediately. Quickly transport a person who shows signals of anaphylactic shock, such as swelling and breathing difficulty, to a medical facility.

If medical care is more than 2 hours away, it may be appropriate to provide preventive care for shock by giving a fully conscious victim cool water or clear juices. You can give an adult about 4 ounces (half a cup, or about 120 milliliters) of water to sip slowly over a 20-minute period. For a child, give half this amount (2 ounces or about 60 milliliters) and for an infant, half of that (1 ounce, about 15 milliliters), over the same 20-minute period. Giving frequent, small amounts, rather than fewer large amounts, minimizes vomiting.

Even in a delayed-help situation, do not give fluids if the victim is unconscious, is having seizures, has a serious head or abdominal injury, or vomiting is frequent and sustained. If you give fluids and the victim then starts to vomit, wait before giving the victim any more to drink. Remember to keep the victim from becoming chilled or overheated.

Head, Neck, and Back Injuries

If you suspect a head, neck, or back injury, the goal and the care are the same as in any other emergency: prevent further injury by providing in-line stabilization (Fig. 22-11).

Caring for a victim with a spinal injury while maintaining in-line stabilization is difficult to do without assistance. Safely transporting a spinal injury victim without special training and equipment is nearly impossible. Therefore, when caring for a spinal injury victim in a delayed-help situation, it is generally

Figure 22-12 Place an insulating barrier between the victim and the ground.

best to stay right where you are and wait for rescue personnel to arrive.

Caring for a spinal injury victim outdoors for an extended period of time may be even more difficult. The victim will not be able to maintain normal body temperature without help. The person will need help with drinking, eating, and going to the bathroom. If you are alone and need to free yourself from maintaining in-line stabilization of the victim's head and neck, place two heavy objects wrapped in clothing next to each side of the head to hold it in line.

Help the spinal injury victim maintain normal body temperature by placing insulation underneath him or her or providing shelter from the weather. If two or more rescuers are on hand, roll the victim on one side to place insulation underneath the body, being careful not to twist the spine (Fig. 22-12).

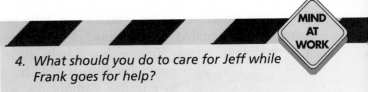

MIND AT WORK

4. *What should you do to care for Jeff while Frank goes for help?*

DIFFICULT DECISIONS

One of the most stressful and emotional situations you can be faced with is dealing with a life-threatening condition when professional help is not easily obtainable. To give a seriously injured victim the best chance of survival, EMS personnel must arrive quickly to provide advanced medical care and to transport the victim

Figure 22-11 Provide in-line stabilization if you suspect a head, neck, or back injury.

to a medical facility. Some victims in delayed-help situations will die because no quick EMS response is available.

In a delayed-help situation, you may be faced with the difficult question of how long to continue resuscitation efforts if the victim's condition does not improve and advanced medical help is hours away. There is no simple answer to this question. In such a situation, you will ultimately need to make your own decision. However, some general principles can help you do so.

As you learned in Chapter 6, the purpose of CPR is to partially and temporarily substitute for the functions of the respiratory and circulatory systems. However, CPR is not designed for and is not capable of sustaining a victim's life indefinitely. Usually, the longer CPR is continued, the less likely it is that the victim will survive.

The victim's survival depends largely on what caused the heart to stop in the first place. If the cause was a direct injury to the heart, such as from a heart attack or from crushing or penetrating trauma to the chest, little chance exists that the victim will survive in a delayed-help environment, whether or not CPR is performed. On the other hand, if the heart is not injured but stops as a result of hypothermia, lightning strike, or drowning, the victim's heart has a better chance of starting. In this case, CPR can limit brain damage in case the heart starts and may even improve the chance that the heart will start.

You learned in Chapter 6 that once CPR is started you must continue to provide care until the victim's heart starts beating or until you are relieved by another trained person, EMS personnel arrive and take over, you become too exhausted to continue, or the situation becomes unsafe. In a delayed-help situation, you may also generally stop if you have performed CPR for 30 minutes without restarting the heart.

The exception to stopping CPR after 30 minutes is if the victim's heart stopped as a result of hypothermia, near drowning, or a lightning injury. In each of these circumstances, continue CPR until the victim's heart starts beating or until you are relieved by another trained rescuer, EMS personnel arrive and take over, you are too exhausted to continue, or the scene becomes unsafe.

PROTECTION FROM THE WEATHER

When caring for a victim in a delayed-help situation, it is critical to protect the victim from environmental conditions such as heat, cold, wind, rain, sleet, or snow. You may need to construct a shelter for the victim using whatever materials you have on hand.

Protecting the Victim

A person who has an injury and is not able to move may develop a heat- or cold-related condition. The fact that you may be comfortable does not necessarily mean the victim is. In cold weather, lying on the ground draws heat away from the body and increases the chances of hypothermia. If it is too hot, the heat from the ground will travel to the body and raise the temperature. If the body's normal temperature is not maintained, the person may slip into shock.

To keep the victim from getting chilled or overheated, provide some type of insulation to protect the victim. If the ground is dry, you can use cloth items such as towels, blankets, clothing, or sleeping bags to insulate the victim from the ground. You can also improvise insulation from dry leaves or grass. If the ground is wet, put a waterproof tarp, raincoat, or poncho between the insulating material and the ground. If the victim is exposed to hot sun, rain, snow, or chilling wind, provide an appropriate shelter.

Constructing Shelter

The following are four basic types of shelters:

- Natural shelters
- Artificial shelters
- Snow shelters
- Tents and bivouac sacs

The type of shelter depends on where you are, the resources you have, and whether you can move the victim safely into a shelter or it is best to construct a shelter over the victim. Natural shelters are structures existing naturally in the environment, such as caves, overhangs, and even large trees (Fig. 22-13, A). Artificial shelters are those you construct of materials, such as small trees or branches (Fig. 22-13, B). An insulated tarp attached to branches makes a good temporary shelter. You

Figure 22-13   A, Natural shelter. **B,** Artificial shelter. **C,** Snow shelter. **D,** A pole tent.

can make a snow shelter by digging out a snow cave, which is easy if it only has to hold one person (Fig. 22-13, *C*). Larger snow caves involve hard work and may take a while to dig. Snow cave shelters are also not advisable if the temperature is above freezing, since as temperature rises, the strength and stability of a snow shelter weakens, making it unsafe. Many people carry a light tent, such as a pole tent or a bivouac sac, that can be easily assembled (Fig. 22-13, *D*). Although tents will keep you dry, they are usually not warm in extreme cold. Bivouac sacs made from Gore-Tex® are better at holding warmth.

A fairly common situation is getting stranded in a car. A car can be an effective shelter. If you are stranded, it is better to stay in your car than to go find help. If you need heat, it is possible to keep the heater on for 15 to 20 minutes each hour. Make sure snow or ice does not block the exhaust pipe and cause carbon monoxide fumes to back up into the car. Leave the window opened a crack to prevent carbon monoxide poisoning. You can also use candles as a source of heat. It is important, especially in the winter months, that you keep your car in good working condition and filled with gasoline and carry a vehicle survival kit. Whether a

VEHICLE SURVIVAL KIT

First aid kit

Sleeping bag

Extra winter clothing

Emergency food

Waterproof matches

Long-burning candles

Pocket knife

Pot or coffee can

Toilet paper

Citizen's band radio

Flashlight with extra batteries

Extra quart of oil

Chains

Snow shovel

Tow chain

Sand or kitty litter

Two jugs of water

Tool kit

Gas line deicer

Flares

Ax

Folding saw

Auerbach PS: *Wilderness medicine*, St Louis, 1994, Mosby.

shelter is natural or artificial, it should be well ventilated to prevent build-up of condensation or toxic fumes.

PREPARING FOR EMERGENCIES

If you live or work in a delayed-help environment or plan to travel to one, develop a plan for how you will respond to emergencies that may arise.

Types of Preparation

There are three general types of preparation—knowledge, skills, and equipment.

Knowledge includes knowing the emergency care resources available and how to access them. It also includes knowing the local geography, including landmarks and hazards. For instance, if you are going on a hiking trip, talk with park rangers or others who know the environment (Fig. 22-14, *A*). Plan your route and decide on check points (Fig. 22-14, *B*). If you are planning a boating expedition, consult the Coast Guard about possible weather hazards for that time of year. If you will be boating on inland waters, also consult with the local authority with control over dam water releases. People in rural areas should meet with their local EMS service and ask about how to access EMS personnel, what to do in the event of an emergency, and estimated arrival time of EMS personnel for their particular location.

A

B

Figure 22-14   Appropriate preparation such as **A,** talking to a park ranger who knows the environment, and **B,** using a map to plan your route.

KIT FOR OVERNIGHT CAMPING

Case

Durable in temperature extremes

Water and dust tight

Sized to meet personal needs

Contents

Scissors

Tweezers

Hypothermia thermometer (reads down to 85 degrees F (29.4 degrees C)

Over-the-counter pain medication

Over-the-counter antihistamine

Antacids

Antibiotic ointment

Sunblock (SPF15 or higher)

Sunburn lotion or cream

Lip protection, such as ointment or cream

Adhesive tape

Roller gauze, 2-inch, 4-inch

Sterile dressings, 4 × 4

Nonstick dressings

Adhesive bandages

Sewing kit (safety pins, needle, thread)

Soap

Cotton swabs

Tongue depressors

Eye drops

Disposable gloves

Allergy kit

Water purification tablets or filter

Knife

Waterproof container of matches, with flint bar or lighter

Spare socks

Heliograph mirror, whistle

Flashlight and spare batteries

Foot powder

Magnifying glass

Sheet of aluminum foil

Nylon cord

Mosquito netting, emergency blanket

Compass

Insect repellent

Skills include proficiency in any language you need to get help; wilderness or survival skills; and technical skills necessary to safely engage in certain activities, such as scuba diving or rock climbing. For instance, if you plan to use a two-way radio, know its operation and how to call for help. Rural inhabitants should know how to safely handle the hazards that they encounter on a regular basis, such as pesticides or farm machinery. Courses are available that address specific situations such as wilderness first aid and farming emergencies.

Equipment includes appropriate clothing for your location and activities, first aid supplies and equipment suitable for your activities and expected hazards, and devices for signaling and communication. Basic first aid supplies are listed in Chapter 3. The contents of a first aid kit should be modified to suit particular needs. For example, boaters should waterproof their kits by placing the contents in a waterproof container. People driving on long trips may want to add flares, a blanket, and a flashlight to their kits.

Ensuring Adequate Preparation

Different delayed-help environments have different characteristics. In addition, your preparation needs will vary with the activities you plan, the weather that is expected, and the special needs or skills of you and your companions.

When planning a trip, several major considerations will help you determine special safety needs. These include—

BEING PREPARED

When you are traveling in a wilderness or backcountry area, the BSA recommends having the following with you at all times:

1. Map, preferably a **topographic map**, of the area in which you will be traveling.
2. **Compass**—and know how to use it before you leave.
3. **Matches** in a waterproof container.
4. 24 hours of **EXTRA high energy food.**
5. **Water,** 1-2 liters (2-3 quarts).
6. Extra **clothes,** such as socks and a sweater.
7. **Rain gear.**
8. A pocket **knife and whistle.**
9. **Sun protection** such as a wide-brimmed hat, sun glasses, and sun screen.
10. **First-aid kit with an emergency blanket.**

- Determining that more than one person in the group knows first aid.
- Maximum anticipated delay in obtaining medical help.
- Total duration of the trip or activity.
- Level of risk associated with the activity and environment.
- Group-related factors, such as preexisting medical or physical conditions.
- Requirements for special equipment and supplies for high-risk or other specific activities.
- Group size. It is best to travel in a group larger than two so that at least one person is always available to stay with the victim.

This information can help you prepare for a trip or activity. The following section details some general principles and ideas for finding out what preparation is needed.

Start preparing early. The sooner you start to plan, the more information you will be able to gather. You will also have more time to act on that information by getting any necessary training and equipment.

Take courses and talk to people with experience. Professionals, such as park rangers and Coast Guard personnel, as well as enthusiasts of the activity you will be engaged in, are good sources of information. You may find experienced people in clubs for those that participate in the activity or in stores that sell equipment for the activity. Ask what preparations they recommend to make your experience safe and enjoyable. If possible, talk to more than one person to get a range of viewpoints.

Look for books and magazines that include information on your intended destination and activity. Find more than one source of written information so that you get more than one author's point of view.

Find out about local weather conditions for the time you will be there. Make sure that you know the environmental conditions you need to be prepared for. An atlas, or reference book, and experienced people may provide you with information about weather-related challenges for the area in which you will be traveling.

Find out about local emergency resources in the area you will be, including how to summon help. Find out if the emergency number is 9-1-1; if it is not, find out what the local emergency number is. Get other important phone numbers, such as hospitals, clinics, and law enforcement agencies. If traveling to a foreign country, find out whatever details you can about the medical care that is available.

Plan your route and write it down. Let others know about your timing, routes, destination, and companions. Letting others know your destination and estimated time of arrival may lessen the response time in the event of an emergency.

Plan for emergencies. Ask yourself, "What

if . . . ?" questions. For example, if you are planning a camping trip that will include day hikes far from a base camp, ask yourself, "What if someone in our group is injured such that the victim can't hike back to camp? Will we have what we need to wait with the victim overnight?" Talk over possible answers with the group. When you decide on a plan, write it down. Writing down emergency plans prevents confusion in the event of an emergency.

Planning for emergencies is an important part of preparation for any trip or activity. Adequate preparation can not only reduce the risk of certain problems, it can help make your trip more enjoyable, whether or not an emergency occurs.

SUMMARY

Emergencies do not always happen where it is quick and easy for you to activate the emergency medical system, for advanced medical personnel to reach the victim, or for the victim to be transported to a medical facility. In these delayed-help situations, you will need to provide care for a much longer time than usual.

In a delayed-help situation, just as in all emergency situations, use *Check-Call-Care*, the emergency action steps, as your basic plan of action. In a delayed-help situation,

however, you generally check the scene and the victim in greater detail before getting help. You need the information from this more detailed check to develop a plan for getting help and caring for the victim. Getting help may involve calling for help, sending for help, leaving the victim alone and going for help, transporting the victim to help, or allowing the victim to recover sufficiently so that he or she can walk to help.

In general, the care you provide the victim in a delayed-help situation is no different from what you have learned in previous chapters. However, you will spend more time caring for the victim. Regularly monitoring the victim's condition while waiting for help and writing down any changes that you find are more important in delayed-help situations. You may also need to protect the victim from heat and cold or construct a shelter if help is delayed for an extended period of time.

If you are planning to venture into a delayed-help enviroment or if you live or work in one, think about how you can reduce the risk of emergencies. Adequately preparing yourself for a delayed-help environment includes early planning, talking to people with experience, reading, finding out about local weather conditions and emergency resources, planning your route, and constructing plans to deal with emergencies should they arise.

MIND AT WORK

Answers to Application Questions

1. The mountains where you, Frank, and Jeff are located cause a delayed-help situation. It will take more than 30 minutes for you and Frank to get help to Jeff. Being on the mountains will also require specially trained rescue personnel to remove Jeff.

2. When checking the scene, you want to check for dangerous conditions, such as loose or slippery rocks. You should be sure the area Jeff is lying on is safe and stable. It appears that Jeff is conscious; however, if his injuries are not cared for, he may develop shock, a life-threatening condition.

3. Jeff slipped and fell. He may have a head, neck, or back injury, and you should not attempt to move him unless necessary. In this situation, since you are trained in first aid, you should stay with Jeff and Frank should go for help.

4. After checking for nonlife-threatening injuries, you should provide care and continue to monitor Jeff. You should take measures to prevent Jeff from getting dehydrated, chilled, or overheated.

STUDY QUESTIONS

1. Match each term with the correct definition.

   a. Tourniquet
   b. Bivouac sac
   c. Wilderness

   d. *Check-Call-Care*
   e. Delayed-help situation

   _____ Basic plan of action to help victim.

   _____ A wide band of clothing placed above a wound to stop all blood flow.

   _____ An emergency situation in which medical care is delayed for 30 minutes or more.

   _____ A lightweight single person shelter made of waterproof and insulating materials.

   _____ A delayed-help environment.

2. List three types of problems that can create a delayed-help situation.

3. List two types of environments that can create a delayed-help situation.

4. List four options for getting help in a delayed-help situation.

In questions 5 through 9, circle the letter of the correct answer.

5. Periodically rechecking the victim's condition while providing care until help arrives is necessary because —

   a. It helps you remember changes in his or her condition.
   b. The victim may become hungry.
   c. The victim's condition may worsen.
   d. The victim needs to be comfortable.

6. The type of shelter that can be built from readily available materials, such as branches and trees, is called a(n)—

   a. Natural shelter.
   b. Artificial shelter.
   c. Snow shelter.
   d. Tent shelter.

7. Flare guns, whistles, and mirrors are examples of—

    a. Hunting gear.
    b. First aid supplies.
    c. Signaling devices.
    d. Ground-to-air signals.

8. To prevent further injury to a person who may have a back injury, you should provide—

    a. In-line immobilization.
    b. In-line traction.
    c. In-line stabilization.
    d. In-line reduction.

9. Which would you do when you are going to leave the victim alone for an extended period of time?

    a. Give the victim instructions to give the rescuers.
    b. Loosen any splints or bandages.
    c. Write down the route you are going to take and the time you are leaving.
    d. Do not leave any food within the victim's reach.

10. In the following scenario, circle the information you should consider before making a plan to get help.

    You are hiking with your hiking club in Greenleaf national forest and are now on a trail about 5 miles from the main road. As you are crossing a stream, a group member slips and falls into the icy water. You all help him out and help him sit on the bank. He is shivering violently in the cool breeze. He says his right knee is very painful and feels as if it is swelling. The sky is overcast and the temperature is about 50 degrees F (10 degrees C). The sun will begin to set in about 4 hours. A group member gives a sweater, which you substitute for the victim's soaked jacket. Other group members provide various dry items of clothing.

11. To keep a victim from getting chilled or overheated, you would

    _____ .

12. Three general types of preparation that can help you plan for going into a delayed-help environment are _____ , _____ ,

    and _____ .

Answers are listed in Appendix A.

HEALTHY LIFESTYLES

CHAPTER 23

A Safer and Healthier Life

WHAT YOU SHOULD LEARN

After reading this chapter, you should be able to—

1. List three general strategies for preventing injuries.

2. List four steps you can take to reduce your risk of personal injury.

3. List two steps you can take to help ensure vehicle safety.

4. List four elements of a fire escape plan.

5. List the three leading causes of accidental home death.

6. Identify 15 ways to make your home a safer place.

7. List five ways to improve safety at work.

8. List 17 ways to improve safety at play.

9. Describe the contents of the current food labels.

10. List in order the food groups shown on the Food Guide Pyramid.

11. List six physical indicators of negative stress.

12. List five risks of smoking.

13. Identify 11 ways to keep alcohol consumption under control.

14. Define the key terms for this chapter.

It was the morning of "Run to the Rescue," a 10K run and 2–mile walk sponsored by the local Red Cross chapter. Rosanna was excited to be entering her first 10K after having completed a few 5Ks earlier in the season. At the registration tables, she was surprised to see a trim gray-haired woman signing up. "Mrs. Gallagher!" she gasped, "What are you doing here? I mean—well, I guess you're here for the walk..." Mrs. Gallagher smiled. "Why, Rosanna, I'm no older than your mother!" After warming up, they joined the crowd at the starting line. Bang! The sea of people began to move out. Rosanna managed to keep up for the first mile, but before long, Mrs. Gallagher had moved so far ahead she was almost out of sight.

Introduction

Disease is the leading cause of death in the United States. Heart disease, the primary cause of death for both males and females, kills approximately 720,000 Americans every year. As a killer, it is followed by cancer, stroke, and **chronic obstructive pulmonary disease (COPD)**. Injury is the fifth leading cause of death for people of all ages and the leading cause of death for people ages 1 to 44 years. The costs of illness and injury in lost wages, medical expenses, insurance, property damage, and other indirect costs are staggering—many billions of dollars a year. But illness and injury are not simply unpleasant facts of life to be shrugged off as inevitable. Often you can prevent them by taking safety precautions and choosing a lifestyle that promotes optimal health.

INJURY

Since the end of World War II, more than 6 million U.S. citizens have died of injuries. Injuries claim thousands of lives each year.

- Approximately 18 million people suffered a disabling injury in 1993—an injury that prevented them from immediately returning to their daily routine.
- Injury is the leading cause of people contacting physicians and the most common cause of hospitalization among people under age 45.
- Injury surpasses all major disease groups (heart disease, cancer, stroke, chronic obstructive pulmonary disease COPD, AIDS-related diseases) as a cause of death for people ages 1 to 44 years.
- Statistics indicate that most people will have a significant injury at some time in their lives. Researchers predict that few will escape the experience of a fatal or permanently disabling injury to a relative or friend. In the few minutes it will take you to read this section on injuries, it is estimated that 2 people will be killed and 170 will suffer a disabling injury. The cost of unintentional injury in 1993 was over $407 billion.

Factors Affecting Risk of Injury

A number of factors affect risk of injury—age, gender, geographic location, economic status, and alcohol use and abuse. Technology also affects the type and frequency of injury. As certain activities, such as skateboarding and rollerblading, gain and lose popularity, the injury statistics reflect the changes.

Key Terms

Aerobic: Requiring additional effort by the heart and lungs to meet the increased demand by the skeletal muscles for oxygen.

Calorie: A measure of the energy value of food.

Carbohydrates: Compounds that contain carbon, oxygen, and hydrogen; the main source of energy for all body functions.

Cardiorespiratory endurance: The ability to take in, deliver, and extract oxygen for physical work; the ability to persevere at a physical task.

Fat: A compound made up of carbon, hydrogen, oxygen, and three fatty acids, a storage form of energy in the body; a type of body tissue composed of cells containing stored fat.

Nutrition: The science that deals with study of the food you eat and how your body uses it.

Obesity: A condition characterized by an excess of stored body fat.

Proteins: Compounds made up of amino acids necessary to build tissues.

Saturated fat: The fat in animal tissue and products.

Sodium: A mineral abundant in table salt; associated with high blood pressure.

Stress: A physiological or psychological response to real or imagined influences that alter an existing state of physical, mental, or emotional balance.

Stressor: An event or condition that triggers the stress response.

- Injury rates are highest among people under age 45. People ages 65 and older and people ages 15 to 24 have the highest rate of deaths from injury.
- Gender is also a significant factor in risk of injury. Males are at greater risk than females for any type of injury. In general, men are 2.5 times more likely to suffer a fatal injury than women.
- Many environmental factors influence injury statistics. Whether you live on a farm or in the city, whether your home is built out of wood or brick, the type of heat used in your home, and the climate all affect your degree of risk. For instance, death rates from injury are higher in rural areas. The death rate from injuries is twice as high in low-income areas as in high-income areas.
- The use and abuse of alcohol is a significant factor in many injuries and fatalities, even in young teenagers. Almost half of all motor vehicle driver fatalities involve alcohol; so do the deaths of many passengers and pedestrians. Over 40 percent of the deaths of 15- to 20-year-olds are the result of motor-

vehicle crashes. About half of these fatalities involve alcohol. It is estimated that an average of one alcohol-related fatality occurs every 22 minutes.
- Alcohol also contributes to other types of injuries. It is estimated that a significant number of victims who die as a result of falls, drownings, fires, assaults, and suicides have blood alcohol concentrations over the legal limit. In one study of emergency department patients, alcohol was in the blood of 30 percent of patients injured while driving or walking on the road, 22 percent of patients injured at home, 16 percent of patients injured on the job, and 56 percent of patients injured in fights and assaults.

Figure 23-1 shows the leading causes of deaths from injuries in 1993.

Reducing Your Risk of Injury

Despite the statistics showing that people of certain ages and gender are injured more than others, your chances of injury have more to do

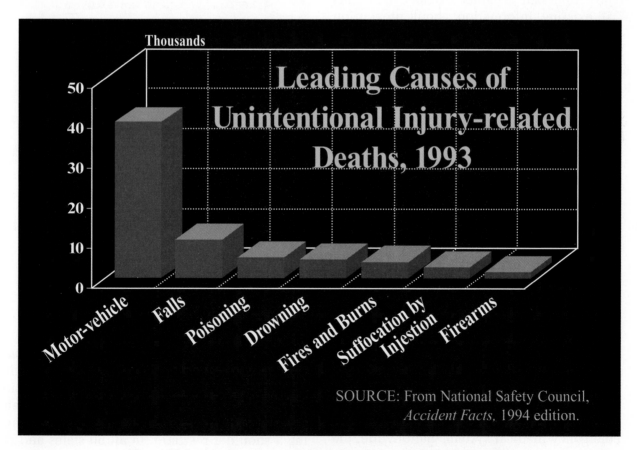

Figure 23-1   Leading causes of unintentional injury-related deaths, 1993.

with what you do than who you are. Injuries do not just happen. Many injuries are preventable, predictable events resulting from the way people interact with the potential dangers in the environment.

The following are three general strategies for preventing injuries:

- Encourage or persuade people at risk to want to change their behavior and to do so.
- Require people at risk to change their behavior, such as with laws requiring people to wear safety belts. Typically, behavior of members of high-risk groups tends to be the hardest to influence, regardless of whether the risk-reducing behavior is voluntary or required. For example, despite the overwhelming number of traffic fatalities in the 15 to 20 age group, teenagers are less likely than adults to wear safety belts.
- Provide products that offer automatic protection, such as air bags, designed to reduce the risk of injury.

The American Trauma Society contends that if existing information about prevention was applied, the injury rate could be reduced by 50 percent. Taking the following steps could significantly reduce your risk of personal injury:

- Know your risk. Complete the Health Check Boxes in this chapter. Note the areas that indicate where you are at risk.
- Take measures that make a difference. Change behaviors that increase your risk of injury and risk injuring others.
- Think safety. Be alert for and avoid potentially harmful conditions or activities that increase your injury risk. Take precautions, such as wearing appropriate protective devices—helmets, padding, and eyewear—and buckle up when driving or riding in motor vehicles. Let your state and congressional representatives know that you support legislation that ensures a safer environment for us all.
- Learn and use first aid skills. Despite dramatic improvements in the last decade in emergency medical systems nationwide, the

VEHICLE SAFETY

The following statements represent an awareness of vehicle safety that can reduce your chances, and the chances of others, of injury in a vehicle crash. Check each statement that reflects your lifestyle.

☐ I put on a safety belt whenever I am a driver or passenger in a motor vehicle.

☐ My vehicle is equipped with an air bag.

☐ I am alert to the actions of other drivers, pedestrians, motorcyclists, and bikers.

☐ I obey traffic rules.

☐ I use turn signals when turning or changing lanes, giving the driver behind me sufficient warning.

☐ I drive a safe distance behind the car in front of me (10 mph = 1 car's length).

☐ I keep my vehicle in good working order.

☐ I do not drink and drive.

☐ I am aware of environmental and weather conditions that increase driving risks.

If you only checked one or two statements, you should consider making changes in your lifestyle now.

person who can often make the difference between death and life is you, when you apply your first aid training.

Vehicle safety

When riding in a motor vehicle, buckle up. Although more automobiles than ever are equipped with air bags, and many have air bags on both the driver and passenger sides, wearing a safety belt is still the easiest and best action you can take to prevent injury in a motor-vehicle collision. Always wear a safety belt, including a shoulder restraint. In all 50 states and the

District of Columbia, wearing a safety belt is a law. Wear a safety belt when you are in the back seat. From 1983 through 1993, it is estimated that 40,138 lives were saved and over 1 million moderate-to-critical injuries were prevented by safety belts. Infants and children should always ride in approved safety seats. Infants weighing under 20 pounds should ride in a safety seat facing the rear of the vehicle to protect the infant's head and neck. For children, motor-vehicle crashes are the major cause of death as a result of injury. All 50 states and the District of Columbia require the use of child safety seats. Unsecured toys and other objects can turn into high-speed missiles in a vehicle crash. Do not leave objects loose in your vehicle.

Do not drink and drive. Plan ahead to find a ride or take a cab or public transportation if you are going to a party where you may drink alcohol. If you are with a group, have a designated driver who agrees not to drink on this occasion. Do not drink if you are in a boat. The U.S. Coast Guard reports that more than 50 percent of drownings from boating incidents involve alcohol.

Fire safety

In 1993, fires and burns caused the deaths of 4000 people in the United States. About 5 percent of these fires were caused by smoking. Fires are also caused by heating equipment, appliances, electrical wiring, cooking, and by many other means. Regardless of the cause of fires, everyone needs to be aware of the danger fire presents and act accordingly.

Plan a fire escape route with your family, housemates, or roommates. The National Fire Protection Association urges that everyone plan and practice a fire escape plan (Fig. 23-2). Gather everyone together at a convenient time. Sketch a floor plan of all rooms, including doors, windows, and hallways. Include all floors of the home.

Plan and draw the escape plan with arrows showing two ways, if possible, to get out of each room. Sleeping areas are most important, since most fires happen at night. Plan to use stairs only, never an elevator. Plan where everyone will meet after leaving the building.

Designate who should call the fire department and from which phone. Plan to leave the

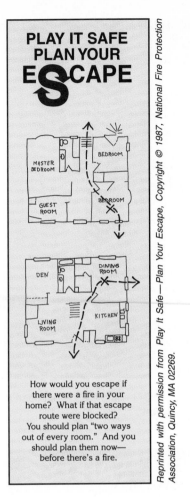

How would you escape if there were a fire in your home? What if that escape route were blocked? You should plan "two ways out of every room." And you should plan them now—before there's a fire.

Reprinted with permission from Play It Safe—Plan Your Escape, Copyright © 1987, National Fire Protection Association, Quincy, MA 02269.

Figure 23-2   Plan a fire escape route for your home.

burning building first and then call from a phone nearby, if possible. Many, but not all, locations in the United States use 9-1-1 for the emergency number. When you travel, take a moment to find out and write down the local emergency number.

Remember and use the following guidelines to escape from fire:

- If smoke is present, crawl low to escape. Since smoke rises in a fire, breathable air is often close to the floor.
- Make sure children can open windows, go down a ladder, and lower themselves to the ground. Practice with them. Always lower children to the ground first before you go out a window.

Figure 23-3 In a fire, do not open a door if it feels hot.

FIRE SAFETY

The following statements represent an awareness of fire safety that can reduce your chances, and the chances of others, of injury from a fire. Check each statement that reflects your lifestyle.

- [ ] I have a fire-escape plan for the place where I live, and I practice it with other people who live there.

- [ ] I have fire extinguishers in at least two rooms in my home, and I and other occupants know how to use them.

- [ ] I have smoke detectors in my home, and I check the batteries every month and change them every 6 months.

- [ ] I keep irons and other heating appliances unplugged when not in use.

If you only checked one or two statements, you should consider making changes in your lifestyle now.

- Get out quickly and do not, under any circumstances, return to a burning building.
- If you cannot escape, stay in the room and stuff door cracks and vents with wet towels, rags, or clothing. If a phone is available, call the fire department—even if rescuers are already outside—and tell the dispatcher your location.

Contact your local fire department for additional safety guidelines. Install a smoke detector on every floor of your home. Eighty percent of homes in the United States have smoke detectors, but half of them do not work because of old or missing batteries, according to the International Association of Fire Chiefs. A good way to remember the batteries is to change them twice a year when you reset your clocks for daylight saving time.

Knowing how to exit from a hotel in a fire could save your life. Locate the fire exits and fire extinguisher on your floor. If you hear an alarm while in your room, feel the door first and do not open it if it is hot (Fig. 23-3). Do not use the elevator. If the hall is relatively smoke free, use the stairs to exit. If the hall is filled with smoke, crawl to the exit. If you cannot get to the exit, return to your room. Turn off the ventilation system, stuff door cracks and vents with wet towels, and telephone the front desk or the fire department to report the fire and your location.

Safety at home

Over 24 million injuries occur in homes each year. The three leading causes of accidental death in the home are falls (32 percent), poisoning (24 percent), and burns (14 percent). Most falls occur around the home. Young children and the elderly are frequent victims of falls. Removing hazards and practicing good safety habits will make your home safer (Fig. 23-4). Make a list of needed improvements. Safety at home is relatively simple and relies largely on common sense. Taking the following steps will help make your home a safer place:

- Post emergency numbers—EMS personnel, fire, police, poison control center, physician, as well as other important numbers—near every phone.

PREVENT ACCIDENTS AT HOME

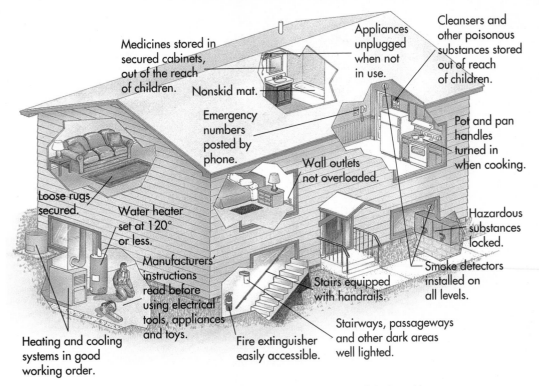

Figure 23-4   Follow home safety practices to prevent injuries at home.

- Make sure that stairways and hallways are well lit.
- Equip stairways with handrails, and have nonslip tread or securely fastened rugs.
- Secure rugs to the floor with double-sided tape.
- If moisture accumulates in damp spots, correct the cause of the problem. Clean up spills promptly.
- Keep medicines and poisonous substances separate from each other and from food. They should be out of reach of children and in secured cabinets.
- Keep medicines in their original containers, with safety caps.
- Keep your heating and cooling systems and all appliances in good working order. Check heating and cooling systems annually before use.
- Read and follow manufacturers' instructions for electrical tools, appliances, and toys.
- Turn off the oven and other appliances when not using them. Unplug certain appliances, such as an iron, curling iron, coffee maker, or portable heater, after use.
- Make sure that your home has at least one working, easily accessible fire extinguisher and everyone knows how to use it.
- Keep any firearms in a locked place, out of the reach of children, and stored separately from ammunition.
- Have an emergency fire escape plan and practice it.
- Try crawling around your home to see it as an infant or young child sees it. You will become aware of unsuspected hazards.
- Turn pot handles toward the back of the stove.
- Ensure that cords for lamps and other items are not placed where someone can trip over them.

This list does not include all the safety measures you need to take in your home. If young

Make Your Home Safe for Kids

Storage Areas

YES/NO Are pesticides, detergents, and other household chemicals kept out of child's reach?

YES/NO Are tools kept out of child's reach?

General Safety Precautions Inside the Home

YES/NO Are stairways kept clear and uncluttered?

YES/NO Are stairs and hallways well lit?

YES/NO Are safety gates installed at tops and bottoms of stairways?

YES/NO Are guards installed around fireplaces, radiators or hot pipes, and wood-burning stoves?

YES/NO Are sharp edges of furniture cushioned with corner guards or other material?

YES/NO Are unused electric outlets covered with tape or safety covers?

YES/NO Are curtain cords and shade pulls kept out of child's reach?

YES/NO Are windows secured with window locks?

YES/NO Are plastic bags kept out of child's reach?

YES/NO Are fire extinguishers installed where they are most likely to be needed?

YES/NO Are smoke detectors in working order?

YES/NO Do you have an emergency plan to use in case of fire? Does your family practice this plan?

YES/NO Is the water set at a safe temperature? (A setting of 120° F or less prevents scalding from tap water in sinks and in tubs. Let the water run for three minutes before testing it.)

YES/NO If you have a gun, is it locked in a place where your child cannot get it?

YES/NO Are all purses, handbags, brief cases, and so on, including those of visitors, kept out of child's reach?

YES/NO Are all poisonous plants kept out of child's reach?

YES/NO Is a list of emergency phone numbers posted near a telephone?

YES/NO Is a list of instructions posted near a telephone for use by children and/or babysitters?

Bathroom

YES/NO Are the toilet seat and lid kept down when the toilet is not in use?

YES/NO Are cabinets equipped with safety latches and kept closed?

YES/NO Are all medicines in child-resistant containers and stored in a locked medicine cabinet?

YES/NO Are shampoos and cosmetics stored out of child's reach?

YES/NO Are razors, razor blades, and other sharp objects kept out of child's reach?

YES/NO Are hair dryers and other appliances stored away from sink, tub, and toilet?

YES/NO Does the bottom of tub or shower have rubber stickers or a rubber mat to prevent slipping?

YES/NO Is the child always watched by an adult while in the tub?

Use this checklist to spot dangers in your home. When you read each question, circle either the "Yes" box or the "No" box. Each "No" shows a possible danger for you and your family. Work with your family to remove dangers and make your home safer.

Kitchen

- YES/NO Do you cook on back stove burners when possible and turn pot handles toward the back of the stove?
- YES/NO Are hot dishes kept away from the edges of tables and counters?
- YES/NO Are hot liquids and foods kept out of child's reach?
- YES/NO Are knives and other sharp items kept out of child's reach?
- YES/NO Is the highchair placed away from stove and other hot appliances?
- YES/NO Are matches and lighters kept out of child's reach?
- YES/NO Are all appliance cords kept out of child's reach?
- YES/NO Are cabinets equipped with safety latches?
- YES/NO Are cabinet doors kept closed when not in use?
- YES/NO Are cleaning products kept out of child's reach?
- YES/NO Do you test the temperature of heated food before feeding the child?

Child's Room

- YES/NO Is child's bed or crib placed away from radiators and other hot surfaces?
- YES/NO Are crib slats no more than 2-3/8 inches apart?
- YES/NO Does the mattress fit the sides of the crib snugly?
- YES/NO Is paint or finish on furniture and toys nontoxic?
- YES/NO Are electric cords kept out of child's reach?
- YES/NO Is the child's clothing, especially sleepwear, flame resistant?
- YES/NO Does the toy box have a secure lid and safe-closing hinges?
- YES/NO Are the toys in good repair?
- YES/NO Are toys appropriate for the child's age?

Outside the Home/Play Areas

- YES/NO Is trash kept in tightly covered containers?
- YES/NO Are walkways, stairs, and railings in good repair?
- YES/NO Are walkways and stairs free of toys, tools, and other objects?
- YES/NO Are sandboxes and wading pools covered when not in use?
- YES/NO Are swimming pools nearby enclosed with a fence that your child cannot easily climb over?
- YES/NO Is playground equipment safe? Is it assembled according to the manufacturer's instructions and anchored over a level, soft surface such as sand or wood chips?

Parents' Bedroom

- YES/NO Are space heaters kept away from curtains and flammable materials?
- YES/NO Are cosmetics, perfumes, and breakable items stored out of child's reach?
- YES/NO Are small objects, such as jewelry, buttons, and safety pins, kept out of child's reach?

CHILD SAFETY

The following statements represent an awareness of child safety that can reduce the chances of injury to your child. Check each statement that reflects your lifestyle.

- ☐ I buckle my child into an approved automobile safety seat even when making short trips.

- ☐ I teach my child safety by behaving safely in my everyday activities.

- ☐ I supervise my child whenever he or she is around water and maintain fences and gates that act as barriers to water.

- ☐ I have checked my home for potential fire hazards and smoke detectors are installed and working.

- ☐ I have placed foods and small items that can choke my child out of his or her reach.

- ☐ I inspect my home, day-care center, school, babysitter's home, or wherever my child spends time for potential safety and health hazards.

If you only checked one or two statements, you should consider making changes in your lifestyle now.

HOME SAFETY

The following statements represent a safety-conscious lifestyle that can reduce your chances, and the chances of others, of injury in your home. Check each statement that reflects your lifestyle.

- ☐ The stairways and halls in my home are well lit.

- ☐ I have nonslip tread or securely fastened rugs on my stairs.

- ☐ I keep all medications out of reach of children and in a locked cabinet.

- ☐ I keep any poisonous materials out of the reach of children and in a locked cabinet.

- ☐ All rugs are firmly secured to the floor.

- ☐ I store any firearms, unloaded, in a locked place out of the reach of children, and ammunition is stored separately.

- ☐ I keep the handles of pots and pans on the stove turned inward when I am using them.

If you only checked one or two statements, you should consider making changes in your lifestyle now.

children or elderly individuals live with you, you will need to take additional steps, depending on the individual characteristics of your home.

For an elderly person, you may need to install hand rails in the bath tub or shower and beside the toilet. You may need a bath chair or bench. Always have an in-tub mat with a suction base if your tub does not have nonslip strips built in. A safe bath water temperature is 101 degrees F (38 degrees C).

Safety at work

Most people spend approximately one third of their day at work. To improve safety at work, you should be aware of the following:

Figure 23-5 Safety clothing and/or equipment are required for some jobs.

WORKPLACE SAFETY

The following statements represent a safety-conscious lifestyle that can reduce your chances, and the chances of others, of injury at your workplace. Check each statement that reflects your lifestyle.

☐ I know the fire evacuation procedures at my workplace.

☐ I know the location of first aid supplies and the nearest fire extinguisher at my workplace.

☐ I wear any recommended safety equipment and follow any recommended safety procedures.

☐ I know how to report an emergency at work.

☐ I know how to activate the emergency response team.

If you only checked one or two statements, you should consider making changes in your lifestyle now.

- Fire evacuation procedures
- Location of the nearest fire extinguisher and first aid kit

If you work in an environment where hazards exist, wear recommended safety equipment and follow safety procedures (Fig. 23-5). Both employers and employees must follow safety rules issued by the Occupational Safety and Health Administration (OSHA). Anytime you operate machinery or perform an activity that may involve flying particles, you should wear protective eyewear, such as goggles. Inspect mechanical equipment and ladders periodically to ensure good working order. Check for worn or loose parts that could break and cause a mishap. Before climbing a ladder, place its legs on a firm, flat surface and have someone anchor it while you climb. Take workplace safety training seriously. Ask your employer about first aid and CPR refresher courses.

Safety at play

Make sports and other recreational activities safe by always following accepted guidelines for the activity (Fig. 23-6).

Each year, about 700 bicyclists are killed and approximately 39,000 suffer disabling injuries. Head injuries cause about 75 percent of all bicycling fatalities. When cycling, always wear an approved helmet. The head or neck is the most seriously injured part of the body in most fatally injured cyclists. Children should wear a helmet even if they are still going along the sidewalk on training wheels. Some states have helmet laws that apply to young children. Look for a helmet approved by the Snell Memorial Foundation or the American National Standards Institute (ANSI), and make sure it is the correct size and fits comfortably and securely. Keep off roads that are busy or have no shoulder. Wear reflective clothing, and have a light and reflectors on your bicycle wheels if you cycle at night. Make sure your

RECREATIONAL SAFETY

The following statements represent a safety-conscious lifestyle that can reduce your chances, and the chances of others, of injury during recreational activity. Check each statement that reflects your lifestyle.

☐ I follow the rules laid down for any sport I take part in.

☐ I wear any recommended safety gear, such as a helmet or goggles, for any sport or activity.

☐ I wear a life jacket when I am in a boat.

☐ I enter the water feetfirst to check unknown water depths.

☐ I keep my recreational equipment in good condition.

If you only checked one or two statements, you should consider making changes in your lifestyle now.

Figure 23-6   Wear proper safety equipment during recreational activities.

bicycle and your child's bicycle are in good condition and the brakes and headlights work. Most bicycle mishaps happen within a mile of home.

With any activity in which eyes could be injured, such as racquetball, wear protective goggles. Appropriate footwear is also important in preventing injuries. For activities involving physical contact, wear properly fitted protective equipment to avoid serious injury. Above all, know and follow the rules of the sport.

If you do not know how to swim, learn how or always wear an appropriate flotation device

if you are going to be in or around the water. If you are on a boat, always wear a flotation device. Never drink and drive a boat and do not travel in a boat whose driver has recently been drinking. Dangerous undercurrents can catch even the best of swimmers in shallow water. Be careful when walking beside rivers, lakes, and other bodies of water. Many drownings happen to people who never intended to be in the water at all.

If you run, jog, or walk, plan your route carefully. Exercise only in well-lit, well-populated areas, and consider exercising with another person. Keep off busy roads. If you must

Nutrition facts	Amount/Serving	% Daily value*	Amount/Serving	% Daily value*	*Percent Daily Values are based on a 2,000 calorie diet. Your daily values may be higher or lower depending on your calorie needs:

Nutrition facts

Serving size 7 slices (28g)
Servings per Container 5

Calories 141
Calories from Fat 57

	Amount/Serving	% Daily value*
Total fat 7 g		11%
Saturated fat 3 g		14%
Cholesterol 0 mg		0%
Sodium 360 mg		15%
Vitamin A 21%	Vitamin C 27%	

Amount/Serving	% Daily value*
Total Carbohydrate 19 g	6%
Dietary Fiber 1 g	4%
Sugars 8 g	
Protein 2 g	
Calcium 1%	Iron 9%

*Percent Daily Values are based on a 2,000 calorie diet. Your daily values may be higher or lower depending on your calorie needs:

	Calories:	2,000	2,500
Total Fat	Less than	65g	80g
Sat Fat	Less than	20g	25g
Cholesterol	Less than	300mg	300mg
Sodium	Less than	2,400mg	2,400mg
Total Carbohydrate		300g	375g
Dietary Fiber		25g	30g

Calories per gram: Fat 9 Carbohydrate 4 Protein 4

Figure 23-7 Food label.

exercise outdoors after dark, wear reflective clothing and move facing traffic. Be alert for cars pulling out at intersections and driveways.

Whenever you start an activity unfamiliar to you, such as boating, skiing, or motorcycle riding, take lessons to learn how to do the sport safely. Many mishaps result from inexperience. Make sure your equipment is in good working order. Ski bindings, for instance, should be professionally inspected, adjusted, and lubricated before each season. An added expense, yes, but so are serious injuries.

REDUCING YOUR RISK OF ILLNESS

The choices you make about your lifestyle affect your health and general well-being. Informed choices can reduce or eliminate your chances of cancer, stroke, cardiovascular disease, COPD, pneumonia, diabetes, HIV infection, and disease of the liver. These diseases are the leading causes of chronic illness and death in the United States.

Nutrition

Nutrition is the science that deals with the food you eat and how your body uses it. Studies indicate that poor diet is a contributing factor to many diseases. Changing your diet, therefore, to make it healthier and more nutritious is one of the lifestyle decisions you may decide to make. This chapter touches on a few basic facts about nutrition; to understand this important subject in more detail, you should take a nutrition course, consult a nutritionist, or at least read a book recommended by a health care provider or a nutritionist. However, learning to interpret the nutrition information on packaged food labels is a basic and important step you can take toward ensuring that you eat a proper diet.

Food labels

Food labels describing a product's nutritional value are required by law on most packaged food and began appearing on many food products in 1993. The labels provide specific information about certain **nutrients,** substances found in food that are required by the body because they are essential elements of a nutritious diet. Weights and percentages are provided so that consumers can evaluate the nutrients as to how they fit as part of a total daily diet.

Food is made up of six classes of nutrients—carbohydrates, fats, proteins, vitamins, minerals, and water. Food labels are now required to list the amounts per serving of the following in a packaged product (Fig. 23-7):

- **Calories**—A *calorie* is a measure of the energy value of food. On some labels, they are called kilocalories or kcalories (1000 calories of heat energy), the term used in nutritional science.
- **Calories from fat**—*Fat* is an important supplier of the body's heat and energy. However, the kind and amount of dietary fat increases the risk of some cancers, coronary heart disease, diabetes, and obesity. Fat should provide no more than 25 to 30 percent of the daily calories in a well-balanced diet—approximately 65 grams per day.
- **Total fat**—The total fat includes the amount of saturated and unsaturated fat. Overconsumption of foods high in fat, especially when they replace healthier foods, such as carbohydrates and fiber, is a major health concern for Americans.

- **Saturated fat**—*Saturated fat* is the fat in animal tissue and products. It should make up no more than 10 percent of daily calories. Saturated fat is solid at room temperature. Eating high levels of saturated fat contributes to high levels of cholesterol in the blood and therefore to coronary artery disease. Foods high in saturated fat include palm and coconut oil, butter, ice cream, milk chocolate, cheddar and American cheese, and beef hot dogs.
- **Cholesterol**—Cholesterol is a waxy chemical substance found in animal tissue. It is not a fat, although it is chemically related to fat. High levels of cholesterol are considered to be a risk factor for cardiovascular disease, as discussed in Chapter 6. Foods high in cholesterol include eggs, shrimp, meat, fish, liver, and kidneys.
- **Sodium**—*Sodium* is a mineral abundant in table salt. The main health problem associated with sodium is hypertension, or high blood pressure. Use salt only in moderation, and check the sodium content of packaged food carefully. Many of them contain surprisingly large amounts of sodium. High sodium content is found in smoked meat and fish, many canned and instant soups, many frozen dinners, and some canned or bottled sauces.
- **Total carbohydrate**—*Carbohydrates* are compounds that contain carbon, hydrogen, and oxygen. In the body, they are easily converted to energy and are the main source of energy for all body functions. Sources of carbohydrates include grain and grain products such as cereal, rice, pasta, baked goods, potatoes, beans and peas, seeds, nuts, fruits, vegetables, and sugars.
- **Dietary fiber**—*Dietary fiber* consists of the carbohydrates that are not broken down by the human digestive process. Soluble fiber, fiber that dissolves in hot water, lowers blood cholesterol levels and has other beneficial effects. Fruit, vegetables, and grains are good sources of soluble fiber. Insoluble fiber adds bulk to the contents of the intestine and speeds the transit time of undigested food through the intestines. Wheat bran, other whole grains, dried beans and peas, and most fruit and vegetables are good sources of insoluble fiber.
- **Sugars**—Sugars are forms of carbohydrates. Sugar should be used in moderation—no more than 10 percent of daily calories. Sugar contributes to tooth decay, and high sugar consumption is considered by some to be a contributing factor to obesity, diabetes, heart disease, and malnutrition. On lists of ingredients, sugar is often hidden by being listed not as table sugar but as corn syrup or sucrose.
- **Protein**—*Proteins* are compounds made up of amino acids and contain the form of nitrogen most easily used by the human body. Protein contains the basic material for cell growth and repair, but if you take in more than the 15 percent of daily calories the body requires from proteins, the excess amount is converted to energy or stored as fat. Sources of protein include milk products, meat, and fish.
- **Vitamin A**—Vitamin A is essential for the growth of the cells of skin, hair, and mucous membranes. It contributes to bone and tooth development and increases resistance to infection. Sources include milk, cheese, butter, eggs, liver, carrots, cantaloupe, yellow squash, and sweet potatoes.
- **Vitamin C**—Vitamin C aids in protection against infection and in the absorption of iron and calcium. It contributes to the formation of bones and teeth and aids in wound healing. Sources include citrus fruits, melons, broccoli, green peppers, spinach, and strawberries.
- **Calcium**—Calcium contributes to tooth and bone formation and general body growth. It helps maintain nerve function, good muscle tone, and the regulation of normal heart beat. Sources include dairy products, dried beans, dark green vegetables, and shellfish.
- **Iron**—Iron aids in the formation of red blood cells, the production of antibodies, and the use of energy. It facilitates the transportation of carbon dioxide and oxygen. Sources include lean red meat, seafood, eggs, dried beans, nuts, grains, and green leafy vegetables.

The label also shows the size of a serving, given as a household measure, such as a piece or cup, followed by the metric weight in parentheses and the total number of servings per con-

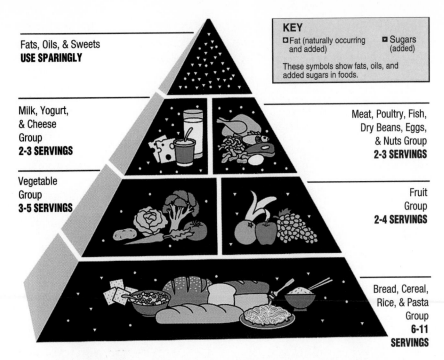

Fats, Oils, & Sweets
USE SPARINGLY

KEY
☐ Fat (naturally occurring   ▪ Sugars
  and added)   (added)

These symbols show fats, oils, and
added sugars in foods.

Milk, Yogurt,
& Cheese
Group
2-3 SERVINGS

Meat, Poultry, Fish,
Dry Beans, Eggs,
& Nuts Group
2-3 SERVINGS

Vegetable
Group
3-5 SERVINGS

Fruit
Group
2-4 SERVINGS

Bread, Cereal,
Rice, & Pasta
Group
**6-11
SERVINGS**

Figure 23-8 Food pyramid. (U.S. Department of Agriculture: *USDA's food guide pyramid,* USDA Human Nutrition, Pub No 249, Washington DC, 1992, U.S. Government Printing.) (From Potter PA, Perry AG: *Basic nursing,* ed 3, St Louis, 1996, Mosby.)

tainer. The term "Daily Value" relates the total nutritional value of the product to a 2000-calorie daily diet and to a 2500-calorie daily diet. For example, using the label in Figure 23-7 on p. 467, a person on a 2000-calorie daily diet consuming one serving of that product would take in 19 grams of carbohydrates. This amount is 6 percent of 300 grams, which is the largest recommended daily amount. The person would also consume 7 grams, 11 percent, of the largest recommended daily amount of fat—65 grams or less.

Water, which is not mentioned on the current food labels, is, next to oxygen, the substance we need most to survive. Water regulates the body temperature through perspiration and carries oxygen and nutrients to the cells as part of the blood. Water lubricates the joints, removes wastes, and aids in respiration by moistening the lungs, which facilitates the intake of oxygen and the removal of carbon dioxide. Most health care professionals advise drinking six to eight 8-ounce (170.5 to 187.3 milliliters) glasses of water a day and more if you exercise regularly or drink alcohol or caffeine.

A healthy diet

A visit to a library will provide you with all the nutrition information you need as to the sources of protein, carbohydrates, including dietary fiber, and other necessary nutrients.

The **Food Guide Pyramid** shows the five basic food groups (Fig. 23-8). The food groups are arranged in a pyramid shape to indicate the proportions in which you should make daily food choices. One of the goals in the development of the Food Guide Pyramid was to recommend that we provide the bulk of our dietary energy from carbohydrates and the least from fats and sweets. The Food Guide Pyramid is a general food guide for planning a well-balanced diet. For information on how to order the "Food Guide Pyramid" brochure, write to the Superintendent of Documents, Consumer Information Center, Department 159-4, Pueblo, Colorado 81009.

Use the following guidelines to help you evaluate your food habits and make improvements in your diet:

- Eat a variety of foods. No single food can supply all the essential nutrients in the amount needed to maintain health. Select foods each day from all the major food groups in the proportions shown on the Food Guide Pyramid.

- Maintain a healthy weight. You need to de-

DIETARY GUIDELINES FOR HEALTHY AMERICAN ADULTS: A STATEMENT FOR PHYSICIANS AND HEALTH PROFESSIONALS BY THE NUTRITION COMMITTEE, AMERICAN HEART ASSOCIATION

1. Total fat intake should be less than 30% of calories.

2. Saturated fat intake should be less than 10% of calories.

3. Polyunsaturated fat intake should not exceed 10% of calories.

4. Cholesterol intake should not exceed 300 mg/day.

5. Carbohydrate intake should constitute 50% or more of calories, with emphasis on complex carbohydrates.

6. Protein intake should provide the remainder of calories.

7. Sodium intake should not exceed 3 g/day.

8. Alcoholic consumption should not exceed 1 to 2 oz of ethanol per day. Two ounces of 100 proof whiskey, 8 oz of wine, and 24 oz of beer each contain 1 oz of ethanol.

9. Total calories should be sufficient to maintain the individual's recommended body weight.

10. A wide variety of foods should be consumed.

Reprinted with permission from the American Heart Association.

termine what a healthy body weight is for you. Check with a physician or health care provider to find out.

- Choose a diet low in fat, saturated fat, and cholesterol.
- Choose a diet with plenty of vegetables, fruits, and grain products. These will supply you with carbohydrates needed for energy, nutrients, and dietary fiber.
- Use sugars in moderation.
- Use salt and sodium in moderation.
- Drink alcohol, if at all, only in moderate amounts. Most alcoholic beverages are high in calories and low in nutrients. Heavy drinking contributes to chronic liver problems, some throat and neck cancers, and many highway deaths (see Chapter 17).

Weight

Many adults are overweight. Some are overweight to the point of obesity. *Obesity,* defined as a condition characterized by excess body fat, contributes to diseases such as heart disease, high blood pressure, diabetes, and gall bladder disease. For males, obesity is defined as body fat equal to or greater than 25 percent of the total weight of the body and for females, it is equal to or greater than 32 percent of total body weight. See your physician or health care specialist for help if you want to have your body fat measured.

Losing weight, especially fat, is no easy task. Calories that are not used as energy are stored as fat. Weight loss and gain depend on the balance of caloric intake and energy output. If you take in more calories than you use, you gain weight. If you use more calories than take in, you lose weight. There are several guides to weight control.

Day-to-day fluctuations in weight reflect changes in the level of fluids in your body. So, if you are watching your weight, pick one day and time per week as weigh-in time. Track your weight loss based on this weekly amount, not on day-to-day differences. Even better, have a body fat analysis done. The term "overweight" does not take body composition into account. **Body composition** is the ratio of fat to all the tissues, such as muscles, that are fat free. One person may weigh more than is termed desirable for his or her height, but the weight may be mainly in muscle rather than fat. Someone else may be within an acceptable weight range but have a large proportion of his or her weight in body fat, which is not healthy.

WEIGHT-LOSS STRATEGIES

Use some of the following strategies to help you lose weight—

- Keep a log of the times, settings, reasons, and feelings associated with your eating.

- Set realistic, long-term goals (for example, losing one pound per week instead of five pounds per week).

- Occasionally reward yourself with small amounts of food you enjoy.

- Eat slowly, and take time to enjoy the taste of the food.

- Be more physically active (take stairs instead of elevators, or park in the distant part of the parking lot).

- Reward yourself when you reach your goals (for example, with new clothes, sporting equipment).

- Share your commitment to losing weight with your family and friends who will support you.

- Keep a record of the food you eat each day.

- Weigh yourself once a week at the same time and record your weight.

- Be prepared to deal with occasional plateaus as you lose weight.

NUTRITION AND WEIGHT

The following statements represent a healthy lifestyle that can reduce your chance of disease. Check each statement that reflects your lifestyle.

- [ ] I eat a balanced diet.

- [ ] I read the nutrition labels on food products to help me eat a balanced diet.

- [ ] I monitor my intake of foods high in fats.

- [ ] I monitor my intake of sodium and sugars.

- [ ] I do not fry foods.

- [ ] I maintain an appropriate weight.

- [ ] If I need to lose weight, I use medically approved diet techniques.

- [ ] For snacks, I eat fruit, vegetables, and other healthy food rather than "junk foods."

- [ ] I drink 6 to 8 glasses of water daily.

If you only checked one or two statements, you should consider making changes in your lifestyle now.

Weight loss or gain should always be combined with regular exercise—another part of a healthy lifestyle. Any activity—walking to the bus, climbing the stairs, cleaning house—uses calories. You even burn off a few while you sleep. The more active you are, the more calories you use. Activity allows you to eat a few more calories and still maintain body weight.

Your eating habits should change as you grow older. A person who eats the same number of calories between the ages of 20 to 40 and maintains the same level of activity during this time will be considerably heavier at 40 than at 20. It is more important as you grow older to eat foods that provide your body with essential nutrients but are not high in calories.

Pregnant women should follow their doctor's advice regarding diet. Severely limiting calories and fat can be detrimental to the developing fetus.

Fitness

Many of us would like to be more fit. In general, fitness involves cardiorespiratory endurance, muscular strength, muscular endurance, and flexibility. You do not need to take part in sports, such as tennis, basketball, or soccer, to achieve health-related fitness. You can achieve fitness for health purposes by taking part in such activities as walking, jogging, swimming, cycling, hiking, and weight training, among others.

Exercise

The "no pain, no gain" theory is not a good approach to exercise. In fact, experiencing pain usually means you are exercising improperly. You achieve the health benefits of exercise when it is somewhat uncomfortable, but not

Figure 23-9   Build exercise into your daily activities.

painful. Be sure to warm up to prepare the body before vigorous exercise and cool down afterwards. Make flexibility exercises part of the warm-up and cool-down process. When possible, add exercises or activities that strengthen the muscles to your fitness routine. Turn your daily activities into exercise (Fig. 23-9). Walk briskly instead of driving, whenever possible. Take the stairs instead of the elevator or the escalator. Pedal an exercise bike while watching TV, listening to music, or reading. Table 23-1 summarizes the contributions to physical fitness of 14 sports and exercises.

Many books and materials are available for those who want to improve their fitness and develop an exercise program. You can become physically fit, regardless of the condition you are in when you start. Set realistic goals and you will see regular progress. A variety of training programs are available. Make a commitment to exercise each week. Whatever activities you choose to achieve fitness, you must exercise regularly and maintain a level of activity to maintain fitness. You should exercise nonstop for a minimum of 20 minutes a day 3 to 5 times a week. The many benefits include loss of body fat, more resistance to disease, an ability to reduce the negative effects of stress, and increased energy. If you have been sedentary or

have health problems, see your doctor before starting an exercise program. It is never too late to start exercising, however. People in nursing homes, many of them in wheelchairs, are able to experience and demonstrate the benefits of flexibility and strength training.

Cardiorespiratory endurance

If you have time for limited exercise only, it is best to build up ***cardiorespiratory endurance,*** the ability to take in, deliver, and extract oxygen for physical work. Cardiorespiratory endurance is the foundation for total fitness. The best way to accomplish cardiorespiratory endurance is through aerobic exercise. The term ***aerobic*** refers to activities that require additional effort by the heart and lungs to meet the increased demand by the skeletal muscles for oxygen. **Aerobic exercise** is sustained, rhythmical exercise, using the large muscle groups, for at least 20-30 minutes within your target heart rate.

Taking part in aerobic exercise can—

- Reduce the risk of cardiovascular disease.
- Develop stronger bones that are less susceptible to injury.
- Promote joint stability.
- Contribute to fewer lower back problems.
- Improve self image.

TABLE 23-1

Rating of 14 Sports and Exercises

Exercise	Cardio-respiratory Endurance (Stamina)	Muscular Endurance	Muscular Strength	Flexibility	Balance	Weight Control	Muscle Definition	Digestion	Sleep	Total
Jogging	21	20	17	9	17	21	14	13	16	148
Bicycling	19	18	16	9	18	20	15	12	15	142
Swimming	21	20	14	15	12	15	14	13	16	140
Skating (ice or roller)	18	17	15	13	20	17	14	11	15	140
Handball/ Squash	19	18	15	16	17	19	11	13	12	140
Skiing— nordic	19	19	15	14	16	17	12	12	15	139
Skiing— alpine	16	18	15	14	21	15	14	9	12	134
Basketball	19	17	15	13	16	19	13	10	12	134
Tennis	16	16	14	14	16	16	13	12	11	128
Calisthenics	10	13	16	19	15	12	18	11	12	126
Walking	13	14	11	7	8	13	11	11	14	102
Golf*	8	8	9	9	8	6	6	7	6	67
Softball	6	8	7	9	7	7	5	8	7	64
Bowling	5	5	5	7	6	5	5	7	6	51

The ratings are on a scale of 0 to 3; thus a rating of 21 is the maximum score that can be achieved (a score of 3 by all 7 panelists). Ratings were made on the following basis: frequency, 4 times per week minimum; duration, 30 to 60 minutes per session.

* The rating was made on the basis of using a golf cart or caddy. If you walk the course and carry your clubs, the values improve.

(Amspaugh DJ, Hammick MH, Rosato FD: *Wellness: concepts and applications*, St Louis, 1994, Mosby.)

- Help control diabetes.
- Stimulate other lifestyle changes.

Target heart rate range

To achieve cardiorespiratory endurance, you must exercise your heart and lungs. To do this, you should exercise at least three times a week for a minimum of 20 to 30 minutes and at your appropriate target heart rate (THR) range. Your **target heart rate range** is 60 to 90 percent of your maximum heart rate. To find your maximum heart rate, subtract your age from 220. To find your target heart rate range, multiply that figure first by 0.60 and then by 0.90. For example, if you are 20 years old, 60 percent of your maximum heart rate would be (220 − 20) × 0.60 = 120 beats per minute (bpm). This figure is the lower limit of your target heart rate range.

To find the upper limit, multiply 220 − 20 by .90, which is 180. Your target heart rate range is from 120 bpm to 180 bpm. You should get your pulse up to between 120 and 180 bpm and keep it there for 20 to 30 minutes. If you are age 20, with an average level of fitness for example, aim for 150 to 160 bpm. Keep below the upper limit. In general, to improve cardiorespiratory endurance, a person must exercise at least 60 percent of his or her maximum heart rate.

As you exercise, take your pulse periodically at the wrist (radial artery) or neck (carotid artery) (Fig. 23-10). Your exercise must be continuous and vigorous to stay within your target heart rate range. As you build cardiorespiratory endurance, you will eventually be able to exercise for longer periods of time and at a higher THR.

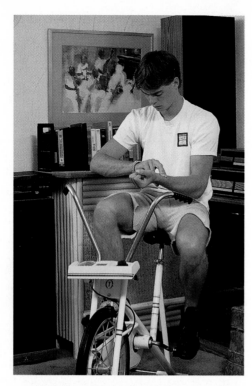

Figure 23-10   As you exercise, take your pulse periodically to see if you have reached your appropriate target heart rate.

FITNESS

The following statements represent a healthy lifestyle that can reduce your chance of disease. Check each statement that reflects your lifestyle.

- ☐ I set realistic exercise goals and aim to achieve them.

- ☐ I exercise regularly for a minimum of 20 minutes at least three times a week.

- ☐ I warm up before exercise and cool down afterwards.

- ☐ I incorporate flexibility and muscle-strengthening activities into my fitness activities.

- ☐ I use aerobic exercise to build cardiorespiratory endurance.

- ☐ I know my target heart rate range and exercise within it.

- ☐ I walk or bike rather than drive whenever possible.

If you only checked one or two statements, you should consider making changes in your lifestyle now.

Stress

Everyone experiences stress. Stress in itself is not harmful. How we deal with what we view as stress is what determines whether it has a positive or negative effect on our lives. **Stress** is a physiological or psychological response to real or imagined influences that alter an existing state of physical, mental, or emotional balance. The reaction to stress can take such varied forms as muscle tension, dizziness, increased heart rate, acute anxiety, sleeplessness, anger, excitement, energy, and even joy. A **stressor** is an event or condition that triggers the stress response. Stressors may be as varied as taking a test, speaking in public, poverty, loneliness, poor self esteem, being stuck in traffic, or winning a prize. A stressor for one person may not be a stressor for another, although some stressors, such as injury or loneliness, tend to stress everyone.

Positive, or "good" stress is productive. Good stress is the force that produces, for example, enhanced thinking ability, improved relationships with others, and a greater sense of control. It can be part of the experience of being in a play, making a new friend, or succeeding at a difficult task, for example. Good stress can help you perform better and be more efficient. Stress judged as "bad" (distress) can result in negative responses, such as sadness, fatigue, guilt, and disease.

Most stressful situations involve either harm and loss, threat, or challenge. Harm and loss situations, for example, include the death or loss of a loved one, physical assault, and physical injury. Threat situations, real or perceived, can be frightening or menacing and make it more difficult to deal with life. They can result in anger, anxiety, or depression. Challenging situations often involve major life changes, such as moving, getting a new job, leaving home, and forming or leaving a close relationship.

The effects of stress

Any stressful situation has an effect on the body. Because it affects the immune system, stress can be a major contributor to disease. The effects of stress on body systems can result in increased susceptibility to headaches, high blood pressure, clogging of the arteries, cancer, and respiratory problems. When someone reacts to stress by over- or under-eating, overusing caffeine or alcohol, smoking, or eating foods high in sugar and fat, for example, the physiological balance in the body is upset.

The first step in learning to deal with stress is to become aware of the accompanying physical and mental signals. Some of the physical indicators of negative stress include severe headaches, sweating, lower back pain, weakness, sleep disturbance, and shortness of breath. Other indicators, both emotional and mental, include depression, irritability, denial that a problem exists, increased incidences of illness, an inability to concentrate, feelings of unreality, inability to relax, and becoming "accident prone." Becoming aware of how your body reacts to stress can help you recognize situations and conditions that are stressful for you.

Managing stress

Stress management is a person's planned attempt to cope or deal with stress. Managing potentially harmful stress may require using a variety of techniques, including using time effectively, evaluating the activities that are important for you, and establishing achievable goals. Perhaps the most difficult form of coping is change. It is especially hard to change an outlook or way of life, even if it has become unproductive and a source of negative stress. The advice and help of a professional counselor can be useful in such situations.

Relaxation techniques can also be helpful in reducing or avoiding the negative effects of stress. A few of these techniques are exercise, yoga, meditation, listening to quiet or soothing music, and relaxation exercises, including deep breathing, and muscle relaxation. **Biofeedback,** another technique, involves using instruments that measure bodily functions, such as heart rate and blood pressure. By receiving immediate feedback on responses such

STRESS

The following statements represent an awareness of stress that can reduce your chance of disease. Check each statement that reflects your lifestyle.

- [ ] I am aware of the physical and mental signals of stress.

- [ ] I know the effects stress has on my body.

- [ ] I would consult a professional counselor if necessary to help cope with stress.

- [ ] I am able to use several relaxation techniques to help manage stress.

If you only checked one or two statements, you should consider making changes in your lifestyle now.

as muscle tension and skin temperature, the person can learn to consciously control these reactions. **Autogenics** uses self-suggestion to produce relaxation, using deep breathing, a conscious effort to relax, and repeated phrases that carry a message of calming. **Imagery** involves using the imagination to create various scenes and wished-for situations. Commercial tapes of various relaxation exercises are available and several books on stress management exist.

Smoking

During the past few decades, studies have made the negative effects of smoking clear. As a result, smoking has been banned or restricted in many work sites and public places around the nation. The nicotine in cigarettes is an addictive substance and a poison. The level of carbon monoxide in cigarette smoke is 400 times greater than the level considered safe in industrial workplaces. The tars are carcinogenic (cancer causing). Nicotine, carbon monoxide, and tars are all inhaled when you smoke.

Next time you are tempted to light up, consider that cigarette smoking is the single most preventable cause of heart and lung disease.

TABLE 23-2

Risks of Smoking

Risks	Results
Coronary heart disease	An estimated 169,000 to 226,000 deaths from coronary heart disease can be attributed to cigarette smoking.
Peripheral arterial disease	Smokers are two to three times more likely to suffer from abdominal aortic aneurysm than nonsmokers. Smokers have more atherosclerotic occlusions.
Lung cancer	Smoking cigarettes is the major cause of lung cancers in men and women. Rates are currently increasing faster among women than men.
Cancer of the larynx	Laryngeal cancer in smokers is 2.0 to 27.4 times that of nonsmokers.
Oral cancers	Use of smokeless tobacco and snuff is associated with an increased risk of oral cancer. Pipes and cigars are also major risk factors. Use of alcohol seems to enhance the possibility of developing oral cancer.
Cancer of the esophagus	Smoking cigarettes, pipes, and cigars increases the risk of dying from esophageal cancer from two to nine times. Alcohol use in combination with smoking adds to that risk.
Bladder cancer	Percentage of bladder cancer attributed to smoking is estimated at 40% to 60% in males and 25% to 35% in females.
Cancer of the pancreas	Smokers have twice the risk of nonsmokers for cancer of the pancreas.
Chronic obstructive pulmonary (lung) disease (COPD)	Between 80% to 90% of more than 60,000 deaths per year from COPD are from smoking.
Peptic ulcers	Cigarette smokers develop peptic ulcers much more frequently than nonsmokers. Ulcers are also more difficult to cure in smokers.
Complications in pregnancy, illnesses in children	Smoking mothers have more stillbirths and babies with low birth weight. The hospital admission rates for pneumonia and bronchitis are 28% higher in children of smoking mothers. Asthma is more common among children of smoking mothers. Prenatal smoking is a risk factor associated with persistent middle-ear effusion in young children.

(Anspaugh DJ, Hamrick MH, Rosato FD: *Wellness: concepts and applications*, St Louis, 1994, Mosby.)

Cigarette smoking causes most cases of lung cancer. Cigarette smoking severely narrows the coronary arteries, giving the cigarette smoker an increased risk of heart attack and sudden cardiac arrest over the nonsmoker. Smokers are at risk for cancer of the esophagus, pancreas, bladder, and larynx, as well. A pregnant woman who smokes harms herself and her unborn baby. The carbon monoxide in cigarettes travels to the fetus through the umbilical cord and into the fetus's circulatory system. Smoking mothers have more stillbirths and babies with low birth weight and respiratory problems than nonsmokers. Inhaling the smoke generated by smokers is a health risk for nonsmokers, including infants and children. Table 23-2 summarizes the risks of smoking.

Those who use smokeless tobacco also face serious risks. Nicotine is absorbed through the membranes of the mouth and cheeks. Chewing tobacco and snuff cause cancer of the mouth and tongue, so these products should also be avoided to help ensure good health.

Your risk of developing the diseases or conditions listed in Table 23-2 starts to go down as soon as you stop smoking and eventually decreases to that of any nonsmoker. Stopping smoking or stopping the use of smokeless tobacco can be difficult, but most ex-smokers and former users say they feel better physically and

SOURCES OF HELP TO QUIT SMOKING

American Heart Association
7272 Greenville Avenue
Dallas, TX 75231
(214) 373-6300
Contact your local heart association

American Lung Association
1740 Broadway
14th Floor
New York, NY 10019
1-800-LUNG-USA
(212) 315-8700
Contact your local lung association

American Cancer Society
1599 Clifton Road NE
Atlanta, GA 30329
(800) ACS-2345
(404) 320-3333
Contact your local cancer society

National Cancer Institute
Cancer Information Service
(800) 4-CANCER

Lungline National Jewish Center for Immunology and Respiratory Medicine
1400 Jackson Street
Denver, CO 80206
(800) 222-LUNG
(303) 355-LUNG (Denver)

SMOKING AND ALCOHOL

The following statements represent an awareness of smoking and alcohol that can reduce your chance of disease. Check each statement that reflects your lifestyle.

☐ I am aware of the risks and negative effects of smoking.

☐ To prevent inhaling second-hand smoke as much as possible, I avoid being around people who are smoking.

☐ I do not use tobacco products.

☐ I drink in moderation or not at all.

☐ Whenever I am in a group driving to a party where alcohol will be served, I make sure the group has a designated driver.

☐ I am aware of the rate at which alcohol passes into the bloodstream.

☐ I do not drink more than one drink per hour.

If you only checked one or two statements, you should consider making changes in your lifestyle now.

---

emotionally. Many programs designed to help the smoker break the habit are available. If you want to quit smoking or know someone who does, the agencies listed in the *Sources of Help to Quit Smoking* may be able to help you.

Alcohol

Alcohol is the most popular drug in Western society. About 100 million Americans drink beer, wine, or distilled spirits. In addition to the hazardous relationship between drinking alcohol and driving, consuming alcohol in large amounts has other unhealthy effects on the body, as indicated in Chapter 17.

A blood alcohol concentration (BAC) of 0.05 percent or higher impairs judgment and reflexes and makes activities like driving unsafe (Fig. 23-11). How much drinking leads to this blood alcohol level? On an empty stomach, an average 160-pound person can reach this level after just two ordinary-size drinks in an hour or less—2 bottles of beer, 10 ounces of wine, or 2 drinks with 1 ounce of alcohol in each. The faster alcohol enters the bloodstream, the faster the BAC increases. A small amount of alcohol enters the body quickly from the stomach, where food slows alcohol absorption. The major portion passes into the bloodstream from the small intestine, where food does not affect absorption. From the bloodstream, alcohol goes directly to the brain and to other parts of the body, such as the liver. Because of the time it takes for the body to process alcohol, you should always limit yourself to one drink per hour.

Only time can make a person sober after having too much to drink. Black coffee and a cold shower may make a person feel more alert, but the body must process the alcohol over time for the impairment of judgment and coordina-

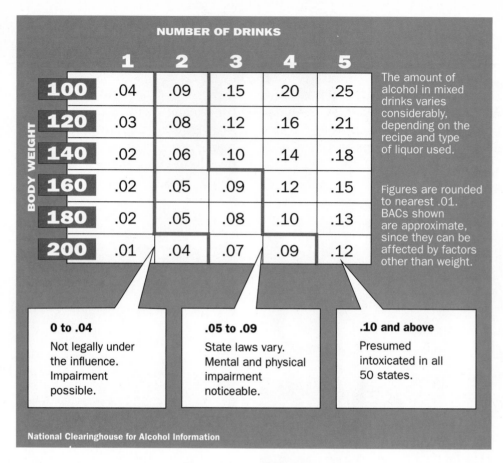

NUMBER OF DRINKS

BODY WEIGHT	1	2	3	4	5
100	.04	.09	.15	.20	.25
120	.03	.08	.12	.16	.21
140	.02	.06	.10	.14	.18
160	.02	.05	.09	.12	.15
180	.02	.05	.08	.10	.13
200	.01	.04	.07	.09	.12

The amount of alcohol in mixed drinks varies considerably, depending on the recipe and type of liquor used.

Figures are rounded to nearest .01. BACs shown are approximate, since they can be affected by factors other than weight.

0 to .04
Not legally under the influence. Impairment possible.

.05 to .09
State laws vary. Mental and physical impairment noticeable.

.10 and above
Presumed intoxicated in all 50 states.

National Clearinghouse for Alcohol Information

Figure 23-11   BAC chart.

tion to pass. Therefore, any group driving to a party should always have a designated, non-drinking driver for the return trip.

Whether hosting a party or participating in one, you can act responsibly by keeping alcohol consumption under control. To do this, remember these general principles:

- Drink slowly. Have no more than one drink per hour.
- As a host, have nonalcoholic beverages available.
- Do not drink before a party.
- Avoid drinking when angry or depressed.
- Eat plenty of food before and while drinking.
- Avoid salty foods—they may make you thirsty and cause you to drink more. As a host, do not provide foods that are high in salt.
- Do not play or promote drinking games.
- When mixing drinks, always measure the amount of alcohol. Do not just pour. As a

host, hire a bartender and give clear instructions about measuring drinks or mix all the drinks yourself.
- As a host, do not have an open bar or serve someone who has had too much to drink.
- Stop drinking alcohol 1 hour before the party is over. If you are a host, stop serving alcohol.
- Do not drink and drive. Have a designated nondrinking driver or call a cab.

For help with an alcohol problem, refer to Chapter 17 for a list of organizations that provide help and support for substance abuse problems.

MIND AT WORK

1. *What might Mrs. Gallagher have done to achieve her current state of fitness?*

SUMMARY

Injury and disease kill over 2 million people a year in the United States. You can help prevent injury and disease by taking safety precautions and making lifestyle choices that promote health. To reduce your risk of injury, it is important to take safety precautions in vehicles, at work, at play, and in your home. To reduce your risk of illness, you need to make choices about your lifestyle. Making healthy choices will reduce your chances of cancer, stroke, heart attack, cardiovascular disease, and other diseases that are the leading causes of chronic illness and death. Eating a healthy diet, exercising regularly, avoiding harmful substances, and managing stress all contribute to a person's health and well-being.

Answer to Application Question

1. To have achieved her current state of fitness, Mrs. Gallagher would probably have eaten a healthy diet, exercised regularly, not smoked, and drank alcohol only in moderation.

STUDY QUESTIONS

1. Match each term with the correct definition.

    a. Carbohydrates
    b. Obesity
    c. Stress
    d. Cardiorespiratory endurance
    e. Aerobic exercise
    f. Saturated fat
    g. Calorie

    _____ A measure of the energy value of food.

    _____ A physiological or psychological response to real or imagined influences that alter an existing state of physical, mental, or emotional balance.

    _____ The ability to take in, deliver, and extract oxygen for physical work.

    _____ The fat in animal tissues and products.

    _____ Activities that require additional effort by the heart and lungs to meet the increased demand by the skeletal muscles for oxygen.

    _____ A condition characterized by excess of stored body fat.

    _____ Compounds that contain carbon, oxygen, and hydrogen; the main source of energy for all body functions.

2. Fill in the blank with the correct word or words.

    The leading cause of death in the United States is _____. The disease

    that is the leading cause of death is _____ _____. The

    leading cause of death for people age 1 to 44 is _____.

3. List three ways to reduce your risk of personal injury.

4. List two motor-vehicle safety guidelines.

5. List four guidelines for what to do in case the building you are in catches fire.

6. When Jake learned that his grandmother had fallen in the upstairs hall, he went to her house to see what he could do to make it safer for her. What hazards might he have discovered in the hall? What could he do to make the hall safer?

7. Your 2-year-old nephew is coming to visit. What can you do to make your kitchen safe?

In questions 8 through 16, circle the letter of the correct answer.

8. Which best describes the purpose of the current food labels?

   a. They compare the beneficial effects of the nutrients listed.
   b. They point out the dangers of fat and sugar.
   c. They provide a way to evaluate the nutritional value of the food product.
   d. All of the above.

9. From which of these food groups should you get the majority of your daily nutrients?

   a. Fruits and vegetables
   b. Milk and cheese
   c. Fats, oils, and sweets
   d. Bread, cereal, rice, and pasta

10. Which of these statements is correct?

    a. You can eat as much fat as you wish as long as it is not saturated fat.
    b. Excess protein is always stored in the body as muscle.
    c. Carbohydrates are the body's main source of energy.
    d. Dietary fiber has no value for the body, since it is not digested.

11. Which of these statements is correct?

    a. To be beneficial, exercise must cause pain.
    b. Only vigorous activities burn off calories.
    c. If you take in more calories than you use, you will not gain weight.
    d. Too much body fat contributes to disease.

12. To improve cardiorespiratory endurance, which form of exercise is most effective?

    a. Strength training
    b. Flexibility training
    c. Aerobic exercise
    d. Vigorous walking

13.   Which of these statements is correct?

   a.   Stress can be positive as well as negative.
   b.   Receiving an unexpected award can cause stress.
   c.   Not all people are stressed by the same events.
   d.   All of the above.

14.   Which is the addictive substance in cigarettes?

   a.   Tar
   b.   Nicotine
   c.   Carbon monoxide
   d.   All of the above

15.   Which of these statements is correct?

   a.   Cigarette smoking contributes heavily to lung cancer.
   b.   If you stop smoking, you remain at the same risk of heart attack.
   c.   The tars and carbon monoxide in cigarettes are harmless.
   d.   Chewing tobacco and snuff are safe because you do not inhale smoke when you use them.

16.   Which is the most effective way to sober up a person who has had too much to drink?

   a.   Give the person a lot of black coffee.
   b.   Put the person in a cold shower.
   c.   Have the person eat a lot of food.
   d.   None of the above.

17.   List four ways in which you can be a responsible host.

Answers are listed in Appendix A.

ANSWERS TO STUDY QUESTIONS

Chapter 1

1. b, c, e, f, d, a
2. (a) Citizen responder (b) EMS dispatcher (c) First responder (d) EMT-paramedic (e) Hospital care providers (f) Rehabilitation
3. (a) Silence when noise is expected; an unusual noise; (b) unusual behavior and appearance; confused speech
4. (a) Fear of doing something wrong; fear of not knowing what to do (b) The presence of bystanders; uncertainty about the victim; fear of disease transmission; the nature of the illness or injury; fear of doing something wrong; fear of not knowing what to do
5. (a) She could call EMS personnel and meet and direct the ambulance. (b) Someone could tell the driver to stop the bus; someone could call EMS personnel after the bus stopped; someone might have information about the person; someone could help calm and reassure other passengers.
6. (a) The immediate care given to a victim of injury or sudden illness until more advanced medical care can be obtained. (b) The most important action you can take in a life-threatening emergency. (c) A sudden illness requiring immediate medical attention. (d) Reasons for not acting or for hesitating to act. (e) A spilled medicine container. (f) Recognizing an emergency and deciding to act. (g) A situation requiring immediate action. (h) A network of community resources and medical personnel that provides emergency care to victims of injury or sudden illness.
7. Screech of tires, crash of metal, car struck telephone pole, leaning telephone pole, dangling wires, stalled vehicle
8. d

Chapter 2

1. Is the scene safe? What happened? How many victims are there? Can bystanders help?
2. Traffic; possible hazardous materials causing fumes; possible fire; extreme weather causing more collisions
3. Your exact location; telephone number from which call is being made; caller's name; what happened; number of people involved; condition of victim(s); help being given
4. Unconsciousness; no breathing; no signs of circulation; severe bleeding
5. a 6. b 7. b 8. d 9. Implied consent
10. Check, call, care

Chapter 3

1. (a) Respiratory (b) airway, lungs (c) circulatory (d) transports oxygen and other nutrients to cells and removes waste (e) skin, hair, nails (f) helps keep fluids in, prevents infection, sweat glands and pores in skin help regulate temperature, helps make vitamin D, stores minerals (g) bones, ligaments, muscles, tendons (h) supports body, allows movement, protects internal organs and structures, produces blood cells, stores minerals, produces heat (i) nervous (j) brain, spinal cord, nerves
2. d, g, c, f, b, a, h, e
3. a 4. c 5. c 6. c 7. b 8. b 9. d

Chapter 4

1. (a) Look for bystanders who can help, look for victims, look for dangers, look for clues to determine what happened. (b) Open the airway, check for breathing, check for signs of circulation, check for severe bleeding. (c) Dial 9-1-1 or the local emergency number. (d) Interview the victim and bystanders, do a head-to-toe examination, ask for consent to give care.
2. Unconsciousness; no breathing; no signs of circulation; severe bleeding
3. Check for consciousness, breathing, pulse, and severe bleeding. If the man is unconscious, have a bystander call EMS personnel immediately. If the man has any life-threatening conditions, have someone call EMS personnel while you give care. If the victim is conscious and has no life-threatening conditions, ask the victim and bystanders what happened, identify yourself, get consent to give care, interview the victim, and do a head-to-toe check for additional problems. Care for any problems you find, and have someone call EMS personnel if necessary. If the victim is not injured and feels able to stand, help the victim to his feet when he is ready.
4. The availability of someone to go with you; that the victim has no conditions that transporting could aggravate; that transporting would not cause additional injury or be painful to the victim.
5. Only when no life-threatening conditions exist; to find injuries or other conditions that may need care.
6. (c) 1, (f) 2, (e) 3, (a) 4, (b) 5, (d) 6
7. Avoid contact with the victim's body substances when possible. Place barriers, such as disposable gloves, plastic wrap, or a clean, dry cloth, between the victim's body substances and yourself. Wear protective clothing, such as disposable gloves, to cover any cuts, scrapes, and skin conditions you may have. Wash your hands with soap and water immediately after giving care. Do not eat, drink, or touch your mouth, nose, or eyes when giving first aid. Do not touch objects that may be soiled with blood or other body substances. Always have a first aid kit handy, and make sure the items in it, such as disposable gloves, are replaced if you use them.
8. b 9. c 10. b 11. a 12. d

Chapter 5

1. b, f, a, g, h, e, d, c
2. High-pitched sounds; skin is unusually moist; fearful; skin has a flushed appearance; shortness of breath; pain in chest
3. Swallowing large pieces of poorly chewed foods; drinking alcoholic beverages before or during meals; wearing dentures; eating while talking excitedly or laughing, or eating too fast; walking, playing, or running with food in the mouth
4. c, a, b
5. d 6. b 7. a 8. a 9. c 10. b
11. d 12. a 13. a 14. b 15. b 16. c
17. 2, 3, 1, 4
18. 4, 5, 2, 3, 1, 6

Chapter 6

1. e, c, g, i, d, b, h, a, f
2. The victim has no signs of circulation.
3. Another trained rescuer arrives and takes over. EMS personnel arrive and take over. The scene suddenly becomes unsafe. The victim's heart starts beating. You are too exhausted to continue.
4. Injury from motor vehicle crashes; drowning; smoke inhalation; poisonings; airway obstruction; firearm injuries; falls
5. Smoking; diets high in fat; high blood pressure; obesity; lack of routine exercise
6. c   7. d   8. d   9. b   10. d
11. b   12. c   13. b
14. Persistent chest pain associated with shoulder pain; perspiring heavily; breathing fast; looking ill
15. 2, 3, 1, 4, 5
16. d

Chapter 7

1. c, g, a, f, e, h, d, b, i
2. Transports oxygen, nutrients, and wastes; protects against disease by producing antibodies and defending against pathogens; maintains constant body temperature by circulating throughout the body
3. Blood spurting from a wound; blood that fails to clot after all measures have been taken to control bleeding
4. Apply direct pressure using your gloved hand. Place a sterile gauze pad or other clean material between the wound and your hand. Elevate the injured area if no broken bones are suspected. Maintain pressure by applying a pressure bandage. If these measures fail to stop the bleeding, apply pressure to a pressure point to slow the flow of blood to the area. Call EMS personnel.
5. Discoloration of the skin in the injured area; soft tissues, such as those in the abdomen, that are tender, swollen, or hard; anxiety or restlessness; rapid, weak pulse; rapid breathing; shortness of breath; cool, moist skin or pale or bluish skin; nausea and vomiting; vomiting blood; abdominal pain; excessive thirst; decreasing level of consciousness
6. Apply ice or a cold pack to the injured area. Be sure to place a cloth or another barrier between the source of cold and the skin to prevent damage to the skin.
7. b, d, c, a
8. Internal bleeding
9. Get ice or a cold pack and apply it to the area. If the injury appears to be serious, call EMS personnel.
10. a
11. Place an effective barrier between yourself and the victim's blood. Wash your hands thoroughly with soap and water immediately after providing care. Avoid eating, drinking, and touching your mouth, nose, or eyes while providing care or before washing your hands.

Chapter 8

1. F
2. Restlessness; fast breathing; drowsiness; pale, cold, moist skin; rapid, weak pulse; unconsciousness; irregular breathing
3. Sudden illnesses; severe injuries
4. Care for any life-threatening problems. Monitor breathing and pulse. If possible, keep Daren still. Help Daren maintain normal body temperature. Reassure Daren. Provide care for specific conditions.
5. d   6. b   7. d   8. d   9. b
10. Shock is life threatening because the circulatory system fails to circulate oxygen-rich blood to all parts of the body, causing vital organs to fail to function properly.

11. Elevating the legs helps to maintain blood flow to the vital organs.

Chapter 9

1. b, f, a, e, c, d
2. b, d, a, c
3. a, c, d, b
4. Swollen, red area around wound; area may be warm or painful, possible pus discharge; fever and feeling ill; red streaks from wound toward heart
5. Hold dressing in place; apply pressure; protect from dirt and infection; provide support
6. Laceration (cut); abrasion (scrape); puncture (penetrates—sharp object); avulsion (torn tissue—may be torn completely away)
7. Heat; electricity; chemicals; radiation
8. Superficial; deep
9. d   10. a   11. d   12. b   13. b   14. a
15. b   16. b   17. c   18. a   19. d   20. b
21. c   22. d   23. c   24. c

Chapter 10

1. h, b, f, c, a, i, k, d, j, g, e
2. Pain; swelling; deformity; discoloration of the skin; inability to use the affected part normally; loss of sensation in the affected part
3. Splint only if you can do it without causing more pain and discomfort. Splint an injury in the position you find it. Splint the injured area and the joints above and below the injury site. Check for proper circulation before and after splinting.
4. c   5. d   6. b   7. d   8. b

Chapter 11

1. c, b, d, a
2. Falling on the hand of an outstretched arm
3. Pain; swelling; discoloration; deformity; inability to use the limb; no sensation
4. Because of loss of sensation may indicate a serious musculoskeletal injury, send someone to call EMS personnel immediately while you stay and care for the victim. Control bleeding; have the person rest; apply ice; immobilize the injured areas; minimize shock
5. Injured lower extremity appears noticeably shorter than the other lower extremity; injured lower extremity is turned outward; severe pain; inability to move the lower extremity
6. Anatomic; soft; rigid
7. d   8. c   9. a
10. Control bleeding. Wear gloves or use a protective barrier. Have someone call EMS personnel. Immobilize the lower extremity, using the ground for a splint if possible. If splinting, check and recheck for feeling, warmth, and color. Monitor breathing and signs of circulation. Minimize shock. Apply ice or a cold pack.

Chapter 12

1. b, a, c, e, d
2. A fall from a height greater than the victim's height; any diving mishap; a person found unconscious for unknown reasons; any injury involving severe blunt force to the head or trunk; any injury that penetrates the head or trunk; a motor vehicle crash involving a driver or passengers not wearing safety belts; any person thrown from a motor vehicle; any injury in which a victim's helmet is broken; lightning strike
3. Changes in the level of consciousness; severe pain or pressure in the head, neck, or back; tingling or loss of sensation in the extremities; partial or complete loss of movement of

any body part; unusual bumps or depressions on the head or spine; blood or other fluid in the ears or nose; profuse external bleeding of the head, neck, or back; seizures; impaired breathing or vision as a result of injury; nausea or vomiting; persistent headache; loss of balance; bruising of the head, especially around the eyes and behind the ears

4. Wearing seat belts, including shoulder restraints; wearing approved helmets, eyewear, faceguards, and mouthguards, when appropriate; preventing falls; obeying rules in sports and recreational activities; avoiding inappropriate use of drugs; inspecting work and recreational equipment; thinking and talking about safety

5. Place the victim on his or her back. Do not attempt to remove any object embedded in the eye. Place a sterile dressing around the object. Stabilize any embedded object in place as best you can. You can use a paper cup to support the object.

6. b	**7.** d	**8.** d	**9.** a	**10.** a
11. b	**12.** a	**13.** d		

14. Do not put direct pressure on the wound. Apply direct pressure around the area of the wound to help control bleeding. Wear gloves or use a barrier. Call EMS personnel if you have not already done so.

15. You know the victim is breathing and has a pulse. If you are able to check consciousness, check for severe bleeding, and find no life-threatening conditions, leave the victim as he is. Send someone to call EMS personnel or call yourself. With the victim still lying on his side, stabilize the head and neck, using in-line stabilization. If the victim's head is severely angled to one side; he complains of pain, pressure, or muscle spasms on initial movement of the head; or you feel resistance when trying to align the head, support the head in the position in which you found it. Maintain an open airway, monitor breathing and pulse, and control any external bleeding. Wear gloves or use a barrier. Keep the victim from getting chilled or overheated.

16. Call EMS personnel. The numbness indicates possible spinal cord damage. Keep the person warm and quiet.

Chapter 13

1. c, a, b, e, d
2. Call EMS personnel. Limit movement. Monitor breathing and circulation. Control bleeding. Minimize shock.
3. Difficulty breathing; severe pain at the injury site; flushed, pale, or bluish discoloration of the skin; obvious deformity; coughing up blood
4. Rib fracture. Have the person rest. Bind the left arm to the left side of the chest. Monitor breathing, skin color, and temperature. Minimize shock.
5. A sucking sound coming from the wound with each breath
6. Severe pain, bruising; external bleeding; nausea; vomiting (sometimes vomit containing blood); weakness; thirst; pain, tenderness, or a tight feeling in the abdomen; organs possibly protruding from the abdomen; with a pelvic injury, possible loss of sensation in the legs or inability to move them
7. d
8. Difficulty breathing; sucking sound when victim breathes
9. Call EMS personnel. Help the victim rest in a comfortable position. Minimize shock. Cover the wound with a dressing that does not allow air to pass through, such as plastic wrap, and leave one corner untaped. Monitor breathing, skin appearance, and temperature.
10. Call EMS personnel; consider applying in-line stabilization; take steps to minimize shock.

Chapter 14

1. e, b, g, f, d, c, a, i, h

2. Changes in levels of consciousness; nausea; vomiting; dizziness, lightheadedness, and weakness; changes in breathing, pulse, body temperature, and skin color

3. Do no harm. Monitor breathing and consciousness. Help the victim rest in the most comfortable position. Keep the victim from getting chilled or overheated. Provide reassurance. Provide any specific care needed.

4. When the seizure lasts more than a few minutes; the victim has repeated seizures; the victim appears to be injured; the person has no known predisposing condition that could have brought on the seizure; the victim is pregnant; the victim is known to have diabetes; the victim is an infant or a child who is experiencing a seizure other than an initial febrile seizure; the seizure takes place in water; the victim fails to regain consciousness after the seizure

5. Control blood pressure; do not smoke; eat a healthy diet; exercise regularly; control diabetes; promptly report any signs or symptoms of stroke to your doctor

6. Check for nonlife-threatening conditions to see if the person was injured during the seizure. Provide any necessary care. Reassure and comfort the victim. Ask bystanders to move away and give the victim room. Stay with the victim until he or she is fully conscious and oriented to the surroundings.

7. Confusion; profuse sweating; pupils of unequal sizes; speech difficulty; weakness or fatigue

8. Call 9-1-1 or the local emergency number. Allow the victim to rest in a comfortable position. Do not give her anything to eat or drink. Stay with her and offer comfort and reassurance until EMS personnel arrive.

9. a	**10.** c	**11.** c	**12.** a
13. b	**14.** a	**15.** c	**16.** d

Chapter 15

1. e, b, f, c, a, d
2. Nausea, vomiting, diarrhea, chest or abdominal pain, breathing difficulty, sweating, loss of consciousness, seizures, and burns around the lips or tongue or on the skin
3. Type and amount of the substance; how and where the substance entered the body; the time elapsed since the poison entered the body; and the victim's size, weight, and age
4. To care for the effects of contact with a poisonous plant—wash affected area thoroughly with soap and water (if the victim is wearing any jewelry that is contaminated or restricting circulation, ask him or her to remove it); if a rash or weeping lesions appear, seek assistance from a pharmacist or doctor about possible treatments; if condition worsens or spreads, call a doctor. To care for contact with other poisons, such as chemicals—flush affected area continuously with water; call 9-1-1 or the local emergency number; continue to flush the affected area until EMS personnel arrive
5. Keep medications and household products out of the reach of children and in secured cabinets. Use childproof safety caps on medications and other poisonous products. Keep products in their original containers with labels in place. Use poison symbols to identify dangerous substances, and teach children what the symbols mean. Dispose of outdated medications and products. Use potentially dangerous chemicals only in well-ventilated areas. Wear proper clothing for work or recreation that may put you in contact with a poisonous substance.
6. Itching and burning hand; swollen finger; red bumps all over the body
7. Rinse the affected area thoroughly with water, and consult a doctor or pharmacist about possible treatments.

8. c	**9.** a	**10.** d	**11.** d	**12.** d

Chapter 16

1. b, a, c, e, d
2. Grasp the tick with fine-tipped tweezers, as close to the skin as possible, and pull slowly, steadily, and firmly. If you do not have tweezers, cover your fingers with some kind of protective barrier, then pull the tick out with your fingers. If your bare fingers come into contact with the tick, wash them immediately. Once the tick is removed, apply an antiseptic to the site. If an antibiotic ointment is available, apply it to the site. Look for signs of infection. If the tick stays in your skin or if a rash or flu-like symptoms develop, seek medical help.
3. Wear long-sleeved shirts and long pants. Wear a repellent. Tuck pant legs into socks or boots; tuck shirt into pants. Wear light-colored clothing. Use a rubber band or tape the area where pants and socks meet so that nothing can get under clothing. Inspect yourself carefully for insects or ticks after being outdoors. If you are outdoors for a long time, check yourself several times during the day, especially in moist, hairy areas of the body. Shower immediately after coming indoors. Keep an eye out for and avoid the nests of wasps, bees, and hornets. Spray pets that go outdoors with repellent and check them for ticks often. Use a repellent if you are in a grassy or wooded area or if the area is infested with insects or ticks. When hiking in the woods, stay in the middle of trails and avoid underbrush, fallen trees, and tall grass. Wear hiking boots. Avoid areas populated with snakes. Make noise so that snakes will avoid you. If you see a snake, look for others. Walk back on the same path. To prevent marine life stings, wear a wet or dry suit or protective footwear in the water.
4. A bite or sting mark at the entry site; a stinger, tentacle, or venom sac remaining in or near the entry site; redness at or around the entry site; swelling at or around the entry site; pain or tenderness at or around the entry site
5. (1) Wash the wound. (2) Immobilize the affected part. (3) Keep the affected area lower than the heart if possible. (4) Call 9-1-1 or the local emergency number. (5) Minimize the victim's movement and, if possible, carry a victim who must be transported or have him or her walk slowly. (6) If the victim cannot get professional medical care within 30 minutes, consider suctioning the wound using a snake-bite kit.
6. Try to get your sister away from the dog without endangering yourself. Do not try to capture the animal. Control the bleeding and apply a dressing. Do not clean the wound. Call 9-1-1 or the local emergency number. In case animal control personnel need to be summoned, try to describe what the dog looked like and the area in which it was last seen.
7. a   8. d   9. b   10. d   11. d   12. d

Chapter 17

1. f, c, d, e, a, h, b, g
2. Difficulty breathing; chest pain; altered level of consciousness; moist or flushed skin; mood changes; nausea; vomiting; sweating; chills; fever; headache; dizziness; rapid pulse; rapid breathing; restlessness; excitement; irritability; talkativeness; hallucinations; confusion; slurred speech; poor coordination; trembling
3. Alcohol; nicotine; caffeine; aspirin; laxatives; sleeping pills; diet pills
4. Use common sense. Keep prescriptions and medications in their appropriate containers. Clearly label all medications including when, how, and how often they should be taken. Throw out leftover prescriptions. Never take another person's prescription or even one prescribed for you at a previous time.

5. Check the scene to make sure it is safe to help the person. Check for any life-threatening conditions. Call EMS or PCC personnel and follow their directions. Question the victim or bystanders to try to find out what substance was taken, how much was taken, and when it was taken. Calm and reassure the victim. Prevent the victim from getting chilled or overheated. Withdraw from the area if the victim becomes violent or threatening. If you suspect that someone has used a designer drug, tell EMS or PCC personnel.
6. b, c, a, d, e, f
7. Containers; drug paraphernalia; signs and symptoms of other medical problems
8. c   9. b   10. d

Chapter 18

1. c, e, d, a, b
2. Air temperature; humidity; wind; clothing; how often you take breaks from activity; how much and how often you drink fluids; intensity of activity; health status
3. Heat cramps; heat exhaustion; heat stroke
4. Changes in body temperature; changes in skin temperature, color, and moisture; headache; nausea; dizziness and weakness; exhaustion; progressive loss of consciousness; rapid, weak pulse; rapid, shallow breathing
5. Refusing water; vomiting; changes in level of consciousness
6. Move the victim away from the heat source. Have the victim rest in a cool place and drink cool water slowly. Loosen tight clothing. Remove clothing soaked with perspiration. Apply wet towels or sheets to the victim's body. Fan the victim. Apply ice and cold packs to the wrists, ankles, armpits, neck, and groin.
7. Frostbite; hypothermia
8. Avoid being outdoors in the hottest or coldest part of the day. Change your activity level according to the temperature. Take frequent breaks. Dress appropriately. Drink large amounts of fluids.
9. a   10. d
11. Lack of feeling in fingers; fingers look waxy and white; fingers feel cold
12. Handle the affected areas gently. Do not rub. Warm the areas gently by soaking them in water no warmer than 100 to 105 degrees F (38 to 41 degrees C). Test the water. If it is uncomfortable to the touch, it is too warm. Do not let the affected areas touch the bottom or the sides of the container. When the affected areas look red and warm, bandage them with a dry, clean dressing and seek professional medical attention. Do not let your friend walk on his thawed feet until all feeling has returned to them.
13. No response to questions; glassy eyes; seems weak and exhausted; does not feel your touch
14. Call the local emergency number. Then look for additional blankets, hot water bottles, and heating pads. Place any available source of heat on the victim after checking for any wet clothing or blankets.

Chapter 19

1. Move a victim only if there is immediate danger, such as a fire, lack of oxygen, risk of drowning, risk of explosion, collapsing structure, or uncontrollable traffic hazards.
2. Dangerous conditions at the scene; size of the victim; your physical ability; whether others can help you; the victim's condition
3. Only attempt to move a person you are sure you can comfortably handle. Bend at the knees and hips. Lift with your legs, not your back. Walk carefully using short steps. When possible, move forward rather than backward. Always look where you are going. Support the victim's head and spine.

Avoid bending or twisting a victim with possible head or spine injury.

4. Walking assist; pack-strap carry; two-person seat carry; clothes drag
5. Reaching assist; throwing assist; wading assist
6. Struggles to breathe; cannot call out for help; arms to the sides pressing down; has no supporting kick; body position is vertical in the water; unable to move forward in the water

7. c   **8.** d   **9.** c   **10.** d   **11.** b

Chapter 20

1. d, c, f, b, e, a
2. Check the scene for safety. Have a bystander call 9-1-1. Introduce yourself as someone who knows first aid. Find out if anyone on the scene is a parent or caretaker of the child and, if so, ask permission to give care. Check the child for life-threatening conditions. If the child is conscious, try to reassure and comfort the child and ask the child's name and address. Have someone try to locate the parents if they are not present.
3. Introduce yourself and explain that you are there to help. Ask the woman her name and use it when you speak to her. Tell her to lie still; try to find out from the neighbor if the woman is generally confused or is taking any medication, if you haven't done so already. Have the neighbor call EMS personnel. Reassure and comfort the victim. Support and immobilize the injured area, probably using blankets and pillows.

4. d   **5.** b   **6.** b   **7.** b   **8.** c

9. Heat-related illness
10. Call EMS personnel.
11. Hearing impaired; confused or mentally impaired; not speak the same language you speak
12. Medication; infection; vision or hearing problems; depression; Alzheimer's disease; mental impairment; shock

Chapter 21

1. h, g, c, e, f, a , d, b
2. Stage 1: Preparation—The mother's body prepares for birth; from the first contraction until the cervix is completely dilated.
   Stage 2: Delivery—Begins when the cervix is completely dilated and ends with the birth of a baby.
   Stage 3: Delivery of the Placenta—The placenta separates from the wall of the uterus and is expelled from the birth canal.
   Stage 4: Recovery—The recovery and monitoring of the mother following childbirth.
3. See that the airway is open and clear. Keep the victim from getting chilled.
4. 1. Is there a bloody discharge?
   2. Has the amniotic sac ruptured?
   3. Is this the first pregnancy?

4. What are the contractions like? (How close together and how strong?)
5. Does she have a need to push?
6. Is the baby crowning?

5. c   **6.** b   **7.** c   **8.** c   **9.** b   **10.** a

Chapter 22

1. d, a, e, b, c
2. There may be no easy way to call for help. There may be no easy way for emergency personnel to reach the victim. There may be no easy way to transport the victim.
3. Wilderness; rural
4. Stay where you are and call, radio or signal for help. Send someone to go get help or leave the victim alone to get help. Transport the victim to help. Care for the victim where you are until the victim has recovered enough to travel on his or her own.

5. c   **6.** b   **7.** c   **8.** c   **9.** c

10. He is shivering violently. His knee is very painful and feels as if it is swelling. The sky is overcast. The temperature is about 50 degrees F. The sun will begin to set in 4 hours. Group members provide various dry items of clothing.
11. Provide some type of insulation.
12. Knowledge; skills; equipment

Chapter 23

1. g, c, d, f, e, b, a
2. Disease; heart disease; injury
3. Know your risk; change risky behaviors; think about safety; take precautions; wear protective devices; wear a safety belt; learn first aid
4. Wear a safety belt including shoulder restraint; do not drink and drive
5. Crawl low to escape smoke. Make sure children can open windows. If you cannot escape down a ladder, be prepared to lower children. Get out quickly and do not return to the building. If you cannot escape, stuff wet towels, rags, or clothing into door cracks and vents. If a phone is available, call the fire department.
6. Poor lighting; rugs that are not fastened down. He could install bright lights, fasten down rugs, place handrails if necessary.
7. Turn pot handles toward the back of the stove; turn off the oven and other appliances when they are not in use; lock up all cleaning products and other poisonous items; clean up any spills promptly; fasten down any rugs

8. c   **9.** d   **10.** c   **11.** d   **12.** c
13. d   **14.** b   **15.** a   **16.** d

17. Stop serving alcohol an hour before the party is to end. Have nonalcoholic beverages available. Do not promote or play drinking games. Do not have salty foods available. Do not have an open bar or serve anyone who has had too much to drink. Measure drinks if you are serving.

Glossary

PRONUNCIATION GUIDE

The accented syllable in a word is shown in capital letters.

    river = RIV er

An unmarked vowel that ends a syllable or comprises a syllable has a long sound, such as the *o* in *open* and the *i* in *silent.*

    O pen   SI lent

A long vowel in a syllable ending in a consonant is marked -.

    snowflake = SNO flāk

An unmarked vowel in a syllable that ends with a consonant has a short sound, such as the *i* in *sister* and the *e* in *reset.*

    SIS ter   re SET

A short vowel that comprises a syllable is marked ˘.

    decimal = DES ĭ mal

The sound of an unstressed vowel, such as the *a* in *ago* and the *o* in *connect*, is spelled ə.

    ahead = ə HED

Abdomen: The middle part of the trunk, under the chest and above the pelvis; contains several organs, including the stomach, liver, and spleen.

Abdominal cavity: An area in the body that contains many organs, including the liver, pancreas, intestines, stomach, kidneys, and spleen.

Abdominal thrusts: A technique for unblocking a completely obstructed airway by compressing the abdomen; also called the Heimlich maneuver.

Abrasion (ah BRA zhun): A wound characterized by skin that has been scraped or rubbed away.

Absorbed poison: A poison that enters the body after it comes in contact with the skin.

Activated charcoal: A substance which, taken internally, is used to absorb and neutralize ingested poisons.

Active drowning victim: A person exhibiting universal behavior that includes struggling at the surface for 20 to 60 seconds before submerging.

Acute: Having a rapid and severe onset, then quickly subsiding.

Addiction: The compulsive need to use a substance. Stopping use would cause the user to suffer mental, physical, and emotional distress.

Adhesive compress: A small pad of nonstick gauze on a strip of adhesive tape, applied directly to small injuries.

Advanced cardiac life support (ACLS): Techniques and treatments designed for use with victims of cardiac emergencies.

Aerobic: Requiring additional effort by the heart and lungs to meet the increased demand by the skeletal muscles for oxygen.

Aerobic exercise: Sustained, rhythmical exercise, using the large muscle groups, for at least 20-30 minutes within one's target heart rate range.

Airway: The pathway through which air travels from the mouth and nose to the lungs.

Airway obstruction: Complete or partial blockage of the airway that prevents air from reaching a person's lungs; the most common cause of respiratory emergencies.

Allergens: Substances that induce allergies.

Alveoli (al VE o li): Microscopic air sacs in the lungs where gases and wastes are exchanged between the lungs and the blood.

Alzheimer's disease: A progressive, degenerative disease that affects the brain, resulting in impaired memory, thinking, and behavior.

Amnesia: Loss of memory.

487

Amniotic sac: A fluid-filled sac that encloses, bathes, and protects the developing baby; commonly called the bag of waters.

Amputation: A type of avulsion injury in which a body part is severed.

Anaphylactic shock (an ə fī LAK tik) shock: A severe allergic reaction in which air passages may swell and restrict breathing; a form of shock.

Anaphylaxis (an ə fī LAK sis): A severe allergic reaction; a form of shock.

Anaphylaxis kit: A container that holds the medication and any necessary equipment used to present or counteract anaphylactic shock.

Anatomical airway obstruction: A condition in which the airway is blocked by the tongue or swollen tissues of the mouth or throat.

Aneurysm (AN u rizm): A condition in which the wall of an artery or vein weakens, balloons out, and may rupture; usually caused by disease, trauma, or a natural weakness in the vessel wall.

Angina (an JI nə) pectoris (PEK tə ris): Chest pain that comes and goes at different times; commonly associated with cardiovascular disease.

Anorexia nervosa: An eating disorder characterized by a long-term refusal to eat food with sufficient nutrients and calories.

Antibiotic: A medicine used to help the body fight bacterial infection.

Antihistamines (an te HIS tə menz): Drugs used to treat the signs and symptoms of allergic reactions.

Antiinflammatory (an te in FLAM ə tor e) drug: A substance used to reduce heat, swelling, redness, and pain in a body area.

Antiseptic: A substance that inhibits the growth and reproduction of microorganisms or germs.

Antitoxins: Antibodies capable of neutralizing specific disease-producing poisonous substances.

Antivenin: A substance used to counteract the poisonous effects of snake, spider, or insect venom.

Arm: The part of the upper extremity from the shoulder to the hand.

Arteries: Large blood vessels that carry blood from the heart to all parts of the body.

Ashen: A grayish color; darker skin often looks ashen instead of pale.

Aspirate: To suck or take blood, vomit, saliva, or other foreign material into the lungs.

Aspiration (as pi RA shun): Sucking or taking blood, vomit, saliva, or other foreign material into the lungs.

Asthma: A condition that narrows the air passages and makes breathing difficult.

Atherosclerosis (ath er o skle RO sis): A form of cardiovascular disease marked by a narrowing of the arteries in the heart and other parts of the body.

Aura (AW rah): An unusual sensation or feeling a person may experience before an epileptic seizure; it may be a visual hallucination; a strange sound, taste, or smell; or an urgent need to get to safety.

Autogenics: A relaxation technique that uses self-suggestion to produce relaxation.

Automated external defibrillator (AED): An automatic device used to recognize a heart rhythm that requires an electric shock and either delivers the shock or prompts the rescuer to deliver it.

Avulsion: A wound in which a portion of the skin and sometimes other soft tissue is partially or completely torn away.

Bacteria: Microorganisms capable of causing infection.

Bandage: Material used to wrap or cover a part of the body; commonly used to hold a dressing or splint in place.

Bandage compress: A thick gauze dressing attached to a gauze bandage.

Biofeedback: A relaxation technique that uses instruments to measure bodily functions, such as heart rate and blood pressure.

Biological death: The irreversible damage caused by the death of brain cells.

Birth canal: The passageway from the uterus to the vaginal opening through which a baby passes during birth.

Bladder: An organ in the pelvis in which urine is stored until it is released from the body.

Blood volume: The total amount of blood circulating within the body.

Body composition: The ratio of fat to all the tissues, such as muscles, that are fat free.

Body system: A group of organs and other structures working together to carry out specific functions.

Bone: A dense, hard tissue that forms the skeleton.

Brachial (BRA ke əl) pulse: The pulse felt at the brachial artery on the inside of the upper arm.

Brain: The center of the nervous system; regulates all body functions.

Breathing emergency: An emergency in which breathing is so impaired that life is threatened.

Breech birth: The delivery of a baby feet or buttocks first.

Bronchi (BRONG ki): The air passages that lead from the trachea to the alveoli.

Bronchioles: The air passage from the bronchi to the lungs.

Bronchitis: A disease resulting in inflammation of the lining of the trachea, bronchi, and bronchioles.

Bulimia: An eating disorder characterized by eating excessively then purging unwanted calories by vomiting or using laxatives.

Burn: A soft tissue injury to the skin or other body tisues caused by heat, chemicals, electricity, or radiation.

Calorie: A measure of the energy value of food.

Cannabis products: Substances, such as marijuana and hashish, that are derived from the *Cannabis sativa* plant; can produce feelings of elation, distorted perceptions of time and space, and impaired motor coordination and judgment.

Capillaries (KAP i ler ez): Microscopic blood vessels linking arteries and veins that transfer oxygen and other nutrients from the blood to all body cells and remove waste products.

Carbohydrates: Compounds that contain oxygen, carbon, and hydrogen; the main source of energy for all body functions.

Carbon dioxide: A colorless, odorless gas; a waste product of respiration.

Carbon monoxide (CO): A clear, odorless, poisonous gas produced when carbon or other fuel is burned, as in gasoline engines.

Cardiac (KAR de ak) arrest: A condition in which the heart has stopped or beats too ineffectively to generate a pulse.

Cardiac emergency: Sudden illness involving the heart.

Cardiopulmonary (kar de o PUL mo ner e) resuscitation (re sus i TA shun) (CPR): A technique that combines rescue breathing and chest compressions for a person whose breathing and heart have stopped.

Cardiorespiratory endurance: The ability to take in, deliver, and extract oxygen for physical work; the ability to persevere in a physical task.

Cardiovascular (kar de o VAS ku lar) disease: Disease of the heart and blood vessels.

Carotid (kə ROT id) arteries: Major blood vessels that supply blood to the head and neck.

Carpals: The bones of the wrist.

Cells: The basic unit of all living tissue.

Cerebral palsy: A dysfunction of the central nervous system in which a person has little or no control of the muscles.

Cervix (SERV ix): A short tube at the upper end of the birth canal; the opening of the uterus.

Chest: The upper part of the trunk, containing the heart, major blood vessels, and lungs.

Child abuse: The physical, psychological, or sexual assault of a child, resulting in injury or emotional trauma.

Cholesterol (ko LES ter ol): A fatty substance made by the body and found in certain foods; too much in the blood can cause fatty deposits on artery walls that may restrict or block blood flow.

Chronic: Persistent over a long period of time.

Chronic obstructive pulmonary disease (COPD): Airway disease, such as emphysema, asthma, and bronchitis, or a combination of the three characterized by difficulty breathing.

Circulatory (SER ku lə tor e) cycle: The flow of blood in the body.

Circulatory system: A group of organs and other structures that carries oxygen-rich blood and other nutrients throughout the body, removes wastes, and returns oxygen-poor blood to the lungs.

Citizen responder: A layperson who recognizes an emergency and decides to act.

Clavicle: The collarbone; the slender, curved bone that extends from the sternum to the scapula (shoulder blade).

Clinically dead: The condition in which the heart stops beating and breathing stops.

Closed fracture: A fracture that leaves the skin unbroken.

Closed wound: An injury to the soft tissues in which the outer layer of skin is intact and soft tissue damage occurs beneath the skin.

Clotting: The process by which blood thickens at a wound site to seal a hole or tear in a blood vessel and stop bleeding.

Concussion (kon CUSH ən): An injury to the brain caused by a violent blow to the head, followed by a temporary impairment of brain function, usually without permanent damage to the brain.

Consciousness: The state of being aware of one's self and one's surroundings.

Consent: Permission to give care, given by the victim to the rescuer.

Contraction: The pumping action of the heart; the rhythmic tightening of muscles in the uterus during labor.

Contusion: A bruise.

Coronary (KOR ə ner e) arteries: Blood vessels that supply the heart muscle with oxygen-rich blood.

Corticosteroid (KOR ti ko STIR oyd): A hormone, made synthetically or in the body, that is used in anti-inflammatory medications.

Cranial cavity: An area in the body that contains the brain and is protected by the skull.

Cravats: Folded triangular bandages used to hold dressings or splints in place.

Critical burn: Any burn that is potentially life threatening, disabling, or disfiguring.

Croup: An infection that causes swelling of the throat around the vocal cords.

Crowning: The point in labor when the baby's head is visible at the opening of the vagina.

Cyanosis (si ə NO sis): A blue discoloration of the skin around the mouth and fingertips resulting from a lack of oxygen in the blood.

Cyanotic: Bluish, as from cyanosis.

Deep burn: A burn that involves the epidermis and the two lower layers of skin, the dermis and the hypodermis, and may destroy underlying structures; it can be life threatening.

Defibrillation (de fib ri LA shun): An electric shock administered to correct a life-threatening heart rhythm.

Defibrillator (de FIB ri la tor): A device that sends an electric shock through the chest to the heart.

Delayed-help situation: A situation in which emergency assistance is delayed for more than 30 minutes.

Dependency: The desire or need to continually use a substance.

Depressants: Substances that affect the central nervous system and decrease physical and mental activity, such as tranquilizers and sleeping pills.

Dermis: The deeper layer of skin; contains the nerves, hair roots, sweat and oil glands, and blood vessels.

Designer drugs: Drugs that are chemically modified from medically prescribed substances to make them more potent or alter their effects.

Diabetes (di ə BE tez): A condition in which the body does not produce enough insulin or does not use insulin effectively enough to regulate the amount of sugar (glucose) in the bloodstream.

Diabetes mellitus (mel I tus): *See* Diabetes.

Diabetic coma: A life-threatening emergency in which the body needs insulin.

Diabetic emergency: A situation in which a person becomes ill because of an imbalance of sugar (glucose) and insulin in the bloodstream.

Diabetic ketoacidosis (KE to a si DO sis): A life-threatening complication of uncontrolled diabetes mellitus.

Diaphragm: A dome-shaped muscle that aids in breathing and separates the chest from the abdomen.

Dietary fiber: The carbohydrates that are not broken down by the human digestive process.

Digestive system: A group of organs and other structures that digests food and eliminates wastes.

Direct pressure: The pressure applied on a wound to control bleeding, for example, by one's gloved hand.

Disability: The absence or impairment of motor, sensory, or mental function.

Dislocation: The displacement or separation of a bone from its normal position at a joint.

Distressed swimmer: A person capable of staying afloat but likely to need assistance to get to shore.

Down syndrome: A condition caused by a genetic accident and characterized by varying degrees of mental retardation and physical defects.

Dressing: A pad placed directly over a wound to absorb blood and other body fluids and to prevent infection.

Drowning: Death by suffocation when submerged in water.

Drug: Any substance, other than food, intended to affect the functions of the body.

Drug paraphernalia (PAR ə fer NAL yə): Devices used to contain or administer various kinds of drugs, such as needles and syringes for drugs that are injected.

Elastic roller bandage: A bandage designed to keep continuous pressure on a body part; the fabric is made of a yarn containing rubber.

Electrolyte (e LEK tro LIT): A substance which, in a solution or in liquid form, is capable of conducting an electric current.

Embolus (EM bo lus): A sudden blockage of a blood vessel by a traveling clot or other material, such as fat or air, that circulates in the bloodstream until it becomes lodged in a blood vessel.

Embryo (EM bre o): The early stages of a developing baby in the uterus; characterized by the rapid growth and development of body systems.

Emergency: A situation requiring immediate action.

Emergency medical services (EMS) professionals: Trained and equipped community-based personnel dispatched through a local emergency number to provide emergency care for ill or injured victims.

Emergency medical services (EMS) system: A network of community resources and medical personnel that provides emergency care to victims of injury or sudden illness.

Emergency medical technician (EMT): Someone who has successfully completed a state-approved emergency medical technician training program. The several different levels of EMTs include paramedics at the highest level.

Emphysema (em fə SE mə): A disease in which the lungs lose their ability to exchange carbon dioxide and oxygen effectively.

Endocrine (EN də crin) system: A group of organs and other structures that regulates and coordinates the activities of other systems by producing chemicals and hormones that influence the activity of tissues.

Epidermis: The outer layer of skin.

Epiglottis (ep i GLOT is): The flap of tissue that covers the trachea during swallowing to keep food and liquid out of the lungs.

Epiglottitis (ep i glot I tis): An infection that causes severe inflammation and potentially life-threatening swelling of the epiglottis.

Epilepsy (EP i lep se): A chronic condition characterized by seizures that may vary in type and duration; can usually be controlled by medication.

Esophagus (e SOF ə gus): The tube leading from the mouth to the stomach.

Exhale: To breathe air out of the lungs.

External bleeding: Bleeding that can be seen coming from a wound.

Extremities: The shoulders to the fingers; the hips to the toes.

Fainting: A partial or complete loss of consciousness resulting from a temporary reduction of blood flow to the brain.

Fat: A compound made up of carbon, hydrogen, oxygen, and three fatty acids, a storage form of energy for the body; a type of body tissue composed of cells containing stored fat.

Febrile (FEB ril) seizure (SE zhur): A seizure caused by a sudden change in body temperature.

Feces: Waste or excrement from the digestive tract that is formed in the intestine and expelled through the rectum.

Femoral arteries: The arteries that supply blood to the lower extremities.

Femur: The bone of the thigh.

Fetus (FE tus): The developing unborn offspring after the embryo stage.

Fibula: One of the two bones of the leg.

Finger sweep: A technique used to remove foreign material from a victim's airway.

First aid: Immediate care given to a victim of injury or sudden illness until more advanced care can be obtained.

First responder: A person trained in emergency care who may be called upon to provide such care as a routine part of his or her job.

Food Guide Pyramid: A pictorial guide to the current five basic food groups.

Forearm: The part of the upper extremity from the elbow to the wrist.

Fracture: A break or disruption in bone tissue.

Frostbite: A condition in which body tissues freeze; most commonly occurs in the fingers, toes, ears, and nose.

Gastric distention: A condition in which the abdomen becomes swollen with air.

Genitals: The external reproductive organs.

Genitourinary (jen i to UR ri nary) system: A group of organs and other structures that eliminates wastes and enables sexual reproduction.

Glands: Organs that release fluid and other substances into the blood or onto the skin.

Glucose: A simple sugar found in certain foods, especially fruits, and a major source of energy occurring in human and animal body fluids.

Good Samaritan laws: Laws that protect people who willingly give first aid without accepting anything in return.

Hallucinogens (hə LOO sin ə jenz): Substances that affect mood, sensation, thought, emotion, and self-awareness; alter perceptions of time and space; and produce visual, auditory, and tactile delusions.

Head-tilt/chin-lift: A technique for opening the airway.

Hearing impairment: Partial or total loss of hearing.

Heart: A muscular organ that circulates blood throughout the body.

Heart attack: A sudden illness involving the death of heart muscle tissue when it does not receive oxygen-rich blood; also known as myocardial infarction.

Heat cramps: Painful spasms of skeletal muscles after exercise or work in warm or moderate temperatures; usually involve the calf and abdominal muscles.

Heat exhaustion: The early stage and most common form of heat-related illness; often results from strenuous work or exercise in a hot environment.

Heat stroke: A life-threatening condition that develops when the body's cooling mechanisms are overwhelmed and body systems begin to fail.

Heaving jug: A homemade piece of rescue equipment for throwing to a victim, composed of a 1-gallon plastic container containing some water, with 50 to 75 feet of floating line attached.

Heaving line: Floating rope, white, yellow, or some other highly visible color, used for water rescue.

Heimlich maneuver: A technique used to clear the airway of a choking victim; see Abdominal thrusts.

Hemorrhage (HEM ə rij): A loss of a large amount of blood in a short period of time.

High blood pressure: A condition, often without any signs or symptoms, of elevated blood pressure; also referred to as hypertension.

Hormone: A substance that circulates in body fluids and has a specific effect on cell activity.

Hospital care provider: The staff that assume responsibility for the care of the injured or ill person while in the hospital.

Humerus: The bone of the arm.

Hyperglycemia (hi per gli SE me ə): A condition in which too much sugar (glucose) is in the bloodstream, and the insulin level in the body is too low.

Hyperventilation: Breathing that is faster than normal.

Hypodermis: A layer of skin located beneath the dermis and epidermis; contains fat, blood vessels, and connective tissues.

Hypoglycemia (hi po gli SE me ə): A condition in which too little sugar (glucose) is in the bloodstream, and the insulin level in the body is too high.

Hypothermia: A life-threatening condition in which the body's warming mechanisms fail to maintain normal body temperature and the entire body cools.

Imagery: A relaxation technique that involves using the imagination to create various scenes and wished-for situations.

Immobilize: Using a splint or other method to keep an injured body part from moving.

Impairment: Damage or reduction in quality, quantity, value, or strength.

Impaled object: An object that remains embedded in an open wound.

Implied consent: A legal concept that assumes a person would consent to receive emergency care if he or she were physically able to do so.

In-line stabilization: A technique used to minimize movement of a victim's head and neck and keep them in line with the body while providing care.

Infection: The growth of disease-producing microorganisms in the body.

Inhalants: Substances inhaled to produce mood-altering effects, such as glue or paint thinners.

Inhale: To breathe air into the lungs.

Inhaled poison: A poison breathed into the lungs.

Injected poison: A poison that enters the body through a bite or sting, or as drugs or medications through a hypodermic needle.

Injury: Damage that occurs when the body is subjected to an external force, such as a blow, a fall, a collision, an electric current, or extremes of temperatures.

Insulin (IN su lin): A hormone produced in the pancreas that enables the body to use sugar (glucose) for energy; frequently used to treat diabetes.

Insulin shock: A life-threatening condition in which too much insulin is in the bloodstream.

Integumentary (in teg YU men tə re) system: The skin, hair, and nails; protects the body, retains fluid, and helps prevent infection.

Internal bleeding: Bleeding inside the body.

Jaw-thrust maneuver: A technique to open a person's airway without moving the head or neck.

Joint: A structure formed by the ends of two or more bones coming together at one place.

Kapok: A fiber used to fill life jackets and other flotation devices.

Kidney: An organ that filters waste from the blood to form urine.

Labor: The birth process; beginning with the contraction of the uterus and dilation of the cervix and ending with the stabilization and recovery of the mother.

Laceration (las ə RA shun): A cut, usually from a sharp object; may have jagged or smooth edges.

Larynx (LAR ingks): A part of the airway connecting the pharynx with the trachea; commonly called the voice box.

Layperson: Someone who does not have special or advanced first aid training or skills.

Leg: The part of the lower extremity from the pelvis to the ankle.

Ligament: A fibrous band that holds bones together at a joint.

Lower extremities: The parts of the body from the hip to the toes.

Lower leg: The part of the lower extremity from the knee to the ankle.

Lungs: A pair of light, spongy organs in the chest that provide the mechanism for taking oxygen in and removing carbon dioxide during breathing.

Lyme disease: An illness transmitted by a certain kind of infected tick; victims may or may not develop a rash.

Mechanical airway obstruction: A condition in which the airway is blocked by a foreign object, such as a piece of food, or a small toy, or by fluids, such as vomit, blood, mucus, or saliva.

Medical emergency: A sudden illness requiring immediate medical attention.

Medication: A drug given therapeutically to prevent or treat the effects of a disease or condition or otherwise enhance mental or physical well-being.

Membrane: A thin layer of tissue that covers a surface, lines a cavity, or divides a space.

Mental (cognitive) function: The brain's capacity to acquire and process information.

Metabolism: The process by which cells convert nutrients to energy.

Metacarpals: The bones of the hand.

Metatarsals: The bones of the foot.

Microorganism (mi kro OOR gə nizm): A bacteria, virus, or other microscopic structure that may enter the body. Those that cause an infection or disease are called pathogens.

Miscarriage: A spontaneous end to pregnancy before the twentieth week; usually because of defects of the fetus or womb.

Motor function: The ability to move the body or a body part.

Motor impairment: The partial or total inability to move or to use a body part.

Mucous membranes: A thin sheet of body tissue that covers parts of the body.

Multiple sclerosis: A progressive disease characterized by nerve degeneration and patches of hardened tissue in the brain or spinal cord.

Muscle: A fibrous soft tissue that is able to contract and relax to create movement.

Muscular dystrophy: A hereditary disease characterized by progressive deterioration of muscles, leading to disability, deformity, and loss of strength.

Musculoskeletal (mus ku lo SKEL ə təl) system: A group of tissues and other structures that supports the body, protects internal organs, allows movement, stores minerals, manufactures blood cells, and creates heat.

Narcotics: Drugs used mainly to relieve pain.

Nerve: A part of the nervous system that transmits information as electrical impulses to and from the brain and all body areas.

Nervous system: A group of organs and other structures that regulates all body functions.

Nitroglycerin: A prescribed medication, often in tablet form, given for the prevention or relief of angina pectoris.

Nutrients: Substances found in food that are required by the body.

Nutrition: The science that deals with the study of food you eat and how the body uses it.

Obesity: A condition characterized by an excess of stored body fat.

Occlusive dressing: A type of dressing that does not allow air or moisture to pass through.

Open fracture: A fracture that involves an open wound.

Open wound: A soft tissue injury resulting in a break in the skin's surface.

Organ: A collection of similar tissues acting together to perform specific body functions.

Osteoporosis (os te o pə RO sis): The gradual, progressive weakening of bone.

Overdose: An excess use of a drug, resulting in adverse reactions ranging from and including mania and hysteria to coma and death; specific reactions include changes in blood pressure and heartbeat, sweating, vomiting, and liver failure.

Oxygen: A tasteless, colorless, odorless gas necessary to sustain life.

Paralysis: A loss of muscle control; a permanent loss of feeling and movement; the inability to move.

Paramedic: A highly specialized EMT.

Passive drowning victim: An unconscious victim facedown, submerged or at the surface.

Patella: The kneecap.

Pathogen: A disease-causing agent; also called a microorganism.

Pelvic cavity: The lowest part of the trunk, containing the bladder, rectum, and female reproductive organs.

Pelvis: The lower part of the trunk, containing the bladder, internal reproductive organs, and part of the large intestine.

Phalanges: The bones of the fingers.

Pharynx (FAR ingks): A part of the airway formed by the back of the nose and the throat.

Placenta (plə CENT ə): An organ attached to the uterus and unborn child through which nutrients are delivered to the baby; expelled after the baby is delivered.

Plasma: The liquid part of the blood.

Platelets: Disk-shaped structures in the blood that are made of cell fragments; help stop bleeding by forming blood clots at wound sites.

Poison: Any substance that can cause injury, illness, or death when introduced into the body in relatively small amounts.

Poison control center (PCC): A specialized health center that provides information in cases of poisoning or suspected poisoning emergencies.

Pregnancy: A condition in which the egg (ovum) of the female is fertilized by the sperm of the male, forming an embryo.

Pressure bandage: A bandage applied snugly to create pressure on a wound to aid in controlling bleeding.

Pressure points: Sites on the body where pressure can be applied to major arteries to slow the flow of blood to a body part.

Prolapsed umbilical cord: A complication of childbirth in which a loop of umbilical cord protrudes through the vagina prior to delivery of the baby.

Proteins: Compounds made up of amino acids necessary to build tissues; contain the basic material for cell growth and repair.

Pulse: The expansion and contraction of the arteries

caused by the ejection of blood from the heart into the arteries as it contracts.

Puncture wound: A wound that results when the skin is pierced with a pointed object, such as a nail, a piece of glass, a splinter, or a knife.

Quarry: A deep pit where stone or gravel was once excavated; when no longer in use, it may become filled with water.

Rabies: A disease caused by a virus transmitted through the saliva of infected mammals.

Radius: One of the two bones of the forearm.

Rehabilitation: The attempted restoration of an ill or injured person to his or her previous state of health.

Reproductive system: A group of organs and other structures that enables sexual reproduction.

Rescue breathing: A technique of breathing for a non-breathing person.

Rescue tube: A vinyl, foam-filled, floating support used in making rescues.

Respiration (res pi RA shun): The breathing process in which the body takes in oxygen and eliminates carbon dioxide.

Respiratory (re SPI rə to re) or (RES pə rə tor e) arrest: A condition in which breathing has stopped.

Respiratory distress: A condition in which breathing is difficult.

Respiratory system: A group of organs and other structures that brings air into the body and removes wastes through a process called breathing or respiration.

Reye's (raz) syndrome: An illness that affects the brain and other internal organs, usually found in people under the age of 18.

Rib cage: The cage of bones formed by the 12 pairs of ribs, the sternum, and the spine.

Ring buoy: A rescue device made of buoyant cork, kapok, or plastic-covered material attached to a line with an object or knot at the end to keep the line from slipping out from under your foot when you throw it.

Risk factors: Conditions or behaviors that increase the chance that a person will develop a disease.

Rocky Mountain spotted fever (RMSF): A disease transmitted by a certain kind of infected tick; victims develop a spotted rash.

Roller bandage: A bandage made of gauze or gauze-like material; generally wrapped around a body part over a dressing.

Saturated fats: Fat derived primarily from animal products; associated with an increased risk of heart disease; the fat in animal tissue and products.

Scapula: The shoulder blade.

Seizure (SE zhur): A disruption in the brain's electrical activity, often marked by loss of consciousness and uncontrollable muscle movement; also called a convulsion.

Sensory function: The ability to see, hear, touch, taste, and smell.

Separation: The moving away from each other of bones at a joint.

Shepherd's crook: A long pole with a hook on the end that can be used to either pull a conscious drowning person to safety or encircle a submerged drowning person and pull the person to safety.

Shock: The failure of the circulatory system to provide adequate oxygen-rich blood to all parts of the body.

Signs: Any observable evidence of injury or illness, such as bleeding or unusually pale skin.

Skeletal muscles: Muscles that attach to bones.

Skin: The tough, elastic membrane that covers much of the surface of the body.

Sodium: A mineral abundant in table salt.

Soft tissues: Body structures that include the layers of skin, fat, and muscles.

Spinal cavity: An area of the body that contains the spinal cord and is protected by the bones of the spine.

Spinal column: The spine.

Spinal cord: A bundle of nerves extending from the brain at the base of the skull to the lower back; protected by the spine.

Spine: A strong, flexible column of vertebrae, extending from the base of the skull to the tip of the tailbone (coccyx), that supports the head and the trunk and encases and protects the spinal cord; also called the spinal column or the vertebral column.

Splint: A device that maintains an injured part in place; to immobilize body parts with such a device.

Spontaneous abortion: A spontaneous or unintentional ending of pregnancy before the fetus can be expected to live, which usually occurs before the twentieth week of pregnancy. Also known as a miscarriage.

Sprain: The partial or complete stretching and tearing of ligaments and other tissue at a joint.

Starting block: Platforms competitive swimmers dive from to start a race.

Sternum: The long, flat bone in the middle of the front of the rib cage; also called the breastbone.

Stimulants: Substances that affect the central nervous system and increase physical and mental activity.

Stoma: An opening in the front of the neck through which a person whose larynx has been removed breathes.

Strain: The stretching and tearing of muscle or tendon fibers.

Stress: A physiological or psychological response to real or imagined influences that alter an existing state of physical, mental, or emotional balance.

Stress management: A person's planned attempt to deal with stress.

Stressor: An event or condition that triggers the stress response.

Stroke: A disruption of blood flow to a part of the brain, which causes permanent damage to brain tissue; also called a cerebrovascular accident (CVA).

Substance abuse: The deliberate, persistent, excessive use of a substance without regard to health concerns or accepted medical practices.

Substance misuse: The use of a substance for unintended purposes or for intended purposes but in improper amounts or doses.

Sucking chest wound: A penetrating chest injury producing a sucking sound each time the victim breathes.

Sudden death: Death from cardiac arrest without any prior sign of heart attack.

Sudden infant death syndrome (SIDS): The sudden death of a seemingly normal, healthy infant that occurs during the infant's sleep without evidence of disease.

Superficial burn: A burn involving only the outer layer of skin, the epidermis, characterized by dry, red skin.

Symptoms: Something the victim tells you about his or her condition, such as "My head hurts," or "I am dizzy."

Syncope (sing kəp ē): A brief lapse in consciousness; see Fainting.

Syrup of ipecac (IP i kak): A substance used to induce vomiting.

Target heart rate range: Sixty to ninety percent of your maximum heart rate.

Tarsals: The bones of the ankle.

Tendon: A cordlike, fibrous band that attaches muscle to bone.

Tetanus: An acute infectious disease caused by a bacteria that produces a powerful poison; can occur in puncture wounds, such as human and animal bites; also called lockjaw.

Thigh: The part of the lower extremity from the pelvis to the knee.

Thoracic (tho RAS ik) cavity: An area in the body that contains the heart and the lungs and is protected by the rib cage and upper portion of the spine.

Thrombus (THROM bus): A collection of blood components that forms in the heart or vessels, obstructing blood flow.

Throw bag: A nylon bag containing 50 to 75 feet of coiled floating line; used as a rescue device.

Tibia: One of the two bones of the leg.

Tissue: A collection of similar cells that act together to perform specific body functions.

Tolerance: A condition in which the effects of a substance on the body decrease as a result of continual use.

Tourniquet (TUR ni kit): A wide band that is wrapped tightly around an extremity to control severe bleeding; used as a last resort measure.

Toxin: A poisonous substance.

Trachea (TRA ke ə): A tube leading from the upper airway to the lungs; also called the windpipe.

Transient (TRANZ e ent) ischemic (is KE mik) attack

(TIA): A temporary episode that, like a stroke, is caused by a disruption of blood flow to the brain; sometimes called a mini-stroke.

Trauma: The violent force or mechanism that can cause injury.

Triangular bandage: A bandage in the shape of a triangle; used to hold a dressing or splint in place or as a sling.

Trunk: The part of the body containing the chest, abdomen, and pelvis.

Ulna: One of the two bones of the forearm.

Umbilical cord: A flexible structure that attaches the placenta to the unborn child, allowing for the passage of blood, nutrients, and waste.

Upper arm: The part of the upper extremity from the shoulder to the elbow.

Upper extremities: The parts of the body from the shoulder to the fingers.

Urinary system: A group of organs and other structures that eliminates waste products from the blood.

Uterus (U ter us): A pear-shaped organ in a woman's pelvis in which an embryo forms and develops into a baby.

Vagina: *See* birth canal.

Veins: Blood vessels that carry blood from all parts of the body to the heart.

Vertebrae (VER tə bra): The 33 bones of the spine.

Vertebral column: The spine.

Virus: A disease-causing microorganism that, unlike bacteria, requires another organism to live and reproduce.

Vision impairment: Partial or total loss of sight.

Vital organs: Organs, such as the brain, heart, and lungs, whose functions are essential for life.

Wheezing: Hoarse whistling sounds made during breathing.

Wilderness: An area that is uninhabited by human beings, uncultivated, and left in its natural condition.

Wind chill factor: A combination of temperature and wind speed.

Withdrawal: The condition produced when a person stops using or abusing a substance to which he or she is addicted.

Wound: An injury to the soft tissues.

Xiphoid (ZI foid) process: An arrow-shaped piece of cartilage at the lowest point of the sternum.

American Academy of Orthopaedic Surgeons: *Basic rescue and emergency care,* Park Ridge, IL, 1990, American Academy of Orthopaedic Surgeons.

American Academy of Orthopaedic Surgeons: *Rural rescue and emergency care,* Park Ridge, IL, 1990, American Academy of Orthopaedic Surgeons.

American Academy of Orthopaedic Surgeons: *Your first response in emergency care,* Park Ridge, IL, 1990, American Academy of Orthopaedic Surgeons.

American Heart Association: *Heart and stroke facts,* 1992.

American Lyme Disease Foundation: A *quick guide to Lyme disease,* 1995.

American Lyme Disease Foundation: A *homeowner's guide to the ecology and environmental management of Lyme disease,* 1995.

Anderson K: *Mosby's medical, nursing, and allied health dictionary,* ed 4, St Louis, 1994, Mosby.

Anspaugh DJ, Hamrick MH, Rosato AA: *Wellness: concepts and applications,* ed 2, St Louis, 1994, Mosby.

Auerbach PS: *Wilderness medicine,* St Louis, 1994, Mosby.

Auerbach PS: *Wilderness medicine: management of wilderness and environmental emergencies,* ed 3, St Louis, 1995, Mosby.

Berkow R: *The Merck manual of diagnosis and therapy,* ed 17, Rahway, NJ, 1993, Regents/Prentice Hall.

Breuss CE, Laing SJ: *Decisions for health,* Dubuque, IA, 1985, William C. Brown.

Canadian Red Cross Society: *The vital link,* St Louis, 1994, Mosby.

Cohn AH: *It shouldn't hurt to be a child,* Chicago, 1987, National Committee for Prevention of Child Abuse.

Dorsman J: *How to quit drinking without AA: a complete self-help guide,* ed 2, Rocklin, CA, 1994, Prima Pub.

Driesbach RH, Robertson WO: *Handbook of poisoning,* ed 12, East Norwalk, CT, 1987, Appleton & Lange.

Getchell B, Pippin R, Barnes J: *Health,* Boston, 1989, Houghton Mifflin.

Green M, ed: *Bright futures: guidelines for health supervision of infants, children, and adolescents,* Arlington, VA, 1994, National Center for Education in Maternal and Child Health.

Guthrie HA, Picciano MF: *Human nutrition,* St Louis, 1995, Mosby.

Hafen BO, Karren KJ: *First aid for colleges and universities,* ed 5, Englewood Cliffs, NJ, 1993, Regents/Prentice Hall.

Hahn DB, Payne WA, *Focus on health,* ed 2, St Louis, 1994, Mosby.

Hauser WA, Hesdorffer DC: *Facts about epilepsy,* 1994, Epilepsy Foundation of America.

Instant health boost: stop smoking, *Glamour,* May 1995, p 48.

Isaac J, Goth P: *Wilderness first aid handbook,* New York, 1991, Lyons & Burford.

Marnell T: *Drug identification bible,* ed 1, Denver, Drug Identification Bible, 1993.

Merenstein GB, Kaplan DW, Rosenberg AA: *Handbook of pediatrics,* ed 17, East Norwalk, CT, 1994, Appleton & Lange.

National Committee for Injury Prevention and Control: *Injury prevention: meeting the challenge,* New York, 1989, Oxford University Press as a supplement to the American Journal of Preventive Medicine, 5:3, 1989.

National Institutes on Drug Abuse: *Anabolic steroids: a threat to body and mind,* National Institutes of Health, No 94-3721, 1994.

National Safety Council: *Accident facts,* 1993, Chicago, National Safety Council.

National Safety Council, Thygerson AL, editors: *First aid essentials,* Boston, 1989, Jones and Bartlett.

Payne WA, Hahn WB: *Understanding your health,* St Louis, 1989, Mosby.

Rice DP, MacKenzie EJ, and associates: *Cost of injury in the United States: a report to Congress 1989,* San Francisco, 1989, Institute for Health and Aging, University of California, and Injury Prevention Center, The Johns Hopkins University.

Rob C: *The caregiver's guide: helping elderly relatives cope with health and safety problems,* Boston, 1991, Houghton Mifflin.

Rodwell SR: *Basic nutrition and diet therapy,* ed 10, St Louis, 1995, Mosby.

Safety IQ: a quiz for the whole family, *Geico Direct,* pp 7-10, K. L. Publications, Spring, 1995.

Schimelpfenig T, Lindsey I: *NOLS wilderness first aid,* Lander, WY, 1991, NOLS Publications.

Seeley RR, Stevens TD, Tate P: *Anatomy and physiology,* ed 3, St Louis, 1995, Mosby.

Simon JE, Goldberg AT: *Prehospital pediatric life support,* St Louis, 1989, Mosby.

Spence WR: *Substance abuse identification guide,* Waco, TX: HEALTH EDCO, 1991.

The White House: *National drug control strategy,* September 1989.

Turkington C: *Poisons and antidotes,* New York, 1994, Facts on File.

U.S. Department of Health and Human Services; Public Health Service; Alcohol, Drug Abuse, and Mental Health Administration; and National Institute on Alcohol Abuse and Alcoholism: *Seventh special report to the U.S. Congress on alcohol and health,* Alexandria, VA, January, 1990, Editorial Experts.

Wardlaw GM, Insel PM: *Perspectives in nutrition,* St Louis, 1990, Mosby.

Wardlaw GM, Insel PM, Seyler MF: *Contemporary nutrition: issues and insights,* ed 2, St Louis, 1994, Mosby.

Weil A, Rosen W: *From chocolate to morphine: everything you need to know about mind-altering drugs,* ed 2, New York, 1993, Houghton-Mifflin Co.

Wilderness Medical Society: *Practice guidelines for wilderness emergency care,* Forgey WW, ed, Merrillville, IN, 1995, ICS Books.

Williams SR: *Basic nutrition and diet therapy,* ed 10, St Louis, 1995, Mosby.

Wyllie I: *The treatment of epilepsy: principles and practice,* Philadelphia, 1993, Lea & Febiger.